Northwestern University
STUDIES IN *Phenomenology &*
Existential Philosophy

Formalism in Ethics and Non-Formal Ethics of Values

Max Scheler

Translated by

Formalism in Ethics and Non-Formal Ethics of Values

A New Attempt toward the Foundation of an Ethical Personalism

MANFRED S. FRINGS
and ROGER L. FUNK

NORTHWESTERN UNIVERSITY PRESS

EVANSTON   1973

Fifth, revised edition originally published in the German under the title, *Der Formalismus in der Ethik und die materiale Wertethik,* by A. Francke AG Verlag, Bern, 1966.

Manfred S. Frings is editor of the German edition of the collected works of Max Scheler.

Contents

170
Sch 26 f

PART II

Foreword

WITH THIS TRANSLATION, Max Scheler's *Der Formalis-mus in der Ethik und die materiale Wertethik* (1913–16) becomes available in English for the first time. The translation is based on the fifth edition (1966) of the German text, which, as well as the fourth edition (1954), appeared as volume II of the *Collected Works* (Bern: Francke Verlag). The *Collected Works* will consist of thirteen volumes when completed.

Formalism in Ethics represents the major contribution of early-twentieth-century Continental philosophy to the field of ethics. It is a work that remains virtually unrivaled in terms of originality, depth, and scope; at the heart of the book one finds Scheler's phenomenological, sociological, and metaphysical explication of the person, personal values, and the foundation of moral obligation in values, as well as his discussion of the relationship of ethics to sociology, religion, and metaphysics. This is preceded, for reasons given by Scheler, by a lengthy critique both of Kant's formal apriorism in general and of specific doctrines of the *Critique of Practical Reason*. But Scheler is not critical of Kant alone. Other sections of this work examine in detail the doctrines of eudaemonism, utilitarianism, and pragmatistic-positivistic ethics. Of course, many of these themes are discussed further in other of Scheler's essays; of special importance is his investigation of American pragmatism, a subject that occupied him for much of his life (see "Erkenntnis und Arbeit" [Bibliog. no. 22]). Scheler emphasizes that the many aspects of this present work cannot be divorced from ideas set forth elsewhere on metaphysics, epistemology, sociology, and the philosophy of religion. (A number of references to passages in other works where these ideas are treated more fully have been supplied by Maria Scheler, the editor of the fourth and fifth editions.)

As we have said, *Formalism in Ethics* is phenomenological. But, as every reader of phenomenology knows, no unanimity concerning the nature of phenomenology itself is to be found as one surveys the works of authors of the phenomenological circle. There were very great differences between Scheler and Husserl, for example. For Scheler, questions of method always remained secondary. Intuitive insight was his primary contribution to phenomenology, and it was in this that he was at his best. Although Scheler, like Heidegger, acknowledged the importance of Husserl's *Logical Investigations*—above all, the sixth—he remained on the whole rather critical of Husserl's work. He was never a student of Husserl in any sense of the term. His primary concern was never the phenomenological investigation of the transcendental ego or the ontological question of Being; it was rather the Being of Man, here and now, in his biological, social, ethical, metaphysical, and religious dimensions—and, ultimately, man as the bearer of love.

No translation is a perfect substitute for the original text. We cite this commonplace, not to justify the errors that may have crept into this work, but to support our refusal to follow the German text slavishly through the employment of awkward and infelicitous neologisms and contrived phrases, though we have undoubtedly not avoided them often enough. It has been our hope that the possession of German as a mother tongue in the one case and English in the other would enable us to avoid the kinds of errors in translation that too frequently distress readers of Continental philosophy.

A few remarks on certain specifics of the translation may be of some help to the reader. We have mentioned that there were differences between Scheler and Husserl; this fact is reflected in their respective terminologies. For example, whereas Husserl speaks of "retention" and "protention," Scheler uses the terms "immediate remembrance" (*unmittelbare Erinnerung*) and "immediate expectation" (*unmittelbare Erwartung*). Such differences are not the products of a simple desire to be different. They are necessitated by the very different starting points of the philosophers. And in many cases Scheler was simply unaware of Husserl's work, as was Husserl of his. We have attempted to preserve these differences and have therefore not employed the terminology that has been used by translators of Husserl's works and subsequently adopted by many English-speaking phenomenologists. To be mentioned here especially is Scheler's phrase *natürliche Weltanschauung*, translated as "natural view of the world." It was years after Scheler's *Formalism* that Husserl introduced the term *Lebenswelt* (lived world) for the same phenomenon. We have retained the phrase that Scheler used throughout this work, although he himself also used the term *Lebenswelt* as early as 1911.

Among other words that deserve attention here, the first is the German adjective *material*, which occurs in the very title. For this adjective we have used *non-formal* and have done so for two reasons. First, the English word *material* corresponds to the German *materiell*, which pertains to matter. However, the German adjective *material* pertains not to matter but to content, and is a technical term. Hence, *materialer Wert* cannot be translated as "material value" if serious confusion is to be avoided. In this text *material* usually pertains, as in the title, to value-content. Unfortunately, there is no adjective form for *content* in English; where we did use *content*, we were often forced to employ circumlocutions. Second, the German *material* is used in this work as the antonym of *formal* in the discussions of both Kantian and other varieties of formalism.

The German word *Gesinnung*, so important in German works on ethics, has been translated as "basic moral tenor." "State of mind," "attitude," and "spirit," used by the various translators of Kant's works, surely do not possess the requisite moral connotation. What is worse, such terms often obscure this very important Kantian concept as well as the fact that Kant's ethics is ultimately a *Gesinnungsethik*.

We could mention many important Schelerian expressions here, but we will restrict ourselves to some examples. We have translated *Tunkönnen* as "able-to-do," *Gesamtperson* as "collective person," *Wertperson* as "value-person." We have not attempted to preserve the similarity between such terms as *Sachverhalt* ("state of affairs") and *Wertverhalt* ("value-complex"), *Streben* ("conation") and *Erstreben* ("striving"). *Erfahren* has been translated as "experiencing," even in cases where the prefix *Er-* is italicized to emphasize the element of finality.

One feature of the text may disturb certain readers, namely, the seemingly excessive use of quotation marks. These marks occur so frequently because Scheler used them not only in all the customary ways but also to indicate that he was discussing *phenomena*. We have generally followed the German text on this matter, even to the point of apparent inconsistency.

The footnotes in brackets that are followed by the notation "*Ed.*" are those supplied by Maria Scheler. Footnote references to works by Scheler are given in shortened form; complete publication information can be found in the Bibliography. Detailed information concerning the posthumous editions of *Formalism*, as well as the relation of *Formalism* to other works of the author, can be found in Maria Scheler's *Nachwort* to the fifth edition.

We wish to express our deep gratitude to Professor David Carr of Yale University, translator of Husserl's *Crisis*, for his suggestions, corrections, and help in the final reading. Our work would have been less adequate without his assistance and advice. We also wish to express our thanks to De Paul University for financial support of the translation. Finally, we would like to thank those who helped in typing the final manuscript: Miss Dorothy C. Chrzanowski, Miss Mary G. Thulin, Miss Anne Brandstetter, and Miss Jane Budny. We alone are responsible for any errors that may remain.

M. S. F.
R. L. F.

Preface to the First Edition

THE INVESTIGATIONS brought together in this special printing appeared under the title "Formalism in Ethics and Non-Formal Ethics of Values" in two parts in *Jahrbuch für Philosophie und phänomenologische Forschung*. The first part appeared in volume I in 1913; the second part, in volume II in July, 1916. The second part of the manuscript was completed three years ago, and most of it was printed then. However, owing to personal circumstances and the turmoil of the war, it could only be published this year. All parts of the work were written prior to the outbreak of the war.

The main objective of these investigations is to establish a strictly scientific and positive foundation for philosophical ethics with respect to all its fundamental problems—but to deal only with the most elementary points of the problems involved. My intention was therefore to lay a *foundation*, not to elaborate the ways in which the discipline of ethics applies to all of concrete life. Even in those passages that touch upon concrete forms of life (e.g., the forms of socialization discussed in part II) it was not my intention to overstep the limits within which strictly a priori essences and ideas and essential interconnections are demonstrable. The reader might get the impression that here and there these investigations descend into the concrete. This descent is attributable not to my own arbitrariness but to the method, which—as Oswald Külpe aptly noted—allows one to broaden significantly the domain of the a priori structures of ideas, even in ethics, beyond the a priori spheres of the formal-practical that have been traditionally recognized since Kant.

The critique of Kant's ethics in these investigations is only a

[xvii]

secondary objective and is found only at the beginning and in a few other places in later chapters. I intended by way of a *positive* discovery of true states of affairs to undertake a criticism of what I consider false in Kant's ethics. I therefore did not intend to discover such true states of affairs only through and subsequent to my criticism of Kant. But even in these sections of criticism it was always my assumption that Kant's ethics, and not the ethics of any other modern philosopher, represents the most *perfect* we have in the area of philosophical ethics—although not in the form of a *Weltanschauung* or a consciousness of faith, but rather in the form of strict scientific insight. It was also my assumption that Kant's ethics, although pointedly criticized, corrected, and supplemented on various occasions, had not yet been shaken to its foundations. The implied unconditional reverence for Kant's work in these assumptions was a matter of course to me, despite the fact that my criticism is not devoid of severity, and despite the fact that it was my intention to discover the *reasons* behind the truth so deeply *felt*, although only felt, by Schiller: that this "excellent man" unfortunately "cared only for the servants and not for the children of the house" (Schiller, *Über Anmut und Würde*). Only through an insight into the reasons contained in the *foundations* of Kant's ethics, not through the conclusions drawn from it, can it be shown, psychologically and historically, that it was the roots of the ethnically and historically very limited (although magnificent and excellent) ethos of the people and state of a specific epoch in the history of Prussia that Kant presumptuously dared to seek in a pure and universally valid human reason.[1]

The present work is the result of lectures on ethics which I have given over a number of years. This may explain the fact that the disposition of the whole of this work lacks the clarity which books that were written uninterruptedly normally have. I apologize for this lack of clarity. But it is quite otherwise with the frequently long excursions into general and specific theories of knowledge and values (e.g., the sections in part I concerning the concepts of the a priori and the formal and the concept of sensation, and those in part II concerning the concept of value and the principles of explanatory psychology). The reader may at times find these painful to read from the viewpoint of style. Yet, given the present deficient status of the foundations of the

1. [See Scheler's "Von zwei deutschen Krankheiten" and "Vom Verrat der Freude" (Bibliog. nos. 13, 19).—Ed.]

discipline of ethics, they appeared to me urgently needed from both a theoretical and a philosophical viewpoint, because of the objective inseparability of the problems involved and because of the roots that ethics extends into the theory of knowledge and the theory of values. Without these excursions the specifically ethical parts of my work would have remained without ultimate foundations. In addition, the achievement of a *systematic* character, which, in my judgment, should belong to any philosophical foundation, including a phenomenological one, required that I demonstrate, throughout this work, interconnections with epistemological views of mine which have not yet been published together in a special volume.[2] There may arise here and there a view according to which phenomenology deals only with isolated phenomena and essences, and according to which "any will to system is a will to lies." I am completely removed from such picture-book phenomenology. For inasmuch as discoverable *states of affairs* of this world *itself* form a systematic interconnective complex, a will to system would not be a "will to lies"; it would, on the contrary, be a will not to notice the systematic character residing in *things* themselves, which is to be regarded as a consequence of a baseless "will to anarchy." To the objective reader this work will in other respects show that I have every reason to detach myself from such kinds of "irrationalism," which at times seek to attach themselves to my coattails.

I owe to the significant works of Edmund Husserl the methodological consciousness of the unity and sense of the phenomenological attitude, which binds together the coeditors of the *Jahrbuch*, men who otherwise vastly differ both in world view and on philosophical matters. The following investigations, too, owe much in their essentials to the works of the editor of the *Jahrbuch*. But I must claim the authorship of and take full responsibility for the manner in which I understand and execute this attitude, even more so, of course, for its application to the groups of problems discussed.

At the end of this text I have proposed some supplementary works which the results of the investigation require according to the idea of system pertinent to sociology and philosophy of religion. These will be submitted separately next year (the major portion of them has already been completed). As to parts of this

2. [See "Phänomenologie und Erkenntnistheorie" and "Lehre von den drei Tatsachen," which stem from the period of *Formalism in Ethics*. They appear in *Zur Ethik und Erkenntnislehre* (Bibliog. no. 29), which is a collection of various works connected with *Formalism.*—Ed.]

text pertinent to other fields, such as the emotive-phenomenological, the moral-critical, and the ethical, the reader is referred to the author's following works: (1) *Zur Phänomenologie und Theorie der Sympathiegefühle* (Bibliog. no. 6); (2) *Abhandlungen und Aufsätze*, Vols. I, II (Bibliog. no. 10); (3) *Der Genius des Krieges und der Deutsche Krieg* (Bibliog. no. 9); (4) *Krieg und Aufbau* (Bibliog. no. 11). Finally, my paper "Ethik" (Bibliog. no. 8) attempts to compare the results of the following investigations and the dominant trends in recent philosophical thought.

Berlin   MAX SCHELER
September, 1916

Preface to the Second Edition

THE FIRST PART of this work has been out of print for some time. The considerable delay in publishing the second edition was caused by the adverse circumstances of our time. The present second edition is an unchanged copy of the first. I refrained from submitting a revised and supplemented edition in which various criticisms of the contents of this work would have been incorporated and evaluated because I saw no reason to change my views on essential points established in the first edition and because this work, already heavily burdened with thought about and digressions into different areas of philosophy, would have been only further complicated by added notes. But the reader's orientation to the contents of this work as well as its connections with other works of mine will be facilitated by a very detailed and exact index of subject matter published by this company. This index has been arranged by Dr. Herbert Leyendecker, who, with rare scholarship, loyalty, and knowledge, devoted himself to this task in a selfless manner. I express my deep gratitude to him.

The reader of this preface will expect a brief explanation of *three* points: the effect this work has had; the place of this work with respect to new works of mine in the *Jahrbücher für Philosophie und phänomenologische Forschung* and those works which are about to be published; and, finally, the relation of the message of this work to the spirit of the *times*, which has changed so much since the manuscript was completed.

I am very happy and satisfied to be able to say that, in general, the effect of the first edition was one of depth more than of broad publicity, and that this book met with criticism that was less than the positive thought which it brought about in the domain of ethics. Apart from scholars of the younger generation who were stimulated by my work, there is J. Cohn's article in *Logos,* Vol. VII, A. Messer's work in the new *Jahrbuch für Pädagogik* (1918), N. Hartmann's contribution in *Die Geisteswissenschaften,*[3] and the contribution of D. H. Kerler in a number of subtle works, especially in "Max Scheler and Ethical Impersonalism"; and O. Külpe, in his *Einleitung in die Philosophie* (8th ed.), has given my work a remarkable position among the new attempts to establish a foundation for ethics. Of greater value to me were the positive stimulations to further my work. These are the wide acceptance of my results, the supplementary ideas and the continuations of my thoughts, and also their simplification and popularization. Witnesses to this are E. Spranger's *Lebensformen* (2d ed.), A. Messer's *Ethik* (1918), H. Driesch's *Philosophie des Organischen* (2d ed.), D. von Hildebrand's work in the *Jahrbücher für Philosophie und phänomenologische Forschung,* Edith Stein's work on empathy, a work written in Russian by N. Losskij, and J. Volkelt's *Das ästhetische Bewusstsein* (1920). I do not know whether the profound and subtle study by A. Meinong, *Über emotionale Präsentation* (1917), in which his ideas on the essence of values and on value-comprehension come closest to my own, has been influenced by me (this study being in marked contrast to his earlier work). No reference is made in Meinong's work to my investigations. On the other hand, I know from personal communication that Mcinong read my work and valued it. In any case I am most happy to know that my ideas and those of this excellent scholar have coincided. In England, G. E. Moore has set forth similar views on many points concerning the problem of values. My attempt to establish "the principle of solidarity" and a new theory of essential forms of human association has had considerable effect in social philosophy. The existence of an objective non-formal order of ranks of values that can become evidential to us has been recognized as valid by many scholars. The criticism of Kant in this work did *not* exercise a noticeable influence on those close to Kantian philosophy, who are mostly preoccupied with themselves, and it inspired no

3. ["Besprechungen," *Die Geisteswissenschaften,* no. 35 (May, 1914). —*Ed.*]

attempt at refutation. Only little attention was given to my important elaborations on the theory of psychological cognition, the kinds of psychological interconnections, and the essence of the givenness of the "lived body," as well as to the epistemological points of my work, especially my new views on the concepts of sensation and excitation. Doubtless the explanation of this is, as H. Driesch has noted, the fact that these are situated in the text within "complexes of thought alien to them." I intend to develop these ideas more precisely in two works on epistemology and the mind-body problem which are now in progress.

The present work occupies a central position among all my hitherto published studies insofar as it contains not only my views on the foundation of ethics but also a number, although not all, of the essential points of departure of my philosophical thought *in general*. The promise at the end of this work to elaborate my ideas on the essence of religion and "the model types of value-persons" in a theory of "the essential experience of the divine" and a work on "models and types of leaders" has been only partially fulfilled in a recently published book, *Vom Ewigen im Menschen*, Vol. I, in which my ideas on "essential experience" in religion may be found in a section entitled "Probleme der Religion." One will also find there a theory on the relationship between "religion and morals" that supplements the present investigations. Volume II of *Vom Ewigen im Menschen* is to fulfill my second promise through a study of "models and leaders." [4] Concrete application of my principles of general ethics to a number of specific problems and to questions concerning our own time will be found in my books *Vom Umsturz der Werte* (2d ed. of *Abhandlungen und Aufsätze* [Bibliog. no. 10]) and *Genius des Krieges*, in my essay *Ursachen des Deutschenhasses* (Bibliog. no. 12), and in my forthcoming book *Schriften zur Soziologie und Weltanschauungslehre* (Bibliog. no. 19). The present work also supplements the new, enlarged edition of my *Wesen und Formen der Sympathie* (Bibliog. no. 18) in terms of an ethical estimation of our emotional life. This book will be followed by a collection of essays entitled *Sinngesetze des emotionalen Lebens*, which contains, among others, "Das Schamgefühl," "Das Ehrgefühl,"

---

4. [Only volume I of *Vom Ewigen im Menschen* appeared (Bibliog. no. 14). The manuscript of "Vorbilder und Führer," found among the author's papers (from the years 1911–21), was published in *Zur Ethik und Erkenntnislehre*, in 1933.—Ed.]

and "Das Furchtgefühl."[5] The well-founded "principle of solidarity" and the interrelated "theory of essential forms of human groups" contained in the present book are to be applied to an assessment of the whole of European modern times, especially with regard to the problem of capitalism, in a future study on solidarism as the basis of social and historical philosophy.

The spirit behind my ethics is one of rigid ethical absolutism and objectivism. My position may in another respect be called "emotional intuitionism" and "non-formal apriorism." The principle outlined in this work, according to which all values, including all possible values of things and non-personal organizations and groupings of men, are subordinated to values of the *person*, takes *such* a significant place in my ethics that I deemed it necessary to use the subtitle *A New Attempt toward the Foundation of an Ethical Personalism*. I am happy to note that ethical absolutism and value-objectivism have made much progress both in Germany and abroad since this book came out, and that the positions of traditional relativism and subjectivism have weakened considerably. It appears that especially the German youth of today have grown weary of all baseless relativisms as well as of Kant's empty and barren formalism and the one-sidedness of its idea of duty. The main thought expressed in Pascal's *ordre du coeur* and *logique du coeur* has been revitalized in our era with its immense *désordre du coeur*. The treason committed against the deepest sources of all moral being and acting, namely, joy and love, which is to be blamed on the false heroism of duty and work prevailing in Germany and German philosophy since Kant, has gradually been revealed as a false direction in our historical ethos.[6] The present study has pursued this treason to its den, and my treatise "Das Ressentiment im Aufbau der Moralen" (contained in *Vom Umsturz der Werte*) is an attempt to discover the historical and psychological bases of this treason. On the other hand, my rigid personalism, with its implicit theory of an "individually and objectively valid good" and the individual moral "destiny" of every person, appears to be even more in opposition to the "socialistic" currents of our time than it was when it was

5. [Of the works in the collection *Sinngesetze des emotionalen Lebens*, only the book on sympathy, *Zur Phänomenologie und Theorie der Sympathiegefühle*, was published by the author himself. "Über Scham und Schamgefühl, from the author's papers, was published in *Zur Ethik und Erkenntnislehre.—Ed.*]

6. [See above, p. xviii, n. 1.—*Ed.*]

first published—also to what is, in my opinion, the limitless stress on "organization" and "community" within Christian churches. In this respect I would like to state the following: Every false so-called individualism, with its erroneous and pernicious consequences, is excluded in my ethics by the theory of the original *coresponsibility* of every person for the moral salvation of the *whole of all realms of persons* (principle of solidarity). What is of moral value, in my view, is not the "isolated" person but the person originally and knowingly joined with God, directed toward the world in love, and feelingly united with the whole of the spiritual world and humanity.

It is precisely because I place all care for the community and its forms in the living *center of the individual person* that I may be allowed to reject most emphatically every direction in an ethos that makes the value of the person originally and essentially *dependent* on his relation to a community and a world of goods that exists independently of him, or that seeks to establish a coincidence between his value and such "relations." Hence, with what is, in my opinion, the bright and clear evidence of the proposition that a *person-value* is higher than all values of things, organizations, and community, I *strongly* oppose any current of a time which, as the British philosopher Herbert Spencer said in his last hours, would finally lead to the fact that "man can no longer do what he wills to do but only what he has been told to do." The most essential and important proposition that my present investigations would found and communicate as perfectly as possible is the proposition that the final meaning and value of the *whole* universe is ultimately to be measured exclusively against the pure being (and not the effectiveness) and the possible perfect being-*good*, the richest fullness and the most perfect development, and the purest beauty and inner harmony of *persons*, in whom at times all forces of the world concentrate themselves and soar upward.

Even a spiritual ground of the world, whatever else it may be, deserves to be named "God" only to the extent that it is *"personal"*; this, of course, is a question which philosophy alone clearly cannot answer (see *Vom Ewigen im Menschen*). The solution to this question can only be *experienced* through a possible answer which the ground of the world *itself* gives to our soul in the mode of the religious act.

Cologne   MAX SCHELER
September, 1921

Preface to the Third Edition

THE THIRD EDITION of this work is, like the second, an unchanged copy of the original text. The reasons for my refusal to make changes in the text are the same as those mentioned in the Preface to the Second Edition. But an index of subject matter has been added, arranged by Dr. Herbert Leyendecker, who displayed great knowledge and conscientiousness in this undertaking. Because of the length of this index and the adverse circumstances surrounding the printing of the second edition, the publisher was not in the position to print the index separately, as planned (see Preface to the Second Edition). The index has been considerably shortened (to about one-third); however, it is hoped that the original will be published at some more favorable time. I must express once again my heartfelt thanks and sincere gratitude to Dr. Leyendecker for his selfless endeavors, for which the reader, too, will be grateful in many respects, as well as for his detailed index of the printing mistakes in the first edition. I also wish to express my thanks to Dr. H. Rüssel, who abridged the original index.

In the Preface to the Second Edition I reported on the effects of this work and the more or less critical continuation of its ideas up to 1921. I also reported on some points concerning the relation of its ideas to other works of mine published *after* 1916 (the year of its first appearance).[7] Here I will add a short supplement covering the time between 1921 and 1926.

It has not remained hidden from view that I have considerably extended my position concerning *primal* questions in metaphysics and the philosophy of religion since the second edition of this work, and have also *changed* my position on so essential a question as that of the metaphysics of the one and absolute being (which I adhere to as before) so basically that I can no longer claim to be a "theist" in the usual sense of this term. This is not the place to make further reference to the positive direction and the most recent results of my metaphysical investigations, especially since lengthy metaphysical works of mine, as well as my *Anthropology,* in large part ready for the press, will give clear

7. [I.e., the edition which contains part I and part II. Part I appeared in 1913 in *Jahrbuch für Philosophie und phänomenologische Forschung.* —*Ed.*]

and distinct information.[8] It appears to me all the *more necessary,* however, to stress here that the ideas in this work not only remain unaffected by the change in my fundamental metaphysical position but *represent some of the reasons and intellectual motives which led to this change.* If changes in this text were to be made, they could be made only in chapter 6, A, section 3, d, "Microcosm, Macrocosm, and the Idea of God." For it was never my intention to establish in this work a *foundation* of ethics on the basis of some kind of presupposition concerning the nature and existence and the idea and will of *God.* To me, ethics is today what it has been, an important part of any metaphysics of absolute being; but metaphysics is not important for the foundation of ethics. Moreover, the changes in my metaphysical outlook are not based on changes in my *philosophy of mind* and of the objective correlates of mental acts; they are based on changes in and extensions of my philosophy of *nature* and *anthropology.*

As to new work supplementary to the present investigation or, better, new research of mine that either extends the thoughts of *Formalism in Ethics* or presupposes them, two other works need to be mentioned. My speech, *Die Formen des Wissens und die Bildung,* is an attempt to apply my theory of an objective order of ranks among values and some propositions about acts of value-comprehension to a more profound grasp of the problem of *"education"* [Bildung] as a form and a process of the personal spirit. My comprehensive work, *Die Wissensformen und die Gesellschaft* (Bibliog. no. 22), in its first part, "Probleme einer Soziologie des Wissens," assumes both the value theory and the act theory of *Formalism in Ethics* as a *foundation* for the idea of a *sociology of culture,* for the theory—based on this work—of the order of historical causal factors (the "real" and "ideal" ones), and for the theory—also based on this work—of the *becoming* of specific *rational organizations* of historical man. In addition, the sociological parts of *Formalism in Ethics* (chap. 6, B, sec. 4, ad 4) are applied to the sociology of culture, especially to the "forms of knowledge," and are confirmed at the same time in this new area of research. In the second part of *Die Wissensformen,* entitled "Erkenntnis und Arbeit," the ranks of values are applied both to the forms of knowledge and to the measures of cognition (knowledge of work, education, and salvation). Moreover, the

---

8. Positive remarks can be found in my *Die Formen des Wissens und die Bildung* (Bibliog. no. 21). [See, above all, the author's notes on the text in the appendix to the above-mentioned work. See also "Die Stellung des Menschen im Kosmos" (Bibliog. no. 23).—*Ed.*]

question asked in *Formalism in Ethics,* whether values are given *before* or *after* the contents of representation (of any kind), is elaborated upon in the part entitled "Philosophie der Wahrnehmung" and is answered as it was in *Formalism* years ago, i.e., they are *pre*given. What is said in *Die Wissensformen* about activities of fantasy (including fantasy of desire) is an important addition to what has been stated in *Formalism in Ethics* concerning "striving and willing." Likewise, my "Philosophie der Wahrnehmung," especially the sections which deal with "environment," "structure of environment," and "excitation," is a supplement to and a confirmation of the same points made in *Formalism in Ethics* (see *Die Wissensformen,* sec. 3, p. 127b).

As to the *scientific effects and the continuations* of this work since 1921, I cannot make detailed references to the very large body of literature (in part supplementary, in part critical, in part popularizing) that I have received during the past years. But reference to some publications may be helpful to the reader: one can evaluate, in both an objective and a subjective sense, a new attempt in value theory and ethics only when one can look over its "fruits." *Formalism in Ethics* has, since 1921, exercised remarkable influence in four areas: the *general theory of values* (axiology), in which, by the way, criticism has been more extensive than in other areas;[9] *ethics* proper and the act theory of the moral mind; *sociology;* and *psychology* and *pedagogy.*

As far as *ethics* proper is concerned, I am most happy to see that my theories are of such value that a man of the rank of Nicolai Hartmann, known for his independence and the scientific rigor of his thought, has written a large work on ethics (*Ethik* [Walter de Gruyter, 1926]) which, as Hartmann states in his Preface, rests on the foundations of non-formal ethics as the "pioneering insight" in ethics since Kant's time. Indeed, I consider Hartmann's work to have furthered the cause of philosophical ethics more decisively than any other work of the last decade of which I am aware, from either within or without Germany, because a large number of his analyses are in part continuations and in part criticisms of the ideas of my *Formalism in Ethics,* and also because he took up the problem of "freedom" in a section unrelated to my work. This is not the place to

---

9. See the book by Rehmke's talented student, J. E. Heyde, *Wert: Eine philosophische Grundlegung* (Erfurt, 1926). This book is valuable, although not exactly polite in its tone. See also D. H. Kerler, *Weltwille und Wertwille* (Leipzig, 1926); M. Beck, *Wesen und Wert* (Berlin, 1925); J. Thyssen, "Vom Ort der Werte," *Logos,* Vol. XV, no. 3 (1926).

describe the qualities of the personal yet *objective wisdom,* standing in *bold relief* in its austerity, courage, and benevolence, which permeates his work, even its very style—qualities most rare in our academic philosophical literature. Nor is this the place to undertake a critical examination of the parts of his work which do not concern *Formalism in Ethics,* or even those which do. I hope to do this at some other time.[10] Yet some very general comments can be made concerning my relation to Hartmann's work.

Hartmann notes in his foreword that "Scheler's thoughts [on non-formal ethics of values] cast new light on Aristotle, although he did not at all intend to do so. This is a surprising test of non-formal value-ethics" (p. vii). I can*not* agree with the esteemed scholar in this respect, much as I am happy to learn that through my *Formalism in Ethics* he came to see something in Aristotle which he had not seen before. I am afraid that he reads things into Aristotle in the old Marburg manner (reminding us of Natorp's Plato and Cassirer's Leibniz, etc.), things that are, in fact, not in Aristotle. For Aristotle does not recognize a sharp distinction between "goods" and "values," nor does he have a concept of value that is independent of the autonomy and degrees of being (i.e., of the measure of the concretization of the entelechial direction belonging to every thing). Aristotle's ethics is in essence an ethics of "goods" and "objective purposes," one that I reject in *Formalism in Ethics* for many reasons. Hence, the non-formal ethics of values belongs *completely* to modern philosophical thought and can serve neither as a springboard for a return to the ancient static objectivism of goods (which in another fashion characterizes Catholic Scholasticism) [11] nor as a basis for a "synthesis of ancient and contemporary ethics" (p. viii). It is only *after* the collapse of ethics of goods and purposes, with their self-reliant "absolute" worlds of goods, that "non-formal value-ethics" *could* come into being. It *presupposes* Kant's *destruction* of these forms of ethics. Non-formal ethics does not

10. I would like to stress here that I consider Hartmann's new analyses of "ideal" and "normative" oughtness a valuable refinement of the analyses of "value and ought" in my *Formalism.* I furthermore consider his elaboration on the relative "strength" of the lower ethical categories and the relative "weakness" of the higher ones an especially *deep* insight of his ethics. This position is largely in agreement with what I say in *Formalism,* namely, that values are all the more unrealizable through willing and action, the *higher* they are in their ranks.

11. Excellent information on this point can be found in the relevant sections of E. Przywara, *Religionsbegrundung—Max Scheler—J. H. Newman* (Freiburg, 1923), esp. chap. 3.

want to be "anti-Kantian" or to go behind Kant in time; rather, it intends to go "beyond" Kant. Non-formal ethics is *more,* not less, historicorelativistic than Kant's, but without giving up the idea of an absolute ethics itself. It is more relativistic in that it regards even the rational humanism of Kant's ethics as only one moment in the history of the human spirit. And it does not at all recognize any constant organization of reason, but only the constancy of the idea of *reason* itself (see chap. 5, sec. 6). Still less can I agree that non-formal ethics would stand its "test" by either casting or not casting new light on Aristotle! Amicus Aristoteles, magis amicus veritas.

Among the reasons which Hartmann gives to show that his work is based on the foundation of the non-formal ethics of values, we find the following remark in his preface:

> With this [*Formalism in Ethics*] the way is shown. But to show a way and to take its course are two different things. Neither Scheler nor anyone else has taken this course, at least as far as ethics proper is concerned—and this fact does not seem to be a matter of chance.

Quite apart from the fact that in the practical world (e.g., in politics) "to take a course" is something more and higher than the mere *showing* of a course, in theoretical matters the *opposite* is true; and does not the rhythm of Hartmann's statement indicate that it is more important to show than to take? Hence I cannot agree with Hartmann in another respect. I would not mention this point at all were we not concerned here with *different directions* taken in my *Formalism* (and other works relevant to ethics) and in Hartmann's *Ethik*—different directions, that is, whose differences Hartmann appears to see within only *one* direction. I do not wish to maintain that the whole of my ethical writings, with its *specific* analyses and conclusions, forms an unbroken continuation of my *Formalism* into the most concrete of problems. Hartmann would be the first to see this if he did not have a much more restricted "concept" of "ethics proper" than I do. And it is in this regard that I wish to put forward some *doubts* concerning his work, which, to put it plainly, can only help.

First, what I fail to see in his work is an analysis of the moral *life* of the *personality* as we find it in all serious processes of conscience and, above all, in all types of moral "acts." Notwithstanding our having learned that we should care about the "objective content" of values, we ought not—if we are to avoid falling back

into an objectivism and ontologism that stifles the *living spirit*—
to neglect the moral *life of the subject* as a problem. In fact, I
reject, in principle and at the very *threshold* of philosophy, a
heavenly realm of ideas and values that is "independent" of the
essence and *execution* of living spiritual *acts*, independent not
only with regard to man and human consciousness but also with
regard to the *essence and execution of a living spirit in general.*
This pertains as much to the theory of knowledge and ontology as
it does to ethics (compare Hartmann's *Metaphysik der Erkenntnis* with my "Erkenntnis und Arbeit," mentioned above, especially
with the part concerning the essence and givenness of "reality").
For this reason I can*not* accept as justified his criticism of my
concept of the person (e.g., my thesis that the person can never
be an "object") and what I call the "collective personality," no
matter how much genuine progress in the non-formal ethics of
values I am inclined to see in his work. Hartmann's return to an
all-too-palpable realistic ontology and value-objectivism appears
to me to be an exaggerated *reaction* to the typical Marburg
excesses of "creative thought" and the "law-bound, pure willing"
that creates values. His ontologism and objectivism are almost
medieval: indeed, they go *behind* even the living substance of
Christianity and its discovery of the eternal right of the living
subjectivity in God *and* man which is *not* objectifiable but *always*
"actual" [*aktual*]. This discovery of the right of the *living spirit*
which has been made in modern times and which goes far beyond this Christian discovery (vis-à-vis antiquity) is precisely
what is questioned in Hartmann's work.

The second point I wish to stress briefly is that Hartmann
attributes too little significance to the *historical* and *social nature
of all* living ethoses and *their* own special orders of values. Man
as a spiritual being *breathes,* as it were, only in history and in
society. One cannot separate the theory of knowledge from the
great problems of the *history* of the structures of the human spirit
(see the preface to my *Die Wissensformen und die Gesellschaft*),
nor can one separate ethics from the *history of the forms of ethos.*
For this reason I do not find the direction of the continuation
of the non-formal ethics of values so much in what Hartmann
calls "ethics proper," i.e., strictly "individualistic" analysis of
virtue in the manner of Aristotle and, even more, in that of the
Stoics; nor do I find this in the particular (and very valuable)
analysis in which values are separated from the structures of
community and history, where they were *first experienced,* and
completely lifted out of time (e.g., Nietzsche's "love of the

most distant"). Rather, I see this continuation more in the *philosophy of the development of moral consciousness* in history and society. Finally, I can*not* approve of the complete and objective detachment of ethical problems—and not *merely* their methodological detachment—from metaphysics, from the "person," and from the *ground* of all things; nor can I approve of Hartmann's "antinomian" stand on ethics and the metaphysics of the Absolute, or philosophy of religion (see his *Ethik*, pt. III, chap. 85, and pt. I, chap. 21), all of which are peculiar characteristics of the magnificent design of his work.[12] If this bond between ethics and the metaphysics of absolute being must not be severed—even Kant did not tear this bond apart with the systematic force that Hartmann has used in those chapters (see also his preface) where he comes close to Nietzsche's "postulatory atheism" (see my essay, "Mensch und Geschichte" [Bibliog. no. 24])[13]—then I do not wish to see the bond with *Kairos*, i.e., the call of the *hour of our* human and historical being and life, severed as completely as it is in Hartmann's work.[14]

Formalism in Ethics and other ethical writings of mine have been elaborated upon and deepened (but in a manner different from Hartmann's) by H. G. Stoker, a South African student of mine. His *Das Gewissen* (Bonn: Verlag Friedrich Cohen, 1925),

12. This pertains, above all, to Hartmann's claim (on behalf of "dignity and freedom") that there *"may"* not *be* any kind of objective teleology (or any teleocliny). But *why* "should" both the world and its ground satisfy this "demand" of a *very* exaggerated concept of the "dignity and freedom" of man? Is one allowed to—indeed, can one—"prescribe" this for what surely is *most* "independent" in us, i.e., absolute being? This is not even possible with regard to processes of life. I must ask the reader to refer to my remarks in "Erkenntnis und Arbeit," esp. the end of chap. 6. [See 1926 ed., pp. 480 ff.—*Ed.*] I argue there in the opposite way; that is, I derive the assumption of a universally valid, formal-mechanical causality of nature (esp. of life and psychic processes) from a mere (arbitrary) *fiat* of man's will to *control,* from the rising bourgeois society and *its* idea of "man" (see also my "Probleme einer Soziologie des Wissens"). I also reject the empty "postulates" of the complete controllability of nature (along with their corresponding "freedom and dignity of man"), just as I rejected Kant's "postulates" of a theistic deity in my *Vom Ewigen im Menschen. Neither* the existence *nor* the non-existence of God has anything to do with human and ethical "*postulates.*"

13. [For the later publication of this, see Bibliog. no. 27.—*Ed.*]

14. [The manuscript includes the following sentence: "*Ultimately ethics is a 'damned bloody affair,' and if it can give me no directives concerning how 'I' 'should' live now in this social and historical context, then what is it?*" The following sentence occurs in the margin: "*The path 'from eternity,' or 'amor intellectualis sub specie quadam aeternitatis,' where one can catch a glimpse of it, to Here and Now must cross an enormous gap. It is precisely philosophy that attempts to bridge it— however indirectly*" (editor's italics).—*Ed.*]

very well received by critical readers, represents, despite the many critical comments one can make concerning some details of my ideas, the most precise and minute analysis on the phenomenon of conscience that we have today (see my preface to his work). This work has also been recognized on various occasions by eminent critics (e.g., K. Groos).

With respect to *sociology* in Germany, *Formalism in Ethics* appears to have had the strongest effect on Theodor Litt, who belongs to a circle of scholars who are much concerned with laying a *philosophical* foundation for the discipline of sociology. His *Individuum und Gemeinschaft* (3d ed., Leipzig, 1926) contains the traces of an energetic and profoundly critical dialogue with all the essential parts of the relevant sections of my work. It is the peculiar form of gratitude of the "dialectical" mind—and Theodor Litt is a dialectical philosopher in the best sense of the nowadays very popular (to my way of thinking, too popular) method of Hegel—that this school of thought is advanced *through* and *by* criticism and, indeed, relative negation (absolute negation is unknown to dialectical philosophy) of the positions of those chosen for such dialogue. But despite (*despite* is almost synonymous with *because* in dialectical thinking) the fact that in almost all cases Litt turns *against* the theses of mine that he cites, I feel especially obliged to thank him for the *service* which he has provided for this book in his work. For I have learned much from his profound study, most of all from those sections in which he "more or less" seeks to bridge the transition *in* man from nature toward spirit (*homo naturalis* toward *homo rationalis* in their essential meanings) by maintaining that the spirit possesses its form of *existence* (metaphysically, its "condition of manifestation") only in certain mutually interrelated acts of a *social* character (see pp. 323 ff.). I am saving the fruits of what I have learned from his work for my *Anthropology* and do not wish to elaborate on them here.[15]

I could not learn as much from E. Troeltsch's critical remarks in his *Historismus* (*Collected Writings*, II, 603 f.). His assertion that my *Formalism* is lacking in reverence for the individuality of the person, peoples, and the hour of history does *not* pertain to me. The concept of an objective and absolute good "for one's own self" is one of the theses of *Formalism in Ethics* (chap. 6, B, sec. 2). Troeltsch was one of the most estimable German philoso-

15. Concerning Litt's opinion of Hartmann and myself in matters of ethics, see his "Ethik der Neuzeit," in *Handbuch der Philosophie*, ed. A. Baeumler and M. Schröter (Munich, 1926).

phers of our time. I owe him much. But the strict and pure philosophy of subject matter [Sach*philosophie*], which lifts philosophic problems above the great world-*chatter,* called the history of philosophy, and considers them *in themselves,* was not his line.

In Spain it was J. Ortega y Gasset, professor of metaphysics at the University of Madrid, who followed both my value theory and my sociological thought. I refer the reader to "Qué son los valores?" *Revista de Occidente,* Vol. I, no. 4, and his two works *El Tema de nuestro Tiempo* (Madrid: Calpe, 1923) and *El Espectador* (Madrid: Calpe, 1921), Vols. I–III. In Japan the sociologist Yasuma Takata published a perspicuous treatise on the sociological parts of my work (*On the Community as a Type* [Fukuoka, 1926]).

As to the effects that my work has had in the field of *psychology,* my ideas on the "ego," the "lived body," the "person," the types of psychic motivation and causality, and, moreover, the laws of the "levels of feelings" have met with recognition and have been continued. Mention should be made of W. Stern (*Wertphilosophie*), A. Grünbaum (see his *Herrschen und Lieben* [Bonn: Verlag Friedrich Cohen, 1924]), Paul Schilder (see his *Medizinische Psychologie* [Springer Verlag, 1924] and *Das Körperschema* [Springer Verlag, 1923]), the Dutch psychiatrist H. C. Rümke (see his "Zur Phänomenologie und Klinik des Glücksgefühls"), and, finally, Kurt Schneider ("Die Schichtung des emotionalen Lebens und der Aufbau der Depressionszustände," *Zeitschrift für Psychologie,* Vol. LIX). V. von Weizsäcker utilizes my ideas on the "solidarity" of personal acts in a work on medical anthropology that is well worth reading, *Seelenbehandlung und Seelenführung* (Gütersloh: Bertelsmann, 1926).

Formalism has had few effects in the area of *pedagogy.* G. Kerschensteiner has engaged in a fruitful dialogue with my work in his very stimulating and truly *constructive* book, *Theorie der Bildung* (Leipzig: Teubnes, 1926).

Finally, I would like to call the reader's attention to a series of lectures, "Moral und Politik" (which I gave at the Hochschule für Politik, Berlin, winter, 1926–27), and a lecture, "Die Idee des Friedens und der Pazifismus" (given at the Reichswehrministerium, 1927),[16] in which the principles established in this work were applied to these themes. These will soon be published. They reveal the direction in which I would like to see the non-formal ethics of values develop.

16. [Bibliog. no. 28.—*Ed.*]

Every truly philosophical work has a "destiny"—for better or for worse, for truth or for falsehood—which is a mixture of the responsibility of the author and the fortuities of comprehension.

May this destiny not weigh so heavily on this work as it has in the past.

Cologne   MAX SCHELER
December, 1926

Formalism in Ethics and Non-Formal Ethics of Values

With Special Attention to Immanuel Kant's Ethics

PART I

Introductory Remarks

IN A MAJOR WORK planned for the near future I will attempt to develop a non-formal ethics of values on the broadest possible basis of phenomenological experience.[1] At present, Kant's ethics, still widely accepted as valid, presents an obstacle to this undertaking. Since I do not intend to deal critically with other philosophers in this planned work but only to utilize their theories to the extent that they cast further light on my own posiive propositions, I wish to take this opportunity to set forth some criticisms of formalism in ethics in general—especially of Kant's arguments in support of it—so that I can clear the way for my work. In the final analysis Spinoza's dictum, "Truth is the criterion of itself and the false," obtains in philosophy. Hence in this work I can accomplish my task only through revealing Kant's erroneous presuppositions by replacing them with correct ones.

It would be a great error, in my judgment, to maintain that any of the post-Kantian versions of non-formal ethics have refuted the Kantian doctrine. Indeed, I am so much of this conviction that I believe that all such versions which take the non-formal values of "life," "well-being," etc., as the starting point of ethical arguments can only serve as examples of the sort of presupposition whose ultimate rejection is precisely the sole merit of Kant's practical philosophy. For, with few exceptions, such versions are at the same time forms of *ethics of goods and purposes*. In my opinion Kant has refuted, once and for all, all ethics

1. [The author's planned "major work" on non-formal value-ethics did not appear. No systematic work on ethics was found among his papers. —Ed.]

[5]

starting with the question, What is the highest good, or what is
the final purpose of all volitional conations? All post-Kantian
ethics, much as they may have served to cast new light on special
moral values and the details of the concrete situations of life,
manage in their principal parts to provide only the background
against which the greatness, strength, and terseness of Kant's
work stands out all the more.

On the other hand, I am of the opinion that this Kantian
colossus of steel and bronze obstructs the way of philosophy toward a concrete and evidential *theory of moral values* (which is
at the same time independent of positive psychological and historical experience), toward the *order of ranks of these values* and
the *norms* based on them. Kant's work therefore bars us from any
true insight into the place of moral values in man's life. As long
as Kant's terrifyingly sublime formula, with its emptiness, remains valid as the only evidential result of all philosophical
ethics, we are robbed of the clear vision of the fullness of the
moral world and its qualities as well as of the conviction which
we might have that this world is something *binding.*

All so-called internal criticism concerning only the consistency of Kant's system would have no value in this respect. The
concern here is rather to detect the Kantian presuppositions, part
of which he formulated, but a large part of which he simply
passed over—probably because he considered them too obvious
to require explicit treatment. The latter presuppositions are for
the most part those he shared with the philosophy of his time or
those he took over uncritically from English empiricism and association psychology. We will encounter both types in the course
of our investigation. Kant research appears to me to have paid
too little attention to them. In addition, I reject the task of "internal criticism" because my concern is not every little flourish
of the work of the "historical Kant," but rather the idea of a
formal ethics as such, for which Kant's ethics is only an example
—although the greatest, most compelling, and most rigorous of
all.

Let us mention those *presuppositions,* whether stated by
Kant or not, which underlie his theories and which we shall examine in separate sections. These can be reduced to the following propositions:

1. Every non-formal ethics must of necessity be an ethics of
   goods and purposes.

2. Every non-formal ethics is necessarily of only empirical-inductive and a posteriori validity.

3. Every non-formal ethics is of necessity an ethics of success. Only formal ethics can treat the basic moral tenor [*Gesinnung*] or willing based upon it as the original bearer of the values of good and evil.

4. Every non-formal ethics is of necessity a hedonism and so falls back on the existence of sensible states of pleasure, that is, pleasure taken in objects. Only formal ethics is in a position to avoid all reference to sensible pleasure-states through the exhibition of moral values and the proof of moral norms resting on such values.

5. Every non-formal ethics is of necessity heteronomous. Only formal ethics can found and establish the autonomy of the person.

6. Every non-formal ethics leads to a mere legalism with respect to actions. Only formal ethics can found the morality of willing.

7. Every non-formal ethics makes the person a servant to his own states or to alien goods. Only formal ethics is in a position to demonstrate and found the dignity of the person.

8. Every non-formal ethics must of necessity place the ground of all ethical value-estimations in the instinctive egoism of man's natural organization. Only formal ethics can lay the foundation for a moral law, valid in general for all rational beings, which is independent of all egoism and every special natural organization of man.

1 / Non-Formal Value-Ethics and Ethics of Goods and Purposes

BEFORE I COME TO THE DISCUSSION of Kant's erroneous identification of goods with values and his opinion that values are to be viewed as abstracted from goods, I would like to point out that from the outset he correctly rejects all ethics of goods and purposes as having false bases. I intend to demonstrate this separately for *ethics of goods* and for *ethics of purposes.*

Goods are, according to their essence, *things* of value [*Wertdinge*]. Kant maintains that whenever we make the goodness or the moral depravity of a person, an act of will, a deed, etc., dependent on their relation to a realm of existing goods (or evils) posited as real, we make the goodness or depravity of the will dependent on the particular contingent existence of this realm of goods, as well as on its experiential knowability. Whatever these goods may be called—for example, the well-being of a given community, state, or church, or the particular level of national or human development of a culture or a civilization—Kant maintains that the moral value of the will would always depend on the way in which it intervened in the "maintenance" or "promotion" of this realm of goods, whether it expedited or hindered, accelerated or retarded, current "trends of development." Any alteration in this realm of goods would be accompanied by a change in the sense and meaning of good and evil. Since such a realm of goods is continuously changing and moving throughout history, the moral value of the human will and being would also have to take part in the destiny of this realm. A destruction of this realm of goods, he holds, would at the same time dissolve the very idea of moral value. Thus all ethics would be based on historical experi-

[9]

ence, which reveals changes in this realm of goods; and hence ethics could have only empirical and inductive validity. We are confronted at once with the relativism of ethics. Furthermore, every good is locked into the natural causal-nexus of real things and can be partially destroyed through the powers of nature or history. If the moral value of our will were dependent on the latter, it would also be affected by these destructions. Thus it would also be dependent on the accidents of the actual course of causality of things and events. But this, as Kant correctly saw, is patent *nonsense*.

Moreover, any kind of *critique* of any extant realm of goods would become completely impossible. We would have to bow before any arbitrary part of such a realm and simply accept whatever "developmental trends" might accompany it. However, it is undeniable not only that we continually criticize this realm of goods, for example, by distinguishing between authentic and inauthentic art, true and sham culture, the state as it is and as it ought to be, etc., but also that we attribute the highest moral esteem to persons who have been radically opposed to the realms of goods of their eras and have battled to replace them with ideal innovations that were quite contrary to these extant realms. And the same remarks equally apply to the "developmental trends" or the "developmental orientation" of any such realm. In *itself* such an orientation can be either *good* or *bad*. The transformation of the religious spirit and ethics of the prophets into both a rabbinical moral legalism and a fabricated cult of prescriptions and transactions between man and God was also a "development." But this was a "development" toward the *bad*, and that will which opposed such a development and finally brought it to a halt was good. Consequently, every attempt to establish an orientation of the development of the "world," of present "life," of human "culture," etc., in order to measure the value of acts of the will according to their significance for the course of that "development"—no matter if this trend of development is progressive in character, tending toward an increase of values, or regressive, tending toward a decrease of values—also carries with it all the traits of that kind of ethics of goods which Kant rightly rejected.

The same holds equally for any ethics that establishes a *purpose*—be it a purpose of the world or one of mankind, one of human conation, or a so-called final purpose—against which to measure the moral value of the will. Any ethics which thus proceeds necessarily degrades the values of good and evil to mere *technical* values subordinated to that purpose. Purposes are justifiable only when the will that posits or has posited them is good. This is true for all purposes, for it is true of the essence of purposes, regardless of what subject may have posited them. This also pertains to certain "divine" purposes. It is only through moral goodness that we can distinguish the purposes of God from those of the devil. Ethics must reject all talk of "good" and "bad" purposes. For purposes as such are never good or bad when considered apart from the values that are to be realized in positing them and apart from the values of the act that posits them. It is not the particular kind of realization of a purpose but the very positing of a purpose that is either good or bad. It is for precisely this reason that one cannot measure good or bad conduct in relation to a purpose, no matter if it furthers or hinders such a purpose. The good person also assigns himself good purposes. But when ignorant of the manner in which purposes have been posited and the phases in which they have come about, we can never discover in their mere *contents* common characteristics which permit us to determine that some purposes are good and others bad. Therefore, the concepts good and bad are surely not concepts derived from empirical contents of purposes. If we know only a purpose itself, but not the manner in which it was posited, it can be good or bad.

Let us refrain from going further into the meaning and the more precise sense of this great insight of Kant, especially since in this context we expect no opposition from those to whom we address ourselves.

Most important to us is the conclusion that Kant drew from this insight. For he believed that he had demonstrated far *more* than, in effect, he had: that an ethics proceeding by correct methods must exclude as presuppositions of the concepts of good and bad and their constitution not only *goods* and *purposes* but also all *values* of a non-formal nature. "All practical principles which presuppose an *object* (material) of the faculty of desire as the determining ground of the will are, without exception, empirical and can furnish no practical laws. By 'material of the faculty of desire' I mean an object whose reality is desired" (*Critique of Practical Reason*, pt. I, bk. I, chap. 1).

Having correctly tried to set aside actual goods in laying the foundations of ethics, Kant also thought that he could exclude from consideration the *values* which represent themselves in goods. But this would be correct only if, instead of finding their fulfillment in *autonomous* phenomena, value-concepts were to be abstracted from *goods,* or if one could derive them only from the actual effects produced by goods acting on our states of pleasure and displeasure. That this is so is one of Kant's *tacit* presuppositions. And the further conclusion that moral right and wrong, good and evil, concern only the formal relations among purposes (unity and harmony as opposed to contradiction and disharmony) presupposes that there is neither *prior* to nor *independent* of an empirical purpose that is posited by a being any phase in the formation of the will in which the *value-direction* of the will in question is given without any determinate idea of a purpose. We claim that Kant erred in drawing these conclusions. It is from *these* errors—and not from Kant's valid rejection of all ethics of goods and purposes—that the first of the above-mentioned erroneous propositions follows, to wit, that every non-formal ethics must necessarily be an ethics of goods and purposes. This, then, is to be demonstrated more precisely.

1. *Goods and Values*

No more than the names of colors refer to mere properties of corporeal things—notwithstanding the fact that appearances of colors in the natural standpoint come to our attention only insofar as they function as a means for distinguishing various corporeal, thinglike unities—do the names of values refer to mere properties of the thinglike given unities that we call *goods.*[1] Just as I can bring to givenness a red color as a mere extensive quale, e.g., as a pure color of the spectrum, without regarding it as covering a corporeal surface or as something spatial, so also are such *values* as agreeable, charming, lovely, friendly, distinguished, and noble in principle accessible to me without my having to represent them as properties belonging to things or men.

Let us first attempt to demonstrate this by considering the simplest of values taken from the sphere of sensory agreeableness, where the relation of the value-quality to its concrete bearer is no doubt the most intimate that *can* be conceived. Every savory fruit always has its particular *kind* of pleasant taste. It is therefore not the case that one and the same savor of a fruit, e.g., a cherry, an apricot, or a peach, is only an amalgamation of various sensations given in tasting, seeing, or touching. Each of these

---

1. See my treatise, "Über Selbsttäuschungen" (Bibliog. no. 4). [See "Die Idole der Selbsterkenntnis" (Bibliog. no. 10), sec. 4.—*Ed.*]

fruits has a savor that is *qualitatively* distinct from that of the others; and what determines the qualitative difference of the savor consists neither in the complexes of sensations of taste, touch, and sight, which are in such cases allied with the savor, nor in the diverse properties of these fruits, which are manifested in the perception of them. The value-qualities, which in these cases "sensory agreeableness" possesses, are *authentic* qualities of a value *itself*. And insofar as we have the ability to grasp these qualities, there is no doubt that we can distinguish fruits without reference to the optical, tactile, or any other *image* except that given by taste; of course it is difficult to effect such a distinction without the function of scent, for example, when we are accustomed to such a function. For the amateur it may be difficult to distinguish red wine from white while in the dark. However, this and many similar facts, such as decreased ability to distinguish among flavors when scent is set aside, show only the very many degrees of competence found among the men in question and their particular habituation to the ways in which they *take* and *grasp* a particular flavor.

What is valid in the sphere of sensory agreeableness is even more so in value-realms outside it. For in the sphere of sensory agreeableness, values are undoubtedly bound most intimately to the vacillations of our states and at the same time to those things which provoke these vacillations in us. It is therefore readily understandable that in most cases language has developed no special names to designate these value-qualities. Rather, language distinguishes them either according to their concrete bearer (e.g., the agreeableness of the scent of a rose) or according to their sensory bases (e.g., the agreeableness of sweetness, the disagreeableness of bitterness).

It is entirely certain that, for example, the aesthetic values which correspond to the terms *pleasant, charming, sublime, beautiful,* etc., are not simple conceptual terms that find their fulfillment in the common qualities of the things which are bearers of these values. This is shown by the simple fact that each time we attempt to determine such "common properties," we find our hands *empty*. Only when we have already classified things according to a non-axiological concept can an attempt to grasp such common properties—of pleasant vases or flowers or noble horses, for example—have success. Values of this kind are not definable. Despite their indubitable objectlike character, we must necessarily have *already* brought them to givenness with things in order for such things to be characterized as "beautiful," "lovely," or "charming." Each of these words brings together, in the unity of an axiological concept, a series of qualitatively discrete value-phenomena; however, they do not include axiologically indifferent properties, which, by way of their constant conjunction, feign an independent value-object.

The above also applies to values belonging to the ethical sphere. That a man or a deed is "noble" or "base," "courageous" or "cowardly," "innocent" or "guilty," "good" or "evil," is not made certain for us by constant characteristics which can be discerned in such things and events; nor do such values *consist* in such characteristics. In certain circumstances a *single* deed or a *single* person is all that we need to grasp the *essence* of the value in question. On the other hand, if the sphere of values is excluded in attempting to establish a common characteristic of, for example, good or evil men, we are theoretically led not only into an epistemological error but also into a moral illusion of the gravest kind. Anyone who has presumed to bind good and evil to self-sufficient *criteria* from outside the domain of values—whether such criteria are demonstrable bodily or psychic predispositions and properties of men or whether they are those of membership in a class or party—and has accordingly spoken of the "good and just" or the "evil and unjust" as if they were an objectively determinable and definable class, has necessarily succumbed to a kind of "pharisaism," confounding possible bearers of the "good" and *their* common characteristics (as simple bearers) with the corresponding *values themselves* and with the essence of these values for which they function only as bearers. Hence the saying of Jesus, "No one is good but God alone" (that is, goodness belongs to God's essence), appears to have but one meaning, namely, to confirm the above state of affairs against the "good and just." Jesus does not mean to say that no man could have properties that are good ones; rather, he means to say that "good" itself never consists in a conceptually definable property of man—as is imagined by all those who wish to separate the good from the evil, like sheep from goats, according to determinably real characteristics of the order of representation. Behavior of this sort constitutes, as it were, the perpetual categorial *form* of pharisaism. In correctly determining a value, it never suffices to attempt to derive it from characteristics and properties which do not belong to the sphere of value-phenomena.[2] The value itself always must be

2. Nevertheless, there are factors of consistency and contradiction as well as many types of connections among valuations. These, however, are not of a logical nature but belong to autonomous laws in the realm of

intuitively given or must refer back to that kind of givenness. Just as it is senseless to ask for the common properties of all blue or red things, since they have nothing in common except their blueness or redness, so is it senseless to ask for the common properties of good or evil deeds, moral tenors [*Gesinnungen*], men, etc.

From the above it follows that there are *authentic* and *true* value-qualities and that they constitute a special domain of objectivities, have their own *distinct* relations and correlations, and, as value-*qualities*, can be, for example, higher or lower. This being the case, there can be among these value-qualities an *order* and an *order of ranks*, both of which are independent of the presence of a *realm of goods* in which they appear, entirely independent of the movement and changes of these goods in history, and "*a priori*" to the experience of this realm of goods.

One could object, however, that we have shown only that values are not, or at least originally are not, properties of things, and that one could instead consider them *powers* or *capacities* or *dispositions* in things capable of *causing*, in sentient and desiring subjects, certain feeling-states or desires. At times, Kant seems to favor this theory, which John Locke first defended. Were this theory correct, all experience of values would without doubt depend on the effects of these "powers," the actualization of these "capacities," or the stimulation of these "dispositions." [3] The order of ranks among values would necessarily be a consequence of real connections among these powers, capacities, and real dispositions. Were this true, Kant would be correct in conceiving every non-formal ethics as necessarily empirical and inductive; for all judgments concerning values would depend on the effects that things, with these powers, capacities, and dispositions, would have on us as beings of a certain real natural organization; and, a fortiori, all judgments concerning the relations of values would

---

values and have their foundation in essential interconnections and essential disagreements among values.

3. This theory should not be confused with one mentioned later, which reduces values to "permanent possibilities" or to a specific order in the course of such feelings and desires, and which also reduces their subjective existence for us, i.e., value-consciousness, to dispositions of feelings and desires or to an "excitation" of such dispositions—just as positivism reduces the thing of perception to an order in the course of sensible appearances and (subjectively) to a nexus of anticipations between them—so that the value is related to actual feelings as the thing is related to contents of sensation. [With regard to this, see below, pp. 241 ff. With regard to the theory of value (Meinong, von Ehrenfels) mentioned in the text, see the author's "Ethik" (Bibliog. no. 8), sec. 2, p. 91.—*Ed.*]

be dependent on these factors. For one can hardly be inclined to classify powers and capacities as "higher" and "lower"; thus the differentiation would have to be established either according to some criterion of quantity or size of power (say, in terms of some special axiological energy) or in terms of a sum of elementary powers of sorts in things, or this differentiation would have to rest wholly with a subject so that higher values, for example, would be those that stimulate desires of greater urgency.[4]

But just as this theory is fundamentally false for colors and their order—for which Locke assumed it to be applicable—so is it false for values. One inquires in vain as to what in all the world such "powers," "capacities," and "dispositions" should consist of. Are we to admit special "axiological powers," or are these powers none other than those which natural science ascribes to things, such as adhesion, cohesion, gravity, etc.? It is clear that in the first hypothesis a pure *qualitas occulta*, an X, had to be introduced, the entire significance of which is given only through the "effect" that it was to have "explicated"—like Molière's *vis dormitiva*. And if we take values to be simple, special cases of effects which certain natural powers have on desiring and sentient organisms—for such powers do *not* seem to consist in effects among things, since natural science can do without such powers—then this thesis, too, fails. In this case values *are not* such powers; they are rather the effects, the desires and feelings *themselves*. However, this leads to a value theory of quite a different type.[5] The same holds for the assumption of obscure "capacities" and "dispositions." Values are *clearly feelable phenomena*—not obscure X's which have meaning only through other well-known phenomena. Yet, if we *take for granted* the value of a process with regard to a feelable datum that we find in this process, we can, in inexact terminology, designate as "value" the not yet completely analyzed cause of that *process*—but *not* the cause of its value. Thus we sometimes speak of the various "nutritive values" of foods, carbohydrates, fats, albumen, etc. Here, however, we are concerned not with certain obscure "capacities," "powers," and "dispositions," but with chemically determined substances and energies (in the sense of chemistry and physics). Here we take for granted the value of nutrition and also the value of the "food," which is immediately given *in*

4. As to feelings, one would have to speak here of a greater degree of excitability, which, however, would not coincide with the intensity of feelings (pleasure, displeasure).

5. I will discuss this theory in pt. II, chap. 5, sec. 1.

the satisfaction of hunger—and which is sharply differentiated from the value of the satisfaction of hunger itself and, a fortiori, from the *pleasure* that usually (but not always) accompanies eating. It is only after a clarification of this that one can ask: By virtue of which chemical properties can a certain ingredient bear this food value for a certain organism, e.g., man, whose condition with regard to digestion, metabolism, etc., is normal (when perhaps for other animals the same ingredient is "poison"), and by virtue of which quantities of this substance does the food value have this or that magnitude? It is completely erroneous to claim that the nutritive value *consists* in such chemical substances or in the presence of such substances and their diverse quantities in a food. One must not confuse the fact that in the things and bodies there are dispositions *for* values—or, better, for *bearers* of values, e.g., for the bearers of the value of "food"—with the totally different contention that the value of these things *is itself* nothing but a certain disposition or capacity!

All values (including the values "good" and "evil") are non-formal *qualities* of contents possessing a determinate order of ranks with respect to "higher" and "lower." This order is independent of the form of being into which values enter—no matter, for instance, if they are present to us as purely objective qualities, as members of value-complexes (e.g., the being-agreeable or being-beautiful of something), or as values that "a thing has."

The ultimate independence of the being of values with regard to things, goods, and states of affairs appears clearly in a number of facts. We know of a stage in the grasping of values wherein the *value* of an object is already very clearly and evidentially given *apart from* the givenness of the *bearer* of the value. Thus, for example, a man can be distressing and repugnant, agreeable, or sympathetic to us without our being able to indicate *how* this comes about; in like manner we can for the longest time consider a poem or another work of art "beautiful" or "ugly," "distinguished" or "common," without knowing in the least which properties of the contents of the work prompt this. Again, a landscape or a room in a house can appear "friendly" or "distressing," and the same holds for a sojourn in a room, without our knowing the *bearers* of such values. This applies equally to physical and psychical realities. Clearly, neither the experience of values nor the degree of the adequation and the evidence (adequation in a full sense plus evidence constitutes the "self-givenness" of a value) depends in any way on the experience of the bearer of the values. Further, the *meaning* of an object in regard to "what" it is (whether, for example, a man is more "poet" or "philosopher") may *fluctuate* to any degree *without* its *value* ever fluctuating. In such cases the extent to which values are, in their *being, independent* of their bearer clearly reveals itself. This applies equally to things and to states of affairs. Distinguishing the values of wines in *no* sense presupposes a knowledge of their composition, the origin of this or that grape, or the method of pressing. Nor are *"value-complexes"* [Wertverhalte] mere values *of* states of affairs. The grasping of states of affairs is not the condition under which they are given to us. It can be given to me that a certain day in August last year "was beautiful" without its being given to me that at that time I visited a friend who is especially dear to me. Indeed, it is as if the *axiological nuance* of an object (whether it be remembered, anticipated, represented, or perceived) were the *first* factor that came upon us, and it is as if the value of the totality of which this object is a member or part constituted a "medium," as it were, in which the value comes to develop its content or (conceptual) meaning. A value precedes its object; it is the first "messenger" of its particular nature. An object may be vague and unclear while its value is already distinct and clear. In any comprehension of our milieu, for example, we immediately grasp the unanalyzed totality and its value; but, again, in the value of the totality we grasp partial values in which individual represented objects [*Bildgegenstände*] are "situated."

Let us not pursue this matter. Detailed investigations are necessary in order to find out how so-called emotive value relates in the *foundation* of givenness to other qualities or, better, properties of contents, such as simple colors, sounds, or their combinations. We are mainly concerned here with the significance of the possible independence of value-comprehension from value-bearers. The same pertains, of course, to value-relations. We can comprehend the higher value of something in regard to something else *without* having an exact and clear cognition of the things that would correspond to the comprehension of the respective value, and without having in our consciousness anything but a merely "meant" thing that we compare with the one present to us.[6]

It clearly follows that *value-qualities* do not change with the changes in things. It is not true that the color blue becomes red when a blue sphere becomes red. Neither is it true that values

6. The latter point obtains for all relations.

become affected in their order when their bearers change in value. Food remains food, and poison remains poison, no matter for which organisms they may be food or poison. The value of friendship is not affected if my friend turns out to be a false friend and betrays me. Nor is the sharp qualitative differentiation of values affected by the fact that it is frequently rather difficult to determine which of qualitatively different values belongs to a certain state of affairs or thing.[7]

But how do value-qualities and value-complexes relate to *things* and *goods*?

It is not merely as *goods* that values differ from the feeling-states and desires which we experience in their presence. They are already different in terms of the most elementary *qualities*. Apart from the erroneous theory of a "thing" as a mere "order in the sequence of appearances," there is the error made by positivistic philosophers who attempt to relate values to factual desires and feelings in the same way that they relate things to their appearances. As value-phenomena (no matter if in the order of appearance or reality), values are *true objects* and are different from all *states* of feeling. In a single given case a completely unrelated "agreeable" is distinct from the pleasure in it. A single case of pleasure in the agreeable—not a series of cases—is sufficient for us to discern the difference between pleasure and being-agreeable. It is also difficult to see how *goods* and *values* are to be distinguished if values are supposed to be analogues of "things," as Cornelius assumes.[8] Are values to be things of a second order? What is this supposed to mean?

One may add, with regard to such theories, that there is as little truth in the assumption that in the natural perception of the world, contents of sensations are "first given" (for it is things that are given, and contents are given only insofar as they reveal to us this thing as a bearer of this or that meaning, and only in the specific modes of appearances which belong by essential necessity to the structure of a *thinglike* unity) as there

---

7. What we have said clearly shows how unfounded it is to regard values as "only subjective" simply because value-judgments frequently contradict each other with regard to the same *state of affairs*. The argument concerned is as unfounded as the well-known arguments of Descartes and Herbart with regard to colors and sounds, and as unfounded as those which arbitrarily posit the unities of the basic colors on the grounds that one often *hesitates* in distinguishing colors of the spectrum, that is, in determining where one color ends and another begins.

8. H. Cornelius, *Einleitung in die Philosophie* (Leipzig: Teubner, 1911) and *Psychologie als Erfahrungswissenschaft* (Leipzig: Teubner, 1897).

is in the assumption that in the natural view of the world, a pure value-quality is "first" given (for a pure value-quality is given only insofar as it reveals a *good* as a good of its specific kind, and only with the specific value-nuances which belong to the structure of the good as a whole). Every good represents a small "hierarchy" of values.[9] The value-qualities that enter into such a good are differentiated in their feelable whatness, notwithstanding their qualitative identity. For instance, a work of art—quite apart from the objective identity of this "good"—is subject to different "opinions" in its history, as rules of preferring among elementary aesthetic values change. It also presents quite different *aspects of value* to various epochs. Nevertheless, such value-aspects are codetermined by the concrete nature of this work of art as a good and by the inner structure of its value. One cannot add up such aspects to arrive at a mere "sum" of simple value-qualities. But the fact that these "aspects"—these value-contents which come to feeling—are mere "aspects" or similarly determined "contents" comes to the *fore* when, in a certain act of our emotive attitude, we pay special attention to *what* is "given" to us in terms of this aspect of the value-totality of this work of art—even more so when we experience the immediate identification of this good in the changes of such aspects and contents. This is the case, for example, when we make clear to ourselves the realm of goods of antiquity in its historically very different "value-aspects."

A *good* is related to a *value*-quality as a thing is to the qualities that fulfill its "properties." This implies that we must distinguish between goods, i.e., "*value-things*," and mere values which things "have" and which "belong" to things, i.e., "*thing-values*." Goods have no foundation in things such that in order for them to be goods they must first be things. Rather, a good represents a "thinglike" unity of value-qualities or value-complexes which is founded in a specific basic value. "*Thinglikeness*," not "the" thing, is present in a good. (If we are concerned with a "material" good, it is not matter but the phenomenon of *materiality* which is present.) A natural thing of perception may be a bearer of certain values, and in this sense a valuable thing. But insofar as its unity as "thing" is constituted not by the unity of a value-quality but by a value that we fortuitously find on the thing, it is not yet a "good." It may be called a "*complex*" [Sache], a word

9. Since values are differentiated first of all according to height, in the case of goods it is better to use the word *hierarchy* rather than the word *structure*, which is used with regard to things.

that we use to designate things insofar as they are objects of a lived relation, itself founded in a value, to an ability to dispose of such things by a volitional faculty. Thus the concept of property presupposes neither mere things nor goods, but "complexes" [*Sachen*]. A *good,* however, is a *value-thing.*

The difference between unities of things and goods becomes clear when we consider that a good is destructible, for instance, apart from the destruction of the thing representing the same real object, e.g., a work of art (a painting) whose colors fade. Also, a thing can be divided, but the same real object as a "good" is not divided but annihilated; or it may be that such a division does not affect the object's character as a good, namely, when the division pertains only to unessential factors. Thus, changes in goods are not identical with changes in the same real objects as things and vice versa.

It is only in goods that values become "real." They are not yet real in valuable things. In a good, however, a value is *objective* (whatever the value may be) *and real* at the same time. There is a *genuine* increase of value in the real world with any new good. Value-qualities, however, are *"ideal objects,"* as are qualities of colors and sounds.

This can be expressed in other terms: Goods and things have the *same originality* of givenness. With this proposition we reject two things. First, we reject any attempt to reduce the essence of the thing itself, i.e., thingness, to a value, or to reduce *unities of things* to *unities of goods.* This has always been the aim of those who have tried to reduce the unity of a thing to a mere unity of an "economical" synthesis of contents of sensation (Ernst Mach), or to a unity of "usability," "controllability," and the like (e.g., H. Bergson), and of those who believed themselves justified in conceiving a thing as a mere "demand" for recognition (with or without empathic emotive contents). According to these theories the simple matter of intuition—independent of values of specific kinds—has no *thinglike* structure at all, but acquires such a structure only through syntheses, which, in turn, are guided by values. Here a *thing* is only a mere *unity of value.* Apart from other errors which one can find in these theories, the *specific* formations of *unities* of things in the natural view of the world are obviously confounded with the *essence* of the form of unities: thingness. Of course, one can avail oneself of values in explicating the formation of units of things, but not in explicating thingness.

From the viewpoint of the originality of the genesis we prefer to say that in the natural view of the world, real objects are "at first" *neither* pure things *nor* pure goods, but *"complexes"* [Sachen], i.e., things insofar as they are of value (and essentially useful); and that from this intermediate field, as it were, the collection moving toward pure things (with deliberate *setting aside* of all values) and toward pure goods (with deliberate setting aside of all thingness) begins.[10]

[Second], from what has been said we also deny that "goods" can be regarded as mere "valuable things." For, according to the essence of a good, its value does not appear to be situated on a thing; on the contrary, goods are thoroughly *permeated* by values. The unity of a *value guides* the synthesis of all other qualities of a good—other value-qualities *as well as* those which do not represent such qualities, such as colors and forms in the case of material goods. The unity of a good has its foundation in a specific value that fills, as it were, the "location" of thingness (but does not "represent" it). Therefore in a world of the *same qualities things* could be quite different from what they are, and yet the *world of goods* could remain the same. In any area of goods the natural thing-world can never be determining or even restricting in the formation of goods. The world is *originaliter* as much a "good" as a "thing." Furthermore, the development of the world of goods is never a continuation of the development of natural things; nor is it determined by their "direction of development."

In contrast to this, any formation of a *world of goods*—no matter how it comes about—is *guided* by an *order of ranks of values,* as is the case, e.g., with art in a specific epoch. The *predominant* order of ranks is thus mirrored within the order of ranks of goods as well as in every single good. Although this order of ranks of values does not univocally determine the world of goods in question, it delineates the *field of the possible,* beyond which a formation of goods cannot proceed. The order of ranks of values is in this sense *a priori* with regard to a world of goods. Which goods are *factually* in formation depends on the energy applied to their formation, on the abilities of the men who form them, on "material" [11] and "technical" advancement, and on a thousand other fortuities. But these factors alone cannot explain the formation of a world of goods—that is, they cannot do so

10. One must not identify this with the *juridical* concept of "state of affairs," which presupposes the distinction between goods and things.

11. All matter is "material" insofar as it is used in the formation of goods independent of their thing-structures.

without the help of such an accepted order of ranks of values as qualities and an activity that aims at these qualities. Existing goods are already under the *domination* of such an order. It is not abstracted from goods, nor is it a consequence of them. Nevertheless, this order of ranks of values is a *non-formal* order, an order of value-*qualities*. And insofar as such an order of values is not absolute but "predominant," it is represented in the rules of preferring among value-qualities which enspirit a given epoch. In the sphere of aesthetic values we call the systems of such rules of preferring a "style," and in the sphere of practical values, a "morality." [12] Such systems reveal growth and development. But this development is *totally* different from that of the world of goods and is a variable independent of it.

What we have wanted to emphasize emerges clearly from what has been said. First, as Kant correctly and pointedly stressed in his proposition (which we generalize here), *no philosophical theory of values* (be it in ethics, aesthetics, etc.) *may presuppose goods, much less things.* But it also becomes clear that it is indeed possible to find a non-formal series of values, with its order, which is *totally* independent of the world of goods and its changing forms, and which is *a priori* to such a world of goods. It also becomes clear that to conclude from this first great Kantian insight that, with regard to non-moral (and non-aesthetic) values, no contents of their *essence* and graded order are *independent* of "experience" (in the sense of induction), and that there is only a *formal* lawfulness among moral (and aesthetic) values, devoid of *all* values as non-formal qualities, is *unmistakably erroneous.*

2. The Relation of the Values "Good" and "Evil" to the Other Values and Goods

We shall discuss later the fallaciousness of Kant's attempt to *reduce* the meanings of the value-words *good* and *evil* to the content of an *ought* (be this an ideal ought of the sort "it ought to be" or an imperative ought of the sort "thou shalt"), or to show that there is no "good" or "evil" at all without an ought, and the similar fallaciousness of his attempt to reduce these values to

12. See my treatise "Über Ressentiment und moralisches Werturteil" (Bibliog. no. 5). [For the expanded version, see "Das Ressentiment im Aufbau der Moralen" (Bibliog. no. 10).—Ed.] Also see Wölfflin, "Der Stil in der bildenden Kunst," *Abhandlungen der preussischen Akademie der Wissenschaften* (1912).

the mere "lawfulness" of an act (of willing) or, more precisely, to the conformity of the act to a law, i.e., to what is "right." [13] Our concern here is to determine the special nature of the values "good" and "evil" with respect to other values and to determine the essential interconnections they have with them.

Kant correctly separates "good" and "evil" from all other values, especially from goods and ills. He says:

> The German language is fortunate to have expressions which do not permit us to overlook this difference. It possesses two very different concepts and equally different expressions for what the Latin language names with the single word *bonum*. For the word *bonum* the German language uses both *good* [*das* Gute] and *well-being* [*das* Wohl = "weal"]; for *malum* it uses both *evil* [*das* Böse] and *ill* [*das* Übel = "woe"]. *Good* and *evil*, however, always signify a relation to the *will* insofar as the will is determined by the *law of reason* to make something its object [*Critique of Practical Reason*, pt. I, bk. I, chap. 2].

But neither his attempt to deny completely the *value*-nature of "good" and "evil" in order to replace them with "according to law" and "contrary to law" nor his assertion that there is a complete *absence of relations* between these values and all other values has any validity.

Of course, if values were only the *consequences of effects of things* on our *sensible feeling-states*, then "good" and "evil" could *not* be values; likewise, the justification for calling something "good" or "evil" could not be conditioned by its relation to other values. And for a rational being or for God there would be no "values" at all, since they would be entirely dependent on the existence of a *sensibly* feeling being; naturally there would be no "higher" or "lower" values, either. Furthermore, unless one wanted to assert that "good" and "evil" are merely technical values for the value of sensible agreeableness, one would even have to assert that the willing of any non-formal value, be it positive or negative, which tends to realize this value could *never* make the will morally good or morally evil. For in this case being-good and being-evil would be wholly independent of the realization of all non-formal values. And, indeed, this is Kant's assertion. It is for him a matter of complete indifference, with respect to being-good and being-evil, whether we seek to realize the noble or the vulgar, the weal or the woe, the useful or the harmful. For the meaning of the words *good* and *evil* is wholly

13. See chap. 4.

exhausted in *lawful* or *unlawful form*. And it is according to this form that we are said to arrange the positing of a value-content with respect to another one.

Let us not further consider the monstrousness of this assertion, which ignores the fact that the purposes of the devil are no less "systematic" than those of God. It is Kant's *first* error to deny that "good" and "evil" are non-formal values. But they are—avoiding all construction—*clearly feelable* non-formal values of their own kind. Of course, there is nothing subject to definition here, as is the case with all basic value-phenomena. All that can be requested is that one attend to seeing precisely what is immediately experienced in feeling good and evil. Nevertheless, we can ask about the conditions of the appearance of these primary non-formal values, about their necessary bearers and their value-ranks, as well as about the peculiarity of reactions when they are given.

Let us examine this question.

Kant is certainly correct in stating that the realization of a certain non-formal value is itself never good or evil. One would have to adhere to Kant's position if there were no *order of ranks* among non-formal values, no order that lies in the essence of such values—and not in *things* which fortuitously carry them. But *there is* such an order of value-ranks. If it exists, it is perfectly clear what relation "good" and "evil" have to other values.

The value "good"—in an absolute sense—is the value that appears, by way of essential necessity, on the *act* of *realizing* the value which (with respect to the measure of cognition of that being which realizes it) is the highest.[14] The value "evil"—in an absolute sense—is the value that appears on the act of realizing the lowest value. The value that appears on the act which is aimed toward realizing a *higher* or lower value, as viewed from the initial value-experience in every case, is relatively good or evil. Since the being-higher of a value with respect to other ones is given in the act of "preferring"[15]—and the being-lower of a value, in the act of "placing after"—the above has the following meaning: [First], morally good is that value-realizing act which, according to its intended value-content, agrees with the value

14. "Good" in the absolute sense is not identical with "good" in the infinite sense. The latter pertains only to the idea of God. Only in God can the absolute *highest* value be considered comprehended.

15. It is not the acts of preferring and placing after that are "good" or "evil," for these are acts of *cognition*, not of *willing*. [See chap. 5, sec. 2.—*Ed.*]

that is "preferred" and disagrees with the value "placed after."
Evil is that act which, according to its intended value-content,
disagrees with the preferred value and agrees with the one that
is placed after. Although it is not in this agreement and disagreement that "good" and "evil" consist, both are essentially
necessary criteria for their being.

Second, the value "good" is the value that is attached to the
act which realizes a *positive* value, as opposed to a negative value,
within the higher (or highest) level of value-ranks. The value
"evil" is the one that is attached to the act which realizes a negative value.[16]

There *exists*, therefore, despite Kant's denial, an interconnection between good and evil on the one hand and the remaining
values on the other. And with this there exists the possibility of a
non-formal ethics that can determine, on the basis of the ordered ranks of the other values, which kinds of value-realizations
are "good" and which are "evil."

For every non-formal value-sphere that is accessible to the
cognition of a being, there exists a definite *non-formal ethics* in
which the laws of preference corresponding to respective value-
contents are to be established.

Such an ethics is based on the following axioms:

I. 1. The existence of a positive value is itself a positive
value.
2. The non-existence of a positive value is itself a negative value.
3. The existence of a negative value is itself a negative
value.
4. The non-existence of a negative value is itself a positive value.

II. 1. Good is the value that is attached to the realization of
a positive value in the sphere of willing.
2. Evil is the value that is attached to the realization of a
negative value in the sphere of willing.
3. Good is the value that is attached to the realization of
a higher (or the highest) value in the sphere of willing.
4. Evil is the value that is attached to the realization of
a lower (or the lowest) value in the sphere of willing.

16. Higher and lower values form an order that is completely different
from the positive and negative natures of values, for positive and negative
values are found at *every* level. See chap. 2, B, secs. 1, 3.

III. The criterion of "good" ("evil") in this sphere consists in the agreement (disagreement) of a value intended in the realization with the value of preference, or in its disagreement (agreement) with the value placed after.

But Kant is correct on one point. It is in essence impossible for the value-contents of "good" and "evil" themselves to be the contents of a realizing act ("willing"). For instance, he who does not want to do good to his fellow man—in such a way that he becomes concerned about the realization of his fellow man's weal—but who merely seizes the opportunity "to be good" or "to do good" in this act, neither *is* good nor *does* "good"; he is truly an example of a pharisee, who wishes only to *appear* "good" to himself. The value "good" appears by our realizing a higher positive value (given in preferring). This value appears *on* the act of willing. It is for this reason that it can *never* be the content of an act of willing. It is located, so to speak, on the back of this act, and this by way of essential necessity; it can therefore *never* be intended in this act. Insofar as Kant denies that there is a non-formal good which could also be the *content* of willing, he is correct. For such a content is always and necessarily a *non*-moral value. However, insofar as he seeks to identify "good" with the concept of duty and what is in conformity with duty, and insofar as he also claims that one must do what is "good" for its own sake in order to be good, and, consequently, that one must do one's duty "out of duty," he falls victim to this pharisaism.

As an adequate proof of his assertion that good and evil are not non-formal values, Kant maintains that these values are wholly different from goods and ills. If one distinguishes value-qualities from goods and ills, as we did, then this proof becomes invalid. Good and evil are non-formal values; but they are, as Kant rightly says, essentially different from all value-*things*. It is only with and through non-moral values that good and evil are still connected with goods and ills. And within these values they are connected also in fact. All that is "good" and "evil" is necessarily connected with acts of realization which take place with respect to (possible) *acts of preferring*. However, good and evil are not necessarily connected with the *act of choosing* in such a way that willing could not be good or evil without a "choice," or, in other words, without acts of conation directed to more than one of the plurality of value-contents given in feeling. On the contrary, the *purest* and *most immediate* good (and also the purest evil) is given in the act of that kind of willing which occurs immediately and *without* a prior "choice" with respect to the preference. Also, in the case where choice does occur, the phenomenon of being-able-to-will-differently can be present without choosing as such. The act of willing that is devoid of choice is by no means a mere drive-impulse (which takes place only where there is no preferring). However, an *act* which realizes a value—regardless of the being that performs the act—is *never* a value-*thing*. Thus "good" and "evil" on the one hand and value-*things* on the other are mutually exclusive.

We must emphatically reject Kant's assertion that good and evil are *originally* attached only to acts of willing. That which can be called *originally* "good" and "evil," i.e., that which bears the non-formal values of "good" and "evil" prior to and independent of all individual acts, is the *"person,"* the *being* of the person himself. We are thus able to give the following definition with regard to the bearers: *"Good" and "evil" are values of the person.* In the first place, it is clear that any attempt to reduce "good" and "evil" to the fulfillment of a law of the ought would make this insight at once impossible. For it is senseless to say that the being of the person is equivalent to "fulfillment of a law," or to "conformity to a norm," or to "correct" and "incorrect." Kant's consideration of the act of willing as the *original* bearer of good and evil is the consequence of his not recognizing good and evil as non-formal values and his seeking to reduce them to the *lawfulness* (or unlawfulness) of an act. For Kant, a being X is a person only through its performing a non-personal rational activity—above all, an activity of practical reason. Thus the value of the person is determined by the value of the will, and not the value of the will by the value of the person.[17]

In the second place, the bearers of specifically moral values are not even the concrete *acts* of the person, but the *directions* of his moral "to-be-able-to"—with regard to his being able to realize the areas of the ideal ought which are differentiated by basic value-qualities. Such areas construed in terms of moral values are *"virtues"* and *"vices."* [18] (This to-be-able-to has nothing in common with dispositional "aptitudes," though there are "dispositions," "aptitudes," and "dispositions for abilities" *for* its specific directions.) The to-be-able-to concerned *precedes* any

17. See chap. 6, B, sec. 3.

18. It is characteristic of Kant that he does not furnish a theory of virtue proper. "Virtue" is only the *sediment* of individual dutiful acts, which alone are originally "good." But, in fact, virtue (and vice) is a foundation for the moral value of *all* particular acts. The theory of virtue precedes the theory of duty.

idea of duty. It is a condition of the possibility of duty. For what is not within the span of a being's to-be-able-to can still be obliging for this being in terms of an *ideal* ought. It can, however, never form an "imperative" for such a being and be named "duty." [19]

In the *third* place, the bearers of "good" and "evil" are the *acts* of a person, including those of willing, and deeds. We shall discuss elsewhere the theme of deeds as special bearers of moral values.[20] Here we will only point out that the consideration of the act of willing to the exclusion of other acts is but another product of the groundless one-sidedness of the Kantian construction. There exists a large number of acts which are by no means acts of willing, but which are nevertheless bearers of moral values— acts of forgiving, commanding, obeying, and promising, to mention only a few.

With the above we have clearly distinguished the essential difference separating "good" and "evil" from all non-formal values that can reside in goods and ills. For the person is not a thing; nor does the person possess the nature of thingness, as is necessarily the case with all value-things. As a concrete unity of all possible acts, the person is *outside* the entire sphere of all possible "*objects*" (including the objects of internal or external perception, i.e., psychic or physical objects); the person is, above all, outside the entire sphere of *thingness*, which is a part of the sphere of objects. The person exists solely in the pursuance of his acts.[21]

From the above one can see to what extent the alternative which Kant intends to submit with regard to the meaning of the words *good* and *evil* is completely groundless. He says:

> If the concept of the good is not derived from a practical law but rather serves as the ground of the latter, it *can* only be the concept of something whose existence promises pleasure and thus determines the causality of the subject in the production of it, i.e., determines the faculty of desire. Now, since it is impossible to see a priori which idea is accompanied by *pleasure* and which by *displeasure*, it would simply be a matter of *experience* to discern what is immediately good or evil [*Critique of Practical Reason*, pt. I, bk. I, chap. 2].

19. See chap. 4, concerning the differences between norms and duty, and between to-be-able and oughtness.
20. [See chap. 3.—*Ed.*]
21. See chap. 6, A, where the concept of the person is developed in detail.

Kant's alternative is possible only through the completely groundless presupposition that all *non-formal* values are reducible to *relations of causality* between things and *our feeling-states,* which are themselves erroneously viewed (as shall be explained later) [22] as having merely a *sensible* nature. It is precisely this presupposition which leads him to the "paradox of method": "namely, that the concept of good and evil is not to be defined prior to the moral law (to which the concept apparently would have to serve even as a basis); rather, the concept must be defined after and through the moral law (as is done here)" (*Critique of Practical Reason,* pt. I, bk. I, chap. 2).

3. Purposes and Values

I have said that there is also indisputable merit in Kant's ethics in that he *rejects* all forms of ethics which view the values of good and evil as determinations of certain *purposes*—indeed, all ethics which view the relation of a person, a deed, or a willing to any purpose or "final purpose" as the constituting condition of a meaningful application of the values of good and evil. For if one could obtain non-formal values from contents of purposes, or if values could be considered of worth only insofar as they were viewed as the *means* for any purpose, any attempt to justify a non-formal ethics of values would have to be rejected *from the very beginning.* This is the case simply because such a purpose (e.g., the well-being of a community) could *no longer* claim to possess *any* "moral value," since the latter would *originate* only *in view of* it and would have a meaning only *through* the designation of a *means* that serves such a purpose. It is only a precise analysis of the relation of the concept of purpose to the concept of value that can show whether Kant is also correct in saying that all *non-formal* values exist in relation to a *will that posits purposes.*[23]

Conation, Values, and Goals. When one speaks of "purpose," a relation to conation [*Streben*] is not necessarily given; [24] conversely, one cannot speak of purposes in all cases of the presence of (any form of) conation. In the most formal sense "purpose" is only a "content" of some sort (of possible thinking, representing,

---

22. [See below, chaps. 3, 5.—*Ed.*]
23. See *Critique of Practical Reason,* esp. pt. I, bk. I, chap. 1.
24. "Conation" here designates the most general basis of experiences that are distinct from all having of objects (representation, sensation, perception), as well as from all feeling [*Fühlen*] (feelings [*Gefühlen*], etc.).

or perceiving) which is given as *to-be-realized*, no matter by what, by whom, etc. Whatever is related to the realization—or, better, the reality—of the content of a purpose in terms of the logical relationship of a condition or a reason is, in a formal sense, a "means" for the "purpose." According to the *nature* of this relation there is no implied *temporal* difference between means and purposes, nor does it matter whether the realizing factor be "conation," "willing," or, in general, something "spiritual." In addition, when we attribute a "purpose" to something, or when we consider parts of something "purposeful" for a purpose, there is no definite purposeful activity that is implied. Nevertheless, it is essential to a purpose that the content concerned belong to the sphere of (ideal or intuitional) *picture-contents* (in contrast to pictureless "values," and that this content be given as "to-be-realized." This does not mean that it cannot be real *at the same time*. The relation to the future does not belong to the essence of purpose. For a real structure [*Gebilde*] can also "have" this or that purpose (which can reside within or outside it). But insofar as a content belongs to a "purpose," it must be present in the *mode of givenness* of the ideal ought-to-be. Hence this to-be-realized is opposed not to that which *is* realized but only to all contents outside the entire sphere of the ought-to-be and the not-ought-to-be which can be viewed *only* as existing or non-existing objects. Therefore, for every application of the concept of purpose, the "ought-to-be" or the "not-ought-to-be" of something, i.e., *the state of affairs of an ought-to-be*, is the foundation.

The frequently heard assertion that the concept of purpose is basically fulfilled only in the sphere of the "psychic" or in that of the human will, and that it is only an "anthropomorphic analogy" to apply this concept also *outside* these spheres, has *no* foundation. One could reasonably speak of purposes in the very absence of a sphere of inner perception with psychic objects. This, by the way, is also Kant's correct opinion. For he defines the purposeful in the most formal sense as "everything whose idea forms the basis of its reality." Nothing of such false restrictions is contained in this. But this definition does contain a reference to the causality of the purposeful which does not belong to its essence. For even when we know that the "idea as the basis of reality" is excluded, we can still speak meaningfully of purposes.

Whenever we speak of *purposes of the will* (or of human purposes of the will), we are concerned only with a special *application* of the idea of purpose, not with its original and sole region of existence and appearance. *What* tends to realize the given, which is to be realized because of its being given as an (ideal) ought-to-be, is precisely *willing,* man, etc. When we say that "the will posits purposes for itself," that "we posit this purpose for ourselves" (and in all analogous formulations), this "positing" never pertains to the *nature* of purpose with respect to this particular purpose; it pertains only to this specific content, as opposed to others, which becomes that purpose to be realized *through us.*

This state of affairs becomes clear when we observe that it is only and exclusively at a definite *level* of our conation that purpose makes its appearance.

It is not the case that in all conation a purpose and the content of a purpose are given.

First of all, one should not refer to purposes in those cases where the phenomenon of "something welling up in us" occurs. Here, in an entirely straightforward manner, we experience the conative movement in one case without yet coexperiencing a certain "away from a state" and a "toward something"; this is so, for instance, in the case of a pure "impulse of movement," in which the moving concerned does not in any sense become a "goal" or something that is *"striven for,"* and in which, a fortiori, no goal is given. With regard to such a state, it is, I say, neither necessary for the state which is the point of departure of the conation to be first apprehended as in some fashion "unpleasant" or "unsatisfying," nor necessary for it to be experienced as a special kind in order for this "welling up," which is directed *toward* our ego (not stemming from it), to come about. There is a class of cases in which it is the initial restlessness of this welling up that first of all directs our attention to our state and makes its unpleasant nature noticeable, whereas it is the objective conditions of the state, e.g., the musty air or the darkness beginning to set in a room, that do so secondarily.

A second type of conation, which is more acutely determined after its initial state, is one that is characterized from the first by an "away from." Let us call this "conation from" [*Wegstreben*], or "conation away" [*Fortstreben*]. This kind differs sharply from a "conation against" some state that is already given as the object of this "against." This "away from," or "conation away from," has no "goal-direction" in its initial movement. It "finds" one, so to speak, while it is "on its way"—without having been initially directed toward one.

There is a very different kind of conation which exhibits from the outset a clear *"direction"* (not coming from the ego but *approaching* it), but which possesses neither a "picture-content" (be it of a meaningful or representative nature, e.g., "nutrition" or a "perceived fruit") nor a "value-content," e.g., a peculiar nuance of agreeable, still less a *representation* of such contents. Rather, this kind is clearly present in those instances which are described by the impersonal grammatical form [in German usage]: "it hungers me," "it thirsts me." Such "directions" belong to conation quite originally. One therefore cannot at all maintain that all conation gets its "direction" *through* so-called representations of goals. Conation *itself* possesses its own intrinsic phenomenal differences of *direction*. There is not simply one kind of conation (or one kind of movement) which divides and differentiates itself through the multiplicity of contents of representation. This common assumption is a completely arbitrary construction. These experiences of conation are rigorously determined by their "direction" in a manner that is completely independent of such contents of representation. This direction distinctly and clearly becomes a part of a *special* kind of consciousness whenever conation encounters a value that corresponds to or contradicts its direction. For it is while we are experiencing, first, the "fulfillment" of conation and, second, the "contradiction" of its "direction" that this "direction" becomes sharply distinguished for us. There can also be an *identity of directionality* in the presence of a plurality of simultaneous or successive experiences of conation that possess entirely different *picture*-contents.

A direction of this kind is not primarily one toward a special *picture-content* or *meaning-content;* rather, it is a *value-direction,* i.e., an experienceable being-directed (which has a special and unmistakable quality) toward a specific value (which, it follows, need *not* be already given as a feelable quality). With this characteristic, conation takes on a coloration that is expressed by the term *desire,* as in "to have a desire" or "to have a liking" *for* something—which is a state of affairs entirely different from all "taking pleasure *in* something," wherein a certain *picture*-content already hovers before us. In the case of a quiet, relatively enduring, and feelable dispositional state, this level of conation is also expressed by "to be disposed toward something."

There is yet another type of conation that differs from the former in that the concept of *goal* is fulfilled in it. *Goals of conation* differ most distinctly from *purposes of the will.* The goal lies in the very *process* of the conation. It is not conditioned by some *act of representation*, but is as *immanent* to the conation as "content" is to representation. We find such goal-directed conation already oriented toward a goal *before* us without our *positing* this goal through central willing (or wishing), which stems from the ego-center. Such *goal-directed* conation, or *striving* [Erstreben], can itself again be *judged* "purposeful" or not. This is the case, for example, with instinctive conations.[25] This "purposefulness" is then *objective*. An organ of an animal can also have this same purposefulness for the preservation of the species or the individual. But it is therefore not an "actively purposeful" occurrence.

With respect to any "goal," two components must be distinguished: the *value-component* and the *picture-component*. They are peculiarly related in that in conation the picture-component can be entirely absent or present in all degrees of "distinctness" and "clarity" when, at the same time, the value-component is already given in a manner that is *perfectly* clear and distinct. Hence the ontic relation between them is such that the value-component founds the picture-component; that is, the picture-component is differentiated *according to* its possible suitability to the realization of the value-component. As far as the first point is concerned, a conation that already has a value "immanent" to it often *fails* to acquire any picture-content because its progress and the development of its picture-content are impeded by the approach of a stronger conation. Thus, when occupied in important affairs, for instance, we may feel a "pull" (perhaps caused by the facial expression of another person) toward a specific direction in our environment [*Umwelt*]; but we do *not* follow it, and so this *picture-content* of what is striven for does not come about. Or it may happen that the "direction" toward a clearly feelable value "fails to fit" into the structure or "system" of our current conations. The conation does not fit into the interconnections of different conations and is "suppressed" by the value of such an interconnection which releases a "counter-conation" rendering the unfolding of its picture-content impossible. This frequently happens when a conation directed to such values is, at the point of its unfolding, given to us as "not right" or "bad." On the other hand, a conation can receive consent from our central ego on the basis of the value-component while

---

25. When, for instance, we look at them "as purposeful in terms of preservation of the species," etc.

the picture-content still varies to a high degree or changes. What we experience in such cases is the "readiness" to make a sacrifice, for example, or to be benevolent toward people—but without having before our eyes those *objects* for or to which we want to do this, and also without having the *contents* of such sacrifices and benevolent deeds in mind. The *resoluteness* with respect to the *value* of what is striven for is in this case clearly distinguished from the *irresoluteness* with respect to the *what* and *for what* (in the pictorial sense).

Let us put aside the more casuistic cases of this type which might be presented. The question remains, then, *how* and *in what way* values or value-components are immanent to conation. Values are given first of all in *feeling* [Fühlen].²⁶ But is feeling the "foundation" of conation, with its "immanent" value, as perception is the "foundation" of perceptual judgment? Do we first feel the values for which we strive; do we feel them *in* the "striving"; or do we feel them only after the striving, by reflecting on what is striven *for*? Nevertheless, it is *not* the case that feeling-states effect conation, or that such feelings (e.g., pleasure) form the *goal* of conation.

Doubtless there are also cases of two sorts in which a feeling-state or a typical process of such a state, interspersed with visceral sensations (a so-called affect), *determines*, for example, a deed. Either an *"initial act* of striving" does *not* come about at all, so that the affect transforms itself into a series of movements without value-directions—as in the case of a purely impulsive action, which probably does not occur in its pure form in experience—or the affect releases some kind of conation. But in the latter case conations are never *univocally* determined by the affect. Hence, people who have similar affective states may, according to their conative dispositions, do entirely different things.

If, however, a feeling, e.g., the *pleasure* of a certain food, is the *goal* of a conation, it can only be so by virtue of its *value* to the individual (or its disvalue, when, for example, it is "sinful" to eat a certain food). Not the pleasure but its *value* is the *immediate* content of the goal.

We must *reject* once and for all the *presupposition of hedonism*, shared by Kant, that man "originally" strives for "pleasure" (or even self-pleasure). In fact, *no* conation is originally more *alien* to man, and none is *later* acquired. This rare

---

26. More details will be provided on the nature of this "feeling" in chap. 5, sec. 2.

(and basically pathological) aberration and perversion of conation (which might have developed here and there into a social-psychic movement), in which all things, goods, men, etc., are given only as possible and value-indifferent "stimulators of pleasure," should not be made into a "basic law." Let us not concern ourselves with this error. For in those cases where pleasure is the goal of conation, it is in terms of its *value* or *disvalue* that pleasure is intended. For this reason the (genuine) ancient hedonism of Aristippus, for example, was *not* based on the proposition that "man strives for pleasure," as many modern people think it was, or on the proposition that such striving is *directed* to pleasure. Nor was it based on an erroneous attempt to reduce the concepts of "value," "good," or "the good" to *pleasure*, in either a genetic or an analytic sense. It was based on the *contrary* opinion that the "natural man" strives for certain *goods* [Güterdinge], such as property, honor, fame, etc., and that precisely therein lies his "folly." Hedonism held that the highest *value*—not distinguished here from *summum bonum*—consists in the very *pleasure* afforded by property, honor, fame, etc., and *not* in such goods themselves. It was thought that only the *"wise man"* who possesses value-*insight* could seek to *rid* himself of the *illusion* which makes us prefer these things to the *pleasure* in them, and that only he could thereby see that pleasure is the highest "value" (a *presupposed* conception which is *not* derived from pleasure), that it and *only* it ought to be striven for. The content of this ethics is false. But in its method it is at least *meaningful* and does not at all share the presupposition that we reject. For, no doubt, the *experience* of pleasure in a value is itself a value; and just as the value is positive or negative, so is the experience of pleasure in it a positive or negative value.

Having rejected these errors, we return to the question of *how* values are given in conation.

In no case is the givenness of a value *dependent* upon conation, either in the sense that a positive value is identical with "to be striven for" and a negative value with "to be striven against," or in the sense that values can be *given* only *in* conation (unless, of course, they are the values of conation itself, felt *in* the act of conation, which are totally different from the values striven for). For we are able to *feel* values (including moral values, e.g., in moral understanding of one another) in the absence of their being striven for or their being immanent to conation. Thus we are able to "prefer" certain values over other ones and to place certain values "after" other ones without simultaneously "choosing" among given conations pertinent to such values. Hence values can be given and preferred *without any* conation. There is also no doubt—when we stick to facts and do not follow empty constructions—that positive values (i.e., values that are simultaneously "given" as positive values) can be rejected, and that negative ones can be striven for.[27] This excludes, of course, the possibility that a value is only the X of striving or counterstriving. There is, however, a frequent *value-deception* in which we attribute a positive value to something *because* it is given in a positive conation, or a negative value because it is given in a negative conation. We tend to *over-estimate* all values for which we possess a positive conation (or, better, for which we experience the "being-able-to-strive-for"), whereas we *underestimate* those values for which we know we cannot strive, although we still *feel* them. In certain cases we refeel them into negative values through a process of deception, a process that plays a necessary role in the *deception of ressenti-ment* of goods and values.[28] Every adjustment of our value-judgments to merely *factual* systems of conations, which is characteristic of sham resignations and pseudoasceticism,[29] is grounded in this *basic form* of value-deception. Thus one can precisely measure how utterly *false* a theory must be in which this form of value-*deception* functions as the normal and *genuine* form of value-comprehension, indeed, even as a productive source of values.[30]

If it is clear that having values is in no sense dependent on conations, we must ask whether it is by virtue of an essential law that every conation (of this level) is founded on a *feeling* of the value-component of its goal-content, or whether values can also appear *originally* in conations and at best be felt as values subsequent to that. In any case it is by virtue of an essential

27. Conation and counterconation have no more to do with value and disvalue than "true" and "false" have to do with positive and negative judgments. It is therefore a precisely analogous mistake to consider a negative judgment only a "false declaration" concerning a true judgment. Both negative and positive judgments can be "true" and "false" with the same originality, depending on whether they agree or disagree with the state of affairs in question. Analogously, counterconation can be "good" as originally as conation can be "evil," depending on whether the value of conation or counterconation is positive or negative.

28. See my treatise "Über Ressentiment und moralisches Werturteil."

29. *True* resignation consists in the renunciation of the striving for a value that is recognized as positive, and this *in* its being positively felt.

30. Thus, c.g., Spinoza's principle. What we desire is good; what we detest is evil. Good and evil are therefore *entia rationis*.

connection that there also *"belongs"* to every value given in conation the possibility of having this value in feeling. For precisely this reason a value striven for can be identified as the "same" value in feeling it. On the other hand, it does not seem conclusive to us that a value-feeling must in fact underlie every conation in the manner of a foundation, as, for example, perception underlies perceptual judgment. We often grasp values only while striving for them, and we would not have experienced them at all had we not done so. Thus it is often the extent of satisfaction of a conation which first clarifies the height of the value for which we strove.[31] But this does not make this "satisfaction" "identical" with this value, as if values were only *symbols* for satisfaction or non-satisfaction. Analogously, we can ask which value (or which good) we prefer to another value (or good), or which value is a higher one, or which good a more valuable one. We can seek to answer this question by way of a "thought-experiment" in which we ask ourselves what it is that we strive for more while listening to the conations which occur as reactions to represented values. We can ask, for instance, which of two persons is more dear to us, which of the two in mortal danger we would save first; or, we can ask which of two meals we would choose, having been given both. But this practical preferring does *not constitute* the height of a value, nor does it *constitute* the preferring in the sense of value-comprehension. It is only a subjective method, serving to make clear to us which value is higher.

Purposes of Willing, Goals of Conation, and Values. Let us now examine the relation of these basic facts to the *purposes of the will.*[32]

As we can see at this point, goals of conation are in *no* way *represented,* let alone judged. This pertains to both value- and picture-components. The goals are given in conation itself, or in the simultaneous or prior feeling of the value-component that enters it. Thus it is not presupposed that conative picture-contents must be primarily "given" in terms of objective experi-

---

31. Often a certain satisfaction, e.g., the presence of a person whom we did not expect or (in negative cases) a death that we wished for without admitting to ourselves that we had this "evil" wish, is what first makes us aware that we strove for the thing in question.

32. [Because this section deals with the relations among purposes of willing, goals of conation, and values, a subtitle has been added. It corresponds to the one above, p. 30.—*Ed.*]

ence, e.g., perception, representation, thinking, etc. Goals of conation are experienced *in* conation, not prior to it. For it is not the contents of representation that differentiate a (uniform) conation into this or that conation (e.g., the conation for food, quenching of thirst, etc.); it is rather the conations themselves that are determined and differentiated by (1) their *direction,* (2) the *value-component* of their "goals," and (3) the *picture-* or *meaning-content* arising from this value-content. In all of this there is *no* intervention of the act of "representation." [33] Of course, the "content of a goal" can become, on the other hand, an *object* of representation or judgment. However, the *inner movement* [Regung] "to go for a walk" now or "to work" now does not presuppose a "representation" of going for a walk and the like in such an instance. We continually strive and counterstrive for things that we have *never* "experienced" *objectively.* The contents, range, and differentiation of our lived conations are in no case distinctly dependent on the contents, range, and differentiation of our intellectual activity of representation and thinking. The latter possesses its own origin and level of meanings. This implies, second, that the *picture-contents* of conation are not its "primary" but, as we have shown, its "secondary" contents, which are *selected in terms of* value-contents from possible "contents" of "consciousness-of-something" not yet differentiated by "conation" and "representation." Only *those* picture-contents that can become the carriers of such a value-content enter into the "goal" of conation as a picture-component.

In contrast to this, the *purposes of willing* are, first of all, the *represented contents* (of a somewhat variable kind) *of goals* of conation. That is, what distinguishes "purpose" from a mere "goal," which is already given "in" conation itself, and in its direction, is the fact that a goal-content (i.e., content already given *as a goal* in conation) is *represented* in a special act. It is only in the phenomenon of "withdrawing" from conative consciousness [34] toward representing consciousness, as well as toward representing comprehension of the goal-content given in

---

33. One who does not see this point (e.g., Franz Brentano, who seeks to ground every act of conation in an act of representation) *intellectualizes* the conative life by falsely construing it as an analogue of *purposeful willing.*

34. Conative consciousness is therefore to be sharply distinguished from mere "consciousness of conation," no matter if the latter is taken as a reflection on conation or even as an "inner perception" of conation in which "consciousness" is, again, an "objectifying consciousness."

conation,[35] that the consciousness of purposes comes to a realization. Anything that is called a purpose of the will therefore presupposes the *representation* of a *goal!* Nothing can become a purpose that was not first a goal! The purpose is grounded in the goal! Goals can be given *without* purposes, but no purposes can be given without previous goals. We are not able to create a purpose out of nothing, or to "posit" a purpose without a prior "conation toward something."

Such a represented goal becomes a "purpose" of our willing (or of any willing) when such a goal-content (namely, its picture-content) is given as *to-be-realized* (i.e., as one that concretely ought to be) or, in other words, as one that is "willed." Whereas conation can stay on the level of the mere value-consciousness of its goal, the kind of willing that is conscious of its purposes is always a willing of something definite in terms of pictures (or meanings), i.e., a willing of a "content" in the sense of a specific *pictorial nature* [Bildhaftigkeit].

Both the factor of the representation of the content of a goal and the factor of what concretely ought to be must be present in the "purpose of the will." If only the first is present, there is only a mere "wish" (which therefore *also* presupposes the *representation* of its goal, in contrast to conation). But "purposes" can never be given in mere "wishes," nor can they be "wished." We may be able to wish that we could posit a certain purpose, or "that we could will in the direction of a purpose" or "wanted to." A purpose, however, cannot be wished for; it can *only* be willed. Wishing for something to be presupposes a conation for something, whereas the wish *phenomenally* lacks the ought-to-be with regard to reality. On the other hand, the representation of what is willed and willing itself are clearly and sharply distinguished in the sphere of "willing." Every willing of a purpose is thus already grounded in an act of representation; but only, however, in the representation of the content of a *goal of conation*, not in any kind of representation. It is this very *separation* that is *not* to be found in conation.

The above is sufficient to give us the insight that the rejection of an ethics of non-formal *purposes*, i.e., an ethics which claims that some *picture*-content, or the representation of it, is "good," does not imply that a "non-formal ethics of *values*" as such must likewise be rejected. For values are neither dependent

35. For more details on the levels of these processes according to intentions, deliberations, etc., see chap. 3.

upon purposes nor abstracted from them, but are the foundation of *goals of conation*, and are hence the foundation of purposes, which are themselves founded in goals. Certainly every positing of a purpose and every purpose must fulfill the requirement of being morally correct, as Kant rightly says. But this morally "correct" is no less dependent on *non-formal* values and their relations, even on values that are already components of goal-contents of acts of conation. Willing, which makes of a goal-content a purpose, can and should "conform" to *them,* and not merely to a "pure law" of the execution of willing. Willing is therefore no less *"non-formally"* conditioned, though it is not conditioned by *purposes* (as is the case with all merely technical willing, which wills the means for the sake of a purpose).

Since the picture-contents of conation (and counterconation) conform to qualities of values that are primarily contents of conation, any ethics which is a non-formal ethics of *values* does not presuppose any kind of "experience" in the sense of "experiences of pictures," and hence also does not presuppose any contents of experiences of this kind. Only purposes necessarily contain such picture-contents. And inasmuch as an act of objective experience (i.e., an act of "representation") enters only into purposeful willing, and not into goal-directed conation, a non-formal ethics of values is *totally* independent of objective experience in general (especially of the experience of the *effect* of an object on a subject). Nevertheless, such ethics is *non-formal* [material] and not formal. A *non-formal ethics of values* is, in contrast to the entire *picture*-content of experience, *a priori,* because both the picture-contents of conations and their relations conform to non-formal values and their relations.

An important remark should be made here. The purpose in willing originates in an act of choosing, whose occurrence is based on value-goals of given conations and has its foundation in these value-contents through the act of preferring among them. All that we have distinguished as various typical cases of conation, which are thus *below* the sphere of central willing "proper," Kant interchangeably calls the sphere of "inclinations" and the sphere of "drive-impulses." In his further discussions he presupposes the *moral value-indifference* of all *"inclinations"* (which I wish to call experiences of mere conations). Just as he identifies (in his theoretical philosophy) the contents of intuition with a "chaos," or a "disordered hodgepodge" of sensations, into which only "reason" (according to its immanent functional laws) brings the form and order lying in all experiences, so also does he identify—or so he says—all "inclinations" and "drive-impulses" with a chaos into which the will, as practical reason, brings, according to its own laws, that order to which, he believes, the idea of "good" can be reduced.

We can at this point reject this proposition of the moral value-indifference of "inclinations." For it is far from being the case that the most basic moral value-difference among human beings is to be seen in *what* they posit as purposes in terms of choices. This difference lies, rather, in the *value-contents*—as well as in their *structural relations* given already in terms of drives (and automatically)—*among* which alone men must choose and according to which they must *posit purposes*. Value-contents and their relations form the *possible field* for the positing of purposes. Of course, one cannot immediately call "inclinations," conation, and welling up [*Aufstreben*] (in our sense) "good"; rather, it is the act of willing in which we choose the (feelably) higher value from the values "given" in conations that we call good. However, this value is already the "higher value" *in* conations themselves, and by no means does this height originate in the value's relation to willing.

Our willing is "good" insofar as it chooses the higher value lying in inclinations. Willing does not "conform to" a "formal law" immanent to it; rather, it conforms to the comprehension, given in the act of preferring, of the being-higher of value-contents given in inclinations.

It clearly follows, then, that the *possible moral* value of willing is dependent on *the kinds* of value-contents present for its choice, and on the value-height which they represent (in the objective order). It is likewise dependent on the fullness of and the differentiation between values.[36] The moral value of a man, which lies in *this* factor, can *never* be superseded by voluntary comportment, nor can it be converted into such—say, as a result of former comportment of this type.[37]

Moreover, the possible moral value of willing is also de-

---

36. It would, of course, be a *petitio principii* to maintain that the "richness" of a moral man could not codetermine the moral value of his willing because he just "cannot help" having it since it was not self-acquired through willing. For the question is whether the content of willing is indifferent to his moral value. On the "self-acquired," see my treatise "Über Ressentiment und moralisches Werturteil." [See below, pp. 78 ff., and "Das Ressentiment im Aufbau der Moralen," sec. 5.—*Ed.*]

37. Nor can this be done in terms of benefits from the hereditary transfer of self-acquired properties of ancestors.

pendent on the *order* of preference in which conations enter into the sphere of central willing.

For it is completely *erroneous* to assume, as Kant does, that the conations which arise automatically, e.g., all that to which "a human being feels tempted," constitute a total "chaos," i.e., a sum of inner occurrences brought about through mere principles of mechanical and associative combinations, which a "rational will," the "practical reason," must shape into an *order* and a *meaningful* structure. On the contrary, it is characteristic of the nature of a man of high moral standing that the involuntary and automatic appearances of his inner conations, and the non-formal values at which the conations "aim," follow an *order of preference,* and that such conations are an already virtually *formed* complex of contents for willing—as measured against the *objective* order of non-formal value-ranks. This order of preference becomes, in the case concerned, the *inner rule of automatism* of conation *itself* and the inner rule of *how* conations enter the central sphere of willing—and all this in different degrees with regard to different non-formal value-areas.

Modern thought-psychology [38] has achieved great merit for having shown that the *automatic* course of normal representations, which occurs independent of acts of judging, concluding, and all voluntary attention, i.e., independent of the entire "apperceptive" sphere, is not intelligible on the basis of laws of association. Rather, this course reveals throughout a logical directedness and a rational goal-directedness that psychologists have described in several ways. It has been said, for example, that the course of representations is under the domination of "superrepresentations," [39] determining units of meanings, [40] or a peculiar regulating consciousness—or that this course is under the domination of a "task" or some other goal of thought. I do not want to analyze here the value of such descriptions. But only in symptoms of pathological flights of fancy [*Ideenflucht*] can we find a successive deficiency of these factors and at the same time an *approximation* of mechanical associations; however, in this case such mechanical associations are, I believe, not actually reached. A close investigation of the seemingly mechanical and associative combination in such special cases, as well as in both day-

---

38. See O. Külpe, *Einleitung in die Philosophie* (Leipzig: Hirzel, 1918), and esp. H. Liepmann, *Über Ideenflucht* (Halle, 1904).
39. This is the thesis of Liepmann, *Über Ideenflucht*.
40. Not, however, in the consciousness of given "meanings."

and night-dreaming, reveals that the combination is determined by such factors as have been mentioned, even though such factors appear strange to normal living or appear to be structured to only a small degree.[41]

The facts of involuntary conations present an entirely analogous case. Here, also, the simple automatism of the "welling up" of conations contains a *sense,* an order of the "higher" and the "lower" (according to the objective order of values); and this sense gets more or less lost only in the rare cases of partial perversions of conation or in those of severe pathological disturbances of the will. Conations build up on each other and follow each other in the sense of a goal-directedness. This can, of course, vary greatly in degree, intensity, and structure; but it is always present.

An ethics like Kant's, which ignores this fact and takes as its starting point a chaos of "inclinations" whose contents and structures are in themselves value-free, and whose form and order are supposed to be subject only to a rational will, naturally leads to errors *of principle.*

---

41. In modern psychology, too, the principles of association become more and more what they are for phenomenology, namely, principles for the understanding of our psychic life which are based on essential interconnections, and which, like mechanical principles, have a purely *ideal* meaning; they can never be fulfilled and confirmed by experience based on observation. [See chap. 6, A, sec. 3, g.—*Ed.*]

2 / Formalism and Apriorism

KANT REJECTS, with complete justification, all ethics of goods and purposes; he similarly rejects, with perfect *right*, all ethics that are based on inductive experience—be this experience historical, psychological, or biological. All experience of *good and evil presupposes* in this sense *the comprehension of the essence* of what *is* good and evil. All questions about *what* men considered good and evil, how such opinion came about, how moral insight is to be awakened, and by which systems of means a good or evil will reveals itself as effective are to be decided by way of experience only in the sense of "induction," but they are *meaningful* questions only insofar as there exists an ethical comprehension of essence in the first place. Even hedonism and utilitarianism, which reduce the good to the greatest amount of pleasure or collective utility, do not derive their principle *from experience;* if they are to make sense of their position, they must lay claim to *intuitive evidence.* Hedonism may prove by induction that *factual* human value-judgments about good and evil factually coincide with what is useful and harmful (according to the level of causal cognition); and insofar as hedonism does so, it may seek to give a theory of the "valid morality" in each case concerned. But this is not the objective of ethics. For ethics does not try to make understandable what is considered good and evil according to "social validity"; rather, it seeks to make understandable what good and evil *are.* It is *not* concerned with *social value-judgments* regarding good and evil, for it is the value-*content* of "good" and "evil" that is the point in question; not judgments, but *what* judgments mean and whereto they aim is the concern of ethics. The question of whether social value-

[45]

judgments possess a moral intention *at all* presupposes the comprehension of the essence of such intentions. No utilitarianism may claim that social-moral value-judgments do in fact "mean" what is useful and harmful, for instance. If hedonism goes even further and subjects the morality of "common sense" [*gesunden Menschenverstandes*] to criticism, it must all the more lean on an intuitive insight, e.g., that utility is the highest of values.

The independence of ethical insight from experience in the sense of "induction" does not have its basis (as Kant says) merely in the proposition that "the good ought to be," whether or not good actions have ever occurred. However correct this proposition may be, it does not go to the *root* of the matter, i.e., it does not explain why experience is the "mother of illusion." It would be equally valid to say that "experience" in the sense of factual moral deeds (as they are recorded in the history of morals) could never determine what "ought" to be, even if the findings of what "ought" to be were nevertheless dependent upon (inductive) experience and this "ought" were to be found in what was *considered* good (or what "ought" to be done) or evil, i.e., in *experienced* value-*judgments* or *judgments* of oughtness. But the discovery of what is good and evil is in this sense *not* dependent on experience. If there had never been a *judgment* that murder is evil, murder would nevertheless have remained evil. And if what is good had never been *considered* "good," it would nevertheless be good.[1] Empiricism fails here, not because oughtness can never be "sifted" out of being (as Kant says), but *precisely* because one can never sift the being of values out of any form of real being [*realen Seins*] (no matter if we are concerned with real deeds, judgments, or experiences of oughtness), and because *their* qualities are independent of real being.

Although Kant's assertion that ethical propositions must be "*a priori*" is true, his statements about how this a priori should be exhibited are both vacillating and vague. He explicitly rejects in this respect the procedure of theoretical philosophy, i.e., the method which takes as its starting point the facts of mathematical natural sciences, or, in other words, "experience" in the sense of the "empirical sciences."[2] On the one hand he proceeds

1. It is precisely in this regard that Kant makes too many concessions to empiricism, e.g., when he presents his moral law as a "formulation" of what has always "obtained" morally.

2. "I cannot, however, take such a course in the deduction of the moral law" (*Critique of Practical Reason*, pt. I, bk. I, chap. 1).

on the basis of analyses of different examples of moral judgments of common sense, which he praises to the same degree in ethics as he rejects it in the theory of cognition; [3] on the other hand he asserts that the moral law is a "fact of pure reason" which is to be exhibited without recourse to another principle. Much as the last assertion points in the right direction, Kant fails to show us how such "facts," on which any a priori ethics must be based lest it remain an empty construction, are to be distinguished from facts of observation and induction, and how their establishment is to be distinguished from that of those which are rightly rejected as a basis. What is the difference between a "fact of pure reason" and a merely psychological fact? How can a "law," such as a "moral law," be called a "fact" (and a "law" is, as we know, a moral foundation according to Kant)? Since Kant did not know of a "phenomenological experience" that exhibits as a fact of intuitive content [*Anschauung*] what is already contained in natural and scientific experience, he can provide *no* answer to this question. For this reason Kant's procedures in ethics acquire a purely constructivistic character—a charge which one cannot make in the same sense against his theoretical apriorism. This peculiarity frequently occurs in expressions stating that the moral law originates in an "autonomy of reason," or that the person endowed with reason is a "lawmaker" of the "moral law" —in contrast to his saying that "it is the inner functional law of pure will" or of "reason as practical" in which the element of this constructivistic arbitrariness is *missing.* Obviously, Kant does not see the range of *facts* on which an a priori ethics, like any cognition, must be based. [4]

However, since Kant holds as an essential state of affairs that only a *formal* ethics can meet the correct demand that all inductive ethics be excluded, how could he have correctly searched for such "facts"? For it is clear that only a *non-formal ethics* is truly based on *facts* as opposed to arbitrary constructions.

The question before us, then, is this: Is there a *non-formal ethics* which is nevertheless "*a priori*" in the sense that its proposi-

3. See esp. his *Groundwork of the Metaphysic of Morals.*
4. Basically, the situation is no better in theoretical philosophy, where one must *not* start with "science" in order to determine the a priori or even the nature of cognition and truth. Here also the first question is: What is given? And the second question is: Which elements of the given of intuition are of *interest* to "science" in contrast to, for example, the "natural view of the world," "philosophy," and art, and why? The a priori cannot be derived as a "presupposition of science"; it is rather to be shown in its phenomenal foundations.

tions are evident and can neither be tested by something that has been found, prior to such testing, by observation and induction nor be refuted by observation and induction? Are there non-formal ethical intuitions?

A. THE A PRIORI AND THE FORMAL IN GENERAL

SO LONG AS AN UNDERSTANDING IN PRINCIPLE has not been reached concerning the manner in which the element of the "*a priori*" of being and cognition relates to the concepts "*form*" and "*formal*," it is not possible to raise the question of the a priori and the formal in ethics.

Let us therefore see what alone may, and should, be called "a priori."

1. We designate as "*a priori*" all those ideal units of meaning and those propositions that are self-given by way of an *immediate intuitive* content in the absence of any kind of positing [*Setzung*] of subjects that think them and of the real nature of those subjects, and in the absence of any kind of positing of objects to which such units of meaning are applicable. The point, therefore, is to leave aside all kinds of *positing,* including the positing of "real" or "non-real," "illusion" or "real," etc. In those cases in which we deceive ourselves—for example, by taking something to be alive when it is not—the intuited *essence* of "life" must be given in the whole of the constituent elements of the deception. If we call the content of such an "intuition" a "*phenomenon,*" such a "phenomenon" therefore has nothing at all to do with "appearance" (of something real) or "illusion." Intuition of this kind, however, is "*essential intuiting*" [Wesensschau], or, as we may call it, "*phenomenological intuition*" or "*phenomenological experience.*" "*What*" this intuition gives cannot be given to a lesser or greater degree, comparable to a more or less exact "observation" of an object and its traits. Either this "what" is intuited and, hence, "self"-given (totally and without subtraction, neither by way of a "picture" nor by way of a "symbol"), or this "what" is *not* intuited and, hence, not given.[5]

An essence, or whatness, is in this sense *as such* neither universal nor particular. The essence red, for example, is given in the universal concept as well as in each perceivable nuance of this color. The differences between universal and particular

5. [See "Phänomenologie und Erkenntnistheorie" and "Lehre von den Drei Tatsachen" (Bibliog. no. 29).—*Ed.*]

meanings come about only in relation to the objects in which an essence comes to the fore. Thus, an essence becomes *universal* if it comes to the fore in a plurality of otherwise different objects as an identical essence: in all and everything that "has" or "bears" this essence. The essence can, on the other hand, also constitute the nature of an *individual thing* without ceasing to be such an *essence*.

Whenever we have such essences and such interconnections among them (which can be of different kinds, e.g., reciprocal, unilateral, conflicting, or, as in the case of values, ordered as higher and lower), the *truth* of propositions that find their fulfillment in such essences is *totally* independent of the entire sphere of observation and description, as well as of what is established in inductive experience. This truth is also independent, quite obviously, of all that enters into causal explanation. It can neither be verified nor refuted by this kind of "experience." We can also say that essences and their interconnections are *a priori* "given" "prior" to all experience (of this kind). However, the *propositions* that find their fulfillment in them are a priori "true." [6] Hence the a priori is *not* dependent on *propositions* (or *even* on acts of judgment corresponding to them). It is not dependent, for example, on the *form* of such propositions and acts (i.e., on "forms of judgments," from which Kant developed his "categories" as "functional laws" of "thinking"). On the contrary, the a priori belongs wholly to the "*given*" and the sphere of *facts*. A proposition is only a priori true (or false) insofar as it finds its fulfillment in *such* "facts." The concept "thing" and the intuited "thingness," the concept equality and the intuited equality, or the being-equal (as distinguished from the being-similar), etc., must be clearly distinguished.[7]

All that is intuited as essence or interconnection can therefore neither be suspended by observation and induction nor be improved or perfected. Nevertheless, the whatness must remain *fulfilled* [erfüllt] throughout the entire sphere of extraphenomenological experience—that of the natural world view and science. It must also be accounted for in this experience, insofar as its constituent elements are analyzed correctly. No "organization" of the bearers of acts can cancel or change it.

6. Here also truth is "correspondence with facts," but only with facts that are themselves "a priori." And propositions are a priori "true" because the facts in which they are fulfilled are given "a priori."

7. It was Husserl who first distinguished category as concept and as content of "categorial intuition" (*Logische Untersuchungen*, II, 6).

Indeed, it is a *criterion* of the *essential*ness of a given content that it must already be *intuited* in the attempt to "*observe*" it, in order to give the observation the desired or presupposed *direction;* and it is a criterion of "*essential interconnections*" that because of the very nature of the state of affairs, it is impossible to attempt to suspend such interconnections by results of observations thought in different ways (representable in fancy) in opposition to real relations. It is also a criterion that in attempting to find such interconnections through an increasing number of observations, we always presuppose the interconnections in the way in which we let one observation follow another. In such attempts the independence of the content of essential intuiting from the contents of all possible observation and induction is clearly shown. Concerning concepts, however, which are a priori because they find their fulfillment in essential intuiting, there is the criterion that in attempting to define them, we are *inevitably* trapped in a *circulus in definiendo.* Concerning propositions, there is the criterion that in attempting to found [*begründen*] them, we are *inevitably* trapped in a *circulus in demonstrando.*[8]

A priori contents can only be *pointed to* [aufgewiesen] by a procedure utilizing these criteria. For neither this procedure nor that of "bracketing," which aims to reveal everything that is not of the essence, can "prove" or "deduce" a priori contents in any form whatsoever. Rather, this procedure is only a means to make them *seen* or to "demonstrate" them in isolation from everything else.

Phenomenological experience, understood in this sense, can be distinguished from all other experience, such as that of the natural world view or that of science, by *two* criteria. Phenomenological experience alone yields facts "themselves" and, hence, immediately, i.e., not in a way mediated by symbols, signs, or instructions of any kind. For instance, one can *define* a specific red in many ways: as *the* color designated by the word *red;* as the color of *this* thing or a certain surface; as a color within an order, such as the order of spectral colors; as the color that "I am just now seeing"; or as the color of a certain wave length and form, etc. This color appears in the above cases as the X of an equation or the X that fulfills the interconnections of conditions. *Phenom-*

---

8. Thus one can show, for example, that all mechanical principles lie in the *phenomenon* of the motion of a mass-point—if the phenomenon is strictly isolated—and that they are at the basis of all *possible* observable motion, i.e., that these principles remain in all possible *observable* variations of motion.

enological experience, however, is the experience in which the totality of these signs, instructions, and kinds of determination find their *basic* fulfillment. It alone gives *red "itself."* It makes a *fact of intuition* out of this X. It honors, as it were, all the bills of exchange on which other "experiences" draw. We can also say that all *non*-phenomenological experience is in principle an experience through or by means of *symbols* and, hence, a mediated experience that never gives things "themselves." Only phenomenological experience is in principle *non*-symbolic and, hence, able to fulfill *all* possible symbols.

Phenomenological experience is at the same time *"immanent"* experience. For only *what* is *intuitively in* an *act* of experiencing (even if this should point to a content beyond itself)— never anything that is *meant* [vermeint] as a content outside of, or separated from, such an act—can belong to it. In principle all non-phenomenological experience *transcends* its intuitional contents, as is the case in the natural perception of real things. In this kind of experience something that is *not* "given" in it is "meant." Phenomenological experience, in contrast to this, contains *no* separation between what is "meant" and what is "given." Taking our *departure*, so to speak, from non-phenomenological experience, we can also express this in the following fashion: In phenomenological experience nothing is *meant* that is not *given*, and nothing is given that is not meant. It is precisely *in* this *coincidence* of the "meant" and the "given" that the *content* of phenomenological experience alone becomes *manifest* [kund werden]. *In* this coincidence, in the very meeting *point* of fulfillment of what is meant and what is given, the phenomenon *appears*. Whenever the given surpasses what is meant, or whenever what is meant is not given *"itself"* and is therefore incomplete, there is no pure phenomenological experience.[9]

2. From all that has been said, it is clear that whatever is a priori given rests on *"experience,"* as does everything else given to us by "experience" in the sense of observation and induction. Thus everything and anything that is given rests on "experience." He who wishes to call this "empiricism" may do so. The philosophy which has phenomenology as its foundation *is* "empiricism"

9. It should be clear that "phenomenological experience" has nothing to do with the experience of "inner perception." What "inner" perception and "outer" perception consist in requires phenomenological clarification. Only "self-givenness" unifies phenomenological experience, and it is a psychological prejudice to maintain that in order for something to be self-given, it must be given in inner perception. [On "phenomenology and psychology," see "Phänomenologie und Erkenntnistheorie."—*Ed.*]

in that sense. It is based on facts, and facts alone, not on constructions of an arbitrary "understanding" [*Verstandes*]. All judgments must conform to *facts,* and "methods" are *purposeful* only insofar as they lead to propositions conforming to facts. But a fact, at least a "pure" or phenomenological fact, does not receive its "determination" through a "proposition" or "judgment" corresponding to that fact; nor is a fact cut out of a so-called chaos of the given. Moreover, the *a priori* given is an intuitive *content,* not something "predesigned" or "constructed," etc., through thinking. "Pure" (or "absolute") facts of "intuition," however, are sharply distinguished from *those* facts that require a *series of observations* (which is in principle endless) for their cognition. The pure facts alone are "evident" in their interconnections—if they are given *themselves.* It therefore is not experience and non-experience, or so-called presuppositions of *all* possible experience (which would be unexperienceable in *every* respect), with which we are concerned in the contrast between the a priori and a posteriori; rather, we are concerned with two *kinds* of experience: pure and immediate experience *and* the experience conditioned and mediated by positing the natural organization of a real bearer of acts. In all non-phenomenological experience the pure facts of intuition and their interconnections function, we can say, as "structures" and "formal laws" in *the sense* that they are *never* "given" in non-phenomenological experience. But this experience *conforms* to them, or happens according to them. However, everything in both natural and scientific experience that functions as a *"form"* and especially everything that functions as a "method" must still become the *"content"* [Materie] and the "object" of intuition in phenomenological experience.

Hence, we expressly reject any given a priori "concept" or "proposition" that does not permit complete fulfillment by a *fact* of intuition. For in this case what is meant is either the nonsense of an "object that by nature is absolutely unknowable" or a mere *sign* or a *convention* in which signs are arbitrarily knotted together. In either case we would be concerned not with *insight* but with blind *positions* [Satzungen] made only in such a way that the contents of scientific experience, for instance, would "follow," or would follow in the "simplest" way. It is equally impossible to attempt to understand the a priori as a "function" or "power" inferred from an interior or exterior observation, a power whose *effect* is to be found in the content of experience. Only this completely mythical assumption that the given is a "chaos of sensations" which must be "formed" by "synthetic functions" and "powers" leads to such curious suppositions. Even if such mythical interpretations of the a priori as a "forming activity" or "synthesizing power" are not under discussion, and if one believes it sufficient to find pure, *objective,* logical "presuppositions" of scientific experience formulated in propositions by means of the procedure of reduction and then calls these "presuppositions" a priori, such an a priori would only be *inferred* and would not be founded in terms of *evidence* in an *intuited* content.[10] But the a priori character of a proposition has *nothing* to do with its provability or unprovability. Insofar as their a priori nature is concerned, it is a matter of indifference whether propositions of arithmetic function as axioms or as provable theorems.[11] For it is in the *content* of intuition, which fills these kinds of propositions, that their apriority has its *roots,* not in the position which they occupy among the postulates and conclusions that are components of theories and systems.[12]

3. From this it is completely clear that the field of the *"a priori–evident"* has *nothing at all* to do with the *"formal."* Nor has the opposition *"a priori"–"a posteriori"* anything to do with the opposition *"formal"–"non-formal"* [material]. Whereas this first distinction is an *absolute* one, founded in the variety of *contents* that fulfill concepts and propositions, the second one is completely *relative* and at the same time related only to *concepts* and *propositions* with respect to their *universality.* For instance, the propositions of pure logic and arithmetic are *equally* a priori (the axioms as well as the theorems that follow from them). But this does *not* preclude our saying that the former are "formal" in relation to the latter, or that the latter are non-formal in relation to the former. For a *plus* of intuitive content is necessary for the theorems to fulfill them. Moreover, the proposition that one of the two propositions, *"A is B"* and *"A is not B,"* is a false proposition is true only on the basis of the phenomenological insight into the *fact* [Sacheinsicht] *that* the being and the non-being of something are irreconcilable (in intuition). Taken in this sense, this proposition has a *content of intuition* for its basis, and the content is not diminished as content because it applies to *any* object. This proposition is "formal" only for the entirely different reason

---

10. [With regard to Kant's "reductive procedures" and his concept of experience, see "Die transzendentale und die psychologische Methode" (Bibliog. no. 3).—*Ed.*]

11. We find all these misconceptions of the a priori in the literature.

12. In this sense, e.g., *every* geometrical proposition is a priori, no matter if it is an axiom or a theorem [*Lehrsatz*].

that *any* object can stand for *A* and *B;* it is formal with respect to two of any such objects. Likewise, $2 \times 2 = 4$ is "formal" for plums and pears alike.

There are, therefore, *within* the total sphere of a priori insight, great differences between "formal" and "non-formal." We shall soon find, too, that there are very significant differences between the (relatively) formal and non-formal a priori in value theory. But those propositions which are least formal in areas of the a priori and which find their fulfillment only through a maximum of non-formal intuitive content (with respect to other propositions) are not, for such a reason, any less *strictly a priori.* The a priori "non-formal" is the essence [*Inbegriff*] of all propositions that are valid in a more special area of objects, in contrast to other a priori propositions, e.g., those of logic. In addition, a priori interconnections between essences occurring only in terms of *one* individual object, and missing in *all* other objects, are thinkable.

On the other hand, one can distinguish the "logical form" and the "non-formal content" in every proposition that is only a posteriori valid, i.e., that is only verifiable by the facts of *observation.* Such propositions have a propositional composition of subject, predicate, and copula, and a *what* that is formed in these "forms." In other words, the opposition "formal–non-formal" intersects the opposition "a priori–a posteriori," but in *no* sense does it coincide with it.

The identification of the "a priori" with the "formal" is a *fundamental error* of Kant's doctrine. This error is also at the bottom of his ethical "formalism," even at the bottom of "formal idealism" as a whole, as Kant calls his doctrine.

4. This error is closely connected with another one, namely, Kant's identification of the "non-formal" (in both the theory of cognition and ethics) with "*sensible* [sinnlichen] content," and the "a priori" with what is "*thought*" or what has been an *addition* to such "sensible content" by way of "reason." Within his ethics the "*given of sensation,*" supposedly brought about by an "effect of things on receptivity," corresponds to the specific *sensible feeling-states* of *pleasure* and *displeasure,* through which "things affect the subject."

This identification, according to which *sensible content* is "*given*" to thinking, is also a mistake in theoretical areas: the concepts of "sensible content" and "sensation" designate nothing whatsoever that determines content as *content*; they simply indicate *how* a content (e.g., a sound, a color with its phenomenal properties) *comes upon us*. For the "sensible" is nothing *in* a color or *in* a sound. These concepts especially require the *most intensified* phenomenological clarification, for it is necessary to find the fact in which the concept of "sensible content" is fulfilled.

As I see it, the πρῶτον ψεῦδος of this identification is that one asks what *can be* given instead of simply asking what *is* given. One assumes in this fashion that nothing "can" be *given* at all when sensory functions (even sense organs and sensory stimuli) for it are lacking. Once entangled in this basically false way of expressing the problem, one must conclude that all such *given* contents of experience which *go beyond* the elements of its "sensible content" and are not congruent with them are something *added* by us or are results of our *"activity,"* a "forming," a "treatment," etc. Consequently, relations, forms, Gestalten, values, space, time, motion, objectivity, being and non-being, thingness, unity, multiplicity, truth, causality, the physical, the psychic, etc., must all, without exception, be reduced to a "forming" or "feeling into" [*Einfühlung*] or some other kind of subjective "activity." For these are supposedly *not* contained in the "sensible content," which alone *"can"* be given to us, and which alone *therefore* (following this line of reasoning) "is" given.

The mistake is that one does not simply ask *what* is given in meaning [*meinenden*] intentionality *itself,* but instead one *mixes* into the question *extra*intentional viewpoints and theories (which may be only natural theories of everyday life) of an objective or even a causal sort. But in this simple question of *what* is given (in an act), one must focus solely on this *what.* Every conceivable objective extraintentional *condition* for the occurrence of the act—e.g., that an "ego" or "subject" performs the act, that the subject has "sensory functions," "sense organs," or a lived body [*Leib*]—pertains no more to the question of *what* is "given" in having a sound or the color red and how this kind of givenness looks than the claim that a main has lungs and two legs pertains to his seeing a color. It is only in the *direction* of the intentional act, *apart* [herausgelösten] from the person, the ego, and the totality of the world in which we are seeing, that we can observe and see the *what* and how it appears. This we do quite independently of the question of how the given can appear or how it occurs to us from the viewpoint of any *real* presuppositions concerning extant things, stimuli, human beings, etc.

In seeing a materially extended cube, for example, I can ask what is given. It would be basically erroneous to answer that the perspectival side of the cube is given, or even that "sensations" of it are given. The "given" is the cube as a *whole*—as a material thing of a certain spatioformal unity that is not split up into "sides" or "perspectival aspects." That as a matter of fact the cube is only *visually* given, and that visual elements in the content of perception correspond only to such points of the seen thing—of all this, nothing is "given," just as the chemical composition of the cube is not "given." Rather, a very rich and complicated series of *ever new* acts (of the same kind, i.e., of natural perception), and a combination of them, is necessary for the "perspectively visible side of the cube" to enter into the experience of it. Let us give a rough sketch of the stratification of such acts.

First, an act of ego-apprehension, i.e., an apprehension of the ego performing the act, as well as a glance at what is given to *this* very ego, must come into play. The cube is still given as before, but with an individual character permeating *everything* given. Second, one would have to apprehend in a further act that the act of perception happens through an *act of seeing* in which not everything appears that was first given, e.g., the "materiality," or the cube's "having an inside." In this act of seeing, there remains only a certain formed, colored, and shaded *shell* of the whole "given," i.e., there is still the *thinglike* (but *immaterial*) object of seeing.

But even at this point the "perspectival side" of the cube, not to mention the so-called content of sensation, is not revealed in the cube's givenness. What is now "given" is this *seen thing of the cube*, i.e., something which, though it does not contain "corporeity," nevertheless does contain *thingness* as a base for form, color, light, and shadows, and which is the *whole* of the extended form in which colors, light, and shadows enter as dependent appearances grounded in the extended *form*. If this "extended form," would change, such partial appearances would change also. I can see "shadows," for example, only in terms of certain qualities of shades of gray which are grasped as *properties of a seen thing*. In very refined margins, shades of colors would change in their apparent contents if the distances and positions of the spatial elements of the seen form were changed by an alteration of the *form-unity*, e.g., if the cube were projected on a plane. For if the coordinate dimension of the localization of the color changes, then its brightness changes also. Moreover, we can establish the fact of a *"seeing"* without necessarily having knowledge of sense organs by way of perception or organic sensations.

"To see" is different from a mere belongingness of the colorful to, say, a perceiving ego; for "to see" is not identical with "to have colors," "to hear" with "to have sounds." Besides, "to see" is also different from mere attention paid to a color. It is a *function* of a definite kind which yields intuition; it has special laws of activation which are completely independent of the organization of the peripheral sense organs. For instance, in "seeing" a plane, the fact that it has another side is *additionally* given, although we do not have a "sensation" of the other side. Consequently, this "*seen thing*" of the cube is by no means the perspectival view of its spatial cube-form. In a seen thing the lines, as "sensed" within the borders of this perspectival side, continue to run *farther* in the *directions* prescribed by the form of cubeness "given" as a whole. This given cubeness is no "synthesis of perspectival sides," nor does it at all "consist" in such a synthesis. The relations of sensed spatial elements are *subordinated* to the seen form according to position, distance, direction of the linear elements, and the order of dimensional depths; and they vary with it. The same positions, distances, and linear directions would vary ever anew if they were parts of a seen thing of the form "sphere." It is in this fact that the space of seen things is sharply distinguished from the space of geometry, which is an artificially *deformed* space.

In order to cut, as it were, the "perspectival side" out of the seen thing on the above bases, a *new* act of experience is required. This cut requires that the existence and the determinateness of the place of the *lived organism* (apprehended as belonging to the perceiving "ego") which performs the act of seeing, as well as *those* parts of the lived organism to which the activation of the visual function is attached, become the object of a *special* act of perception. For example, the fact that I see by way of some activation of my eyes, rather than my ears, lies neither in the intuition of the *function* of seeing nor in that of the seen *thing*. We know only through an "experiment" of a natural type (which we all make early in our lives) that our seeing a seen thing stops when we close our eyes, and that with the movement of our eyes (accompanied by organic and muscular sensations), or with increased distance between the seen thing and the lived body bearing our eyes, there occur manifold changes in the properties of the seen thing. But it is always necessary that a seen thing, in the above sense, be already "given," and that it be "given" in determinate size-*qualities*, if such possible distinctions of variation (e.g., toward the "bigger" or the "smaller") are to be set off—insofar as the factual variations are conditioned by the mere facts of natural perspectives, distances, position, and distance from the organ or its felt strata. (This size-*quality* is, of course, no measurable size; it is wholly dependent on the extent to which the seen thing partakes in the spatial occupation of the *entire* visual space concerned, and therefore it is also relative to the participation of the other seen things in visual space.) It is only through a perception of the relationship of the fact of the seen thing given in separate experiential acts to my lived body [*Leibes*] and eyes and the above "experiment" that the variations of the seen thing come to stand out from the "perspectival side-view." I can know what a perspectival side of a body is only *if* this variation is given. Thus it is in a specific act that the naïve starting point of a sensualistic epistemologist can be given: the "perspectival side-view of this cube." However, it is still a long way from here to "contents of sensation."

Phenomenologically, *"contents of sensation,"* i.e., those immediately *given* as contents of a "sensation," are only those which in their coming and going imply some variation of our experienced *lived-body* [leiblichen] states. Such contents are not "inferred," either by means of an analogy to genuine and immediately given "contents of sensation" or by means of a causal conception of a stimulus and the subsequent reaction in an organism. And among such contents we do *not* find *any* sound, color, or qualities of smelling and tasting, but hunger, thirst, pain, lust, and tiredness, as well as all *"organic sensations"* faintly localized in specific organs. These are the *prototypes* of "sensation," sensations that one *"senses"* [*die man* "empfindet"]. All sensations which occur with the activation of sense *organs* and which simultaneously change with the organs' changed activations also belong, of course, to this category.

For the sake of *linguistic convenience* one can also designate as "contents of sensation" *all* elements of outer perception which can partake (in their appearing and disappearing) in a change of the state of the lived body. This can be done, not because they *are* themselves sensations, but because their realization is regularly accompanied by genuine sensations (in the ear, eye, etc.) of a psychophysical individual, and because every alteration of the simplest *contents* of intuition, e.g., a color and a plane, is coordinately attached to an *alteration* of the sensory state of the *lived body*, including the organ, according to sound, for instance, or satiation, brightness, or Gestalt.

In this *enlarged* sense, "sensation" is not a specific *object,* nor is it a *content* of intuition, like "red," "green," or "hard," or a small "element" of a composite fact, like part of a mosaic. It is only a *direction of variation* of the outer (*and* inner) world of appearances when it is experienced as *dependent* on a *present lived body* of an individual. This would be the *essence* of "sensation," and everything that can vary in this direction is de facto "sensation." [13]

Thus understood, a "content of sensation" is *never* "given" in any sense of the word. Only through an act of comparing a plurality of appearances that are still given with a plurality of states of the lived body can one determine what can be changed in appearance on the occasion of changes in the lived states. Strictly speaking, sensation in this enlarged sense is only a name for a "variable relation" that obtains between a state of the lived body and appearances of the outer (or inner) world. Its content is only the *final point* of the defined relation between the lived body and appearances *in* the appearances. If states of the lived body or states of organic sensations in sense organs are in a process of change, those elements of an appearance are "sensed" through whose variation the *entire* appearance is changed.

A "pure" sensation is therefore *never* given. It is always a specific X, or, better, a *symbol,* with which we describe those dependencies. The pure sensation of red, as a specific quality, intensity, brightness (e.g., of color geometry), is never "given," since only the color of an object, codetermined by the so-called sense-memory, can be given. Color is already demarcated and determined by the previous visual commerce that has taken place with this object.

No presumptive construction of the contents of intuition out of "sensations" could *ever* be a philosophic task. On the contrary, the task lies in a maximal purification of the intuitive contents through elimination of the organic sensations which always accompany these contents and which are the only "genuine" sensations; and it lies as well in peeling off those characteristics of contents of intuition which, far from being contents of "pure" intuition, are contents that are *received* only by their entering into a fixed union with organic sensations, thereby serving as a "symbol" for an expected change in the state of the lived body.

13. [For a discussion of sensation, excitation, and organism, see below, pp. 138 ff. See also the author's later work, "Erkenntnis und Arbeit" (Bibliog. no. 22), sec. 5.—*Ed.*]

Whatever is valid in theoretical areas is valid in terms of a far-reaching analogy for *values* and *willing*.

In theoretical areas the "givens" are, according to the natural attitude, things; in matters of values and willing, *goods*. The values that we *feel* in goods, as well as the "feeling of values" itself, are only secondarily given. Independently, and thirdly, however, there are the *feeling-states* of pleasure and displeasure, which we reduce to the effect that goods have on us (and this effect can be understood causally or as an *experienced* stimulus); last of all, there are the states of specific *sensible* feeling which are interwoven with feeling-states (the "feeling-sensations" [*Gefühlsempfindungen*], as Stumpf aptly calls them). These feeling-states are experienced in a special manner in that we view different parts of the spatialized and organically structured lived body (present to us in inner perception) and connect the given peripheral feeling-states with the qualities of agreeableness in terms of a (more or less conscious) *thought*-connection or with the qualities that are interwoven in goods. For the values of the *agreeable* are *distinct* from their accompanying sensible feeling-states (e.g., the agreeableness of sugar is distinct from the pleasant feeling of it on the tongue). Consequently, what in the "material" of feeling corresponds to *sensible* feeling-states as a *related object* so that the variation of these states *depends* on the object, or what in this sense is the "sensible content" (which, strictly speaking, should not be so *called*) of the value-content as such, is never given *in* this material, let alone primarily given —as if goods stood before us as mere "causes" of such states. A sensible feeling-state in our lives is *in* and *on* the world of values and goods and is, in our action and conduct in this realm, welded to our lived body as a secondary symptom. This is the case in sensory enjoyment and even more so in *those* value-spheres that are *above* the agreeable, i.e., in spiritual and vital value-ranks. A special *intention* toward these states, a deflection from the objective emotive *direction,* is not only rare but at the same time a comportment leading to disease.[14]

Analogous remarks hold true for *conation* and *willing.* Kant asserts that *no* willing determined by a *material* (and not by a "law of reason") is *a priori* determined, because in his view it is determined by the contingent *reaction* of our *sensible* feeling-states to the content which is realized through willing. But this has *no* factual basis whatsoever.

14. See my treatise "Über Selbsttäuschungen" (Bibliog. no. 4).

The stronger and more intense willing is, the more we are *lost* in the *value* (to be realized) and the pictorial contents given in willing; in cases of the most intense willing, the *willed-through-us* of the content is *least given*. It is precisely in cases of weak willing that the *willing* of contents with "exertion" becomes most distinct. Being completely "lost" in one's projects and their realization is a typical attitude of the daring man of action, e.g., the man of great enterprises—in the highest form, the man of heroic character.[15] But this phenomenon, before us in a macrocosmic view, shows itself microscopically in every intense act of willing. This act is always characterized by its *drawing* us *beyond* the ideas of the reactions it evokes in our states, especially in our sensible states. For instance, we do not notice that we hurt ourselves during a dangerous kind of work, or that feelings of tiredness and even pain protest against it. All passionate willing, especially its highest forms, leaves simultaneous sensible feeling-states, or those to be expected, completely outside the sphere of givenness. These facts make it understandable that among persons of very powerful will, and especially among energetic groups in history, the very consciousness of the *departure* of willing from the "ego"—let alone its reaction *on* the ego—was developed least. They experienced the effectiveness of their will as "grace" (e.g., the energetic English Puritans, like Cromwell and

---

15. One can easily confuse this with the tendency characteristic of the non-energetic dreamer, that is, the tendency to take mere wish-contents of fantasy and daydreaming as if they were given as real in consciousness, a tendency most pronounced in illusion and hallucination. In other words, what is merely wished for or practically striven for is *anticipated* in its existence, and its reality is relished and enjoyed in advance. This is the case, for instance, when we live in the reality of the content of a purpose contained in a plan which we started to realize but which requires much more of us than we feel able to do. Conversely, the tendency to anticipate what has been wished for and what has been only halfway accomplished and to relish it in advance in one's feelings can bear negatively on the energy to realize it. To some extent we find this in persons who are always planning [*Projektemacher*]. The "realization of wishes" applied by Freud and his school to contents of dreams, the effect of the wish on contents of remembrance, and the effect of the wish on contents of expectation are relevant in this connection. In contrast to this, the strong-willed person "lives" in his projects *as* "projects," as contents "to be realized," but they do not acquire this *token* reality; at the same time this person has a cold-blooded outlook toward the real, which is given to him in its causal nexus in sharply distinguished intentions. Whereas in the former case the anticipated project is already relished and enjoyed "as real," in the latter case it has the dynamic effect of bringing before the eyes an entire network of means within the field of possible control (which is then to be analyzed in deliberations). It is a hallmark of the strong-willed man to distinguish *sharply* the real from the non-real and to live fully in his projects.

his circle), or they felt themselves to be completely tools of God (e.g., Calvin, as God's "instrument"), or they experienced the stages in their life-development as "fate" (e.g., the energetic Arabs and Turks, Wallenstein, and Napoleon), or they viewed themselves as having furthered and released only developmental tendencies (e.g., Bismarck). Theories about "great men" have never come from great men, only from their *beholders*.[16]

The primarily given *content* is not a possible repercussion of that which is willed on the sensible feeling-state (or a vital or spiritual one). Rather, to the same degree as an expectation or representation of the feeling-state occurs, there is an impediment, a limitation, or perhaps a "postponement" of willing the content concerned, so that it turns into a content which is merely wished or not even willed anymore. Therefore the effect of feeling-states on the content of willing is *in essence negative and selective*. Of the primary willed content, it is not the *what* but *what* we "no longer" will that is *primarily* determined by feeling-states.[17]

Kant directly reverses the facts when he presupposes that all contents of willing are *determined* by experiences of pleasure and displeasure. Even when the idea of "law" is determining for willing, "law" is still the *content* of the will (at least of the pure will); it is not determining as a law that is the law *of* the pure will, i.e., a law *according to* which willing took place. The realization of the "law" is willed as *one* of the possible contents of will. It is for this reason that all willing has its foundation in *contents*, which can nevertheless be a priori insofar as they consist in *value-qualities* according to which *pictorial contents* form themselves. Willing is therefore not in the least determined by "sensible feeling-states."

No less erroneous is the identification of the "a priori" with the *"rational"* (or *"thought"*), which corresponds to the identification of the "non-formal" with the "sensible" (as well as the a posteriori). We saw earlier that the a priori is first a "given" of an

16. It would be the greatest of errors to identify this phenomenon of strongest *willing* (ecstatic willing, as it were) with the facts of mere wellings up and instinctive strivings simply because both are experienced as *not* coming from the ego. They are opposite extremes of the continuum of facts of striving, whose center is represented by the "I will" (as experience). The first fact is by all means a most central willing and, indeed, a willing proper of the "person"; as the point of departure for all acts, it is totally different from the object of inner perception or the "ego." See chap. 6, A.

17. See chap. 3.

intuition, and that the propositions which are "thought" in judgments can be called a priori only insofar as they find their fulfillment in the facts of phenomenological experience. Even in theoretical cognition, then, the a priori is by no means something merely and primarily "thought." Indeed, no doctrine has obstructed the theory of cognition more than the one proceeding from the presupposition that a factor in cognition *must* be *either* a "sensible content" *or* something "thought." How can one bring to fulfillment, on this presupposition, concepts such as thing, real, force, equality, similarity, effect (within the concept of causality), motion, space, time, quantity, number, or—and this is our concern here—the value-concepts? There must be for them a *datum* of intuition—to be sure, *not* a datum of "sensible" character; otherwise these concepts—including the essential interconnections obtaining among them, for instance, the principles of mechanics—would have to be "fabricated" [er*dacht*], i.e., posited out of nothingness by "thinking." This presupposition alone *always* implies an unsatisfactory solution to the problem of cognition. Whatever such a solution may be (more sensualistic or more rationalistic), it will doom cognition to the degree that it has *content* [Inhalt], which here obviously means "sensible" data or the cognition based on them, since such content is "*subjective*" and "*relative*" to the organization of man. Cognition is doomed to become *bare* of content—in the final analysis, to become mere relations that are relations of nothing—to the degree that it is reduced to purely *logical* factors.

But the identification of the "a priori" with "thought," and "apriorism" with "rationalism," as Kant would have it, leads to yet another basic fallacy, one that is especially detrimental to ethics.

For it is our *whole* spiritual life—and not simply objective thinking in the sense of cognition of being—that possesses "pure" acts and laws of acts which are, according to their nature and contents, *independent* of the human organization. The *emotive* elements of spirit, such as feeling, preferring, loving, hating, and *willing*, also possess original a priori contents which are not borrowed from "thinking," and which ethics must show to be independent of logic. There is an a priori *ordre du coeur*, or *logique du coeur*, as Blaise Pascal aptly calls it.[18] Since its introduction by the Greeks, the term *reason*, or *ratio*—especially when placed in opposition to so-called sensibility—has always designated

---

18. Here we cannot elaborate upon the meaning of this great idea. See chap. 5, sec. 2. [See also "Ordo Amoris" (Bibliog. no. 29), which was written between 1916 and 1917.—*Ed.*]

only the logical side of spirit, not the *non-logical a priori* side. Thus Kant reduces "pure willing" to "practical reason," or "the" reason insofar as it is practically effective, and with this he misconceives the *originality* of the act of will. Willing appears merely as an area of application for logic, not as having a lawfulness of the *same originality* as that of thinking. It may well be that the same ultimate phenomenal content fulfills, for example, the principle of contradiction as well as the impossibility of "to will and not to will the same thing," or to strive for and to detest the same thing. This, however, does not make the latter a mere "application of the principle of contradiction" to the concepts of striving and detesting. The latter is a basic principle independent of the former, sharing (in part) only an *identical* phenomenological basis with it. Thus *axioms of values* are wholly independent of logical axioms and are not mere "applications" of the latter to values. Logic and a *pure doctrine of values* [reine Wertlehre] stand *side by side.* Though Kant wavers on these questions, he becomes all the more firm in his position that all feelings, even love and hate, basically belong to the "sensible" sphere; he excludes them from ethics because he cannot assign them to "reason." [19]

This wholly unfounded restriction and limitation of the "a priori" also has its roots in his identification of the a priori with the *"formal."*

Only with the final dismissal of the ancient prejudice that the human spirit is *exhausted* in the contraposition of "reason" and "sensibility," or that everything must be subordinated to the former *or* the latter, is the structuration of an *a priori non-formal ethics* made possible. This groundless dualism, whose erroneous implications compel one to neglect and misinterpret the *peculiar properties* of whole classes of acts, must in every respect vanish from the door of philosophy. The *phenomenology of values* and the *phenomenology of emotive life* are completely independent of logic, having an autonomous area of objects and research.[20]

19. It is this prejudice that led Kant to the monstrous opinion that love and hate are "sensible feeling-states."

20. Ultimately the apriorism of love and hate is the irreducible foundation of *all* other apriorisms (but we cannot demonstrate this here). It is the foundation of a priori cognition of being, as well as of a priori willing of contents. It is in the apriorism of love and hate, not in the primacy of either "theoretical" or "practical" reason, that the spheres of the theoretical and the practical find their ultimate phenomenological unity. Franz Brentano has maintained something like this. But we will not pursue this point. [See "Liebe und Erkenntnis" (Bibliog. nos. 11, 19).—*Ed.*]

Kant therefore has no grounds for his assumption that any utilization of "feeling," "loving," "hating," etc., in the sense of basic moral acts is an *erroneous deviation* of ethics toward "empiricism" or the "sensible," or a false basis in the "nature of man" for the cognition of good and evil. For feeling, loving, hating, and *their* laws obtaining among them and their correlative contents, are no more "specifically human" than are acts of thinking, no matter how they may be studied as *belonging to* man [am *Menschen*]. Their *phenomenological* analysis, which consists esssentially in setting aside both the specific organizations of the bearers of acts and all positing of real objects so that the *essence* of these *act-classes* and their *contents* can be discovered, is distinguished from all psychology and anthropology as the phenomenological analysis of thinking is distinguished from the psychology of thinking. A *spiritual* level also exists for this analysis, one that has nothing to do with the sphere of the sensible or the sphere of the vital or of the lived body, which is to be sharply distinguished from the sensible sphere. The inner lawfulness of these act-classes is as independent of *their* lawfulness as the laws of thought are of the activity of sensations.

Hence, contrary to Kant, we recognize an *emotive apriorism* as a definite necessity, and we demand a new division of the false unity of apriorism and rationalism that hitherto has existed. An "emotive ethics," as distinct from a "rational ethics," is not at all necessarily an "empiricism" that attempts to derive moral values from observation and induction. Feeling, preferring and rejecting, loving and hating, which belong to the totality of spirit [*des Geistes*], possess their own a priori contents independent of inductive experience and pure laws of thought. Here, as with thought, *there is* the *intuiting of essences* of acts and their correlates, their foundations, and their interconnections. In both cases there is "evidence" and maximum exactness of phenomenological findings.

5. In what concerns the concept "a priori" as such, we wish to distinguish the facts of the a priori—i.e., the facts of essences and their interconnections, which are independent of induction —from attempts to make the a priori *understandable* or even to explain it. In all areas of philosophy Kant's a priori is closely related to two principles (to which a fundamental metaphysical world view and a fundamental position of the philosopher correspond). These principles we reject as groundless assumptions.

First, according to his theory of the "*spontaneity*" of thinking, every "synthesis" in appearances must of necessity be produced by understanding (or by practical reason). Thus the a priori of interconnections between objects and states of affairs [*Sachverhalten*] is reduced to a "product" of a "spontaneous activity of connecting" or of a "pure synthesis" operating in the "chaos of the given." The "form," to which the a priori is falsely restricted, is, or is supposed to be, the result of a "*forming activity*," of a "forming" and a "synthesizing." Indeed, this theory is so closely interwoven with his theory of the a priori that, for many people who read Kant with no other view to bring to bear, the two have seemingly become an inseparable whole. But this mythology of productive rational activity has nothing to do with apriorism; it does not rest on intuition, but is a *purely constructivistic explanation* of the a priori contents of objects of experience, an explanation based on the very *presupposition* that only a "disordered chaos" is "given" (on the one hand, so-called sensations; on the other, "drives" or "inclinations"). This presupposition is also the *basic error of sensualism,* which was most distinctly developed by Hume. And it is *Kant's* error, for he borrowed it from the English on blind faith.[21] If the "given" were a "chaos" of impressions (or impulses or drives), and if, in the *contents* of experience, there *nevertheless* were interconnection, order, form, some organized structure, which cannot possibly— as Kant correctly saw—stem from associative combinations of impressions and their inner correlates, then the hypothesis of such "synthetic functions" and "combining forces" (whose lawfulness would be the "a priori" quite independent of this) would at least *suggest itself.* If the world is pulverized into a medley of sensations and man into a chaos of drives (which, though this is inconceivable, are said to be of service to the bare *preservation* of man's existence), then there naturally is a need for an actively organizing principle which leads back to the contents of natural experience. In short, *Hume's notion of nature required a Kantian understanding,* and *Hobbes's notion of man required a Kantian practical reason,* insofar as these theories were to be brought back to the facts of natural experience. But *without* this erroneous presupposition of a Humean nature and a Hobbesian man there is *no* need for such a hypothesis and *hence* no need for an interpretation of the a priori as a "law of functions" of such organizing activities. The a priori is, then, the *objective structure* [*sachliche* gegenständliche Struktur] of the large areas of ex-

---

21. H. Bergson has also stressed this in his *Matière et Mémoire* (Paris: Alcan, 1900).

perience itself to which certain acts and functional relations among them "correspond," without its having been "brought into" or "added to" this structure by such acts.

Ethics especially has suffered from the above presuppositions, perhaps more so than theoretical philosophy. Kant's presuppositions (barely spelled out as such) that man apart from practical reason is a mere "natural being" (for Kant, equal to a mechanical bundle of drives), that all love for the other is reducible to self-love, and even that all love is reducible to egoism,[22] presuppositions frequently expressed in Hobbes's *terminology* (e.g., in his *Anthropology*), do have this same origin. Without them, however, the compulsion to assume a "practical reason," one that will inform this chaos, breaks down.[23]

[Second], we have reached a point where apriorism is so deeply conjoined with a final, hardly expressible attitude of Kant's view of the world that his philosophy becomes most dangerously connected with a highly individual tendency of his. This "attitude" I can only describe as a basic "hostility" toward or "distrust" of the given *as* such, a fear of the given as "chaos," an anxiety—an attitude that can be expressed as "the world outside me, nature within me." "Nature" is what is to be formed, to be organized, to be "controlled"; it is the "hostile," the "chaos," etc. Hence this atttiude is the opposite of *love* of the world, of trust in and loving *devotion* to the world. Strictly speaking, this attitude belongs only to modern times, which are permeated by a *hatred of the world,* a hostility toward the world, and a distrust of it, and by the *consequence* of this hatred: namely, the limitless need for activity to "organize" and "control" the world, which this combination of apriorism and the theory of a "forming," "lawmaking" understanding (and a "will of reason" that brings drives into an "order") has *psychologically* caused. And all of this has culminated in the mind of an ingenious philosopher.

Apriorism must be freed completely from this association with affectations that are more than questionable in their his-

---

22. For Kant, self-love and egoism are the same.

23. At the *bottom* of all this lies an attitude of Puritan Protestantism, a *distrust* in principle of one's own "nature" (to the extent that it is not subject to systematic, rational self-control) and all its impulses. (This attitude is mirrored in Kant's theory of "radical evil.") Here we also find the *distrust* in principle of other men insofar as relations among men have not assumed *contractual* legal forms (a tradition of Puritan Protestantism). These attitudes were basic in the formation of many of the theories of the English moral philosophers. See "Über Ressentiment und moralisches Werturteil" (Bibliog. no. 5) and Max Weber's excellent treatise on capitalism and Calvinistic ethics.

torical origin and value, and from association with the resulting hypotheses. Interconnections are, like essences, *"given."* They are not a "product" of "understanding." They are *intuited,* not "made." They are original *thing*-interconnections [Sach*zusammenhänge*], not laws of objects just because they are laws of acts apprehending objects. They are "a priori" because they are grounded in *essences* [Wesenheiten], not in objects and goods. They are a priori, but not because "understanding" or "reason" "produces" them. The λόγος permeating the universe can be grasped only through *them.*

Our explication of the a priori is of great significance for *ethics insofar* as it sharply distinguishes *moral cognition, moral comportment,* and *philosophical ethics,* all of which Kant confounded.

The actual seat of the entire value–a priori (including the moral a priori) is the *value-cognition* or *value-intuition* [Wert-Erschauung] that comes to the fore in feeling, basically in love and hate, as well as the *"moral cognition"* [sittliche Erkenntnis] of the interconnections of values, i.e., their "being-higher" and "being-lower." This cognition occurs in *special* functions and acts which are *toto caelo* different from all perception and thinking.[24] These functions and acts supply the only possible *access* to the world of values. It is not only in "inner perception" or observation (in which only the psychic is given) but also *in* the felt and lived affair with *world* (be it psychic, physical, or whatever), *in* preferring and rejecting, *in* loving and hating, i.e., in the course of *performing* such intentional functions and acts, that values and their order flash before us! The a priori content lies in what is given in these manners.[25] A spirit limited to perception and thinking would be absolutely *blind* to values, no matter how much it might have the faculty of "inner perception," i.e., of psychic perception.

Moral *willing* and, indeed, *moral comportment* have their foundation in this value-cognition (in certain cases, moral value-cognition), with its own a priori content and its own evidence, in such a fashion that every willing (indeed, every conation) is primarily directed toward the realization of a value given in these acts. *Only* insofar as this value is factually given in the sphere of moral cognition is willing morally evidential, in con-

24. [See chap. 5, sec. 2.—*Ed.*]
25. This obtains *also* with respect to the psychic and one's own psychic life. In this case we relate to ourselves feelingly (in inner intuition), lovingly, etc., but *not* perceivingly or observingly.

trast to "blind" willing, or, better, blind impulses.[26] A value (or its position) can be given in feeling and preferring in various degrees of adequation up to its *"self-givenness"* (with which "absolute evidence" coincides). If a value is self-given, however, willing (or choosing in the [special] sense of preferring) becomes necessary in its *being,* according to laws of essential interconnections. And it is in this sense alone that Socrates' dictum [27] is restored—that all "good willing" is founded in the "cognition of the good," and that all evil willing rests on moral deception and aberration.[28] But this sphere of moral cognition is completely independent of the sphere of judgments and propositions (including the sphere in which we comprehend relations of values in terms of "assessments" or valuations [*Werthaltungen*]). Both assessments and value-estimations fulfill themselves in the value given in *feeling* and are only in this sense evident. It is therefore quite obvious that the Socratic dictum cannot apply to mere conceptual and judgmental knowledge of a value or a moral value.

If all moral comportment is built on the basis of moral *insight,* all ethics must go back to the facts lying in moral cognition and their a priori interconnections. I said, must go back! For moral cognition and insight are not "ethics." *Ethics* is only the judgmental formulation of what is given in the sphere of moral cognition. And it is philosophical ethics if it restricts itself to the *a priori* content of the evidentially given of moral cognition. Moral willing does not have to pass through *ethics* at all—by which, obviously, no human being becomes "good"—but it must in principle pass through *moral cognition* and insight.

Kant is completely mistaken about these basic states of affairs. For it is clear that both the willing of a good and the assessment of "what" is good can be called a priori (as derived)

26. Although there is a value given in blind impulses, this value is not felt first.

27. All mere *judgmental* "knowledge" of what is "good" is without fulfillment in a felt value. For this reason such knowledge of moral norms is *not* determining for willing. Even the feeling of what is good determines willing only if the value is given adequately and evidentially, i.e., only if it is self-given. What is wrong with Socrates' formulation (not with his *knowledge* of the good, whose *power* over willing was so clearly demonstrated by his death) is the rationalism which implies that the mere concept of what is "good" has the power to determine the will. With this, all known objections against his famous principle are disposed of.

28. Not on "error," but on *deception* in feeling itself, i.e., in preferring. Only where a judgment on valuation takes place can evil willing also rest on "aberration" [*Verirrung*], which is distinct from, and not a type of, theoretical "error."

only insofar as they are directed toward the *a priori fact* residing in the value-content of moral cognition or are fulfilled in it. However, since Kant reduces the a priori to "forming" and "acting," willing is on the one hand turned into something which supposedly has its own "a priori lawfulness," so that the product of the will's activity leads to judgment *and* moral cognition, and it is on the other hand determined by the idea of the "law" or of assessment, so that such willing is "right." In either case Kant fails to see the total sphere of moral cognition and, along with it, the proper *seat* of the ethical a priori. In theoretical philosophy he erroneously derives the a priori from functions of judgment instead of from the content of intuition as the basis of all judgments; and here, in ethics, he derives the a priori from functions of willing instead of from the *content of moral cognition* as it occurs in feeling, preferring, loving, and hating. For this reason also, the fact of *"moral insight"* is completely unknown to him. In its place there is the *"consciousness of duty,"* which is, as we shall see, anything but insight itself, even though it can also be *one of the possible forms* of the automatic *subjective* realization of a content of such possible insight. But it can occur, as we shall also see, only when moral insight in the full sense is missing.[29]

Now, on Kant's grounds, it is also impossible for us to know in our own case and with respect to others whether comportment is good or evil. Experience simply gives us non-formal, empirical, sensibly conditioned "intentions," which are, as such, morally indifferent. The *form* of their being-posited is never given. This stands to reason if one situates the a priori in the *function* of willing rather than in the feelable *content* of willing.[30] For Kant, therefore, there exists only a negative criterion of the moral good: good willing occurs *against* all "inclinations" in question. There is never a *positive insight* that willing may *be* good. But since, as he himself states, there always remains the possibility of a secret interplay of "inclinations," there is no *evidence* at all here. Though one cannot accuse Kant of having made this "against inclinations" a constituent element of good willing,[31] one can blame him for making it a constituent element of the

29. See below, p. 191.
30. Analogously, Kant cannot show how the a priori of the understanding—*if* it exists as he maintains—is to be known and discovered, that is, whether in an a priori or an empirical-inductive fashion.
31. But one can blame his basic moral tenor, which is thoroughly "rigorous" in the sense of Schiller's epigram.

cognition concerned with the question of whether willing is good—a cognition that has only the character of approximate probability. It is also in this regard that Kant is historically an heir to the Puritan tradition, in which there existed no criterion for the question of the "chosen" and the "condemned," just as for Kant there is no criterion for the question of "good" and "evil." With this, the individual who broods over morals faces a seemingly endless task.

Finally, ethics has arrived at an impossible position since it does not possess an autonomous source of cognition. Even if there is such a law of the functions of the will and "pure willing," Kant has failed to show how it is possible to know "pure willing" and to formulate it in ethics. On the one hand he operates on the basis of analyzing common moral judging—something that philosophical ethics must not do on terms other than *heuristic* ones (in conformity with Kant's own findings)—and on the other hand he states that one should not operate on this basis! Where, then, is the *source* of the cognition of the a priori of willing? Are we expected to believe that ethics itself is moral comportment? No clarification of this point can be found on the basis of his presuppositions.

6. Kant's explanation of the a priori in terms of the "synthetic activity" of mind, which we reject, is also closely related to two interpretations of the a priori, the *"transcendental"* and the "subjectivistic," which must be distinguished from each other.[32]

In the transcendental interpretation there is supposedly a law according to which "the laws of the objects of experience and cognition (and also of willing) conform to the laws of the experience and the cognition (and the willing) of the objects."

In all areas of its investigations phenomenology distinguishes three kinds of essential interconnections: (1) the essences (and

---

32. Kant *never* made the mistake of the "psychologistic" interpretation of the a priori, according to which "facts of inner perception" are of necessity "misplaced" in or "empathized" into outer experience because "inner perception" is immediate and evident and outer perception is not! And he *never* made the mistake of identifying "acts of reason" with *psychic experiences,* not even with so-called experiences of a "species-consciousness." Indeed, one of the historically important merits of Kant's philosophy is his *rejection* of these psychologistic mistakes, which at present are gaining a great deal of ground in Fichtean and Humean variations. And, at least in his ethics, Kant did not fall victim to an anthropological interpretation of the a priori, which is quite independent of the above-mentioned interpretation; but he did fall victim to it in his theoretical philosophy.

their interconnections) of the *qualities* and other *thing-contents* [Sachgehalte] given in acts (thing-phenomenology) [*Sachphä-nomenologie*]; (2) the essences of *acts themselves* and their interconnections and relations of foundation (phenomenology of acts or foundational orders); and (3) the essetnial interconnections *between the essences of acts and those of things* [zwischen Akt- und Sachwesenheiten] (e.g., values are given in feeling, colors in seeing, sounds in hearing, etc.).[33] Acts themselves can in no sense become known as objects, since their being consists solely in their pursuance and being acted out, although one can bring to reflective intuition their different essences in the pursuance of different acts.[34] There is, however, not the slightest reason to *select* from these three essential interconnections only the *third* and to assume generally, with Kant, only a unilateral essential interconnection, i.e., that a priori laws of objects must *"conform"* to laws of acts. Rather, there are in principle (apart from the other two kinds of essential interconnections) *mutual* interconnections of essences between specific kinds of acts and things [*Sacharten*] (for example, between "inner perception" and the "psychic," and between the "psychic" and "inner perception"; between "outer perception" and the "physical," and between the "physical" and "outer perception"). The great and important problem of the *"origin"* of (all kinds of) cognition is itself only a *part* of the total problem of a priori essential relations, i.e., that part of the a priori relations of foundations which obtains be-

---

33. These would not be "essential interconnections" if "hearing" and "seeing" were not *functions* of (uniform) sensation comprehended in reflection, and if these terms meant only "consciousness of colors or sounds" (apart from the consciousness of the cooperation of eyes and ears in the acts of seeing and hearing). But this is not the case (though, e.g., B. Natorp falsely maintains this in his *Einleitung in die Psychologie*). Rather, one must show that—apart from the givenness of functions in reflection—these essential interconnections possess, independent of their *contents* (colors, sounds), a certain lawfulness in their *variations*, for example, a lawfulness of scope (of so-called sensible attention), perspective (in seeing), and the "ability to look over" contents quite independent of the intensities of hearing and seeing, and a lawfulness with regard to special *possibilities of disturbances*, etc. All of these variations are independent of contents and sensations, of organs like eyes and ears, as well as of the *general* variations of attention (which meet *all* contents of consciousness in like manner). Nor does it matter here whether sounds and colors are in fact seen and heard or whether they are "seen" and "heard" in fantasy or remembrance.

34. "Reflection" is possible vis-à-vis specific essences of acts. But it has nothing to do with inner perception or observation, still less with inner observation. Any "observation" does away with acts. [See chap. 6, A, esp. sec. 3.—*Ed.*]

tween acts (as act-essences). But this question is by no means *"the"* problem of apriorism, to whose solution other important central problems must conform. There is *no* such thing as an "understanding that prescribes laws to nature" (laws that are not *in nature itself*) or a "practical reason" that impresses its "form" on bundles of drives! [35] We can only "prescribe" (whether we do so "generally" or "individually" does not matter here) the signs and combinations of signs (conventions) that we employ in designating things (the functions of signs being presupposed)! [36] Kant's apriorism necessarily leads to a confusion of a priori propositions and concepts with signs. For such propositions cannot be fulfilled by any intuitive content! What can they be, save mere conventions from which one can perhaps deduce the "results of science" in the simplest fashion? We will avoid the consequence of turning philosophy into a "wisdom of words" only if we realize that the a priori content of essences must be found in *things* themselves [Sachen *selbst*], and that all propositions and concepts of understanding find their fulfillment in this content.

The a priori contents of essences by no means conceal *objects* and their *being*. (According to Kant's position there remains the idea of objects which do not conform to the a priori functional laws, namely, the idea of "things in themselves"; his position, however, must restrict itself to the "objects of possible experience," or to the so-called world of appearances.) Rather, in the a priori content of essences the absolute being- and value-content of the world is *opened up,* and the distinction between "thing in itself" and "appearances" breaks down.[37] For this distinction is only a consequence of the "transcendental" interpretation of the a priori, which we have rejected.

But there does exist a lawfulness of the "conforming" in a

35. The problem concerning the "origin" of cognition is completely independent of the one concerning the *genesis* of the cognition of a specific thing-reality by a real subject in objective time. "Foundation" concerns only the *order* of the structure of acts, *not* their real temporal sequence.

36. To put it plainly, what "understanding prescribes to nature" are merely the *conventions* of scholars.

37. The relativity of the "being" of the natural way of looking at the world, as well as (in another sense) the "being" of science and its "nature of manifestation," remains unaffected by this. This relativity is based not on any supposed "relativity of cognition" but on the specific *goals* and *purposes* which these two kinds of cognition possess and which are effective as selective factors on the given. [See "Phänomenologie und Erkenntnistheorie" and "Lehre von den Drei Tatsachen."—*Ed.*]

sense quite different from Kant's; for the *essential relations* remain fulfilled in all "experience" in the sense of "observation and induction," as well as in all "experience of the natural view of the world" and "natural understanding." Real things, goods, and acts, and their real interconnections, are what "conform" to the a priori content of experience (in the sense explained before). But this basic law that obtains between *essences* and the *real* has nothing at all to do with Kant's erroneous "Copernican turn."

7. Kant's *subjectivistic* interpretation of the a priori is different from his profound, but false, transcendental one. The subjectivistic interpretation appears in varying degrees throughout his works, which thus lend themselves to many explanations. What concerns us here is the separation of the true "apriorism" from all "subjectivism."

In connection with this we are now confronted with Kant's attempt either to reduce the a priori evidential to the so-called *necessity* and *universality* of judgment (or of "assessments" in the area of values, or of willing in ethics), or to see in them criteria for the existence of a priori insight.

Two points are essential for all kinds of "*necessity*," no matter how "objectively" one uses this concept, distinguishing it—with Kant—from all "subjective mental constraint," "habits," etc. The first point is that the meaning of this term pertains solely to *propositions* (e.g., the relation between premise and conclusion), not to facts of intuition (except *derivatively, if* they fulfill propositions of this kind). The second point is that necessity is a *negative* concept, insofar as "only that whose opposite is impossible can be necessary." As I tried to show before, a priori insight is first of all *factual* insight, first given not in "judgments" but in *intuition*. And, in addition, it is a *positive* insight into the factual state of affairs of an essential interconnection. These considerations separate a priori insight from all kinds of "necessity" by an unbridgeable gulf. Whenever we speak of "necessity," we must presuppose as *true* those propositions *according* to which propositional relations are necessary, e.g., the proposition that two propositions of the form "*A is B*" and "*A is not B*" cannot both be true and the well-known propositions concerning premises and conclusions. These propositions must *be true*, and it is erroneous to state that they *define* "truth" in the sense that "true" propositions would be those following from them. But it is clear that *these* propositions and their *truth* cannot be reduced to any "necessity" that would differ from mere "mental constraint." They are *true because they are a priori evident*. It is because the being of something contradicts its non-being in intuition that the above proposition is true. "*A* is *B*" is false if "*A* is not *B*" is true; and it is necessarily false because the above proposition is true, i.e., a priori evident. It makes no sense to reduce *insight itself* to "necessity."

If it is our problem to comprehend that the contradictory of a proposition is impossible, we must ask *how* we comprehend that it is impossible. If we refrain from starting with propositions pertaining to combinations of propositons, there is only one possibility: the contradictory is impossible if the proposition is *true*. This demonstration is the only possible one for all propositions referring back to essential interconnections and also to those of pure logic! Such propositions are "evidentially true"; and those propositions whose opposites contradict evidentially true propositions (including the principle of contradiction, which is not necessary but is "evidentially true") are "necessary."

We must therefore consider it wrong to reduce the nature of "truth" or the nature of the "object" to the "necessity" of judgments or propositions or to the "necessity of a connection of representations." If one says, We are concerned not with "subjective mental necessity" but with "objective necessity," the adjective *objective* always *presupposes* the *objective thing* or the *truth* as objective. The necessity of a proposition is "objective" only if the proposition is based on an a priori *fact,* in which case the proposition is "necessarily" valid for *all* "cases" containing this fact.

The above remarks apply especially to the a priori in the areas of values and ethics. For all "necessity of oughtness" has its foundation in the *insight into a priori* interconnections obtaining among *values.* Values are never based on the necessity of the ought! Thus, only what *is good* can become "duty"; or it is *because* it is good (in the ideal sense) that it necessarily "ought" to be.[38] It is the insight into the *a priori structure of the realm of values* (which is independent of all experience of goods and all posited purposes) that, in the sphere of the "ought" and judgments, permits the "necessity" of the ought and the judgments. On the other hand, it is as false to place the necessity of oughtness (or even that of "duty") *before* the insight into *what* is good as it is to think that an object (and, in another sense, the idea of "truth") can be reduced to the "necessity of a connection of representations" (or to mental necessity).

38. [See chap. 4, sec. 2.—*Ed.*]

"Objective necessity" itself contains the "subjective" element, in that the necessity is constituted in the attempt to *negate* a proposition based on an essential interconnection. It is only in this attempt that the necessity springs forth. This necessity still contains, apart from this attempt, the aforementioned *relations of essence* that must be *sustained* in all non-phenomenological experience; and, consequently, propositions based on them cannot be proved or destroyed by inductive experience! *These propositions are valid for all objects of this essence because they are valid for the essence of all these objects.*

Needless to say, "universal validity" has nothing to do with the a priori, for "universality" in no sense belongs to essence [*Wesenheit*]. There are individual essences and essential interconnections between individual elements. We have stressed elsewhere that universality in the sense of a validity "for" all subjects having a certain "understanding," or for the human species, has nothing to do with the "a priori." [39] There can very well be an a priori for only *one* individual's insight, or one that only one individual *can* have! A proposition based on the a priori is "universal" only for those subjects who *can* have the same insight (all universality is essentially "for" someone, whereas the a priori does not at all imply such a "for" relation).

Subjectivism becomes erroneously intertwined with the a priori not only when one (exclusively) interprets the a priori as a primary "law" of acts but also when one considers it a law of the acts of an "*ego*" or a "subject," e.g., as the form of the activity of a "transcendental ego," a so-called consciousness as such, or even a "consciousness of a species"! For the "ego," including the "egoness" in all individual egos, is only an "*object*" (in every sense of the word) for acts, especially for acts having the nature of "inner perception." We meet the ego only in this perception, not in an act of, say, "outer perception." The ego, as "egoness," is also part of an essential interconnection in terms of the nature of the specific act-form of inner perception. Even if we consider egoness as *such*—putting aside all individual egos and their "conscious contents"—it is still a *positive content* of intuition, not merely a "correlate" of a logical subject having empirical experiences as its predicates. The ego is a possible term [*Glied*] in essential interconnections in that there belongs to every "ego-being" a "nature-being," to all "inner perception" the act of "outer

---

39. [See "Das Ressentiment in Aufbau der Moralen" (Bibliog. no. 10), sec. 5.—*Ed.*]

perception," etc. But the ego is neither the *point of departure* for the apprehension nor the producer of essences.[40] It is not an essence which unilaterally "founds" all other essences or even all essences of acts. In the lived pursuance of outer perception, nature *"itself"* is *immediately* given, not a "representation" or "sensations" that belong to an ego. The *act-direction* of outer perception is given in "reflection"; no ego from which its emanation is experienced is given.[41] It is only while one is conscious of himself as the *very same person* who is performing acts in every act of inner perception, in which his ego appears, *and* in every act of outer perception, in which nature, like the ego in the former case, is given immediately, that he can say, "I perceive this tree." In this statement the *I* is neither "the I" nor the individual "I" of the one speaking (in contrast to nature), but solely the "I" in contrast to the "thou," i.e., the individual speaking person as opposed to another person. It is not "an ego which perceives the tree," but a man who has an ego and is conscious of his being the same person in the pursuance of both outer *and* inner perception.[42]

It is also of the greatest significance for the a priori of ethics that no activity of an *"ego,"* a "consciousness in general," etc., be set forth. In this area also, the ego (in every sense of the term) is only a *"bearer"* of values. It is *neither a presupposition* of values *nor* a "valuing" subject through which values exist or through which values are comprehensible. It is a curious fact that the "subjectivism" of that theory of the a priori which we reject *degraded* the moral value of the *individual* ego to the greatest extent and, indeed, made of this value a *contradictio in adjecto*.[43]

40. "Materiality," too, is given to us in *every* act of outer perception. It is not "concluded," "thought into," or even "believed," no matter how much theories on matter may vary.

41. The so-called independence of outer objects from the ego is a *consequence* of the "self"-givenness of physical objects. But the essence of these objects does not consist in an "independence from the ego" that is given primitively.

42. Concerning the point that this "very sameness" is the "person" as fundamentally different from the "ego," and that the idea of the person is not based on the ego, but that this idea represents the concrete form in which alone acts can exist, see chap. 6, A.

43. Precisely because the "individual ego" coincides here with the totality of *empirical* experiences (which are supposed to make one individual ego different from another), and because the *moral* value of the ego is supposed to consist in its being determined by a transcendental ego, the individual ego *as* an individual ego must be on the wrong track. (This resembles the thinking of Averroes and Spinoza, namely, that the "individual" *perforce* sins because he is an individual.) But in fact the so-called empirical experiences of an ego are given abstractly and inade-

For it *must* appear from this interpretation that there are, from the outset, no essential values of an individual ego, no "individual conscience," no good for *one* individual and *only* for *him*. If the a priori is the "form of activity" of "consciousness in general" or of a "transcendental ego," the individual ego is at once, in this case, necessarily an empirical obscuration of such a transcendental ego, a being founded in experience (in the sense of observation or sensible experience).[44] Moreover, its moral value is absorbed by the formal a priori and its bearer, the transcendental ego.[45]

8. Let us turn to a final point in the misunderstanding of the a priori: its relation to the concepts *"innate"* and *"acquired."* Since it has been stressed, perhaps more than was necessary, that the difference between the a priori and the a posteriori has nothing to do with the question of "innate" or "acquired," we do not want to repeat ourselves at this point. The concepts of "innate" and "acquired" are causal-genetic ones and are therefore not applicable when we are concerned with a *type of insight.*

For anyone who has at all understood the difference between a priori and inductive givenness in experience, it goes without saying that failure is inevitable in any attempt to reduce the a priori to "inherited dispositions" based on experiences that first belonged to our phylogenetic "ancestors" (see, for example, Spencer), or to traditional compulsions of combinations of ideas which became fixated during historical development and which preserved themselves because their purposefulness determined actions toward the "useful" (as so-called pragmatism fancies).

Because the problem of the "innate" and the "acquired" is not at all touched upon by the question of the a priori, and because it continues to bear fully on the *realization* of a cognition (a priori or a posteriori) by an individual of a specific natural organization, it is not to be precluded that a priori insights become

quately as long as one does not see the individual ego to which they belong. And "the" ego is not an individual ego only as what moves a lived body. [See chap. 6, A. On "individual conscience" and "individual good," see chap. 6, B, sec. 2.—*Ed.*]

44. See the end of my treatise "Über Selbsttäuschungen."

45. Two basic interconnections of essence—basic for ethics, too—are to be distinguished from this erroneous interpretation of the a priori. These two alone deserve the place which Kant attributes to transcendental apperception. The first interconnection is that between the *nature* of the *act* and the *nature* of the *object!* This, too, is a mutual interconnection which excludes the possibility of "unknowable" objects and "unfeelable" values, etc. The second interconnection is that between *act* and *"person"* and *object* and *"world."* [See chap. 6, A, sec. 3.—*Ed.*]

factually realized by men in *all* these ways (*heredity, tradition, acquisition*). It would be an abuse of the philosophical insight concerning the basic difference between the a priori and the "innate"—now, finally, an accepted fact—to assume that the "a priori" is therefore only an "acquired" or "self-acquired" insight. For the realization of an a priori insight can *also* depend on *innate dispositions*—just as the color sense represents a "disposition" [*Anlage*] (having broad latitudes of variation), without the a priori of the geometry of colors being thereby affected. In this sense it is perfectly possible that the *capacity* for a priori insight is "innate," i.e., inherited.[46] This capacity can also be inherited in a limited fashion, e.g., in only a certain race, such that other races do not have the "a priori insights" concerned. For to say that there is a "universal human disposition" to the attainment of a priori insights has no more to do with the nature of the a priori than does a specific determination of its factual attainment. The genuine "a priori" has nothing in common with a so-called universal human rational disposition as a solid stock of "forms" or "ideas" (which is the idol of the philosophy of the Enlightenment). Likewise, a type of insight as a type of essence [*Wesensart*] has nothing in common with the *factual distribution of the capacity* for this insight within a natural species. In the same sense the a priori insight that comes upon us [*zugeht*] though "tradition" does not lose its a priori character. But, of course, something does not *become* an a priori insight because it comes upon us through tradition or heredity. Neither does it *lose* its character for that reason. The a priori most certainly *can* come upon an individual through these kinds of vehicles. The "self-obtained" or "self-found" belongs not at all to a priori insight.

If Kant frequently equates "a priori cognition" and the "self-obtained," it is because he holds that the a priori in an object is rooted in the *form of activity* of the mind, and that it primarily represents a law of "synthesis." If the a priori is not an original *content of intuition* (and, in a derivative sense, a proposition fulfilled by such content), but is instead a form of activity (e.g., a form of judgment), it necessarily follows that one can perform this "activity" only by himself, and that it must be "self-obtained." We have already rejected this interpretation of the a priori; hence, this conclusion breaks down for us.

46. Today it is out of the question to speak of "innate" in the rationalistic sense, which is to reduce the capacity for a priori insight to a gift that God bestowed on the soul.

We are confronted here with a completely different series of problems. We may sum them up as the problem of the factual and purposeful *economization of activities* leading to "a priori insight." Among these problems, however, "self-obtainment" is only *one* such activity. For instance, there is a large and most important complex of problems involved when we want to discover what the role of the factual interaction of heredity, tradition, education, authority, one's own life experience, and the formation of conscience resulting from these is in the acquisition of such insights; also, when we want to find out what is most expedient in the economical-technical sense in order to let the moral "a priori evidential" factually come upon man. This complex of problems has nothing to do with the question of *what is thus evidential.* But this complex must *not* be divided by this false identification and be decided in favor solely of the "self-obtained."

This point is of special importance for ethics. For ethicists close to Kantian philosophy presuppose as a matter of course that a *genuine* moral insight is a *self-obtained* one, as if everyone were "able" to see what is morally "evident" in the same way. They are, of course, correct insofar as they reject any attempt to replace the *insight* into *what is good* by an "authority," be it "God's will," "inherited instincts of a species" or a "race," the moral "tradition," or orders of an "authority." But the proposition that only *insight* into the good can originally determine what is good (and, consequently, all norms for willing and acting) has nothing in common with the question concerning which factors of activity in their interactions lead to the evidentially good in the most expedient manner. Nor has this proposition anything to do with the question concerning what tradition, heredity, authority, education, and self-obtained experiences may *add* to this.[47] To get the opposite impression, one must presuppose the formalistic, subjective, transcendental, spontaneous interpretations of the a priori.

We have assumed, as we said before, that, in general, moral *cognition* is fundamentally different from *willing*, and that it is the foundation for the willing of the good; and we have assumed that the seat of the ethical a priori is in the sphere of *moral cognition, not* in that of willing. If the moral good were a "concept" (not a non-formal value) which came into existence only

47. On heteronomy and autonomy, see chap. 6, B, sec. 3, where the significance of tradition and authority in the acquisition of moral insight is discussed.

through reflection on an act of willing or on a special form of willing, then, of course, ethical cognition, as *independent* of moral willing, would be impossible. And since one can only "will" his own will (and since one can only "obey" another's will unless there is psychological suggestion), moral cognition must in this case be self-obtained (i.e., obtained from one's will). Otherwise there would have to be blind obedience to commandments, in which case one could not know whether or not they (as acts of will) rest on moral insight. However, such an alternative rests on the aforementioned erroneous presupposition.[48]

B. The Non-Formal A Priori in Ethics

In the following I wish to show that the formal and the a priori do not coincide at all within the *value–a priori*. I also intend to point out the *basic kinds* of a priori essential relations. But I shall not mention all of these basic kinds, for this would be equal to developing a positive ethics, which is not the task here.

1. *Formal Essential Interconnections*

We can designate as (pure) *"formal"* a priori interconnections all those that are independent of the types and qualities of values, as well as of the idea of a "bearer of values," and all those that have their foundation in the essence of values as values. They represent a pure axiology which in a certain sense corresponds to logic. Within this axiology one can distinguish a pure theory of *values* and a pure theory of *valuations* (corresponding to the logical "theory of objects" and the logical "theory of thinking").

A first essential fact is that all values (such as ethical, aesthetic, etc.) fall into two groups: *positive* and *negative* (as we may call them for the sake of simplicity). This fact lies in the *essence* [Wesen] of values; it is independent of our being able to feel specific opposites of values (i.e., positive and negative

---

48. For this reason the autonomy of moral cognition and the autonomy of moral willing and action are basically different. Thus the act of obedience is an autonomous act of the will (in contrast to succumbing to suggestion, emotive contagion, or a tendency to imitate), but it always follows the insight of *another*. This act is also an evidential act when we have the insight that the person giving the order possesses a higher degree of moral insight than we do.

values), such as beautiful-ugly, good-evil, agreeable-disagreeable, etc.

In addition, there are "axioms," already discovered by Franz Brentano, which a priori fix the *relation of being* to *positive* and *negative* values.

> The existence of a positive value is itself a positive value.
> The existence of a negative value is itself a negative value.
> The non-existence of a positive value is itself a negative value.
> The non-existence of a negative value is itself a positive value.

It is also necessary to mention the essential interconnections obtaining *between values* and the (ideal) *ought*. First, there is the proposition that all oughtness must have its foundation in values—i.e., only values ought or ought not to be—and there is the proposition that a positive value ought to be and a negative value ought not to be.

We must also mention the interconnections which are a priori valid for the *relation of being to the ideal ought*, and which regulate their connection with *right* and *wrong*. Thus the being of what (positively) ought to be is right, and the being of what ought not to be is wrong; all non-being of what ought to be is wrong, and all non-being of what ought not to be is right.[49]

There are other interconnections that belong here: the *same* value cannot be both positive and negative; every non-negative value is a positive value; every non-positive value is a negative value. These propositions are not *applications* of the principles of contradiction and excluded middle; for here it is not a question of relations between propositions at their foundations, but one of essential interconnections. Nor are these interconnections the same as those obtaining between the being and non-being of values, as if they simply concerned the being and non-being of values. Rather these interconnections obtain among the values *themselves*, independent of their *being or non-being*.[50]

And it is to these interconnections that the *principles of valu-*

---

49. The ideal ought has as little to do with duty and norms as rightness has to do with what is "correct." The last pertains only to *comportment* which corresponds to what a norm demands.

50. These interconnections are the foundation of a purely formal theory of values which stands at the side of pure (formal) logic as the science of objects in general.

ation correspond: it is impossible to hold that the *same* value is both positive and negative, etc.

I would like to emphasize that Kant's principles represent only a special case of these formal principles of valuation. However, they are (erroneously) related only to the moral sphere, and they are (also erroneously) related not to valuation but directly to willing; but they are in fact valid for willing (indeed, for conation in general) simply *because* they are valid for the valuation at the foundation of willing (and conation). For Kant's "moral law," in its different formulations, means one of two things: either that it is necessary to avoid a contradiction in the positing of purposes (expressed subjectively and normatively, "to contribute to the establishment of a realm of purposes in which every purpose exists with every other one without contradiction"), or that it is necessary to uphold the *consequence* of willing (i.e., to be "truthful" to one's self), to will the same thing under the same conditions (i.e., the same conditions of "empirical character" and "environment"), etc.[51] Kant, however, does not see the following: (1) that it is altogether *impossible* to gain the idea of the good from these "formal" laws, and that the value "good" represents only an *area of application* of these formal value-laws (valid for all values), an application which presupposes "good" and "evil"; (2) that these laws, like laws of logic, are based on *intuitive* essential interconnections; (3) that these laws are as fundamentally valid among *values* as they are among valuations; (4) that they are laws of *value-comprehension* (as laws of acts), not originally laws of the will.

On the other hand it appears that Kant was (negatively) right in claiming that these formal laws are *not* mere applications of logical (theoretical) laws—i.e., laws to be applied to moral comportment insofar as it is an object of *judgment*—but *immediate* laws of moral comportment, though in his case primarily of willing, not of valuation. This appears to imply that reason becomes "*directly* practical" through these laws.

But Kant is completely mistaken about the meaning of these "laws" (and, by the way, about the meaning of the laws of theoretical areas also). The principle of contradiction is valid for being, not because it is valid for the "thinking of being"; rather, it pertains to the thinking of being because the essential interconnection fulfilling it is fulfilled in all *being* (including factual

51. Recently Theodor Lipps appropriately stressed that Kant's moral law is basically only the principle of identity and contradiction in the sphere of the will.

thinking). This principle states that "*A* is *B*" and "*A* is not *B*" cannot both be true propositions in the sphere of propositions. For it lies in the nature of *being* to exclude this possibility. Only through the *disagreement* [Widerstreit] of one of these propositions with being can both of them be *meant* in judgments. If they are true propositions, there must be a difference between the *A* of one proposition and that of the other (*A* and *A'*), or between the two *B*'s (*B* and *B'*), or between their connection. As far as judgments are concerned, however, it is impossible to state that "*A* is *B*" and "*A* is not *B*" insofar as the *same A* and *B*, as well as the *same* kind of connection in judgment, is meant. Whenever it appears that such a judgment has been so made, different kinds of judging are concealed under the same *formulation*. For the *propositions* "*A* is *B*" and "*A* is not *B*" cannot (*salva veritate*) agree with each other a priori, because *being* excludes this possibility. One must never admit, then, that there are judgments of this form! The principle of contradiction states, among other things, that there are *no* such judgments.

An analogous state of affairs holds in the area of *values*. One can "value" the same things positively and negatively, but only because of *different complexes of values* [verschiedenen Wertverhaltes] intended in the same thing. If there is the *same* complex of values in the intention of "valuation," only the *formulations* of the valuations can be different. Hence the essential interconnection that the same complex of values can never be of both positive and negative value is also fulfilled in all complexes of values that lie at the foundation of all "inclinations" (to use Kant's terminology). It is an evident proposition that we cannot at the same time *desire* and *despise* the *same* value-complex. If this seems to happen, there are *different* value-complexes hidden behind the supposedly identical intention of valuation. This law also pertains to the most spontaneous "caprice" in value-estimation. For value-*estimations* [Wertschätzungen] are also objects of feelable complexes of values. For instance, we may be sad about the disvalue of our negative value-estimation of high positive values, namely, "that we made a valuation in this manner." Therefore, it is not an alleged contrariness between the "logic" and the "non-logic" of value-estimations which represents the moral "struggle" of life, but a genuine contrariness between the immanent logic of the value-complex of the central notion of "good" and the logic of the remaining value-complexes or between the logic of value-estimations of good-being and the estimations of other kinds of value-being. This moral struggle is not a kind of "disobedience" to propositions, as Kant asserts, having (falsely) conceived the principles of identity and contradiction as norms of our judgments (and willing). Let us give some examples. He who wants different things in identical situations, e.g., in a legal case involving a friend and in an identical one involving a foe, does not "violate" these laws, as Kant maintains he does. Rather, he is in a state of deception concerning the range of the applicability of these laws. The same holds for someone (having only the same rights as another) who allows himself to do something that he denies the other in an identical situation, or for someone who changes a decision without giving specific reasons (which belong to the state of affairs in question). In these examples the one concerned considers situations (with regard to friend and foe) as different when they are the same, he takes his own situation to be of a different value than that of the other, and he takes the state of affairs to be changed when it is the same. If he falls into *deceptions*, his *evil* will must be considered the cause. This cause can never consist in "disobedience" to these laws, which, on the contrary, he *necessarily* fulfills.

2. *Values and Bearers of Values*

There exist a priori interconnections *between values* and their *bearers*. I will give only some examples.

Only persons can (originally) be morally good or evil; everything else can be good or evil only *by reference to persons*, no matter how indirect this "reference" may be. All properties of the person that vary (according to rules) with the *goodness of the person* are called virtues; [52] those that vary with the person's being-evil are called vices. Acts of will and deeds are also good or evil only insofar as acting persons are comprehended with them.[53]

But a person can never be "agreeable" or "useful." *These* values are *essentially thing-values* and *values of events*. Conversely, there are no morally good or evil things and events.

First, all aesthetic values are in essence values of *objects*. Second, they are values of objects whose posited reality (of any

52. The person is a continuous actuality. The person experiences virtue in the mode of the "being-able-to" of this actuality in regard to something which "ought" to be done.

53. Whether they are comprehended as special *bearers* of moral values or as mere "*signs*" of the goodness or badness of the *person* is a difference implied in this general determination.

form) has been suspended; such objects are there as *"appearance"* [Schein], even if the reality-phenomenon is a partial content of the given "picturelike" appearing object, as is the case in a historical drama. Third, they are values of objects because of their *intuited picturelikeness* (in contrast to merely "thought" objects).

Ethical values, on the other hand, are those whose bearers can never (originally) be given as "objects," since they belong in essence to the sphere of the *person* (and act-being). For neither the person nor acts can ever be given to us as "objects." [54] As soon as we tend to "objectify" a human being in any way, the bearer of moral values disappears *of necessity.*

Second, ethical values are those belonging to bearers as *real,* not to merely (appearing) pictorial objects. Even in a work of art in which such values may occur—for example, in a drama—the bearers must still be given "as" real bearers (notwithstanding the fact that these bearers given "as real" are given as a part of the aesthetic, appearing pictorial object).

Ethical values are not necessarily attached to bearers that are intuited pictorially. They can also pertain to bearers that are only *thought.*

As moral values are, by their essence, borne by persons, the values "noble" and "vulgar" (or "bad" [*schlecht*]) are, by virtue of their essence, borne by "living beings" in general. That is, the important values of this series (completely overlooked in Kant's dualism) are, by virtue of their essence, "values of life," or "vital values." Hence they pertain not only to man but also to animals and plants, i.e., anything that is alive. But they do not pertain to things, as do the values "agreeable" and "useful." [55] *Living beings* are not "things," still less corporeal things. *They represent an irreducible type of categorial unity.*[56]

3. *"Higher" and "Lower" Values*

In the *totality* of the realm of values there exists a singular order, an *"order of ranks"* that all values possess among themselves. It is because of this that a value is *"higher"* or *"lower"*

---

54. If an action is objectively given, insofar as it is the bearer of values it must be given through the mediation of the idea of the person (even merely one person), which can never be given to us as an object.

55. One does speak of noble jewels and noble wines, but only in an analogous sense, as when one speaks of having had a "beautiful" meal.

56. Here I cannot prove that the unity of life is not a "thing-unity" (still less a "corporeal unity").

than another one. This order lies in the *essence* of values themselves, as does the difference between "positive" and "negative"
values. It does not belong simply to "values known" by us.[57]

The fact that one value is "higher" than another is apprehended in a special act of value-cognition: the act of *preferring*.
One must not assume that the height of a value is "*felt*" in the
same manner as the value itself, and that the higher value is
subsequently "preferred" or "placed after." Rather, the height of a
value is "given," by virtue of its essence, only *in* the act of preferring. Whenever this is denied, one falsely equates this preferring
with "*choosing*" in general, i.e., an act of conation. Without
doubt, choosing must be grounded in the cognition of a higher
value, for we choose that purpose among others which has
its foundation in a higher value. But "preferring" occurs in
the absence of all conation, choosing, and willing. For instance,
we can say, "I prefer roses to carnations," *without* thinking of a
choice. All "choosing" takes place between different deeds. By
contrast, preferring also occurs with regard to any of the goods
and values. This first kind of preferring (i.e., the preferring between different *goods*) may also be called *empirical* preferring.

On the other hand "preferring" is *a priori* if it occurs between

---

57. On the other hand, one cannot reduce this division to one of positive and negative values or to one of "greater" and "smaller" values.
Brentano's axiom that a value which is the sum of the values W_1 and W_2
must be a higher value (a value to be preferred, according to his definition) than W_1 or W_2 is not an autonomous value-proposition but only the
application of an arithmetic proposition to values, indeed, only to symbols
of values. It cannot be that a value is "higher" than another value simply
because it is a sum of values. For it is characteristic of the contrast between "higher" and "lower" values that an infinite magnitude of a value,
say, the agreeable (or the disagreeable), never yields any magnitude of,
say, the noble (or the base) or of a spiritual value (of cognition, for
instance). The *sum* of values is to be preferred to single values; but it is
an error on Brentano's part to assume that the higher value is in this
case to be identified with the one to be "preferred." For preferring is
(essentially) the *access* to the "higher value," but in individual cases it is
subject to "deception." Besides, the "greater value" in this case pertains
only to the act of "choosing," not to the act of "preferring." For the act of
preferring always takes place in the sphere of a value-series that has a
specific "position" in the order of values. Finally, I cannot agree with
Brentano when he leaves it up to *historical relativity* to determine what the
non-formal ranks of values actually are, when, for instance, he does not
wish to decide (see the notes to his *Vom Ursprung sittlicher Erkenntnis*)
whether an "act of cognition" is of higher value than an "act of noble
love" (as Aristotle and the Greeks held) or whether the opposite is the
case (as the Christians held), in other words, when he does not make a
decision on the basis of the non-formal values themselves. [See chap. 5,
sec. 2. On the invariability of the order of ranks of values and the variability of rules of preferring, see chap. 5, sec. 6.—*Ed.*]

different *values themselves*—independent of "goods." Such preferring always encompasses whole (and indefinitely wide) complexes of goods. He who "prefers" the noble to the agreeable will end up in an (inductive) experience of a *world of goods* very different from the one in which he who does not do so will find himself. The "height of a value" is "given" not "prior" to preferring, but *in* preferring. Hence, whenever we choose an end founded in a lower value, there must exist a *deception of preferring*. But this is not the place to discuss the possibility of such a deception.

But one may not say that the "being-higher" of a value only "means" that it is the value "preferred." For if the height of a value is given "in" preferring, this height is nevertheless a relation in the *essence* of the values concerned. Therefore, the *"ordered ranks of values"* are themselves absolutely *invariable*, whereas the "rules of preferring" are, in principle, variable throughout history (a variation which is very different from the apprehension of new values).

When an act of preferring takes place, it is not necessary that a multiplicity of values be given in feeling, nor is it necessary that such a multiplicity serve as a "foundation" for the act of preferring.

Concerning the former point, there are those cases where, for example, a deed is given as preferable to others *without* our thinking of these other deeds or our representing them in detail. It is only the consciousness of "being able to prefer something else" that must accompany the act.[58] Also, the consciousness of height can accompany a felt value in the absence of the *factual givenness* of the related value with respect to which the felt value is higher.[59] It suffices that this other value is indicated in a specific "consciousness of direction." This is precisely the case when preferring is most *definitive* (without there having been any prior indeterminate attitude), and when at the same time the height of a felt value is given in maximal degrees of evidence. Moreover, there may be given, in the act of preferring, the fact that "there exists a value higher than the one given in feeling" without the givenness of this value *itself* in feeling.[60] The height

---

58. The same obtains in the case of choosing.

59. It is characteristic of "determined" preferring, in contrast to "wavering" preferring, that the other values belonging to the same series are barely given.

60. Thus we often realize that we could have done something "better" than we did without this "better" being given to us.

of a value *B*, in contrast to a value *A*, can be "given" in *preferring B* to *A, as well as* in the act of placing *A after B.* Nevertheless, these two methods of apprehending the same relation of value-ranks are basically different. True, it is an a priori interconnection that both types of acts can lead to the same relation of ranks. The difference exists nonetheless. It is distinctly manifest in human characters! For there are moral characters who are specifically "critical"; they may, in extreme cases, become "ascetics." These persons realize the height of a value principally in the act of "placing after." In contrast to these persons, there are positive types of characters who principally "prefer," and to whom the "lower" value shows itself only from the "platform" that they ascended in the act of preferring. Whereas the former strive for "virtue" by means of a battle against "vice," the latter bury and cover vices under newly acquired virtues.

As an act, "preferring" must be sharply distinguished from its kinds of realization. The realization may consist in the special activity that we experience in its execution. This is the case in a clearly *conscious* preferring, accompanied by a *"deliberation,"* among several values given in feeling. The realization may also occur, however, quite *"automatically,"* so that we are not at all aware of any "activity." In this case a higher value comes to us as if it were coming "by itself," as in "instinctive" preferring. Whereas in the former case we must labor to reach this value, in the latter this higher value "draws" us toward it, as it were. Such is the case in "enthusiastically" devoting oneself to a higher value. The act of preferring is in both cases the same.

Since all values stand essentially in an order of ranks—i.e., since all values are, in relation to each other, higher or lower— and since these relations are comprehensible only "in" preferring or rejecting them, the "feeling" of values has its foundation, by essential necessity, in "preferring" and "placing after." The feeling of values is by no means a "foundation" for the manner of preferring, as though preferring were "added" to the values comprehended in a primary intention of feeling as only a secondary act. Rather, all *widening* of the value-range (e.g., of an individual) takes place only "in" preferring and placing after. Only those values which are originally "given" in these acts can *secondarily* be "felt." Hence, the *structure of preferring and placing after circumscribes* the value-qualities that we feel.

Therefore the order of the ranks of values can *never be deduced or derived.* Which value is "higher" can be comprehended only through the acts of preferring and placing after. There exists here an *intuitive "evidence of preference"* that cannot be replaced by logical deduction.

But we can and must ask whether or not there are *a priori essential interconnections* between the *higher* and *lower levels* of a value and its *other* essential properties.

We can find, in this respect, different characters of values—already to be found in everyday experiences—with which their "height" seems to grow. But these may be traced back to *one* factor.

It appears that values are "higher" the *more* they *endure* and the *less* they partake in *"extension"* and *divisibility*. They are higher the *less they are "founded"* through other values and the *"deeper"* the *"satisfaction"* connected with feeling them. Moreover, they are higher the *less* the feeling of them is *relative* to the *positing* of a specific bearer of "feeling" and "preferring."

1. Since time immemorial, the wisdom of life has been to prefer enduring goods to transient and changing ones. But for philosophy this "wisdom of life" is only a "problem." For if it is a matter of *"goods,"* and one understands *"endurance"* in terms of the objective time in which they exist, this proposition makes little sense. "Fire" or "water" or any mechanical accident, for example, can destroy a work of art of the highest value. As Pascal states, a drop of "hot water" can destroy the health and life of the healthiest being; a "brick" can extinguish the light of a genius! "Short-lived existence" certainly does not diminish the height of the value of the being concerned! If one were to take "endurance" in this sense as a criterion for the height of values, one would fall into a type of deception characteristic of the nature of certain "moralities," especially of "pantheistic" ones. The everyday saying that "one ought not to fasten his heart on transitory things," or that the "highest good" is one of no temporal change, finds a philosophical formulation, so to speak, in all types of moralities. Spinoza, for example, holds this at the beginning of his "De emendatione intellectus".[61] Don't fall in love with anything, neither with a human being nor with an animal, neither with family, nation, or homeland nor with any positive structure of being or of value, for they all are "transitory." So runs this weary wisdom! It is anxiety and fear of the possible destruction of the good in question that drives the moralist into an ever growing "emptiness." Because of his fear of losing positive goods, he can-

---

61. The idea of God becomes a mere "idea of being," and values are to be reduced to a mere "fullness of being," which he calls perfection.

not, in the end, find *any* of them.[62] It is certain, however, that the objective endurance of goods in time can never make them more valuable.

The aforementioned proposition takes on a very different meaning if it is the higher *values* (and not goods) that, in their relation to lower values, are given as *"enduring"* by a phenomenal necessity. *"Endurance"* is, of course, basically an *absolute* and *qualitative phenomenon of time.* It has nothing to do with an absence of "succession." Endurance is, *eo ipso,* a positive mode, i.e., a mode of contents filling time as well as succession.[63] Whatever we may call "enduring" in this sense of the term may be relative (with respect to something else); however, endurance itself is not relative but a phenomenon absolutely different from "succession" (or change). A value is *enduring* through its quality of having the phenomenon of being "able" to exist through time, no matter how long its thing-bearer may exist. "Endurance" already belongs to something of value, in the particular sense of "being of value." This is the case, for instance, when we execute the act of loving a person (on the basis of his personal value)! The *phenomenon of endurance* is implicit in both the *value* to which we are directed and the experienced value of the *act of love;* hence there is also an implicit *"unceasing endurance"* [*Fortdauer*] of these values and this act. An inner attitude which would correspond to expressions like "I love you *now*" or "for a certain time" therefore contradicts the essential interconnection concerned. But there *is* this essential interconnection, no matter how long *in practice* love toward a real person may last in a span of objective time. If, on the other hand, this factual quality of the love for a person is in practical experience *not* filled in terms of endurance, so that we "do not any longer love" at a certain time, we tend to say, "I was mistaken; I never loved this person; there were only common interests that I held to be love," or "I was deceived by this person (and his value)." For there belongs to the

62. The axiom that the existence of a positive value is itself a positive value is obviously falsely interpreted to mean that *existence* is always a positive value. Something analogous occurs when pessimism falsely interprets the proposition that the non-existence of a negative value is itself a positive value to mean that non-existence is always a positive value.

63. It is false to maintain, as, e.g., David Hume does, that time belongs only to a "succession" of different contents, i.e., to assume that if the world consisted of only one and the same content, there would be no *time,* and that "duration" therefore consists only in the relation of two successions of different speeds. "Duration" is no mere difference of succession but a positive quality that can be intuited without any appearance of succession.

essence of a genuine act of love a *sub specie quadam aeterni.* This shows us, too, that the mere de facto endurance of a partnership does not at all prove that love is the bond on which it rests. For a partnership or a bond of interests and habits can last for any length of time—as long as, or longer than, a factual "love between persons." Nevertheless, it lies in the *essence* of a *bond of interests,* as opposed to love and *its* implicit values, i.e., in the essence of such an intention and its own implicit value— namely, the value of usefulness—to be *"transient."* Something sensibly agreeable or its respective "good," which we enjoy, may last for any length of (objective) time. Likewise, the factual *feeling* of the agreeable. But it belongs to the *essence* of this value, as opposed to, say, the value of health, even more to the value of "cognition," to be given "as variable." This variableness is implicit in any act of apprehending the value of agreeableness.

All this becomes clear in considering the qualitatively and basically different *acts* in which we feel values and the very *values* of these experiences.[64] Thus, it lies in the *essence* of "blissfulness" and its opposite, "despair," to *persist* and "endure" throughout the vicissitudes of "happiness" and "unhappiness," no matter how long they may last in *objective* time. Likewise, it lies in the essence of "happiness" and "unhappiness" to persist and endure throughout the vicissitudes of "joy" and "suffering," [65] and in the essence of "joy" and "suffering," in turn, to persist and endure throughout the vicissitudes of (vital) "comfort" and "discomfort." And, again, it lies in the essence of "comfort" and "discomfort" to persist and endure throughout changes in sensible states of well-being and pain. In the very "quality" of these feeling-experiences there also lies, by essential necessity, *"endurability."* Whenever, to whomever, and however long they are factually given, they are given as "enduring" or as "varying." Without having to wait for any experience of factual endurance, we experience in them a certain "endurability" and, with this, a certain measure of temporal "extendedness" in our souls, as well as a personal "permeation" by them as belonging to their *essence.*

No doubt, therefore, this "criterion" of the height of a value is of significance. For the lowest values are at the same time essentially the *"most transient"* ones; the highest values, at the same time *"eternal"* ones. And this is quite independent of any empirical "hebetability" of mere sensible feeling or similar fac-

64. The experience of values and the value of this experience are, of course, to be distinguished.
65. Taken as phenomenological unities.

tors which belong only to psychophysical characteristics of special *bearers*.

But whether or not this "criterion" can also be considered an original criterion for the height of a value is another question.

2. There is also no question about the fact that values are "higher" *the less they are divisible,* that is, the *less* they must be *divided* in *participation by several.* The fact that the participation of several in "material" goods is possible only by dividing these goods (e.g., a piece of cloth, a loaf of bread) has this final *phenomenological* basis: the *values* of the *sensibly agreeable* are clearly *extensive in their essence,* and their felt experiences occur as localized and as extensive in the body.[66] For example, the agreeableness of sweet, etc., is spread over sugar, and the corresponding sensible feeling-state over the "tongue." From this simple phenomenological fact, based on the essence of this kind of value and this particular feeling-state that corresponds to it, it follows that *material "goods"* can only be distributed when they are *divided,* and that their value corresponds to their material extension—to the extent that they are still unformed, i.e., when they are "pure" material goods. Thus a piece of cloth is, more or less, double the *worth* of one-half of it. The height of the value conforms in this case to the extension of its bearer. In strict contrast to this there stands a "work of art," for example, which is "indivisible" and of which there is no "piece." It is therefore essentially impossible for one and the same value of the value-series of the "sensibly agreeable" to be enjoyed by several beings *without* the division of its bearer and of the value itself. For this reason there are also, in the *essence* of this value-modality, "conflicts of interest" relative to the striving for a realization of these values, and relative to their enjoyment—quite independent of the amount of goods (amount being important only for the socioeconomic value of material goods). This, however, also implies that it belongs to the *essence* of these values to *divide,* not to unite, the individuals who feel them.[67]

The most extreme opposite of these values, the values of the *"holy,"* of *"cognition,"* and of the *"beautiful,"* etc., as well as their

66. *Extensive* does not mean "in a spatial order" or "measurable." A pain in the leg or a sensible feeling is, according to its nature, localized and extensive, but it is in no way ordered spatially or "in" space.

67. "Cofeeling" is least possible in feeling these values. It is not possible to cofeel a sensible pleasure as one can a joy, or to cofeel a pain (in the strict sense) as one can a sorrow. See *Zur Phänomenologie und Theorie der Sympathiegefühle.* [See Bibliog. nos. 6, 18. The relevant section is pt. A, chap. 2.—Ed.]

corresponding spiritual feeling-states, have a totally different character. There is no participation in extension and divisibility with these values; nor is there any need to divide their bearers if they are to be felt and experiencd by any *number* of beings. A work of spiritual culture can be simultaneously apprehended by any number of beings and can be felt and enjoyed in its value. It lies in the essence of values of this kind to be *communicable without limit* and without any division and diminution (even though this proposition seemingly becomes relative by reason of the existence of their bearers and their materiality, by the limits of possible access to these bearers, e.g., in buying books, or the inaccessibility of material bearers of a work of art). Nothing *unites* beings more immediately and intimately, however, than the common worship and adoration of the "*holy*," which by its nature excludes a "material" bearer, though not a symbolic one. This pertains, first, to the "absolute" and "infinitely holy," the infinitely holy person—the "*divine*." This value, the "divine," is in principle "proper" to any being just because it is the *most indivisible* value. No matter how men have been *divided* by what came to be considered "holy" in history (e.g., wars of religion, denominational quarrels), it lies in the *essence* of the *intention toward the holy to unite and join together*. All possible divisions are based solely on *symbols and techniques,* not on the holy *itself*.

Although we are concerned here, as these examples show, with essential interconnections, the question remains whether the criteria of extension and divisibility reveal the basic nature of "higher" and "lower" values.

3. I maintain that a value B is the "*foundation*" of a value A if a certain value A can only be given on the condition of the givenness of a certain value B, and this by virtue of an essential lawful necessity. If this is so, the "founding" value, i.e., the value B, is in each case the "*higher*" value. Thus the value of what is "*useful*" is "founded" in the value of what is "*agreeable*." For the "useful" is the value of something that reveals itself as a "means" to something agreeable, not in terms of a conclusion, but in terms of immediate intuition. This is the case with regard to "tools." Without the "agreeable," there would not be the "useful." Again, the agreeable, i.e., the agreeable as a value, is "founded" by essential necessity in a vital value, for instance, the value of health; feeling the agreeable (or its value), however, is founded in the value of the feeling of a living being (e.g., the feeling of its vitality and strength) which comprehends this value of the

agreeable through sensible feeling. Even the purely vital, subjective *"life-value"*—as independent of all spiritual values—is *not* exhausted in the feeling-states of agreeableness. Rather, this value *governs* all qualities and degrees of the values of the "agreeable" felt by a being. This proposition is an essential law, quite independent of all *inductive experience* that concerns, for example, the relations between factual health and disease on the one hand and feelings of pleasure and displeasure among human beings on the other. This essential law is independent of the fact that many diseases of the lungs, for example, as well as specific phases in death by suffocation and the euphoria of paralysis, are accompanied by strong pleasure-feelings, and the fact that the tearing out of a fingernail (despite the insignificance of the existence of the nail for the whole process of life) causes more pain than the removal of the cerebral cortex (despite the mortal danger involved). For there is *evidence* that the value of the agreeable of *diseased* life is *subordinated* to the same value of *healthy* life, even if the acceptability of this value is equal in both cases, or even greater in the diseased. Who, among possible victims, would "envy" a paralyzed being for its euphoria? The above cases show only that we must draw a line between the vital well-being of a total organism (as a bearer of the life-value) and that of its parts, e.g., organs, tissues, etc. (as bearers of life-values). The lower limit of the value of life, or "death," necessarily coincides with the nihilation of the value of the agreeable (or the entire sphere of "agreeable" and "disagreeable"). Hence, a *positive value of life* is the foundation of this value-series.

No matter how independent of *spiritual* values (e.g., values of cognition, beauty, etc.) the value-series of the *noble* and *vulgar* may be, it remains "founded" in these values. Life *has* these values in fact only insofar as *life* itself (in all its forms) *is* a bearer of values that take on certain heights in an absolutely objective scale. But such an "order of value-ranks" is comprehensible only through *spiritual* acts that are not vitally conditioned. For instance, it would be an "anthropomorphism" to consider man the most valuable living being if the value of this value-cognition, with *all* its values (including the value of the cognition that "man is the most valuable living being"), were "relative to man." But this proposition is "true," independent of man, "for" man ("for" in the objective sense of the word). *Life simpliciter* has a value, apart from the differentiations among vital value-qualities, only insofar as there are spiritual values and spiritual acts through which they are grasped. If values were "relative" to life alone, *life itself would have no value.* It would be a value-indifferent being.

However, *all* possible values are "founded" in the *value of an infinitely personified spirit* and its correlative *"world of values."* Acts which comprehend values comprehend absolutely objective values only if they are executed *"in"* this world of values, and values are absolute values only if they appear in this realm.

4. The *"depth of contentment,"* too, is a criterion of the heights of values. This depth accompanies the feeling of a value-height. But the height does not *consist* in this depth. Yet it is an essential interconnection that a *"higher* value" yields a *"deeper* contentment."[68] "Contentment" here has nothing to do with *pleasure,* much as "pleasure" may result from it. "Contentment" is an *experience of fulfillment;* it sets in only if an intention toward a value is fulfilled through the appearance of this value. There is no "contentment" *without* the *acceptance* of objective values. On the other hand, contentment is not necessarily linked with *"conation."* It is different, for example, from the experience of fulfillment in the realization of the desired or of the expected, even if such realizations may be considered special cases of contentment. The purest form of contentment is given in peaceful feeling and in a fully felt "possessing" of a valuable good; i.e., it is present when "conation" is at rest. Furthermore, it is by no means necessary that conation *precede* contentment as its condition. "Contentment" is implicit in the pure comprehension of values, no matter if such values were given "to be realized" antecedently in conation or in a movement of willing. But we must distinguish again between the "degree" of contentment and its *"depth,"* which alone concerns us here. The contentment in feeling one value is deeper than the contentment in feeling another value if the former proves to be *independent* of the latter while the latter remains dependent on the former. For instance, it is a quite peculiar phenomenon that sensuous enjoyment or a harmlessly trivial delight (e.g., attending a party or going for a walk) will bring us full "contentment" *only* when we feel "content" in the more central sphere of our life, where everything is "serious." It is only against this background of a deeper contentment that a fully content laughter can resound about the most trivial joys. Conversely, if the more central sphere is not content, there arises a "discontentment" and a restless search for *pleasure values* that

68. H. Cornelius (*Einleitung in die Philosophie* [Leipzig: Teubner, 1911]) has attempted a subtle reduction of the higher value to the value of deeper contentment.

at once replace a full contentment in feeling the lower values concerned. One can even draw a conclusion from this: the many forms of hedonism always reveal a token of "discontentment" with regard to higher values. There exists a reciprocal relation, then, between the degrees of *searching* for pleasure and the depth of contentment in a value of the value-series in question.

Nevertheless, on whatever essential interconnections the above four criteria of value-heights may rest, they do not give us the *ultimate* meaning of value-heights. Is there another such criteriological principle, then, one that can bring us nearer to the meaning of "being-higher," and from which the above criteria may be derived?

5. Whatever "objectivity" and "factual nature" are attributable to all "values," and however *independent* their interrelations may be of the reality and the real connections of goods in which they are real, there is yet another distinguishing element among values that has nothing to do with apriority or aposteriority: this is the *level* of the "*relativity* of values," or their *relationship* to "*absolute* values." [69]

The basic mutual interconnection between the act and its correlate implies that we must not presuppose any objective existence of values and their types (let alone of real goods that bear values of a certain kind) unless we can find types of acts and functions *belonging* to the experience of such types of values. For instance, for a non-sensible being there are no values of the agreeable. Indeed, such a being may know that "there are sensibly feeling beings," and that "they feel values of the agreeable"; and it may also know the *value* of this fact and its exemplifications. But the *value* of the *agreeable itself* does not exist for such an imaginary creature. We cannot assume that God, like men and animals, has a *lived experience* of all values of the agreeable. In this particular sense I maintain that the values of the agreeable and disagreeable are "*relative*" to a "sensibly feeling being," just as the values of "noble and vulgar" are relative

69. Because a "relative" value is relative does not mean that it is a "subjective" value. For instance, a hallucinated body-thing is "relative" to an individual, yet this object is not "subjective" in the way that feeling is. An emotive hallucination, for example, is *both* "subjective" and "relative" to the individual. And a "real" feeling is "subjective," but not "relative," to an individual, even when only the individual concerned has access to the cognition of its reality. On the other hand a mirror image, as a physical phenomenon, is "*relative*" to the mirror and the mirrored object, but it is not relative to the individual. [On "relativity" (*Daseinsrelativität*), see "Idealismus—Realismus" (Bibliog. no. 25) "Phänomenologie und Erkenntnistheorie," and "Erkenntnis und Arbeit."—*Ed.*]

to "living beings" in general. In strict contrast to this, however, I maintain that *absolute values* are those that exist in "pure" feeling (and preferring and loving), i.e., they exist in a type of feeling that is *independent* of the *nature* of sensibility and of life as such. This feeling possesses its own functional characteristics and laws. Among the values belonging to this feeling are *moral* values. In *pure* feeling we may be able to "understand" the feeling of sensible values (i.e., in a feeling manner) without performing sensible feeling-functions through which we (or others) enjoy the agreeable, but we cannot feel them in this manner. From this we infer that God can "understand" pain, for instance, but that he does so without feeling pain.

Such relativity of the being of *kinds* of values has, of course, *nothing* to do with another relativity: that of the *kinds of goods* that are the *bearers* of such values. For kinds of goods are, *in addition*, relative to the special factual psychophysical constitution of the real being that has such goods. The fact that the same object can be poisonous for one species and nutritious for another, for instance, or that something may be agreeable to the perverted drives of one living being and "disagreeable" or "harmful" to the normal drives of another being of the same species, determines only a relativity of values *in relation to* the *goods* in question. But this relativity in no way represents an ontic relativity of the values themselves. It is one of a "second order" only, which has nothing to do with the relativity of the above-mentioned "first order." One cannot reduce this relativity of *kinds* of values to that of goods (*in relation* to kinds of values). Both orders are essentially different. There are even "a priori" interconnections holding among relative values, but there are none holding among goods.[70]

Taking the words *relative* and *absolute* in *this* sense, I assert it to be an essential interconnection that values given in immediate intuition *"as higher"* are values that are given as *nearer* to *absolute* values *in* feeling and preferring (and not by way of deliberation). Entirely outside the sphere of "judgment" or "deliberation" there is an *immediate* feeling of the "relativity" of a value. And for this feeling the variability of a relative value in comparison with the concomitant constancy of a less "relative" value (no matter if variability and constancy pertain to "endurance," "divisibility," "depth of contentment") is a *confirmation*,

---

70. That there must be "goods" for *all* values is the one *absolute* interconnection here.

but not a *proof*. Thus the value of the cognition of a truth, or the value of the silent beauty of a work of art, has a *phenomenal detachment* from the concomitant feeling of our *life*—above all, from our sensible feeling-states. Such a value is also quite independent of an estimative deliberation about the permanence of such beauty or truth with regard to the "experiences of life," which tend more to detract us from true absolute values than to bring us nearer to them. In living an act of pure love toward a person, the *value* of this person is detached from all simultaneously felt value-levels of our own personal world of values when we experience these as connected with our sense and feeling of life. Again, this value is also quite independent of any estimative deliberation about the permanence that an act of pure loving may have through happiness and sorrow, the inherent or accidental fate of life. *Implicit* in the very kind of the given value-experience there is a *guarantee* (and not a "conclusion") that there is here an absolute value. This *evidence* of an absolute value stems neither from an estimative deliberation about the permanence it may have in practical life nor from the universality of a judgment which holds that "this value is absolute in *all* moments of our lives." Rather, it is the *felt absoluteness* of this value that makes us feel that a defection from it in favor of other values constitutes "*possible* guilt" as well as a "falling away" from the height of value-existence which we had just reached.

Whereas the "relativity" of values to goods (and therefore also to our psychophysical constitution) is found by judgment and syllogism—by comparisons and induction—*this kind of relativity* and *absoluteness* is *given in emotive immediacy*. In this area judgments and the allied acts of comparing and induction tend more to cover the immediacy of the fact of the self-given "relativity" or "absoluteness" of a felt value than to make it clear to us. There is a *depth* in man that always silently tells him what the "relativity" of felt values is,[71] no matter how much he may seek to cover it up by means of judgments, comparisons, and induction.

The essential (i.e., *original*) characteristic of a "higher value"

---

71. In theory, a "skeptic" or an "anthropologist" is the one who feels that he *actually* "knows" nothing. Socrates, on the other hand, *knows* and also feels that he *must know* "that he knows nothing." In morals, someone is a skeptic or an anthropologist who (secretly) feels "that his values are not the highest." Jesus, on the other hand, says, "No one is good"; with regard to the "absolute" value, he feels that *no one* is its bearer except God.

is, then, its being *less "relative"*; of the "highest" value, its being an *"absolute"* value. All other essential interconnections among values are grounded in these criteria.

4. The A Priori Relations between Heights of Values and "Pure" Bearers of Values

We expect an ethics first of all to furnish us with an explicit determination of "higher" and "lower" in the order of values, a determination that is itself based on the contents of the essences of values—insofar as this order is understood to be independent of all possible positive systems of goods and purposes. It is not our aim at this point in the discussion to furnish such a determination. It will be sufficient here to characterize more fully the *kinds* of a priori orders among values.

In this respect we find two orders. One contains the heights of values in their ordered ranks according to their *essential* [wesenhaften] *bearers*. The other is a *pure non-formal* order in that it exists only among the ultimate units of the *series of value-qualities*, which we shall call value-modalities.

We shall discuss here the first order mentioned, which can also be called a relatively *"formal"* order when compared with the second.

I will first give a brief survey of values with respect to their *essential* bearers.

a. Values of the Person and Values of Things [Sachwerte]

The values of the person pertain to the *person* himself, *without any mediation. Values of things* pertain to *things* of value as represented in "goods." Again, goods may be material (goods of enjoyment, of usefulness), vital (all economic goods), or spiritual (science and art, which are also called cultural goods). In contrast to these values there are two kinds of values that belong to the human person: (1) the value of the *person "himself,"* and (2) the values of virtue. In this sense the values of the person are *higher* than those of things. This lies in their *essence*.

b. Values of Oneself [Eigenwerte] and Values of the Other [Fremdwerte]

The division of values into *"values of oneself"* and *"values of the other"* has nothing to do with the former division, values of the person and values of things. For values of oneself and values of the other can be values of persons and values of things, as well as "values of acts," "values of functions," and "values of feeling-states." Values of oneself and values of the other have equal *heights.*[72] It is, however, a valid question (which we shall not discuss here in detail, since we are concerned with *kinds* of a priori relations) whether the very *apprehension* of "values of the other" is of higher value than the apprehension of a value of oneself. It is certain, however, that the act of realizing a value of the other is of *higher* value than the act of realizing a value of oneself.

c. Values of Acts, Values of Functions, and Values of Reactions

Other bearers of values are *acts* (e.g., acts of cognition, love, hate, will), *functions* (e.g., hearing, seeing, feeling), and *responses* and *reactions* (e.g., "to be glad about something"). The last also contain responses to human persons, like cofeeling, revenge, etc., which, in turn, are distinguished from "spontaneous" acts. All of these are subordinated to the values of the person. But they, too, possess a priori relations among their own heights. For instance, the values of acts as such are *higher* than the values of functions, and both are *higher* than the values of mere "responses." Spontaneous manifestations of comportment are of higher value than reactive ones.

d. Values of the Basic Moral Tenor [*Gesinnungswerte*], Values of Deeds, and Values of Success

Values of the basic moral tenor and values of deeds (both are moral values as opposed to *"values of success"*), as well as the bearers of values between them, such as "intention," "resolve," "performance," are bearers of values having a specific order of heights (apart from their own special contents).[73] But this order will not be further discussed here.

e. Values of Intention and Values of Feeling-States

All values of intentional experiences are *higher* than those of mere *states* of experience, such as sensible or bodily feeling-states. The heights of the values of experiences correspond here to the heights of the experienced values.

---

72. Eduard von Hartmann correctly proves that values of the other can function as higher values (i.e., higher than proper values) only in ontological pessimism, i.e., when *being* itself is a *disvalue* (see *Phänomenologie des sittlichen Bewusstseins*). If we were to agree to this (false) presupposition, we would give in to this pessimism.

73. [On the basic tenor and deeds as bearers of values, see chap. 3. —Ed.]

f. Values of Terms of Relations, Values of Forms of Relations, and Values of Relations

In all relations among human persons there are, first, the persons themselves as bearers of values, second, the forms of their relations, and, third, the relations as given experiences within this form. All these are bearers of values. Thus there are the persons as *"terms"* of, say, a friendship or marriage relation; then there is the *"form"* of such a relation, and, finally, the (experienced) *"relation"* of persons within such a form. For instance, the value of the form of marriage, which is historically quite independent of specific experiences in this relation and *their own* proper values (e.g., "good" or "bad" marriages, which are possible in *all* "forms"), is to be sharply distinguished from the value of the relation obtaining among persons *within* this form. But this relation *itself* is also a specific bearer of values whose value does *not* coincide with the values of the relational terms or form.

Any *"life-community"* is, as a moral bearer of values, governed by the a priori value-relations obtaining among these kinds of values. We will not go into this further at this point.

g. Individual Values and Collective Values

The distinction between individual values and collective values has nothing to do with the above bearers of values or the distinction between "values of oneself" and "values of the other." If one turns to values of oneself, such values may be individual values or collective values proper to one as a "member" or "representative" of a "social rank," "profession," or "class"; or they may be values of one's own individuality. This holds also for values of the other.[74] This division does not coincide with the distinction drawn among values of relational terms, values of relational forms, and values of relations. Here we have differences among bearers of values that lie in the whole of an experienced "community," by which we mean only a *whole experienced* by all its "members." Such a life-community is not a factually existing (more or less) artificial unit of mere elements which act among each other objectively and conceive their unit as a unit. We shall

74. Thus love (in the Christian sense) is always *individual love*, both as *self*-love and love of the *other*, which is also called love of one's neighbor, but not as love for one who is a *member* of the class of workers, for example, or a "representative" of a collective group. The "social consciousness" of the working class has nothing to do with "love of one's neighbor." The latter pertains to the worker, but only as a human *individual*.

call this latter unit of human beings a *society*. Now, all "collective values" are "*values of a society*." Their bearers form not experienced "wholes" but majorities of a conceptualized class. Life-communities, however, may also function as "*individuals*" vis-à-vis "collectives," e.g., an individual marriage, a family, a community, a people, etc., as opposed to the totality of marriages or families or communities of a country or the totality of peoples, etc.[75]

Between individual values and collective values in general there are a priori value-relations.

h. Self-Values and Consecutive Values

There are values which retain their value-character independent of all other values. There are also values which by essence possess a *phenomenal* (intuitively feelable) relatedness to other values which is necessary for their being "values." The former I call *self-values;* the latter, *consecutive values*.

But we must remember that all things representing themselves as "*means*" for *causal* productions of goods, and all mere *symbols* of values (insofar as they are *only* that), have *no immediate* or *phenomenal* value and are not independent bearers of values. The so-called value of a mere "means" attributed to a thing (in the form of a "judgment") [76] is attributable to it only by virtue of a calculating act of thinking (or an association) through which this thing represents itself as a "means." Symbols *for* values (e.g., paper money) have no phenomenal value. Therefore, we do not call the value of a "means" or a "symbol" a consecutive value. *Consecutive values* are still *phenomenal* value-facts. Any kind of "*tool-value*," for example, is a genuine consecutive value, for there is intuited in this value of the tool a true *value*. Of course, this value always implies a "reference" to the value of the thing produced by this tool, but this former value is phenomenally "given" *prior* to the value of the product. It is not derived from the given value of the product. We must therefore sharply distinguish the value which something "has as a means" or "can have as a means" from the value which pertains to the means *insofar as it is intuitively given "as a means,"* and which is attached to its bearer no matter whether or not it is, in fact, used as a means, and no matter to what degree it is used.

75. [On "community" and "society," see chap. 6, B, sec. 4, ad 4.—*Ed.*]
76. But not in the form of an assessment, which presupposes given values.

All specifically *"technical values"* are also, in this sense, genuine, consecutive values. Among them, the "useful" is a (genuine) consecutive value with regard to the *self-value* of the "agreeable." Among higher values, also, there are self-values and technical values; and for every kind of higher value, there exists a special realm of technical values.[77]

A second basic kind of consecutive values (besides "technical" values) consists of *"symbolic values."* These are not the same as pure "symbols of values," which are not (phenomenal) bearers of values. An example of a true symbolic value is a regimental "flag," in which the honor and dignity of a regiment are symbolically concentrated. It is precisely for this reason that a flag possesses a *phenomenal value* that has nothing to do with its cloth value, etc.[78] In this sense all "sacramental things" (*res sacrae*) are also genuine symbolic values, not mere symbols of values. Their special *symbolic* function of pointing to something holy (of a special kind) becomes here, again, another *bearer* of a special kind of value (independent of symbolic things). It is this that raises them above mere "symbols for values."

Self-values and consecutive values also have their own a priori relations between their being-*higher* and being-*lower*.

In contrast, symbols of values serve only for (always artificial) *quantifications of values* and for measurements of *larger* and *smaller,* which have nothing to do with the *height* of a value.[79] But we shall not dwell on the problem of measurements of values or the question of how one can speak of a "sum of happiness" and the like.

5. *A Priori Relations of Rank among Value-Modalities*

The most important and most fundamental a priori relations obtain as an *order of ranks* among the systems of qualities of non-formal values which we call *value-modalities*. They consti-

77. See chap. 2, sec. 5.
78. Likewise, a king's colors or a priest's chasuble.
79. As pure qualities, values are not measurable. In this respect they are like the *pure phenomena of color and sound*, which become indirectly measurable through their *bearers* and their quantities (through the mediations of the phenomena of light and sound and their relations to extension and spatiality). Values of the *same* modality can be made *indirectly* measurable by measuring their bearers in such a way that their magnitude-units, which assume a just-noticeable difference in value, are used as units of measurement and designated with a certain *symbol of value*. By counting and treating such *symbols* numerically, we achieve an indirect value-measurement.

tute the *non-formal a priori* proper in the intuition of values and the intuition of preferences. The facts of these modalities present the *strongest* refutation of Kant's formalism. The ultimate divisions of value-qualities that are presupposed for these essential interconnections must be as independent of all factual goods and the special organizations of living beings that feel values as is the order of the ranks of the value-modalities.

Rather than giving a full development and establishment of these systems of qualities and their implicit laws of preferring, the following presents an explanation through examples of the kinds of a priori orders of ranks among values.

1. The values ranging from *the agreeable to the disagreeable* represent a sharply delineated value-modality (Aristotle already mentions them in his division of the ἡδύ, the χρήσιμον, and the καλόν). The function of *sensible feeling* (with its modes of enjoying and suffering) is correlative to this modality. The respective feeling-states, the so-called feelings of sensation,[80] are pleasure and pain. As in all value-modalities, there are values of *things* [Sachwerte], values of *feeling-functions*, and values of *feeling-states*.

This modality is *"relative"* to beings endowed with sensibility in general. But it is relative *neither* to a specific species, e.g., man, *nor* to specific things or events of the real world that are "agreeable" or "disagreeable" to a being of a particular species. Although one type of event may be agreeable to one man and disagreeable to another (or agreeable and disagreeable to different animals), the difference between the values of agreeable and disagreeable as such is an *absolute* difference, clearly given prior to any cognition of things.

The proposition that the agreeable is preferable to the disagreeable (*ceteris paribus*) is not based on observation and induction. The preference lies in the essential contents of these values as well as in the nature of sensible feelings. If a traveler or a historian or a zoologist were to tell us that this preference is reversed in a certain kind of animal, we would "a priori" disbelieve his story. We would say that this is impossible unless it is only *things* different from ours that this animal feels are disagreeable and agreeable, or unless its preferring the disagreeable to the agreeable is based on a value of a *modality* (perhaps unknown to us) that is "higher" than that of the agreeable and the disagreeable. In the latter case the animal would only "put

80. [See below, p. 332, n. 114.—*Ed.*]

up with" the disagreeable in preferring the value of the extra
modality. There may also be cases of perverted drives in this
animal, allowing it to experience as agreeable those things that
are *detrimental* to life. The state of affairs in all of these examples, as well as that which our proposition expresses, namely,
that the agreeable is preferable to the disagreeable, also serves
as a *law of understanding* external expressions of life and concrete (e.g., historical) valuation (even one's *own*, e.g., in remembering); our proposition is a *presupposition* of all observation
and induction, and it is "a priori" to all ethnological experience.

Nor can this proposition and its respective facts be "explained" by way of evolutionary theories. It is nonsense to say
that values (and their laws of preference) "developed" as *signs*
of kinetic combinations that proved purposeful for the individual
or its species. Such a theory can explain only the accompanying
feeling-*states* that are connected with impulsive actions directed
toward things. But *the values themselves* and their *laws of
preferring* could *never* be thus explained. For the latter are independent of all specific organizations of living beings.

Certain groups of consecutive values (technical values [81] and
symbolic values) correspond to these self-values of the modality
of the agreeable and the disagreeable. But they do not concern
us here.

2. The essence of values correlated to *vital feeling* differs
sharply from the above modality. Its thing-values, insofar as
they are self-values, are such qualities as those encompassed by
the *"noble"* and the *"vulgar"* (and by the "good" in the pregnant
sense of "excellent" [*tüchtig*] as opposed to "bad" rather than
"evil").[82] All corresponding consecutive values (technical and
symbolic) belong to the sphere denoted by *"weal,"* or *"well-
being."* [83] They are *subordinated* to the noble and its opposite.
The feeling-states of this modality include all modes of the
feelings of life (e.g., the feelings of "quickening" and "declining"

81. They are in part technical values concerning the *production* of
agreeable things and are unified in the concept of the "useful" (*values of
civilization*), and in part values concerning the enjoyment of agreeable
things (*luxury values*).

82. One also uses "noble" and its opposite with respect to vital values
("noble horse," "noble tree," "noble race," "nobility," etc.).

83. "Weal" and "well-being" therefore do not coincide with vital values
in general; the value of well-being is determined by the extent to which
the individual or the community, which can be in a good or a bad state, is
noble or *base*. On the other hand, "weal" is superior as a vital value to
mere "usefulness" (and "agreeableness"), and the well-being of a community is superior to the sum of its interests (as a society).

life, the feelings of health and illness, the feeling of aging and oncoming death, the feelings of "weakness," "strength," etc.). Certain emotional reactions also belong to this modality—(a certain kind of) "being glad about" or "being sad about," drive reactions such as "courage," "anxiety," revengeful impulses, ire, etc. Here we cannot even indicate the tremendous richness of these value-qualities and their correlates.

Vital values form an entirely *original* modality. They cannot be "reduced" to the values of the agreeable and the useful, nor can they be reduced to spiritual values. Previous ethical theories made a *basic mistake* in ignoring this fact. Even Kant tacitly presupposes that these values can be reduced to mere hedonistic ones when he tries to divide all values in terms of good-evil on the one hand and agreeable-disagreeable on the other.[84] This division, however, is not applicable even to values of "well-being," let alone the vital self-value of the noble.

The particular character of this modality lies in the fact that "*life*" is a *genuine essence* and not an "empirical generic conception" that contains only "common properties" of all living organisms. When this fact is misconceived, the uniqueness of vital values is overlooked. We will not go into this in further detail here.

3. The realm of *spiritual values* is distinct from that of vital values as an original modal unity. In the kind of their *givenness*, spiritual values have a peculiar detachment from and independence of the spheres of the lived body and the environment. Their unity reveals itself in the clear evidence that vital values "ought" to be sacrificed for them. The functions and acts in which they are apprehended are functions of *spiritual* feeling and acts of *spiritual* preferring, loving, and hating. They are set off from like-named *vital* functions and acts by pure phenomenological evidence as well as by their *own proper lawfulness* (which *cannot be reduced* to any "biological" lawfulness).

The main types of spiritual values are the following: (1) the values of "*beautiful*" and "*ugly*," together with the whole range of purely aesthetic values; (2) the values of "*right*" and "*wrong*" [*des* Rechten *und* Unrechten], objects that are "values" and wholly different from what is "correct" and "incorrect" according to a

---

84. See *Critique of Practical Reason*, pt. I, bk. II, chap. 2. The hedonists and the utilitarians, like Kant, make the mistake of reducing this value-modality to the agreeable and the useful; the rationalists make the (equally erroneous) mistake of reducing it to spiritual values (especially the rational ones).

law, which form the utlimate phenomenal basis of the idea of the objective *order of right* [Rechtsordnung], an order that is independent of the idea of "law," the idea of the state, and the idea of the life-community on which the state rests (it is especially independent of all positive legislation); [85] (3) the values of the *"pure cognition of truth,"* whose realization is sought in *philosophy* (in contrast to positive "science," which is guided by the aim of controlling natural appearances).[86] Hence *"values of science"* are consecutive values of the values of the cognition of truth. So-called *cultural values* in general are the consecutive (technical and symbolic) values of *spiritual* values and belong to the value-sphere of *goods* (e.g., art treasures, scientific institutions, positive legislation, etc.). The correlative feeling-states of spiritual values—for instance, the feeling-states of spiritual joy and sorrow (as opposed to the vital "being gay" and "not being gay")—possess the phenomenal quality of appearing *without mediation.* That is to say, they do not appear on an "ego" as its states, nor does an antecedent givenness of the lived body of a person serve as a condition of their appearance.[87] Spiritual feeling-states vary *independent* of changes in vital feeling-states (and, of course, sensible feeling-states). Their variations are directly dependent upon the variations of the values of the *objects themselves* and occur according to their own proper laws.

Finally, there are the reactions belonging to this modality, including "pleasing" and "displeasing," "approving" and "disapproving," "respect" and "disrespect," "retributive conation" (as opposed to the vital impulses of revenge) and "spiritual sympathy" (which is the foundation of friendship, for instance).

4. Values of the last modality are those of the *holy* and the *unholy.* This modality differs sharply from the above modalities. It forms a unit of value-qualities not subject to further definition. Nevertheless, these values have *one* very definite condition of their givenness: they appear only in objects that are given in intention as "absolute objects." This expression, however, refers *not* to a specific or definable *class* of objects, but (in principle) to *any* object given in the "absolute sphere." Again, this modality

---

85. "Law" is only a consecutive value for the self-value of the "order of right"; positive law (of a state) is the consecutive value for the (objective) "order of right" which is valid in the state and which lawmakers *and* judges must realize.

86. We speak of the value of "cognition," not of the value of "truth." Truth does *not* belong among the values. [See chap. 4, sec. 1.—Ed.]

87. See chap. 5, esp. sec. 8.

is quite independent of all that has been considered "holy" by different peoples at various times, such as holy things, powers, persons, institutions, and the like (i.e., from ideas of fetishism to the purest conceptions of God). These latter problems do not belong to an *a priori phenomenology of values* [apriorische Wertlehre] and the theory of ordered ranks of values.[88] They concern the *positive representations of goods* within this value-sphere. With regard to the values of the holy, however, *all* other values are at the same time given as symbols for these values.

The feeling-states belonging to this modality range from "blissfulness" to "despair"; they are independent of "happiness" and "unhappiness," whether it be in occurrence, duration, or change. In a certain sense these feeling-states indicate the "nearness" or the "remoteness" of the divine in experience.

"Faith" and "lack of faith," "awe," "adoration," and analogous atttiudes are specific reactions in this modality.

However, the act through which we *originally* apprehend the value of the holy is an act of a specific kind of *love* (whose value-direction *precedes* and *determines* all pictorial representations and concepts of holy objects); that is to say, in essence the act is directed toward persons, or toward something of the *form of a personal being, no matter what* content or what "*conception*" of personhood is implied. The self-value in the sphere of the values of the "holy" is therefore, by essential necessity, a "*value of the person.*"

The values of things and forms of worship implicit in cults and sacraments are consecutive values (technical and symbolic) of all holy values of the person. They represent genuine "symbolic values," not mere "symbols of values."

Since we intend to stick to the most elementary points, we shall refrain from showing how these basic values are connected with the ideas of person and community. We shall likewise refrain from showing how one can obtain from these values the "*pure types of persons,*" such as the saint, the genius, the hero, the leading spirit of civilization, and the *bon vivant,* and their respective technical occupations (e.g., the priest), as well as the *pure types of communal forms of togetherness,* such as the community of love (plus its technical form, the church), the community of law, the community of culture, and the life-community

---

88. Thus, e.g., an oath is an affirmation and a promise with reference to the value of the holy, no matter what is holy to the man concerned, no matter by what he swears.

(plus its technical form, the state), and the mere forms of so-called society.[89]

As we have stated, these modalities have their own a priori order of ranks that precedes their series of qualities. This order of value-ranks is valid for the *goods* of correlative values because it is valid for the *values* of goods. The order is this: the modality of vital values is *higher* than that of the agreeable and the disagreeable; the modality of spiritual values is *higher* than that of vital values; the modality of the holy is *higher* than that of spiritual values.

A more detailed attempt to found these propositions cannot be undertaken at this point.

89. [On the "pure types of persons," see chap. 6, B, sec. 4, ad 6 b. See also "Vorbilder und Führer" (Bibliog. no. 29). On the "pure types of community," see chap. 6, B, sec. 4, ad 4.—*Ed.*]

3 / Non-Formal Ethics and Ethics of Success

ANOTHER OF THE ESSENTIAL INTERCONNECTIONS mentioned at the beginning of our investigation is, in Kant's terms, the following: *only a formal ethics is able to locate the values of good and evil within the basic moral tenor, whereas every non-formal ethics must of necessity be an "ethics of success,"* i.e., an ethics which makes the value of persons and of acts of willing—indeed, of all acting—dependent upon the experience of the practical *consequences* of their efficacy in the real world.

First of all, there is no doubt that the moral value of the person and his acts and acting is entirely *indifferent* to the *success* of moral deeds. Therefore, any attempt to introduce the concept of the *"basic moral tenor"* as a merely auxiliary concept designating solely a "constant disposition" for a certain kind of positive or negative success of deeds, and, hence, to consider its value as a merely *dispositional value*, must fail in the presence of the unequivocal clarity in moral feeling as well as the moral judgments founded on the contents of this feeling. It is, in principle, nonsense to make the moral relevance of practical acting dependent upon a calculation of probable consequences based on real states of affairs and their causal relationships. The *"basic moral tenor,"* if it is to possess a moral value, must allow of an immediate demonstration as a *confirmable fact* within the formation of an act of will. Whether there can be yet *other* dispositions "for" a basic moral tenor is a totally different question.

But what is Kant's notion of this *"basic moral tenor"*? First, he correctly distinguishes between this "basic tenor" and "intentions." He expressly states that it is not intentions as opposed to success which serve as the original bearers of moral good and evil, but that it is this "basic moral tenor in which intentions are posited." Hence it is only the *"form of positing an intention."* Precisely for this reason, according to Kant, it cannot itself have any *"material,"* as intentions undoubtedly do. Moreover, since the material of willing and conation rests *of necessity* on the relationship between what is willed and our sensible states of pleasure [*Lust*], and since pleasure is first represented necessarily as a (not yet intended) success of some kind of acting in the world, or as some excitability resulting through the world, any consideration of the "material" of willing necessarily implies, says Kant, that *"success"* is a standard for this material.

My critique of these propositions begins with the concept of the *basic moral tenor.* Kant rightly stresses that the "basic moral tenor" is to be distinguished from mere *"intention"* and, of course, from anything done "on purpose" [*Vorsatz*]. It is a phenomenal fact that we can remain within the *same* basic moral tenor with respect to one and the same state of affairs while our intentions continually change. Likewise, whatever we plan to do on purpose may vary while the intention remains the same. The basic moral tenor is certainly one level *lower* than intentions. As Kant correctly saw, the formation of intentions is *dependent* on the individual's fortuitous life-experiences and, consequently, also on the success of deeds or on dispositions that have been established by previous deeds (even those of our ancestors, in which case the dispositions coincide with "inherited disposition"). But clearly we find the *phenomenon* of the basic moral tenor in cases where there is yet no formation of intentions, e.g., intentions with respect to someone else. If, for instance, someone asks us to do something special for him, the *first* thing that we experience is an act of conation aiming in the direction of either "positive values" or "negative values" with regard to this person. This happens whether or not we have formed the intent to do this special favor in some manner or other. We say in such a case that there is a difference in "basic moral tenor" between us. In this case the basic moral tenor is certainly an *experienceable fact;* and it is *more* than a mere "mode" or "form" of conation, because a *direction toward certain positive or negative values* is already clearly given in it. Only within the *scope* of this can a formation of intentions take place. Much as Kant is correct in regarding the *"basic moral tenor,"* and not intentions, as the *original* bearer of good and evil, he is mistaken in asserting that it is on the one hand unexperienceable and on the other a mere "form" of the position of intentions. For, according to Kant, only posited *intentions* are experienceable; and since the *basic moral tenor* is supposedly only the "form of their position," it *cannot,* strictly speaking, *ever be experienced.* This, however, is not at all the case. We do *not* have to *compute* the basic tenor that we have toward someone by *comparing experiences* of our comportment toward him in different phases of our lives. Yet this is precisely what the theory of dispositions asserts. Rather, we are *aware* of the basic moral tenor, its *endurance,* and its *independence* of changing life-experiences. Nevertheless, the basic moral tenor is an object of *"experience,"* though of a *different* kind from that of inductive experience. For this very reason there can be a community of individuals of the *same* basic moral tenor and the domination of one basic moral tenor in a certain group of human beings. The concept of a "conscious *community* of one and the same basic moral tenor" would be a contradiction in terms if it were unexperienceable and at the same time a bearer of moral values.[1] Nor is it a mere *form* of the positing of intentions. If this were the case, it could have only the predicates of *"according to law"* and *"not according to law."* Moreover, Kant maintains that its nature consists in the lawful form of the sequence of intentions, as opposed to a person's being pushed toward intentions without rules when lacking a basic moral tenor, and hence he concludes that an "unlawful moral tenor" could not exist at all. Thus, "willing the good" coincides with "willing morally according to the basic tenor." This, however, is by no means true. Undoubtedly there are *good* and *evil* moral tenors, as well as lawful and unlawful ones. And within the former kinds there again exists a large number of special qualities, such as benevolent, loving, revengeful, distrusting, and trustful. Although these are *genuine* qualities of a moral tenor, they are nevertheless *independent* of the *intentions* that exist within the scope of such qualities, and independent of all intentions that may originate in fortuitous experiences (of the associative sphere, with its implicit possibilities of connections). Lawful and unlawful basic moral tenors represent only *one* pair among the qualities mentioned that a basic moral tenor can have. For this very reason alone, an ethics that seeks to locate the moral value of willing in its basic moral tenor does *not* coincide with a *formal* ethics.

---

1. All communities would then have the outer form that is built on the idea of the "contract" alone.

If the basic moral tenor is the principal bearer of the moral values within the realm of act-values, one must also attribute a moral value to every *other* level of the act of willing and to deeds as well. The moral tenor is *not* the *sole* bearer of moral values, but only the bearer that must have moral value *insofar* as intentions, deliberateness [*Vorsatz*], resolve, and deeds are to be of moral value. Kant himself says that the basic moral tenor is the original, but not the sole, object of moral values. But his theory implies that everything *outside* this original moral tenor and everything that follows from it—indeed, everything that can normally follow from it—must be subject to a mere *natural mechanism* (including a psychic mechanism). This would imply, too, that all other levels in the willing of deeds that are added to the basic moral tenor, as it were, are *not* novel bearers of moral values. It is true that the moral value of the basic moral tenor is the *foundation* of the moral value of a deed. Without a good moral tenor there is no good deed. Nevertheless, the *addition* of a deed (and its special quality) to a good moral tenor determines also a new *bearer* of a moral value, one that is *not* contained in this tenor.

The recognition of this proposition is, of course, dependent on the recognition of a *non-formal specification* of the basic moral tenor—a recognition which is in *no* way the result of a response to the success of a deed on the part of the person, but which, on the contrary, is independent of such a response. For if the basic moral tenor were nothing but an awareness of lawfulness or unlawfulness in which the positing of a content would follow intentions, then any *content* of intentions, any *deed*, and especially anything done *on purpose* could emanate from either a good or an evil moral tenor. The moral tenor could not at all *determine* the contents of such levels up to a deed. On the basis of this disconnection of the basic moral tenor as the original bearer of the values of good and evil, a deed *as such* cannot function as a bearer of these values. A deed must then be an *addition* to the moral tenor similar to a natural process lying beyond all influences of the will. And, like any natural process, a deed would be morally indifferent. It would also be necessary to conclude from this that one can never *judge* a human being on the basis of his deeds, or even his intentions. For in this case *any* intention and *any* deed could come from a "good" or an "evil" moral tenor. People whom we praise for always having "shown love to us" and who we think are "our best friends" could, on the above premise, have a moral tenor contrary to that which we think they must have. Again, an inveterate criminal whose life consists of an uninterrupted chain of bad deeds could be a man of "good moral tenor." Hence we would be confronted with the Calvinistic doctrine, according to which no determinable reason can be given for a distinction between the deeds of the "chosen" and those of the "rejected." True, the ancient proposition that *"only* God can see into man's heart" does have an educational justification when one considers moral judgments that are formed all too quickly. But to place the bearer of moral value beyond sight and recognition—which is a consequence of the Kantian theories—is to proceed in a way that is different perhaps only in *words* from any ethical skepticism.

But this is not the case. The basic moral tenor, i.e., the directedness of willing toward a higher (or lower) value and its content, contains a *non-formal value-quality* [Wertmaterie] that is independent of success, even of all further levels of an act of willing. Therefore the basic moral tenor does not unilaterally determine intentions, something done on purpose, or deeds. But whatever *can* become their content is nevertheless dependent on the value-content of the basic tenor in that the peculiarity of its content determines what *can* become in a special case of intention, something done on purpose, or a deed. Hence the importance of the basic moral tenor consists in the delineation of *a non-formal a priori field* for the formation of possible intentions, acts done on purpose, and deeds, *including* the kinematic intention that directly guides a deed. The basic moral tenor permeates all levels of a deed up to its success with its own value-content. Therefore it can come to an *appearance* in a deed and can be *intuitively* given without our having to "conclude" anything. It is peculiar to the basic moral tenor to remain *constant* throughout changes in the qualities of conation, as well as throughout differences in the conation's intention toward *reality.* Its *content* appears not only in intentions, acts done on purpose, and deeds, but also in wishes and their expressions. It permeates the fantasy-world of conation far into reveries and dreams. It may even appear outwardly in cases where all ability of willing and acting disappears, as in abulia and apraxia, in an *expressive phenomenon,* in smiling, in gestures, etc. Indeed, the expressive phenomenon often gives clearer witness to the moral tenor's directedness, insofar as we often recognize it in this phenomenon, than do speech, deeds, etc., which may hide its genuineness. It is likewise efficacious in the significant process of the *formation* of intentions, often called *"moral deliberation,"* which consists in an inner emotive probing and scrutiny of possible intentions and their values. Granted there are great differences between the contents of mere fanciful wishes or factual intentions and things done on purpose (also with regard to the moral values involved). For instance, a human being may fancy himself a criminal, whereas in real life he is a most righteous person. But in this case we would also find that intentions are dependent on the basic moral tenor permeating *both* sides of the conative life. A wish, as a *sign* of the "moral tenor," is also subject to moral arbitration [*Beurteilung*], whereas willing and deeds are also *independent* bearers of moral values, though they can of course function as "signs" of the basic moral tenor.

We claim, then, that the "basic moral tenor" can determine the formation of intentions. It belongs to its essence to *endure* throughout all changes in intentions concerning the same state of affairs. However, this does not mean that the basic moral tenor itself cannot change. Whenever the *basic moral tenor* changes, there is *no* way to reduce this change to the fact that acts of willing and deeds have had a success *different* from the intended one. Nor can such a change in the tenor be reduced to a formation of new intentions. Rather, variation in the tenor is *primary* and *independent* of all formation of intentions. Hence, change in tenor yields a new *direction* in one's whole life, as in cases of moral "conversion." Only what, in the formation of further volitional activity, is proven to be a *dependent* factor by a different kind of *acting can* become an object of *"education"* [*Erziehung*]. For it is this acting alone, to be sure, which can be reached through mere educational measures. On the other hand, it is *essentially* impossible to influence or change the "moral tenor" by education—a point that Kant correctly stresses. Educational measures which have as their objective a change in the moral tenor can only *hide* its true nature in a person, i.e., they can only lead to *mendacity* in the basic moral tenor. Herbart's serious misunderstanding of the "phenomenon" designated by Kant's concept of the basic moral tenor led him to believe that it could be replaced by enduring dispositions of will and deed to be brought about by education. If it lies in the essence of the "basic moral tenor" to endure (i.e., with respect to intentions, acts done on purpose), this, of course, has nothing to do with a certain *span of time*. A basic moral tenor may last only one moment.[2] On the other hand, there is not the slightest guarantee in the mere duration of deeds, even in the formation of intentions of certain positive value-directions during one's whole life, that these intentions and deeds do not have the purpose of hiding one's "genuine moral tenor." The true nature of all pharisaical moral correctness consists, to be sure, in just *this*. Association psychology, the special application of which in this area leads to a complete misunderstanding of the "moral tenor," as well as Herbart's ideas, arose from a pragmatic (i.e., an educational-pragmatic) prejudice that spirit and soul *must* be such that they can be controlled and directed limitlessly by an educator. True, one can *separate* controllable elements from the psychic life by this principle and weigh them in their dependencies in order to show an educator, statesman, etc., how he must proceed in his work. But it is completely false, and even ridiculous, to equate this "picture" with *facts* of the spirit. If the moral tenor were only an outcome of different deeds, it would be possible, of course, to influence it by education or even gradually to "make" a basic moral tenor according to some previously desired form. However, since the moral tenor is what *governs* deeds, including those deeds attempting to hide it, such educational procedures are nonsensical. We must accept what Kant pointedly says—namely, that "good intentions superimposed on an evil moral tenor result in nothing but deception [*Schein*]."

Since the basic moral tenor is not a disposition but an *actual intuited* givenness, it is also to be differentiated from what is commonly called a person's "*character*." In general, the character of a person is understood to be the constant cause for his individual actions as first encountered from without, so to speak. The "character" is but a merely hypothetical assumption about something that is *never* given to us but only *assumed* in induction to be of a certain quality so that the explanation of a deed in question can become plausible. If, for instance, someone acts contrary to our *previously held assumptions* about his "character," a *new* picture of his character will replace the old one. But this does not hold for the moral tenor. For it is not inferred from deeds at all; it is, rather, *intuited in* deeds (including the entire range of the expressions of this person). It has often been said, and with justification, that though we may be acquainted with

2. For this reason the "moral tenor" has nothing to do with any "inborn moral character" of a man (Schopenhauer).

many of a person's deeds, it is often the trifle which suddenly reveals his *true* moral tenor. The automatic expression is often a much better indicator than the arbitrary language which may contradict both deeds and expressions. Moreover, in cases where we think that we know a person's moral tenor, we do not change our *picture* of it when we come to know his further actions, as we do in the case of character mentioned above. Rather, we admit to ourselves that we do not yet understand his deeds, since they contradict his moral tenor as it is known to us. We say, then, that we must *analyze these deeds more carefully*. Hence we correct our opinion of his deeds on the basis of *our picture of his moral tenor*, which is now proven to be *independent* of his deeds as a fact of *intuition that cannot be inferred* from those deeds. The evidence here is not an inductive certainty but a genuine *insight*.

It is for the above reasons that the moral tenor is accessible to us even in cases in which a person's deeds, decisions, and intentions would lead us to entirely *opposite* conclusions concerning his moral tenor on the basis of deviations from the normal formation of intentions, decisions, and deliberate resolve. If, for example, a person's formation of intentions is affected by perverted desires, he can intend to hurt someone even though his moral tenor is an amiable one (which shows itself in the fact that he may also intend to hurt himself). There are also cases of severe organic cerebral diseases in which the normal formation of intentions and of what is done on purpose disappears. Here, also, we can trace a diseased person's good or evil *moral tenor* despite the numerous interruptions and perturbations on the paths connecting a moral tenor with factual deeds. For the moral tenor is *not* disturbed or destroyed or changed by a mere psychic *illness,* no matter how grave, no matter how deeply such disturbances may be located in the levels leading to actual deeds. A close examination of these facts would reveal to us that there must exist an *ultimate* bearer of a value of the will that *cannot be influenced by diseases,* even when we consider the great differences in moral character among diseased persons and the various types of diseases to which such persons may be subjected.[3]

We mentioned above that it is not only the phenomena of expression but also *deeds* which allow us to intuit a person's

3. It is precisely for this reason that there is a sharp distinction between "ill" and "morally bad," between "healthy" and "good," no matter how difficult it may be to make the distinction in individual cases.

moral tenor. In this sense a deed represents only a *symbolic value for the moral tenor*. But this is not to deny that a deed *as a deed* possesses its *own* value. An example may clarify this point. The ethics and the notion of the basic moral tenor that we are criticizing here would maintain the following in regard to this situation: If a paralyzed person happens to see someone drowning, he is *no less* moral than someone else not paralyzed who actually rescues the man—provided, of course, that the paralyzed person has the *will* to come to the rescue. In both cases the *same* type of moral tenor can be present, and hence the two men would be of equal moral value. But it would be too much to assert that the same act of willing with its moral value is present in the "paralyzed" person. For this *cannot* be the case, simply because in his situation there is *no* possibility of a "willing-to-do." Much as the paralyzed man may *"wish"* to perform the rescuing act, he cannot "will" it. Concerning his relation to this willing-to-do and its value, he is in the same situation as someone absent from the scene who has the "same moral tenor" and recognizes the fact that drowning people ought to be rescued. Hence we are *not* faced with the *same moral state of affairs* in these two cases. The paralyzed person is, of course, not at all subject to moral reproach. But neither is he subject to any part of the moral praise that belongs to the rescuer. Any opinion that would refute the above view and regard the moral tenor as the *only* bearer of moral value must be reduced to the *ressentiment* of "disabled" people. Moreover, an ethics which locates moral value *exclusively* in the basic moral tenor does not recognize that there are clear cases of *deception* possible with respect to the basic moral tenor. We can, for example, be mistaken for a long time about our moral tenor in relation to someone else. But this false moral tenor quickly dissolves as soon as we are placed in a situation that commands us to *realize* this tenor in a *deed*. In this case we are subject to *deception* in the case of our own basic tenor. [Two propositions follow from this]: The evidence of the factual moral tenor is *independent* of a willed deed determined by the moral tenor. In contrast to deceptive simulation of a moral tenor, a *genuine* one *necessarily* (although not univocally) determines a *willed deed corresponding* to itself. Since this interconnection is essential, one not only can but must insist that the moral tenor is "confirmed" [*sich . . . bewähre*] in a deed. This *"confirmation"* in a deed is a unique category based on the above interconnections. Although this "confirmation" cannot *replace* the *evidence* of a moral tenor existing before a deed (pragmatism falsely holds that it can), it nevertheless has this special importance: it shows the *untrue* moral tenor when a genuine one is missing and when a pretended one that corresponds to it is at hand; or, in other words, it reveals to us the irreality of its supposed evidence. Yet a confirmation of the moral tenor of a deed does not *necessarily* point to the moral tenor itself (when the value of a deed exists as a mere self-value). The "confirmation" therefore must not be construed as subsequent justification through success. It is for this reason also that whenever the idea of confirmation played a great role (e.g., in Calvinism), it was *not* understood in this manner. On the other hand, "confirmation" is not a *basis of the cognition* of the nature of the moral tenor, as if it presupposed judgments and conclusions. "Confirmation" lies, rather, as a fact between the moral tenor and a deed; that is, the deed is experienced as a *confirmation* of the moral tenor in a special and practical experience of *fulfillment*. Therefore the role that confirmation plays for us is not smaller than the one it plays with regard to others. It is in this confirmation that we can become inwardly *certain* of an evident moral tenor. On the other hand, the lack of confirmation, or the omission of what lies in the moral tenor, determines an immediate and practical consciousness of *conflict* in which our moral tenor is revealed to us as imaginary.

I wish to return to the example of the paralyzed person. I maintained that he is not in a *position* to will the rescue of the drowning man because he is not in a position to *will* the rescue. He may be "prepared" to will, but not in reality. But in another case a different interpretation is possible, namely, when he *experiences* his paralyzed state on the occasion of such an event. For then he would have the experience of resistance, setting in against his kinematic intention and the subsequent graduated series of kinematic impulses, as an experience of the practically "impossible." In that case there is an attempt to act on his part which is equal to a factual deed of rescue (at least insofar as a moral evaluation is concerned).

The ethics subject to our criticism completely reverses the true state of affairs when it views the mere objective content of willing as the factor that reveals the moral tenor in a deed, instead of seeing that a deed is immediately directed toward the realization of a specific value, and that a deed *emanates* from a moral tenor and is at the same time guided by it. Kant's proposition that a truly good person is, in the case of a rescue, the one who is concerned only with doing his duty, but not "as if he were concerned with the reality of the well-being of the other," comes close to the implicit error under discussion. This proposition virtually reduces the false ethics of the moral tenor to absurdity. For a will "not concerned with" the reality of its content is, as Sigwart stresses, a will that "does not will what it wills." [4] The comportment that Kant asks for is entirely impossible. Moreover, his proposition presupposes the false opinion that if this comportment were to become the content of willing, it would be morally valid "to show" [*an den Tag zu legen*] a moral tenor (to us or to others), by way of a helpful deed, "on the occasion of" someone else's suffering. This, however, is a de facto pharisaism which makes the mere realization of a *picture* of a good will (e.g., the wish to will so), or the realization of the *judgment* that the willing "is good," the content of willing.[5]

Let us now proceed to furnish a precise analysis of the levels contained in the unity of a *deed* [Handlung] and of those *causal factors* which can determine the variations in the contents of these levels.

The following elements in a deed must be distinguished: (1) the presence of the situation and the object of the deed; (2) the content to be realized by the deed; (3) the willing of this content and its levels, leading from the moral tenor, through intentions, deliberation, and resolution [*Vorsatz*], to decision; (4) the class of activities directed toward the lived body leading to movements of the members (the *"willing-to-do"*); (5) the states of sensation and feelings connected with these activities; (6) the experienced realization of the content (the *"performance"*); and (7) the states and feelings posited by the content realized. No doubt the sixth belongs to a *deed*. But the causal effects of a deed, which can be *inferred* on the basis of an *assumption* of the realization of the content (*before* or *after* a deed), do *not* belong to a deed. A *deed* must be sharply distinguished from its *effects;* for the latter, unlike the realization of a deed, are not experienced in a deed itself.[6] If one considers a deed or its ultimate component of realization as a mere "effect" of willing, a *false* ethics of the moral tenor is introduced at once. Whereas a deed with its ultimate element (its experienced realization) is a *bearer of moral values,* its

4. See C. Sigwart, *Vorfragen der Ethik.*
5. We are confronted with the same thing when, e.g., someone says, "Act so that you can make the judgment 'I am good,' or so that you can esteem yourself."
6. On the other hand, in *"success"* the objective occurrence is the "fulfillment" of execution. This character of "fulfillment" is missing in the mere *causal effects* of an action.

causal effects can *never* be regarded as such. If a deed were a mere "effect of willing," it could not be considered a bearer of moral values. The realization of a deed, however, is a "part" of it, belonging to its *unity*. This difference must not be taken as only a "relative" or "arbitrary" one. For *whatever* is *experienced as belonging* to my deed, and whatever is phenomenally manifested as its simple effect, can never be "relative." Objective causal relations that are *taken into consideration* in a deed have *nothing* to do with this fact. It may be that a *content of willing*, i.e., what I will to be *real*, represents a remote effect of what I am realizing in acting—e.g., an effect that I previously "calculated." But this effect does not belong to my *deed,* nor is it the "success of my deed" [*Handlungserfolg*]; it is, rather, the "success of my speculation and calculation." At the beginning of a deed, then, *this* very content is "given," not as *content* of the will-to-do, but as the "consequence of this doing," which is not contained at all in the *phenomenal content* of acting. The fulfillment (or non-fulfillment, i.e., conflict) consists in the execution with respect to the *will-to-do* (when I *experience myself as doing what* I will to do), not in the execution with respect to *what* I will to be *real*. This distinction is clearly manifest in the differences between a *misdeed* [Fehlhandlung] and the mistakes and errors that we make in our calculations concerning causal relations in which we are about to be engaged, or concerning the means and tools that we use in such an engagement. The nature of a *misdeed* consists in my not actually experiencing my doing what I will to do, not in my not accomplishing what I will. One may think of "mis-taking" something, as opposed to an object's being something other than what I took it for.

The primary questions here are the following: What is the relation of the *content* of willing to the *content* of the performance of doing? What is the relation of the content of willing to the object *at which* our action is directed, i.e., what we may call the *"practical object,"* as opposed to objects of theoretical experience?

Concerning the first question, Kant's thesis would, in our terminology, imply the following:

1. *Every content of the will,* insofar as it is content and not the mere *form* of willing, always has its foundation in the content of *success* and therefore "stems" from the content of success. Hence a non-formal ethics would of necessity have to be an ethics of success.

2. The elements in the content of success which can become

elements in the content of willing are always *those* which produce *states of pleasure* through repercussions on the acting person.

In the first assumption Kant follows the "empirical" theory of the will, as it has been called.[7] This theory maintains that successive states of pure reflexive movements (e.g., the pleasure of an infant as effected by the reflexive movements of sucking, which cause the milk to go through the mouth into the stomach) induce a "willing" of such movements. This state of affairs is supposedly made possible through the reproduction of the *picture* of the movement (given in "kinematic" and "organic sensations" that are coposited in the respective movements and induced by them). For it is only on the basis of this theory of the will that Kant can reasonably conclude that every non-formal ethics is necessarily an ethics of success.

It is precisely this presupposition of his that we reject. For the content of the will does not "originate" in the supposed manner—namely, as a "representation" of what determines a pleasurable effect or (in the case of an initial reflexive movement) a reaction of that kind. Nor is the "will-to-do" simply a reproduction of such a reproduced "kinematic picture" or a "regulative consciousness" of a plurality of such pictorial sequences.

The phenomenon of *willing* contains nothing more than a conation in which a *content* to be *realized* is given. Herein lies the difference between willing and all mere "welling up" and "wishing." Wishing is a conation that does *not*, in its intentional nature, aim at the realization of a content.[8] A child may *"will,"* for example, that a star fall into his lap. He may truly "will" this. This kind of willing is quite different from the *"willing-to-do."* The latter is only a special case of willing, namely, *a willing to do something.* It is true that the *willing* of a content alone does *not*, in principle, bring success if such willing does not change into a will-to-do. This we know from the earliest of our *experiences.* If such willing could ever coincide with the reality of what is "willed," our subsequent experiences would show that the reality of the willed did not stem *from willing* itself. The *reality* of the

7. Kant does not go so far as to dissolve *conation* into representations, feelings, and sensations. It remains moot, however, whether he ever saw that conation is *not* based on representation, and that a content can be given with equal originality in both striving and representation. In any case such content is possible for him only by way of the success of movements and the effect of such success on sensible states of pleasure.

8. It is distinguished as well by many factors not considered here.

willed fails to come to be unless a *will-to-do* has come into play. This fact is only very gradually noticed in childhood, as well as throughout the development of man. For the coincidence of the willed with its realization makes many human beings to this day firmly believe that the mere will can make rain and sunshine, or that it can hurt or kill (e.g., conjuring [*Anwünschen*]). Even an educated person feels something like "guilt" if something which he had "willed" to happen occurs accidentally, e.g., the death of a person. Only after the experience that connects the *possible* causal realization of a content of the will "through willing" (and not its realization in general) to a previous will-to-do does conation having its content *outside* the experienced "*being-able-to-do*" obtain the "character of a *wish*." But all central conation (wishing also belongs to this, for there is no such thing as "it wishes in me," comparable to "it thirsts me" or "it hungers me" [*according to German usage*]) is "first of all" the *willing* of a content. It is only *after* the experienced connection of the willing of the only possibly successful to the willing-to-do, and only *after* the experience of the *inhibition* exercised by the being-able-to-do on a part of "willing," that this part can become a "mere" *wish*. It must be considered a reversal of the facts when one attempts to understand "willing" on the basis of "wishing," claiming that willing is only (1) the wish that something come to be and (2) the allied wish that it come to be through me,[9] or that willing is wish (1) plus the wish of "doing it," or that willing is wish (1) accompanied by a (first of all "accidental" and "reflexive") kinematic movement of the body realizing its content. Even a "wish" that something should happen "through me" remains a "wish" and does not become a "willing." It is "*willing*," not wishing, that is (with regard to acts) the *basic* and central conative act-experience. An original object of willing can become an object of wishing if the object of the will *failed* with respect to the "being-able-to-do" (and its implicit spheres of contents). It is this "placing after" of what is originally given as an object of the will that makes it an "object of wishing." This state of affairs is quite obviously suggested by some well-known kinds of deception which occur in a long-sustained willing of a content that, despite the failure of this willing in the sphere of the being-able-to-do, leads to the *phenomenon* of its realization (including the "conviction" of its realization). A case like this can be found in the volitional fulfillments (or, in the objective sense, fulfill-

9. See Theodor Lipps, *Vom Fühlen, Wollen und Denken.*

ments of wishes) of fancy, illusions, dreams, and hallucinations. This can also be found, for example, in cases of "delusions of amnesty" in a criminal (most often one who has been imprisoned for life) who expresses the firm conviction that he *has* been granted amnesty and indicts his guards for keeping him imprisoned. All such cases show that if an original willing is not reduced to a "wish," despite the experienced failure of the willing in the sphere of possible acting, the reality of the willed *must* emerge at least as a *phenomenon* (in the form of a "delusion") when the content of willing itself is retained. For the fact that the will posits the reality of the willed, *insofar* as there is no (effective) objection against this, must be considered to obtain in the above case, because the objection is not noticed.

If, however, in a normal case the aforementioned "rejection" of an *originally* given willed content occurs with an objection in the sphere of the being-able-to-do, the result of that experience is a cessation of any *further* acts of willing, though the given "willed" contents—i.e., what continues to be such a content because it is *not* touched by this objection—do not cease to be codetermined by the original willing or, better, by the non-formal values that correspond to its "moral tenor." In other words, at this stage *everything* against which there occurs an experience of the *"not-being-able-to-do"* or of "weakness" [*Ohnmacht*] in factual doing is immediately removed from the original volitional content by increasing degrees. (We shall return to this phenomenon later.) [10] Therefore it is *not even* the entire range of the given contents of the "being-able-to-do" (let alone the "success of deeds") that "restricts" the *original content* of willing; nor does this range *positively* "determine" the content of the will. Rather, the being-able-to-do only *selectively acts* on the originally given content of willing, with the result that a great deal of the originally willed content is *no longer* "willed" and its realization is *"renounced."* Both an individual's and a community's willing develops in a fashion typical of this law. A primary phenomenon of all psychic maturity is to be seen, for instance, in the continuous *restriction* of willing to the *sphere of the "being-able-to-do."* The soaring plans and fanciful "dreams" of children and adolescents (though at such ages they are not experienced *"as"* dreams) are abandoned during adulthood. Volitional fanaticism is replaced by an increase in "compromises." The same phenomenon can be seen in the history of any political, religious, or

10. [See chap. 4, sec. 2, c.—*Ed.*]

social group. In all practical areas the history of man shows a gradual differentiation of original volitional aims. This differentiation takes place at the "threshold" of what "can be done" and is accompanied by a continuous restriction of objectives. The more primitive man is, the more he believes himself capable of *anything* by mere *willing*, from controlling the weather and making gold to all forms of "magic." From the original volitional aims, "possible" ones are only gradually *filtered*, and within this sphere of what can be done there is again a gradual filtration of what can be realized through this or that kind of acting. The outcome of increasing "experience" is always this—it makes one "prudent," as the saying goes. But the outcome is not "willing" or "willing this or that." Experience is neither productive nor creative. It is first of all *negative* and *selective* within the *span* of *original* volitional contents determined by the contents of specific *value*-qualities. Above all, experience teaches a prudent "resignation" from original volitional contents; it is *not* a *positive source* of their creation.

We must keep two points in mind here. First, we must remember the evidential fact that the *primary* intention of willing always remains directed toward the *realization* of a state of affairs or a "value-complex" when an original volitional content is proven possible and is realized by acting and deeds (as in normal cases of willing). Only *secondarily* is an intention of "willing-to-do" (with its partial functions) connected with this realization. If I will to have my lamp on this desk rather than on the other, it is this *state of affairs* which is primarily willed, namely, "that this lamp be at this place." It is *neither* "carrying" the lamp nor even the necessary kinematic intentions and impulses (nor directing a servant to carry the lamp, in which case *my* will, not the servant's, is realized). I do not "will" to perform a "movement" when I take my hat off the shelf and put it on, for I will "to have my hat on my head." Of course a "movement" can be a willed state of affairs, e.g., in gymnastics, etc. But even if it were a question of the same movement, the two cases would remain different. He who slays someone wills "to slay him," not to "move" his arms and the ax in a certain way. There are two entirely different cases here. On the one hand willing is primarily directed toward a *state of affairs*, whereupon the will-to-do (as a special *kind* of willing) ensues without any hindrance; on the other hand it is the *doing itself* which is the primary *state of affairs* of willing. Thus a common arsonist, e.g., an envious farmer, wills that his neighbor's rich and attractive farm "cease to exist." He wills its destruction. A pathological arsonist, however, wills perhaps only "to set fire." A common thief wills to possess another's property. The will "to steal" in turn rests on this will to possess and, on this, the will-to-do. In contrast, the kleptomaniac wills "to steal." Again, there is a type of businessman who wills "to be rich," and so he makes his bargains and his money. But there is also the more "capitalistic" type of businessman who wills "to do business" and to make money, and who only thereby becomes rich. (Of course there is also the rare type who wills "to enjoy" and so wants to be rich. According to Kant's theory he would be the only type of businessman.) In all of the above cases the willed state of affairs and the will-to-do are different. They remain different even when the content of a state of affairs itself becomes a type of acting, as in stealing, making money, sacrificing oneself (sacrificial mania), etc. For here also the "willing-*to-do*" is different from the *willing* "of such doing." It is also clear that the relation between the willing of a state of affairs and the will-to-do is not one of "means" to "ends." Such a relation can hold only between *states of affairs,* never between the willing of content and the will-to-do. Nevertheless, there is a *foundational* order between the willing of a state of affairs and the will-to-do (namely, the will-to-do is founded in the willing of a state of affairs). This order of foundation is an evidential one, not the result of mere thought.

Hence the willing of a state of affairs (even when a will-to-do is involved) must by all means be considered the *primary* content of willing. In the strictest sense of the term, a *"deed"* is the *experience of the realization of such a state of affairs in acting,* i.e., the *special unity* of experience that represents a *phenomenal unity* which is *totally* independent of all objective causal events belonging to it and independent also of the consequences of the deed.

Second, as we said before, an experience of the being-able-to-do vis-à-vis *temporally* and *genetically earlier* volitional contents (e.g., the "soaring plans of a youth") would efface and obliterate contents only. This, however, must not be construed to imply that *all* later volitional contents are genetically "contained" in earlier ones. For we are concerned here with a *law of the origin of acts* and a *law of the foundation of contents.* These laws are fulfilled in *all phases* of the genetic and real volitional development of an individual in a *uniform* fashion. Of course we can find during maturation *ever new* contents in willing which were *not* present in earlier phases of development, for the source of original willing streams *incessantly*. The volitional moral tenor has nothing to do with an "inborn character" (despite what Schopenhauer asserts).[11] Also, the experience of the being-able-to-do influences selectively the contents of volitional aims *continuously*. What we mean to say, then, is this: the *possible* volitional goals, which can fulfill a volitional moral tenor and its non-formal and basic value-direction (which is, in principle, variable, but *independent* of the experience of the being-able-to-do and, especially, the experience of success), can be *selected* (by their nature) by this experience, but can *never* be positively determined by it.[12] Accordingly, the value-*contents* which co-determined these earlier volitional contents that were later "pushed back" as mere wishes remain determining factors for *such* willing whose contents proved to be realizable by acting. As was shown earlier, we can see that a "volitional moral tenor" permeates *both* spheres, i.e., the spheres of wishing and those of willing, *independent* of any empirical genesis of volitional experience.

As far as this being-able-to-do is concerned, only the first level of the selection of volitional contents, i.e., those of "pure willing" (which is independent of all possibilities and impossibilities of doing), has been given. There are other selecting factors to be added here.

Before turning to these factors, I wish to stress one point. The *determining* factor of "volitional contents" insofar as they are *picturelike* contents of *intentions,* that which selects the volitional contents from the sphere of the a priori "possible," i.e., the picture-contents corresponding to the *value-qualities* of the moral tenor, is, in fact, the experience of *"being-able-to-do"* or *"not-being-able-to-do"* (i.e., "volitional power" or "volitional weakness"). It is not (despite what Kant says) the *factual* doing or its success. We shall discuss this later. Here we only wish to emphasize that this selection is in *no sen*se a mere *consequence* of *factual acting,* as is, say, an "excited disposition" to repeat a factual act, like the consciousness of being "able" to do something that one *did* before. On the contrary, man has a *being-able-to-do consciousness* pertaining to certain contents which is *not* medi-

11. The volitional tenor is subject to changes in the life of an individual; but it is only *primitively* changeable.

12. It is easy to see that if this law of the origins of volitional acts is valid, there *must* be a "tendency" toward development in the direction mentioned as a consequence, i.e., toward the withholding of original volitional contents (not only value-complexes but also states of affairs based on these value-complexes).

ated by such reproduction. In this consciousness the to-be-able "itself" is phenomenally given as a special *kind* of conative consciousness (and not as an object of thinking that "we can do something"). The presence or absence of such a consciousness and its opposite, i.e., *"weakness"* (which is a *positive* experience of the *not*-being-able-to-do), is a *determinant* of the *willing-to-do*.[13] Second, this experience is a completely *simple* fact; it is not assembled from the consciousness of the ability to perform the partial acts, such as the kinematic ones into which acting splits up.[14] The being-able-to-do may be compared to the general feeling of being alive [*Lebensgefühl*], which has nothing to do with a sum of sensible feelings. Just as the general feeling of being alive has its *own* laws of variations (along with their modifications of "strength," "vitality," "healthiness," "illness," "growth," and "aging") and never represents a *sum* of sensible feelings, although it codetermines the occurrence of these feelings and their special qualities,[15] the *being-able-to-do* is likewise first a *unitary* and *peculiarly lawful* varying experience of the *whole* individual. The being-able-to-do is therefore wholly independent of reproductions of states of sensation and feelings connected with the factual movements of limbs during the performance of a deed (or those initially caused by them). One who has a firm and full consciousness of being-able-to-do experiences *from the very outset* states that differ totally from the kind mentioned. Such a person *acts* differently, since he "trusts" himself differently. Hence *this* "being-able" can be neither increased nor decreased by "exercise" or "habituation." According to its nature it determines the very *ability* to exercise for specific activities or to accustom oneself to them.

The problem of what *leads from the willing-to-do to acting* pertains to *two* experiences. (Since we cannot give a more de-

---

13. This "being-able-to-do" is also an independent bearer of values and an object of forms of value-consciousness (and of "self-consciousness"). It is independent of the values of factual actions (of the same content). Its value is higher than factual acting (with its possible "dispositions"). See chap. 4, sec. 2, c (on Kant's theory of freedom).

14. There is here a "being-able-to-do" which pertains to the *values*, not to the *power*, of actions. This is the case when we say, "This man could do something like that (e.g., something bad)," or, "He could do anything." We know, quite independent of our factual actions, what we are "able to do" (with respect to good and bad). "Virtue" becomes a moral tenor only when its value-content has moved into this "being-able-to-do" (in the sense of the last form). Virtue is a moral tenor of a specific kind, both *ready for* and *able to do* a deed.

15. See chap. 5, sec. 8.

tailed analysis of this process here, we will mention only the major elements.) These two experiences bring about a continuous transition toward the factual occurrences of the *objective* movements in which deeds as seen from the *outside* consist.

There are a number of viewpoints in traditional psychology which have in common a failure to account for the "phenomenon" of the *unity* of a deed. Such viewpoints deny the *continuity* of this phenomenon and imply that a deed is composed of an "inner act of will" and objective movements of the limbs which are simply added to it *in time*. This movement is then said to make itself known to us by its *effects* (or accompanying appearances), such as a sequence of tactile, articular, and positional sensations, etc. Or such viewpoints imply that an inner act of the will is followed by a "kinematic representation" of the limbs. This representation could only be a reproduction of an already *performed* movement of the limbs, and thus it would basically have to be purely reflective. According to such viewpoints, then, there is *no* such thing as a genuine experience of "moving" which follows the willing-to-do; the "kinematic representation" is simply followed by the movement itself. They deny (as did Hume) that there is an *efficacy* of willing (as willing-to-do) which acts on our lived body and *issues forth into movement*.[16] I have shown elsewhere [17] that such a kinematic *picture* (as a reproduction of already performed movements which is ultimately reflective) can be found only in cases in which kinematic *intentions* are missing—for instance, when idiotic children learn to write. A normal child can *immediately* transform the seen Gestalt of a letter on the blackboard into a kinematic intention (and, gradually, into the necessary kinematic impulses). His hand and arm are *not led* in order to aid the reproduction of the sequence of sensations thereby released. Kinematic intention is an *intuitive phenomenon* within the kinematic effectuation and its variations which are necessary to transfer a given state of affairs (viewed as a value-complex) to the state of affairs (value-complex) that

16. This problem plays only a small part in Hume's work because he denies the phenomenon of "effecting." Jurisprudence has at times been led to erroneous assumptions by this false psychological theory. One refers to this theory as the "intellectualistic theory of the will." If this theory is followed through, it either makes *every dolus* a *dolus eventualis* or leads to a rejection of the *dolus eventualis* precisely because *every dolus* is then a *dolus eventualis*, i.e., it leads to the effacement of the difference between willing with the *foresight* that there are illegal consequences and willing the illegal fact.

17. [See "Über Selbsttäuschungen" (Bibliog. no. 4) or "Die Idole der Selbsterkenntnis" (Bibliog. no. 10), sec. 4.—*Ed.*]

is willed in the willing-to-do. Thus we possess an *immediate insight* into the connection of factors which lead from a seen (most simple) Gestalt-unit given in tactile sensation to a depiction [*Darstellung*] of the *same* Gestalt in a movement. We do *not* learn this connection by the *execution* of movements or by the *empirical* coordination of a seen or touched Gestalt with the sequence of kinematic *sensations,* as we might think is the case in the drawing of a picture. For we can *immediately* identify a seen Gestalt drawn in red lines with a Gestalt made with the hand in the air. In the order of places in [pure] *extensionality* as such, there is an intuitable identity between the temporal rhythm of the motion producing a Gestalt and the special places and positions of immobile points which (objectively) lead to the unity of the Gestalt. The kinematic intention is therefore completely *independent* of all so-called kinematic *sensations* and their reproductions, which can exist only in single peripheral organs that are quite dependent upon the initial positions which organs have with regard to one another, as well as upon the positions which the body has with reference to external objects in regard to which objective motion takes place. Kinematic intention is neither a mere *rule* governing the succession of different organic sensations (in the sense of motion through different organs) nor a rule governing such rules of succession which is sustained throughout the varying positional manifolds of the organs in relation to an external body, and which thus represents what remains of prior experiences. For the *same* content of the will-to-do can be realized in the *same* kinematic intention through quite *different* organs (e.g., by hands and fingers, by the leg, the foot, and the hand) and also through their cooperation. (We know, for instance, that the basic Gestalt of a person's handwriting is unchanged even if he loses his hands and learns to write with his feet.) The kinematic intention is also independent of the special character of the entire organic cooperation necessary in executing a motion—e.g., in moving away from a car that is (at a certain angle) a meter away from the position of my body, which, depending on the car's original position and my own, must demand quite different types of cooperative movements (and separation of movements) of my organs. The successions of organic sensations that follow organic movements in both cases differ sharply in their special characteristics.[18] More-

18. The opposite of a uniform kinematic intention with regard to kinematic impulses is experienced, *prior to* the experience of the execu-

over, the kinematic *intention* is also independent of the distance of my lived body from the object in regard to which the movement occurs. The kinematic intention in the representative imagination of a motion to be performed is the same as that in the actual motion. The "place" of its appearance, its point of departure, is not any determinate spot in my body, nor is it the place of the bodies of my environment toward which objective movement is directed. All that kinematic intention yields is a special kind of picture of the *directional variation* of possible motion which is still indeterminate in terms of distance and in terms of the size of the movable body. In this directional variation *the object on which the performance of acting occurs,* or the object to be changed by the will-to-do, is joined together with *the content of the will-to-do.* The variation prescribes the motion through which this is possible. But this variation is not mechanically effected (by environmental stimuli or by traces of previous kinematic organic processes and their mutual cooperations): rather, it is dependent on the point of departure (the situation) and the object and content of the will-to-do, and it varies with these. It accounts for the *unity* and the *proper directionality* of subsequent kinematic *impulses* that it specifies in accordance with the position of the body with regard to the environmental body and its distance from that body and in accordance with the organs in their mutual relations (insofar as these relations are in a fixed order). The kinematic *impulse,* too, is an *experienced datum that precedes* objective motion. The "movement" of the arm that I lift or drop is given in this movement itself. Hence we are in no way dealing with a movement that is reported back to consciousness. The impulse stands out clearly as a special experience when, for instance, the objective execution of the movement is "obstructed." Here it is not the case that a kinematic intention is simply present while so-called kinematic sensations are missing (i.e., there occurs a disappointment of the expectation of these sensations). Rather, we experience a *positive* obstruction *prior* to our noticing that the movement fails to occur. We experience a "with-standing" of our organs against the impulse. The experience of impulses is also clearly given when the organ is fastened so that it is immobile, e.g., when a finger that

---

tion of the movement, as a "movement going astray" [*Fehlbewegen*]. For instance, someone shooting at a target knows before seeing the target (after shooting), and even before feeling the movement of the finger that triggers the shot, whether or not he hit the center of the target (and, if he did not, by how much he missed it).

is to be moved to the right has been fastened in that way. As far as the outer aspects of acting are concerned, so-called kinematic sensations serve solely for the specification of impulses that are necessary throughout given intentions, given modes, given distances, and given positions of the body with regard to objects and to given fixed organic relations in the organism and the altering spatial relations of the organs themselves in their present positions (within the limits of their possible movability and co-movability and the separability of their motions). So-called kinematic sensations are actually sensations of successive changes [*Wechsels*] in organic *positions*.[19]

We must now turn to the factors which I previously called *situation* and *object of a deed*,[20] or the "objective relational link of the deed," in which the "volitional content" is realized or the execution of a certain "act of willing" is determined (i.e., one by one, the formation of an intention, the positing of something to be done on purpose [*Vorsatzes*]). All willing occurs in reference to such a "situation," a world of (*practical*) "objects." Kant asserts that it is such objects (which he does not clearly distinguish from objects of cognitive or "representational" experience) that determine all content of the will by their efficacy as it is experienced in a sensible feeling (i.e., apart from the mere form of law), or that determine the reproduction of sensible feeling-states effected by such objects. The following will implicitly deny this assertion.

We must clearly see that any "practical object" in this sense has *its foundation* (1) *in a value-object* and (2) *in an object that corresponds to the value-content of the basic moral tenor of the will-to-do.*

Such "objects" are *value-things* or *goods* (and affairs [*Sachen*]), not primarily things of *perception* (or representation). For every conation has its *immediate foundation* in value-feeling (in preferring or in loving and hating) and its contents. Its foundation does not lie in an (objective) pictorial content that, in addition, would have to be "represented" or "perceived." [21] Two points are implied here: All willing "of something" presupposes the *feeling* of the (positive or negative) *value* of this "something." A value can therefore *never* be a *consequence* of willing,

---

19. It is only by virtue of the unity of impulses going through the positions of our organs that these successions are grasped as "kinematic sensations."
    20. [See above, p. 121.—*Ed.*]
    21. [See chap. 1, sec. 3.—*Ed.*]

for what phenomenally sets willing in motion is never a feeling-state, but always the value-object given "in" feeling. Insofar as there is no difference in value between objects, they can determine no difference in willing. It is only in the unities of "value-things" and "complexes of values" that objects can become "practical objects."

An important proposition follows from this: *Objects which for pure willing are possible objects for the realization of complexes of values* (and states of affairs founded in them) *are selected according to and on the basis of* those *values* which permeate the *moral tenor* of this willing. That is, the practical "world" in which pure willing "intervenes" by intending a realization of value-complexes already possesses the lineaments of the *value-structure* of the "basic moral tenor" of the bearer of this willing. The bearer's changing "feeling-states" in relation to this "world" are irrelevant here. His *willing* certain *value-complexes*, and the *"world"* in which he "wills" them to be *realized*, always *"fit"* one another in a certain sense. For both are dependent on the value-qualities and their "order" which lie in his "moral tenor." [22] It is precisely in the basic moral tenor that a priori value-consciousness and the center of all willing according to its ultimate value-contents *coincide*. But the value-complexes of pure willing (or of its value-projects), even though they contain only the *same* value-qualities (and their order) as the value-complex of the "practical world," are not "derived" from the practical world. Their givenness is *independent* of this "practical world," also. For any *specific* value-complex that we will can very well conflict (or coincide) with "given" value-complexes. Only the value-*qualities* are identical in both cases. Insofar as this applies to pure willing (independent of the sphere of the will-to-do), the relation is expressed in acts of *"approval"* and *"disapproval."* [23] These acts are neither "acts of the will" nor acts of "value-cognition" (like feeling and preferring). They are acts in which the *identity* of both the values of value-cognition and the willing that is directed toward the reality of values is constituted in an immediate and intuitive fashion.

Therefore, if the world of "practical objects" is *determined* by

22. All "perceiving" and "representing" and, in general, the cognitive consciousness of the world are first of all independent of this "practical world." We do not agree with Fichte when he writes, "What kind of philosophy one has depends on what kind of man one is."
23. We can "approve" and "disapprove" of both our own willing and that of others, as well as the "project" of a willing, independent of their real execution.

values (and the a priori practical objects by a priori values), within this sphere of value-objects a content given as a volitional object in a *singular* experience is given only in the *with-standing* of willing. If one were to allow a terminology in which the word *objects* means only pictorial objects and not "value-objects" (or, better, value-unities), the "object" and that which "with-stands" would have to be considered as *two separate kinds* of givens.

This with-standing is a phenomenon given only in conation —and, moreover, only *in a willing*.[24] Only in *this* phenomenon is practical reality given.[25] But practical reality is always at the same time a value-reality (affairs [*Sachen*] and value-things).

It is hardly worthwhile mentioning in this context that there is no such thing as a "sensation of with-standing." That which "with-stands" is given only in an intentional experience and only in willing. It "constitutes" a "practical object." The phenomenon of "with-standing" consists in a tendency directed "against" willing. The experienced point of departure of this tendency is the value-object, which is the foundation of the practical object. The phenomenon of with-standing appears only *where* there is an object (if the object is, for example, in space).[26] It only appears "on" the value-object in the case of non-spatial objects, as is the case in the experience of this with-standing in other willing—for instance, that of the state. This phenomenon has nothing to do with the phenomena of "pull" or "push," which originate in the value-*qualities* of a thing [*Sache*] or a value-thing. These latter phenomena can already be given in feeling (as when we say that "we feel repelled" or that "something repels or attracts in our feelings"). But if we experience them in conation itself, they are already founded in the phenomenon of with-standing.

If a phenomenon of with-standing is "given," it is in the pure

24. Mere "wishes" have no such with-standing because the absence of the realization of their contents is also phenomenally given in them. An aspiration "finds" a factor of with-standing, but it is not given "in" it.

25. The question whether the phenomenal "consciousness of reality" *as such* rests on this experienced "with-standing" and whether a world of mere "pictorial contents" lacks a distinction between "reality" and "non-reality" must be set aside here. [See "Erkenntnis und Arbeit" (Bibliog. no. 22), sec. 6, and "Idealismus—Realismus" (Bibliog. no. 25).—*Ed.*]

26. If I hold a stick horizontally against a wall, the with-standing is given in the *wall*, not in the hand or the "tactile sensations" of the hand. Lotze has already stressed this. The extent to which the *feeling* of with-standing (a "sensation" of this is nonsense) varies depends on the *experienced with-standing*, which is itself *also* determined by the (phenomenal) magnitude of the action or by the experienced exercise of force. If the force exercised is large, with-standing is, *ceteris paribus*, small, and vice versa.

willing in which it is "given" that we find its "*seat.*" In other words, it is not *necessary* that a determination of its point of departure be given—whether this point lies, for example, in the "ego," in the "lived body," or in objects existing independent of the body (and given as existing). This can be seen in the fact that we are often in doubt as to where the experienced withstanding has its "seat" (in the above sense)—in a lack of willing something [*Sache*], in a lack of will-to-do (with equal willing and with-standing of the thing), or in an abundance of the withstanding of the thing [*Sache*] (with equal willing and will-to-do). However, the phenomenon of "with-standing" is given independent of these seats. But we can say with certainty that a normal person is inclined to place a given phenomenon of withstanding, first (and *ceteris paribus*), in the *object* that exists apart from his ego and lived body,[27] second, in his lived body, and, third, in his psychic sphere. The reversal of this order is at least "pathological." If a person asks whether "this with-standing lies in his willing," the question itself betrays an objectification of the state of affairs "that he thus willed." This objectification does not increase but decreases willing. The same would hold were one to ask whether he "willed to do" the willed with sufficient energy, or whether he *could* do that which is to be realized through his will (and which is given as such). This objectification of the being-able-to decreases the *experiencing* of it. It is in attempting to reach the phenomenon of with-standing in such a reverse order that we meet the phenomenon of "hesitation"; its extreme opposite is the "audacity" of willing, in which withstanding is localized to a special degree in the *being* of a thing [*Sache*] alone. A driver about to run into a tree who does not "will" to avoid the crash and to make a turn by handling his steering wheel accordingly, but who instead deviates from this aim by paying attention to "pressing his hands against the steering wheel" (i.e., if he experiences the obstruction from "within himself" and not from the tree), is in the greatest danger of crashing into the tree.

A *will-to-do* and its *content* (which is always distinct from the content of primary willing)[28] is immediately determined by

27. I have stressed the biological purposefulness of this order of "misplacing" the factor of with-standing in "Über Selbsttäuschungen." [See *ibid.*, sec. 4.—*Ed.*]

28. For example, "I will the possession of a good" in primary *willing;* "willing to buy," "willing to steal," "willing to rob," "willing to have oneself receive a present," etc., are contents of the "will-to-*do.*"

the *with-standing* of the primary *practical object* against my willing the existence of a specific value-complex according to the immanent evaluative moral tenor. This determination does *not* lie with a feeling-*state* that occurs as the effect of the primary volitional object acting on my feeling (as Kant assumes it does). Therefore the primary source of the *will-to-do* is not a feeling-state (neither is a feeling-state an objective of willing). It is the experienced with-standing of practical objects or "things" [*Sachen*] vis-à-vis pure willing. The content of the will-to-do is always dependent on two factors: (1) the *willed value-complex* (state of affairs) and (2) the special nature of the *with-standing object*.

A will "*to do* something specific," however, is called a volitional "*intention*" [Absicht].[29]

The large number of complex levels of this with-standing and their contents as they are encountered in volitional life are facts of "*practical experience*," i.e., the "experience" we make (only) in willing. It is experience in the *a posteriori* and *inductive* sense of the term. To this extent, as Kant correctly saw, the *content of intention* is codetermined by such "experience." Nevertheless, this does not reduce the extent of his error. For Kant not only fails to see that both the content of volitional intention and the with-standing object are already *a priori* limited by the content of non-formal values in the *basic moral tenor;* he also mistakenly places the nature of this "experience" *in sensible feeling-states* that are effected in us by objects, or in the effect on our feeling-states of what we have already done. Thus he also fails to see the *level of experience* under discussion. Man is not the passive creature that Kant supposes him to be. Man does not require things around him to effect sensible feeling-states in him so that the will is supplied with content and is subsequently determined by a selection of such contents that yield the greatest amount of *pleasure* and the least amount of displeasure. *Such sensible feeling-states have their foundation in* and are subsequent to *the experienced phenomena of with-standing* which man's willing "meets" (and they conform to their kinds and extent). The *primary content* of our practical experience is to be seen in the dynamic relationship between "effecting and suffering," "winning and succumbing," "overcoming and yielding." The intentional content of our will-to-do is determined by the (experi-

29. There are no "intentions" in the sphere of wishing, nor are there any in the sphere of pure willing. Every intention is an intention to *do* something.

entially) experienced with-standing in pure willing, not by the success of factual deeds.

The above phenomena of with-standing must be *fundamentally* distinguished from those which we find in the *already comprehended* and given contents of a volitional intention, i.e., the phenomena of with-standing "in the service of" the will-to-do and the execution of an intention. It is on this level that that which "with-stands" becomes resisting *states of affairs*, i.e., *things,* in regard to which we now set out *to do something on purpose* [Vorsatz] (and to make a decision). The *effectiveness* of (phenomenal) *things* on our *states* begins to play its role only in this formation of new contents—first of all, the content of what is done on purpose [*Vorsatzinhalte*]. It is only with what is done "on purpose" that the will has an immediate connection with empirical reality, and that we consequently have a bodily *presence* with the things that are the immediate objects of our acting; and it is only here that the *place* and *time* of our acting, which remain in principle unaccounted for at the level of "intention," are necessarily accounted for as part of the phenomenon. With this we gain some basis for a possible consideration of sensible feeling-states as such—namely, those that are effected by the *things* which are the objects of deeds, as well as those effected by their *success.* For these feeling-states are phenomenally connected with the phenomenal presence of a *lived body* (first, the ego-body, to which a bodily lived body [*Körperleib*] always corresponds by essential necessity).

It is this (possible) consideration of the role of sensible feeling-states in the determination of volitional contents that Kant adopts as necessary at the *level of the formation of intentions*, even at the level of the moral tenor. But we believe that the above shows his position to be unjustified.

Let us add that if one speaks, as Kant does, of the effect of things on our "sensibility," and if one maintains, along with Kant, that the moral will must posit its purposes independent of such efficacy, with the implication that this can occur only according to a "formal law" (because all contents of purposes are supposedly based on such an efficacy), one must seriously ask which *level* of "things and objects" he has in mind. Are we concerned here with things in themselves? Or are we dealing with "things" of natural experience, i.e., those of *representational* experience (without special value-experiences)? Or are we speaking about those "things" without qualities which belong to the sciences (physics and chemistry) that supposedly exercise this efficacy (the physical stimuli)? Is this efficacy a lived one, or is it one of the objective order? Moreover, are such "sensible feeling-states" that supposedly determine volitional contents released by natural things and their perception, or by complexes of sensations that unleash the "stimuli" understood to be effective on our sense organs?

All this poses a series of significant questions which, if not answered, leave Kant's theory without a determinate sense. While it is not possible in this context to pose these questions in precise formulations, let alone to solve them, we shall show the direction in which the solution to these problems can be sought.

One point must be clarified at the beginning. The "things" of our deeds and acting, which we always refer to when, for example, we trace certain deeds of human beings (or dispositions toward them) to the *"milieu"* of such human beings, have nothing to do with Kant's "thing in itself" or with scientific objects (through the supposition of which science "explains" natural facts). The sun of the milieu of human beings is not the sun of astronomy. Neither stolen meat nor bought meat is a sum of cells and tissues and their chemicophysical processes. The sun of the milieu is different at the North Pole, in moderate zones, and at the equator, and its beams are felt as different beams. Such *milieu-things* possess, first of all, two characteristics. (1) They lie in the "directionality of the natural world view," and it is there that they can be found. (2) As objects of action they are *value-units* and *things* [Sachen]. Although there are many things that have an "effect" on me in the *objective* sense —for instance, electrical and magnetic currents, rays of many sorts that I do not sense, etc.—they belong to my "milieu" no more than something I inherit belongs to my "tradition." *Only what one effectively experiences belongs to one's milieu.*

Hence the "milieu" is only what I experience as "effective" on me. Anything "effectively experienced" is precisely something whose variation in any form corresponds to a variation of some form in my experience—no matter whether or not I can show this variation as one of a *specific* thing and the variation of my experience as a variation of a *specific* experience, and no matter whether or not the "effectively experienced" has been *perceived* in any form. Hence the "sun of the milieu" has no more to do with the sun of astronomy than it has to do with the "representation" and the "perception of the sun." A "milieu-thing" belongs to an *"intermediate sphere"* lying between our perceptual content and its objects on the one hand and those objectively thought objects on the other. For not only can we experience changes in our environment without knowing what it is that has changed in the perceived (e.g., the removal of a picture from a room in which we live); but we also frequently experience the *effectiveness* of *something* that we do *not* perceive. It often happens that the addition or the absence of such an effectiveness turns us to the direction from which it came and thus enables us to perceive the effecting object, be it in the form of "representing," "fancying," etc. Thus there belongs to the momentary "milieu" not only the series of objects that I perceive (either through sense or through representation) while I am walking in the street or sitting in my room, but also everything with whose *existence or absence,* with whose being so or other than so, I practically *"reckon,"* [30] e.g., the cars and people that I avoid (when I am lost in thought or when I fix my sight on a man far away). A sailor, for example, is able to "reckon" with an oncoming storm from changes in his milieu without being able to say which *specific* change (e.g., in the formation of clouds, in temperature, etc.) serves as a sign. Throughout all comprehensions of objects (both in the perception of present and past objects) we possess the ability to *"take practical account"* of things, which implies an experience of their efficacy and of changes in it that is *independent* of the *perceptual* sphere. It is this same "practical accounting" which experientially determines our acting in such a way or otherwise, and which is itself "given" only in such experienced alter-determinations—but not before, as a "reason" for them. It is in this fashion that we also experience the "honor" of our own person, based on human esteem, as a unity of efficacy. The same holds true for the love of our parents, without any necessity that the acts and the persons who execute them be *given* in this experience. Indeed, this experience is of such a nature that the *unity* of this efficacy sets itself off as a *special* one as soon as it suddenly ceases to be—i.e., when love and esteem are withdrawn from us. Also, when we *treat* something as the "same thing" or

---

30. This phenomenon appears in peculiar isolation in abnormal states. This is the case when persons suffering from hysterically limited fields of vision "reckon," in their movements and orientations, with objects beyond the given field of vision. We do not find this phenomenon when this limitation is organically conditioned, for which reason organic limitation, even when it is less severe than hysterical limitation, destroys the ability of orientation, whereas hysterical limitation influences it only a little. This is also the case in nervously conditioned blindness to certain words or letters of a word, although these words or letters must somehow be "given" if they are to be excluded from the visual picture.

as something different, or when we treat a human being "as someone he is not," we are not necessarily involved in an intellectually perceived "identity," "difference," or "being-something" that precedes this "treating"; nevertheless there is an intentional experiencing here, not simply an objective occurrence.

It is only on the assumption of this phenomenon that we can come to a perfect understanding of the nature of all specifically "practical experience," which the *"practical man"* likes to hold up before the *"theoretician,"* be it practical experience in a craft, in an area of art, or in educational and political activities. Through this phenomenon we can also come to a perfect understanding of the immediate differentiation of the practically "essential" from the "inessential," a differentiation that can escape even the greatest thinkers (in theory) in a certain area. The "practical man" in this sense is surrounded, as it were, by thinglike units representing a realm of graduated and qualitatively differentiated efficacies independent of their being perceived. They are already differentiated and structured as points of departure of possible acting. The practical man "learns" to "handle" these units without needing to have any *theoretical* knowledge of the laws that govern such units. However, this "practical learning," this progressive logicalization of acting, is something quite different from the mere practice and habituation which occur only on the other side of deeds (and combinations of movements) that have already been performed. There occurs, rather, a progressive mastering of quite a *new* series of facts and situations, although independent of previous theoretical knowledge. What is practically inessential always subordinates itself to what is practically essential in the very *kind* of givenness involved—and not by way of a choice made *from* what is given. This subordination is, as it were, automatic insofar as it represents itself immediately as a feeble value-relief for acting. Let us mention another case: There is something like "practical" obeying and "disobeying" of laws, but not of laws which "control" natural acting as natural laws control, in the sense that natural acting would conform "to" them in an objective manner. The laws that we have in mind are not at all given as laws (in a form of perception, of "being conscious of . . ."); they are *experienced* as fulfilled or broken *in* the execution of acting. And it is only in these experiences that they are given. In this sense the acting artist is "controlled" by the aesthetic laws of his art without "applying" them; nor does he realize their fulfillment or violation only in the effect, i.e., in the work of art produced. In this sense, too, it belongs to the essence of the "crime" that he who breaks laws experiences himself as breaking them while acting; these are laws with which he reckons in *practice*, whether he or others are concerned, without having to have the slightest *knowledge* of such laws, and without having to have "thought" about them. On the other hand, he who knows the laws and still breaks them is definitely not a "criminal." The mere "breaker" or "enemy" of a legal system is no "criminal," for he accords it no practical recognition.[31] The criminal, although he does not necessarily have to recognize laws in a special act of "recognition," nevertheless *effectively experiences the laws* in his willing and acting, and *thus "recognizes them practically"* (thus he expects others to follow the law as a matter of course, not in a special act of "expectation" that he experiences). He is a criminal because he rises against that whose domination he effectively experiences, and it is this *experienced contradiction* that makes him different from a mere "breaker" of laws. Let these examples suffice.

Let us now turn to an explanation of the importance that these practically effective objects of our environment have for the possible determination of the *act of willing* and the *deed* (i.e., at their different levels).

This question is often posed in a popular form: To what extent does the "milieu" explain man's acting and doing, or, conversely, to what extent does he influence and create the milieu? Does the milieu explain the "hero"? Or will "everything around him become tragedy," as Nietzsche thinks?

In this form the question is not posed scientifically. One must decide to what extent one or the other case holds, i.e., according to the *essence*, independent of empirical explanations of specific deeds coming from a specific milieu.

For we must determine which factors, be they inside us or outside, are still determining factors in the *formation* of the "milieu"; likewise, we must determine at which level of a volitional deed the "milieu" *itself* remains a determining factor. One thing is clear in this context: that which we call "*milieu*," or the value-world as effectively experienced in practice, does not undergo alterations [*wechselt nicht*] in content simply because we

---

31. H. von Kleist's novel, *Michael Kohlhaas*, subtly shows how the hero becomes less and less an apparent criminal and more and more an enemy of the system of laws which makes him appear a "criminal." Kohlhaas gradually withdraws his involuntary "practical recognition" from the order under which he lives until, like an enemy in war, he confronts the system; and for this reason he begins to lose the nature of the "criminal" in his truly objective *deeds against the laws*.

travel or change our residence, etc. Although the objects that we meet during such changes do undergo alterations, the milieu *itself*, with its *structure*, through which any thing is a milieu-thing (not only a "value-thing" but also a "thing of the environment"), remains completely *constant* throughout such bodily changes of place. Whenever our bodies change their positions, the structure of the milieu remains as constant as the differences in spatial dimensions—like those of front and back, above and below—although ever new things are given in such dimensions. For the same value-qualities are the foundation of our different evaluating attitudes (or attitudes toward value-complexes). It is in their order of ranks which govern our "inclinations" that we approach altering empirical reality. A Philistine remains a Philistine; a Bohemian remains a Bohemian. Only that which carries with it the value-complexes of their attitudes becomes part of their "milieu." Human beings belonging to a specific social rank, race, ethnic group, or occupation, and even individuals, carry with them the structure of their own milieu. To a forester, a hunter, and someone taking a walk, the same forest represents different "milieux." In principle, the forest provides a milieu for a deer which differs from that for a human and, again, for a lizard living in it. One point must be kept in mind: if we say that the same forest provides different milieux for someone taking a walk, a hunter, etc., we do not imply (1) that they merely have different *interests* in this forest, (2) that they execute vis-à-vis the forest *acts of attention* which are merely of different levels, or (3) that these different persons *perceive* (while the directions of their lives are identical in terms of both the feeling of value and practicality) the same contents (in either sensible perception or representation, etc.) and consequently merely *observe* different aspects of the contents.[32] Rather, for all of these kinds

32. Attention must be paid to the difference between *individual* (or what stands in its place, a man, a Mongol) and *environment*. This distinction has nothing to do with that between *"ego"* and *"outer world,"* i.e., between psychic and physical spheres. This distinction between "individual" and "environment" is *psychophysically indifferent*, for every individual has both in his environment and in himself a "psychic" and a "physical" part. To the former belongs all things that he experiences as alter psychic and as effective on him without his having to perceive them: all thoughts and feelings that he does not experience "as" his own, as endowed with the quality of his individuality. (This sphere, by the way, coincides with what can be explained by the principle of association.) To the physical part there belongs his body-thing as it is given to him in the phenomenon of outer perception (in the practical milieu given with its positive and negative value-elements). Therefore, the distinction between the *organic body* and surrounding bodies has nothing to do with the distinction be-

of possible givenness in the acts mentioned, there must be an object that *belongs* to the "milieu" from the beginning so that the object *can* become a content in such acts with all their possible and potential degrees of adequacy. We can also say that from the outset all such acts—"taking interest," "passive and active attention," "perceiving"—find the milieu to be something like a *firm wall* that they cannot penetrate. They meet the milieu as something whose contents already represent every *possible* material for those contents that vary according to the kinds and degrees of acts. This may be shown here in brief:

1. Let us first turn to *attention*. It is correct to distinguish active from passive attention. Insofar as attention appears "in" conation, it is active attention, as clearly seen in the phenomenon of "searching for." In the phenomenon of suffering something that "imposes" itself, attention is passive. The latter breaks down into the qualities of "being attracted" or "being pushed away." This difference in attention is not a relative one; e.g., it is not relative to the temporal order of the sequence of perception and consciousness of activity. The difference is to be seen, rather, in the phenomenal point of departure of the given activity, whether it is experienced as coming forth from the ego or as approaching

---

tween individual and environment, for it holds *within* the sphere of the objects of outer perception and divides the phenomena of this sphere (according to the relation of dependence on organic bodies and inanimate bodies) into physiological and physical (in a wider sense) phenomena. (Nor does this distinction have anything to do with the real relation of soul to soul.) Furthermore, this distinction has nothing to do with the relation between the psychic, immediately experienced ego and the spheres of the psychic body and the ego-body (the seat of all organic sensations and instinctive striving, e.g., "becoming hungry"), for the difference obtains *within* the sphere of inner perception and divides the phenomena of this sphere (according to the relation of dependence on the ego and the ego-body) into the phenomena of pure and physiological psychology, purely psychic phenomena, and those of the "inner sense." (See "Über Selbsttäuschungen.") But the unity of the lived body is *given as a totality*, as an immediately intuitive and identical content, i.e., completely independent of outer and inner perception (and not through the *constant coordination* of outer and inner perception of the same "lived body"). It is precisely this totality that is the essential opposite of "environment." And opposite this uniform "lived body" (not the body-thing) stands the sphere of the *"person"* (as the psychophysically indifferent unity of acts). (See chap. 6, A, sec. 3.) But the opposite essential term (on the object side) with regard to the person is not an "environment" but a "world," of whose content "environment" represents only the domain of contents significant to the unity of the lived body and experienced as effective. Hence these opposites are to be sharply distinguished: (1) person and world, (2) lived body and environment, (3) ego and outer world, (4) body as thing and inanimate body, (5) soul and body-ego.

it. Now there can be little doubt that the milieu has no foundation in the variations of "active attention." Inasmuch as active
attention, with respect to a hallucinated object or even an illusory
one, can vary in all its subdivisions, such as observing, having regard to, keeping in sight, and noticing, and inasmuch as active
attention can also vary throughout the degrees of observing, having regard to, and keeping in sight *without* any change in the
contents of the objects concerned, it does so a fortiori with regard
to objects of the milieu. Of course, once a milieu is *given*, very
different aspects of things may become part of the increasing
or decreasing content of such functions. An individual is alterna-
tively attentive to this or that of its milieu. It "seeks" this or that
in it. A hunter, for instance, keeps in sight and notices this and
that trait, this and that process. But he *never thereby* enters the
milieu of one who just takes a walk through the forest! It should
also be clear that the milieu is given in experienced effectiveness,
never in seeking; one can "seek" different things *in* it, and one
can have regard to and notice this and that in it. The milieu is
obviously a firm wall to such activities and their degrees. "Passive attention," the imposition of objects with their qualities of
attraction and repellence,[33] presupposes at least the perception of
these objects. But this is not true, as I have shown, with respect
to the milieu-object! Passive attention presupposes even more.
First, it presupposes an objective factor in the object, its "conspicuity." This "conspicuity" (for example, of posters, clothes, or
other elemental forms; brightness and darkness are given *before*
different colors, including black and white; the Gestalt of a line
is given *before* its thickness, thinness, and color; the rhythm of
sequential sounds is given *before* their melodious form; the similarity of a Gestalt is given *before* the similarity in size of the
elements of the Gestalt) is at once a determining factor as a
measure of the degree of this "imposition." Whatever "imposes" itself on an individual must first be divided into the (general) degrees of conspicuity of the elements contained in it, no matter
which structural unit is concerned. Second, the *direction of taking interest* belonging to the individual concerned must be taken
into consideration in determining the degree of this "imposing."
What we call "interest," however, has nothing to do with a strong
degree of passive (or even active) attention. Nor is it a result of
a mere accumulation of such experiences of activity with respect
to a thing. For acts of attention (active and passive) may at times

33. All "feeling" of this is secondary.

fortuitously bring to our sight an appearance in which we take interest. But this act of "taking interest" is *not* given in any of the degrees of attentive experiences. It is a *novel* experiential quality, one that builds on the membership of an object in a unity in which we "have interest." [34] Thus the slightest sounds that have a significatory function toward her child condition the awakening of a mother from a deep sleep by the interest in her child and his state; but these same sounds *without* this significatory function "toward the child," though with the same value of liveliness or the same abilities (or even greater ones) to draw the mother's passive attention, *cannot* condition the mother's awakening. During the variations of attention (active and passive) it is the *direction* of interest that governs us. Its content (which is always a value-content) *guides* the direction of the acts concerned, no matter how high the degree of attention may be. To hold that an increase of attention in a student would also increase his interest in specific objects is the worst theory of education imaginable. [35] On the contrary, one must evoke interest in the object; the attention will then increase by itself. For example, I go to a party "out of interest" in a person. My attention may then turn to this or that. It may turn toward the hostess out of mere politeness when she is talking to me, though the person in whom I have a specific interest may be standing next to me. Although the hostess talking to me is subject to active and passive attention, the interest in the person concerned lies behind these experiences of attention and is experienced in a lived manner. The hostess and all that she says to me (which may draw my attention in greater or lesser degrees) is only one element within the sphere of my interest. Each of her gestures and words that has even a remote significatory function toward the object of my interest, namely, the person next to me, will thereby gain a passive attention in disproportionate fashion. Moreover, could I have come into the situation enabling me to perform these acts of attention concerning the hostess without this interest? Without doubt, "attention," with all its levels, is not conditioned by a value-feeling. As such it is *blind to values*. For I can be "attentive to" things and traits without comprehending any values in them! But that in which attention moves is always a phenomenally given *value-unit*, i.e.,

---

34. "Having interest" is an experience that has nothing to do with the so-called true interests of my person (which someone else can explain to me). But this experience does condition the direction of taking interest.
35. See William James, *Psychology* (New York: Holt, 1892).

a value-whole to which the object of my attention belongs in an emotively felt fashion.

Experiences of attention occur *within* "units of interest" and their corresponding units of values. *They* cannot break or change the structure of these units and their divisions. All possible attention oscillates within the frame of the *directions of interest,* which are the determining factors. Attention is imprisoned and captured within them.

2. Can *interest* determine the milieu? Interest in things originally presupposes the *perception* of these things and thus presupposes that their "efficacy" is experienced. Let us look at how something may catch my interest. This process presupposes that an object in which I take interest is already there for my conative life, i.e., that it is effective. The same thing-units taken from a definite part of the real world can possess such an efficacy for two individuals. Nevertheless, the directions of interest toward such thing-units (including those one "has" in them) can be very different. For instance, to two farmers negotiating over a farm, the same milieu is given in their considerations of the land, the stables, the buildings, etc. (insofar as the two come into question as farmers). That is, the same thing-units, tailored to their work and its field of acting, will become *alive* and *effective* on them in their considerations. And they will certainly be quite different from those of someone painting a picture of the farm. But the *different* interests that they have in conducting business with one another will yield quite different partial contents of their milieu, as well as different stresses and unimportances in the meaning of the contents that come to the threshold of their acts of noticing. The seller of the farm is attuned to advantages, the buyer to disadvantages.

Thus the milieu is something already *found* in interest. Interest makes selections from the different parts and perspectives of the *milieu-objects,*[36] and precisely for this reason it *cannot* determine the milieu.

3. Finally, I have said that the milieu-object also determines the *perception* of things (always, of course, within the limits of what can enter into our conative life as perceivable contents). The milieu is not only the intuited whole of the background for

36. What is otherwise called milieu is, in its temporal extension, *tradition,* i.e., history as living and effective in us, which *excludes* the conscious recollection of effective events and constitutes the *object* of historical science.

all contents of *perception* but also a reservoir, as it were, *from which* perceptual contents are taken. Thus objects in my room are efficaciously experienced not only when they do not belong—passively or actively—to my sphere of attention, but also when they are not *perceived* at all; nevertheless, their *variation* would *also* experienceably vary the *totality* of my experiences.

What is "efficacious in the milieu" therefore encompasses the perceptual sphere as a wider horizon, just as the perceptual sphere encompasses the sphere of interest, and the latter the sphere of attention. What lies in the perceptual sphere remains founded in milieu-objects. For, of the perceptible, we perceive in fact only those contents of real things (in the sense of the "natural world view") which are properties and qualities for the unity of efficacy of a milieu-thing, or which can at least have *some symbolic function.* The determination of the meaning and the "point of departure" of this uniformly experienced efficacy in a pictorial fashion is, depending on its magnitude and kind, identical with the condition of *what* is perceived. For this reason the perceived content of the milieu, with its structure and units, is the *exact counterpart* [Gegenbild] of such efficacious units in our conation! They are the "forms of resistance" that condition the "contents of objects."

The same holds true for the *"sensible contents"* occurring in the milieu. The milieu is *not* the sum of all that we sensibly perceive; rather, we can only sensibly perceive *what belongs to the "milieu."* [37]

It is the (twofold) one-sidedness contained in the methods of investigating so-called sensations, combined with an epistemological error, that is responsible for the apparent paradox in what we say. One aspect of this one-sidedness consists in the belief that it is not necessary to look into the real *uniform function* of the sensible totality of sensations of a living individual and this totality's biological significance and lawfulness. On the contrary, one simply concentrates on the question of what the determining function of sense organs, taken as disconnected from the lived body and its uniform process, *would* be for so-called

37. The *complete* content of things, events, etc., of the "natural way of looking at the world" is the "milieu" of the species "man" (the milieu emptied of all special interests). The peculiar "forms" of the "natural view of the world" represent the structure of the milieu of living beings in general. It is not this content but its very "structure" that is "a priori" for all "scientific experience"; but this is *not* the case for philosophy, i.e., absolute cognition. [See "Phänomenologie und Erkenntnistheorie" and "Lehre von den Drei Tatsachen" (Bibliog. no. 29).—*Ed.*]

sensations on the occasion of physical and chemical causes that stimulate the sense organs. Certainly this method—based on the useful fiction that there are such sense organs existing by themselves, sense corridors as well as localized terminals for them in a center, and that there are "complexes of sensations" existing by themselves which are dependent on stimulations of the terminals —is of great *economical* importance for knowledge of the laws that obtain here, given this fictitious presupposition. But this method tells us *absolutely nothing* about *what* a uniform living being *factually* senses in one of its lived moments, and it fails to indicate why such a being senses rather than that—for instance, why it does not sense what it *should* sense according to the results of this method *if* it *were* a mere collection of eyes, ears, tactile organs, and their prolongations to their respective parts in the brain. Nor does this method explain why different living beings have this range of qualities and modalities of contents of sensations and no other. But if this method of investigation assumes philosophical aspirations, it is bound to conceive of ultimate being as a chaos of "sensations" which no one senses and for whose special "complexes" all things, organisms, egos, etc., are only summarizing "symbols"—a being which is factually *never* given. Such philosophy necessarily ends up resembling that of Mach.

The fact is, however, that sensations are primarily *given* to a living being only *insofar* as they *function as pointers* to *things*, i.e., only insofar as they point to things of the *total milieu*. Whatever is not related to this function is *not* "given" at all. Qualities of sensations (and specific cases of other properties they might have) are given in concrete cases of organic sensations, but only *within the limitations* of the unities of functions, e.g., functions of visual and auditory acts, in which they are able to play a role. These functions work *in practice* only if they serve in acts like spying and eavesdropping and any of *their* units and objects in order to make objects manipulable according to interests that *guide* spying, eavesdropping, or initial feeling [*Spüren*] (e.g., touching). In the different species we find specific kinds of qualities representing an alphabet, as it were, by which "living words" of milieu-things become *representable*. Of course, just as all literary works, from Homer to Goethe, etc., are only "instances" of possible permutations of the sounds and letters that enter into a language, so also qualities of sensations are "elements" of which the great "poem" of our environment consists. But just as certainly as one who knows only such sounds and letters knows nothing at all of world literature and its "ultimate being"' and has nothing of such literature "given" to him, so also those to whom "sensations" are "given" not only have no world given but also have *nothing* of the world. The same is true of the relation between sensible feelings and the world of values.

Thus the *functions* of which the *uniform* "sensing" of a living being is composed—"hearing," "seeing," "initial feeling," etc.— are only *partial functions* of its "sensing," despite their own laws as opposed to the relational laws obtaining for stimulation, organ, and sensation; i.e., they are something *through* which a living being has its *uniform* sensory function. The content of sensation is not, however, a "sum" of what a being sees, hears, smells, and tastes, but a *whole* with whose variation the contents of these partial functions also change.[38] On the other hand, this content which enters a being's uniform sensation represents only a possible partial content of milieu-things (as the hearing of what has been overheard, the seeing of what has been spied on); and this partial content corresponds to the direction of interest in them. For we perceive *more* (in perception) than what we sense, even uniformly, and the milieu that we experience is always *wider* and *fuller* and given as more efficacious on us than what we apprehend and perceive. The uniform direction of interest of a uniform living being determines even the sensuous content of perception, though not the perceptual content, which must be given already for "interest." [39]

38. For this analytic method, this state of affairs can be seen in recently employed facts of changes in visual contents with simultaneous hearing, independent of variations in the things seen and heard. On the relations between "inner" seeing and hearing and simultaneous actual seeing and hearing, see Urbantschitsch, *Über subjektive Hörerscheinungen* (Leipzig, 1908). A *uniform* acting together of sense-functions in the direction of the hallucinated thing and its significance, which is in any case independent of simultaneous organic excitations, is revealed in a series of facts that show how sense-functions cooperate in hallucination— for example, when the hallucinated optical trumpeter makes the (hallucinated) sound of the trumpet while putting the trumpet to his mouth (Pick), or when the form of an (optically) hallucinated chair reveals spatially solid forms to the sense of touch. On these points, see W. Specht, "Zur Phänomenologie und Morphologie der pathologischen Wahrnehmungstäuschungen," *Zeitschrift für Pathopsychologie*, Vol. II, nos. 1, 2, 4.

39. One must not raise a certain objection to the points made, namely, that *we hear many sounds that we are not "listening" to,* that we have sensations of many things that do not "interest" us, etc. This objection is tantamount to misunderstanding our propositions empiricistically. It is true that we can have auditory sensations without hearing, and visual sensations without seeing (as hysterical blindness and deafness show). Also, visual and auditory contents may impose themselves on us when their things and events are neither listened to nor looked at. But they must

This division of sensibility into senses and the senses into sense organs constitutes a completely justified area of investigation—provided such investigation remains aware of its purposes and does not have philosophical aspirations. However, there is a second reason behind the paradoxical appearance of our proposition, namely, a profound epistemological error, an error which Kant also presupposes and which has enjoyed an uncontested position in philosophy since Descartes. It has also misled the physiology of senses, even in its most concrete problems (until a short time ago). This error consists in falsely founding the *concept of excitation* on those phenomena and categories which are constitutive of the facts and objects of the *physical sciences* (according to the sense of "nature" as everything *independent* of "life"). Only a phenomenological investigation of the foundation of the concept of excitation (in regard to both the excitation of *reaction* and the excitation of the *senses*) can clarify such an error.[40]

This error is ultimately based on a philosophical presupposition that consists in assuming that the whole world of physical objects and their reality is the result of an inference (a causal inference, be it "conscious" or "unconscious") which serves to "explain" pictorial representations and perceptions. This implies that physical reality is a purely mental construction that is contrived to explain certain "contents of consciousness"—first of all, "sensations." Here physical reality does not have its intuitive foundation in a proper *series of phenomena* of its own kind, which is to be *distinguished* from the series of phenomena in which "excitations" have their foundation, although both series of phenomena lie within the sphere of "outer perception." Physical reality is conceived as an "excitation" for psychic phenomena

---

belong to the *unity* of the act of seeing and hearing which belongs to our *species* (or "race," etc.) in order to become factual sensations (in contrast to consequences of possible "fictional" presuppositions). And they must belong to the unity of the act of listening and looking (of our *species*) in order to be given in hearing and seeing. We are not dealing with the question of what the real individual experiences of this or that real thing. We are examining the order of the foundation of acts as *such*, no matter *who executes them,* no matter how they realize themselves in individuals, for example, actually or dispositionally. Perhaps the son's or the grandson's hearing was preceded by the father's or the grandfather's listening so that the listening is given to the son as only an inherited "disposition" whose actual experience is not experienced by him again. We only wish to state that an act of "listening" founds every act of "hearing," no matter through what *real* causality this order of foundation of acts is transmitted.

40. [See the section on natural facts and sensible contents in "Lehre von den Drei Tatsachen."—*Ed.*]

(i.e., those of "inner perception"). Helmholz, for instance, holds that even appearances of colors are "facts" of "inner perception." [41] And since "psychic phenomena" (i.e., such "appearances of colors"), as "psychic," do not belong at all to the domain of physiological problems, physical determinations of colors must, according to Helmholz, be presupposed in physiological investigations of the sense of color. The physiology of colors does not possess its own *phenomenal* facts as points of departure, but is only an "application" of physical optics to the special case of light rays hitting organic bodies. This false point of departure and method, from which Hering first broke away, is only *one* (relatively secondary) example of the lack of insight into the phenomenological foundation of the "concept of excitation," so important for *all biology*.

One must first sharply distinguish between *inner* and *outer* perception, their corresponding spheres of phenomena, and their specific forms of unity and diversity.[42] This distinction is *not* relative to the lived body or to one specific lived body; it rests on a difference in "perceptual" direction, which can be shown in phenomenology. This distinction would *still* remain, even if we were to *bracket* completely the lived body (and what is "inner" and "outer" in relation *to it*).

Both directions of perception yield *only* such phenomena as can appear in them alone. In principle, they yield such phenomena (depending on the kind of perception involved) with equal "immediacy" and "mediacy." The levels of immediacy and mediacy, the distinction between the "real" and "appearance" and "illusion" [*Schein*], are the *same* in both. As perceptions, they possess the *same* evidence, and in both spheres there is an "a priori" and an "a posteriori." They also encompass the kinds of acts of knowledge that we distinguished earlier (i.e., theoretical comportment directed toward valueless objects), as well as acts of *value-feeling* and *preferring*, etc. Furthermore, they encompass acts of conation and willing. For I can be directed toward the ego and its value in a feeling manner as well as in a willing manner.[43]

41. For a refutation of this curious assertion, see I. Lieferung, *Über den Farbensinn*, and Ewald Hering, *Grundzüge der Lehre vom Lichtsinn* (Leipzig: Engelmann, 1911).

42. [See chap. 6, A, sec. 3, f, and Über Selbsttäuschungen" or "Idole," sec. 2.—*Ed.*]

43. I comport myself feelingly, willingly, and perceivingly (e.g., as a psychologist) in the sphere of being-given-to-myself (or ego-givenness in general). If, for instance, I want to control myself, my ego is not given in

But *within* the spheres of outer and inner intuition (and also in feeling and willing, as values and resistances) two *different* series of phenomena are given. These two series do not, however, represent themselves as different through their objective relational dependencies, but are immediately experienced as "different." They are, on the one hand, those series which are still *dependent* on the lived body, experienced, as it were, as belonging to it, and, on the other, those which are experienced as *independent* of it. The latter constitute the ultimate "facts" of the cognition of psychology and physics; the former, the facts of the (enlarged) physiology of the inner and outer senses. *Every* fact of outer perception therefore contains two components, one of which possesses an experienced symbolic relation to a fact or process in the lived body, the other a relation to the physical (inanimate) world. For instance, the phenomena of the sensation of temperature are distinct from those of objectively given "warmth." We phenomenally distinguish our being "warm," "cold," "hot," from the phenomenon of its being "cold" or "warm" here; i.e., we distinguish our being "chilly" from the temperature of the room around us, our fever from the heat in the room. It is therefore incorrect to assert, as Mach did, that we get the concepts of *objective* temperature from a *sensation* of temperature, be it by way of an inference from effect to cause or by way of a convention or a definition.[44] In addition, there are *intensity-relations* among phenomena, e.g., brightness and darkness in relation to spatial extension, and warmth and coldness in relation to spatial extension (which are, of course, not measurable with objective scales). Such relations are the very *presupposition* of the physical definitions of light and temperature. This is not the place to show that the phenomena of distance, as well as those of nearness (e.g., the mutual "touching" of two bodies—of one body with the lived body or of one lived-body part with another part), are experienced *in part as related to the lived body, in part as not related to the lived body.*

For this reason the concept of excitation is not a merely hypothetical concept contrived for purposes of explanation; it has a *phenomenological* foundation as *primitive* as the concept of a physical process. Therefore it is as incorrect to define excitation

---

perception as an "object" (in the pregnant sense); it is given as a "withstanding" factor in willing.

44. See the section on the concept of temperature in E. Mach, *Die Principien der Wärmelehre* (Leipzig: Barth, 1919).

merely as a kind of physical process that strikes an organism as it is to define, conversely, the physical process merely as a hypothetical excitation for the sensation of the reaction of an organism.

One should consider the following. In the strict sense of the terms it is nonsense to say that "ether waves hit the eye." The mistake lies in submitting the appearance of light to a mechanical reduction while retaining the natural view of the world and its reality for the "eye." But where there are ether waves, there no longer are "eyes"; even the organism itself is only a *part* of the continuous motion coming from the sun to my brain! Visual excitations are beams of light, not "ether waves." And again, there are countless physical movements going through an organism, but without being "excitations." Only what changes the states of a lived body or posits changed reactions in an organism can be called an excitation. The objective concept of excitation must always be related *to the unity of a lived body* and *its* variations according to its phenomenological foundation in experienced "efficacy."

For this reason the *experienced efficacy* of an object on my *acting* has nothing to do with those movements which in turn produce movements in my organism. Where such movements exist, there is no organism as an independent unity, but only a *complex of all cosmic motions* that is (arbitrarily) selected. A deed is always determined through concrete *units of things and events in the natural world view* which are effectively experienced; it is *never* determined by molecular and atomic complexes. A deed—irrespective of how it realizes itself mechanically through the mediation of such reflexes, chain reflexes, tropisms, directional movements, etc.—is a phenomenologically *uniform* act, which can *never* be resolved into the sum of such "movements."

The totality, or the *uniform whole,* of the world (or, when specified as the outer world, "nature") which is effectively experienced by a living being constitutes that being's *"environment"* [Umwelt]. In order to have a correct foundation of the science of biology (and especially physiology), one must always begin with the *basic relation of an organism to its environment.* This relation *constitutes* the essence of a life-process. It consists in the *dynamic variations* that are the condition of changes in an organism *as well as* of changes in the environment. Such changes are therefore always conditioned *simultaneously* by the variations in processes "between" organism and environment.[45] Hence an "environment" belongs to any unit of life, just as an "organism" does. It is wrong in principle to regard an organism as a counterpart of inanimate nature and its objects, and "environment" as a merely subjective "representation" and "sensation" "originated" by the real effects of inanimate nature on an organism. It is equally wrong to conceive of the "adaptation relationship" between organism and environment as a unilateral adaptation of the organism to its environment (or vice versa, as a certain kind of vitalism holds). One should conceive of *each* as a dependent variable of the *processes of life* in its uniform occurrence. And it is completely erroneous to construe the adaptation as an adaptation to *inanimate nature,* instead of to the "environment," as if the astronomical sun were an object to which, for example, a worm or an Eskimo would have to "adapt" himself.

The Russian physiologist Pavlov did *philosophy* a great favor by recognizing the narrowness of traditional physiology and demanding that this science broaden its scope so that the relational dependencies between the variations of an "environment" and the physiological processes could be impartially examined—*without* first asking which physical and chemical actions produce physiological functional changes. It is his exclusion of both the "psychic" and the "physical" that brings to the fore the *purely* biological and physiological "problem."[46]

45. This also applies to every initial state and every final state of a process of life and to *their* changes through changes in the *process* of life. The final state is therefore never univocally conditioned by the initial state.

46. From this it clearly follows that it is not only an error of observation but also one of philosophical relevance to *reduce* changes in the "organizations" of living beings to ever increasing "adaptations" to their "*milieu*" in the theory of their evolution. The genuine "traits of adaptation" of organisms (e.g., the leaves and roots of aquatic plants and plants growing in the desert or on mountains) leave proper "traits of organization" quite *unchanged.* For such organisms can never be conceived as a mere agglomeration of adaptations. Within one organization, to which there always corresponds a milieu-structure, individuals or subclasses of this organization can adapt to their *milieu* to quite different degrees. But one can never reduce a change in the structure of the milieu (which is always accompanied by changes in organization) to "adaptation," for example, an *enlargement* of the milieu. *Its* causes at any rate are of another *type* (not merely different in *degree*) than those of variations of adaptation. One who fails to see this point will be led into a false *anthropomorphism* by considering man's environment *basic* to all other organizations and by examining their adaptations to *man's* environment, which is not *theirs*. A worm's or a fish's environment is not at all "contained" in the human environment. The environment of different animals is

A final basic mistake in the traditional and widely accepted concept of excitation consists in taking the *essence* of "excitation" to be so-called *excitations of senses* or *excitations of sensation,* instead of viewing the concept in terms of the *reactions* that are effected by an "excitation" (i.e., according to its original meaning in language). Thus one gradually comes to the conclusion that even colors and sounds, for example, "do not exist" as qualities independent of an organism and its excitations, but that they are only "movements" that are to be "translated" into the "language" of these qualities, or even to be "produced" and "made" in quite a mythical fashion (some explain these qualities in terms of "specific energies" of the nerves, others in terms of the so-called soul and its "nature"). Likewise, *values* are supposed to be "subjective appearances," which, "strictly speaking," are only the names of changing states (sensible feelings) of the lived body. But processes of life, organisms, and the environment are *not* factors in the production of "sensations" and sensible feelings; an organism is no factor "for" sense organs; the environment is no factor "for" being perceived. Rather, *sensing* (of any type of qualities) and *feeling* (of any type of values) stand solely in the *service* of the uniform processes of life. Sense organs serve the basic vital processes, e.g., nutrition, propagation, etc.; and the kind and structure of perceiving serve to illuminate the environment. In other words, it is not seen that the *sensing* of qualities alone and the *feeling* of values (*conation* toward goals), but *not* the contents concerned, are conditioned by excitations, or

---

always fixed by special procedures. (See J. von Uexküll; *Umwelt und Innenwelt der Tiere.*) It is only between the environment of an organization and its *members* that there are different adaptations. Spencer's primary mistake in biology and the theory of knowledge is his idea that the world of organizations is related to the environment of *man* and that changes in higher organizations are to be reduced to a mere adaptation of organisms to this "environment." The *activities* of life (and its *directions* and their changes) that alone *determine* environment fall by the wayside. There is one natural object *common* to all (outer) environments of organizations (including man), but it is an error to think of this common natural object in terms of *those* categories and forms of manifolds that are necessary for the mechanical conceptualization of natural appearances. We do not wish to deal here with the question of which categories and forms are constitutive of this common natural object, although this is a question of great importance. In my forthcoming work, *Arbeit und Erkenntnis,* this question will be treated in detail. [On "organism and adaptation," see below, chap. 5, sec. 5. The above-mentioned "forthcoming work" did not appear; the essay "Erkenntnis und Arbeit" is based on a manuscript of 1925. For earlier works by the author on the problem of pragmatism, see the notes to "Phänomenologie und Erkenntnistheorie," in the appendix to *Zur Ethik und Erkenntnislehre* (Bibliog. no. 29).—Ed.]

that sensation still belongs to the *reactions* of life. Instead, one tries to reduce reactions to mere sequences of "organic sensations," which are considered in terms of the nature of outer "sensations." Who cannot see this mistake! There are no "sensations" like these independent things about which there is so much talk. There is *sensation* (a special case of vital reaction), and there are *qualities* that are sensed. It is (in the development of individual and general life) only the increasing differentiation of sensation in its functions, such as hearing, seeing, tasting, etc., which determines that ever new and richer units of pictorial qualities *approach* life from the sphere of the universe. Similarly, it is the increasing differentiation of feeling which determines the *approach* of ever new and richer units of value-qualities. It is not that a poor and inanimate universe of uniform motion conceals and hides itself more and more from developing life; on the contrary, this universe shows ever more richly differentiated kinds of reaction that permit the fullness of qualities existing *in itself* to come to "light."

It is not that a value*less* universe hides itself from developing life, masking itself as merely subjective sensible feelings; on the contrary, the realm of values *opens* itself up more and more to differentiating feeling.

Let us return from this excursus to our original question. We can see that: (1) Objects that become determining factors in *acting*, i.e., *milieu-objects*, can become such objects only if they are *already* cut out of the totality of world-facts *on the basis* of the *value-directions* of the *portion of life of the lived body* and its immanent rules of preferring.[47] The *milieu* of a being is therefore the *precise counterpart* of its *drive-constellation* and its structure, i.e., its *make-up*. The fullness and emptiness of the *milieu* (when world-facts remain the same), as well as the prevailing values in such facts, are dependent on these *drive-constellations and directions*. (2) The occurrences of *sensible feeling-states* are *dependent* on the *primary drive-manifestations* which are stirred up by *milieu-objects* that are themselves *selected through drive-constellations*. Sensible feeling-states are not causes but *consequences* of these stimulations.[48]

47. I.e., *those* facts which would be "given" in "pure" outer and inner perception, value-taking, and willing *not* conditioned by a lived body and its drives.
48. I find solid proof of this fact in all experiences of the origin of perversions. They all show that the primary factor is always the perversion of *drives*, not that of sensible feeling. It is because the drives of nutrition

On both points Kant presupposes the *contrary*. Concerning the first point, he believes not only that the *stimulations* of drives are consequences of the effects of the milieu, but also that the material drive-*constellations* are such consequences. This in turn leads him to believe that all drives are to be regarded finally as mere specializations of *one* formal basic drive: the drive of self-preservation, which is split into a plurality of drives through the effects of outer objects. In fact, however, every living being possesses an *ordered structure of levels of drives* with non-formal value-constellations that are *independent* of the effects of milieu-objects, but nevertheless *determining* for them. A living being already provides a "plan" for possible goods through its own kind of drive-constellation, a plan that does not rely on a living being's experiences in a milieu, but that corresponds to its bodily organization.[49] Such constellations of drives, no matter how they are to be explained, *cannot* be reduced to any uniform drive like that of "self-preservation." [50]

Second, Kant assumes that drive-excitations are caused by a sensible feeling-state vis-à-vis a milieu-object, and that this feeling-state determines an object in its effect on a lived body. Hence he must come to the false conclusion that all non-formal contents of drives, i.e., value-qualities toward which a drive is directed, are determined not only by experience (of inductive form) in general—which would be correct—but also by the experience in a milieu.

This bears on his *ethics* in that he must as a consequence divide the whole of value-facts into *formal laws* and *sense-pleasure*. And from this it follows that the *fullness* and *structure* of the drive-life of a human being, as opposed to the will's accomplishment in "ordering" it, do not represent a factor in the *evaluation* of a human being.

These conclusions follow from all of the above: (1) The *basic moral tenor possesses a realm of non-formal values which*

---

or sex are perverted that the perverted person feels "pleasure" in what disgusts a normal person. In all beginnings of perversion there are negative feelings implicit in striving; feeling only gradually *follows* the perverted drive.

49. We will discuss elsewhere the immense importance of the drive-constellations of "races," which *cannot at all* be reduced to the changing milieux of the groups concerned, as well as their significance for morals. This will in general provide broad confirmation of what we have said.

50. The reproductive drive in all living things is stronger and more original than the drive of self-preservation. It was only the increasing drive-perversion of a small section of Western European history that prompted the mistaken assumption that the opposite is the case.

is independent of all experience and any *success in deeds*. The basic moral tenor determines the *world of values of the person*. The act of willing within the value-direction of a person's moral cognition may be called a "self-positioning" [*Selbstellung*]. (2) The *"drive-constellation,"* however, presupposes the experience of some *lived-body organization*. If such an organization is given, the *material of drive-stimulations* is possible only within the scope that the *milieu allows* as conditioned by a *drive-constellation*.

It becomes clear that a fundamental error in Kant's philosophy in general is no less fundamental in his ethics. I refer here to his prejudiced point of departure, namely, *mathematical science* on the one hand and *British association psychology* on the other. Both led Kant to believe that the basic biological concepts, the "categories" of biology, can be derived from mathematical science, and that "life" is not at all a basic phenomenon; these also led him to believe that drives can receive their contents and directions only from the contents of the sphere of sensible feeling or from the genetic products of this sphere insofar as they can be explained by the principles of association and reproduction. In ethics this error implies that it is only the *success* of acting, taken in the sense of the repercussion of what is realized in acting on a sensible feeling, that can furnish material for drives; and because this repercussion is in any case indifferent to a man's value, drives and their directions as well as their contents are indifferent to his value. Kant failed to see a fact that is fundamental in ethics, namely, that a *basic* value-difference among men is determined by which objects *can* have an effect on their possible comportment and, hence, *can* give rise to sensible feeling-states; and he failed to see that there are differences among those things in which different men *can* experience "pleasure."

PART II

4 / Value-Ethics and
Ethics of Imperatives

*1. Unsatisfactory Theories of the Origin of the Concept of
Value and the Essence of Moral Facts*

EVERY KIND OF COGNITION is rooted in experience.
Therefore ethics, too, must have its foundation in "experience."
But the question concerns the essence of the experience that
yields moral cognition, and the essential elements that such experience must contain. If I assess a deed of mine or the comportment of one of my fellow men as "good" or "evil," either in recollection or prior to its execution, what kind of experience is it that
renders the material for the judgment? It does not help to begin
the investigation with an analysis of propositions of assessment
which are formulated in language. So-called assessments are no
different from other judgments with respect to logical form. The
question here concerns the *fact-material* which corresponds to
"assessments," how this material comes upon us, and the factors
of which it consists. One must inquire into the immediately given
facts that fulfill the predicates of such propositions as this deed
is "distinguished," "vulgar," "noble," "base," "criminal," etc., and
into the ways in which such facts come upon us.

Nothing looks more paradoxical at a superficial glance than
the assertion that there are such things as moral "*facts.*" One is
inclined to admit that there are astronomical, botanical, and
chemical facts to which theories must "correspond" in some way
or another. But what can "moral facts" be? Let us momentarily
refrain from considering the universal difficulty with the concept
of "facts" in general: whether every fact is a certain mental con-

struction, an X-something, which supplies an answer to a pre viously formed concept, question, or hypothesis, or whether there are genuine and *pure* facts. One can still see, apart from this question pertaining to the essence of a fact, a distinct difference. Whatever the case may be, the question is not the same for both "moral facts" and other kinds of "facts." Looking at nature, I perceive stars, plants, animals, and bodies in various forms of composition. Looking into myself, I perceive an ego, conation, willing, and sensations in a complex of interwoven manifolds. In a thinking fashion, I comprehend numbers, for instance, and many relations among them, in a sphere that can be called the being of ideal objects. But where can I find moral facts? Surely an ego or a willing can be good or evil, noble or base. But do I see this in the same manner as I see, in inner perception, the factors that lie in *willing:* conation, affirmation, the "it ought to be so," and the sensations of muscular tension that always accompany these factors? And is it not the case that a law, an institution, even the order or disorder in my room—things, in other words, that do not occur at all in myself, and which cannot appear in inner perception—can be connected with predicates that refer to the moral, such as "just," "unjust," "orderly," and "disorderly"? If I thus scrutinize the entire world, it seems that I find no "moral facts." Indeed, in how many areas have "moral facts" been sought in the history of philosophy?

Many thought they could find them in "inner experiences." But it is unsatisfactory to assume that there are many feelings of what is "seemly" or "unseemly," for instance, or of "repentance," or of "sin" and "guilt." Do I perceive *that* which we call seemly and unseemly, *that* which we call repentance, guilt, and sin, as *belonging to* and *in* such feelings? Is a feeling itself "seemly" or "unseemly"—just as it may be strong, weak, pleasant, or unpleasant, or just as it has this or that quality? Certainly not. If we were to have in our hands *that* which we call "repentance," "guilt," or "sin," and if we were to know *what* it really is, then it would be meaningful to talk about the feelings that we have and find in ourselves on the occasion of repenting and knowing ourselves to be of guilt, just as we can determine a representation A and a representation B by saying that representation A is "of Bismarck," and that B is "of Moltke." In both cases, however, we *leave* what we find in inner experience and move toward *objects* that do not lie in lived experiences. Therefore the psychologist or the researcher whose sphere of investigation is inner experience does not concern himself with whether his facts are "moral" or "immoral." Everyone knows that the psychologist must *reject* these differences as they impose themselves. There is *no* psychological division between good and bad feelings. It may be that the world of ethical concepts depicts everything possible as inner being and happening, so that a certain feeling of displeasure appears as "repentance," "guilt," and the like, just as a "tree" or a "house" appears in a certain complex of colors, forms, and shadows. Then, as a psychologist, one must not fix his gaze on *these* conceptual differences if he is to locate his objects. "Moral facts" therefore do *not* lie in "inner perception."

Are they to be found in the realm of "ideal objects," where numbers, "the" circle, and "the" triangle are? Plato thought so. This assumption is correct in one sense only. There is an ideal meaning-content of "the good" which I can bring into my consciousness with a good man and a good deed, just as I can do this with the ideal species "red" in a seen red color, i.e., the "red" in a certain shade of red. But the difference appears when we ask if objects can be found *only* in this realm and not elsewhere. Numbers and triangles are given only in this realm. I cannot intuit them as I can red or green. There is only *one* number 3, no matter how many operations I must perform to arrive at it, and no matter with which symbols I designate it. But red and green, as well as the tones D and C, are also to be found in another sphere. I can intuit red without looking in the direction of the meaning "red." This does not mean that an "undetermined" color becomes red only when subsumed under its concept. A seen red can have thousands of shades that do not enter into the sphere of meaning. Conversely, anything that does *not* fall under the meaning of a seen triangle does not belong to the sphere of *triangularity*: it is the "deviations" from it, e.g., different colors, etc., that are not triangular at all. Is Plato correct in saying that the "good" is of the same nature as the triangle or the number 3? Are noble, magnanimous, just, etc., differentiated as value-qualities, as the shades of red are differentiated as *intuitive* contents, or are they only "exemplifications" of the single "good" whose differences lie only in complex acts of willing, deeds, human beings, etc., as bearers of qualities such as noble, magnanimous, just? Can I not see any type of kindness that I meet in experience as a special and *peculiar* fact without looking at the idea of "kindness as such"— however *possible* it may be in such a case to think of the essence of "kindness"? This is beyond doubt. "Morality" does not lie in the realm of ideal meanings *alone*. It is not in the light of such ideal meanings alone that "premoral facts" *become* moral ones. There are *originaliter* moral facts that are distinct from the sphere of the meanings of moral concepts. Plato, too, fell victim to the deception of the ancient and historically very effective division of spirit into "reason" and "sensibility." On the assumption that moral values—indeed, all value-facts—are comparable to straight lines and triangles in that they do *not* belong to the sphere of *contents of sensation,* one concludes that they are only "meanings comprehensible through reason." Yet a child feels the kindness of his mother without having even vaguely comprehended an idea of the good. And how often do we feel that our enemy possesses a noble moral quality while we stick to our negative judgment of him in the sphere of meanings, so that the appearance of his noble quality passes us by without a change in our intellectual convictions concerning him? Moral facts, as opposed to the sphere of meanings, are *facts of non-formal intuition, not* of sensible intuition, if by "intuition" we mean immediacy of the givenness of an object and not necessarily a picturelike content.

There is another analogy that must be done away with, one that claims justification on its own terms. It is often emphasized that, like mathematical concept-words, the words which express moral values possess no correlates in the contents of experience that *adequately* correspond to them. Just as no real cube is a perfect cube, so also, it is claimed, "no one is good but your Father in heaven"; i.e., the existence of "moral facts" as independent of the sphere of meanings is denied because moral words refer not only to something "fictionally ideal" but also to the *"ideal"* that real human beings and deeds can only "approximate." Thus, later Platonists (like Augustine, Descartes, and Malebranche) asserted that one could not comprehend the kindness of a certain human being without referring to the idea of *total kindness,* or the idea of *God*—just as one could not comprehend a finite straight line without referring to the idea of an absolute infinite line as a measure of sorts, and taking the finite line as a "part" of the latter. Yet the assertion that all values are "ideal" must be rejected. There are values *of* the ideal and *of* the factual; but a moral value as such is *never* an "ideal" of something that itself is *not* yet a value. Here one cannot see which direction of "idealization" one should take in order to arrive at a *value* from properties—say, of human beings—which are value-indifferent. A value must be *caught in intuition* if it is to be idealized, and it makes no difference whether we are concerned with a finite or infinite object of the quality concerned. Nor is it permissible to dissolve the differences between moral value-qualities, such as the essential difference between good and evil, into mere *degrees of approximation* of an "ideal" of the "good" or "all kindness." Socratic-Platonic intellectual idealism was mistaken at the out-set in denying values of the bad, with their manifold qualities, as positive facts, and in identifying the bad with that which is the *greatest distance* from the highest good, or "the good," as well as in equating the bad with "appearances" (μὴ ὄν as opposed to ὄντως ὄν). But values of both the good and the bad occur at *all* levels of being, if one wishes to distinguish levels of being. However, one cannot identify the "good" with the ultimate level of being (the ὄντως ὄν, as Plato says) nor can one regard the bad as only a relative level of being.

Modern rationalism (e.g., that of Spinoza, Leibniz, Wolff) commits the same error in using the unclear concept of "perfection" for this purpose, identifying the more perfect with a "higher degree of being," and absolute perfection with the *ens realissimum*. Perfection presupposes value-facts, and, if applied to something, it assumes a meaning only when a certain value-property in a thing in relation to which this thing is perfect has been comprehended.

But if moral value-facts do not belong to the sphere of pure meanings, where are they, and how are they to be found? Before responding to the question, let us consider another theory on the matter. This theory holds that there are absolutely *no* genuine fulfillments of the words *good, noble,* etc., *neither* in the sphere of meanings *nor* anywhere else, and that we are concerned here with *human inventions* that have their original existence only in words of language. According to this theory such words have no intentional function at all, but are only *expressions* of feelings, affects, interests, and acts of desire. The first of these assertions was held in its most radical form by Thomas Hobbes. It is also behind many statements made by Nietzsche, e.g., his claim that there are no moral phenomena, only moral interpretations of phenomena.

Despite basic differences in the interpretation of "ideas" and "meanings," this opinion shares more with Platonism and its schools than it realizes. For in both this theory and Platonism, autonomous *value-facts*—and *moral* value-facts in particular—are *denied*, and the entire sphere of the moral is pushed over into the sphere of an unintuitable area of thought. In the later theory, *"interpretation"* replaces eternal ideas that are only comprehensible through meanings. Initially such interpretation grows unarbitrarily out of the factual conations, interests, and needs of a group; later it supposedly falls victim to more or less *arbitrary* definitions and conventions. There is no *knowledge* of the morally valuable, but rather the *fixation* of what is to be called that; it is not evidence and truth but *purposefulness* that decides moral conflict.

The central point of this theory is its claim that there is no such thing as a definite moral experience. Words designating values—especially moral values—and propositions and moral evaluations containing such words are not considered words and propositions reflecting *facts* or words and propositions having an intentional cognitive function in relation to such facts; they are considered mere expressions of reactions to extant emotive and conative processes, processes which are *not* comprehended as psychic facts of *inner perception*. At a higher level of development such words and propositions become *arbitrary expressions* of a *readiness* to *act* in a certain situation. Hence they are not forms of communication of something known; they are, rather, means to *guide* our deeds and those of others in a certain direction. Accordingly, *praise* and *reproach precede* moral *value-cognition*. Propositions such as "This deed is good" (or "This personality is good," etc.) are not based on value-cognition. On the contrary, the concepts of good, bad, etc., follow only from reflection on the acts of praise and reproach as well as on their directions and laws. Praise and reproach, however, are only the immediate expressions of the fact that the praised (reproached) lies in the direction of a present and factual conation (counter-conation) in the one who is praising (reproaching).[1]

Ethical *nominalism* must be clearly *distinguished* from the psychological doctrine which holds that "moral facts" are found in the sphere of inner experience ("psychologism") and in the feelings and conations, etc., that one comprehends *there*. For nominalism asserts the opposite, namely, that there are no such "facts," and that *definitions* and secret and hidden *conventions* govern our moral evaluations.

Ethical nominalism does not maintain that a proposition such as "This man's conduct is good" is different only in words from the proposition "I find in myself, or there is in me, a feeling

---

1. See my criticism of Adam Smith's ethics of sympathy. His ethics takes as its starting point the cofeeling of a neutral onlooker and his praise and reproach. See *Zur Phänomenologie und Theorie der Sympathie-gefühle* (Bibliog. no. 6), pp. 1–9. [See *Wesen und Formen der Sympathie* (Bibliog. no. 18), pt. A, chaps. 1, 2.—*Ed.*]

of satisfaction with regard to this deed"; it maintains that the first proposition *expresses* a certain *feeling—without* intending to. If I say, "Ouch," after experiencing pain, this *ouch* does not relate to this pain as does my saying that I feel pain; rather, it expresses the pain. This *ouch* does not contain an intention to "communicate" my pain, though it may well be that someone else can use it as a datum for the cognition of the pain; it is, rather, the immediate expressive consequence of the painful experience. Likewise, propositions such as "This is good," "This is bad," do not, according to this theory, reflect the contents of inner experience as taking place or as having taken place; nor do they tell someone about them. They simply *express* certain acts of feeling and desiring. Any proposition predicating a moral value or disvalue is always the expression of a desire or a feeling. We do not desire something because we have the insight that it is good; rather, we call something "good" because we desire it (Spinoza, Hobbes, et al.). It is by reference to a factually executed act of willing—be this an act of our own, a societal will, an authority, God, etc.—that *sense* is given to an assertion like "This is good."

Involuntary utterances of desire and feeling, which constitute the most elementary sense of so-called value-judgments, are later replaced by *voluntary "enunciations"* of such acts with the intent to invoke the same desire and feeling in others. In the various modes of wishing, giving orders, advising, recommending, etc., enunciation is something different from "communicating," which is also different from merely "giving expression." Enunciation is different from "expression" in its factor of *willing* a certain movement or speech, as well as in its intention with respect to fellow men, which does not, however, necessarily imply a certain group of men. "Enunciation" is generally directed to a *"social environment"* and its objects. Thus an edict or a resolution by an authority is not "communicated" but "enunciated" (or "promulgated"). More significant is the fact that enunciation has a much higher degree of generalization than communication. In a wish such as "I wish you to do this" or in an order such as "You shall do this," "Do this," or "This you shall do," I enunciate my *immediate* will. That is, I do not realize in terms of an act of reflecting that "I wish this," that "I will this," or that "I order this" in order to "communicate" these states of affairs to someone else in the form of a judgment. Rather, it is the very wish and the willing itself that is enunciated in such propositions of wishing and giving orders. All communication refers to contents of a judgment. i.e., to states of affairs. This is not the case in enunciating wishes and orders. It is also not the case that I intend to make someone else understand, grasp, or comprehend a state of affairs—for example, that I intend to make him see that this or that wish and conation is in me. On the contrary, it is my intention *to move his willing* and to determine his conation and move it in a certain direction. This moving and determining of the other's willing is not mediated by an act of objective understanding of my wish and conation; it is, rather, an immediate "postfeeling" or "postconation" which immediately follows upon the word-comprehension of the enunciation.[2]

The nominalistic theory, however, reduces the communication of *value-judgments* to such *enunciations* of wishes and acts of the will. "Thou shalt do this" can have many meanings, as we will see. It can be a form of *expressing* my will that one do this. But it can also be a linguistic mummification of a *value-judgment:* "It is good and objectively demanded that you do this," or "Your doing this is positively valuable." But such an original difference is *denied* by nominalism. Furthermore, according to this theory value-predications do not mediate a type of moral cognition; they only express *wishes* and *orders* in a hidden manner. In this theory there are no communicated cognitions of a fact demanding recognition, but only hidden *solicitations* to will in a certain direction (as distinct from the immediate); i.e., value-predications are linguistically acts of *orders*, also, and are this *only* because they accompany the consciousness of expecting others or a certain authority to approve or praise what has been ordered. "Moral experience," which according to this theory does not exist, is therefore replaced by an observation of struggling, victorious, and yielding volitional impulses that in many ways mutually determine each other; and this observation must *precede* any determination of what is good or evil. The names used for moral values in propositions which predicate them as *properties* of certain volitional acts, deeds, or persons—e.g., "good," "evil," "noble," "base"—are therefore only *symbols* for the quality and the degree of *success* which, under average circumstances in a given volitional sphere, an act of will and a deed will have after such approval or disapproval. Hence *no* specific *factual state of affairs* corresponds to these names. They are only names for summing up deeds viewed from the standpoint of the result that one

2. Concerning the differences between "postfeeling" and "cofeeling," see *Zur Phänomenologie und Theorie der Sympathiegefühle*, pp. 9 f. [See *Wesen und Formen der Sympathie*, pt. A, chap. 2.—Ed.]

would have to expect in a certain case. A moral evaluation can therefore *never* be of *guidance* in our acting and willing; for in the final analysis it is nothing but a symbolic expression of factual relations of power among volitional acts.

It is clear, then, that according to *these views* ethics can have only a twofold task: to reduce all valid value-judgments to factually present conations and volitions and their real relations of power, and to *define* as precisely as possible the content of a will on the presupposition of a specific will (e.g., the will of God, the will of the state, the "collective" will, etc.). It is only this content that is the "good"; all that contradicts this content is "evil." Accordingly, any endeavor to determine the value or simply the justification of *this* will has *no sense*. For according to this theory no isolated act of the will possesses a specific value. The act obtains its value only through *relating* the isolated act to *other acts of will*, where *one* among these acts of will is taken as a measure for all the rest. And it is the command coming from this will (be it expressed in a concrete form or in terms of a general rule [norm]) that permits the definition of "good" and "evil" through the content of the command. From this it follows that all of the kinds of changes in moral value-judgments in individuals and in history are but symbolic expressions for the victory of one will over another. It is *never* progress in *moral cognition* that changes deeds, but only a new praxis that makes one call the ends of others' wills good or bad. A moral genius is an "inventor," not a discoverer. He neither cognizes nor shows ways. He acts and draws people with him. The moral codex is nothing but a compilation of the ends and directions of *his* willing put together at a later time.

Are things really as ethical nominalism would have them be? Are there no moral facts? Are good and evil merely arbitrary determinations and interpretations of facts which rest on a kind of conventional measure for human deeds that is similar to the conventional units of measurement in physics?

It is not our intention to examine the nominalistic doctrine *as a whole*.[3] We would, however, like to stress that a large part of the argument of ethical nominalism is not *substantially* different from the reasons for which nominalistic philosophy rejects the objective and real validity of concepts, propositions, and formulations of laws. Not only moral laws but also laws of nature have

3. I wish to refer to Husserl's classical critique of the nominalistic theory in his *Logische Untersuchungen*, Vol. II.

been described as aids for the most economical ordering of the contents of sense-perception (just as the former have been described as a means for ordering our deeds); even the principal laws of logic and mathematics have been subjected to attempts to explain them in terms of definitions and conventions; the existence of certain *magnitudes* in nature as independent of arbitrarily chosen units and methods of measurement have been denied by identifying the existence of "magnitudes"—even the concept of magnitude itself—with what is measurable according to an arbitrary rule. There is even a philosophy that rejects autonomous acts of meaning which are conjoined with words and which are fulfillable in the sensible and non-sensible contents of intuition, including the most simple theoretical statements. This philosophy identifies meaning—taken objectively—with a *rule for applying* an identical word-symbol to sensibly given facts. It is maintained that in a simple judgment like "This is red," and not only in a judgment like "This is beautiful," the word *red* has no relation to a specific act of a meaning that finds its fulfillment in viewing or representing this color; and that, at first, only this sensible red itself and the respective pronounced acoustic complexes are given. Such complexes are originally devoid of meaning; but because these acoustic complexes are bound firmly with the sensible content and always recur on the occasion of the sensible content, they are said to acquire the function that we call the meaning of the word *red*.

Let us disregard the reasons with which the nominalistic theory tries to support these and other theses and turn to the question of the extent to which ethical nominalism can make its case from the nature of the facts of this area *without the presupposition* of the nominalistic doctrine as a whole.

First, we can find a clear and sharp difference between emotional and volitional expressions and the respective statements and value-statements. There is a *difference in essence* rather than a difference in degree or in mere qualities of an expressed feeling between, on the one hand, an emotional expression—e.g., "Ah," when we suddenly come across a painting or when a landscape opens up before us during a walk, in which cases admiration, surprise, and the like find expression—and, on the other hand, statements like "This painting is beautiful," "This landscape is lovely." This *ah* neither *means* nor *signifies* anything; it merely expresses a feeling-state. The statements, however, both mean and signify something, namely, something lying *in* the painting and the landscape. When I make such a statement, I am not directed toward my feeling-state; nor do I live in one. For I am directed toward those contents, and I live in those objects. No matter how many feeling-states may enter into the comprehension of the "beautiful" and the "lovely" *in* those objects, and no matter in how many ways they may be expressed, they are nevertheless in *no* way *meant* in the sense that the beautiful and the lovely in the things are meant. The same is true for the statement "This is red." If, on seeing a thing, I make this statement, I do not *mean* that certain muscular sensations occur in my eyes while seeing the red thing. Likewise, the expression of enthusiasm over a noble moral deed or the expression of indignation over a base deed, as contained in "Phooey," is different in *essence* not only from the judgment "This is noble" or "That deed is base," but from the *prelogical comprehension* of these qualities that lie in the facts themselves. This enthusiasm and this indignation may or may not be justified, but they always have their foundation in the comprehension of the *value-contents* lying in the objects. For I admire not the landscape but its *beauty*, which flashes out clearly or vaguely. Even a simple observation in one single case in point will show this. He who finds this unsatisfactory may see this fact even more clearly in the *independence* of value-comprehensions from such feelings, which somehow express themselves, and in the independence of their mutual alterations. The feeling-state of the ego that is connected with value-experience and the expression of the state may diminish to a zone of indifference *without* any diminution of this *value* or of the degree of the comprehension of this value or our beginning to dwell in it. Thus we can coolly confirm the value of an ability, even a moral value of an enemy, without enthusiasm and expression of it. Yet such value is *fully* given. The *value* can also remain constant before our eyes while our feeling-state and its expressions undergo manifold changes. A thousand different feeling-states—joy, anger, ire, pride, or feelings of being offended—may fleet by us while facing a person whom we value and hold in high esteem, but without the involvement of our value-consciousness —let alone the value itself. Such states are tied not to certain values but to concrete situations, to which our *bodily* thereness always belongs, too. A value-statement does not express a conation. We can comprehend values that are in no way realizable by any possible conation, e.g., the sublimity of the nocturnal sky and stars, the morally valuable personality of a human being; similarly, there are values that are known upon comprehension not to lie at all in the direction of the conation present to us, values that we at the same time know ourselves in fact to resist.[4]

There is also an essential difference between the *enunciation* of a wish or desire with the intention of directing the will of another and the *communication* of a value-judgment or even the mere *allusion* to (and "indication" of) a present value, no matter how much this difference lies hidden behind the double meaning of "you ought to." Indeed, we comprehend many moral traits of men by means of communication in historical studies or in art without having any *conation* or disposition toward them! And how poor our world of values would be if values were only *X*'s of factual and possible conation! For the plain fact is that we act vis-à-vis values just as we do vis-à-vis colors and sounds. In these cases we intend a common and therefore an objective world, and we distinguish it from the subjectively different abilities of comprehension, as well as from the degrees of interest with which we turn to its parts. Just as we hear the same sound and see the same color and make judgments about them, so also do we intend to feel the same values and to make judgments about things according to them. This is the case when we speak about the goodness and ability of a man or the inviting character of a deed. We are not bothered by any metaphysics which holds that the above is nothing but an "illusion"—e.g., a mechanistic metaphysics which denies, in addition, the identity of colors and sounds in perception and remembrance—for we adhere to the groundwork which must precede all such metaphysics. A value-statement is therefore not a hidden solicitation or an order to will and to act in a determinate way. Every value-statement is directed toward a content that is capable and needy of adequate intuitional cognition. There are propositions which *mean* or signify something *objectlike,* as in statements like "This man is good," but which are not expressions or enunciations of wishes and conations.

It would be difficult to understand how nominalism could ever arrive at its theory that values are only signs pointing to areas of axiologically indifferent facts were it not the case that there are facts which nominalism believes it can best clarify in terms of its own theory. We are concerned here with every kind of *deception in moral cognition* that in fact rests on differences in *interest.*

4. See my elaborations on true and untrue asceticism in "Über Ressentiment und moralisches Werturteil" (Bibliog. no. 5). [See *ibid.,* sec. 3.—*Ed.*]

Every observer of life knows that the *same* properties of men, the same deeds and kinds of comportment, give rise—not infrequently to an extreme degree—to expressive forms of both *approval and disapproval.* We do not mean a difference in *judgment* that can be explained in terms of different *states of affairs* which A and B find with regard to the same person or deed, nor do we mean different "sides of the state of affairs," with each fixing his attention on a different side. We mean those differences that concern identical "sides," identical *states of affairs.* And we do not mean the differences in judgment concerning complicated concrete facts where this or that *component part* more strongly influences a final judgment. We mean those evaluations which concern diverse (abstract) *kinds* of comportment that are detached from their concrete relations with other deeds and properties in which they appear. This is the case, for instance, when someone calls a certain kind of deed "frivolous" and someone else calls it "bold," or when one calls a certain kind of deed "humble" and "meek" and another calls it "cowardly" and "servile," or when one calls a personality trait "proud" and another calls it "haughty" or "conceited." One can ask if "bold," "frivolous," "humble," "meek," "proud," "servile," "cowardly," and "haughty" designate specific independent *facts*, or if they are applied to the same matters only in terms of their *praising and disapproving functions.* It appears that the decisive factors in the application of an expression of praise or disapproval are in such cases the various attitudes of *interest* with which those who judge face these matters. One can see this very well in judgments made about the same people or events by different political, economical, ecclesiastical, and social "parties." [5] And here one can indeed ask whether there is any objective difference between modesty and humility and cowardice and servility *on the basis* of which some properties *deserve* praise and others disapproval, or whether it is not the case that the sole *difference* among such expressions consists in a *praising and disapproving function—* ultimately in an *invitation* to praise or disapprove (as is easily implied in such a function), as well as in a *defense* against other deeds. If this were the case, moral value-statements would only symbolically depict a play of *interests* that exists concerning deeds, men, and even kinds of deeds and traits of character. Moral value-statements would only be a kind of *language of signs* for them, and to imply that such signs mean anything more

5. For this reason the above theory has been held for the most part by politicians.

than stimulations of interest as a whole would be to devise a kind of mythology. However, when we have the *same* value-statement with regard to a state of affairs, the reason would not be one and the same *value-object* as detached from all conation and interest and comprehended by all in the same manner, but only an existing *uniformity* among interests themselves.

This area of facts most clearly shows the errors of ethical nominalism. For not only can these facts be understood in terms of an *objective theory of values;* they in fact *require* it. It is necessary to ask why men mummify their interests and desires in value-judgments instead of giving expression to them. Why do they disguise their interest in a certain kind of deed in propositions saying that to act in this way is "good" or "bad," praise*worthy* or blame*worthy*? Nominalism cannot explain this; it can only say that such behavior is a sheer miracle! Why, for example, is a group that is bound together in a trade-union which is on strike inclined to regard those workers who do not strike as morally bad rather than as men with different interests, or why do the members of a trust that determines prices also regard an entrepreneur in this way when he remains an outsider and continues to sell under trust prices? We do come to an understanding of this if we assume that there are independent and qualitatively differentiated moral value-facts. Since it is of the *essence* of *moral values* as autonomous objects that are independent of the processes of their real comprehension to demand recognition from all, it is very *advantageous* and extremely *"useful"* to attach expressions of *moral* praise to persons and deeds that conform to the interests of those who judge and expressions of *moral* disapproval to persons and deeds that do not; but it is not useful simply to say that one shares the same interests with them. It is very beneficial to one's own interest to tell someone serving this interest that he is a *"morally good"* man, and it is very detrimental to one's interest to tell him that he is serving such an interest. For in doing this we make *use* of the demand for universal recognition that belongs essentially to all moral values, but we do so on behalf of our *private interest;* and we silently solicit *all* others to serve this interest with the same comportment in order to be morally praised by us. No matter how deep-seated in our "nature" this *pharisaism* may be which calls only what serves its own subjects or party good (and its opposite evil), it is *possible* only because there *are* autonomous moral values, and because these are somehow comprehended in a concrete case. In such cases, however, they are *not perceived* or "given" in the object itself, but are merely *"represented"* and "judged" and thus fancied to be in the matter concerned; and we still comprehend them as autonomous facts—but *where they do not exist.* It is precisely in the fact that the illusion of the good can be so useful, the fact, as they say, that "even hypocrisy pays homage to virtue," that the *independence* of value and virtue from interest appears *most clearly.*

Because the presence of moral values demands both *praise and disapproval* from all, not because moral values are mere symbols for relations and conflicts of interest, it is useful and even of the highest *interest* to apply words designating values to cases of greater contrasts in interest. *Interest* therefore does not "account for" the pure feeling of moral values, their pure objective intuition; on the contrary, it *deceives* it. Interest does not explain moral experience, only moral *deception.* Here and elsewhere it is methodologically wrong to explain the normal case by analogy to the illusory.[6] For a long time this has been a common practice in modern philosophy, e.g., the attempt to explain perception through the conditions used to explain hallucination, calling it *hallucination vraie,* or the attempt to reduce the phenomenon of volume to those elements that are also in a plane (those elements of a specific form and distribution of light and shade which suggest volume). The matters of fact of normal perception are no more made understandable by this than is the *phenomenon* of volume. For an *existence* that is different from the deceptive content is *presupposed* in both cases. If I take the painful effects and subsequent displeasure which result from excessive enjoyment to be "repentance," or if I take the weight of a past experience that I cannot "manage" to be "guilt," or if many people—as a modern poet puts it—use the expression "sin" only as a mythical term for their "wicked affairs," it is presupposed that the phenomena of repentance, guilt, and sin are therein given, even if they are merely illusions introduced into the components of experience by people who think that they "perceive" something which, in fact, they only *"represent."*

From the above we get a clearer view of the significance of *utilitarianism* in ethics, which is at first difficult to see. If one proceeds, not from moral phenomena, but from the acts of praising and fault-finding or approving and disapproving, and from their linguistic expressions and enunciations within a "society"

6. See "Über Selbsttäuschungen" (Bibliog. no. 4), p. 113. [See "Die Idole der Selbsterkenntnis" (Bibliog. no. 10), sec. 3.—*Ed.*]

(which we regard as something moved by mere "interests," as opposed to a "community"), the utilitarian principle will *always necessarily* be fulfilled in the contents of such praising and fault-finding judgments, i.e., in *what* is *praised* or *blamed*—that is, insofar as *no* moral positive value is praised and no negative value blamed whose possession or non-possession on the part of any bearer has a *positive* or *negative* significance for the sum of the interests of the society in question. It is clear that the collection of *rules* concerning such societal praising and disapproving, which we call the "socially acknowledged morality," can *never* contradict the utilitarian principle. It is equally clear that what is praised and blamed can never be *derived* from the utilitarian principle. It must also be all too obvious to the utilitarian that the proposition "The moral is the useful" cannot be converted into the proposition "The useful is the moral," as if all useful deeds were in fact praised as moral.[7] This peculiar fact becomes understandable with a strict separation of moral values from acts of approving and disapproving and from those of praising and fault-finding. It is far from being the case that the *unity* of moral *values themselves* depends, as the utilitarian believes, on the useful and its opposite (for if this were so, the above proposition would have to be convertible); even in a socially acknowledged morality, only the autonomous qualities of values are in fact *intentionized*. But the kinds of comportment which correspond to these qualities are socially praised or blamed only *insofar* as they are *at the same time* useful or harmful to the interests of the society. In other words, usefulness and harmfulness function here as the *threshold* of possible *social praise and disapproval,* but they do not function in the least as the *condition of their existence* or as the factor that determines the *unity* of the values in question as "moral" or "immoral."

It is therefore a grave mistake on the part of the opponents of utilitarianism to condemn the theory totally and absolutely without attempting to determine precisely *in which respects* it is wrong. In fact, the utilitarian theory is the only correct and true theory about those contents which existing moral values find— indeed, *can* find—*socially praiseworthy and blameworthy.* It is the *only correct* theory of the *social valuation of good and evil.* It is not because of some "nadir of socially acknowledged morality"

---

7. The idea of "limes-usefulness," recently presented by von Ehrenfels, does not change anything in this respect.

—in a certain historical period—that only those bearers of moral values and only those deeds that are "useful" or "harmful" to the society are praised or blamed. It belongs to the *essence of all socially acknowledged morality* to proceed in this way, and *only in this way*. This is no "historical imperfection" of a *certain* socially acknowledged morality, but an *everlasting essential limit* of this morality and of *exclusively social* praise and disapproval, one that keeps it within limits.

The "most ideal and perfect" morality could be such only insofar as its rules of praising and disapproving judgments pertain *factually* to what is morally valuable and valueless—where the present morally valuable lies within the *limits* set by the above "threshold" of *social* praise and disapproval. A socially acknowledged morality becomes "imperfect" only when its judgments of praise and disapproval and their rules fail to pertain to adequate moral values and disvalues, when the usefulness or harmfulness of a certain comportment becomes in itself *sufficient* for it to be designated good or bad, when the *merely* useful or harmful is expressly intentionized "as" good or bad. It is with *this* that genuine "pharisaism" begins. If, on the other hand, one wants to apply the name "pharisaism" to the fact of this "threshold" itself, then the ideally perfect socially acknowledged morality must be designated "pharisaical" in essence. Utilitarianism thinks it has given us a theory of good and evil *itself;* but in fact it has only gives us a (true) theory of the *social praise and disapproval* of good and bad, and therein lies its error.

If one disregards this error for a moment, utilitarianism appears to be the charming and beautiful *enfant terrible* of every possible socially acknowledged morality and to have the eminent significance of revealing the secret that such moralities so quickly seek to hide. The utilitarian's comportment *itself*, i.e., the comportment in which the utilitarian thesis is *established* and *represented*, is as such not merely "utilitarily" valuable, but *morally valuable* to the highest degree. For it is by no means "useful" to *pass off* "as" useful the kinds of comportment of men which are only useful (and not morally valuable) and to call them that. This practice is "harmful" to the highest degree; on the contrary, it is useful to the *highest degree* to represent such kinds of comportment as "good" or even as the very essence of the "good." The utilitarian is therefore very different from the pharisee who means "useful" when he says "good." However, the utilitarian *contradicts* himself here. By executing such a harmful deed—

which is, however, *at the same time* as morally *good* and *true* as one that passes off the useful and harmful, which constitute the limits of all social praise and disapproval, as *what they are* and not as the "good"—the utilitarian fails with respect to his own principle of the good and the bad and as a consequence should have to call his own comportment "bad." For nothing is more harmful than to be a utilitarian, and nothing more useful than to be a pharisee.

But the opposite also holds (above all, in the case of the mostly superficial and "ingenuous" critics of utilitarianism): He who accepts the utilitarian point of departure, arguing that the concept and essence of the good and the bad can be gained only through reflection on the *judgments of social praise or disapproval,* but who denies the utilitarian thesis, even with "emphasis and moral scorn," yet *with* them thinks that there is no good or bad *outside* the objects of these social judgments—that is, he who misunderstands the *threshold* and its law by (correctly) maintaining that moral value-facts are phenomena separate from the values of the useful while equating them with what "society" praises and blames—by doing so acts, as it were, *very usefully* and by no means as an *enfant terrible,* but at the same time highly *immorally* and *pharisaically.* For he is practically a utilitarian and theoretically an "idealist," whereas the utilitarians—as men like Bentham and the two Mills show—are practically idealists (and not only with respect to the point that we made) and only theoretically utilitarians.

Therefore the denial of a special moral experience and its reduction to homemade signs for processes that are in themselves value-free are *not possible*.

There is another opinion which, though different from nominalism, has in common with it the denial of autonomous ethical value-phenomena. According to this view, assessments concerning willing, deeds, etc., do not encounter values in willing, deeds, etc., *themselves* to which they must conform; on the contrary, a moral value is to be seen only *in* or *through* the *assessment,* if indeed it is not the assessment which *produces* the value. Just as "true" and "false" are concepts resulting from reflection on affirmative and negative judgments, so, it is claimed, "good" and "bad" are abstracted through reflection on acts of moral assessment. Such acts are supposedly not conditioned arbitrarily or through the mechanisms of conation, but are the result of an immanent and *original* lawfulness according to which a certain assessment (others say a certain "approval" or "disapproval," "loving" or "hating") is characterized as "correct" or "incorrect" (Herbart, Brentano). It is the task of *ethics*, therefore, to bring these *laws* and *types* of *assessments* to light, and to seek the "measures" and "ideas" *from which* an assessment ensues. This theory, first set forth by Herbart (who borrowed from Adam Smith) and then further developed by Franz Brentano and his school, is similar to nominalism on at least one point: it makes moral values the results of some sort of judgmental behavior.[8] One of the main points of this theory is, according to Herbart, that moral values are not *in psychic* processes, and that it is necessary to investigate them according to the *causal* laws of their genesis. But it is held that in *this* investigation no values can be found. Accordingly, a certain feeling becomes one of, say, guilt only when I consider myself guilty in an assessment; without such a judgment the feeling is an entirely value-free object.

According to this view, ethics no longer has to deal with the question of freedom. Willing and acting may be causally determined, and I may be able to make their occurrence completely comprehensible and plausible; but the *assessment* judges them no less clearly and distinctly.[9]

A closer look reveals that such attempts at solving the problem are as untenable as those of genuine nominalism. Even if there were a class of acts called assessments, which differed totally from judgments, it remains to be seen what such acts intend, at what they aim, and in what *state of affairs* their intendings find fulfillment. And if we concede that there is a class of laws of "assessments" which yield "correct" or "false" assessments, a class of laws different from logical laws, such "correctness" would be the *same* in all correct assessments, and hence we could not understand how *different* ethical value-qualities, e.g., "innocent," "benevolent," "noble," etc., could come about. "Feelings of evidence"—in which, according to some, this correctness is supposedly represented, if it does not consist in them —would have to be as qualitatively *diversified* as the values

8. According to Adam Smith, it is the praise and reproach of the "neutral onlooker" that can, by sympathetic participation in comportment, lead to self-criticism by a so-called conscience (but in fact through psychic contagion, as I showed). See *Zur Phänomenologie und Theorie der Sympathiegefühle*, pp. 2–3. [See *Wesen und Formen der Sympathie*, pt. A, chap. 1.—Ed.] Herbart misplaces this "neutral onlooker" in the inner spheres of the person, and his "ideas" are therefore at the same time original forms of self-assessment.

9. See Windelband's lectures, *Über die Willensfreiheit* (Tübingen: Mohr, 1914), and "Normen und Naturgesetze," *Präludien* (Tübingen: Mohr, 1911).

given in them. Or it would be necessary to attribute the same diversity to the "being-required" of deeds which are characterized "as" valuable in such feelings. But this would only move things from light into darkness, and the unity of the laws concerned would be lost. Furthermore, it is difficult to see how the reference to an *act of assessment* could ever yield the concepts *"good"* and *"evil"* instead of the concepts *"correct"* and *"incorrect."* It is not this *act* which is intended as "good" or "evil"; it is, rather, the *willing* or the *deed* or the *person* at which this act is directed. Deception is undoubtedly possible here: a moralistic judge can find himself and his sentence "morally good" and praiseworthy when he "judges" us rigorously and severely; he *speaks judgingly about* good and evil and believes himself to be "good" and even takes his judgment to be a "good deed." [10] But this is in fact pharisaic. The *assessment* of something moral is by no means a *moral* act. It is a judgmental act with a non-formal value-predicate. This theory is often connected with the demand that one should so live, act, and be that he can "pass" judgment on himself, "esteem himself." If one takes these propositions strictly according to their meaning, he finds the basic error that we discussed earlier. True moral willing and being are replaced by willing designed to enable us "to pass a favorable *judgment* on ourselves," i.e., so that our intellectual *picture* of ourselves comes out well. Herbart expressly says that it is not *willing* itself but the mere *picture* of "such willing" that is assessed by "conscience." But this viewing of a mere "picture" is a basic trait of a mode of pharisaism, namely, *"self-righteousness."* We are not concerned here with a common pharisaism in which the "picture" is formed by someone else, e.g., the "picture" that "society" or "public opinion" could have of me or, in the case of a religious pharisee, the "picture" that "God" could have of me; we are, rather, concerned with the "picture" that "I must have of myself." In contrast to a self-righteous person, a person of true *humility* feels *uneasy* about his "picture" of himself as a "good"

---

10. Someone may believe that he can diminish his felt guilt by blaming himself rather harshly and by gazing (vainly) at the *goodness* of his act of blaming. If a judge sentences "justly," he does not for this reason act "justly" in the sense of a *moral* value-predicate. He only judges according to what *is just* by law. And this judgment can, in turn, be "correct" or not. But one cannot speak here of a *volitional act,* which alone can be "just" or "unjust," for example, an act in which someone returns a good of his own accord because he considers his possession of it "unjust" to the other.

person and *is* "good" in his uneasiness.[11] A moral act of willing is *not* good or evil because a correct or incorrect assessment is or "can be" made of it. In its execution there is a *value-quality* in which every possible assessment must find its fulfillment. If good and evil belonged only to the sphere of judgment, there would be no *independent facts* of the moral life, and the construction of a pleasant picture would not be possible in factual lives of *any* kind. In his willing, the moral man tries to *be* good; but he does *not* try to be good in order to "judge" that "I am good." "Act so that you can have esteem for yourself" can make good sense, namely, when this "esteeming" functions as a basis for the cognition of one's possible moral *being,* but not when the ability to judge that "I am good" or the ability to esteem becomes the end of willing. Besides, a moral act can be executed *without* judgment on this act. A judgment neither "makes" nor "structures" anything. Indeed, the best are those who do not *know that* they are best, those who, with Paul, "do not dare to judge themselves."[12]

Nor is it plausible to assume that there are special acts of assessment which differ from acts of judgment. Yet that must be the case if the expressions "good" and "evil" are fulfilled by referring to those acts and their correct or incorrect execution, or, as it is said, if they are abstracted from such execution. In judgments like "*A* is good" or "*A* is pretty," the conjunctive unity of subject and predicate and what is posited in the complete judgment—as well as the inseparable belief, or the absence of a belief, in what has been posited—possess the same elements as judgments like "*A* is green" or "*A* is hard." The sole difference here consists in the *contents* of the predicates.

Moreover, it *cannot* be said that so-called value-judgments express an "*ought*-connection," a should-be, instead of an ontological connection, or that "good" and "evil" represent only different kinds of this "*ought*." Nor can it be held that some experienced "ought" functions as a necessary foundation for a value-judgment. The meaning of propositions like "This picture is beautiful" or "This man is good" does not imply that this picture or this man "ought" to be something. It is beautiful; he is

---

11. [See the analysis of humility in "Zur Rehabilitierung der Tugend" (Bibliog. no. 10).—*Ed.*]

12. I Cor. 4 : 4. See also "Über Ressentiment und moralisches Werturteil," p. 305. [See "Das Ressentiment im Aufbau der Moralen" (Bibliog. no. 10), sec. 3.—*Ed.*]

good. They "ought" not to be this (or anything else). Such judgments give simply a *factual state of affairs,* and under certain circumstances also *one of the ought,* as in the judgment "He ought to be good." This "ought" only signifies that the subject is not the factual, empirical man, but the man in his "ideal." Prior to this particular judgment, an *"idealization"* that follows the lines of this man's nature takes place, and to *be* good is in this case valid for the *ideal.* Or, better, this man is one who ought-to-be-good. Such idealization, however, is not an outcome of a judgment. It must have taken place prior to the judgment. The fact that value-judgments cannot be reduced to judgments expressing an ought reveals the plain fact that the field of value-judgments is much wider than that of the ought. We can make value-statements in cases where it would make no *sense* to say that the bearers "ought" to be this or that. This is the case with all aesthetic predicates of objects of nature. Even in the moral sphere the ought is restricted to single acts of *doing* a deed. As Schopenhauer has observed, an "ought-to-will" is nonsense. In the case of deeds one can of course ask whether a proposition like "This deed is good" simply means that "this deed ought to be done," or that "there is a demand that it be done." This, however, is not the case when "good" is attributed to a man, i.e., a *person* in his *being.* Any ethics based on an "ought" must, as an ethics of the ought, err with respect to the true *value of the person* and indeed must *exclude* it; such an ethics can validly retain the person only as an X of possible *doings* that ought to be done.[13]

The truth of the matter lies in the opposite direction. Whenever we speak of an ought, the comprehension of a *value* must have occurred. Whenever we say that something ought to happen or ought to be, a *relation* between a positive value and a possible real bearer of this value, such as a thing, an event, etc., is cointuited. That a deed *"ought"* to be presupposes that the "ought" is grasped in the intention of the value of the deed. What we are saying is that this ought is based essentially on a relation between value and reality, not that the ought "consists" in this relation.

With regard to the principle that *every ought has its foundation in a value* (and not vice versa), it can be objected that there is an ought or ought-to-be of contents which do not *exist* (or do not "yet" exist), and that such an ought therefore cannot have a

13. See chap. 6.

value. Value-statements are, according to this objection, restricted to something existing, whereas ought-statements are not. But this apparent objection is groundless. For it is not true that value-statements pertain only to existing objects, though they can pertain *also* to them. As was seen in the first chapter, values are not concepts abstracted from empirical, concrete things, men, or deeds; nor are they abstract, "dependent" moments of such things. They are *independent phenomena* that are comprehended independent of the peculiarity of contents, as well as of the being-real or the being-ideal and the non-being (in this twofold sense) of their bearers. Hence one can attribute a factual value to non-factual contents. For example, that a competent rather than an incompetent man should be the minister has, as a state of affairs, a value, even if the competent man is in fact not the minister. And it is only because this has value that it "ought" to be so. The ought always has its foundation in a value that is viewed in terms of its *possible* being-real, i.e., in a value that is considered in light of this relation. Insofar as this and only this is the case, we shall speak of an "ideal ought." In contrast to this ought, there is an "ought" that also possesses a relation to a possible *willing whose content is to be realized* (the "ought of duty").[14] The first kind of ought is contained in the proposition "Injustice ought not to be"; the second, in "Thou shalt not do injustice." Thus a value does not *consist* at all in the ought-to-be of something. For if this were so, there would have to be an infinity of different modes and kinds of ought, namely, as many as the different contents of values. Because values not only span existing and non-existing things but also concern the *transition* from non-existence (of a value) to (its) existence (the value of the "ought" itself), the ideal ought is restricted to existing and non-existing contents and is founded in such a "transition." In contrast, the "ought of duty" is founded *exclusively* in non-existing values. It is here that the ought reveals its derived and restricted nature. Hegel correctly states that an ethics which has its *foundation* in the concept of the ought (e.g., Kant's ethics), even in the concept of the "ought of duty," and which regards the ought as the primordial ethical phenomenon, cannot do justice to the *factual* world of moral values. He also correctly observes that as soon as the mere content of the ought of duty is realized, i.e., as

14. [These remarks obtain for every normative ("real") ought. See chap. 4, sec. 2.—*Ed.*]

soon as an imperative, a commandment, or a norm is fulfilled in deeds, this very content ceases to be a "moral" fact.[15] However, we must be careful not to conclude from the frequent application of the expression "ought" to some non-existing future event, being, or acting that the relation to the future, as we find it in "tasks," belongs to the essence of the "ought." The ought does not (necessarily) concern our striving toward the future. One can also speak meaningfully of an "ought-to-be" with regard to the present and the past. Kant also uses the term in this sense when he says that the categorical imperative commands what ought to be, "even if this has not happened, even if it never will happen." In fact, the ought is not abstracted from a factual being or happening, say, from a feeling in inner perception or a consciousness of "necessity"; it is an autonomous mode of the *givenness* of *contents* that do *not* have to be comprehended first in the modes of the givenness of *extant* being in order to be comprehended as something that ought to be or ought to be done. Contents of the ought-to-be need not be contained in the area of extant being, no matter to what extent the contents of these two realms "coincide." *Nevertheless,* the ideal "ought" essentially retains its foundation in the relation between value and reality, whereas the ought of duty retains a *direction* toward the realization of a non-real value. Hence it is nonsense to say that a realized value "ought" to be according to duty.[16] The ought of duty is therefore something that is added to a certain realm of values insofar as they are considered as lying in the direction toward their realization by way of a possible *conation.* But values do not *consist* in an ought-to-be [Gesolltsein], as a kind of false subjectivism maintains.[17] Values are not "necessitations" exercised by a so-called transcendental ego or subject on an empirical ego; neither are they "voices," "calls," or "demands" which are addressed to "empirical man" from outside. Such hypotheses are constructed interpretations of simple matters of fact which favor a questionable subjective metaphysics. Rather, all norms, imperatives, demands, etc.—if they are not to be understood as

15. See Hegel, *Die Phänomenologie des Geistes.*
16. This is the very sense of Kant's rejection of eudaemonism. He states that since men do strive for happiness, it makes no "sense" to say that they ought to. It is only in the sense of the *ideal* ought that one can say, "So it is, and so it ought to be."
17. One should similarly repudiate the attempt to reduce the concept of existence to an ought or a being-required, etc. (an attempt to be found in the thought of Fichte), as if the existence of something meant that it ought to be recognized, believed in, etc.

arbitrary orders—have their foundation in an autonomous *being*, the *being of values*.

It is also necessary to reject the assertion that values "are" not, that they only *"obtain"* [gälten]. Propositions "obtain" only when they are in themselves *true*, insofar as the propositions and meaning-contents are related to possible assertions.[18] This, of course, also holds true for propositions that attribute a value to something [*Sache*]. But values therefore cannot be regarded merely as "obtaining," as if they sprang out of this "obtain." Values are facts that belong to a specific mode of experience, and therefore, according to the essence of the truth of such valid propositions, they must agree with such *facts*.

It is even less tenable to hold that aesthetic, ethical, and theoretical statements are three coordinated kinds of "assessing" acts that attribute to certain isolated contents or relations of contents the values "good," "beautiful," "true." [19] For here a plain, theoretical, factual judgment becomes subjected to the viewpoint of a "critical" assessment so that the complete expression of some theoretical judgment "*A* is *B*" would be, "The conjunction *A-B* is true." And forms like "*A* is good" and "*A* is beautiful" would then be equal and coordinated to this form. But there are two considerations worthy of note in this regard: (1) Is it not a bit strange that a theoretical judgment does not contain the predicate "true," and that this predicate appears only and exclusively after a preceding doubt or conflict; and is it not strange that it then does not pertain to the same state of affairs, but to a state of affairs insofar as it has been judged in another judgment? Is it not strange that on the other hand both aesthetic and ethical assessments *must* of necessity contain such a value-predicate? In a theoretical judgment the asserting function of the copula, or the function of what it linguistically represents (verbal endings, etc.), suffices to coexpress the claim to the foundation of a state of affairs [*Sachgegründetheit*] and, in this sense, "truth." Insofar as the above three coordinated modes of assessing are concerned, is it not to be expected that the theoretical judgment contains of necessity the element "true," or, if this is not the case, that aesthetic and ethical statements are of neces-

---

18. The truth of propositions does not consist in their "obtaining," whether this "obtaining" refers to the subjects or to the objects which such propositions mean and in which they are fulfilled. These relations of "true propositions" are the foundation of truth, but they do *not* constitute truth itself.

19. [See the critique of Windelband's theory of assessment in "Ethik" (Bibliog. no. 8), sec. 3.—*Ed.*]

sity characterized by a special *sign of conjunction* and so require no special value-predicate? But neither is the case. Can one charge language with such an inadequacy to thought? I do *not* believe so.[20] (2) In this case the "proper" predicate would always be "true," and the "subject" would always be the *connection of an A with a B*, whereas in value-statements an object *A* would simply be called good, beautiful, etc. A theory which, by making use of impersonal and existential propositions, seeks to free a most elementary form of a judgment from its obligation to imply some kind of *relationship* between terms, and which regards a two-termed judgment, "attributing" a *B* to an *A*, as a mere continuation of a one-termed judgment in which one term is "recognized"—that is, an *A* is simply "recognized" or "posited"—cannot find any great fault in what we have said.

In reality, apart from the question of the truth of this opinion, which I hold to be completely indefensible, there is clearly a difference here; for good and beautiful always signify characteristics of an object in a judgment, whereas it simply does not make sense to say of a tree or a man that it is "true" in the same way that we say it is "beautiful" or "good." On the other hand, it appears quite clear to me that a claim to truth, which is implicit in the mere assertion of any theoretical judgment, and not solely because of a possible assessment of this assertion, is *not* missing in propositions like "*A* is good" or "*A* is beautiful." This is sometimes accentuated in certain propositions, e.g., "It is true that *A* is beautiful or good." But they have this element only insofar as this "It is true that . . ." contains this *simple* claim to truth. Otherwise we would be concerned with an infinite number of "critical" assessments. Therefore the demand of *truth also* pertains to and exists for value-statements. Value-statements must, like any judgment, be logically "correct"; i.e., they must correspond to the formal rules of the formation of judgments and must, in addition, show some agreement with some kind of "facts" in order to be true.

There are no special rules of aesthetic and ethical "assessments" or aesthetic and ethical inferences which differ from rules of logic. At least no such rules are known to me. But there are laws of aesthetic and ethical *valuations* of value-complexes.

---

20. In phrases like "true advice of a friend," "true friend," and "true God," the term *true* stands for "genuine" in contrast to "not genuine," a concept that presupposes value-essences. "*Genuineness*" is the self-givenness of the value, in contrast to value-deception. True value-judgments are founded in the feeling of genuine values.

And such laws are not forms of judgment and inference, but laws of experiencing specific *facts and contents* that give unity to ethics and aesthetics and the conviction of this experience.[21] On the other hand, one cannot put logic on a level with a value-science of ethics and aesthetics simply because it, too, is concerned with the value of "truth." For truth is *not* a "value." Of course it makes good sense to attribute a value to acts of *searching*, the investigations into truth.[22] One can also attribute a value to the *certainty* of the truth of a proposition, just as one can speak of the values of probabilities. The *knowledge* of truth, too, is a value; but truth as such is *not* a value. It is, rather, an idea, distinct from all values, which is fulfilled when the meaning-content of a judgment (formulated in a proposition) coincides with the facts of a state of affairs and when this coincidence is itself given in evidence. In this sense a value-statement must also be "true," but it can also be "false." However, it makes no sense to demand that a theoretical judgment be "good" or "beautiful," or to attribute such predicates to it.

One question remains unanswered here: What is the relation between a state of affairs that fulfills a value-judgment and a state of affairs that fulfills a theoretical statement with respect to one and the same object? In other words, what is the relation beween a *value-complex* [Wertverhalt] and a *state of affairs* [Sachverhalt]? It is necessary to ask whether the former is necessarily founded in the latter, or if the former can be given as an

---

21. There are laws of *approving* and *disapproving* (of value-complexes) which on the one hand presuppose the experience and its own laws of values themselves and on the other hand represent contents and facts for the sphere of judgment, but which are completely independent of the laws of judgments.

22. *Truth* is by no means only the "ideal" of this seeking and research, nor even an ideal that we "posit for our will" (as Sigwart says in his *Logik* [Tübingen: Mohr, 1911], Vol. II). There are also truths which are not "ideal." There can be a "search for truth" only to the extent that we have brought the *being*-true of a proposition to fulfillment in an *evidential* manner. After this, we can "search for" this moment, which was seen in a meaning-complex, in the area of other facts, questions, and propositions. Ever so many "activities" of the mind must precede this so that we can find something true (also volitional activities); but the *insight* into the truth is always a sudden flashing out, bare of degrees, and it always has the character of *receiving*, not of accomplishing, making, building up, etc. After the printing of this text, I discovered that Emil Lask's views on these problems are similar in many ways to my own. See Lask, *Die Logik der Philosophie und die Kategorienlehre* (Tübingen, 1911), esp. the excellent chap. 3, sec. 2. But I do *not* share Lask's opinions on "Kant's Copernican turn" and the meaning of the existence of the object as object.

independent fact, or if, conversely, a state of affairs must be founded in a value-complex in order to be given. This question can be resolved only after we have carried value theory a good deal further than we have at this point in our discussion.

As I mentioned before, the assessment theory of moral values cites as one of its justifications the claim that there *are no* moral values to be found in the real *psychic processes* which are represented in inner perception and in thinking interpretations and supplements of the perceived, and that it is a *measure,* a *norm,* or an *ideal,* introduced from *without,* that makes the distinction between good and bad possible. Psychic facts of willing and behaving are said to be completely *"value-free"* objects; neither a description of them nor an investigation into their causal genesis can yield anything concerning their value. Only a norm can do this. On the other hand, the clearest insight into the causal determination of volitional acts cannot eliminate the assessment or the legitimacy of the assessment of psychic facts. Even the most precise understanding of a bad deed in terms of individual, social, psychic, and physiological causes does not make it any better.

This opinion mixes truth and falsehood in a curious fashion.

Let us assume for a moment that this theory is correct. It is necessary then to ask *where* in all the world we can find the *"measure"* or *"norm"* that is to be introduced into psychic processes in order to make our moral distinctions possible. I can see only two possibilities. Do measures and norms lead us back to such psychic processes, e.g., to special facts of the ought, a feeling of obligation, or a command experienced in one's inner being? Is such a fact less "value-free" than the other facts, and is it not, like other facts, a *necessary* result of psychic development, of which the structure and orientation vary according to the causal conditions of its occurrence? With what right, and on the basis of what *new* "measures," are *these* facts chosen from the totality of psychic diversity as the measure of other facts? If it is claimed that this new measure has its own *independent* province, where does it come from? What can it be but an arbitrary order? So we return to an experienced ought or an experienced duty! Why *must* (in the ideal sense of ought) this experience be one that ought to be? Why "ought" we to obey this consciousness of duty? Why should causal understandings come to a stop at *this* point? And why cannot this consciousness of duty be reduced, e.g., to a coercive inclination, based on hereditary factors or social suggestion, which is independent of or even opposed to the direction

of our individual conations, and which has a certain purposefulness in terms of the preservation of a form of community? Why
does one call a halt to causal understandings at this point? It
can only be done arbitrarily! The proposition "It ought to be so!"
can only be drawn arbitrarily from some kind of *factual* experience of oughtness. From birth, everyone finds himself surrounded
by factual forces that impose norms. Which norm is he to
recognize? There would be no difficulties if he were to say that
he recognizes that norm which, according to his insight, is the
one that, when followed, realizes the values that are, according
to his insight, the highest possible. Yet it is supposed to be the
norm that determines a value! Furthermore, if one accepts or
rejects orders and norms coming from without according to the
measure of an "inner necessitation," is such necessitation less
"blind" because it happens to be an "inner" one? Should one not
be allowed to ask how it has come about within him, just as one
can inquire to his advantage about a compulsive neurosis whose
origins remain hidden in memory, or about an inherited drive
that one experiences as an outside power opposed to his individual ego and its interconnections of inclinations and willings?

Here it does not matter at all if an experienced necessitation
or order pertains to only *one* concrete deed or if it pertains to
comportment for which conditions have been coposited in some
degree of *universality*. Neither the nature of an order nor the
nature of blind necessitation is spirited away by the universality
of what ought to be done. *"Duty"* is the name of an order experienced concretely in an inner fashion, not an order prescribed
by someone else; *"norm"* is the name of an inner necessitation
pertaining to the general character of comportment (so that
comportment is first understood in terms of a *concept*). But
neither the concept of "duty" *nor* that of "norm" can serve as a
point of departure for ethics. Nor can they function as a "measure" that would make the distinction between good and evil
possible.

Ethics *cannot* be regarded as having its foundation in the
idea of duty. This becomes clear when one dismisses the somewhat magical character which Kant confers upon this idea, and
refuses as well to adopt a pragmatistic standpoint concerning
what the *"ethos of duty"* has in effect brought about. There are
four points to the analysis. First, duty is a *"necessitation"* or a
"compulsion" in two directions. It is a necessitation or compulsion against *"inclination,"* i.e., against everything that "wells up
in me," everything that is not an experienced conation coming

from myself, such as hunger, thirst, spontaneous erotic inclination, etc. Duty is also a necessitation or a constraint with respect to individual *willing,* i.e., with respect to that conation which does *not* have the nature of inclination, but which comes from me and is experienced and executed by me as a "person." *Both* directions of necessitation belong to "duty," *not* merely the first, as the Kantians one-sidedly maintain. Thus it becomes clear that the content of a mere "ought" or the content of what is demanded in terms of value first becomes "duty" when it meets an opposing and rising inclination, and also when it is posited *against* or at least *independent of* an individual's will. Whenever we have the evidential *insight* that a deed or a will is *good,* we do *not* talk about "duty." Indeed, whenever this insight is totally adequate and ideally perfect, it determines willing *unequivocally,* without any factor of compulsion or necessitation that might come between insight and willing.[23]

This suggests a second characteristic of the idea of duty. By virtue of its essence, willing according to duty prunes, as it were, moral considerations based on such an *insight,* or at least it develops *independent* of insight. The ought contained in the idea of duty is not based on a clear and evident feeling of the value of willing or the value of a deed, and its "necessity" is the experience of a blind inner commandment—whether or not what is commanded in this "duty" coincides with a factual and *evidentially* preferred value. Our life-experiences reveal again and again that the representation of "duty" comes into play *precisely* when our moral considerations based on insight begin to *weaken,* or when our moral considerations *fall short of* resolving a situation that is too complicated, or when they do not suffice to avoid an important responsibility with strong moral consequences. By saying, "This is my duty," or, "This is simply my duty," one goes further toward cutting off the spiritual endeavor for *insight* than toward giving the insight gained an expression. General von York, for instance, did not do "his duty" at Tauroggen, for he did much more than what his military consciousness of duty dictated. He followed a higher moral insight. There is an element of *blindness* in the necessitation of duty which belongs to it essentially. If the meaning of duty is not *arbitrarily* redefined, and if the significance of the word itself is analyzed, it becomes clear that a kind of commanding voice appears in "duty" which, like

23. With regard to the restitution of Socrates' principle, see above, p. 69. Here also "necessity" reveals its negative nature. Acting from duty is always given as "not-being-able-to-act-differently."

the orders of an authority, *lacks* additional "grounds" and is *not* immediately evident. "Duty" is an authority from within. Its "necessitation" is subjectively conditioned. It is *not* founded objectively in the essential value of the *matter of fact* [Sache]. Its necessitation remains subjective, even *when* this compelling impulse is given as a "universally valid" one, as in cases where we know that everyone should act as we do. A universally valid inner impulse of compulsion, because it is given as "universally valid," is *not* an "objective" insight (in the genuine sense of the term *objective*). On the other hand, the consciousness that this or that deed or comportment is objectively "good" only for *me* and for no one else [24] does not imply that this comportment is not grounded in an *insight* into its objective value of preference.

Third, duty is a command that comes *from us* and resounds *in us*, in contrast to other kinds of orders coming "from outside." But, as we have said, this does not eliminate the "blindness" of the command. Obedience to an order of an outside authority *may* rest on *insight into the value of obedience* and the value of the authority which surpasses our own value, and in this case our willing and our acting are based on insight; conversely, obedience to an "inner" duty *may* be *blind* in the sense that we may simply follow this peculiar necessitation. The mere "from within" does not give the idea of duty any higher dignity. Even commands resounding in us by way of social suggestion, but without a consciousness of this suggestion, appear to come "from within" and frequently contradict "inclinations."

Fourth, duty possesses an essentially *negative* and *restrictive* nature. I am not referring simply to the common idea that a consciousness of duty *proscribes* more than it *prescribes*.[25] It appears to me that even when the content of duty is given to us in the sense of a "commandment," this content is also given as a content in relation to which other contents are "impossible." Our obligations follow first from a scrutiny of *what ought not to be* (in the sense of the ideal ought-not-to-be). Duty is *more* an invincible assertion in relation to manifold criticisms of our conations and impulses than something *intuited as positively good*. Duty shares this characteristic with "necessity," including *objectively* founded necessity, which has nothing to do with the mere feeling of compulsion or with causal necessity. In this case "necessity" is also that "whose opposite is impossible," or that

24. See chap. 6, B, sec. 2.
25. See Sigwart, *Logik*, II, 745, and also Paulsen's ethics.

which continues to assert itself in any attempt to think or will something different. But in both cases "necessity" is distinguished from a plain *insight into the being* (or the value) of a fact, a state of affairs, or a value-complex. Insight does *not* require the thought of even a possible opposite. Nor does moral insight require an attempted counterwilling against a willing whose value is in question.

Moral insight differs from mere *consciousness of duty* in all of these aspects. The content which imposes itself on us as a duty, which comes to us as a morally evidential and good content, and which is therefore a *true* and *genuine* duty, is also an object of moral insight, in contrast to a merely imagined duty. Thus an ethics of insight should not be, as it frequently is, confused with an ethics of duty. They are in opposition to each other.

But this is not to say that the "consciousness of duty" possesses no specific significance in terms of the *path* that leads to moral insight. But, as it will be shown, listening to the orders of an *authority* and attending to what *tradition* tells us are of no lesser significance. They all are irreplaceable means for economizing the moral insight that has been accomplished. But their possible worth in the ideal realization of moral insight must itself remain an *object* of moral insight.

What we have said about "duty" applies to the "*norm*" as well. The question of whether ethics has to look for norms or for natural laws, as it is often put, does not exhaust existing alternatives. But we will return to this point.

It is not simply that this theory [26] cannot respond to the question of where the "measure" that is to be applied to volitional processes is to be found; the facts do not exist in the way that the theory maintains.

It is asserted that nothing like a value is found in the objects themselves, e.g., in the processes of the will or in the entire range of kinds of comportment. These are supposedly *value-free* complexes of simple elements of psychic life, which are determined by psychology (according to their number and nature). Only *assessments* according to a norm or an ideal put (or can put) value on them. But if one disregards the presuppositions of genetic theories and examines the facts of the moral life, these assertions cannot hold. When we feel inclined to do a deed, we have a consciousness (we will not characterize it more precisely here) of the rightness or wrongness of the deed *apart* from any

26. [See above, p. 180.—*Ed.*]

assessment of it. It is not necessary that this deed be already performed, nor is it necessary that a will be present. It can, for example, be a matter of some content which belongs only to *wishing,* and which we only *represent* as willed or wished, e.g., when we read a drama. It can also be a matter of a deed that we never before have performed. In this refined way of hearing such facts of consciousness, in the ability to notice them and in the practice of listening, there is, first of all, what we call "conscience," which is *not* contained in acts of assessment. Here there is also a broad range of types of deceptions that have nothing to do with mere errors made in assessments of something, e.g., the false subsumption of a fact thus known under a concept. If, for example, I feel genuine repentance about something I did yesterday, or if I only feel its unfavorable effects with an accompanying displeasure, or if I only use my past deeds to indulge my penchant for self-torment, or if I wallow with secret delight in the sweetness of my sins, the differences are *not* differences in assessment, nor are they differences in *causal* interpretations of the same feeling-state. What we have here, beyond the sphere of judgment, are basically different *facts.* The nuances of values are *in* the experiences themselves. It is not possible to hold that these experiences are given first as "value-free" objects—even for a moment—to which one subsequently attributes a value through a new act, or to which one adds a value through a second experience.

This becomes even more apparent when the very *value* of a process is *clearly* and *distinctly* comprehended although the process *itself* is only unclearly and indistinctly present, or when the process is only present in a certain direction of consciousness in *"intending,"* or when it lies hidden, as in a capsule, while its value is spread out clearly and fully in emotive consciousness. But in any assessment the more or less *full* presence of the *process* bearing the value is necessary. If we can clearly comprehend values *without* the presence of a bearer, the consciousness of a value *cannot* have its foundation in an assessment. Thus a man may be given a task that promises the realization of a high value. He sees this value clearly and distinctly; it may strain and unleash his entire energy! He may elevate himself in terms of the value of his task! But the *pictorial* or *conceptual content* of his task may continue to vacillate while its *value* or the value to be actualized in this task does not! The idea of *what* he has to do may at times recede, but the value of what he has to do will continue to cast its light on him and may, so to speak, illuminate his present life. This value of his task is now of central significance to him; it disengages him from a multitude of insignificant attachments to mores, as well as from habits that formerly bound him, so that his *factual* present *life* is acted out in a different manner than it would have been had the feeling for this value *not* existed. Moreover, there is a striking phenomenon that is familiar to anyone who knows how to grasp moral stirrings at their origin: We may feel a "deep contentment" over the day's deeds without really knowing the particular deed or comportment toward which this contentment is directed; and we may feel the pressure of "guilt" with a direction toward "yesterday" or toward a certain human being without representing to ourselves what lies in this direction. The value of the deed is in such cases *very* clearly and distinctly present to us. But we merely *seek* the deed itself, perhaps locating it subsequently in this direction.

The claim that the pictorial content to which a value is attached must have been given once before and that it has only been forgotten is surely a *slanted* interpretation of this and similar phenomena. For here there is a law governing all act-qualities in which objectivities can become present in consciousness (including, for example, perceiving and expecting): namely, that we can possess with *full* evidence the values of the object *without* its being given to us with the same degree of evidence or with the same degree of fullness in its "meaning," and that we can do this independent of the sphere of remembering. We can, for example, possess with full evidence the beauty of a poem or a painting without being able to say to which *factors* this value is attached, e.g., color, design, composition, rhythm, musical characteristics, speech-values, picture-values, etc. The same holds for all "phenomena of fulfillment" that occur when we encounter in experience a thing which has the value that we were looking for. Such value-intentions vary independent of pictorial variations, but the former guide the latter. Indeed, there is a large group of values which dissolve increasingly the more we analyze their bearers. This is known to anyone who has for some period dealt scientifically with the world of sounds, and who listens to a composition with such an analytical attitude. This attitude and this analysis of a picture similarly disturb the comprehension of the respective art-value (not only in technical analysis but also in the analysis of the aesthetic object of the picture). But, on the other hand, when the appearance of a value seems to be attached more to a close analysis of the object, as with the sensuous pleasures (e.g., in the case of gourmets), it is not the analysis of the object concerned but this "seeking" for a more refined *value*-differentiation, e.g., of the bouquets of wines or the savory qualities of a dish, that leads *secondarily* to an analysis of the objects concerned and their sensory qualities.

What we have said reveals the erroneous presuppositions that lead to the positions of those scholars who would find the origin of ethical values in "assessment" and in a law of assessment according to certain "ideas" or "norms." In many cases the point of departure is the principle that *psychic processes themselves contain no values.* If a value is attributed to them (as in all moral judgments), it must—so these scholars hold—have been attributed from without or "assigned" to them, and this can be done only through an act of assessing on the basis of a "measure," an "idea," or a "purpose," none of which, however, can be extracted from psychic happenings. But there is an error in the presuppositions of these researchers because, as we stated before, they cannot tell us *where* in all the world such a "measure," "norm," or "purpose" comes from, or why it is not *arbitrary* (as in the case of physical measures) to choose any particular measure (e.g., a meter). As I see it, the error is this: these researchers never ask how one arrives at the *specifically psychological* assumption of *value-free psychic processes* (an analogous question is to be posed with respect to the values of outer objects). If one directs his attention to this, he soon finds that there is *no addition* of values to the value-indifferent given of the psychic (as content of inner intuition), but that there is, on the contrary, a more or less *artificial diminution* (not an addition, but a subtraction) of the originally given by virtue of the express *absence* of certain acts of feeling, loving, hating, willing, etc., which results in *value-free* objects. All *primordial* comportment toward the world—i.e., vis-à-vis not only the outer but *also* the inner world, vis-à-vis not only others but also our own ego—although not precisely a "representational" one of *perceiving* [Wahrnehmung], is nevertheless, even according to what we have thus far gathered, a *primordial emotional* comportment of *value-ception* [Wertnehmung]. And this does not imply, as these scholars believe, that we primarily "perceive" feelings, conations, etc. For this would again presuppose the very error that we are fighting and would also be the opposite of what is in fact correct. As every psychologist knows, and as the latest subtle analyses of "the noticing of feelings" have shown with respect to the precise levels of "noticing" that are possible,[27] the act-modifications of paying attention that are possible vis-à-vis feelings or other emotive happenings are *not the same* as those that are possible vis-à-vis pictorial contents. In other words, in the sphere of inner intuition, or, better, "intuitive inward directedness," our primordial attitude is neither exclusively nor primarily one of perceiving but one of *value*-ceiving and *value*-feeling as well. And we add, it is only because this is the case that we *can understand* why we are unable to "observe" a feeling as we can a picture in memory or imagination. What is primary in *experiencing* life [Er-*leben des Lebens*] must be secondary in *experienced* [gelebten] life (where "perception" belongs necessarily to comprehension), and it cannot be comprehended in the same act-modifications of attention.

That values are not somehow added is clearly shown by the fact that anyone who is not schooled in psychology—who has not yet *learned*, as a psychologist has, to perform perceptual acts of *experiencing* [Er-*lebensakte*] which have been *separated* from the concrete *totality* of act-performances and to *withhold* emotive acts of experiencing—finds it very *difficult* to observe without valuing and to think psychologically. Just as it is difficult for someone learning to draw to pay attention to visual objects and their perspectival foreshortening and shifting instead of the material thing as it is primarily given in the natural view of the world, so has it become difficult in the history of cognition, as in the case of any individual, to *disregard* the primary *cogiven* value-qualities of psychic experiences by suspending the *experiencing* acts of feeling which are necessarily bound up with such value-qualities.

It is precisely here that the necessity of a *simultaneous* phenomenological grounding of both psychology and ethics becomes most apparent. The above theories, which find it necessary to add a "measure" to the sphere of the psychic, stem from the *presupposition*, established *without* phenomenological investigation or foundation, of a (value-free) "psychic sphere." This presupposition leads them to ask how values can be attributed to the psychic. But value-phenomena are, in their essence as value-phenomena, thoroughly independent of the distinction between the psychic and the physical. And those values that lie

---

27. See Moritz Geiger, "Über das Beachten von Gefühlen," *Münchener Philosophische Abhandlungen* (1911), Festschrift für Theodor Lipps.

in psychic experiences are likewise independent of the factual complex *of* "psychic experience" presupposed by descriptive psychology, to say nothing of real and explanatory psychology. If the psychic is understood as everything that can be comprehended in the act-direction of inner intuition ("intuition" in the sense of all immediate kinds of givenness), it is necessary to say that the values of psychic experience are *given in them.* It is even necessary to say that these values are given *primordially* with respect to their other determinations. A disvalue is *immanent* to an impulse of revenge, for example, apart from any assessment of it. Thus a genuine experience of fellow-feeling has positive value. In this sense any experience has an immediate and intuitive nuance of value in "feeling," and it is not true that we are led to values by way of a definite "order" or by a lack of experiences that could balance another experience or obstruct its effects [28] or analogous relations. If we construe the "psychic" not as what is given generally in inner intuitive direction, or, as we prefer to say, the *full psychic life* (which is sharply distinguishable from the *acts* of *experiencing* this life), but as a *component* of this "full life," a component that remains "given" even when we expressly *suspend experiential* [er-*lebenden*] emotional acts, i.e., when we suspend emotive and practical attitudes concerning our ego (or alter egos), then of course *no* value is given in this "psychic." Only a "feeling" of some kind is given. Such feelings may be called "value-feelings" (e.g., "feelings of respect") only because *values themselves* were immediately given in the primary givenness of this "full life," values without which the feelings could not be called value-feelings. And it is this final "psychic," i.e., this "full psychic life," *minus the given values* that is the material from which psychological description and observation—and psychological knowledge in general—takes its point of *departure.* All causal psychology *presupposes* this observation and description, and must a fortiori disregard all possible values of psychic processes.

It was the long-standing misunderstanding of this rather complicated state of affairs that led to a search for "measures," "norms," and "laws of assessment" which were to be attributed to the value-indifferent sphere of the psychic, and which were to have given it a value. But no one could explain where in all the world such measures and norms were to be found. This

28. As Lipps holds in *Die ethischen Grundfragen* (Leipzig: Voss, 1912), p. 64.

search also occurred insofar as one tried to avoid *arbitrary* acts of commanding or theories like those of Nietzsche: values are "made" or "interpreted into" value-indifferent phenomena; there are no "moral phenomena," only "moral interpretations" of phenomena. It became necessary to pose the (*unsolvable*) problem of how the values of psychic experiences come about. First, acts of *experiencing* [Er-*lebens*] psychic life were confused with experienced psychic life (or only the difference between momentary actual life and its immediate continuation in immediate retentive memory was seen—a difference that has *nothing at all* to do with the above). Second, this "fully experienced life" in which values themselves are still given was confused with the remnant that remains, after an *express suspension* of emotional acts of *experiencing* [Er-*lebnisakte*], as an object of "inner perception" (or immediate memory). Instead of tracing values of experiences back to primordial facts of givenness that appear in value-*experiences* [*Wert*-er-*lebnissen*] (which is the *only* place of their appearance, and this by essential necessity), some tried to *reduce* such value-*experiences* to mere values of experience (value-*experiences*, by the way, relate also to the extrapsychic, e.g., the physical, with the same originality, and they can occur in both outer and inner intuition, in both the intuition of the other and that of oneself). Values of experience were then traced back to assessment according to the "measures" and "norms" of a more or less conventional morality, measures that are represented as "principles" from which this code of rules could be logically inferred. But such a reduction of an extant morality, or even of extant institutions of law and the science of them (see, for example, Hermann Cohen's ethics), to its "principles" can achieve no more for us in ethics than the question of how "mathematical natural science" is logically and objectively possible can achieve for us in epistemology.[29]

The theory of assessment, as it was first developed by Herbart, also remains unclear about how such assessments, which are performed according to his "ideas of pleasing volitional relations," can become even *possible* practical determining grounds for willing. For if all volitional processes are rigorously determined causally, and if, as is undoubtedly the case, it belongs to the *essence* of "assessment" to occur only *after* a given act of will ("after," not in the sense of temporal succession, but in the sense

29. See above, pp. 46 ff.

of the temporal *order* of the origination of acts), then it should be possible simply to *set aside* all assessing acts in which the psychic is said to gain its value and to do so without any change in the factual process of the volitional act. In this case a world *with* morals [*Sittlichkeit*] and one *without* them, apart from such accompanying acts of assessing and the laws that they follow, would be identical. Herbart's theory of assessments necessarily shares this most paradoxical consequence with any other theory of this type. (This consequence cannot be avoided when performed assessments enter into real psychic life and its causal process as real terms through reproduction and association, because assessments are *subsequent* to volitional acts by an *essential* and *original necessity,* and also because they can never play a *causal* role in acts of willing by their entering into this real causal process.) We escape such a consequence, which, no doubt, led Herbart to incorporate ethics into aesthetics, because we are attempting to found psychology and ethics *simultaneously* in a phenomenological fashion. If in this "full life" values and immediate phenomena of motivation of willing and conation are given in value-experiences *without* the addition of some possible assessment, then the remnant that is left as the "psychic" of psychology through a suspension of emotional acts of *experiencing* must *differ* in each case according to the kind and nature of the value-experiences. And, a fortiori, the *real* processes of *experience* (which are derived from psychic facts and are transcendent to immediate intuition) and their real causal connections must be *different* in each case. In practice this means that a man who feels values livingly and adequately, and for whom a certain value flashes out in its own rank in the act of preferring, will provide a psychologist or one searching for causal explanations (even himself, if he adopts the proper attitude) with *data* quite *different* from those provided by one who does *not* have this value given to him in this manner.

Value-ception, as we have tried to show, *precedes* all representational acts according to an essential law of origins. Its evidence is largely independent of the evidence of representations. Before a "psychic experience" even becomes percept*ible* (in the sense of psychological "perception," i.e., with suspension of emotional acts of *experiencing* and as value-indifferent being), before it becomes not only "perceptible" for an individual but "perceptible" in general according to the *essential laws* of the origins of acts, this full *experiencing* [Er-*leben*] (with its emotional acts) has already codetermined its being and non-being, its being-so or other-than-so. A detailed phenomenological analysis of so-called stirrings of conscience shows that a subtle, tender, and alert "conscience" is something *essentially* different from Herbart's representation of it: a cold and strange "judge," one who is always "too late" according to his nature. If, unlike the psychologist, we do not look at an already *lived* life or an already *lived* process of the will, but harken instead to the manner in which such an act and its project comes about, we will find, as stressed before, that the values of conative stirrings are already given at their point of "origin," at which such strivings as well as the direction of the project, not to mention the presence of a definite *project,* are not yet *fully* experienced. It can happen, for example, that the evidence of the "evil" in a conative impulse nips it *in the bud* and thus *excludes* it from the realm of what is observed by the *psychologist.* This "nipping in the bud" has as little to do with a possible "displacement" or an "active rejection" of the impulse concerned as with a mere "inner turning away" from it or a deviation from its being noted or noticed. For both this rejection and this deviation from attention *presuppose some* degree of formation of this conative process and a *given* project, as well as a passing over of the "nucleus" to which we refer here. A true feeling of shame, for example, does not appear primarily as a shameful reaction to certain things that cross one's mind; fewer things cross the mind of the more shameful person than cross the mind of one who is less so.[30] Therefore, if we relate "feeling of something" to the "something" of *pictorial* objects, we can and must say that the *values* of the pictorial objects are *pre*felt. That is, according to the law of origins the values of pictorial objects are already given at a level where the pictorial objects are *not yet* given. This is valid also for all possible pictorial objects of the inner perception of our experiences. And this "prefeeling" can occur in perception, remembering, and anticipation. In the last case this *"having a prefeeling* of something" is also directed toward the future, but it does *not* coincide with the above-defined meaning of prefeeling. For this "prefeeling" is in like manner present in the refeeling of past experience. The value is in this case prefelt *in* a refeeling.

It will be seen that this fundamental fact of our spiritual life

---

30. See "Das Schamgefühl" (Bibliog. no. 6). [This essay of 1913 was published under the title "Über Scham und Schamgefühl" in *Zur Ethik und Erkenntnislehre* (Bibliog. no. 29).—Ed.]

sheds a great deal of light on the obscure questions of the problem of freedom.[31] And it will also become apparent that there is little truth in the assertion so closely related to the assessment theory of moral values that the causal determination of acts of will does not affect their moral value, that causal determination matters as little as it does in the case of aesthetic values, e.g., the beauty of a gem, where such a gem is a necessary product of causal laws. It does not appear necessary to me to state explicitly that this assertion completely *contradicts* the facts. The reasons for this will become clear later, in another context.

2. *Value and the Ought*

a. Value and the Ideal Ought

Within the ought in general, I have distinguished between the *"ideal ought"* and the ought that represents a demand and an order imposed upon a conation. Whenever we speak of "duty" or "norms," we are concerned not with an "ideal" ought but with a specification of it as something that is *imperative*. This second type of ought is dependent on the former, because every duty is *also* an ideal ought-to-be of an act of the will. If some content of the ideal ought is given and is referred to a conation, it will *issue* a demand to this conation. Such an experience of a demand *is* therefore not the ideal ought itself, but its *consequence*. This *demand* is *stressed* by the inner command of a knowing-oneself-to-be-obliged, or by commanding acts coming from without, such as "orders," "advice," "counsel," and "recommendations."

The specific form *"Thou shalt* do so-and-so" can give expression to different acts. Under certain circumstances it *may* merely communicate (but in an inadequate way) that the speaker wants someone to do something. But this inadequate form of speech would then mean: "I communicate to you that I want you to do this." There are two factors here: first, the assertion that the action of the other corresponds to the *demand* of an *ought*,[32] and,

31. [The author's intention (expressed here and elsewhere in this work) to discuss the problem of *freedom* was not carried out, most likely because of concern for the size of the present work. Writings on the problem of freedom which were found among the author's papers stemming from the period of *Formalism* were published in *Collected Works* (Bibliog. no. 31), Vol. X. On the problem of the freedom of the will, see "Ethik," sec. 5.—Ed.]

32. Whether this assertion corresponds to a conviction is another matter.

second, the immediate expression and enunciation of the will of the person who speaks that the other, hearing this demand, act in a certain way. In the strictest sense of the term, *ought* in this sense pertains only to the *orders of an authority.*

An "*order,*" therefore, is *never* a mere communication of the fact that the person who orders wants this or that; rather, it represents an act in its own right by which the sphere of the will and powers of the other is *influenced* in an immediate fashion and without such "communication." Hence the ultimate form of an order is one that makes no allowance for the existence of the other's will, as when we say, "you do this" ("suggestive order").

"Genuine orders" are to be clearly distinguished from so-called *pedagogical orders,* which are essentially only *illusory orders* analogous to the "illusory questions of pedagogues" [*Scheinfragen*]. In reality, only *advice* underlies pedagogic propositions that express orders. The nature of advice is contained in the form: "It is best for you to do this, and I want you to do what is best for you." The difference consists in this: In advice we are not concerned with what is good or bad, what ought to be or ought not to be with respect to a will in general, but only with the willing of this *individuality.* Moreover, the volitional act in advising does not imply that an action, which (ideally) "ought" to be, should be "eventuated" by the one addressed, but that he *should do this action* (through a free act of his will). For the limitation of all pedagogic orders consists in the fact that they are justified only insofar as the educator is convinced that his pupil is mature and developed enough to have done what *he* ordered. An educator who cannot be convinced that his mature pupil would freely do what he feels obliged to "order" must abandon the education of the pupil.[33]

In addition to this illusory order in education there is another

---

33. The attempts of a large number of philosophers of the Enlightenment to reduce an authoritative order (be it of the state or of the church) to a mere pedagogical *illusory order* (pedagogical theory of authority) is as much *nonsense* as the opposite attempt to invest the educator with *authoritative* orders, as in Herbart's theories of education. Just as the pedagogical question, in which the *form* of the question is only a means to actualize some knowledge in the pupil (or a means to establish what he knows), does not "ask" anything, so also the pedagogical order, in which the *form* of the order is a means to *awaken* central volitional intentions and to lead such intentions to their adequate projects (in Socrates' sense), is not a genuine order. See A. Riehl's profound work on the "pedagogical genius" of Socrates (*Zur Einführung in die Philosophie der Gegenwart* [Leipzig: Teubner, 1913]).

kind of pointing out what "ought" to be done. This is "advice," "counsel," and "recommendation." Although fundamentally the above pedagogic order is (objectively) only "advice," its effectiveness is nevertheless tied to this "illusory form" of giving orders. When, for example, it is applied in mass education, it does not pertain to what is good for an individual, but is tied in its contents to the *typical* development of a human being. It is otherwise with *true* advice, which represents itself immediately as advice, and within which the *"advice of a friend"* can be distinguished from "the advice of an authority" (e.g., the "evangelical counsel" of church authority). The advice of a friend passes immediately to the *individual.* It is a communication of what one believes to be the best for this individual in a specific situation *and,* at the same time, an expression of one's will that this individual choose the best. In the second case, advice is given to certain *types* of people. The type cannot be "defined"; still less can the individuals concerned be *designated* by the authority. It is, rather, the *concern of everyone* to decide for himself whether or not he belongs to the type to which the advice is addressed, i.e., whether or not he is "called" to follow the advice. It is therefore possible for someone who is not called, but who follows such advice, to act worse than he would have, had he not followed it.

But there is still an *expression of will* in "advice." Advice is not a *mere* communication of what someone else should ideally do. In contrast to this, moral *"counsel"* is only an assist that helps one to see morally what should or should not be; it is *not* an expression of will. A *"recommendation"* communicates what one holds that someone else should do, but *without* an expression of will or any immediate assist that would help him gain moral knowledge of what is recommended. Finally, the mere *"proposal,"* which pertains not to something that ought to be done, but to the mere *technique* of the *realization* of what ought to be, is to be distinguished from all of these.

It is from the situation in which something is given as an (ideal) ought and, at the same time, as something that "can" be done that the concept of *"virtue"* springs. Virtue is the immediately experienced *power* to do something that ought to be done. The concept of *vice* originates in the immediately comprehended contrariety of an (ideal) ought and what can be done, or, in other words, in the immediate comprehension of *not-being-able-to-do* or *impotency* vis-à-vis something that is given as an ideal ought.

If, as Spinoza and Guyau (and many others) hold, the ought

were merely the consciousness of a higher "ability," there would be no virtue, but solely "proficiency" [*Tüchtigkeit*]. If there were no immediate fact of the "ability to do something," whose factual execution is never experienced or acted out, and if every "I can do what I ought to do" were merely a "postulate" (as in Kant's proposition "You can, for you ought") which is based on an immediate, experienced ought, but which is intuitively unfulfillable, there would again be no virtue, but only a (dispositional) *"facility" to repeat* one's duty *once* it has been done.

The willing and doing of an ideal ought is *"meritorious"* if the content of the ought *exceeds* in value the content of generally valid "norms." Something ideally given as ought-not-to-be is *"permitted"* if an immediate "not-being-able-to" is given for the abstention; but it must be a "not-being-able-to" that is *not in contradiction* with *universally valid* norms. The opponents of the concepts of "meritorious" and "permissible" maintain that something is either according to duty or not, and therefore there can be nothing like permissibility or meritoriousness. For both concepts, they say, presuppose heteronomy, that is, the uncritical acceptance of an authority's commandments of duty. But this would be the case only if the "ideal" ought-to-be had its foundation in the inner necessity of the *consciousness of duty* rather than in objective value-*insight*. Since this is not the case, this assertion, as well as the doctrine of the so-called "infinity of duty," are indefensible.

Let us return to the *relation between the ideal ought and values*. This relation is fundamentally governed by two axioms: anything of positive value ought to be, and anything of negative value ought not to be. The interconnection set up in these axioms is not reciprocal but *unilateral:* every *ought has its foundation in values*, but values are *not* founded in the ideal ought. According to our other axioms it is easy to see that, of all values, only those resting on the *being* (or *non-being*) of values enter into an immediate relation with the ought. These axioms are the following: "the being of a positive value is itself a positive value"; "the being of a negative value is itself a negative value," etc. *Values* are in principle given *indifferently* with respect to existence and non-existence. On the other hand, every ought is *related* to the sphere of the existence (and non-existence) of values. This is apparent in our use of language. We can say, "It was good to act thus in this case," whereas we cannot say, "This *had* to have been so," but only, "This *should have* been so."

That is, the ought is not so indifferent with regard to the possible being and non-being of its content as a value. Every ought is therefore an *ought-to-be* [Seinsollen] of something. Hence there is no special category of "ought-being" [*Soll-Seins*] which is such that the essence of values like "good," "beautiful," etc., *plus* the value of the being of such values, as another part of this essence, could replace the being of these values! [34] Thus it becomes clear that whenever we say that something "*ought* to be," this something is comprehended—in the same act—"as" non-existing (or "as" existing, in the case of an ought-not-to-be). But the ought is, as we stated before, totally independent of any relation to the *future*. The ideal ought-to-be and ought-not-to-be also pertain to both present and past. Kant is right, therefore, when he says that "the good ought to be, even if it has *never* happened anywhere." Thus any attempt to reduce the ought to a factual "development" is mistaken. This pertains to all well-known evolutionary theories of ethics which would derive "what ought to be" from a factual "evolutionary tendency" of the "world" (Hartmann), "life" (Spencer), or "culture" (W. Wundt), and which would specify those events, wills, or actions that lie in the *direction* of this development as things that ought-to-be, and those that oppose this direction as things that ought-not-to-be. For a "world" in which the ought-to-be *occurs* is quite different from one in which this does not happen, one that also "develops" *differently*. Evolutionary ethics will always be the ethics of the tale of the seven Swabians, each of whom wants one of the others to lead the way. For possible directions of development are themselves things that ought or ought not to be. But it is wrong to assume that the concept of development can be determined as a series of changes aiming at the realization of a positive (or negative) value; and it is especially wrong to attribute a purpose to the *essence* of development. For these characteristics are applicable only to the concepts of "progress" and "regress" *within* development, which themselves have nothing to do with the essence of development. Development is merely an increase in the *fullness* of a totality, that is, an increase that cannot be conceived as a summation of divisible spatial and temporal contents (of any kind). There is no value-concept contained in it. It is for precisely this reason, and this reason alone, that the "direction" of development (a concept that does not presuppose a value or a

34. It appears to me that this was G. Simmel's assumption in his *Einleitung in die Moralwissenschaft: Eine Kritik der ethischen Grundbegriffe* (Stuttgart: Cottasche, 1911).

purpose or even the concept of an "end") can itself be a bearer
of positive *and* negative value-predicates. If, on the other hand,
development were founded in a value (in Rickert's sense), there
could be no "development" of negative value (and no decadence
of positive value); every development would be *eo ipso* of positive
value. But it belongs to the essence of a content which is given
as one that positively ought to be, to be given as *non-existent*
at the same time and in the same act. Although we sometimes
say, "It is so and ought to be so," we are then concerned with
two distinct acts through which only the *objective* identity of
something that ought to be and something that exists is stated.
Second, in such cases the proposition "It is so" refers not to the
value of the being in question, but only to the state of affairs
bearing this value. We never say, "This is good and ought to be
so"; but we do say, "He is unhappy and ought to be so," or, "He
defends himself and ought to do so." Our position here is simply
that the *non-being* of the *value* to which the ought refers is presupposed in all propositions of the ought-to-be (or the being of
the disvalue, in propositions of the ought-not-to-be). There are
also propositions in which this "ought to be so" is merely an
inadequate expression for the proposition "It is rightfully so."
"Rightness," however, consists in the coincidence of a value that
ideally ought to be and the existence of this value.[35]

Since there is no being of oughtness [*Sollsein*] whose *content*
is mere being, there is always an "ought-not-to-be" opposed to
the "ought-to-be." This "ought-not-to-be" must be qualified as a
different quality of oughtness. It is to be sharply distinguished
from the ought-to-be of a non-being. Of course, being and non-
being can also belong to the *contents* of an ought, either an

---

35. I do not wish to elaborate here on the very important class of
propositions of the form "It is rightfully so that . . ." and "It is not rightfully so that . . . ." But I wish to stress: (1) Rightness and its opposite
are the ultimate phenomenal starting points of all studies of "right" and
the idea of the "order of right." (2) The idea of right has its basis not in
rightness but in the opposite of rightness, so that "rightful" or "according to the order of right" is *everything that does not include the opposite
of rightness.* Hence (according to an exact reduction) the order of right
can never state *what* ought to be (or *what* is right), but only and simply
what *ought not to be* (or what is not right). Everything that is positively
legislated in the order of right is, when reduced to pure complexes of
rightness and its opposite, a complex of what is *not within the domain of
rightness.* This complex is governed by "right" and its "order." (A law is
only a technique for realizing the order of right.) (3) Rightness and its
opposite are *bearers* of values, but they are *not* the source of these values.
(4) That comportment is "correct" whose being is right.

ought-to-be or an ought-not-to-be. Positive values apply to the ought-to-be; negative ones, to the ought-not-to-be.

The ultimate sense of any positive proposition, e.g., "There ought to be justice in the world," "Indemnifications ought to be paid," necessarily contains, therefore, a reference to a *disvalue,* i.e., a reference to the non-being of a positive value.[36] It follows from this that the ought can *never* itself determine *what positive* values are. It can only determine positive values as opposites of negative values. *Every* ought (not only the ought-not-to-be) is directed toward the exclusion of disvalues, but it does *not* posit positive values!

The proof of this (very important) proposition can be found in what we have already said. If all acts of the ought pertain to values given *"as"* non-existing (no matter if they factually are), positive propositions of the ought must pertain to "values given as non-existing." But the axiom holds that the being of a positive value is itself a positive value, and that the non-being of a positive value is a *disvalue.* Therefore it follows (syllogistically) that all positive propositions of the ought pertain to *negative* values as well. And since positive propositions of the ought also contain, verbally and according to their mode of formulation, names for positive values, e.g., "The good ought to be," positive values can be meant only as the opposites of evils, as X, Y, and Z, the *opposites* of the evils to which we factually turn our attention.

There is no "value-necessity"; there are only essential interconnections of values. But there is a "necessity of the ought." This necessity of a positive oughtness is, however, always the oughtness of the non-being of the opposite of a positive value. This state of affairs is entirely similar to that of theoretical necessity, e.g., "B belongs to A." Such necessity means that the opposite is impossible.

Hence every proposition of the ought "rests" on a positive value that it cannot contain. For what "ought to be done" is originally never the being of good, but the non-being of evil.

Hence a proposition of the *ought* can never contradict the *insight* into what is positively good, nor can such insight be subordinated to such a proposition. If, for instance, I know what is good for me, I care not at all about what "I ought to do." For

---

36. A fortiori the presupposition of the ought-not-to-be is a reference to a negative value, namely, to the being of a disvalue.

the ought presupposes my knowing what is good. And if I immediately and fully know what is good, such feeling-knowing *immediately* determines my willing without my having to go through an "I-ought-to."

Hence an ethics which rejects the idea of *duty* as its point of departure and adopts instead the *ideal* ought must also assume a negatively *critical* character in accordance with the above axiomatic relations between the being of values and the ought. The entire attitude of this ethics is such that it attains positive values by *referring* to *negative* values as their opposites. But if there is an inclination here to confuse ideal oughtness with the ought of duty, or to *derive* the ideal ought from the ought of duty, a peculiar kind of negativism and an anxiety in the presence of all existing moral values, as well as in that of the *realization* of the good in deed and history, are the necessary results. It is precisely this attitude that Hegel so pointedly describes in his discussion, in *The Phenomenology of Mind,* of the tenets of Kant and Fichte. If an "ought-to" [*Gesolltes*], in the sense of the ought of duty, belonged to the essence of the good, and if it *consisted* therein, the good as *realized* would necessarily *cease* to be the good and would become something morally indifferent. The good would be so firmly secured in the region of the ought that it could not enter into the sphere of existing being without losing its essence. To be sure, Goethe's paradox would hold: "He who acts is always without conscience." Only a departure from that idea of *value* which is *indifferent* to the existential sphere *and* the sphere of the ought, and which *founds* every ought, can enable us to escape the basic fault of this critical and ruinous negativism against all extant values. One must also be extremely careful to avoid construing values as belonging originally to an *existential* sphere, as if they were abstracted from present facts, men, actions, goods, etc., instead of viewing them as originally indifferent to being and oughtness.[37] This mistake necessarily leads to that adoration and justification of the historical to which Hegel, for example, finally succumbed, a position which is no less mistaken than the one that he so pointedly criticized. All "evolutionary" ethics shares this mistake with him.

b. The Normative Ought

The ideal ought in "the good ought to be" becomes a *demand* when its content is simultaneously experienced in conation in

37. See chap. 1, sec. 1.

terms of its possible realization.[38] The question "Why should I do what ought to be?" is possible on this basis alone. If the ought in general were only and originally a "demand" or an experienced imperative, as both Rickert and Lipps have described it, this question could never be asked, and the problem of the "binding force" of propositions of the ought would not exist. But the answer to this question is that there is also an *ideal* ought for the being of a particular *conation* and *willing*. Schopenhauer's remark that there is no sense in speaking of an ought-to-will because it only makes sense to speak of an ought-to-do pertains to *normative* oughtness, which implies the experienced relation to a willing. But it does *not* pertain at all to the ideal ought in general.

In order for the ideal ought to become a demand for a will, an *act of commanding*—however it reaches the will, be it by an authority or by tradition—is always *presupposed*. This also pertains to the concept of *duty*. Herbart has correctly stressed that *every* idea of duty is based on the obligation of an order. It makes *no* sense to speak, as Kant does, of a duty that is floating in the air, as it were, a duty vis-à-vis no one, and which is not imposed by the order of an authority.[39] It also makes no sense to speak about "*self-obligation*," as Herbart also correctly stated. There are duties "to oneself," but there is no "self-obligation," as if the obliging and what is obliged were the same thing. In the statement "I oblige myself to do this," one merely says that he recognizes a duty to do or achieve something with respect to someone else (whether this pertains to himself or the other).

According to the nature of the ideal ought, one can speak of an ought only when a value is given in its non-being; so, according to its nature, an *imperative* pertains to a posited value to which a conation is related, but not in original intention. When, on the other hand, this is the case, it makes no *sense* to speak of "duty," "norm," or "imperative." However, on the basis of what we have said, this implies that an (ideal) *ought-not-to-be* of a *conation* is the foundation of every imperative proposition. Throughout history, therefore, proscriptions have always preceded prescriptions (e.g., the Decalogue). Commandments, too, give values whose realization they prescribe; such commandments are founded in the intuited *possible counterconation*

38. [See above, pp. 185 ff.—*Ed.*]
39. One cannot "give orders to oneself" or "obey oneself"; one can only "resolve to do something," which can at times act as a "constraint" on willing. One can also "make a vow to oneself," but only "before" another (e.g., God).

ıinst the realization of the values. Since such counterconation
ıtself *bad*, commandments also are based on this *intuition of
e bad*.

From this we can see that any imperativistic ethics—for
example, one which takes its point of departure from duty as the
ultimate moral phenomenon and attempts to derive the ideas
of the good and the bad, of virtue and vice, only from it—has a
merely *negative, critical, and repressive* character from the outset. A constitutive distrust not only of human nature but also of
the essence of moral acts in general is the very *presupposition*
of all its tenets.

Still, it is completely wrong to assume, following a position
which Schopenhauer helped to make popular, that all *religious*
ethics, especially those which trace good and bad back to God,
must have an *imperativistic* character, and, therefore, that
Kant's imperativistic ethics is only a consequence of an enduring
conception, hidden even from himself, of the divine will as the
foundation of moral law. But this is true for only some religious
ethics, e.g., Jewish ethics and the Scotistic theology of Scholasticism, which trace the ideas of good and evil to a will that gives
laws—the will of God.[40] In direct contrast to this are those ethics
which hold that the good lies in the *"essence of God"* rather than
in the *will* (Thomas Aquinas) and those most profound opinions
according to which all good comportment is *"in"* God (*amare "in"
deo, velle "in" deo, credere "in" deo*). Comportment of this kind
is such that the act of moral insight as executed by man and the
moral will that follows it are lived and given as factually distinct from the act of God, whereas according to its *content* the
act is immediately experienced and given as identical to and
coincidental with the content of the divine acts of cognition and
will. All normative "laws" and all imperatives are then to be
regarded as "derived" from the *intuitive content* of good and
bad as it is given in such a basic religious relation, and as leading
back to church *authority*. Therefore it is erroneous to emphasize
this coincidence in *content* of divine and human acts (which,
in contrast to pantheistic views, always presupposes *two different* real acts) to the point of a real identity, so that, as is the

40. But Kant also does this to the extent that he reduces the idea of the
good to the idea of *willing according to law* (not God's law, but that of
"autonomous" rational willing), instead of reducing the idea of the good
to a *non-formal value*. August Messer seems to have overlooked this in his
valuable comparison of Thomistic and Kantian ethics (*Kants Ethik* [Leip-
zig, 1904], pp. 291 ff.).

case in pantheism, God himself "thinks," "wills," "loves," etc., in man, just as it is a mistake to consider the volitional act of finite man a mere act of *"obedience"* to divine *imperatives* and *commandments,* as is still presupposed in the case of the Ten Commandments.[41] Strictly speaking, only church authority can "command," and if it lets God himself give commandments, it only conceals its own responsibility for the moral value of its acts of commanding under the idea of God.

All imperatives, even the categorical imperative, if there is one, are *justified* imperatives only when they pertain to an ideal ought and, indirectly, to the value belonging to it. They therefore remain *objects* of propositions of being-right and being-wrong.

Indeed, there is here a peculiar essential relation, one that often is overlooked, between the *being-right* and the *being-wrong* of commandments or prohibitions and the *willing* to which they pertain. An order is a commandment (or a prohibition) when the content of the order is simultaneously given as an ideal ought-to-be to the person who is ordered. And the first condition of the being-right of the commandment is that this being-right which is given to him "as" an ideal ought-to-be must also be an objective ought-to-be, i.e., the ought-to-be of a good. This condition alone is not sufficient for an order to become a commandment or a prohibition—that is, a justified commandment, etc. The second condition is that he who gives orders in terms of commanding or prohibiting must also have *seen* a conative tendency *"against"* that ideal ought-to-be, i.e., a tendency of counterconation, or a conative tendency toward the ideal ought-not-to-be, in the being who is given the commandment or the prohibition. And a *commandment* or a *prohibition* is (objectively) "right" only insofar as this is in fact the case. If, on the other hand, an insight into the fact that such tendencies are *missing* is possible, but commandments and prohibitions are *nevertheless* given, the *act implicit in commanding* (and *forbidding*) is *itself a bearer of a moral disvalue or something evil*—even when the ideal ought-to-be is commanded. Furthermore, it belongs to the *essence* of such acts to *intend* the realization of evil or the cancellation of a present good, despite their character as prohibition (or commandment). And it is not incidental but essentially necessary

41. It remains moot whether Moses appeared merely as the ambassador of God, *announcing* God's "laws" in obedience to him, or whether through his knowledge of God's will he prescribed what corresponds to God's will as a "norm."

that the understanding of these acts by someone else entail something like "moral defiance." Even when both subjects have the same insight into the ideal ought-to-be of what is commanded, it is the *commandedness* or *prohibitedness* of this content, which is "unjustified" in the above sense, that effects a *counterreaction* of defiance, a reaction which is also directed against the *content* to the extent that it is inseparable from the form of commandedness. The good person, who would have done the good "of his own accord" [*aus freien Stücken*] because he had *insight*, is now put on the *defensive* against the imperativistic form of the posited content in question, and this gives rise to a tendency toward the bad. The autonomy of *insight* thus comes into conflict with the very idea of "duty." [42] In this sense every commandment or prohibition that is unnecessary and, hence, *unjustified* necessarily brings about a tendency to produce the bad and is itself a bad volitional act in that it implies an offense (precisely because commandments and prohibitions necessarily involve the possibility of an excitation against the ideal ought-to-be). This is the case when a good is commanded or when an evil is forbidden. If, for example, something that lies in the direction of our love is commanded, such a commandment is itself experienced as a grave offense.[43] Let us only mention that prohibitions suggest to a "pure heart" the evil which they forbid, and bring an evil as a possible project closer to the will.

An ethics which recognizes only what is "commandable" as "*good*" and only what is "prohibitable" as "*evil*" (as Kant once rejected the moral value of love because it cannot be "commanded") makes that demand which belongs to the essence of all norms—namely, that they be doubly "justified"—basically unfulfillable, no matter if one commands himself or another. The "pragmatism" of this ethics is, morally speaking, as impractical as can be; for the moralist of this view does not notice that with his "norms" he only tends to *produce* factually what he so strongly forbids, nor does he notice that with his commandments and imperatives he prevents free moral persons who will the good—not because it is commanded, but because they *see* it—from doing what they see. To make the medication of commandments and prohibitions our normal moral nourishment is nonsense.

42. [On "duty and insight," see above, pp. 191 ff.—*Ed.*]
43. Ibsen showed the subtleties of this problem in his drama, *Lady from the Sea.*

The relation between norms and values has, moreover, a consequence that is not only basic for ethics in general but also of greatest importance for the history of morals. *All imperatives* and *norms* can *vary* historically and with different groups, even when the *same values* are recognized; and they can continue to vary, even when the same propositions of the *ideal ought* are affirmed. For the significance of norms is not determined *merely* by the contents of propositions concerning the ideal ought (still less by recognized values); it is codetermined by the *original value-direction* of the *conation* to which these norms are addressed. If this direction coincides with an ideal ought, *no* imperative ensues. Only when they are opposed are there imperatives. Indeed, this possibility of variation in imperatives with the same values (and with the same propositions of the ideal ought) may even permit imperatives of *opposite* meanings to have their foundation in them. Let us take, for example, the imperatives that can be formulated on the basis of the principle that "the value of oneself is equal to the value of the other." We can find in history that completely opposite *norms* have been recognized as consistent with this principle: love your neighbor more than yourself; attempt first to be someone so that you can give others something from yourself. In his fable of the bees Mandeville tried to show that culture and well-being develop only when everyone unscrupulously seeks to further his own interests. Rückert's saying, "A rose that adorns itself also adorns its garden," contains this idea, namely, that service to others has value only when he who serves has already furthered himself and his own value to the highest degree. Along such lines of thinking, the questions of value and the problem of the "imperative" are often badly confused. If these things are separated, it becomes clear that, depending on the original direction of conation, completely *opposite imperatives* can and must ensue. No doubt there are men who by nature find it difficult to *comprehend* the values of others, or at least find it more difficult than to comprehend their own; and it is a fortiori difficult for them to act in accordance with the direction of the ideal demands resting on these values. On the other hand, there are also men who suffer from a pathological urge to sacrifice, who must make some effort to push themselves over to *their own values*. It is clear that for the first type the imperative "Turn toward the values of others, and care, above all, for others" is necessary, and that for the latter the opposite, "Attend to yourself and care for yourself before you care for others," is necessary. Kant was certainly mistaken in maintaining that the command to seek the highest self-happiness makes no sense *because* everyone already seeks it by natural inclination.[44] It is beyond doubt that there are types of men to whom this proposition is *not* applicable. Friedrich Nietzsche's imperatives, e.g., "Become hard," "Look out for yourself," etc., must be seen as having this psychological disposition as their basis.

What we have said implies that we are *never* entitled to infer what moral *norms*, as they are found in history, command in terms of the dispositions of a people. W. Rathenau appropriately states:

> From the laws of a people one should infer something about its dispositions only *ex contrario*. Divine unity had to be so often and so strongly impressed upon Israel because the people were deeply inclined toward polytheism. Exaggerated veneration of parents among cruel peoples leads us to assume that they used to maltreat and do away with the aged [*Reflexionen*, p. 235].

If there are commandments or prohibitions for one people which do not exist for another, it *may* be that doing what is commanded or what is contrary to what is prohibited is felt to be of value by the first and not by the other. But it *may* be the case that one people already does everything that the commandments or prohibitions require, and hence they do not need norms. The frequent appearance of commandments and prohibitions often indicates that the immediate feeling for the values to which the commandments and prohibitions refer has been *obscured,* or at least that conation has taken a course which is opposed to value-feeling. Commandments and prohibitions relating to reproduction, for example, are always signs of the *declining* character of the reproductive drive, one of the ultimate drives of life; this can be seen in the later Roman population policies. A similar state of affairs exists concerning the "norms" of the modern movements of moderation and restraint.

Hence, in a population that consists of diverse parts—for example, different races with different original vital dispositions—there may be entirely *different* "norms." But this does not mean that the *same values* and the same *propositions* of the ideal *ought* are not recognized by all members of the community. It does *not* follow from the identity of values and their order of ranks that the same moral norms must be valid for "all men,"

---

44. See pertinent remarks by Henry Sidgwick, *Methods of Ethics* (London: Macmillan, 1907).

or even for all members of a people. There may well be quite different laws or any number of laws of exception in the presence of the *same* moral values and the same order of ranks, but nothing can be said against the objectivity and identity of moral values because of this state of affairs. He who would prove ethical skepticism by simply considering changes in moral norms throughout history, even the amount of change in one people, can *easily* do this; but he misses the point, because norms are *not* the ultimate facts of moral life.

Moreover, as we have shown, norms are totally different from all (merely pedagogical) *advice* and technical *proposals*. True, norms can *change* along with commanding willings and the conation to which they pertain. In this they differ from propositions of the ideal ought, which are completely independent of existing natural laws, and which can also be considered valid for men of a nature quite *different* from ours. Norms change along with changes in any one of these factors. Yet they are still *independent of the causal insight* into nature with which technical proposals, for example, vary; and such proposals can of course vary greatly with respect to the *same norms*. Pedagogical advice can also vary greatly with respect to the same norms. It is therefore *not* possible to reduce the variational possibilities of norms with respect to values and forms of an ideal ought, which we assert, to this very different variational possibility proper to pedagogical advice and technical rules which are directed toward the accomplishment of a purpose, e.g., that of general well-being.[45]

45. Since the contents of *norms* rest on two factors—namely, the factor of the ideal ought, which itself is based on values, and the factor of the direction of conation—norms cannot be genetically-psychologically (or biologically) explained insofar as their contents alone are considered. What can be explained, though, is simply the *selection* of norm-giving contents from the ideal contents of the ought-to-be (which correspond to known axioms of a given domain of values and its order)—not the *contents* of a norm, but only the *norm-giving* [Normierung] of these contents and no others.

Here we cannot fully explain the difficult relationship between normative laws and "*natural laws*," but it requires a thorough investigation. We do want to say that it is not correct to consider normative laws results of the lawfulness of the natural psychic process (as Laas tried to show). Nor is it correct to side with Sigwart (*Logik*, Vol. II) and Windelband ("Normen und Naturgesetze"), and to consider the principle of natural lawfulness a norm for the "willing to think" of nature or a postulate of the will for the "comprehensibility" of nature (as H. Poincaré holds in his *La valeur de la science*). Things are much more complex than these simple explanations would have it. For the principle that expresses what is (most formally) "*according to law*" [Gesetzmässigkeit] in the sense of

We hold that every imperative ought presupposes a *conation* to which an order (as commandment or prohibition) based on the ideal ought pertains. Every duty is an immediate obligation to *do* something, and to do it with respect to a specific person. We cannot be obligated to perform an *act of will* as we can be obligated to do something. Nevertheless, an obliging imperative is a "determining factor" in volitional decision with regard to

---

unequivocal dependencies of a series of any variations (factors of otherness) is an a priori component common to both normative and natural laws (which has its foundation in the nature of objects and variations in general). Hence there is not a "transference" of *nature's lawfulness* [Naturgesetzlichkeit], understood as one of objects of thought, to the *lawfulness of norms* [Normgesetzlichkeit], understood as volitional withstanding. Nor is there, conversely, a transference of the latter to the former. The idea of what is "according to law" is a priori to both series of laws.

What we have called "nature's lawfulness" in the widest sense is the *application* of this highest a priori principle to appearances in the spheres of the inner world and the outer world and in the spheres of the lived body as objects of thought. In this sense there is an infinite domain of functional dependencies among such appearances, a domain that is not affected by the differences among these spheres, differences that are in themselves only special cases of psychic, psychophysical, lived-body-physical, and lived-body-psychic dependencies (each indivisible). Nor is there here the condition that dependent variations must be *temporal* variations, i.e., "changes," or that functional dependencies would have to be of spatiotemporal contiguity (or, better, "contiguity in the pure expanse in general"). Rather, on this level *all* spatiotemporal determinations enter into the contents of dependent relata. To this "lawfulness in nature" there corresponds a series of factors of the ideal ought which are no less dependent on laws and which presuppose the *idea* and *essence* of conation in general, but not a *factual* conation of a certain determined direction, as in the case with "norms." Undoubtedly, norms are subject to *both* types of laws, and in principle the selection from the ideal ought of contents of norms can be "explained" in terms of this "lawfulness in nature." The latter possesses a third level only in the (formal) *mechanical lawfulness in nature*, where we find the part of functional dependencies of the inner world and the outer world that satisfies the condition that *the interdependent elements must be contiguous with each other in extension.* The *latter dependencies* alone are (formally) *mechanical* and, after the division has been made between inner and outer world (with their own manifolds), separate into *associative-mechanical* and *natural-mechanical* dependencies. We will not demonstrate that in these two forms of dependencies the essence of *"lived body"* and the principle of similarity are presupposed, i.e., that the factors of similarity in appearance are not reducible to *identitas partium* (in the sense of spatiotemporal parts). [See chap. 6, A, sec. 3, g.—Ed.]

Norms are certainly not explicable through this "mechanical" lawfulness or through association psychology. Indeed, one can show that the very assumption of such lawfulness in nature requires *one* type of norm: the norm which gives the order to *control* nature (in the above sense). For both the *mechanical view of nature* and its counterpart, *association psychology*, select from the objective and a priori functional dependencies *"willing-to-do."* [46] And this is why, as Kant has *correctly* seen, it is out of the question to reduce the concepts of norm and duty to the relation of a mere means to a given purpose. The positing of a purpose should (in the ideal sense) follow the codetermination of the norm or the obliging imperative.

It is, however, of greatest importance to see that every obligation, as well as every norm, refers to the act of willing-to-do.

---

of variations only those dependencies that can have significance as points of departure for conduct to control nature in the attempt to control the series of appearances through the will of an embodied being (although not necessarily man qua man). In my view association psychology (in the strict sense) is that science which rests on the *principle of association by contiguity.* Both the associative-psychological and the mechanical "sides" of nature therefore have a significance conditioned by the *possible existence of life and lived bodies.* Contrary to Hume, one cannot derive the idea of the laws of nature (as physical laws) from presupposed *laws of association* by contiguity and similarity. Nor, contrary to Kant, can one derive even *one* of the laws of association (especially the law of similarity) from the lawfulness (of a transcendental understanding), presupposed for outer nature, of time-sequences in appearances and spatial reciprocities. But one can explain *both* (formal) *mechanical lawfulnesses* with the premise of the universal principle of functions in all variations of appearances and the premise of the principle of similarity, which is not derivable from the two and which already functions in the *formation* of the natural view of the world as a form of comprehension of the outer world and the inner world or as a principle of selection of appearances entering into them. (See chap. 6, A, sec. 3, g.)

If, however, the *norm of control over nature,* as a norm that gives possible *orientation* to the psychic and the physical, precedes mechanical laws as their foundation, *any* attempt to explain norms and their historical changes in terms of association psychology, or to interpret their changes as consequences of increased control over nature through increased knowledge of mechanical nature, is *from the very beginning* impossible. On the contrary, from a historical viewpoint it is the new *will to control nature* of our era that is responsible for the significance assigned to mechanical-physical and mechanical-psychic theories. And just as the norm of control over nature necessarily and essentially precedes those mechanical principles, so also the search for these laws in appearances is historically conditioned by the factual appearance of this norm as a conscious principle.

From the above it clearly follows that an increase in the knowledge of mechanical laws can only explain changes in *technical rules* concerning how one is to proceed from this norm to "control nature." This norm, like any other true norm, is inexplicable, even with an *infinite* increase in knowledge of *this* kind. (See my treatise, "Über Ressentiment und moralisches Werturteil.") All attempts to *reduce historical changes in norms to changes in knowledge of mechanical nature* (Spencer, Paulsen, et al.) have as their presupposition the (historically non-existing) identity of norms with norms of modern times. This also pertains, of course, to those attempts which consider norms technological rules for the increase of human well-being or the maximization of life, etc.

Kant, therefore, *was completely correct* to separate the *essence* of norms from all possible technological rules.

46. See chap. 3.

This appears to contradict many writers, especially ecclesiastical ones, who speak of *"duties of faith"* and the *"duty of love."* If this manner of speaking is to be understood in the way that one understands talk concerning obligations of the will, it must be *rejected,* as Kant rightfully stressed.[47] This indeterminability by imperatives or norms belongs to the essence of the act of faith and the act of love. Strictly speaking, there can be no "obligation" for faith or love. But the concepts of the duty of faith and the duty of love can have sense if they are taken to mean that a norm or an imperative exists only for the purpose of putting oneself through an act of will into a *situation* in order to execute an act of faith or love. We can, for example, say: Concentrate your attention on the contents of the dogma of your church; try to live spiritually in this dogma; above all, bring yourself into the cognitive situation that is the presupposition of an act of faith. But there can be no "duty" to execute the act of faith *itself.* So also can we point out the values of one man to another who does not see them, and we can ask him to try to immerse himself in these values more deeply than ever before. But we can *never* "oblige" him to love this person. If one speaks of "duties of love," [48] the act of love is replaced by *doing good* [Wohltun] and, in the extreme case, by "goodwill" [*Wohlwollen*] (if one does not mean mere deeds [*äussere Werke*]). The great danger in these word-combinations of "duty of faith" and "duty of love" is that certain works or certain outer and visible displays

---

47. See esp. *Religion innerhalb der Grenzen der blossen Vernunft.*

48. Catholic writers like to speak of the *"law of love";* for example, they hold that Jesus has replaced the old "law" with a new one, that this "law of love" is higher than the old law (of Moses) but still contains it. If they understand by this that love is nothing arbitrary and not a causally produced feeling-state (in Kant's sense), but something which cannot be reduced to anything else, this manner of speaking is fully justified. Should this mean, however, that there is a "norm of law" which commands love and which Jesus established and joined to existing norms and raised above all other norms in such a way that there is no law "of" love (subjective genitive) but only the law to love (= ought to love), this manner of speaking is *nonsense.* The validity of Protestant criticism against the "law of love" depends on the sense of the term. This criticism is not justified in the former sense, but is justified in the latter. Nevertheless, it is most deplorable that the thrust of much of this criticism is such that *both totally* miss the phenomenon of the act of love. In clinging to the idea of a norm to love, i.e., a law to love in the second sense, Luther classified love under what he called works of law [*Gesetzeswerke*] and thus arrived at his idea of *sola fides.* And his opponents countered with this idea of a new "law of love" (in the second sense). Thus, in both Catholic and Protestant conceptualizations the act and the law of love (in the first sense) sought a place of rest in vain.

of the existence of these acts—the symbolic deeds of a cult, for example—will replace the spiritual acts that alone originally bear these names. Anyone who does not understand the expression "duty of faith" in the figurative sense that we have discussed must succumb to the deception which consists in taking an *external expression* of an act of faith—e.g., the act of confessing faith, if not, indeed, going to church or some other action of a cult—for this "faith." For one can, in fact, be "obliged" to do such things. Thus if these concepts are taken in this *false* sense, we are confronted with that error for which Protestant writers have frequently censured Catholic ecclesiastical morals, namely, the danger of mere sanctification through works. There is also another danger here. No doubt there is something like "willing to believe" or "willing to love," which, however, has nothing to do with faith or love; even the presence of such willingness always indicates a *lack* of faith and love. In speaking of the duty of faith and the duty of love in this false sense, one also paves the way for the deception which consists in equating the will to believe and the will to love with faith and love *themselves,* as well as in regarding them to be of equal value.

As Kant correctly observed, the acts of faith and love "cannot be commanded." But his *conclusion* that an act of love has no moral value *because* it cannot be commanded is totally *erroneous* and is comprehensible only in terms of the false presuppositions that are basic to his entire ethics.

Kant's interpretation of the principle "Love God above all and your neighbor as yourself" in his *Critique of Practical Reason* (pt. I, bk. I, chap. 3) annuls every trace of the meaning of this proposition. First he says, "For, as a command, this principle demands reverence for a law that *commands love* and does not leave it up to just any kind of choice." According to this interpretation, the act of love which raises man not only above this or that imperativistic "law" and its spheres of validity but also *beyond* and toward Jesus (in that he who lives according to him, as the Gospel says, realizes *eo ipso* all values that the "law" entreats and at the same time a value that is *superior* to all laws and what they command and prohibit) is again *sub*ordinated to the *"law."* Jesus appears as someone who merely gives new content to the same "legislation of God," which is also present in the legislation of the Decalogue. This account fails to recognize that from the beginning this principle posits a *new and fundamental relation* between God and man, a relation whose meaning lies beyond "command" and "obey": that men are the children of

God. Indeed, according to Kant the act of love has its foundation in the act of *"reverence"* for the law, whose mere *content* is supposed to be "love." Thus the act of reverence appears to be more basic and hence more valuable than the act of love.[49]

But in fact this principle cannot be considered a "norm" that "gives an order," for it does not make any sense, as Kant himself subsequently says, to want to "order" or "command" love. Still, this principle says that he who so acts (i.e., he who loves his neighbor as himself) realizes the highest moral value, and that such comportment is of ideal oughtness. Insofar as this proposition is directed toward a subjective will, it is meant not as a norm that commands, but as an invitation to *follow.*[50]

Kant continues his interpretation by saying that "love of God as an inclination (pathological love) is impossible; for he is not an object of the senses." Here Kant's doubly erroneous concept of love becomes most apparent. For he thinks that love is a derivative of "sensible feelings" and a mere "feeling-state," like sensuous pleasure derived from an object. We have refuted this

---

49. On the foundational relations between acts and the heights of values, see chap. 2, B, sec. 3.

50. Here again Catholic and Protestant (Lutheran) *polemics* often miss the point of the matter. Lutherans object to the opinion that Jesus gave "a new law," that apart from the importance of his sacrifice and mission as Savior, he was *also* a "teacher of morals" and a "moral lawgiver." But since they recognize the moral in general (an autonomous phenomenon as opposed to religion) exclusively as norm and justice of the law (exactly as many of their opponents do), they (necessarily) deny the Jesus of a purely moral significance independent of his religious significance. They conceive of Jesus exclusively as the Son of God, whose atoning blood gives those who trust and believe in him justification before and conciliation with God. Now, it is correct that Jesus *neither* "experienced" a new moral law in the sense of a "norm" *nor* "detected" or "established" one. But the fundamental *moral significance* of Jesus (essentially independent of the religious one, but in his person organically conjoined into a concrete unity) will be missing for anyone who bases moral value on norms and squeezes *moral effectiveness* from person to person into the alternative: *either* moral significance consists in its practical-moral effectiveness (i.e., in willing and actions), *or* it consists in norms stemming from this effectiveness. But moral effectiveness from person to person, *infinitely superior* to all these kinds of effectiveness, consists in the fact that the pure and immediate vision of the pure value and pure being of the person invites free *"following."* There is only *one* ideal content of the ought (not the normative ought) that helps us to bring the phenomenon of Jesus to the fore: *he himself.* And for this reason all "imitation" of his actions and all "obedience" to his supposedly new norms, as well as the above-mentioned denial of his original moral significance and morally effective significance, are nothing but a going-out-of-his-way. (See chap. 6, B, sec. 3, on autonomy and heteronomy, and chap. 6, B, sec. 4, ad 6 a.)

double error elsewhere.[51] If, like Kant, one takes the term *incli-nation* to mean an immediate movement toward a value (without a prior norm or commandment), and not a *sensuous drive*, then "love of God," i.e., a *spiritual* act which is called that, is indeed very "possible," even though God is not an object of the senses. Indeed, one must assert the opposite, that love of a *mere* "object of the senses" is something nonsensical.[52] If someone says that he "loves a meal," for instance, he is concerned with comportment totally different from what he has in mind when he says that he loves a person. Here we have not considered the fact that Kant has in mind only the phenomenon of the love of God, not the highest Christian phenomenon of "love in God" (*amare in Deo*). In the latter, man rises above all laws, even the laws of God (if God can be thought of as a "legislator"), by virtue of the fact that he knows himself to have the immediate power of an essential identity with the spiritual principle of life (with simultaneously differentiated real acts), through which all "commandments" find their only possible (and also necessary) justification.

If this principle were first of all a "divine commandment," as Kant holds, this commandment could be obeyed only out of fear (of punishment) and hope (for reward) insofar as it does not presuppose *love* and *veneration* of the highest Lord, i.e., as acts which are by far superior to all "reverence." [53]

51. For positive elaborations on love, see *Zur Phänomenologie und Theorie der Sympathiegefühle*, pp. 52–76. [See *Wesen und Formen der Sympathie*, pt. B, chap. 1, sec. 2–chap. 4.—Ed.] See also "Über Ressentiment und moralisches Werturteil."

52. See *Zur Phänomenologie und Theorie der Sympathiegefühle*, pp. 70 ff. [See *Wesen und Formen der Sympathie*, pt. B, chap. 1.—Ed.]

53. As to the phenomenological differences between *love* and *reverence*, see *Zur Phänomenologie und Theorie der Sympathiegefühle*, p. 48. [See *Wesen und Formen der Sympathie*, pt. B, chap. 1.—Ed.] Concerning veneration, see my treatise on the feeling of shame. [See "Über Scham und Schamgefühl."—Ed.] In contrast to love, whose movement involves the immediate feeling of the (qualified) height of a value, "reverence" *presupposes* the feeling of a given value and an *assessment* of its object, which obviously is not the case with love. Love based on reverence (for a mere "law," independent of the person who posited this law) or reverence for a law "which commands love" is the most extreme nonsense that rationalism ever set forth in ethics. A legal norm can only require and sustain "reverence" by virtue of the value to which the norm's basis in an ideal ought can be reduced, insofar as it is not the personal value of the one who establishes the norm that requires reverence. But to have reverence for a law because it is a "law" is something which cannot move and has never moved a feeling being in a pure fashion. Or else it would be the case that every natural law, e.g., Ohm's law, would require "reverence." He who asserts that he has reverence for a law only because it is a law and

If this principle were a commandment or a new law of a norm that Jesus established—the "law of love," as several theologians say—one would have to concede that Luther was right in excluding love from the ultimate relation between man and God, reckoning it to be among "the impossible works," and in taking faith alone as the standard of this basic relation. For the error that we find in Kant's work is the presupposition of Luther's criticism of traditional theology and morals, even though Kant draws *moralistic,* while Luther draws *anti*moralistic, conclusions from it,[54] and even though Luther denies Christ not only as a "lawmaker" but also as a "moral model," attributing to Christ only his purely religious meaning as "Savior."

Kant continues:

> [Love] is indeed possible with regard to men, but it cannot be *commanded;* for no man can love another simply on an order. Hence it is only *practical love* which can be understood in the core of all laws. In this sense to love God means to *like* to follow his commandments; to love one's neighbor, to *like* to do all duties with regard to him.

What is correct in this passage is what we have already stressed, namely, that love cannot be commanded. One who begins with the presupposition of imperativistic ethics and holds without doubt that "only what can be commanded is of moral value," and, moreover, that the good is what is commanded by a law, must of course conclude that love has no moral value. At the same time we are given only one alternative: either this principle is not meant as a law, as *we* assert, *or* it is in itself nonsense. Instead of concluding that this principle as a "commandment that orders love" is nonsense, as Kant's logic with its pre-

---

because the law has the form of an order exaggerates the object of reverence *much* more than he admits. His analysis is insufficient. And one who says that he is concerned here with the law of the good (or the law of moral values) must not derive the idea of the good from a law and a norm and *in addition* require reverence for this law. There can be reverence for the imperative form only if, in addition to the assessment, the *value* for the sake of whose realization something is commanded is *feelably given.* If, on the other hand, there is only the assessment and nothing else—without any feelable fulfillment and with only an empty value-intention—there is only "respect." And if this (empty) value-intention is also missing, there remains only a slavish contagion of conations through the mere form of orders as such, which surely has nothing to do with "reverence."

54. Because these conclusions are precisely the most important thing, it is totally incomprehensible to me why people continue to speak of "Luther and Kant" in the sense of a moral community of mind.

suppositions would require, Kant attempts to *reinterpret* the term *love so arbitrarily* that in the end the most barren moralism is interpreted into this evangelic principle. He says that although love cannot be commanded, *"practical love"* can. But there is no "practical love," strictly speaking, i.e., as a species within the genus. If there were, it would be senseless to affirm something about practical love which must be denied with regard to love as such. There is no "practical love" as a special quality of love, only love that leads to practical ways of comportment. But the *latter* cannot be commanded, either. On the other hand, things other than love can lead to practical ways of comportment, too, e.g., "goodwill" as well as "good-doing." The latter can be commanded.[55] But both are basically different from the act of loving, and they can exist without being consequences of love. We have "goodwill," e.g., toward men who serve us or are useful to us. Good *deeds* [*Wohl*taten], however, can also be consequences of vanity and the desire for fame. But in the sense of the evangelic principle, goodwill and good-doing have only as much moral *value* as there is *love* in them. On the other hand, love does not necessarily lead to goodwill and good-doing. One can also become angry, and hurt another out of love, if the pain and suffering inflicted are seen as leading to the *salvation* of the person.[56] But love is directed not to the *well-being* of someone but to the highest *value* of his person. It is directed to his "well-being" only if his value is thereby enhanced. There is therefore no justification for Kant's replacing love with goodwill or good-doing in this evangelic principle and hiding this behind the equivocation of "practical love." Moreover, "to love God" does not have the same meaning as "to like to follow his commandments," "to love men," "to like to do one's duty with regard to them." Since duty is, by its nature, independent of inclination and disinclination, this "to like" is a secondary factor that does not matter in the fulfillment of duty. If this "to like" is present, it rests only on the *love* of the persons involved, either the one who decreed the commandments or the one to whom one has the "duties"; but such duties are then *only ideal oughts* and are not given as "duties." We like to do our "duties" to those we love, and he who loves God likes to comply with God's commandments. But at this moment there are no longer any "commandments." It is wholly impossible, however,

55. On goodwill and love, see *Zur Phänomenologie und Theorie der Sympathiegefühle*, p. 41. [See *Wesen und Formen der Sympathie*, pt. A, chap. 11.—*Ed.*]
56. See "Über Ressentiment und moralisches Werturteil."

to identify this love with the mere consequences of one's "liking to do one's duty." [57]

Kant continues, completely eliminating the *entire* meaning of this principle through his conflicting reinterpretations of the evangelic words:

> The commandment which makes this a rule cannot require us to *have* this moral tenor, but only to *strive* for it. For a commandment which tells us that we ought to like to do something is contradictory, because a commandment becomes unnecessary if we already know what we are obliged to do and, moreover, are aware that we like to do it.

Everything that Kant says here about his previous contradictory elaborations concerning an "order" to "like to obey commandments" is correct. But instead of concluding that love of God and one's neighbor is therefore *not* identical with "liking to obey commandments," he seeks to correct his previous mistake with a new one, replacing "loving" in the sense of "liking to obey commandments" with a mere *striving* for love or a *willing* to love. With this, Kant recovers the only bearer of the moral good that he recognizes as "original": the will. This almost unbelievable change in meaning to which Kant has subjected these powerful words should become apparent at *first* glance. "Love God above all and your neighbor as yourself" has now become "Strive to like obeying God's commandments and fulfilling your duties to your neighbor."

Here we must reconsider in another respect the basic errors of imperativistic ethics: Only what can be commanded or prohibited is of moral value. Anything that cannot be commanded or prohibited is of no moral value, because man does (or does not do) it of his own accord, or because the acts concerned— e.g., the acts of faith and love—are such that they cannot be commanded or prohibited. These propositions are comprehensible only in light of a pragmatistic attitude which admits moral values only to the extent that man can *intervene* in the moral

---

57. It comes to us as an even greater surprise when the passages mentioned proclaim the following nonsense: To say that we should *love* our neighbor as ourselves is *not* to say that we should first love and then, by means of this love, perform acts of good-doing, but that we should do good to our neighbor and that this will effect in us love for him. In other words, good-doing is to effect love! Good-doing that is effected by vanity or by a motive to keep a useful servant is said to effect love! Kant cannot show us how to turn straw into gold. For this is the same as saying: Genuflect as much as possible, for then you will become a pious man.

world and *change* it through *orders*. But pragmatism is not the sole victim of this prejudice. Kant shares this view, and ecclesiastics often make this basic mistake, too.[58]

The concepts of good and evil are far from being dependent in any way on given norms and obligations. On the contrary, it is necessary to check to what extent the content of *any* imperative or *any* established norm of the will *ought to be in the ideal sense,* and to what extent its establishment is *justified* and *valuable.*

As to the first of these prejudices, that which has moral value is done not only according to duty but, as Kant further specifies, also *"from duty,"* i.e., in obedience to the command of duty. This theory of Kant's has often been called a *"rigorism,"* and it has been debated whether this rigorism is really present and to what extent it can be justified. Following what we have established, we can easily solve the old problem of the relation of the actions of the *"beautiful soul,"* who wills and does what ideally ought to be "by inclination" rather than "from duty," to actions "from duty," to which alone Kant attributes moral value. For we can say that this "beautiful soul" is in this respect not of equal value but of *higher value.*[59] Let it be conceded, by the way, that at least within the realm of logical fundamentals Kant did not make the error that Schiller attributes to him in his well-known distich. Kant does not imply that virtuous conduct as such is conduct *against* an inclination. For according to Kant's fundamental principles, not only can the contents of inclination and duty coincide (which is a matter of course), but the action corresponding to an inclination can also be simultaneously given as coming "from duty." Insofar as Kant's descriptions lead us to conclude that a morally good action must be one *against* inclination, this would have to be attributed more to the atmosphere and pathos of his description than to the objective sense of his propositions. One should not conclude from the fact that the peculiar cognitive certainty of man concerning his actions "from duty" becomes more sharply defined when actions are *against* inclinations, that the objective sense of the moral good is such that actions "from duty" are always against inclinations. Doubt-

58. On resentment as the source of this moral deception, see "Über Ressentiment und moralisches Werturteil."

59. That the so-called beautiful soul (with his unpleasant air of inactive romanticism, in contrast to the *belle âme*) is supposed to act in terms of "sensuous drives" because he does not act "from duty" shows the poverty of Kantian concepts which prompts the reduction of all "inclination" to "sensuous drives."

less there are scrupulous men who, in order to make sure that every possible action is done from duty, prefer to act against their inclinations rather than according to them, even if what corresponds to inclination could in fact have been done from duty. From this scrupulousness, which in itself is no moral advancement (for to be *conscious* of being good is not at all a moral value), one easily slips to something that has even less claim to moral significance. I am referring here to a certain kind of cruelty against oneself and one's inclinations which, owing to a peculiar value-illusion, is savored as something especially "good" and "noble." I do not believe that Kant can be said to be entirely free of this inclination, or that his ethical conceptions are not influenced by it to a certain degree, at least in the *pathos* of their description. Be this as it may, the reproach which those who favor the "beautiful soul" would bring upon Kant remains fully valid. For even if one holds that actions of duty and inclination can generally coexist, as is the case when one refers to someone's doing his duty "gladly and willingly," or "with joy," according to Kant such an action of a beautiful soul can be no *more* than *equal* in value to the action of a man of duty. But from a correct point of departure in ethics, namely, from values, this action is not of equal but of *higher* value. Of course, *in principle* Kant cannot admit this, because the term *good* supposedly derives its *meaning* from the concept of an ideal ought, if not from the concept of the dutiful and the "from duty," as can be seen in many passages. The good from "mere inclination" is therefore a *contradictio in adjecto*.

In addition, Kant falls victim to an error that we have discussed elsewhere.[60] He makes the moral value of an action dependent on its *cost*, on the *sacrifices* made by the one who acts. In an example of *ressentiment*-illusion from his discussion of correct moral instruction in the "Methodology" of the *Critique of Practical Reason*, he says, "Virtue is worth so much here only because it costs so much, not because it brings us something." I have elsewhere shown that it is one of the kinds of value-illusion, based on *ressentiment*, to hold that something is more valuable because its realization requires more power, labor, endeavor, etc. Anyone who believes, for example, that a treatise of his is especially valuable because he worked so hard on it, or that he loves someone because he sacrificed so much for that person, be-

---

60. On resentment as the source of the theory of costs [*Kostentheorie*], see "Über Ressentiment und moralisches Werturteil."

cause he "did" so much for him, or that a faith is true and valuable because so many men died for it as martyrs, falls victim to this form of value-confusion. Thus it is certain that values cannot be reduced to sacrifices and costs, no matter which values are in question. On the contrary, it is quite clear that sacrifices and costs—i.e., devotion to values, especially values of oneself—are valuable only to the extent that they preserve or realize evidentially higher values or, if values of the same height are in question, a greater number of values. Expended costs and sacrifices can *never* "establish" or even "confirm" that these values are "higher." Any theory of morals which denies this basic proposition, either explicitly or through its reasoning processes, is based on negativistic *ressentiment* and inauthentic sacrificial mania, if not on a pathological love of inflicting pain and cruelty on oneself. The manner in which Kant presents the example of Anne Boleyn and Henry VIII, speaking as he does of advances from "approval" to "admiration" and "veneration" when this "upright man" is increasingly threatened and tormented, cannot be said to be free of this psychological motivation. For it cannot be doubted that this man would have been just as good and upright without these increasingly severe tests of his uprightness and all that it cost him to maintain it. At most one can say that in this case the purity and uprightness of his will would not have been *revealed* to others to such a degree (perhaps not even to himself). Obviously Kant confuses this revelation of moral values with moral values themselves. If things were otherwise, if the moral value of such comportment *consisted* in suffering such tests and sacrifices, then, as Guyau has remarked, morality would disappear as societal conditions become more orderly and customs less demanding. For, to the degree that this is the case, there are fewer opportunities for men to undergo such tests. Indeed, it would be necessary to demand that there be enough mean and base men to torment others until their "virtue" is completely revealed. But when the condition of a revelation of a good moral tenor—even to oneself—is confused with the condition of a good moral tenor, it is but a secret vainglory to *pass* as morally good.

Though cost and sacrifice are not the foundation of the values that they serve, this theory of sacrifices does contain one correct point; but it does not lie in the direction in which it is most often sought. When we ask ourselves questions like "Which of two things is more valuable to me?" or "Which of two persons do I like better?" we often undertake a *thought-experiment*, asking ourselves, "Which thing would I sacrifice for the other?" or, "Which of the two persons would I rescue first if both were drowning?" In asking such questions, we begin with the presupposition of an evident state of affairs, namely, that one should sacrifice a lower value for a higher one, and that one wants to sacrifice the lower value when the higher value is completely evident. We then proceed to find out, as this consciousness of "being able to sacrifice something" appears, which of the two values is higher for us. However, this procedure does not signify that this consciousness of being-able-to-sacrifice *creates* values and *determines* their *heights*. We are concerned, rather, with a *clarification* of our own given and accepted *valuations*. One who makes the mistake (as the Stoics and Kant did) of assigning the highest value to "being able to represent oneself as good" and "being able to esteem oneself," instead of to the unreflected *being*-good,[61] must also make the *other* mistake of construing the means that one utilizes in order to come to better knowledge of his value as a constituent of this value. But precisely for this reason *both* mistakes must be avoided.

What we have just said does not appear to exhaust the significance of cost and sacrifice in terms of our value-judgments of other men. We know with certainty only that moral value and the ideal ought-to-be have nothing to do with the endeavor required for their realization. For if their contents are *given* as *well-delineated*, the morally higher *personality* is precisely the one who endeavors and sacrifices the least for the realization of the content. He who has the least withstanding against the good is the best. But it is quite a different state of affairs when we are concerned with an *imperative*, an obliging norm to be obeyed, and an obligation, and when a *plurality* of persons is given a commandment. In this case the value which is the basis of the norm is independent of that norm and of obedience to it. Furthermore, the value of obedience to the imperative is always the same, no matter how much those who obey this order have to overcome in terms of their resistance to this order. But the *actions* in which the value of obedience is realized may differ in value in that that action which overcomes more resistance is more valuable. Here valuation appears paradoxical indeed: a person is more valuable the *less* the "*execution* of obedience" to

61. Note what has been said on this point in part I. [See above, pp. 27, 120–21.—*Ed.*]

the law costs him. The value of "obedience" is always the same, but the "action" is more valuable as it "costs" *more*. This curious paradox in our value-estimations of the *outcome* of obedience is clarified when we see that such "costs" enter into the question of value-estimations only when *persons of the same moral ability* or the same "virtuousness" are presupposed. And since, as we have shown, every imperative essentially presupposes a reference to something of negative value, for an imperative has no "meaning" so long as there is an "inclination" to the action that the imperative demands, and since every justified imperative presupposes an adverse striving against the content of its ideal ought-to-be, and not against a commandment, one can see that the action in which "obedience" is performed becomes all the more valuable as greater resistance is overcome, that is, overcome solely through the *form* of the imperative in which the ought-to-be is given here. Whenever we disregard the *relation* between possible executions of obedience and already existing, rightfully presupposed imperatives and seek to determine values by looking at the moral values of the person himself without the aid of an imperative, there is necessarily no consideration of *cost* or *sacrifice,* nor can one avail himself of them.

One can speak of *"true"* sacrifice only when it serves an intention toward a value that is *given as higher,* i.e., one that is a higher value and is *given* as such independent of a will to sacrifice. In addition, the sacrificed good must be given as a good of a *positive* value. In my treatise on *ressentiment* I pointed out that it is precisely this aspect of true sacrifice which distinguishes *true* asceticism from the illusory asceticism of *ressentiment.* The latter is characterized by the fact that either before or at the moment of denial we *devalue* what we deny ourselves and then regard it as something of *no importance.* For a Christian, for instance, a *free* renunciation of possessions, marriage, and self-will for the sake of higher goods represents a morally valuable act only when such goods are positive.

For this reason J. Henry Newman has described true asceticism as "admiring the earthly while denying it to ourselves." But a person fraught with *ressentiment* does not admire the earthly at the moment of denial; on the contrary, he devalues it. He says: "All of this is nothing." "It has no value." "These are things of no importance." In reality, poverty is an evil and possession a good, and in true asceticism it is only the free act of renunciation of possessions which are presupposed as having positive value and felt as such that is a higher good; the asceticism of *ressentiment* declares poverty a good and possession an evil.[62] Renunciations stemming from *ressentiment* are made not for the sake of a higher good; it is, rather, impotence, the inability to gain possessions, which is falsely *represented* as a positive act of renunciation. Here we can also clearly see the consequences of the spurious theory of sacrifices that we discussed above.

c. Ability and Ought

We mentioned earlier that there is an ultimate, irreducible modality of conation called "to-be-able."[63] This particular *to-be-able* as an act of *experience* [Erlebnisakt], in which conative contents can be originally given in an "I can do something," differs completely from a mere consciousness *of* being able to do something. In the experience of this to-be-able, a content is *immediately* given as below our volitional powers. There have been repeated attempts to analyze this "to-be-able" in terms of a *representation* of something to be done or executed, plus the memory of our having realized this content before and an expectation of realizing the same again on a given occasion. That is, in order to know that I am "able" to do something, I must remember actions already performed or reproduce similar earlier impulses, and "to-be-able" is nothing other than the expectation that I *shall* on an occasion do again what I did before. But this intellectual analysis of the "to-be-able" is based on a completely erroneous view. It is *because* we have the *immediate* consciousness of "being able" to do something *that we expect* that we *shall* do it. But this to-be-able does not *consist* in the above operation. For this reason the to-be-able is, as a phenomenon, completely *different* from mere *existing dispositions* and "faculties" to do or to effect something. Of course there are dispositions for the emergence of an earlier consciousness of a certain to-be-able of an individual; but this *presupposes* the to-be-able as a type of striving experiencing, and this is anything but a disposition.

The autonomy and peculiarity of this to-be-able is especially manifest in the special kinds of contentment, joy, and pleasure that we take in the mere to-be-able-to-do something. But this pleasure has nothing to do with the pleasure that we might expect from the realization of what we know we are able to do. Nor is it the pleasure in doing what we can do. It is, rather, the

62. We leave undecided here whether the economic theory of costs also has its origins in resentment.
63. See above, pp. 126 ff.

pleasure in the *to-be-able* of such doing. This is apparent in cases in which we do *not* realize something, e.g., a certain gratification, and do not even strive to realize it, *because* we are aware that we *can* do so at any time. On the other hand, being conscious of *"not-being-able-to-do"* something, or the awareness of impotence (which is a thoroughly positive experience),[64] does not consist merely in knowing in advance that we lack that pleasure which comes from the realization of what we were able to do or from its execution. Striving for wealth or economic power cannot be understood if it is reduced to the memory and expectation of the factual joys and enjoyments that come from wealth, or to the enjoyment of profits and work and reproductions of the enjoyment. The mainspring is no doubt the acquisition of the consciousness of economic ability and power, the ability to rule, shape, order, and control the market, which a businessman or industrialist experiences in the presence of his possessions.[65] The contentment that comes from being "able to" is much deeper and nobler than the enjoyment of manifold realizations of what one was able to do. Nor is the consciousness of to-be-able some "copy" or "reproduction" of facts of consciousness that were conjoined with earlier actions and deeds. For we often experience a consciousness of "I can do this or that" with regard to contents that we never before have realized, in completely *new* situations, when facing the novel and unique tasks which life puts to us. On the other hand, the factual realization —indeed, the stimulation of a real disposition to such a realization, insofar as this disposition is in us and within our factual powers—often depends on the fact *that* this consciousness of to-be-able is markedly present. Educators have rightly stressed that

64. Impotence is not a striving to be able to do something which has no success. It is a quality of being-able-to-do, not the absence of it.

65. A quite different matter is *avarice*, which Theodor Lipps cites as an example of joy in ability. He says that the miser piles treasure upon treasure in order to increase his awareness of his ability to buy, enjoy, and possess, and thereby denies himself the awareness of factual possession and enjoyment. This example completely fails to lay bare true ability and true pleasure in ability. For avarice consists precisely in the attitude of taking pleasure in money *as* a mere means to anything that may provide pleasure or be "agreeable." The miser's attitude is definitely hedonistic, although perverted in that the pleasure in the agreeable (and in the goods tied up with this value) shifts to the pure means to the agreeable. He experiences satisfaction, not *in* his ability (to buy, possess, etc.), but in his being conscious of the mere presence of objective conditions of buying, possessing, etc., and in the intellectual consciousness of a present disposition to be able to buy. Avarice stems from a conjunction of lust for pleasure and the inability to acquire pleasure or the means to it.

one should concentrate on increasing the consciousness of this to-be-able in pupils, encouraging them to develop it in their own ways. A man may have many hidden abilities that are not realized because he does not have the correct *consciousness of to-be-able,* a consciousness of the power of his will. Comportment that corresponds to the description of "to-be-able" furnished by association psychology—i.e., when we doubt whether we can do something so long as we do not remember an earlier action similar to it—is in fact *pathological* comportment. The interposition of a "Can I?" before every "I will do this" is especially pathological. A person for whom the formation of a consciousness of to-be-able requires the reproduction of earlier actions suffers from a diseased form of hesitating that can take on any form, depending on the area (speaking, etc.) in which the lack of experience of to-be-able occurs. It should be emphasized that this "to-be-able," in the sense of being able to act, has nothing to do with the memory or the reproduction of complexes of organic and kinematic sensations that accompanied earlier movement of the limbs in a certain action. Nor can the absence of a consciousness of to-be-able (to will, to do) in any manner be reduced to the absence of the above.

The independence of this to-be-able is also manifest in the fact that, as a "power" seen by others, it exercises an influence which differs significantly from the mere *expectation of the execution* of the action for which the power is present; it also differs from the mere expectation of displays of force. Thus "power" and "force" are to be sharply distinguished from one another, in contrast to the current confused use of these terms. Irrespective of the situation, he who needs the *least* amount of force to impose his will on someone possesses the greatest amount of "power." The influence of the look of someone taming a lion, where the lion's force is much greater than that of the one who tames him, no doubt consists in the power of his will as it appears in the glance. No authority (e.g., state, church) is thinkable without power. But the power of an authority increases as the force required to enforce its orders decreases.

In the history of philosophy there have been a number of views concerning the relation between this to-be-able and the ought (which is construed here as the real ought, since we are concerned only with ought in the sense of "obligation").[66]

There have been many attempts to reduce the *"ought"* to a

66. [See above, pp. 210 ff.—*Ed.*]

consciousness of being able to do something, even to a "higher ability," as this appears on the average in factual actions. In an interesting chapter of *Morality without Duty and Obligation,* Guyau tried to prove that all consciousness of "obligation" is only the consciousness of being able to do those actions of *higher* value as present conations and intentions intend them. According to this view we have the peculiar consciousness of an "obligation" to do something when we become aware of an ability and a power that have not yet entered into the present interplay of our motives. At least we must perceive such an *ability* in others in order to know that we are obligated in the relevant respect. This is basically the view of most of the ancient thinkers, too. Aristotle, for example, determines the good in general as that for which a being possesses a peculiar "faculty," one belonging only to this being. He thus concludes that in the case of man, whose peculiar "faculty" in contrast to that of animals and plants is rational activity (*anima rationalis*), the good is represented in rational activity. Such a methodological procedure is based on the proposition that every ought must be reduced to an ability.[67] More recently, Spinoza held this view in a more rigid and one-sided way.[68] He traces the bad and the evil to an absence of power and freedom and says that everyone ought to do what he can do. In theology omnibenevolence is reduced to omnipotence, and the bad and the evil of this world are justified through the claim that a world which lacks them does not contain everything that is *possible,* which in turn can be created only by an *omnipotent* Being. The extent to which Spinoza knew this joy in ability as such becomes apparent in his famous saying, "Blissfulness is no reward of virtue; it is virtue itself." For no doubt this blissfulness means this particular joy as conjoined with the highest consciousness of power and freedom. From this, Spinoza also derives a significant principle for *pedagogy:* All true education must avoid weaning persons from their mistakes; it must not adopt the form of a prohibition and a "You should not do this." Rather, it should draw a pupil's attention to *new* faculties that are in him, whose activation makes the mistakes in question disappear. Hence it is not this "you shall not," but a "you can" that is the *basic form* of education. According to this theory there is little value in attempting to reform a drinker through

67. To those familiar with this theory, it goes without saying that faculties in Aristotle's philosophy are generally not dispositions or "real conditions for" but real potency.

68. [See "Spinoza: Eine Rede" (Bibliog. no. 27).—*Ed.*]

admonitions, good counsel, etc. We can accomplish the reform by encouraging him to develop new interests as well as his latent faculties, by pointing to the positive aims of life in whose pursuance a drinker's vice disappears and is, as it were, covered up. William James recently made this basic idea of Spinoza's a principle in his theory of the "education of the will."

The same view is held by no less a man than Luther, although he expresses it in religious and theological language. The presupposition of his entire opposition to the Catholic theory of justification is that man can will the *good* and can do *good*, and that he can do so by way of disposition only if he possesses the consciousness of the *power* and the *ability* for the good through his consciousness of a benevolent God, i.e., through his consciousness of being justified before God "by faith alone." To those who regard this justification as wholly or in part a consequence of obedience to divine command and "the law," Luther explicitly states, "A debere ad posse non valet consequentia." It is not only the negatively expressed content of this proposition that is his conviction; his basic theory of the relation of faith to good works and even to morality in general is in fact based on the proposition "A posse ad debere valet consequentia." Every *true* moral "ought" is for him the consequence of the consciousness of power and ability that comes from the forgiveness of sin through faith in Jesus' suffering for us and the atoning power of his blood.

Kant's opinion is in direct opposition to the above views. It is distinctly and clearly expressed in the famous proposition: "You can, for you ought!" According to section 6 of the *Critique of Practical Reason,* this proposition implies that our knowledge of the unconditional-practical comes from consciousness of the practical law, not from the experience of freedom; that is, we become more conscious of our "ability" the more we become aware of our *duty.* We are never to ask about the range of our power in order to find its limits and subsequently to determine what we ought or ought not to do. On the contrary, we must first listen to the "voice of practical reason," which obliges us categorically to act in a certain way, so that we then reach the point of *assuming* as a postulate that we can do what we ought to do. Kant undoubtedly did not mean that the consciousness of ability follows from the consciousness of duty as a simple theoretical inference. He would admit Luther's proposition that I cited above so long as this *non valet consequentia* is understood as a simple logical conclusion. For the freedom that he demonstrated in the third antinomy of the *Critique of Pure Reason,* or believed to have demonstrated, as "theoretically possible" on the basis of the division of man as a thing in itself (*homo noumenon*) and man as a phenomenon (*homo phenomenon*) is, in its *positive* sense of being "able" to do something, only the consequence of a "postulate" that is based on the categorical imperative. But even in this sense his proposition is not justified. It is, of course, a justified *pedagogical* practice to increase the consciousness of ability by giving a pupil orders and by telling him, "You must be able to do what you ought to do," "You must not even ask whether you can," etc., while denying him permission to examine his ability. But this has nothing to do with the *evidential insight* that it is nonsense to impose a command or a prohibition upon a being whose range of ability does not encompass the commanded or the prohibited. On the basis of what reason do we not expect obedience to moral laws on the part of animals, if it is not our knowledge that they are unable to realize them? Values and propositions of the ideal ought-to-be are as independent of ability and inability as commands and prohibitions are dependent (in terms of unique, essential interconnections) on ability.

We must recognize, above all, that the experience of the *ideal ought* and the experience of *ability* have their foundation in equally original, ultimate intuitions that are independent of each other. We must recognize that it is *completely* impossible to reduce one to the other.

It is as impossible to reduce the consciousness of "*duty,*" for which such an experience is in any case a presupposition, to an inward development of a higher *ability* as it is to regard ability as a mere postulatory consequence of an immediately given consciousness of duty. Kant errs in the following:

> [Our knowledge of the unconditional-practical] cannot come from freedom, for we cannot be *immediately* conscious of it, since our first concept of it is negative; nor can we infer it from experience. . . . *Therefore* it is the moral law, of which we are immediately conscious and which presents itself first, because reason represents this law as a determining factor not to be outweighed by any sensible condition and, indeed, independent of such, that leads in fact to the concept of freedom.

It is false to claim that we are less capable of a consciousness of our freedom of ability, for it is as immediate as our experience of the ought. For this reason the concept of *virtue,* i.e., the immediate consciousness of an ability to do something that is experienced as ideally obligatory, is a *meaningful* concept. If both immediate experiences did not exist—if, as Kant maintains, ability were not an immediate fact of experience, that is, if the experience of the ought were the only immediate experience and ability were only "postulated"—then "virtue" would merely be a disposition to do our duty. Virtue would not be an autonomous ethical category.[69] On the other hand, if there were no immediate ought-experience of something, but only a reproduction of an experience of ability, insofar as the *content* of the latter is present in a moment of life as a conative project and an immediate *ability* to do this content is not experienced, virtue and *aptitude* would indivisibly merge. Virtue, however, is not aptitude for anything but willing and doing something that is given and experienced as ideally obligatory.

If the *experience of the ideal ought* of a content and the experience of the ability to do of a content are *equally original* and essential facts that can be *equally* fulfilled in *intuition*, then "duty" and "norms," i.e., all *contents* that confront a person in their imperativistic character, presuppose a possible experience of ability with respect to the content that assumes the imperative form.[70]

69. Virtue and all of its qualifications are immediate facts of experience and hence, unlike dexterities, can never be reduced to habits.

70. We postpone our discussion of the interrelation of these problems with the problem of freedom. [See above, p. 203, n. 31.—Ed.]

5 / Non-Formal Value-Ethics and Eudaemonism

IN OUR INTRODUCTORY REMARKS we mentioned that it is one of Kant's basic theories that every non-formal ethics must be *eudaemonistic,* i.e., an ethics which either regards pleasure as the highest value (or the "highest good") or somehow reduces the facts and ideas of the values of good and evil to pleasure and displeasure. Therefore, according to this theory, only a formal ethics, which, as a rational ethics, eschews all references to the emotive life, can avoid those errors to which all imaginable forms of eudaemonism lead (we agree with Kant on the errors to which they lead, as we have stressed a number of times before). We have rejected this thesis of Kant because it does not reflect the facts. It is deeply rooted in his impoverished conceptions of the emotive life and the nature of values as well as the relations among values. It would make little sense to undertake an elaborate critique of these conceptions at this point, for in so doing we could not consider the more subtle theories that recent scholars have developed on this matter—theories that would also be refuted by the facts. I shall therefore attempt in the following to consider these facts only to the extent that the context demands.

Although Kant did not undertake a special study of pleasure and value, it follows from his work that, for him, the fact that a thing has a value means that man attributes a value to it in the form of a judgment. This, he holds, occurs when a thing's effects on the psychophysical organism cause a state of *pleasure* in man. We showed in the last chapter that a value and its givenness cannot be reduced to an act of judgment. According to

[239]

Kant, man strives *eo ipso* for pleasure insofar as he strives and wills—if his will is not guided by the moral law. Kant treats this proposition as if it were a law of nature; and only on this basis can he say that it makes no sense to claim that one "ought" to strive for pleasure, since everyone does so already. It appears to me that this law of nature, that man strives for pleasure and nothing else, is twofold: on the one hand, it is the *objective law* that the course of conation always has a tendency to go from a state of less pleasure to one of greater pleasure (or, from one of greater displeasure to one of less displeasure); on the other hand, it is the *law of the intention* of conation—that is, it also expresses the fact that pleasure is intended in conation. Hence, it is both an absolute and a relative law, an objective natural law and a law of the intention of all "striving for." Moreover, Kant does not draw either a factual distinction, which would be relevant to his ethics, or a value-distinction between striving for one's own and striving for someone else's pleasure. But it is clear that in his view striving for someone else's pleasure (mediated through feelings of sympathy) can be genetically reduced to striving for one's own pleasure in someone else's pleasure. This is a clear consequence of his assumption that all pleasures and displeasures as feelings—irrespective of what they are "in"—are *qualitatively* of the same kind and not different in *depth*, and that the genetic basis of pleasure and displeasure, i.e., that from which all pleasure and displeasure is derived, is *sensible* pleasure and displeasure. I have shown elsewhere that it belongs to the essence of sensible pleasure to be extended and localized on the body (in contrast to the sphere of vital feelings and pure psychic and spiritual feelings), and that one cannot enter into someone else's sensible feeling [*nicht nachfühlbar*], anticipate it feelingly [*nicht vorfühlbar*], or share it with him [*nicht mitfühlbar*] in an immediate fashion.[1] I have also shown that such feelings can be given as felt only in actuality and as one's own. There is no immediate "feeling" of these feelings in others, only a (judgmental) knowledge of someone else's sensible pleasure and displeasure and the subsequent reproduction of one's own earlier situations of a similar type and, in turn, a subsequent "reawakening" and "vague continuing" of such feelings. There is no "sensible sympathy." There is, at best, a contagion through sensible feelings. Since Kant considers all feelings relevant to ethics to be

1. See *Zur Phänomenologie und Theorie der Sympathiegefühle* (Bibliog. no. 6), p. 9. [See *Wesen und Formen der Sympathie* (Bibliog. no. 18), pt. A, chap. 2.—Ed.]

sensible feelings—with the sole exception of the feeling of respect, which he calls a spiritual feeling, "effected by the moral law"—all feelings of sympathy, under which he also subsumes love and hate,[2] are excluded as morally relevant determining grounds of willing and acting and as bearers of moral values.[3] Kant's presupposition that all feelings except "respect" are of sensible origin is the reason why he does not draw any essential distinction in terms of quality or depth between sensible pleasure, joy, happiness, and bliss. It is for this reason, also, that he finds both Aristotle's eudaemonism and Aristippus' hedonism to be not only theoretically wrong (we agree) but also equal in value as attitudes of life. Taking all of this together, one can say that on Kant's presupposition man as independent of the rational and formal moral law is an absolute egoist and an absolute sensual hedonist, and that he is this indiscriminately in all of his impulses. Of course, as Kant sees it, any *ethics* that is established through recourse to emotional *experience* [*Er-leben*] must for this reason be a *hedonism*, for *apriority* in the emotional sphere is entirely out of the question.[4]

All of these presuppositions of Kant are without foundation (as the following will show in detail), and, from a historical point of view, they are uncritical assumptions that he borrowed without scrutiny from the sensualistic psychology and ethics of the English and the French—a literature which can be understood in terms of the structure of the experience of eighteenth-century Western European man, but which has no foundation in facts.

1. *Value and Pleasure*

If one renounces this error of reducing the being of values to oughtness, norms, imperatives, and types of assessments, the curious poverty of philosophical alternatives leads one back to the theory that the *value*-being of something is some type of *"relation"* between an object and experiences of *pleasure* and *displeasure*.

A most elementary form of such a theory holds that the attri-

2. *Zur Phänomenologie und Theorie der Sympathiegefühle*, p. 45. [See *Wesen und Formen der Sympathie*, pt. B, chap. 1, sec. 2.—*Ed.*]

3. For this reason, too, commiseration, mercy, etc., are, for Kant, not emotive units of experience which can be phenomenally manifested. They are only dispositions or "natural dispositions" to certain drive-impulses and actions, which therefore cannot possess moral value.

4. See above, pp. 63 ff.

bution of value-being to an object, an action, etc., is nothing but an inadequate expression of the fact that an object evokes pleasure through its efficacy on man and his ego. In this case the "relation" is an empirical causal one, and an a priori theory of values is, of course, impossible. Since we often judge things and actions to be positively or negatively valuable when they are not at that moment causing pleasure, it is maintained that the thing in question has at least an ability, disposition, or power to give rise to such experiences. I have shown in part I that however complex this theory may be, it is untenable in the face of any phenomenological examination.[5] Let us add a few more points:

1. A value is not a "relation" that is added to other relations, e.g., "equal," "similar," "different." Values may serve as a basis for a relation, but they *are* no more relations than red and blue are. And for this reason, too, a value-experience, i.e., an experiencing of values, is not an experience of a relation. The value of a jewel and its value for me (affective value) are clearly distinguished in natural language, namely, when we distinguish the value of the thing *in itself* from the value that it has *only* for *me*.[6] It is essential to all "bartering" that the things in question have the same value objectively, and that this equality be "given" to those who barter; *but at the same time* it must be given to them that thing S (which B possesses) has a higher or greater value "for A" than "for B," and that thing S_1 (which A possesses) has a smaller value "for A" than "for B." That is, the relation of the valuable things to A or to B, which is expressed here by the term *for*, becomes a new bearer of value that is added to the bearer of the thing-value. Therefore, not only can a value function as the foundation of a relation; it can also belong to the relation itself. True, we frequently *mistake* the mere value of the relation of a thing to the feeling that we have of its value, or even the mere value of its possible usefulness to us, for the value of the thing itself. This is one of the most important sources of value-illusions. But as soon as this state of affairs is given to us, we can see this illusion as an "illusion." We then say, "This thing is good, but I don't care for it," or, in other cases, "I don't take any pleasure in it." The extent to which we can comprehend types of values, the breadth or narrowness of our ability to feel values, is itself an object of a consciousness and perhaps of the value-consciousness that we have of our special nature and

5. See above, pp. 15 ff.
6. Aristotle made this appropriate distinction in the introduction to the *Nicomachean Ethics*.

organization. It often happens that a value, e.g., the value of a work of art, comes to us in a more adequate form of givenness through another value, but only through a refeeling of the feeling of the value concerned; and we often realize through this that our ability to feel the type of value in question is very narrow indeed.

2. If values in general are to be subsumed under a category, they must be characterized as *qualities,* not as relations. Without a doubt it belongs essentially to these qualities to be given originally only in a *"feeling of something."* But this is not to say that values consist in any relation to feeling-states, either actual or "possible" ones. A value-quality is no more a feeling-state or a relation to one or merely the (unknown) X of a feeling than the quality "blue" is a visual sensation or a relation to a sensible state or an unknown X of a specific visual act. The vacillating feeling-states that are effected in us by things—whether in terms of experience, in the sense that we feel their efficacy, or in terms of objective causal effects (e.g., the anxiety that we might have from a respiratory defect of which we are unaware)—pass by our valuations and their qualitative material without any influence. True, our feeling-states may generally detract us from valuing comportment, as is occasionally the case in hypochondria and all those phenomena that we have come to call *"egotism,"* i.e., all types of conative attitudes directed toward one's own feeling-states. But even when our environment appears to be given in fact merely as a *source of excitation* for our changing feeling-states—as in cases of objective value-blindness—the parts of this environment are still phenomenally clothed with value. In this case, however, it is not the values of objects but the value-qualities of our feeling-states that illusively appear in things. It is the *locations* of the values of objects and objective value-being in general which remain given. In such locations the value-qualities of our vacillating feeling-states now appear, and they more or less completely conceal the value-qualities of the things concerned. We then believe that our "food is bad" because we feel bad; today we see a "questionable" affair in rosy light because something else has made us happy. Culpable *"egoism"* is, however, different from this. The egoist is directed, first of all, toward things and values of things, not toward his ego or feeling-states. Still, he does not live in the fullness of the values of things, human beings, or actions; nor does he, when feelingly directed toward himself, live in the values of his ego and experiences. He lives solely in the value of the experienced *relation* of

thing-values or self-values *to himself.* The egoist's point of view in selection, according to which *his* feeling singles out every possible value (without an intervening intention or judgment), becomes the value of *his* feeling or comprehending or understanding the values of things (the egoism of enjoyment); or, in the case of a more common form of "practical" egoism, it is his "needing" or "using" things because of their values. It is not the value of his moral goodness or of any aptitude of his; rather, it is the value of *his* being the bearer of the values. A typical "egoist" is not one who experiences the value of things fully in order to enjoy, possess, or use them. He is one whose full experience in this respect is obstructed by the egological concentration on his experiencing (not on what is experienced). Even the full experience of the values of his own self, indeed, especially the experience of them, is obstructed.[7] But the claim that values are given in a "feeling of something" does not imply that values exist *only* insofar as they are felt or can be felt. For it is a phenomenological fact that in feeling a value, the value is given as *distinct* from its being felt—and this is true in any *single* case of a feeling-function. For this reason the disappearance of this feeling does not cancel the being of this value. Just as we are conscious at every moment of knowing many things without knowing them in actuality at the moment, and just as we are conscious as well of many things that can be known but are conscious of our not knowing them, so also do we feel many values that we know, which belong to the world of our values, and also an infinite number of values that exist without our having felt them in the past or our feeling them in the future.[8]

3. We have already disproved in detail the nonsense that man strives "first" for *pleasure* (in the intentional sense of striving toward), and that values are capacities and powers in things which evoke pleasure (or displeasure).[9] Man strives "first" for *goods,* not for the pleasure in goods. The possible givenness of

7. In this sense Nietzsche is right: "Every man is farthest from himself."

8. This phenomenon is clearly manifest in veneration of the world. Veneration is not a feeling which merely *adds* to a given value-series without any change in the object. Rather, veneration renders to every good a dimension of *depth* in value, for in every phase of its feeling penetration of its value-qualities it "foreshadows" ever richer and higher values. Veneration yields a peculiar consciousness of the objective value-fullness and "inexhaustibility" of the object given in veneration. [See "Zur Rehabilitierung der Tugend" (Bibliog. no. 10) and "Über Scham und Schamgefühl" (Bibliog. no. 29).—*Ed.*]

9. See above, pp. 15 f., 35.

the value of the efficacy of goods follows the possible givenness of goods *themselves* and remains, of course, within the limits of given goods. Even when, on the basis of an artificial attitude, pleasure becomes the end of striving—as Aristippus, for example, advises the sage—the pleasure hovers above this striving "*as a good.*" Just as things of our environment are not given to us as stimuli of sensory perception (e.g., through an "unconscious causal inference"), so also are goods not given as causes of what we feel in them. And perception is no more a group of states of sensation (and its derivatives) than the feeling of goods is a group of states of pleasure. The series of states of pleasure and displeasure which a being can experience is in principle strictly tied to the *sphere of feeling* and to possible units of goods given in this sphere, goods *bound* together by the *value*-qualities of these units. This proposition holds for intended states of pleasure and displeasure as well as for states that are passively suffered. If we call a thinglike value (no matter if it is a good or an evil) a value-thing, we can say that all possible states of pleasure and displeasure are within the scope of the feelability of the value-qualities that occur as properties and as representatives of these value-things and their range. Let us use an earlier example. The foundation of the concept of the *nutritive value* of a substance is the phenomenological datum that is given to us in these things as the *correlate of appetite* and disgust in terms of "inviting" and "attracting," or in terms of "disgusting" and "repelling." Any objective chemicophysiological investigation and measurement of the so-called nutritive value of substances and their components (i.e., the optimum quantity of their energy that can be used to build up an organism) rests on this foundation. To *replace* the value-differentiating function of "appetite" with such investigations would be not merely ridiculous but impossible. For the very *problem* of such an investigation cannot be meaningfully posed without referring to and presupposing such emotively felt value-differentiations. Appetite and disgust are by no means drive-impulses, no matter to what extent they may be based on such impulses in their expressions. They are *value-directed functions of* (vital) *feeling.* They are therefore wholly different from hunger, which is a non-directional urging accompanied by burning and searing stresses of pain and organic sensations; hunger can neither yield a value-difference nor have an opposite ("appeasement of hunger" being only a state during the satisfaction of this drive). Appetite and disgust are also different from the impulse of the drive to eat and its opposite, the impulse to vomit, which are *consequences* of appetite and disgust. Needless to say, the variations of appetite and disgust and their degrees are independent of the variations and degrees of hunger. I can be disgusted by a meal even when I am extremely hungry, and I can have all degrees of appetite with little or no hunger. Although the impulse to eat and the impulse to resist the disgusting normally follow appetite and disgust, they can become separated from this foundation. We then speak of perversion. But appetite and disgust are never perverted in this case. We know from experience that they do not cease expressing themselves—for example, during the onset of a drive to eat something that is disgusting. What is disgusting remains "disgusting" to the perverted person, too. Both appetite and disgust, like any "feeling-of," can "deceive"; but they cannot "pervert." For they are functions of cognition, not of striving and desiring. It is clear that the sensible feeling-states produced by food as it is moved over the tongue and gums, with its good or bad taste in terms of its sweetness, bitterness, sourness, saltiness, etc., and the enjoyment of these qualities of feeling (which can be given more or less objectively or more or less as states) have nothing at all to do with the *being-valuable* of the food as it is given in appetite or disgust. Nevertheless, (1) the qualitatively different good or bad flavor that is bound up with qualities of taste and their combinations normally and *ceteris paribus* only arises within limits insofar as both appetite and disgust have already made their *pre*felt expression (concerning those feeling-states); and (2) the given qualities in question are present only within those limits because, for the organization of the being concerned and its corresponding environment, it is *these* qualities which can possess representative significance for those nutritive things contained in the common sphere of appetite and disgust. Appetite and disgust *pre*decide, as it were, which of such sensible feeling-states are to come about. And *they* immediately condition a "striving for." But in no way do they condition those feeling-states or whatever has the power and disposition to release or effect them. The givenness of value and the value-difference of the objects concerned *precede* in principle the experience of feeling-states which the objects effect and are the *foundation* of these states and their completion.

This interconnection of value, value-feeling, and feeling-states is valid for all levels of non-formal emotional areas belonging to them—up to the highest ones. Feeling-states are in principle always given as (1) *effected,* or (2) effected by things, actions, etc., which are *present* to us as bearers of values. This is the case no matter how this experienced efficacy may differ from objective and real efficacies—for example, we may "shift" a feeling-state onto something, i.e., experience it as effected by something that is in fact not its cause. But we must note an important difference. Values and goods by no means have objectively real efficacy. However, values *as* values, goods *as* goods, and not merely things, are *experientially* efficacious or motivating. They "*attract*" and "*repel.*" This does not mean, as it could easily be interpreted, that we desire or detest them only in terms of drives, or in terms of regarding this "driving" as centripetal. There is a marked difference between "I am thirsty," "I am hungry," and "I long for . . ." and the experienced attraction and repulsion that come from goods *themselves.* Attraction and repulsion are not ego-centripetal but are bound up with the lived body and belong to me in a wider sense (although they do not stem from the psychic ego). The *laws of motivation* which hold between values and goods and the powers of *attraction* and *repulsion,* and which are based on this difference, are independent of feeling-states, although they condition *them,* too. But the nature of a good does not *consist* in an attraction that is effected by a valueless thing. The beauty of a landscape or a human being and being spellbound by this beauty are clearly differentiated experiences, the former being the foundation of the latter. Beauty "is" not the experienced efficacy of a (value-free) landscape; it is its *beauty* that has an effect, whose efficacy is transformed into the changes of a feeling-state.[10]

We must mention a second attempt to reduce the phenomenon of value to a relation, namely, a relation to the feeling of pleasure or displeasure (a relation considered analogous to the relation to a plurality of desires or dispositions of them). At least the mistake of construing these "relations" as causal relations is not made here. This doctrine has been established for both an emotional theory of values and a desire theory of values. Since we have rejected the latter in principle, let us turn our attention to the former. This theory was developed principally by H. Cornelius, though it was set forth earlier and in a more articulate manner by F. Krüger. It is a copy of the positivistic conceptions

10. A phenomenology of "temptation" and of the "demand for atonement," starting with the "blood shed," would have to clarify this more precisely. Something given as evil can "tempt" us and work its charms on us, even though there is no desire for it, even though willing resists its experienced efficacy.

of the thing and its givenness.[11] This theory holds that values are neither feelings nor dispositions in things which enable things to awaken feelings. They possess a constancy (to which Krüger gives special emphasis, and rightly so) that experiences of pleasure do not have. The actual feeling (or the actual desire) that a thing (experientially) evokes stands in opposition to the axiological sign (positive or negative) that the so-called valuation of the thing assigns to it. We can take displeasure in goods and enjoy evils. But, supposedly, as soon as we consider what a value-judgment brings to fulfillment, i.e., what corresponds to the "valuation" (which plays a role analogous to that of perception), we do not find *any* what-content given in this thing itself. We cannot find it here, just as we cannot find something similar in the case of the "thing." The nature of value is constituted only by the *order in sequences* of certain experiences of pleasure (or desire) which come about under normal circumstances; this is also true in the case of the "thing," inasmuch as the thing is only the order of sensual contents that come about under normal circumstances in the various possible perceptions of the same individual or of different individuals. Whereas experiences of pleasure are, by their nature, *actual* [aktuell] and at the same time *individual,* values as the constant order of these experiences are *permanently enduring* and *interindividual* in the flux of actual experiences of pleasure. The givenness of values, however, consists not only in the fact that the thing produces actual feeling-states and desires, but also in the fact that the thing stimulates dispositions which it had formerly aroused through its effects on our feelings and desires, and in the fact that it leads us to expect experiences of pleasure (or desire) in the course of the experience during a varied examination of the thing. The nature of the *givenness* of the value is constituted by the interconnection of present subtle tensions of expectation which are based on the arousal of the dispositions mentioned.[12]

It appears to me that there are cogent reasons against this attempt, which in a deeper and more serious way seeks to reduce experiences of value to experiences of pleasure.

1. According to this theory we must have a *plurality* of ex-

---

11. [See above, p. 15, n. 3.—*Ed.*]

12. The meaning of the words *good, distinguished,* etc., is supposed to be fulfilled in these, just as according to Cornelius logical meanings of words are fulfilled in excitations of dispositions of similarity of previous perceptions, whereas the logical "meaning" itself is supposed to constitute this "area of similarity" of the objects.

periences of pleasure in the same thing in order to establish the difference between value and pleasure. But in fact we find that when a thing which was quite unknown to us evokes pleasure, we are confronted with two *distinct* facts: "agreeableness" and "the pleasure in this agreeableness." Indeed, this difference is already clearly given when we feel the pure value itself as a quality *apart from* the givenness of anything, e.g., a thing of our total environment, to which such a value could be attached. In this case it is difficult to say *which* dispositions of feeling are evoked, since the value is not given as a property of a thing or a good. For we are told that it is the arousal of the dispositions of experiences of feeling of the *same* thing that should constitute value-consciousness!

2. This analogy between value and thing does not agree with the facts, because the analogy holds only between "thing" and "*good*," i.e., a value-thing, which we earlier differentiated sharply from a thing-value and the value-quality itself.[13] Even if this theory were otherwise correct, it could only show how value-qualities become *properties* of things, not how experiences of pleasure become points of departure for the givenness of values.[14] Besides, it appears to me that one must not presuppose a thing-unit if a value is supposed to be the strict *analogue* of the thing. But this is the presupposition if the dispositions of feeling to be aroused are determined as those which the "*same thing*" aroused earlier. But *neither* a good *nor* the thinglike unity of value-phenomena is, in fact, dependent on the thing. Nor are they founded in a thing. If, however, a thinglike unity is not presupposed, that is, if there is only a "constant order in the sequences of sensible contents," as this theory maintains, it becomes necessary to ask the following question: The dispositions of *which* of the previous experiences of pleasure, or the arousal of *which* of these dispositions, are to bring to givenness the supposed *given and specific* value? There are many such experiences of feelings and their dispositions, and it appears to me that no guided and vague arousal of such a great number can ever give us the specific and *well-delineated* qualities of values which we in fact feel—which we even feel as *different* from each other when we abstract from their representative functions in different goods and kinds of goods and bring the pure whatness of these values to givenness.

3. At first glance this theory appears to have a great advan-

13. [See chap. 1, sec. 1.—*Ed.*]
14. See above, p. 15.

tage in that it enables us to explain the attribution of a positive value to, e.g., things that we do not actually desire and do not regard in terms of actual reactions of pleasure. But we encounter a great difficulty if we recall the indubitable fact that actual experiences of feelings can directly *conflict* with the contents of our concurrent value-consciousness. This is the case when we say: "True, this work of art is valuable, but I do not take any delight in looking at it; I do not like it"; or, "True, this man is very able and virtuous, but I cannot suffer him," etc. Statements like the above are entirely *different* in sense from: "True, this thing is very valuable, but I cannot take any pleasure in it *at this moment* (i.e., in my present state); I am *at this moment* not in a position to enjoy it," etc. In such cases one can say that the reproduced feelings "prevail" over the actual feeling. But when such positive experiences of feelings *cannot* be shown to exist, and when we bring to expression a *continuing* affair-complex of feelings in regard to a thing so that this complex conflicts with our value-consciousness, this is not the case. And doubtless there are such cases. Indeed, they are the origin of new feelings. We can be sad, for example, because a beautiful thing leaves us cold, because it hardly moves us, or because a special kind of evil continually attracts us. Precisely because there are synthetic relations of exaction between affair-complexes of values and reactions of feeling (e.g., a value-complex *A* "that a friend arrived" "exacts" a "rejoicing"; a *B* "exacts" sadness) whose absence is the source of negative feeling-states (we are sad because we cannot rejoice when that is demanded, etc.), it is apparent that there is no necessary relation between the *factual* sequence of our experiences of feelings on the one hand and our value-consciousness on the other. This theory also fails in that we can be quite conscious not only of our momentary failure to desire or enjoy something, but also of our not being "able" to enjoy something, even though it can have positive value in feeling.

4. Even more decisive is the fact that our experiences of pleasure and displeasure *themselves* have value. Not only is there a joy in the base and a displeasure in the noble; there is also a base joy and a noble sadness, etc. Our experiences of feeling are bearers of values of certain kinds. But according to the above theory it would be impossible to say that there are not only value-experiences but also *values of experiences*. In addition, the value-consciousness of a thing or a man would have to disappear to the extent that we bring earlier experiences of feeling and

those expected (which are supposedly constituted only in the "dispositional excitation" of this consciousness) to givenness, i.e., to *explicit* remembrance and expectation. But if they are exhausted in the constitution of value-consciousness, they cannot then be given in consciousness (along with their attached values) without obliterating value-consciousness. Moreover, the value-consciousness of a thing and the specific value-consciousness of *that* value which "for us" consists in our expecting the thing in various degrees of expectation-tension (be it because this thing is near or far, or because this thing is important or unimportant "to us") remain *clearly distinguished* in their givenness. They do *not* mix, though according to this theory one would have to assume that they do.

5. Assuming for the moment that this theory is correct, what *ethical consequences* follow from it? It is of great interest to compare this theory with the classical hedonism of Aristippus. He does not reduce value to pleasure. On the contrary, for him pleasure is the highest of values, the *summum bonum*. But according to this theory (and for this reason it must be called "ascetic"), pleasure is never a value.[15] Still, it is supposed to make values possible, to ground them. But here a positive value *is* merely a symbol for possible experiences of pleasure; it is a "check" for them, a "note" that is not "covered" by pleasure, and ultimately it is reduced to nothing. Nevertheless, ethics must rule that this "check," this "note" for pleasure, is to be preferred to pleasure *itself!* I must admit that this appears paradoxical to me. If pleasure itself is not a positive value, how can the check for it possibly be a positive value? How can a mere mechanism that postpones pleasure have a positive value, or how can this postponement itself *be* a positive value, if what one postpones has no positive value? I can well understand that *if* pleasure is a positive value, one should postpone it so that the greatest possible pleasure ensues. But I do not understand how the postponement of something, whether this occurs automatically or arbitrarily, can represent a value if the postponed thing itself has no value. If this theory in fact describes an automatism in human nature, I can find it correct for the philosopher to say only this: "An inherent automatism has the tendency to make you believe, in the course of your mental development, that the mere *postponement* of pleasure is a value and something to

15. For Felix Krüger, the highest value is "valuing."

strive for; it leads you to view a symbol, or a check that is not and cannot be covered,[16] as something solid. Wake up! Fight this deceiving automatism which cheats you out of every present moment and makes you continually reach for nothing." Surely Aristippus would have said this, and I think he would have been right. This theory clearly betrays the tendency of a specifically *modern* type of experience whose nature I have described elsewhere.[17] It is the tendency of a blind *work*-conation which is ultimately based on a quite earthly and hedonistic valuation of things *and* on an ascetic displacement of pleasure—a tendency that undoubtedly constitutes one of the driving forces of complicated modern civilization. Ethics (as well as psychology) has *no* reason to justify this in an ethical theory. As a genealogy of morals, ethics must trace this type of experience and its causes back to certain concrete *historical* origins; it must show —and I think that it can be done—that this type originated in a stratum of people who "progressed" toward a pseudoascetic contempt for the enjoyment of pleasure, which their work originally served to augment. This stratum of people, with a deep-seated *ressentiment* against an advanced civilization of luxuries, a civilization that was stripped of higher values as it developed, and from which these people, because of their natural disposition, felt excluded, took up this civilization's modes of valuating (by contagion), and their working activities were originally directed toward meeting the requirements of this civilization.[18] We refrain here from going into this question into detail.[19]

Thus, whatever "relation" one would establish between pleasure and object, it is never possible to derive the fact that *there are values* from such a relation. All such attempts encounter value-facts as *primordial phenomena* that do not admit of any further explanation. For this reason Kant's assertion that every non-formal ethics is a "eudaemonism" is fundamentally false.

---

16. For pleasure itself is *not* a value, and hence it is immoral to strive after it.

17. See "Über Ressentiment und moralisches Werturteil" (Bibliog. no. 5), p. 348. [See "Das Ressentiment im Aufbau der Moralen" (Bibliog. no. 10), sec. 5, 3 a.—*Ed.*]

18. Werner Sombart furnishes much information in support of our theory in *Luxus und Kapitalismus* (1913), especially in his chapter on the origins of large cities.

19. I have rejected the empathic theory of values elsewhere. See *Zur Phänomenologie und Theorie der Sympathiegefühle*, p. 5, app., and "Über Selbsttäuschungen" (Bibliog. no. 4), p. 127. [See *Wesen und Formen der Sympathie*, pt. C, chap. 3; pt. A, chap. 2 (beginning). See "Die Idole der Selbsterkenntnis" (Bibliog. no. 10), sec. 4.—*Ed.*]

Indeed, one must say the opposite, that *only* a *non-formal ethics* is in a position to come up with the *decisive* argument against every form of eudaemonism. For feeling-states of all kinds neither are nor condition values; they can at best be *bearers* of values. The practical hedonist, who in practice seeks his pleasure in things or goods, in people, and in his own or others' actions (and who is to be distinguished from the "egoist" in the afore-mentioned sense), can only strive for pleasure *as* the bearer of a value or, more precisely, as the object of his enjoyment. Con-sidered ethically, he may be wrong; this, in fact, is our opinion. But his error does not lie in his attributing a positive value to pleasure; it lies, rather, in his putting this value in the wrong rank in the order of values. In particular, he does not see that all values of feeling-states are *eo ipso* subordinated to values of the person, of acts, of virtues, and of functions, and that the being and non-being, as well as the quality and depth, of values of feeling-states ultimately vary in a fashion that is dependent on them.[20] The happiness of a man is of as much positive value as the *person* who is happy. Indeed, a practical hedonist does not see that there is but *one* safe means to *by-pass* the positive value lying in pleasurable states themselves, one safe means *not* to realize it: namely, to *intend* it and to strive for it. And this is the tragic phenomenon implicit in his attitude. Not only does he cheat himself out of the *higher* values that he sacrifices for pleasure; but he also cheats himself out of the positive values in pleasure *itself!*

It is now more important than ever for us to see how values as primordial phenomena are given.

2. *Feeling and Feeling-States*

Until recent times philosophy was inclined to a prejudice that has its historical origin in antiquity. This prejudice con-sists in upholding the division between "reason" and "sensibility," which is completely inadequate in terms of the structure of the spiritual. This division demands that we assign everything that is not rational—that is not order, law, and the like—to sensibil-ity. Thus our *whole emotional life*—and, for most modern philosophers, our conative life as well, even love and hate—must be assigned to "sensibility." According to this division, *everything* in the mind which is alogical, e.g., intuition, feeling,

20. See chap. 5, secs. 8–10.

striving, loving, hating, is dependent on man's *psychophysical organization*. The formation of the alogical becomes here a function of real changes in organization during the evolution of life and history, and dependent on the peculiarities of the environment and all their effects. Whether there are original as well as essential differentiations in rank among the essences of acts and functions at the base of the alogical of our spiritual life, that is, whether these acts and functions have an "originality" comparable to that of the acts in which we comprehend objects in pure logic—in other words, whether there is also a *pure intuiting and feeling, a pure loving and hating, a pure striving and willing,* which are *as* independent of the psychophysical organization of man as pure thought, and which at the same time possess their own original laws that cannot be reduced to laws of empirical psychic life—this question is not even asked by those who share this prejudice. Since no one asks this question, no one asks whether or not there are a priori interconnections and oppositions among the objects and qualities to which those alogical acts are directed, or whether or not there is an a priori lawfulness of these acts which corresponds to such interconnections and oppositions.

The consequence of this prejudice is that ethics has in the course of its history been constituted either as absolute and a priori, and therefore rational, or as relative, empirical, and emotional. That ethics can and must be both absolute *and* emotional has rarely even been considered.

Very few thinkers have tried to undermine this prejudice (and then nothing more than that, for none has managed to elaborate an opposing viewpoint). Two such thinkers are Augustine and Blaise Pascal.[21] Throughout Pascal's works we find an idea which he calls *ordre du coeur* or *logique du coeur;* it runs through them like a golden thread. He says, "Le coeur a ses raisons." To him this means that there is an eternal and absolute lawfulness of feeling, loving, and hating which is as absolute as that of pure logic, but which is not reducible to intellectual lawfulness. Pascal uses a sublime vocabulary when he speaks of those men who have partaken intuitively in this order, expressing it in their lives and teaching. He speaks of their small number as compared with the geniuses of scientific knowledge, and he believes that the rank of these men is to the

21. With regard to Augustine, see A. von Harnack, *Dogmengeschichte* (Freiburg: Mohr, 1898), and J. Mausbach, *Die Ethik des hl. Augustinus.*

rank of geniuses as the rank of geniuses is to that of average men. For Pascal, the person who most perfectly comprehended and lived this *ordre du coeur* was Jesus Christ.

It is strange to see how these remarks of Pascal have been misunderstood by so many of his interpreters! One of them thinks he means that "the heart, too, has its say when reason has spoken"! This is a well-known opinion, and it is held by philosophers, too. We are told, for example, that "philosophy's task is to furnish both reason and the heart with a satisfactory world view." That is, the word *reasons* (*raisons*) is taken somewhat ironically. Supposedly Pascal does not mean to say that the heart *has* reasons or that there is anything which is *truly equivalent* to "reasons" in its rank and meaning, i.e., "*ses*" *raisons,* or its *own* reasons not borrowed from understanding; rather he means that one must not always seek "reasons" or their "equivalents," but must occasionally let the "heart" speak—blind feeling! But this is the exact *opposite* of what Pascal means. The stress of his proposition is on *ses raisons* and *ses* raisons. That there is a complaisance of the conscientiousness of thinking with regard to so-called needs of the heart, or that the so-called world view is "complemented" by assumptions which feelings and "postulates" suggest—even "postulates of reason"—when reason cannot provide an answer: surely Pascal's proposition does not imply any of this! On the contrary, there is a type of experiencing whose "objects" are completely inaccessible to reason; reason is as blind to them as ears and hearing are blind to colors. It is a kind of experience that leads us to *genuinely* objective objects and the eternal order among them, i.e., to *values* and the order of ranks among them. And the order and laws contained in this experience are as exact and evident as those of logic and mathematics; that is, there are evident interconnections and oppositions among values and value-attitudes and among the acts of preferring, etc., which are built on them, and on the basis of these a genuine grounding of moral decisions and laws for such decisions is both possible and necessary.[22]

We shall take up Pascal's idea at this point.

First, we must distinguish between the intentional *"feeling of something"* and mere *feeling-states*. This distinction in itself does not yet bear on the content given in intentional feelings, i.e., when we regard them as organs for comprehending values.

22. [See "Ordo Amoris" (Bibliog. no. 29). See also above, chap. 2.—*Ed.*]

There is original emotive intentionality. Perhaps this is most apparent when both a feeling and feeling it occur simultaneously, when a feeling is that toward which feeling is directed. Let us consider a feeling-state that is indubitably sensible, e.g., a sensible pain or state of pleasure, or a state that corresponds to the agreeableness of a food, a scent, or a gentle touch, etc. Given such facts, such feeling-states, the kind and mode of feeling them is by no means yet determined. There are changing facts involved when I "suffer," "endure," "tolerate," or even "enjoy" "pain." What varies here in the functional quality of *feeling* it (which can also vary by degrees) is certainly not the *state of pain*. Nor is this variation to be found in general attention, with its levels of "noticing," "heeding," "noting," "observing," and "viewing." Pain observed is almost the opposite of pain suffered. In addition, all these kinds and levels of attention and interpretive viewings may freely vary to any extent within such qualities of feeling without any dissolution of the feeling itself. The limits of the feelable variations of the givenness of pain are quite different from those of a feeling-state in its relation to excitation and different also from the degrees of such a state. For this reason the ability to suffer or to enjoy has nothing to do with sensitivity to sensible pleasure and pain. An individual can suffer the same degree of pain more or less than another individual.

Hence feeling-states and feeling are totally different. The former belong to contents and appearances; the latter, to the functions of reception. This becomes clear when we heed the differences that are obviously present.

All specifically sensible feelings are, by their nature, states. They may be "connected" with objects through the simple contents of sensing, representing, or perceiving; or they may be more or less "objectless." Whenever there is such a connection, it is always *mediate*. The subsequent acts of relating which follow the givenness of a feeling connect feelings with objects. This is the case, for instance, when I ask myself: "Why am I in this or that mood today?" "What is it that *causes* my sadness or joy?" Indeed, the causal object and the feeling-state can enter perception or memory in terms of quite different acts. I relate the object and the feeling-state in such cases through "thinking." The feeling itself is not *originally* related to an object, e.g., when I "feel the beauty of snow-covered mountains in the light of the setting sun." In some cases a feeling is connected with an object through association or through a perception or representation of it. Surely there are feeling-states which at first appear to be without any relation to an object. I must then find the cause that produces the state. But in none of these cases is a feeling related *of itself* to an object. It does not "take" anything, nor is there anything that "moves" toward it, nor is there anything in it that "approaches me." There is no "signifying" in it, nor is there any immanent directedness in it. Finally, a feeling can, after it has frequently occurred in my lived body in connection with outer objects, situations, or changing experiences, become a *"token"* of these changes. This is the case, for example, when I recognize the beginning of an illness by the presence of specific pains because I have learned that these are connected with the onset of such an illness. In this case also, a symbolic relation is mediated only through experience and thinking.

However, the connection between *intentional feeling* and *what* is therein felt is entirely different from the above connection. This connection is present in all feeling *of* values.[23] There is here an original relatedness, a directedness of feeling toward something objective, namely, *values*. This kind of feeling is not a dead state or a factual state of affairs that can enter into associative connections or be related to them; nor is such feeling a "token." This feeling is a goal-determined movement, although it is by no means an *activity* issuing forth from a center (nor is

---

23. Hence we distinguish: (1) The feeling of feelings in the sense of feeling-states and their modes, e.g., suffering, enjoying. I wish to add that apart from vacillations in the modes of an identical feeling-state, the feeling of the feeling-state itself can approximate a zero point. Very strong affectations of fright (e.g., on the occasion of an earthquake) often produce a virtually complete absence of feeling. (Jaspers' *Allgemeine Psychopathologie* [Berlin: Springer, 1913], which I just received, gives some good descriptions of this.) In these cases sensitivity remains intact, and there is no reason to assume that the feeling-states are not *present*. What occurs in extreme cases is a marked increase in the *intensity* of the feeling; there is complete fulfillment by it, which makes us for a moment "feelingless" with respect to this feeling. We are put into a state of rigid and convulsive "indifference" toward it. In this case it is only when the feeling goes away, or when our complete fulfillment by it begins to disappear, that the feeling becomes an object of feeling proper. The rigid indifference begins to "dissolve," and we feel the feeling. In this sense the feeling of a feeling-state "relieves" and takes away the state of pressure. I have pointed out elsewhere that in a similar way true cofeeling with the suffering of another *frees* us from infection by this suffering. [See *Wesen und Formen der Sympathie*, pt. A, chap. 2, sec. 3 (toward the end).—*Ed.*] (2) The feeling of objective emotional characteristics of the atmosphere (restfulness of a river, serenity of the skies, sadness of a landscape), in which there are emotionally qualitative characteristics that can also be given as qualities of feeling, but never as "feelings," i.e., as experienced in relatedness to an ego. (3) The feeling of *values*, e.g., agreeable, beautiful, good. It is *here* that feeling gains a cognitive function in addition to its intentional nature, whereas it does not do so in the first two cases.

it a temporally extended movement). It is a punctual movement, whether objectively directed from the ego or coming toward the ego as a movement in which something *is* given to me and in which it comes to "appearance." This feeling therefore has the same relation to its value-correlate as "representing" has to its "object," namely, an intentional relation. It is not *externally brought together* with an object, whether immediately or through a representation (which can be related to a feeling either mechanically and fortuitously or by mere thinking). On the contrary, feeling *originally* intends its *own* kind of objects, namely, "*values*." Feeling is therefore a meaningful occurrence that is capable of "fulfillment" and "non-fulfillment." [24] Consider an affect in contrast to this. An affect of anger "wells up within me" and then "takes its course in me." The connection of anger with the "about" of my anger is not intentional or original. A representation or a thought or, better, the objects in these that I first "perceived," "represented," or "thought" are what "cause my anger." And it is later—even though in normal cases very quickly—that I relate this anger to these objects, and then always through a representation. Surely I do not "comprehend" anything in this anger. Certain *evils* must be "comprehended" beforehand in *feeling* if anger is to be aroused. It is quite different when I "rejoice in something," or when I "am sad about something" or "enthusiastic about something," or when I "am merry" or "despondent." The use of the words *in* and *about* shows that in this rejoicing and sadness the objects "about" which I am glad, etc., are not first of all comprehended. They already stand *before* me in that they are not only perceived but also charged with the value-predicates which are given *in* feeling. The value-qualities in value-affair-complexes *demand* certain qualities in emotional "reactions of response" of the same type, and these reactions in a certain sense "reach their goal" in the value-qualities. They form complexes of understanding and meaning, complexes of their own kind which are not simply empirically contingent or dependent on the individual psychic causality of individuals.[25] If value-

24. For this reason all "feeling of" is in principle "understandable," whereas pure feeling-states are subject only to observation and causal explanation.

25. These interconnections of meaning between value-complexes and emotional reactions constitute the *presupposition* of *all* empirical understanding (including social and historical understanding) and enter into the understanding of other men and our own empirical experiences. They are therefore *laws of the understanding* of the psychic life of others that must be added to the "laws of the universal grammar of expression" in

demands appear to remain unfulfilled, we suffer as a result, e.g., we are sad because we cannot be happy about an event to the degree that its felt value deserves, or we cannot be as sad as the death of a beloved person "demands." Such peculiar "manners of conduct" (we do not call them acts or functions) have "direction" in common with intentional feeling; but they are *not* intentional in the strict sense of this term, if we understand *intentional* to indicate only those experiences that can *mean* an object and in whose execution an objective content can *appear*. This occurs only in emotional experiences, which, in a strict sense, constitute value-feeling. For here we do not feel "about something"; we immediately feel *something*, i.e., a specific value-quality. In this case, i.e., *in* the execution of feeling, we are not objectively conscious of feeling itself. Only a value-quality comes "upon" us from within or without. A new act of reflection is required if this "feeling of" is to become objective, thus enabling us to reflect subsequently on *what* we "feel" in the already objectively given value.

Let us call these feelings that receive values the class of *intentional functions of feeling*. It is not necessary for these functions to be connected with the objective sphere through the mediation of so-called objectifying acts of representation, judgment, etc. Such mediation is necessary *only* for feeling-states, *not* for genuine intentional feeling. During the process of intentional feeling, the world of objects "comes to the fore" by itself, but only in terms of its *value*-aspect. The frequent lack of pictorial objects in intentional feeling shows that feeling is originally an "objectifying act" that does not require the mediation of representation. Indeed, if we were to undertake an analysis of the formation of natural perception and natural world views, of the formation of the general laws of the development of units of meaning in the language of children, of the differences in the structuration of meanings in the principal language groups, and of the development of shifts in meaning of words and their syntactical structuration in positive languages (which is not our task here), we would see that *units of feeling* and *units of values* play a guiding and fundamental role in the world views expressed in these languages. Of course one overlooks these facts—indeed, even the task of setting them forth—if he assigns the entire

order to make understanding possible (see *Zur Phänomenologie und Theorie der Sympathiegefühle,* p. 7). [See *Wesen und Formen der Sympathie,* pt. A, chap. 2.—*Ed.*]

sphere of feeling to psychology *originaliter;* and then he can never see that part of *the world and the value-content of world* which *comes forth in* feeling, *in* preferring, *in* loving and *hating.* He sees only what we find in inner perception, i.e., in "representational" comportment, *if* we feel, *if* we prefer, *if* we love and hate, *if* we enjoy a work of art, *if* we pray to God.

It is necessary to distinguish emotional functions from the experiences that are based on *"preferring"* and *"placing after."* The latter constitute a *higher* stage in our emotional and intentional life, and *in* them we comprehend the ranks of values, their being higher and lower. "Preferring" and "placing after" are not conative activities like, say, "choosing," which is based on acts of preferring. Nor is preferring (or placing after) a purely feeling comportment. It constitutes a special class of emotional act-experiences. The proof is that we can "choose," strictly speaking, only between actions, whereas we can "prefer" one good to another, good weather to bad, one food to another, etc. Moreover, this "preferring" occurs immediately on the basis of the felt value-material and independent of its thing-bearers. It does not presuppose pictorial goal-contents or contents of purposes, whereas choosing does. On the contrary, the contents of goals in conation—contents that are not contents of purposes, which, as we saw, presuppose a reflection on preceding contents of goals and belong only to willing within conation—are *formed* with the cocondition of preferring.[26] Therefore, preferring belongs to the sphere of *value-cognition, not* to the sphere of striving. This class of experiences, experiences of preferring, is in the strict sense intentional; these experiences are "directed" and sense-giving, but we classify them with loving and hating as *"emotional acts,"* in contrast to intentional functions of feeling.

Finally, *loving* and *hating* constitute the highest level of our intentional emotive life. Here we are farthest from all states. The difference between them and reactive responses is marked even in language: we speak not of loving or hating "about something" or "in something," but of loving or hating *something.* The fact that we frequently hear people assert that love and hate, like anger, rage, and spite, belong to the "affects," or that love and hate belong to feeling-states, can be explained only by the peculiar lack of learning in our age and the complete lack of phenomenological investigations of these matters. There is also the opinion that love and hate are preferring and placing

26. [See chap. 1, sec. 3.—*Ed.*]

after. This is not so. For preferring always presupposes a *plurality* of felt values in intention. This is not the case with love and hate, in which even a *single* value can be given. I have discussed elsewhere how love and hate are to be characterized, and how they relate to feeling and preferring on the one hand and to striving and its modes on the other.[27] Here I simply want to reject the theory that love and hate are "reactive responses" to the different heights of felt values that are given in preferring. We call love and hate *spontaneous* acts, in contrast to reactive responses (e.g., revenge). In love and hate our spirit does much more than "respond" to already felt and perhaps preferred values. Love and hate are acts in which the value-realm accessible to the feeling of a being (the value-realm with which preferring is also connected) is either *extended* or *narrowed* (and this, of course, independent of the present world of *goods*, i.e., real valuable things, which are not presupposed in the plurality, fullness, and differentiation of felt values). In speaking of this "extension" or "narrowing" of the value-realm given to a being, I do not mean to imply in the least that values are created, made, or destroyed by love and hate. Values cannot be created or destroyed. They exist independent of the organization of all beings endowed with spirit. I do not mean to say that the nature of the act of love is such that it is directed in a "responding" fashion to a value *after* that value is felt or preferred; I mean, rather, that, strictly speaking, this act plays the *disclosing* role in our value-comprehensions, and that it is only this act which does so. This act is, as it were, a movement in whose execution ever *new* and *higher* values flash out, i.e., values that were wholly unknown to the being concerned. Thus this act does not *follow* value-feeling and preferring, but is ahead of them as a *pioneer* and a guide. And we must therefore attribute a *"creative"* role to this act to the extent that the range and nature of feelable and preferable values of a being, but not the existing values themselves, are concerned. Hence *all* of ethics would reach its completion in the discovery of the laws of love and hate, which, in regard to the degree of their absoluteness, apriority, and originality, go beyond the laws of preferring and those obtaining among their corresponding value-qualities.[28]

Let us return to the discussion of intentional feeling. Allow

---

27. See *Zur Phänomenologie und Theorie der Sympathiegefühle.*
28. As to the concepts of the absolute and the relative a priori, see "Phänomenologie und Erkenntnistheorie" (Bibliog. no. 29).

me one historical observation. In my opinion there have been two major periods in the history of philosophy in which erroneous theories have been set forth on this point—though erroneous in very different ways.[29] The first of these periods continued up to the nineteenth century. We find that the theory of intentional feeling was widely held until then. Spinoza, Descartes, and Leibniz shared this theory, though with modifications. None of these thinkers or their disciples identified the whole of the emotional life in its kind of givenness with, if I may use the expression, a pain in the stomach. If this is done, values of course cannot be found. It is likely that there never would have been any astronomy if the sun, the moon, and the stars that appear in the night skies had been regarded as statelike "complexes of sensations," i.e., as phenomena which are on the *same* level of givenness as a pain in the stomach, and which are "dependent" on the appearance of a pain in the stomach in different ways only to the extent that they differ from each other. Only in an age in which the confusion of hearts, the *désordre du coeur*, has reached the degree that it has in our own could the totality of our emotive life be considered a process of causally moved states which follow each other without meaning or ends, and only in such an age could our emotive life be denied "meaning" and intentional "contents." The error of these great thinkers was their assumption that feeling, loving, hating, etc., are nothing ultimate and original in spirit, and that values, on the other hand, are not ultimate and irreducible phenomena. Like Leibniz, they held that intentional feeling is simply "dark" and "confused" conceiving and thinking; the object of such confused and dark thought is constituted in evident and rational relations. According to Leibniz, for example, maternal love is a confused conception of the fact that it is good to love one's child. "Good" and "evil" are reduced to *degrees of perfection of being*. These thinkers also interpreted intuitive qualities, e.g., colors and sounds, in an analogous way. To the philosophers of that age these qualities are—metaphysically— effects of things on a so-called soul, which, on the basis of completely incomprehensible "faculties" (truly "occult" qualities), represents these contents when certain movements occur and then ("falsely") projects them. This theory, especially in the case

29. I wish only to touch on these matters. Dietrich von Hildebrand has treated in detail the historical development of the theory of feeling and value in his "Die Idee der sittlichen Handlung," *Jahrbuch für Philosophie und phänomenologische Forschung*, Vol. III.

of Locke, is only a subsequent metaphysical construction. Epistemologically, these qualities are, according to these thinkers, a "confused" and "dark" (unclear) knowledge of those movements themselves. There is not only a causal relation but also a cognitive relation between quality and movement. In the other principal area of philosophic problems, namely, the *question of values*, there was the corresponding attempt to resolve values somehow into mere "degrees of being"; and the concept of "perfection" proved to be the means. For Spinoza, the "best" world is the one in which there is a maximum of being. He says that God necessarily permits evil and mischief *because* a world *without* them would be less "perfect" and would not contain "*everything* possible." Leibniz criticizes Spinoza on this point, but he does not reduce perfection to a fundamental and accepted idea of a *value*. He reduces it to the concept of *being*. Hence "God's" necessities of being are our emotional necessities of values (just as God's *vérités de raison* are our *vérités de fait*). Assuredly God has not let "everything possible" come into being, as Spinoza asserts; God has *chosen* what, in addition to its "possibility in itself," is also "compossible" with other possible things. For Leibniz, it is not only possibility but also compossibility that is the condition of being. But when Leibniz says that God created "the best of all possible worlds" (i.e., the most perfect) according to a *principe du meilleur,* he gives us the following explanation: the most perfect world among possible worlds is the one in which there is a "*maximum of things compossible.*" Hence the reduction of values to being is achieved again, although by a number of detours.

This theory corresponds *exactly* to a theory of feeling in which feeling is nothing but a confused cognition in the sense of rational knowledge.

At the beginning of the nineteenth century (after Tetens and Kant) the *irreducibility* of the emotional life was gradually recognized.[30] But since the intellectualistic attitude of the eighteenth century was maintained, *everything* emotional was degraded to *states.*

If we compare these two basic conceptions with what we said earlier, we can see that each contains something correct as well as something incorrect. The first contains the correct insight that there is an *intentional* "feeling of," and that there are, in addition

30. See the passages in Hildebrand, "Die Idee der sittlichen Handlung," which cite early writings of Kant in which one can find traces of a doctrine of intentional feeling.

to feeling-states, emotional functions and acts in which something is given and which underlie autonomous laws of meaning and understanding. What is erroneous here (as in the case of the sensation of the qualities of sounds and colors) is the assumption that feeling can be reduced to "understanding," and that there is only a difference in degree between feeling and understanding. In the second theory the assumption that emotive being and life cannot be "reduced" to "understanding" is correct, but the implicit denial of intentional feeling and the abandonment of the entire emotional life to a descriptive psychology and its causal explanations is wrong. It hardly needs to be said that the concession of some modern psychologists that feelings (e.g., of different kinds of pain, of fatigue, appetite, fear, etc.) possess a *purposeful* character for life's activity and its guidance, and that these function as *signs* of certain present or future states to be further enhanced or avoided, has nothing to do with their *intentional* nature or their cognitive functions. Nothing is "given" in a mere signal. The modes of the feeling of life must therefore be reinvestigated on the basis of our basic thesis.[31] And in this it will be shown that mere emotional states are, strictly speaking, only sensible feelings, but that vital feelings and pure psychic and spiritual feelings *can* always exhibit an intentional character, and that the purely spiritual ones exhibit it essentially. It will also be shown that the functions of feeling-states as "signs of something" (e.g., the various kinds of pain) are always mediated by a true intentional feeling, and that they do not rest on a mere associative connection, which supposedly is the only objectively purposeful one. Inasmuch as a conspicuous intentional character can be attributed only to spiritual, psychic, and vital feelings, precisely the same mistake accounts for the misunderstanding of these feelings. And hence they were treated for the most part as analogues of sensible feelings, whose nature as feeling-states is apparent. For example, the fact that the refined interplay between spiritual feelings of self-value and their numerous modes enables us to see the value of our person was completely misunderstood. Likewise, the entire sphere of *value- and feeling-illusions*, which, according to this theory, resolve themselves into mere deficient phenomena or perversions, or which are confused with mere errors, was entirely overlooked.

31. I assigned this task to myself in *Beiträge zum Sinn und den Sinngesetzen des emotionalen Lebens*, pt. I, "Das Schamgefühl." [See above, p. xxiii, n. 5.—Ed.] See also *Zur Phänomenologie und Theorie der Sympathiegefühle*.

3. The Meaning of the Thesis of the "Relativity" and "Subjectivity" of Values

Thus far our analysis has shown that values are irreducible, basic phenomena of emotive intuition. Nevertheless, we are confronted with the thesis of the *relativity* and *subjectivity* of all values, especially moral values, a thesis that has strong support from philosophers in almost all parts of the modern world. Therefore we must dwell on this thesis, on its meaning and supposed justification, as well as on the psychic and historical causes of its presentation.[32]

What do those who speak of the subjectivity of values mean by that? The proposition in question may mean that it *belongs* to all values by essential necessity to be given through a special kind of "consciousness of something," namely, "feeling." In this sense the proposition is correct. Our point of departure is the ultimate principle of phenomenology: namely, that there is an interconnection between the essence of an object and the essence of intentional experiencing.[33] This essential interconnection can be grasped in any random case of such experience. This does not imply (as Kant says it does) that the laws of objects must "conform" to the laws of acts which comprehend objects, and that these laws of the comprehension of objects are also laws of objects which are comprehended. In this sense the interconnection would be unilateral. Moreover, we do not accept an absolute ontologism, i.e., the theory that there can be objects which are, according to their nature, beyond comprehension by any consciousness. Any assertion of the existence of a class of objects requires, on the basis of this essential interconnection, a description of the kind of experience involved. In other words, according to their essence, values must be able to appear in a feeling-consciousness.

The above does not imply, however, that values are "appearances in consciousness" if by this it is understood that they appear only in inner intuition. According to what we said elsewhere, this second concept of consciousness presupposes the first.[34] A fortiori

---

32. [The words *and "Subjectivity"* have been added to the title of this section in accordance with its content. See chap. 5, secs. 5, 7, where the author discusses the difference between the "subjectivity" and the "relativity" of values, which was touched upon before.—*Ed.*]

33. [See above, pp. 71 ff.—*Ed.*]

34. [See "Über Selbsttäuschungen" ("Idole"), sec. 2.—*Ed.*]

it does not imply that values belong to "intuition of the self," be it inner or outer intuition of the self; that is, it does not imply that in order to comprehend values of the other (psychic or physical ones), one must first feel them in himself [an ihm]. In history and the affairs of life we continually comprehend values which are *not* and never were given in us [an uns]. For example, whenever one historical epoch reads its values into the value-complexes of an earlier epoch, we have a basic form of historical illusion. Thus we understand the values of, say, the psychic activity of another which are not comprehended through a consideration of our own psychic being. We are able to do this because we neither infer nor empathize with the alter psychic, but perceive it in the phenomena of expression.[35]

I have also rejected the claim that the being of values presupposes a "subject" or an "ego," be this a so-called transcendental ego or a "consciousness in general," etc.[36] The ego is, in *every* possible sense of this term, always an *object* of intentional experiencing and hence of a "consciousness of" in the first sense. The ego is given *only* in inner intuition [Anschauung] and is only a certain *form* of the multiplicity of phenomena that appear in the direction of inner intuition. Insofar as the being of values is concerned, it does not matter whether an ego "has" or "experiences" values. The "ego" (or, in the formal sense, egoness in general) is an object of value-consciousness. It is not an essentially necessary point of origin of value-consciousness. With this we also reject all theories which hold that values can be reduced to a "transcendental ought," or an inwardly felt necessity, and that moral values can be reduced to what "conscience" tells us. The being of values no more presupposes an ego than does the existence of objects (e.g., numbers) or nature as a whole. In *this* sense the theory of the subjectivity of values must also be rejected.

This rejection applies equally to any theory that restricts values, according to their essence, to *man*, his "psychic" (anthropologism *and* psychologism) or psychophysical (anthropologism) organization, i.e., any theory that seeks to posit the being of values *as relative to* these. This is complete nonsense; animals, too, feel values (certainly the values of the agreeable and the disagreeable, the useful and the harmful, etc.). Values *exist in*

35. I tried to prove this in the appendix to *Zur Phänomenologie und Theorie der Sympathiegefühle*. [See *Wesen und Formen der Sympathie*, pt. C, chap. 3.—Ed.]

36. [See chap. 6, A, secs. 1–2; see also above, p. 77.—Ed.]

all nature apart from the comprehension of values. In this area, too, we must not take natural *science,* which deliberately seeks to *disregard* values and is itself guided by a selection of elements of outer intuition that is founded in the *value* of possible control over nature, as our point of departure. Aesthetic values of nature, for instance, are not borderline cases of works of art (as Hegel thought they were), as if the beauty of a sunset were only a "picture" not yet painted but nevertheless conceived *as* a "work of art." It will perhaps be objected that there are many factual realities in nature which are value-*indifferent.* And one could say that in this sense value is relative to what is useful to man. But the question is, Is this because indifferent things have no value at all, or is it because we cannot *feel* their values? Let us recall the immense differences among the wide range of value-qualities that individuals, peoples, races, and ages possess, as well as the enormous possibilities of refinement that man has in this regard! Malayans in Sumatra, for example, have only one word for agreeable or pleasant and one for disagreeable or unpleasant. We cannot conclude simply from this lack of words that there is a lack of a value-consciousness, nor can we do this with respect to the names of colors.[37] But it may be inferred from the comportment of these people that they feel far fewer value-qualities than we do.

But where can we find a criterion of the difference between the values that are "relative" to us in their *being* and those that are relative to us only in their *feelability,* insofar as only one being of values is at all certain? The capacity for the development of value-feeling is unlimited for both historical man and the individual; man as a species, too, is a transitional link in the development of universal life. In developing his feeling, he *advances into* the full range of present values.

For example, the wretchedness of the world of values belonging to the great masses of our culture and times does not rest on a general human subjectivity of values. It rests on other grounds, which determine in part man's natural view of the world in general and in part the common views of men of our civilization.[38]

The man of the natural standpoint customarily becomes aware of feelable values only insofar as they are *signs* for *comportment* that is guided by his bodily drives and needs. It is this

37. See A. Marty's interesting work, *Die Frage nach der geschichtlichen Entwicklung des Farbensinnes* (Vienna: C. Gerolds Sohn, 1879).
38. See "Über Selbsttäuschungen," pp. 140 ff. [See "Idole," sec. 4.—*Ed.*]

possible "symbolic function" that feelable values have for the changing satisfactions of his needs and interests, and not the being of values, that prevents a *clear awareness* of values.[39] The less we take active possession of our spiritual person, the more values are given as mere signs for goods that are important in terms of our bodily needs. The more we live "in our stomachs," as the apostle says, the *poorer* in values the world becomes, and the more values that are still given become present to us only within the confines of their possible symbolic functions for vital and sensuously "important" goods. And it is in *this* factor alone, and not in values themselves, that a subjective element in the givenness of values can be found. Moreover, for *societal* man, values exceed the borders of his instinctive attention only when their possible *bearers* are so limited and rare that they demand work and labor for their realization (a factor also connected with the degrees of their divisibility), or when the goods of those values are not only "possessed" in general but also possessed by one man *more* than another "by comparison." [40] Thus absolute progress in the standard of life of a social class in history is not noticed as an increase in its amount of goods; only the difference between this class and other classes is noticed. It is not what one has but what one does *not* have (when everyone has equal political and legal prospects for the kinds of goods in question) that comes to our attention. The same is true for the value-consciousness of the inventions and goods of civilization which are "thankfully" accepted and feelingly stressed as values in the transition from the old to the new, but which are otherwise used thanklessly —almost like air or space. The fact that *value-differences* are "first" given as values, that even mere *symbolic differences* for

39. The manifold beauty of subhuman nature, the aesthetic values of the physical appearance of many kinds of animals (designs, feathers, scales, etc.), as well as the values of their singing, are of course at the *service* of propagation and courtship because they are *signs* of the biological values of these animals. But it would be complete nonsense to derive from sexual exigencies not only the selection, preservation, inheritability, and fixation of these values, but also these very qualities themselves. Even if one *could* conceive of the origin of the bearers of these values in the addition of the smallest factors, one could not do so in the case of the *values*. In addition, the curious *coincidence* of what we as men find to be "pretty" and what entices a female animal (despite the *immense* differences between the organizations involved) shows the objectivity of these values. See Oliver Lodge's valuable elaborations in his *Leben und Materie* (Berlin, 1908).

40. On the "ambitious" person, i.e., the one whose consciousness of self-value is *constituted* only in the comparison of himself with others, who thinks "nothing" of himself as long as he is not "more" than someone else, see below [p. 353, n. 140.—Ed.]

value-differences are first given *as* values (e.g., an exaggerated esteem for names and titles, etc.), constitutes the *subjective* factor of *our* value-consciousness (the human, "all too human" in our comportment) that increasingly impoverishes the comprehension of factual values and goods. But values are not for this reason "subjective." It is only because this attitude corresponds to an *extraordinary* degree to the predominant structure of the value-experience of the man of the *capitalistic system of competition* (just as the mechanistic conception of being corresponds to the predominant structure of the experience of being) that those people in its bond, i.e., those not able to objectify it *merely* as *one* historical experiential structure among others, made this competitive system into a metaphysics of values and consequently declared values *in general* to be "subjective." Here the experienced structure of values represents the cumulative *guilt* of historical men, not a "natural law" of the mind or the human mind. The principles according to which the series of vital values and the values of utility (which are relative [*daseinsrelativ*], in contrast to spiritual and holy values) are distinguished from social and economic values are not conditions of our, or even *the*, value-consciousness alone, but conditions of *values themselves*.[41]

Who does not see that there is *another*, quite different direction in which values can be given to man, provided he can hold his spirit above the fog of the perspective of interest of his own "time"? We turn to the inner *content itself* of this direction by gradually freeing ourselves from the symbolic values of certain things for our actions and for other already existing goods, and by freeing ourselves also from the value-symbols of goods and parts of goods; and we arrange our actions and productions of goods according to the *purely* felt *realm of values* of this direction (instead of having our value-comprehensions restricted and structured by *their* existing directions). Moreover, in this direction, because the principle of *solidarity* would gradually outweigh the individualistic principle of competition and envy, goods become all the more esteemed the less they are capable of being "possessed" (and the more they are indivisible in essence). And among the goods that can be possessed, those will become most esteemed which are most valuable in terms of their *vital* significance, no matter what their quantity, e.g., air, water, and, in a certain sense, earth; and they are more esteemed in larger quanti-

41. [On "relativity" and "divisibility" of values as measures of their height, see chap. 2, B, sec. 3.—*Ed.*]

ties, because the feeling of pleasure in these values of goods, or the joy in them, can be complemented by the feeling of the value of shared pleasure and shared joy. In this direction, too, the value of a person which surpasses my own value would be given *in itself;* and *values themselves,* and their increases (and decreases), not only the mere differences among them, would be given. Finally, in this direction all value-feeling and its culture, as led and guided by the tenet that there *are* still *infinitely* more values than anyone has ever felt or grasped, would continue to unfold with ever more seriousness, accuracy, and determinateness. And this process would be accompanied by an increasing awareness that it is only the *overcoming* of the experienceable structure of natural man and its one-sided structure in our age that can give us *access* to existing, objective values, that can break the walls barring us from them so that the light of day, as it were—or, as Fechner appropriately put it, the day's view—can reach the feeling eyes of our spirits.

For the person, the world of values *opens up* the more he and his comportment are of value. The devout soul always gives silent thanks for space, light, and air, and for the existence of his own arms, limbs, and breath; and everything that is "value-indifferent" to others is populated with values and disvalues. The Franciscan saying, "Omnia habemus nil possidentes," expresses the *direction* toward such a liberation of value-feeling from the aforementioned subjective limitations.

4. The Relativity of Values to Man

We must therefore expressly reject every so-called human ethics. This is what Kant rightly did, by the way, in showing that the moral law is valid for "rational persons" in general and for man only insofar as he is the bearer of reason. *"Mankind"* as a real species is *one* object among others in which we comprehend values and whose values we assess. It is *not* in any form a "necessary subject" of such value-comprehending, as if good and bad were only what is contained as an emotive direction in human "species-consciousness." Nor is it a "principle" of moral value-estimations so that good and bad are merely what furthers or obstructs a "developmental tendency" in mankind as a real species. The modern theory of evolution, which portrays mankind as a result of a developmental process of life on earth, and which places man (with the totality of his psychophysical dispositions), as a result of nature that is affected by all the accidents of earthly environment, within the framework of all of nature, has made *impossible* once and for all the idea that "men" as "men" are special and unique psychic or physical natural agents.[42] This idea is basic not to practical but to theoretical philosophy, and it is basic to Kant's theory (e.g., he considers the forms of intuition, space, and time, as valid only for "man"). Mankind is, like any race, people, or individual, changeable in principle, and its psychophysical constitution is a product of the universal development of life. How could mankind contain a *"source"* or a *"principle"* of moral valuation? Mankind possesses a positive moral value only insofar as it consists of *good* men. A man who lets himself be moved by a "human-species-consciousness," i.e., one who is obedient to herd instincts, is by no means "good." For "mankind" could change quite arbitrarily for the worse without being *able* to notice the accompanying changes in its species-consciousness—insofar as this consciousness is the source of moral values. Just as a measuring rod that shrinks with its object always gives the same measurement, so also would the measure of a species-consciousness adjust so that no matter what the factual corruption of "mankind," the estimation would remain the same.

Nevertheless, we do find the peculiar *essence* of moral values through *feeling;* and feeling is found *with* [am] man, as are all laws pertaining to acts of value-feeling, preferring, loving, hating, etc. But we do not find these in a way that differs in principle from the way in which we find propositions and laws of arithmetic, mechanics, physics, and chemistry. These, as well as propositions valid for all life, are found "with" man. Thus we also find the essence and idea of the "person" with man (and, above all, with men of a certain kind). In all such cases man qua man is the locus and the occasion, as it were, of the occurrence of feelable values, acts, and act-laws, which are by themselves totally *independent* of the special *kind* of organization involved and its existence. One can also prove the law of falling bodies "with" man when a man falls freely through space.

For this reason it makes no difference in terms of the evidence and objective validity of our value-comprehension (e.g., the acts that can be determined as belonging to moral *insight*) whether *all* members of a particular species in fact possess such acts, or whether there are also races and peoples that do *not*

42. [Compare this section with the author's "Die Stellung des Menschen im Kosmos" (Bibliog. no. 23).—*Ed.*]

have such specific insights, as some ethnologists assert.[43] Nor does it matter at *which* level of historical life-development such acts appear. The main point is that *wherever and insofar as they exist,* these acts and their objects obey laws that are as independent of inductive experience as are the propositions concerning the geometry of colors and sounds. Indeed, our present-day knowledge of the probable origin of "mankind" (in the natural sense) seems to indicate that moral qualities and acts do *not* correspond to any "universal human" disposition. To my way of thinking, our positive knowledge of this origin fails to indicate that mankind constitutes a racial unity *in the sense* that all races go back to one and the same animal level. It is more likely that the various races can be traced back to different kinds of animal organisms that are the common predecessors of both mankind *and* the primates. Even if the "polyphyletic" hypothesis of human origin were valid, what would correspond in reality to the concept *"man"* would not be a real, uniform species (which would presuppose consanguinity), but a general object that would break up into a *plurality* of racial units as soon as its real correlate was thought. Hence it is not only possible but probable that there are *kinds of acts* and corresponding *kinds of values* within certain races that we do *not* find in the rest of humanity. But this does *not* bear on the objectivity of these phenomena and the essential necessities of their interconnections. If this holds for values and the acts in which they are comprehended, it holds a fortiori, of course, for the networks of *norms* that guide actions. For all *"norms"* presuppose the ability to realize what is commanded in them. Despite his denial of this proposition in the well-known "You can, for you ought," Kant does not claim that the moral law in its "universal validity" can be extended to animals. But it is not necessary for different races to be equally able to realize the contents of the ideal ought, even when they are able to comprehend and intuit the same values and their interconnections. It is precisely the objective, *non*-formal ethics that does *not* preclude differences among norms in different races.

It is therefore also possible that certain moral value-qualities will be comprehended for the first time in history, and that they will appear first, for example, in the feeling insight of a *single individual.* The evidential comprehension of such a quality and the fact that it represents a value higher than those known up to

---

43. See the remarks by Carl Stumpf in his speech, "Vom ethischen Skeptizismus" (1908).

this point have, for this reason, nothing to do with the universality and the magnitude of the dissemination of this comprehensibility or with the so-called *"universal validity"* of norms.

But it is necessary to distinguish three things: first, the factual *universal possession of dispositions* to *comprehend* certain values; second, what is morally valid for a given group of people or what is morally *"universally accepted,"* no matter if all the members of this group possess the ability to comprehend the universally valid values or not; third, those values whose recognition is universally "valid," no matter if they are factually "universally valid" or not. In this sense "universally valid" is by nature based on an ideal ought, in contrast to the two other kinds of universality, whereas "universally accepted" merely implies the opinion of the ideal ought that factually governs the universal *judgment.* But in this "universally valid" we find a reference to universally disseminated dispositions and propensities for *being able to comprehend* this ought. We do not mean to say that for a norm to be universally valid, there must be propensities for the *realization* of the ought in a group of men "for" which or for whose members the recognition of certain values is universally valid. Insofar as Kant denies *this* point, one must agree with him. Nevertheless, there must be propensities for the consciousness of being able to comprehend the contents of the ought in question. In this sense it must be within the "power" of the beings concerned to comprehend the ought as such. It makes no sense here to say that the value of humility or forgiveness is "universally valid" for animals, too. And in this sense it may very well be that values and contents of the ought accessible to certain people are not "universally valid" for all mankind. Although the universally valid in the strict sense presupposes the evidential truth of the relevant proposition, this does not suffice to make a proposition "universally valid" without a reference to its comprehensibility.

Kant's application of the concept of the universally valid in morals appears to be twofold. First, the moral law as a *law* is universally valid for all rational beings. Second, the universality of a maxim appears in the *content* of the moral law insofar as that willing is "good" which is universally valid when generalized in a maxim, i.e., that willing which can be a principle of general legislation. None of these Kantian applications of the concept can be supported; for although the moral law is "universally valid for all rational beings," Kant unwittingly presupposes that all "men" *are* "rational beings," and he therefore concludes that the moral law is in fact valid for all men. This is quite obvious when he says (with eighteenth-century pathos) that "one must respect the humanity in every man," that "man" must never be merely a means but always at the same time an end (a proposition that can claim validity only for the rational person). Although Kant carefully avoids restricting the validity of the moral law to man, the form of his pathos, more than the reasons that he gives, manifests this "humanistic" idea, which in no way corresponds to our positive ethnological, historical, and evolutionary knowledge of man.[44] Still less can one support the second application of the concept of the universally valid (as the following will show with more accuracy). It is quite possible for *one* individual to have full evidence of the content of an ought which refers only to *him* and which is valid only in this particular "case." And it is quite possible for this individual, who is completely aware of this content, to know at the same time that this content is *not* appropriate as a principle for *universal legislation,* that it is neither "universal" with regard to similar situations or "cases" nor "universal" with regard to all men, and that it is evident *only* to this particular individual and *only* in the case in question. In all of this the insight into the objective nature of the ought does not become "subjective," but remains in principle quite objective. We will later reject as completely erroneous Kant's attempt to make the universalizability of a maxim a *criterion* for the moral *justification* of its content and even for its "being-good." [45]

It must be considered most fortunate that within the problematic of the philosophical ethics of our times the very question of treating values as relative to man, especially the concept of moral value, i.e., so-called human ethics, is more or less *precluded.* The present problematic, we are glad to say, faces the following alternative: (1) Moral values and moral laws can be reduced to values which are in their feelability *relative to life* and represent in the objective sense constructs of *life-values,* or the norms belonging to them can be reduced to general laws of life, e.g., adaptation and the hereditary transmission of the useful, i.e., laws that are valid for man, not *as* man, but as a *living* being (laws that are of course conditioned in their *application* by the special organization of man and his environment). (2) *Within* mankind, at some level of being and development, there appears an *entirely new, essential kind* of values and acts by which man

---

44. See the pertinent remarks in Max Steiner, *Die Lehre Darwins in ihren letzten Folgen* (Berlin, 1908), pp. 142 ff.
    45. [See esp. chap. 6, B, sec. 2.—*Ed.*]

begins to partake in a realm which is to be called extrahuman and divine in its positive sense, and which bears within itself qualities and interconnections that are *independent* of and *beyond* all values and interconnections to be found *within* the general vital realm. The first opinion is held by Spencer, Fouillée, Guyau, Nietzsche, certain racial ethicists, and some others. In their opinion one must construe ethical values and laws merely as *special cases of life-values and laws of life,* namely, those which are set off from the rest of life-values by the specifically human organization. In other words, at least this much has become clear in the present-day problematic: moral values are either *less* or *more* than merely "human"; in any case they cannot be something specifically human. In this one can perhaps see the *greatest* change in the foundation of the ideas in ethics since the time of humanism. In that epoch there was no theory of evolution that encompassed man, nor was there any precise knowledge of the immense *inequalities* among human races or any ethnography or science of history built on the insight into such differences. "Man" was something firm and stable. The concept of man was, in a way, involuntarily idealized, and a real species was subsumed under this ideal concept as a correlate, which today seems possible only on the basis of insufficient knowledge of the facts. This resulted in the pathos of the "universally human," "humanity," the "truly human," etc., which since Nietzsche has been opposed more and more by the merely human and the "all too human."

5. *The Relativity of Values to Life*

The thesis of the relativity and subjectivity of values must be taken much more seriously if it is interpreted to mean that all value-being (including moral values) is relative to *life,* and that a pure mind, i.e., one that does not function within a possible organization of life, has no values at all, or if it is maintained that the being of values is *necessarily* tied to a specific sphere of *vital* feeling and striving. This thesis is held by Kant with respect to all *non-formal* values. According to him, good and evil are not *values;* they are verbal designations that supposedly refer to the conformity and opposition of willing to law. But this, too, is erroneous. If values were relative to life, it would be impossible to attribute a specific value to life *itself.* Life in this case would be a value-indifferent fact. But this cannot be. Life is an object of valuation not only as this or that living being (insofar as beings incorporate more or less life) but also as an *essence*. Indeed, it is an evident proposition (Malebranche has referred to it as such) that the living has *ceteris paribus* a higher value than the inanimate and therefore, quite independent of human cognition, demands *different* comportment than the inanimate does. This pertains to all objects in which the phenomena of life appear, even to the most primitive plants and animals. It is very surprising to see, for example, that H. Spencer would reduce the value of life to the degree to which a system is able to preserve itself, as if a chemical atom were of more value than a living being! [46] But the life-value is in fact an ultimate, undeniable value-quality, just as life itself is an irreducible, primordial phenomenon.

It is also clear that if life (in whatever sense) were the source of our mind, of our intuition, loving, hating, value-feeling, and their laws and forms, this "life" would be something entirely different from that life which we intuitively encounter in the natural view of the world and in scientific and philosophical biology (and thus it would be an equivocation to call both by the same name), or it would have to be taken as a completely transcendent and indeterminable *X*, because this "life," which is still given in our experience, has already passed through laws and forms of precisely *that* mind which is to be made comprehensible *through* this life. Just as that understanding or perception whose contents and laws are in this sense relative to life, say, a result of drives and exigencies, etc., could never *know* life *as an object,* so also feeling and preferring, loving and hating, as relative to life, could not *value* life itself. Such a mind could neither prefer life to death nor sacrifice it for something higher than itself. For this reason the thesis that values and value-being are relative to life in general cannot be maintained. Even if we regard "vital values" as a special and uniquely characterized modality, or as values for which the facts and appearances of life function as bearers, it remains true that values in general (and their value-being) exist [*bestehen*], and that they are *not* conditioned by any reactions of factual living beings. Nevertheless, it may very well be that a class of such existing values "belongs" in peculiar fashion to life (in terms of an essential interconnection). This can come about in two ways: on the one hand because things of the essence of life are their *necessary* bearers, and on the other be-

46. See Paul Hensel's pertinent remarks in his *Hauptprobleme der Ethik* (Leipzig, 1913), lecture 3.

cause such values can be given in the specific form of the *feeling of life*, i.e., vital feeling.

The fact that there is this irreducible *kind* of value which is essentially tied to the essence of life was stressed earlier.[47] It is of greatest importance for all of ethics to see its originality and not to confuse it with the "useful" or "values of mind." In particular, it is impossible to reduce vital values to the *useful*.[48]

Let us pay tribute to two French scholars who saw this and its significance for ethics: the philosophers Fouillée and Guyau.[49] All ethics of the seventeenth and eighteenth centuries, including the ethics of Kant and Spencer, was dominated by this false conception of life that developed in the wake of Cartesianism. This conception of life and its corresponding psychology were based on an application of basic concepts and principles of mechanics, especially the *principles of preservation,* to the phenomena of life. There were attempts to reduce all kinds of sympathy, for example—through any number of mediations—to egoism, and all appearances of growth, unfolding, and development to mere epiphenomena of processes of preservation in the smallest units of life, which, in turn, by their socializations in certain organic units, were supposed to provide an image of "growth," "unfolding," and "development." We cannot show here how deeply these ideas have influenced even our basic conceptions of cellular and developmental theories, for example. In any case, the ethical errors involved appear upon closer examination to be merely *special* errors resulting from a false conception of life. It is to the credit of the above-mentioned scholars that such errors have been left behind, at least in *ethics*. Fouillée and Guyau also correctly saw that there is an entire *system of values* and corresponding moral norms which come from the nature and essence of *life itself* and do not require any reference to values *higher* than vital values or values of the mind and corresponding acts or even the divine. The relations of the unity of life, the feeling of life, and the tendency of all life to sensible feelings and impulses institute, in fact, an order of ranks as well as a conscious-

47. See above, p. 106.
48. See "Über Ressentiment und moralisches Werturteil," p. 351. [See "Das Ressentiment im Aufbau der Moralen," sec. 5, 3.—*Ed.*]

49. See Alfred Fouillée, *L'Evolutionnisme des idées-forces* (Paris: Alcan, 1906); J. M. Guyau, *Esquisse d'une morale sans obligation* (Paris: Alcan, 1898). [Compare the remarks in this section pertaining to Spencer's moral theory, and the evaluation of vitalistic ethics (Guyau, Fouillée, Nietzsche) in section 4, with the author's "Ethik" (Bibliog. no. 8).—*Ed.*]

ness of oughtness, obligation, and certain norms, the constitution and derivation of which require no reference to specific acts of the *mind,* their laws, and their form of existence—the personality. Vital values are values of the series noble-base, of power, well-being, etc., which we emphasized earlier. But as soon as these scholars considered life-values to be the *highest* values, and as soon as they thought any ethics assuming values higher than life-values to be wrong, they, too, fell victim to error. These scholars surpassed Nietzsche, who shared with them the vitalistic principle in ethics, with their deep insight into the fact that love, sympathy, devotion, and striving for sacrifice essentially belong to life as much as does the tendency to growth, development, and power. Without doubt Nietzsche was well beyond the error that life is primarily a "preservation of existence," but he did make a mistake in assuming that life is exclusively *self*-preservation and, in his opinion, *self-growth.* At *this* point he incorporated all the errors of a false and one-sided biology and psychology like those maintained in the *specific* Darwinian formulation of the principle of the "*struggle for existence.*" But whereas the earlier moralists and biologists (as I have shown elsewhere) did not surrender the positive value-estimation of feelings of *sympathy* and love (e.g., Spencer and Darwin), even though they reduced them to a mechanism of self-deception and illusion,[50] Nietzsche, for his part, drew the *conclusion* that is fully *justified* on the basis of *his* false presupposition, which he shared with them—namely, that all feelings of sympathy and all morals of love and sympathy based on feelings of sympathy and the still-acknowledged value-estimations of the morality are consequences of declining life. As a matter of fact, the correct conception of life as a tendency to "power" does not preclude the possibility that participation in and sympathy with other life-processes also belong to the *original* tendencies of life. From this very union comes the idea of a *unified power-striving* of living beings and the idea of mutual support in the acquisition of power; and this has as a consequence the highest possible efficacy of this tendency to power.

Let us return to the question of "*egoism.*" Even the most simple facts of the experience of life show that "egoism" is not an original vital tendency from which the feelings of sympathy could have developed through the *mediation* of the idea and feeling of a growing solidarity of interests, such that these feel-

---

50. See *Zur Phänomenologie und Theorie der Sympathiegefühle.* [See *Wesen und Formen der Sympathie,* pt. A, chap. 8.—Ed.]

ings of sympathy supervene genetically upon an original egoism; on the contrary, they show that egoism is based on a *loss,* on a *removal* of the *feelings of sympathy* that belong *originally* and naturally to all life.

It is well known that the theory which would derive feelings of sympathy from an original tendency toward self-preservation in all living beings has taken many different forms. Starting with the quite naïve opinion that all one's valuings and doings are based on the calculation of one's own advantages, some tried to attribute this "development" of sympathetic feelings to an egoism that is ever more indirect and less and less guided by conscious deliberations. John Mill, who maintained that everyone at birth has only the simple tendency to preserve his existence, tried to show that the association of another's states of pain and their expressions with one's own similarly experienced injuries leads, little by little, to a striving for the diminution of the other's pain, even when this pain is not connected with one's own: when the primary link in the chain of associations (one's own injuries and pains) is missing, a striving to diminish the other's pain is supposed to occur, even though this pain is not connected with one's own experience. Spencer goes even further: he admits that there exists in the individual an innate disposition to fellow-feeling; but he locates the automatic process through which (according to Mill) sympathy is developed in the history of the ancestors of the being in question. But all these attempts assume the same basically false principle in its *entirety.* Moreover, Spencer turns human history more or less upside down when he reads the state of "society," *in concreto* the trait that characterizes modern society, namely, the predominance of individual egoism, into the original "communal formations," whose essence is characterized by precisely that principle which I have elsewhere called the principle of solidarity.[51] The experience of life shows that it is first certain experiences—e.g., *disappointment* in an original trust, the experience of illness which directs all attention to one's own body, etc.—and the simultaneous *rationalization* of certain vital experiences that lead to the phenomenon of "egoism." This also holds for historical epochs: communities become diseased or senile to the degree that egoism becomes their ruling principle. I should like to stress that what I have said concurs *exactly* with correct and objective biological observations. The tendency

---

51. See "Über Ressentiment und moralisches Werturteil," p. 359. [See "Das Ressentiment im Aufbau der Moralen," sec. 5, 3, b, 1.—*Ed.*]

toward preservation in a *species* becomes all the stronger and all the more dominant in comparison with the tendency toward preservation in the individual when there are no *special* conditions of adaptation prescribing actions to preserve and increase a certain *fullness of total life* through longer individual life spans rather than through shorter life spans with increased propagation. The ages of species, as well as the relation between life spans and reproductive tendencies, whatever it may be, are represented as appearances of adaptation. For this reason the preservation of a species is by no means a sum of the successful preservations of individual existences; it is based in principle on a *primary tendency* in living beings that precedes the preservation of individuals. The drive of reproduction and propagation *precedes* the drive of preservation; and only to the degree that the drive of propagation meets certain obstructions is an increased drive of preservation formed in individuals. In an objective sense the organic bearer of the energies of propagation does not appear as a part of the individual (e.g., the germ cell as *one* cell among many of which the organism is composed); rather, the organic individual appears as "part" of the bearer of the energies of propagation inasmuch as the individual is already predetermined by the part. This principle—which in Weismann's theory of the continuity of the germ plasma is expressed in only one of its possible formulations and by no means coincides with this theory—remains valid, no matter what one thinks about the heritability of those characteristics which an individual *acquires* during his lifetime. For the *ability* to acquire is itself a capacity restricted to certain kinds of animals.

What is true of the relations between the drive of self-preservation and the drive of sacrifice, between egoism and sympathy, and between individual- and species-preservation within a specific species remains true even when we consider the interrelations among species, among higher units of life, or, indeed, among larger organic realms. Every theory that seeks to derive all organic progress from a so-called *struggle for existence* merely represents another formulation of that incorrect conception according to which life is a "tendency toward self-preservation" in individual organisms. In examining the historical development of this theory, one finds that it is characteristically based on a transfer of concepts derived from human civilization to the extrahuman world and, when applied to man, on a transfer of concepts derived from a modern, Western European, industrial civilization to earlier forms of humanity. Haunted on the one hand by a vision of the poverty of the masses and the accompanying struggle of the workers for higher wages and more food in an industrialized England, and prepared on the other hand by his Calvinistic dogmatism to regard nature as "poor" and "needy," as too small for the powers of vital drives, an orthodox preacher came up with the idea of man's necessarily competitive struggle for food and other well-known theories connected with this, which are expressed in Malthus' laws of population. Darwin extended this idea to all organic life. The very genesis of this idea can lead one to suspect that the theory of the struggle for existence as a necessary condition of progress in life is nothing but a mere *projection* of specific historical conditions of man onto the whole of organic nature. Darwin, who concentrated on this struggle as the struggle of men around him, as well as the struggle of man with plants and animals, never consciously and clearly posed the problem of the *proportion,* in all organic nature, of the tendency toward mutual *solidarity* and support, dedication and sacrifice, to the *principle of struggle* founded on the egoism of the preservation of existence. One cannot say, as is so often said, that *both* factors (i.e., struggle and support, competition and solidarity) occur in nature, and that they do so in mixtures, precluding any determination of which is the stronger, the more dominant, and the more characteristic. The problem is to determine which of the two tendencies is the *foundation* of the other. A priori there are two possibilities. It could be that the principle of struggle is predominant to the extent that the criteria enabling us to establish a classification and systematic of living beings are profound and fundamental, and that the principle of mutual support is predominant when the criteria enabling us to establish such a systematic are secondary and derived—and it could be vice versa. Even before asking which of the two possibilities is true, we can decide in which special case of the two we can speak of the "predominance" of one principle over the other. The question is resolved, it seems to me, because we can say that the principle of struggle is the image of the fundamental aspect of organic nature only when this struggle increases with the depth and importance of the criteria for this classification, and that the principle of support and solidarity appears to be realized only when such criteria for a system are more derived. If these presuppositions, which I regard as undeniable, are taken into account in this factual question, I believe that the fundamental aspect of nature will take on traits different from those that Darwin depicted. The more *penetrating* the criteria for the division become, the more significant the principle of solidarity becomes in comparison with that of struggle. And thus we can say that the total aspect of life is *inner solidarity and unity, but outward struggle and discord.* If we begin with the most marked differences among the living beings that we know, i.e., between plants and animals, the struggle is in this case totally *sub-ordinated* to the principle of solidarity. The different forms of nutrition for each realm preclude struggle, or at least make it quite secondary in importance. The vegetal forms of nutrition condition those of animals. If one thinks further along these lines, it becomes apparent that the principle of struggle gains significance only to the degree that the beings and units entering into this struggle (e.g., forms of adaptation and varieties of a species, species among each other, or individuals within a certain form of adaptation and variety) are already encompassed by a *higher unit* of a basic criterion of classification which, in relation to a unit of the same order or more of such units, is in the *predominant* relation of mutual support and solidarity.

A second observation can be made in support of this. I pointed out earlier that Spencer in particular made the fundamental mistake of taking *man's milieu* and *its* corresponding forms of thinking as the object of adaptation that is basic to *all* species.[52] Hence his whole theory of evolution is *one* huge anthropologism. He proceeded as if *all* life were faced with the task of *adapting* to man's milieu; and he failed to see that on the basis of the *same world-givenness* (as a correlate of pure reason and pure intuitive givenness) species select quite different milieux from the entirety of the (phenomenally reduced) world according to their organization, and, furthermore, that the "nature" of our mechanical physics and chemistry lies *within* the limits of the *structure* of man's milieu (no matter how much it may extend beyond the special *contents* of the natural view of the world).[53] Consequently, Spencer believed that he could reduce organizational differences among living beings to the increase and accumulation of adaptational characteristics of different origin that are to be found in individual organs of living beings. Apart from the great differences between Spencer and Darwin with regard to *how* this adaptation takes place, the role of the selection of the best-adapted variations, and the role of the heredity of functionally acquired properties, they *shared*

52. [See above, p. 155, n. 46.—*Ed.*]
53. See "Phänomenologie und Erkenntnistheorie." [The manuscript found among the author's papers contains no remarks on Spencer.—*Ed.*]

the above mistake. The following should be clear: a basic condition for the possibility of a *competitive struggle* is that this struggle take place in a given milieu-structure which is *common* to the units of life in this struggle, or, in other words, that this milieu-structure present *common elements*. When this is not the case, there is of course no common ground for the struggle. As I asserted earlier, however, if it is the case that the primary tendency of life is to be seen, not in the adaptation to a given milieu, but in the *transcending* of a given milieu, in extending it and conquering something new in it,[54] then the principle of *struggle* can become active only to the extent that this primary tendency *stagnates* and the mere tendency of adaptation to a given milieu becomes predominant in its stead. If this is the case, the struggle for the goods in this milieu is of course a necessary consequence. But if this is not the case, the units of life in question, to the degree that they develop and extend their milieux, will make this struggle redundant or will reduce it; and they will be able to live side by side in the whole of the universe with its abundantly rich table.

In addition to this there is another observation which is partly directed against the principle of the relativity of moral values to life, but which concurrently poses the question of whether, according to this principle, "man" *retains the value* that biological ethics also attributes to him. If by "life" we understand only an *earthly* organic world, natural laws put limits upon life. As individuals and species are destined to die, so is earthly life itself, whether because of a decrease in the distance of the earth from the sun and a resultant increase in temperature, or because of the general natural law of the transformation of all energy into heat and the diminution of energy-differences. Life appears to battle this tendency naturally (as Bergson and Auerbach showed), but *earthly* life is ultimately powerless in this endeavor. From a macroscopic view, earthly life lasts hardly a second in the history of the universe, and all products and works coming from it *alone* are contained in this second. If earthly organisms were not mere bearers in which life *as such* appears according to its own proper laws, just as magnetism appears in positively or negatively charged bodies,[55] and if life *consisted* only in properties and activities of organisms, it would be odd to demand the abandonment of so much vital and

---

54. [See Über Ressentiment und moralisches Werturteil," sec. 5.—*Ed.*]

55. I borrow this image from Oliver Lodge, *Leben und Materie* (Berlin, 1908).

sensuous happiness (which is undeniably entailed by ethical norms) for the sake of a trivial prolongation of this world-second (which is as long as "life" in this sense lasts), a prolongation that could be attained by the commission of so-called moral actions (i.e., in this case actions that "further life") and the omission of immoral actions. Moreover, the idea of the decline of life itself would in this case also imply the *cancellation* of all moral values—an idea that clearly contradicts all consciousness of the *meaning* of moral values.

In addition, the degree to which living forms are independent in existence with respect to others indubitably deserves a positive value-estimation. The more dependent on others such forms are, the more they must be exposed to perils and injuries, and the earlier they will meet their destiny in earthly life in the sequences of death, which, in the end, is the destiny of earthly life itself. But our earthly organic nature is such that the greatest degree of independence (among the larger realms) belongs to plants. Animals cannot nourish themselves without green plants, which provide organic nutrition from inorganic material. Within the realm of animals, however, man as carnivore is more dependent than any other. To this we must add the general principle that the more *differentiated* a being is in its nature, and the more the conditions of its life are therefore tied to *specific* conditions, the more *improbable* is the occurrence of those specific conditions in the whole of nature and its development. If we apply this to man, we see that he who distinctly lacks the life-value of an independent biological existence is the one who can endure.[56]

What we have said implies that the proposition that man is the most valuable being in nature—insofar as this proposition has an *objective* sense and is not the result of mere anthropomorphic self-love—*cannot* be justified at all from the viewpoint of biological values. Neither his two chief abilities, which *alone* lead to civilization (his ability to devise variable signs for mutual understanding and his ability to make artificial tools), nor what he has produced (civilization itself, with all its "progress") can raise man above this biological verdict. As is well known, Spencer and Nietzsche drew quite *different* conclusions concerning the assessment of the *value of civilization* from the presupposition that biological values are the "highest values." Whereas Spencer thought that he could justify civilization on this presupposition

56. [Compare this entire section with "Zur Idee des Menschen" (Bibliog. no. 10). See also "Die Stellung des Menschen im Kosmos."—*Ed.*]

and attempted to show that the "progress" of civilization could heal all the wounds that it inflicted, Nietzsche went more in the direction of negating the value of civilization and came to the point of venerating what he finally called "the blond beast." Spencer's conclusions are the consequences of his errors in *principle* concerning the nature of life. In *this* respect, and this respect *alone*, Nietzsche's solutions are in principle *more* justified. But *both* err in their *presupposition* that life is the highest value. In fact, man and civilization, insofar as they are to be measured against *biological* values, represent a kind of *faux pas* which life has taken in its evolution on earth. If there are no values *higher* than biological ones, it is necessary to call man a "diseased animal" with and in spite of his civilization. And as a consequence, man's thinking, too, becomes a form of his disease. Here I say nothing other than what Kant has said:

> If, for a being endowed with reason and will, the genuine purpose of nature were his preservation and well-being, or, in one word, his happiness, nature would have come upon a rather bad arrangement in selecting *reason* in this creature to carry out this purpose. For all the actions that he has to perform with this purpose in mind, the entire rule of his comportment would be much more exactly predelineated by *instinct*, and this purpose could be much more securely preserved in this way than it ever can be through reason.[57]

If, on the basis of our present positive knowledge of the evolution of life, we consider the means which nature uses to create higher organizations, we can see that conscious choice, reason, etc., have no place among such means. No matter what our conception of the causes of evolution, whether it be only in terms of the general power of natural breeding and selection or, in addition, in terms of life's immanent tendencies to higher organizations and the cumulative effect of the inheritance of properties functionally acquired, "reason"—even in the latter case—plays no role. For what is called "function" in physiology has nothing to do with mental factors. Thus human "reason" cannot be viewed as an especially valuable biological means; on the contrary, among the well-known and effective means of natural breeding, which can be seen already in the vegetal realm, it is the *least valuable*. In fact, if nature could succeed in "preserving mankind" only through a refinement of instruments like reason and

---

57. See *Groundwork of the Metaphysics of Morals*, chap. 1.

conscience, which are *biologically inferior* to instincts and automatisms, this would only show that nature had lost all other more useful and valuable means for the preservation and increase of life. Furthermore, conscious reason, irrespective of what it does for the preservation of man through the substitution of *artificial* adaptation, has a directly *harmful* effect on all psychophysical automatisms and instincts which further life and which, in comparison with their abundance in higher animals (e.g., insects), appear as remnants in man. For we must consider it a law that automatic life-activities (including psychic ones) become *disturbed* and diseased to the extent that they are performed consciously and are accompanied by conscious selections and attention.

Of all those estimations which make man the most valuable —insofar as they are supposed to go beyond the expression of his self-love and to be in accord with objective facts—the most nonsensical (i.e., Spencer's) is the one that measures the value of a living system in terms of its ability to preserve itself. For in that case—according to the rule of economy—man, with his highly differentiated nervous system, must compare with more simply equipped beings as the mountaineering enthusiast who climbs only with a very large and complicated apparatus (crampons, ropes, snow-glasses, etc.) compares with the mountaineer who climbs with a simple alpenstock. But since the simply equipped mountaineer is the better climber of the two, man must be regarded—according to this measure—as a lower being because no *higher values* are realized with his complicated constitution than are realized without it. In order to prove that these values in man are "higher" values, it is necessary to *disregard* values that are conditioned by man—indeed, vital values in general.

It could be objected that man is the "highest" of beings even in terms of true vital values *themselves;* for he is the *most powerful* living being, the being that has the greatest latitude in its activities as well as the largest milieu! But the question concerns *how* man acquires this power! And there is no doubt that his *vital* organization does not account for this. For his *artificial* tools and his ability to make them are what endow him with this increased power. There is a twofold value-relationship between the vital refinement and the degree of development of this capacity for civilization: (1) there is a need for making tools only when the vital developmental ability to grow an organ (for the realization of the same value) is *missing;* (2) civilization and a capacity for it, which is only one vital capacity among others, develop only to the degree that further *purely* vital development *stagnates,* and hence also to the degree that the type of species concerned manifests a "fixed" character. Thus, "understanding," taken as this ability to make artificial tools, is an advantage only if one *presupposes* a *deficient* vital organization or one that is in need of artificial surrogates (precisely because it is *fixed*). One must recognize that it is incorrect in principle to view tools as extensions of organs; such a viewpoint leads to a subversion of the order of values (as I have shown elsewhere).[58] Although one can view the refinement of understanding, in contrast to instincts, for example, as a result of vital development, i.e., the growth of the ability to make tools, one cannot regard the tools and the actions that produce them as an extension of *vital* power. This refinement of understanding is, rather, the consequence of a *stagnating* life, i.e., the consequence of a vital deficit. Man has become the "understanding animal" for precisely the same reason that *within* mankind the vitally *weak* become bearers of "prudence," "calculation," "craftiness," "foresight," and artificial rationalizations of existence; and it is for this reason also that craftiness often becomes a substitute for powers of self-defense among higher animals. Hence man's *impotence* in the *vital* sense, his unique neediness, the stagnation of the processes of differentiation in peripheral organs, and, above all, the *fixation* of his vital *ability* to develop—the fact that he is, as Weismann says, "the most fixed animal"—are what lead to the development of his talent for civilization. Man did not *continue* to grow and develop *organically* in an ever "richer milieu," as all life before him did—for instance, by growing new sensory functions and developing sensitivity to new qualities. He only artificially extended his latitude with respect to *things* having the same qualities that are within a *stable milieu;* he *"adapted to"* his milieu without *"extending"* it (i.e., without the extension that takes place as one species advances to a more organized one). One could say that man has fallen in love with his milieu. Indeed, one can maintain that the growth and "adaptation" reached by mere civilization has as its consequence a *decrease* in vital abilities. Thus the sense of smell diminishes more and more—so also memory, as writing and printing are employed. Civilization creates *more* sensuous needs than it can provide means to satisfy,

58. See "Über Ressentiment und moralisches Werturteil," p. 362. [See "Das Ressentiment im Aufbau der Moralen," sec. 5.—*Ed.*]

and it produces *more* diseases than it can treat and heal through progress in medicine and hygiene. It becomes the cause of a decrease in propagation through the diminution of fertility that follows in its wake, and this decrease cannot be compensated for by possible prolongations of life through science and hygiene. Civilization as a whole sets the impotent against the strong and *sustains* their propagation; for the "impotent" are not subject to dying out, as is the case in nature, but to *degradation* under the domination of the strong. Yet this *degradation* has no value in terms of vital exigencies, for only the *exclusion* of propagation has such a value. And since their propagation is not excluded, civilization necessarily causes the impotent to increase in number and permits *their* values *to dominate* more and more.

If what we have said shows that the proposition "Man is the most valuable living being" is *biologically* unjustified, it becomes clear that it is only on the basis of *other* values, i.e., values "higher" than *biological* ones, that this proposition can have an objective sense. And here we reach the aim of this investigation: whenever we value "man," we in fact *presuppose* values that are independent of vital values—*the values of the holy* and *spiritual values*. That is, man is the "highest being" insofar as he is the *bearer* of acts that are *independent* of his biological organization, and insofar as he *sees* and *realizes* the *values* corresponding to these acts. It is only on the presupposition of values of the holy and spiritual, values which are superordinate to and independent of biological values, that man is the most valuable being. The novelty that issues forth in him or at a certain point in his development consists, as it were—from a biological viewpoint—in an *abundance of mental activity*. It is as if in him and his history there were a fissure in which an order of acts and contents (values) makes its appearance—an order that is above *all* life, and yet, at the same time, a novel *unitary form* of this order which must be seen as the *"personal"* (in contrast to ego, organism, etc.), whose bond is *love,* which is the foundation of pure *justice.* However, the idea of this unitary form as the ultimate bearer of the value "holy" is the *idea of God,* and the realm of persons belonging to him and their order is "God's realm." But with this we come to a curious result. "Man" as the being of "highest value" among earthly beings and as a moral being becomes comprehensible and phenomenologically intuitable only on the presupposition of the idea of God and *"in the light"* of this idea! We can even say that, correctly viewed, he *is* only this movement, the *tendency* and the *transition* to the *divine.* He is the bodily being that God intentionizes and the point at which the realm of God breaks through, and he is that being in whose acts the being and value of the world is first constituted. How nonsensical it is to look at the idea of God as an *"anthropomorphism,"* when, on the contrary, it is in the *theomorphism* of his most noble exemplars that the unique *value* of his "humanity" lies! Thus man's intention beyond himself and all life constitutes his *essence*. And precisely this *is* the essential concept of "man": He is a thing that *transcends its own life and all life*. The core of his nature—apart from all special organization—is in fact this movement, this spiritual act of transcending himself! "Human" ethics and "biological" ethics both fail to see this.

But it is again historico-developmental biology that testifies to the *unity* of the truth by justifying the results of philosophy. All positive investigations into the origins of man in a biological sense—the morphological and physiological comparisons of races in connection with the comparison of races and primates, as well as paleontology—vacillate between the polyphyletic hypothesis on the one hand, i.e., the theory that man does *not* represent a *closed unity* of consanguinity, and the monophyletic theory on the other. Thus the unity of the definition of man as a biological species is itself questionable.[59] And hence there is less justification for the ethical presupposition of a unitary moral disposition in "man" (when this concept is taken naturalistically). In any case, there is no precise, essential border between man and animal when this problem is considered from the biological point of view. The entire problem of the *meaning* of the theory of evolution for philosophy is tied up with the consequences that follow from it. Naturalism thus concludes that man is only a higher animal, and that his spirit and moral insight are also products of animal development. The mistake in this theory is its assumption of a unitary biological concept of "man"; it *presupposes* this concept, *instead of* seeing that the *main result* of this theory is the *biological indefinability of man*. However, we conclude that because there is *no* essential concept of man for biology, the unique *borders of nature* and the unique *frontier of value*, which become a problem when we consider the earthly beings that reveal life, lie *not* between man and animal, which together systematically and genetically represent a continuous

59. Quenstedt said, "If Negroes and Caucasians were snails, zoologists would consider them two species."

transition, but between *person* and *organism,* between *spiritual being* and *living being.*

With this at least the problem of "man's place in the universe" is clearly circumscribed—a problem that every ethics must take into account, and one that Augustine, Malebranche, and Pascal posed in such a profound way. With regard to the mistaken attempts of a certain philosophy to credit man as a *natural species* with specific "dispositions" to language, morality, and reason, and even to a so-called immortal soul-substance, *we expressly deny that these attempts have any sense.* We assert that within the continuous evolution from animal to man, here and there (i.e., not necessarily "everywhere"), *acts* of a certain *being* and *laws* of acts and values of a certain *being* and their *interconnections* come to appearance, which we first exhibit in their essential contents in order to show that they belong *in principle* to an *order above* the *biological* order, and of which we have a sufficient number to foreshadow the *being* of a world of values and persons, which here and there flashes into the human environment, but which is not of biological origin.[60]

Let us consider the source of the error which leads to the opinion that "man" is, even from a biological point of view, the most valuable being. This can be seen most clearly in the case of Spencer's argument. Instead of placing every species and order of living beings in the kind of milieu that corresponds to its organizational structure, and instead of regarding the conditions of adaptation of all members of a species only in terms of the milieu that corresponds to *their* organizational structure, Spencer made the mistake of making man's milieu basic to *all* species and judging the degree of the conditions of adaptation in terms of man's milieu. This also led him to reduce organizational differences to differences among characteristics of adaptation to *man's* milieu, and this is the basic error of his epistemology! When he reduced categories of the understanding and a priori elements of morality to "*adaptations*" acquired by ancestors, which are, in turn, supposedly made innate in individuals through heredity, he presupposed as the "nature" to which this adaptation is to take place that kind of nature which is already determined in its structure by precisely these categories. For, if that *to which* adaptation takes place is not to be this unknown transcendent X, which his agnosticism asserts—an "adaptation" that can never be proved—but is, rather, to be nature given to us by the natural

---

60. [See "Die Stellung des Menschen im Kosmos."—*Ed.*]

view of the world and science, then *that* nature, already marked by those categories and already a *result* of "adaptation" cannot have been at the same time an *object* of an adaptation. There are only two possibilities here: either one must, with Kant, renounce any further biological derivation of forms of understanding and regard such forms as something absolutely *ultimate* and, indeed, as a "metacosmic" foundation of the universe (as O. Liebmann has pointedly said),[61] *or* one must regard such forms as biologically derived, but as determining *man's* milieu only vis-à-vis the fullness of *other* milieux and analogous systems of categories. Spencer's view, however, rests on a trait of thinking which one must call anthropomorphism. For from the beginning he relates all vital organizations to man and his milieu, and, without saying so, subordinates all organizations to man's milieu. Thus his reasoning proceeds here just as it does in his ethical relativism concerning the history of human value-estimation. As I have shown elsewhere,[62] he relates all values to values of *latter-day* Western European man and considers historical value-estimations as merely technical differences in the ways of realizing *these* values—though in fact differences among *value-estimations and morals themselves* hold sway. On the other hand, he furtively considers "man" the goal in the entire development of life, and he draws into the course of this development all *those* values and *those* forms of change which in fact guided only the formation of *human civilization.* He gives us a *picture* of life and its development which shows only how a possible tool could begin to make organisms *if* it were confronted, like a machine, with the task of making such organisms. He should have seen, however, that an understanding that is derived from life for a certain species, namely, the human species, can never explain life itself —as a part can never explain a whole—and that life must necessarily remain transcendent to such understanding. Bergson, too, has incisively pointed out this last error in Spencer's theory.[63]

If I say that man is the bearer of a tendency which transcends all possible vital values and which is directed toward the "divine,"

61. What are referred to here as "forms of understanding" are *not* the acts corresponding to propositions of pure logic, but the structures of thought which are *contingent* on them and which lead to a mechanical picture of the universe. See "Phänomenologie und Erkenntnistheorie." [See *ibid.*, sec. 5. See also "Lehre von den Drei Tatsachen" (Bibliog. no. 29).—*Ed.*]

62. [See "Über Ressentiment und moralisches Werturteil," esp. chap. 5. On ethical relativism, see below, chap. 5, sec. 6.—*Ed.*]

63. See "Introduction" to *L'Evolution créatrice* (Paris: Alcan, 1908).

or if I say, in short, that he is a being that seeks God, I imply no predication having as its subject an already definable unity of man, be it of a biological or a psychological nature. It is precisely such a unity that I expressly deny. According to his essence man is, rather, only the living X of this seeking, an X that must be conceived as still completely *variable* with regard to all possible psychophysical organizations so that the organization of factual earthly man represents only *one* actualized possibility among all the possibilities for which this X affords an infinite field of play. If a parrot manifested this tendency, he would be more "comprehensible" to us than any single member of a primitive people who lacked this transcendence of vital values. And this parrot could be called man with more justification, despite its different organization, than this particular member of a primitive people *without* this tendency. From this member we could find, in principle, *continuous* transitions to animals; for the divisions and limits can only be set by an *arbitrary act* of our understanding.

In trying to intuit the *essence* of man, it is not the idea of God in the sense of an extant and positively determined reality that is presupposed; rather, it is only the *quality* of the divine, or the *quality* of the holy, that is given in an infinite fullness of being. On the other hand, whatever takes the place of this essentiality (in the historical time of earthly man and in the changing beliefs of positive religions) cannot be presupposed in any sense. Yet this idea of God is not an empirical abstraction from diverse positive representations of gods that in different positive religions are objects of worship and cults. The ultimate (i.e., the highest) *value-quality* in the order of ranks of values originally *guides* the formation of all positive representations, ideas, and concepts of "God." Of course, when we investigate them historically and psychologically, we undoubtedly find that these representations and concepts of God contain a large number of "anthropomorphic" elements which are characteristically connected with the fortuitous contents of the peoples' lives. Certainly, Mohammed's God has the character of a fanatic and sensuous sheik roaming about the desert, and Aristotle's God has the character of a self-sufficient, contemplative Greek sage who is satisfied with his own wisdom. The particular and concrete expressions of the Christian idea of God, too, possess characteristics of Christian peoples, if we look at their religiosity and not at mere dogmas; and these characteristics change in time with the changing historical levels of development. Indeed, the Christian God of the Germanic tribes more or less has blue eyes and the temperament of a Germanic duke to whom one belongs by trust and without a contract. This God is quite different from the Romans' regimental religious representation of God. Such considerations can be extended *ad libitum*. It is the task of the history of religion and the psychology of religion to show in detail the different factors that have determined these objective representations of the divine and to point out those elements of their representations that have determined them in characteristic fashion—for example, the character of a people, forms of cults, definitions of priests, stages of science and philosophy, etc. Apart from these points, however, within specifically *religious* experience—in a collective sense "revelation," in an individual sense "grace"—it is first through an experience of the personality of a model saint that the idea of the divine is filled with positive, intuitive content which cannot be derived from philosophy and which has the full objectivity that corresponds to this independent type of experience. A theory of religious cognition must discover how the uniform whole of what is intuited and experienced in "revelation" receives its original form of language and thereby becomes communicable, how this becomes secondarily transformed into rigid dogmas through traditions and ecclesiastical organizations, and how the conceptions of such dogmas become more precisely defined and systematized in their contents by the changing science of theology. However, it is *our* concern, above all, to show that there is an *a priori value-idea* of the "divine" which does not presuppose any historical or inductive experience, and which is wholly *independent* of the above sources of positive religious experience and even more independent of those colorations added to determinations of positive religious representations by the special characteristics and historical life-contents of different peoples. And we want to show that this a priori value-idea of the divine has *no* foundation in the existence of a world and an ego.[64]

With the above we appropriate the core of the truth contained in a philosophico-religious line of thought which dates back to the times of Augustine, and which has been called ontologism. In this line of thought it was not only the quality of the divine but also the existence of God as a specific "substance" that was regarded as immediately and intuitively given. The comprehension of the existence of God, too, was not taken to

64. [See "Probleme der Religion" (Bibliog. no. 14).—*Ed.*]

presuppose the existence of the world or a certain constitution of it or an inference from this world to its ultimate cause or the nature of this cause (as in the "teleological" proof). The truth in this theory consists in the fact that there is an ultimate element of an immediate and intuitable nature in all religious object-ideas. We must reject, however, the view generally connected with all forms of ontologism to date, namely, that we are also able to comprehend this existence in the sense of a substantial reality (of God) in this way. This necessarily requires the specific religious and positive experience of a revelation. If this is not recognized, ontologism must of necessity become a nebulous mysticism which believes that it can destroy all positive representations of religion by measuring them against the empty idea of an infinite being. We also disagree with historical ontologism in that it considered the idea of an infinite being to be this intuitively given ultimate element of all positive religious representations and also attempted in many insufficient ways, especially through the mediation of the unclear concept of a "most perfect being," to extract value-predicates from this idea. It is to be objected here that this ultimate intuitable element possesses the character of a final, irreducible, and, in the order of ranks of values, evidentially highest value-quality, which is precisely the value of the infinitely holy. This moment of value is therefore not a predicate of a given idea of God, but the *nucleus* around which all conceptualizations and pictorial representations of the real are secondarily formed. What guides the formation of *ideas* of God and *concepts* of God are peculiar nuances of *value-qualities* of the divine that are given only in feeling and in the intentionality of love for God. In the end, any God is thought and represented in ways corresponding to the primary given nature of his value. Here we have the solution to Pascal's profound paradox: "I would not seek Thee, had I not already found Thee." This "found" refers precisely to the possession of the value-being of God through the spiritual eyes of one's heart and love; it refers to the flashing out of this quality *in* the execution of these emotive acts. And this "seeking" refers to the conceptualization and representation that takes place in accordance with this already "found." This point concerning the divine substantiates a law of the foundation of acts which is not merely valid for the divine alone, but which corresponds to an earlier proven [*erwiesenen*] proposition, to wit, that *values of things* are *given* to us *prior to and independent of pictorial representations.* For this reason there can be *agreement* among individuals and groups with regard to this substance—that is, this nucleus of the idea of God—even though their conceptualizations differ greatly. The latter change and fluctuate according to levels of culture, and it is a matter of course that the God of a farmer's wife is different from the God of a theologian. Nevertheless, the ultimate *religious* content of truth can be the same for both. There are more people who similarly grasp God through love than there are people who similarly conceptualize God. Anyone who fails to appreciate this proposition turns precisely what alone can and should found a deep unity and agreement among men—and, what is more, what *constitutes* the *unity* of mankind (in a moral sense), as we showed—into necessary and insurmountable differences among intellectual levels of culture; from the beginning he transforms it into an object of dispute and intellectual strife and, consequently, an issue of terrible religious struggles, of which the great religious wars are examples.

I hope that the above remarks on the phenomenology of the idea of God will not be confused with those subjectivistic and romantic conceptions of a religion of feeling—for example, that which Schleiermacher leaned toward. A religious idea of an object cannot have its foundation in a feeling, i.e., in a subjective feeling-state. I cannot see the slightest meaning in Schleiermacher's proposition that religious dogmas are "descriptions of pious feelings." [65] Piety is subjective comportment with respect to a positively represented or thought divine object, and it can be the same or quite different with all possible ideas of deities and God among different individuals. There certainly were both pious and impious fetishists. Zeus can be worshiped with and without piety. The fact that the Christian God was worshiped after Zeus cannot be interpreted to mean that there was an increase or change in piety.

6. *The Historical Relativity of Ethical Value-Estimations and Its Dimensions*

It has always been one of the major claims of formal ethics and its formal a priori that its presuppositions alone can explain historical variability and differences in moral value-estimation among different peoples and races, and that they can do so without drawing any skeptical conclusion from this historical varia-

65. [See the critique of Schleiermacher's philosophy of religion in "Probleme der Religion."—*Ed.*]

bility. And, on the other hand, it is held that every non-formal
ethics necessarily leads to ethical skepticism because all non-
formal value-estimations would prove to be historically relative.
If good and evil consist in no special content of value-estimation
and willing, but only in the mere laws of willing, then any such
content can of necessity be good and evil, and the fact that
history supports this corresponds to what we must expect from
this presupposition.

Apart from the errors in these presuppositions [66] and their
consequences that we have pointed out, there are other false assumptions behind them which can be completely clarified only
by a positive insight into the *dimensions of the relativity of
value-estimations.* Such a task would have the eminent significance of providing us with an a priori apparatus of concepts for
our historical understanding of all human value-estimations, an
apparatus that could yield an intelligible order in this realm of
value-estimations and their contents, which at first appears like
a palette daubed with paint. Of course, one who from the outset
views values only as a reflex of causal processes of feeling-states
and states of sensations will not *seek* an intelligible order of this
kind in the past; rather, if he is not a pure skeptic and content
with the fact that there is this change, he will seek a direction
only in the process of the development of these value-estimations.
Indeed, if man had construed the constellations as mere complexes of sensations, he never would have distinguished the skies
and their history from the history of knowledge of them, and he
never would have worked in the field of astronomy. But it appears
to me that our very young "historical age," in which mere piles
of facts were first accumulated, is not at all in a position to judge
from history alone on this important problem. At least it is not
in a position to make a judgment on the degrees of sense and
harmony that may lie in historical value-estimations and their
systems (of "taste," "style," "conscience," "morals," etc.) without
the help of a wide range of phenomenological concepts concerning the possible dimensions of relativity in these value-estimations. It may well be that this "palette daubed with paint," when

66. That is, (1) of the confusion of changes in values with changes in
estimations of units of goods and actions bearing these values, (2) of the
false inferences of changes in values from changes in norms, (3) of the
erroneous inferences of deficient objectivity and insight from deficient
universality, (4) of the failure to see that it is in the moral value-
estimation of "willing" and "action" (in contrast to being) and of norms
and duty (in contrast to virtue) that there is a truly non-formally variable
moment.

seen from a correct distance and with proper understanding, will gradually assume the interconnection of sense of a grandiose painting, or at least of the fragments of one. And in this painting, one will be able to see mankind, mixed as it is, beginning to take possession, through love, feeling, and action, of a realm of objective values and their objective order, a realm that is independent of mankind as well as of its own manifestations; and one will be able to see mankind draw this realm into its existence, as happened in the history of knowledge, e.g., the knowledge of the heavens.[67]

In a study of historical moral facts, it is necessary first of all to make a sharp distinction between the stages of intellectual insight into outer and inner causal connections of things on the one hand, and value-estimations in general and moral ones in particular on the other. It is likewise necessary to indicate what belongs to the techniques of action. For instance, the fact that the people living on an Asian island consider smoking to be as bad as murdering a king and have therefore made it a crime punishable by death does not imply any deviation on their part from our value-estimations. This is not the case, for example, when tobacco is considered a lethal poison. The estimation of the vital welfare of the people is the same as it is among us. Many of the differences in this respect, which ethical relativism claims as its justification, are resolved when we discover the superstitions and intellectual errors or deceptions that condition such differences.[68] Analogously, it is necessary to look into historical changes in morally significant institutions and types of actions in order to discover whether these changes rest on the changes in moral or other value-estimations, or on changes in the realm of goods. A relatively practical devaluation of economic goods can rest on a diminished development of the feeling for goods of this type. It can also rest on a peculiar abundance of nature or on the affective dominance of values given as higher (e.g., religious values, like "voluntary poverty"). A morally sig-

67. What is said here is meant only as an illustration, for only goods, and not values, should be compared to stars.
68. See Stumpf, "Vom ethischen Skeptizismus." Still, this has to be established in every case. Henry T. Buckle's principle (*The History of Civilization in England* [London: Richards, 1904])—namely, that *all* historic changes are effected by intellectual progress alone, that in the domain of mores everything remains the same—is completely misleading. This principle has a counterpart in Darwin's assertion that sympathetic feelings are consequences of social instincts and intellectual development. See *Zur Phänomenologie und Sympathiegefühle*, p. 33. [See *Wesen und Formen der Sympathie*, pt. A, chap. 8.—Ed.]

nificant reason for this can be found only in the last case. A transition to (factual) monogamy can be the result of a decrease in the number of females in relation to males, the result of increasing poverty, or, indeed, the result of such remote things as the introduction of cow's milk for the nourishment of children.[69] In such cases there is certainly no moral significance to the transition, and moral polygamy is by no means overcome by it. In addition, it is necessary to distinguish sharply between variations in partial and whole artificial forms of the expressions of moral value-estimations and moral feeling itself, e.g., between variations in decorum and those in the feeling of shame.[70] Again, other variations that have been regarded as moral ones prove, when analyzed, to be dependent on an increasing or decreasing solidarity of interest among groups—e.g., the result of extended periods of peace throughout history or of an increase in the ability to suffer (which has nothing to do with an increase in the ability to participate in another's affective state or with an increase in abilities of fellow suffering, but which is only a consequence of an increasing effeminacy in civilization). Still other variations are simply variations in aesthetic feeling.

In order to *compare* peoples or other groups in terms of their moral values, it is first necessary to *reduce* such peoples or groups to the *same* conditions in terms of their intellectual culture, their techniques of action, the levels of expression of their value-estimations and their extramoral estimations, their degrees and types of solidarity of interest, their ability to suffer, etc.[71] For the variations and developments of moral value-estimations are in principle never direct consequences of all the other variations; and, more particularly, they are not consequences of the level of intellectual culture. A very highly developed, differentiated intellectual culture can have very primitive moral feeling, and vice versa; the increased dovetailing of interests, which is the driving wheel of civilization, with the resulting security of life, property, and commerce, can go hand in hand with a very low level of moral culture.[72]

It is necessary to get behind all the costumes and disguises in which the moral value-sphere appears to us in history in order

69. In this way the nursing time, during which the woman is to remain untouched, is shortened.

70. A number of examples of such confusions can be found in my essay, "Das Schamgefühl."

71. These points are only examples and are not meant to be exhaustive.

72. See *Zur Phänomenologie und Sympathiegefühle*, p. 99. [See *Wesen und Formen der Sympathie*, pt. B, chap. 6, sec. 4.—Ed.]

to find the material of problems concerning the dimensions of the relativity of morals.

Within this material, however, there are five strata which must be sharply differentiated for all historical considerations of moral affairs.

First, there are variations in *feeling* (i.e., "cognizing") values themselves, as well as in the *structure* of *preferring* values and *loving* and *hating*. Let us take the liberty of calling these variations as a whole variations in the "*ethos*." [73]

Second, there are variations which occur in the sphere of *judgment* and the sphere of rules of the *assessment* of values and value-ranks given in these functions and acts. These are variations in "*ethics*" (in the broadest sense of the term).

Third, there are variations in *types* of unity of *institutions, goods*, and *actions*, i.e., the quintessences of institutions, goods, and actions, the unities of which are founded in moral value-complexes, e.g., "marriage," "monogamy," "murder," "theft," "lying," etc. These types must be clearly differentiated from the (positive) definitions that are valid on the basis of mores and positive law, i.e., what shall *obtain* as "marriage," "monogamy," "murder," or "theft." Yet these types lie behind these changing definitions as the foundation of the definability of these things. They represent unities of *states of affairs*, but as such they can be distinguished only on the basis of certain *value-complexes* as these or other, the same or different, unities. Thus murder is never = killing [*Tötung*] a man (or killing with intent and deliberation), a lie never = conscious statement of an untruth, etc. The essence of such unities of states of affairs is such that in each case a peculiar, morally negative value-complex which is basic to each case must be given if such an action is to become a lie or murder. Variations of this kind can be called variations in existing *morals*, to which a science of morals corresponds.

Fourth, and very different from all of these variations, are variations in *practical morality*. Practical morality pertains to the value of the factual comportment of men, that is, comportment on the basis of norms which belong to the relations of value-ranks recognized by *these men*, and which correspond to

73. To the ethos there corresponds: (1) in the *intellectual* sphere, the *Weltanschauung* (= structure of looking at the world, which every man and every people has, no matter if they "know" this reflectively or not); (2) in the *religious* sphere, the structure of a living faith, with its contents, which is to be distinguished from the dogmatic and theological (i.e., normative, defining, and judgmental) wording of the contents given in faith, the former being the foundation of the latter.

their own structures of preferring. The value of such practical comportment is completely relative to its *"ethos"* and can never be measured by an ethos of another epoch or that of another people. Only *after* we take possession of an ethos of a certain age can we judge the actions and types of comportment of the people of that age; such judgment also requires preliminary knowledge of their unities of moral *types*.[74] On the other hand, we can assess historical being and action *itself* (in terms of a refeeling understanding of the ethos of the epoch). In so doing, we can disregard the principles of the *ethics* of this age, as well as the factual assessments made by people in this age and the instances which they regarded as authoritative.[75] On the other hand, an action that is "bad" in relation to the ethos of its age can nevertheless be absolutely "good" if the acting person surpasses, in *his* ethos, the ethos of his time. Indeed, according to the nature of the relation between morality and ethos, and not according to the fortuitous immorality of contemporaries or their insufficient ethics, the *moral genius,* who is superior to the ethos of his time, i.e., who has made a new advance into the realm of extant values by being the first to comprehend a higher value, is assessed and judged as morally inferior by the extant ethos, "legitimately" and *without* deception or error. The broad transitions in the history of an ethos are therefore replete with individuals who are necessarily victimized by this *tragic* which is essentially immanent to moral development itself, but not because they are subject to the moral disapproval of a historian.[76]

Fifth, and finally, it is necessary to distinguish the variations in moralities from variations belonging to the areas of *mores* and *customs*, i.e., forms of action and expression whose validity and practice are rooted solely in (genuine) traditions, and whose nature is such that a deviation from them presupposes an act of willing. Mores and customs *themselves* can be morally good and evil, and their origins can almost always be found in morally immediate and relevant acts and actions. They can "transmit" what is morally of positive and negative value. An action against mores, insofar as it is without reason, i.e., without insight into

74. It is not, as Hegel maintains, moral assessment in general but the direct moral assessment according to the ethos and the morality of one's time that makes historical representations like Schlosser's so intolerable.

75. Thus the killing of Socrates, for example, remains judicial murder, even though he was "legally" sentenced by the Greek people.

76. See "Zum Phänomen des Tragischen" (Bibliog. no. 10), esp. the remarks on the concept of "guiltless guilt." The eternal source of "tragic" guilt in general lies in the fact mentioned above.

their moral deficiency, is practically immoral because the ethos is already coeffective in the very *selection* of actions within a tradition and is also the measure of practical morality. With this insight, however, it becomes moral.

ad 1. Variations in Ethos

Both the *relativistic* non-formal ethics of goods and purposes and *formal* ethics have failed to see that there are variations in the *ethos itself* which have nothing to do with an adaptation of a given ethos to the changing realm of goods that belongs to civilization and culture (yet they cocondition their formation) or with an adaptation of an ethos to the entire reality of nature (including dispositions of peoples). *Ethical relativism,* which believes that not only moral value-estimations but also values themselves and their ranks are in development, has its origins in retrospectively *applying* moral values abstracted from present-day factual value-estimations to moral subjects of the past, and in mistaking what is in fact a variation in the ethos for a better adaptation of willing and acting to that which corresponds to present-day value-estimations or their supposed unity (e.g., general welfare, development of culture, maximum intensity of life, etc.). Relativism fails to see the even more radical "relativity" of moral value-estimations which consists in variations in the contents of an immediate value-consciousness and its governing rules of preferring. It fails to see even the *changes* in *moral ideals themselves* (and not merely changes in the application of this value-consciousness to changing groups, actions, institutions). According to the relativist all change is explained by the fact that at different times different groups of a society (at times warriors and farmers, at other times researchers and workers) or different human qualities (courage, audacity, and energy, or industriousness, thriftiness, and diligence) served to realize the value of general well-being, for example, and that estimations of preferences occurred accordingly. The relativist does not doubt that this value (or any other that he would put at the top) has always been the highest value, and that from it and in terms of it he can derive and explain value-estimations by taking into account the life-reality in question, i.e., dispositions, stages of technology, intellectual insight; nor does he doubt that at the highest level the men of the past only lacked a *clear theoretical awareness* of the meaning of their value-estimations (i.e., a true *ethics*).

Every future investigation into the manifold systems of moral value-estimations that are found in history must radically rid itself of this presupposition. It must look into the great *typical forms of ethos itself*, i.e., the experiential structure of values and their immanent rules of preferring, which lie *behind* both the morality and the ethics of a people (primarily those of larger racial groups); and it must proceed with the aid of concepts drawn from this historical material, concepts which the theory of the *dimensions of the relativity of value-estimations* provides.[77] It is necessary to investigate the extent to which the ethos also conditions ways of looking at the world [Welt-anschauung],[78] i.e., the structure of knowing world-experiencing as presupposed in all judgmental activities, especially the formation of the levels of the experienced relativity of the existence of objects. It is not the changing *ideas* about love and justice that must be investigated, but the forms of *moral attitudes themselves* and their experienced order of ranks; not the action that is considered noble or useful or conducive to well-being, but the rules by which such *values themselves* were preferred or placed after.[79] Who would not be convinced by a detailed analysis that the ethos of

77. There is to be mentioned here the problem of how the large families of language form *value-units*—the faces, as it were, which the world of values assumes by and through meanings of words, and the structure which this world acquires by and through syntax. A detailed investigation of this promises most fruitful results. I hope to develop an exact indication of the methods of such investigations (with examples) in a planned work on the foundations of historical cognition.

78. Here I do not use the term *Weltanschauung* as it is frequently used, i.e., to indicate a premature termination of the essentially infinite scientific process through some ultimate conceptual result of a science, from which derives what today is called monism, energetics, pan-psychism, etc. In this sense of the word Husserl was correct in rejecting all "philosophy of *Weltanschauung*" (see his *Philosophie als strenge Wissenschaft*). I use the term *Weltanschauung* in W. von Humboldt's and W. Dilthey's sense (if I understand it correctly), namely, to characterize the kind of selection and structurization which factually governs both a whole cultural unit and a person, and with which the person receives the pure whatness of physical, psychic, and ideal things (no matter whether the person knows this reflectively, and, if he knows it reflectively, no matter how he has arrived at this knowledge). In this sense of the term every historical phase of a "science" is always already *conditioned* by a *Weltanschauung* and an ethos with regard to goals and methods. Therefore, a science *never* changes a *Weltanschauung*. See my address, "Die Idee des Todes und das Fortleben," and my "Phänomenologie und Erkenntnistheorie." ["Die Idee des Todes" was never published by the author. The manuscript found among the author's papers (from the period ca. 1912–13) was posthumously published under the title "Tod und Fortleben" (Bibliog. no. 29).—*Ed.*]

79. For a concrete example, see my "Über Ressentiment und moralisches Werturteil."

the ancient Indian caste system and religion is radically different as ethos (and not as ethics or as adaptation to the changing historical realities of this people) from the ethos of the Greeks or from that of the Christian world? The Romans before Ennius found usury more reproachable than theft, and the old German moral and legal value-estimation deemed plundering better than theft; who would not admit that this points to basically different rules of preferring for certain kinds of the vital values (courage, manliness) and the value of usefulness—and not to changes in value-estimations of different actions according to the same rule of preferring? Of course, there is also a change in the simple adaptation of an ethos to changing historical realities, a change that is expressed, for instance, in changing positive definitions of *what* is considered profiteering, theft, or robbery. But these are as different from the variations in the ethos as are ethical theories, any number of which can be found within *one* ethos. The ethos lives *in* the structure of this historical life-reality itself and is therefore not an adaptation to this reality. It serves as the basis of this reality and has also guided the construction of the non-arbitrary forms of its structure. We must learn to distinguish moral change in the ethos, which is one of the *first* order, from differences in adaptation—just as the history of art has at last begun to *separate* typical basic forms of the artistic representative penetration into the world of intuition, which is guided by a specific structure of aesthetic value-experiences, from differences that are based on changing abilities and levels of artistic technique and available materials, as well as from the objects determined by the ethos and world view of a ruling class as objects to be glorified in art, and also from consciously "applied" aesthetic and technical laws.

Nevertheless, this *most radical* relativity of moral value-estimations gives us no reason to assume a relativism of moral *values* themselves and their order of ranks.[80] One can only say that a complete and adequate experience of the cosmos of values and its order of ranks, and, with this, the representation of the moral sense of the world, is *essentially* connected with the *co-operation* of the different forms of ethos which unfold historically according to its laws. It is precisely a correctly understood *absolute ethics* that strictly *requires* these differences—this value-

---

80. By way of analogy, I could say that the discovery of new geometries with different axiomatic systems, which is to be sharply distinguished from the discovery of new propositions within each system, does not make geometry any more relative than it was from the very start.

perspectivism of values among peoples and their times and this openness in the formative stages of the ethos. Because moral value-estimations and their systems are more manifold and richer in their qualities than the diversity of mere natural dispositions and realities of peoples would allow one reasonably to expect, one must assume an objective realm of values which our experiencing can enter only gradually and according to definite structures of the selection of values. On the other hand, the origins of *ethical relativism* are to be found in the fact that it takes values to be mere *symbols* of its own culturally dominant value-estimations of certain goods and actions (or even mere theories about these) and arbitrarily construes all history simply as the increasing technical adaptation of acting to factual values that are posited in its own age and taken to be absolute and thus as "progress" toward such values. Thus value-relativism always rests on an absolutizing of value-estimations which depend on the idiosyncrasies and culture of the observer concerned. That is to say, it rests on the narrowness and blindness of the horizon of moral values, an outlook that is conditioned by a deficient sense of awe and humility vis-à-vis the realm of moral values and its expanse and fullness. It rests on the arrogance of taking only the moral value-estimations of one's *own* time as a "matter of course," without scrutiny, and assuming that these values underlie all times; or of "empathizing" one's own experience into men of the past instead of indirectly overcoming the narrowness of this pride by understanding the types of ethoses of other times and other peoples in an experience of the objective realm of values, shaking off the blinders that the value-experiences of one's own time impose.

Formal absolute ethics makes a mistake of a different type. Since it does not recognize an *ethos* between ethics and practical morality, it recognizes no changes in the ethos.[81] It is satisfied with the establishment of a simple "new formula" for a (latent) ethos that is supposedly constant and always of the same type, as if men at all times equally "know what is good and evil." By not recognizing the very "historicity" of the ethos *itself*, which it possesses as a form of experiencing values and their orders or ranks, formal ethics is necessarily led to the assumption that at any time there must be the possibility of a complete ethics that would *exhaust* moral values and the mind comprehending them. Such an ethics, it is assumed, must culminate in a so-called

81. See above, pp. 67 ff.

absolute moral principle—thus, in *one* proposition. All other variations in the moral-historical world must therefore be accounted for either through variations in *practical morality* (through which unhistorical and moralistic obtrusiveness in praising and blaming alien states of culture, as in the German Enlightenment, receives a philosophical justification) or through inexplicable variations in the *nature* of human *drives*, which provide new and changing, but morally indifferent, "material" for this "formula." Like ethical relativism, this theory ignores the inner history of the *ethos itself*, i.e., the central history *in* all history.

But what are the *special dimensions* in which this change in the ethos takes place? The most radical form of renewal and growth of the ethos occurs in the movement of *love* and its power, in which "higher" values (with regard to existing ones) are discovered and disclosed. This happens first within the limits of the highest value-modalities, which we mentioned earlier,[82] then within those of the others. Thus it is to the *moral-religious genius* that the realm of values opens up. In such a variation the rules of preferring among old and new values become altered by themselves. Although the rules of preferring among the old values and their mutual objectivity are not necessarily affected, the old realm of values as a whole is nevertheless relativized.[83] It is now a matter of blindness or deception to prefer the old values to the new, and it is practically "evil" to live according to the old values as the highest ones. The virtues of the old ethos now become "glittering vices." *But* the rules of preferring among old values are *not* affected by this. It remains "better" to retaliate, for instance, or even to seek revenge, than to prefer one's own usefulness (in regard to retaliation) or the common weal to the value of retaliation and revenge—even when these are subordinate in their value to forgiveness as the most valued and therefore the *only* morally "good" comportment in cases of experienced offenses and guilt. The rules of preferring that belong to an old ethos are not abolished as a new ethos "grows." Only a relativizing of the whole of the old ethos occurs.

It is necessary to distinguish these variations from the experience of a relation of being-higher among qualities of values

---

82. [See chap. 2, B, sec. 5.—*Ed.*]

83. I know of no more grandiose evidence for such a discovery of a whole realm of values which relativizes an older ethos than the Sermon on the Mount, whose very form repeatedly announces evidence of the relativizing of the old values of the "law": "But I say unto you, . . ."

in the same value-modality that are already given, as well as from the experience of types of values that manifest themselves as higher or lower according to their essential interconnections with their bearers.[84] For, as we have already seen, it is in preferring that the synthetic relations of higher and lower values are constituted. In this dimension of reciprocal change it is, above all, the regions of value that become more sharply delineated—for instance, aptitude from virtue, the values of noble and base from those of good and evil, values of the person and his moral tenor from those of action and success.

Finally, there are variations in the fullness of the *differences* through which individual value-qualities (negative and positive ones) are generally feelable and then secondarily distinguished in language. This measure of the differentiation of value-feeling itself and the different levels of approval and disapproval which are based on it, finally, of assessments, permits us to see what we may appropriately call *the level of moral culture.*

But apart from the above kind of variation in the growth of the ethos, i.e., the variation in which a disclosure of the realm of objective values and their order occurs, there are also in history all those forms of value-*deceptions* and *deceptions* in preferring, as well as *falsifications* and *overthrows* which are founded on *such* deceptions and which pertain to earlier forms of ethical assessment and standards that had conformed to the objective ranks of values. I discovered one such deception in my study of *ressentiment.* Only a systematic study of these kinds of emotional deceptions will teach us to observe also those which lie in the history of the ethos and to distinguish *falsifications of values* from mere false ideas about their bearers, as well as from practical immorality. Principles of value-judgment in an age, in the sense of a dominant or acknowledged *"ethics,"* can rest on such deceptions; and they can be overtaken and judged accordingly by those whose *ethos* did *not* fall victim to such deceptions. It is important, therefore, to investigate not only the genealogy of deceptions but also the forms of their dispersion. Furthermore, it is necessary to distinguish between attitudes toward values themselves and attitudes toward the contemporary historical reality, i.e., between attitudes toward the factual bearer of values and attitudes toward the world of goods. Let us consider the example of the relations between vital values and values of utility. Norms that come from vital values alone undoubtedly

84. See chap. 2, B, secs. 2–4.

require in principle an aristocratic structure of society, i.e., a structure in which noble blood and character-values of heredity belonging to such noble blood possess political prerogatives.[85] But norms coming from values of utility dictate an equalization of biological value-differences among groups. Values of utility taken by themselves at least tend to political democracy—irrespective of the extent to which they permit the formation of "class differences" in a democracy, i.e., the formation of individual groups based primarily on property differences. However, it does not follow at all from these two essential relations between vital values and values of utility (further exploration of which we cannot permit ourselves here) that the vital-aristocratic ethos *must* lead to the justification of a certain historically positive, factual ruling minority—for example, the minority of a present "ruling class"—or that the utilitarian-democratic ethos *must* lead to the justification of a present factual rule of the people— that is, majority rule and election by majority. The ethos of a ruling minority (even of a positive nominal "nobility") can have traits that are in essence those of a utilitarian-democratic ethos,[86] and the ethos of subordinate classes can have traits of a vital-aristocratic ethos. The values of a ruling and factual minority can very well be in essence those of a "majority."[87]

ad 2. Variations in Ethics

By the *"ethics"* of a time (in the broadest sense) we mean the judgmental and linguistic formulation both of values and relations of value-ranks which are self-given in emotional intentionality and of the principles of assessment and norm-giving founded on values and their relations of rank. Through procedures of logical reduction we can show that such principles are the general propositions from which the content of individual acts of assessment and norm-giving can be logically derived.

Within the domain of ethics two things must be sharply distinguished: the ethics that is "applied and used" by moral subjects (and here we must distinguish the explicitly "recognized"

85. The basic reason why Herbert Spencer becomes an advocate of modern democracy through his principle of a maximum of life is that he tries to reduce vital values to those of utility.

86. Note, for instance, the fact that the greater part of the French nobility, whose domination and privileges were destroyed by the French Revolution (see W. Sombart's proof in his *Luxus und Kapitalismus*), was not a nobility at all but rather a self-made nobility of retailers, i.e., descendants of the very groups that took away its rights.

87. L. Schmidt (*Ethik der alten Griechen*) tries to depict the ethics of the Greeks in this way.

from the tacitly "recognized," which can be *very* different, the former being always far more rigid and strict than the latter) and the groups of ethical principles that are discovered by logical procedures for which an "applied ethics" furnishes the material. That is, the ethics of a natural-practical view of the world expressed in natural language (e.g., the homespun wisdom of sayings and traditional maxims) is to be distinguished from a more or less scientific, philosophical, or theological *ethics* that seeks to "justify" applied ethics and to "ground" it in the highest of principles, "principles" which do not have to be *known* by the subjects of an applied ethics. Whereas ethics in the first sense is a constant factor accompanying every ethos, ethics in the *second* sense is a relatively rare phenomenon. *Its origin is always connected with processes of disintegration in an existing ethos.*[88] Of course, such a "scientific" ethics has no value *beyond* the intuitive evidences of its ethos (nor is there even a possibility of a critique of its ethos). It also has no cognitive value which would go beyond the principle that gives the most economical formulation (on the basis of formal logic and its laws) of what lies in the facts of an applied ethics. It only *formulates* the predominant and traditional opinions about moral values. It cannot subject them to criticism, because they are its factual basis. If one of its principles logically leads to a conclusion that contradicts existing and applied ethics, its principle, not the existing ethics, is "false" and must be modified until the facts follow from it. It is thus no surprise that this "scientific" ethics has derived about the same number of rules of assessment and norms from its diverse "principles" as existed at the time—precisely those which already obtained. This fact shows that the content of the conclusions drawn was already fixed as an existing ethics *prior* to so-called conclusive confirmation. Ethics deserves to be called *philosophical* ethics in the proper sense not only when it deals with the derivation of applied existing ethics from principles, but also when it begins to measure the applied rules of assessment, after they have been logically ordered and systematized, against the contents of the *ethos,* and when it critically evaluates these rules on the basis of "intended" essential evidences in the ethos. In addition, philosophical ethics is concerned with a critique of these "intended" evidences of the ethos of its

---

88. H. Steinthal has pointed out in his ethics that among the Greeks and the Romans the scientific reflection on matters of ethics increased as their ethos dissolved. One could say similar things about the Christian ethos in relation to Christian ethics.

time in terms of the pure *self-givenness* of moral values and value-relations.

The forms of ethics (in both senses of ethics) can *deviate* from the contents of an ethos to any degree. One must never conclude anything about the ethos itself from ethics.[89] Possible ethical *"aberrations"* (in the applied ethics of the "assessment") and *"errors"* (in scientific ethics) must be sharply distinguished from emotional *"deceptions,"* which belong to *the ethos* of a certain time and its group, and which lead to the predominance of a false ethos, with its corresponding "illusory values," in which the absolute order of ranks of values appears in "subverted" form. In comparison with deceptions in an ethos and their correlates, the "illusory values," all errors of ethics are quite minimal. Even the highest ethical "truth," which would consist in the coincidence of ethics and ethos (in contrast to their conflicting with each other), could never guarantee the absence of such deceptions in an ethos.

ad 3. Variations in Type

Ethical relativism can easily justify its theses if it does not distinguish between unities of *types* of value-complexes and the states of affairs that are unified by them on the one hand and the *quintessences of things, actions, and men,* which by definition are to be considered bearers of such value-complexes, on the other. Let us consider types of *actions,* e.g., theft, adultery, and murder. It is clear that under different positive systems of holding property, the *same* factual actions must appear either as theft or as legal acquisition (rather than theft); likewise, under different systems of marriage (polygamy, monogamy, and their numerous subdivisions), the *same* actions must appear either as adultery or as good and legal behavior. But this does *not* exclude the possibility that, apart from their unlawfulness, theft and adultery—if we enucleate only *essences,* which give all their definitions unity—always appeared to the authentic ethos as evil. Value-estimations of murder are also of great interest in terms of the problem concerning the relations between values of the person and the vital values of human life. W. Wundt states:

Intuitionism can come to terms with the changeableness of conscience only by doing violence to the facts. The simple fact that

89. One must not draw conclusions with respect to practical morality, either.

there have been peoples and periods that considered murder to be not a crime but a praiseworthy deed, and for reasons that we would reject, is a sufficient testimony.[90]

My first reaction to this statement was one of utmost astonishment. I saw in it—little as Wundt may have meant this— a grave assault on the honor of historical mankind, with which we are united by the bond of moral solidarity. In order to find out whether Wundt's judgment is correct, and whether there are quite different *actions* that only sporadically have been felt or judged to be murder, we must ask what, in fact, the *essence* of murder is, and *what* constitutes the *identical type* of this value-state-of-affairs. This consideration (here presented only peripherally and incompletely) may also provide a methodological example that will assist us in seeking out such types.

One remark is necessary before we begin. It may be that Wundt came to his astonishing conclusion because he used a definition of murder like that which one finds in the present penal code of Germany. Yet this seems unlikely. Wundt would then have regarded as murderers all Germans who in 1870 defended their national border and, in so doing, killed men with intent and deliberation; and he would have viewed hangmen similarly. Although there exists a morbid, spurious, and aberrant emotional pathos among certain groups of our time which regard war as "mass murder," we can be sure that Wundt was far from being influenced by this in his philosophical judgments. There is a definition of murder in old Teutonic moral and legal opinion which, if we disregard its simple nature, could have induced Wundt to say that until relatively recently murder was a permissible action in Germany. For at that time murder was something like what we today call assassination, whereas all open attacks (that is, where the attacked were armed and were expected to defend themselves) and the subsequent killings (with intent and deliberation) were not regarded as murder. We cannot approach history with our latter-day concepts of this type of action in order to check Wundt's thesis. For such "relativism" would again be merely the consequence of the *absolutism of latter-day ethics*, indeed, of present positive law, about which we spoke above.

From the times when human beings were sacrificed to deities and in sacred services, through the times of deeper and more spiritual ideas of sacrifice, which belong to the core of the

90. See Wundt, *Ethik*, 4th ed., III, 59.

Christian religion, to the present time, in which it is considered "good" to devote one's life to spiritual values (of cognition, faith —be it in dangerous work or as martyr—freedom, or patriotism), the value of human life was not given to any ethos as the "highest" value. That human life is "not the highest of goods" corresponds to humanity's common ethos. This fact is undoubtedly incomprehensible to all biological ethics.[91] For according to this ethics, all values that are "higher" than life in its most valuable form, i.e., human life, must be illusions; or, as Friedrich Nietzsche says, their acceptance must be a symptom of declining life, and they themselves "values of *ressentiment*" of the disadvantaged of life, or it must be a result of false obsessions with values that were mistakenly considered absolute because their relativity to life was not known. But this basic conception fails in the light of the clear fact that the value of human life is *not* the highest value, and that the being of other values (those which belong to the modalities of the spiritual and the holy—among these, values of oneself and values of the other, individual and collective values, values of the person and of states of affairs) is preferable to the being of this value.[92] One cannot see how on this biological basis murder can be different in value, not merely in degree, but in *essence*, from killing a man or, indeed, any living being.[93]

91. This is not the case in the ethics of Wundt, who finds the highest principle of moral value-estimation in the "promotion of spiritual goods of culture."

92. The reply that what is involved here is only the sacrifice of individual life for the life-community or the sacrifice of vitally weakened life for strong life, the vulgar for the noble, etc., does not hold. Such an opinion does not do justice to the intentions that people who are ready to make sacrifices factually have. Nor does the opinion hold in those cases in which a whole people is ready to die, for example, for its freedom and honor; this opinion even *contradicts* the ethoses of all eras, which require sacrifices of this kind *first* from the strong and noble—even sacrifices for weakened or lower life.

93. It is true that the Indian ethos (and especially the Buddhist ethos), which prescribes benevolence "toward all things alive" and derivatively toward human life, relativizes this difference. But this is because in this ethos love and benevolence are only a way "toward the deliverance of the heart" (Buddha's Sermons). This contradicts biological ethics, which regards the value of life not only as a positive value but also as the highest value, whereas the Buddhist ethos considers the value of life a negative value. The full moral meaning of the Buddhist idea of love is not "toward a positive value" but "away from oneself." Concerning the feelings and values that ground the moral relatedness to living nature and their underivability from our moral-human relations, see *Zur Phänomenologie und Sympathiegefühle*, pp. 55 ff. [See *ibid.*, pt. B, chap. 1, sec. 2. On the Buddhist idea of love, see "Liebe und Erkenntnis" (Bibliog. no. 11).—*Ed.*]

Even these considerations show that not any action in which a man is killed can be regarded as "murder." Nor can one call institutions permitting such actions institutions that legitimate murder. Certainly this type is based on the state of affairs *that a man has been killed by an action.*" Without it there is no murder. This fact alone implies that if the unity of *"man"* is not given in the idea of man or in the term, it is nevertheless given in emotive understanding, and that this unity is clearly separated from sympathetic relations with animals, say, cattle or domestic animals of a certain group. One must have intuited this "being-human" if he wants to speak at all of murder. A group or a tribe which does not possess this idea or does not comprehend this being-human in factual men, e.g., in strangers, cannot be guilty of murdering them, just as he who mistakes men for animals or trees and shoots at them cannot be guilty. There would also be no murder in cases of a pathological defect in this kind of understanding. A first condition for determining whether "murder" is permitted here or there is a pre-examination of the range of this understanding of being-human and the degree of givenness of the idea in general within different factual groups. If, for example, this ability to understand extended only to members of a tribe, etc., then the killing of a member would be "murder," but not the killing of an outsider. The killing of a man is *not* murder; it is only its presupposition. In cases of murder the *value of the person* in a being "man" must be given in intention, and a possible intention of action must aim at *its* annihilation. Let us consider some examples.

Perhaps Wundt was thinking of the institution of sacrificing humans to gods, i.e., to beings considered absolutely holy. Was such an institution a legitimation of "murder"? Certainly not! It rested on diverse superstitions, e.g., that by sacrificing humans, one could do service to *both* the gods and the sacrificed humans or fulfill the just demands of the gods. In the first place it was the most handsome and noble youths and virgins, as well as the most beloved, who were chosen to be sacrificed. The intention was hardly to annihilate the being of the *person* concerned, or the "let it be annihilated," which belongs essentially to murder. There was rather the cointention, implicit in the intention of love and favor, of the *affirmation* of the being of the person. How else could there be a genuine *sacrifice*? Even in cases of fulfilling a legal demand under certain conditions (with regard to strangers or prisoners) or of "reconciliation with gods," the intention of annihilation, which is essential to murder, was missing. But the sacrifice of the being and life of a man for *any* utilitarian needs or for the sake of convenience was always proscribed by *every* ethos. Of course, this institution could have been abused for egotistical purposes, for example, to gain favor for oneself or one's family from the gods,[94] the priests, or the people in power, to get rid of a hated enemy, or to secure one's possessions or wife, etc. But under the dominance of this institution such actions and the implicit moral tenor were considered evil and impious. Yet, the law of preferring, according to which life-values are to be subordinated to values of the holy and spiritual values, encompassing those of rightness, was *fulfilled* through this institution—although under superstitious presuppositions. For not only did all of these cases lack the intention of hate and its essential correlate, the annihilation of being; but the actions themselves contained no intention toward the cancellation of being. Frequently the killings in question were nothing but "removals" to a higher sphere of being and value, to heavenly dwelling-places; they were presents to the gods in the form of the very *lived body* of the sacrificed. But this was never understood to be the annihilation of the person himself; such annihilation is precluded by the very idea and essence of *sacrifice,* which includes *devotion* to a positive and valuable being. An act of sacrifice in which the sacrificed is annihilated is a *contradictio in adjecto.*

This holds analogously for capital punishment. Of course, capital punishment is (morally) murder whenever it is committed with the intention to annihilate being, i.e., whenever the life of a man is equated with his being, and the continuation of his life is not intuitively given (and is without "proof").[95] For punishment is the administration of an evil and the spoliation of a good. Punishment which annihilates the punished is not punishment. *"Punishment"* presupposes that the life of the punished is a good *for* him as a person whose existence is not affected by the removal of this good. Annihilation of a human being, say, for the well-being of society, is (ethically) murder.[96] Only when there is the intention of not annihilating the person,

---

94. See the completely erroneous interpretation of these facts in Herbert Spencer, *The Inductions of Ethics* (London: Appleton, 1892), chap. 10.

95. On the different kinds of givenness of the afterlife of the person, see my speech "Die Idee des Todes und das Fortleben."

96. See Bismarck's well-known speech before the Prussian Parliament, which touches on this point, so important in ethics.

and when *his right* is also realized in the realization of the order of right,[97] is there no factor of murder involved.[98]

Why is it that killing in wars or in duels is not murder? In cases of killing people in wars (including wars of aggression) there is first of all no givenness of *persons* in what is called the enemy. The individual is given only as a member of a collective thing, "the enemy," which is a complex of vital power. The other nation may well be an object of hate and revenge, but not a person belonging to it. Of course, the state of war can be misused, for example, when one kills a personal enemy or robs and personally enriches himself by killing certain persons. Here, of course, we are concerned with common murder. But whenever persons are given in war, the intention toward the negation and annihilation of these persons is so little given that, on the contrary, the principle of *chivalry* demands not only that the person expose himself to the same kind and degree of danger as he affords but also that he *affirm the favor* of the *person* of the enemy, in its value and its existence, the better and more courageously he fights and defends himself. A certain measure of positive valuation of the enemy is connected with the very agreement to duel.[99]

Murder, we said, presupposes the givenness of a human being as a *person* and as a bearer of possible *values of the person.* The value-complex that underlies murder is essentially connected with the intention to annihilate the person. Thus it is understandable—indeed, it is clearly consequential—that whenever men are killed who are not given "as persons" or "acknowledged" as such, there is no murder. This is the case, for example, with the erstwhile Indian custom of burning widows. The institution is understandable only when the personality (or the "soul,"

97. Thus the killing of the heretic not only served the salvation of the whole, but also was intended to facilitate the purification of his *own* soul.

98. I hope there will be no objections to this based on a misunderstanding to the effect that according to my presuppositions belief in the afterlife of the person would preclude murder. For the question is not what someone "believes" (even with his whole life), but what someone *intends* in an action. The question, therefore, is not how this intention arises, for example, from an intended purpose of robbery, revenge, etc., but what precisely is contained in the center of the intention of the action itself. Its content may be the annihilation of the person, even with such faith. If a person is not given where persons could be given according to the level of moral configuration, we have not murder but homicide [*Totschlag*].

99. We do not want to make a decision here regarding the moral justification of war or individual combat—a problem in itself—or capital punishment. Our concern is to clarify the idea of murder alone.

among the believers in Mohammed) of the woman is denied *at the same time*. A wife was "considered" something that belonged to a male personality. By virtue of the same reasons the ancient Roman *paterfamilias* could kill his children, and the free Roman could kill his slaves—the former his children, "just as he could cut off one of his own limbs," and the latter his slaves, just as he could do away with "things" (Mommsen). In either case there was no givenness (or legal recognition) of the personality of the killed. The child was only a member of the paterfamilias. This *pater* did not desire to annihilate himself as a person in killing the child. He only "hurt himself." The child's acts of will were regarded only as partial acts of the will of the person of the father. The slave, however, was given as a thing. His person and his will were "in the master" (Aristotle). The absence of the givenness of the person also accompanies institutions that maintained the size of a population or the distribution of male and female individuals (killing the newborn, exposing children, etc.). Either the newborn were not given as personalities, but only as animated bodies (in feeling), and the actions involved were therefore experienced as dutiful self-afflictions of the families for the sake of preserving the power of the state and obeying the will of the state; or the unity of personal value (and its autonomous will) was *not* given in human individuals, but in units like family, tribe, gens, state. In these cases the value-complex of murder is *missing*. Abortion is also the killing of a human (a living being), but it is never considered murder (a fact that no "biological" ethics can explain). Abortion was and is not considered murder, because the embryo is not given as a personality. In Rome, as is well known, the embryo was not considered an independent human unit of life, and abortion, as directed to the "viscera" of the mother, was not punished. Abortion was not "killing." During the times of the Roman emperors, abortion was eventually recognized as killing and was consequently punished, but it was—and to this day is—distinguished from murder.

The above is meant to be only an example. But the example shows that there is an *interconnection* between a certain intention in an action and a sharply delineated *value*-complex, i.e., a certain *type* of "acting" and "action" which is held to be evil in every authentic ethos and nowhere "permitted," let alone considered "laudable." But, in contrast to this uniform type, the changing *positive* unities of what obtains and the definitions that provide the conditions for qualifying something as **murder** (according to the degree of moral culture, etc.), i.e., as an actual case of this essential type, are of importance only with regard to the pragmatic criteria concerning what is to be *considered* murder, i.e., a factual realization of this type of unit of acting. Ethics must not content itself with these changing criteria (e.g., the definitions in our penal code or the prevailing opinion about what is "considered" murder). Ethics must tell us what murder *is,* what its *essence* consists in. If a correct attempt is made to solve this difficult problem, the material that apparently proves the "relativism" of such types of evil and good deeds will eventually disappear. The thesis of *relativism* can be held only by one who clings to the changing clothes of these types; who does not see their core because of the covering; who believes that definitions can make such essences *comprehensible,* or even *create* them; or who takes this or that type of covering for their essence.[100]

On the other hand, our example may also show that there is no foundation to the assumption by formal ethics that the proposition *"murder is evil,"* like all non-formal moral value-judgments, has only a factual and relative meaning insofar as it minimally presupposes—or so it is believed—a human organization. Formal ethics must consequently assume that murder can also be good if the murderer merely accepts the soundness of

100. If one grasps the essence of murder, one will realize that *suicide* is *genuine* murder, in contrast to martyrdom or the annihilation of one's body [*Selbstentleibung*]. For the essence of murder lies in the act-intention of annihilating the person and his value in killing him. This pertains to both one's own and another's person, for one's own value is not lower than that of the other. Genuine suicide occurs when the intention is directed toward the non-existence of the person because of a loss of goods whose values are subordinate to the value of the person. These may be spiritual or vital goods, useful or agreeable things (possessions, social freedom, enjoyment of life, etc.). Conversely, *martyrdom* occurs when life, with all its goods, is given away for the higher good, when the preservation of the *spiritual person,* with his *self-values,* is given away for values of faith and cognition (given as "absolute" values). It is precisely the one who commits suicide who affirms the essence of "life" as the highest value (above which he knows no other value), and in his action he (supposedly) annihilates his *being* "as" a bad factual concretization of the value of life affirmed by him as the highest value. In contrast to this, the martyr gives *his* life, given to him as a *positive* value, for a good which to him is essentially *"higher"* than life in general. In affirming *his* life, he negates "life" as the "highest" value. It does not appear to me to make any difference whether he "lets" himself be killed or whether he kills himself, as long as true "self-love," i.e., care for the salvation of his person, as opposed to the self-hate of suicide, leads him by the hand. In the martyr's case there is only the "annihilation of the body," which is, from a moral point of view, totally different from suicide.

"the maxim of his action as a principle of universally valid legislation." For if *no* specific content of intention is evil, *any* intention can be good. And why should someone who elevates his self-hatred and misanthropy to a general principle, and who thereupon establishes a kind of "metaphysics" which holds that the non-being of persons is better than their being, not act out his hate with an awareness that everyone should do likewise? There are cases which approach this possibility. Does one really mean to say that in such cases murder is a morally good deed? It is wrong to conclude that because murder implies killing, which can only be committed against living organisms, the above proposition loses its meaning for "rational beings" in general. Because the *"lived body"* is not an empirical abstraction from earthly organisms but an *essence* and a form of existence which is independent of organisms, the above assertion would also be wrong if the essential nature of "murder" implied the annihilation of a lived body. The above proposition would be "valid" wherever there are embodied personal beings. But what constitutes the ethical core of the value-complex is in fact the volitional intention of one person to annihilate the value of the person in another. In comparison with this core, "killing" itself is only the form of realization that this intention possesses within the realm of embodied personal beings. And therefore this proposition is absolutely valid within *every* possible realm of persons. And it follows from the moral nature of God that he, too, *cannot* will this annihilation—although his omnipotence makes the annihilation of the person *possible*.

We will not undertake an investigation into the special dimensions of relativities among *moralities, mores,* and *customs,* or analogous investigations into the *order of laws*. But we wish to stress that the history of law, too, must include an investigation into the dimensions of relativity in the formations of laws as its basis if it is to be conducted in the correct way.[101]

7. *The So-called Conscience-Subjectivity of Moral Values*

We stressed earlier that the concept of the "subjectivity" of values means something other than the relativity of values to existence. But despite our lengthy treatments of both problems,

---

101. A. Reinach made an excellent attempt to distinguish the absolute from the relative in this sphere. See his "Die apriorischen Grundlagen des bürgerlichen Rechts," *Jahrbuch für Philosophie und phänomenologische Forschung,* Vol. I, no. 2.

the discussion would be incomplete if we did not comment on *another* form of the theory of the subjectivity of moral values, one that takes its departure from *conscience*.

No assertion today is taken more as a "matter of course" or enjoys more universal repute than the assertion that moral value-judgments are *"subjective"* because they are based on declarations of "conscience" and because the recognized *"principle of freedom of conscience"* precludes correction of a declaration of conscience by another instance of insight.

1. Among the reasons leading to a theory of the subjectivity of moral values, there is first of all the fact that objective values are *more difficult* than other objective contents to comprehend and assess. "More difficult" here means that the motives of deception that must be overcome in comprehending moral values are more numerous and stronger than in cases of theoretical cognition. It is therefore much easier to *confuse* contents of objective value-cognition with what our interests suggest. This is so because the comprehension of values presupposes a more difficult struggle against *our* interest and because a successful struggle occurs much less frequently than in normal cases of cognition, not because values are symbols for interests and their conflict, as ethical nominalism asserts. The reason for this fact is that our cognition of moral values is more immediately connected with our *volitional* life than is our theoretical cognition.

This circumstance conditions a number of motives of *value-deception*, which are far more common than other motives of deception. Strangely enough, ethical skepticism is far more common than theoretical and logical skepticism. Nevertheless, the differences among theoretical views of the world [102] are as great as, or perhaps even greater than, differences among existing moral systems. What is the reason for all of this? As I see it, in single cases our differentiating *consciousness* reacts in a more subtle way in what concerns moral values than it does in what concerns theoretical differences among our views and judgments. And the reason for this, in turn, is our tendency to *overestimate* in general the consonance of ethical value-judgments. This overestimation stems from our tendency to justify and excuse our actions by saying that "someone else has acted in this way." Even children habitually justify their actions in this fashion. Discrepancies in the area of values, much more than those in the

102. E.g., of the heavens.

area of theory, make us uneasy, and it is this *uneasiness* that makes such differences in value-judgments *more conspicuous* than those in theoretical judgments. Skepticism is then a consequence of the *disappointment* over our failure to find the expected or sought-for consonance among value-judgments; and this disappointment stems from our weakness, our inability to stand alone when it comes to questions of moral values, which prompts anxious looks in search of someone who might feel and think as we do. Hence we come readily to the proposition: All moral values are *"subjective."*

This tendency to look for social support is so strong that it led Kant to the mistake of trying to establish mere universalizability of a maxim of the will as the measure of moral correctness. The universalization of a maxim that itself commands a *good* is, of course, desirable (insofar as this maxim is not meant originally only for one individual or a class of individuals). Nevertheless, its universalizability from case to case and from man to man does not *make* it morally good in the least! Indeed, as we shall see, there is evidence in a strictly objective insight which shows that a certain kind of willing or acting or being is good *for only one* individual, e.g., for "me," and that it cannot be universalized. Furthermore, we shall see that the more adequate (i.e., the more "objective") moral insight into pure and *absolute moral values* of a being and comportment is, the more it must *necessarily* possess the character of being restricted to individuals.[103] Not only is the exclusion of the universalizability of a "maxim" possible without prejudice to the objectivity and obligatory character of the insight; but it *must* be possible to the degree that we are concerned with ultimate, evidential, and fully adequate insight into the absolute good, and not merely with rules governing the suppression of impulses that dim and distort the mere capacity for this insight. Of course the idea of a declaration of conscience that is binding only for the individual, and whose content is, "This is good for *you,* and *you alone,* no matter what the good for others may be," must be rejected as *self-contradictory* if one falsely believes that the objective and evidential value of the good can be reduced to the mere possible *universalizability* of a maxim. And in *this* case an insight into what is good *"for me"* to do or to will must have the character of a "subjective fancy" or a subjective impulse, devoid of any insight. But in fact the opposite is true. This skeptical tendency

103. See chap. 6, B, sec. 2.

that seeks social support, and this *primary* distrust of true objectivity and insight into the moral good, are what lead to nomism, i.e., the doctrine according to which only the idea of a possible *universally valid* norm allows insight into the good, including "the good for me." The universal validity, as well as the capacity for universalization, of a value-estimation is now supposed to be a kind of substitute for assessments that cannot find fulfillment in intuitively given and evidentially objective values. From a psychological and historical point of view such a procedure is a clear expression of the origin of the value-judgments forming our present code of morals; i.e., their origin is in groups that were instinctively and emotionally weak and possessed with a *désordre du coeur*.[104]

Therefore a feeling and an awareness of inferiority in the presence of objective values are what lead to a kind of act of revenge against values in general and culminate in the proposition: "All" values are "merely" subjective! What led to the supposed "subjectivity" of values, or the interpretation of their true objectivity as "universally valid subjectivity," is a deep-seated and secret experience of impotence—that is, an experience of the inability to realize values and to be somebody through recognizing them—and the subsequent feeling of depression.

2. The prevailing opinion concerning the *subjectivity of values* is nowadays hidden behind the pathos of a term that in a sense summons all the moral tendencies of modern times as if by the call of a trumpet: this term is *freedom of conscience*. We also admit that by this term people mean something great and important, something that must be maintained and preserved. But before we "stand" or "fight" for it, let us permit ourselves to ask what freedom of conscience is.

Auguste Comte, who numbers the principle of the freedom of conscience (together with the principle of the sovereignty of the people) among the fundamentals of what he calls the "metaphysical," "negative," and "critical" epoch, which, in his judgment, is the least significant and the least essential of the epochs that he distinguishes in world history, and which is, according to his conviction, to be replaced by the "positive" epoch, asks this question: Is there among the sciences that provide us with strict insights perhaps something like a freedom of acceptance and rejection? Can we find it in mathematics, physics, chemistry,

---

104. See "Über Ressentiment und moralisches Werturteil," p. 342. [See "Das Ressentiment im Aufbau der Moralen," sec. 5, 2.—*Ed.*]

or even biology? In all domains men accept the results of the sciences and trust and believe in the judgments of the scientists. Comte maintains that this axiomatic deviation in morals as it is expressed by the principle of the freedom of conscience, according to which everyone should have the right to determine what is good and what is evil, can be regarded only as an expression of the inner *moral anarchy* of the metaphysical-critical age. He avers that the principle of the freedom of conscience is neither positive nor creative, but a *dissolving and negative principle* that must be replaced in the "positive age" by an objectively binding insight into good and evil.[105] His observation contains a strange admixture of the true and the false. It is true, no doubt, that the principle of "the freedom of conscience" is frequently used in a way which merely expresses the conviction that there are no possible *objective solutions* in moral matters like those which we are willing to admit in what concerns problems of theoretical cognition. Comte, too, sees through the *désordre du coeur* of this time. But the analogy which he draws between moral cognition and the sciences that he mentions is erroneous (as we see immediately); and in rejecting the false interpretation and application of this principle, Comte also rejects the proper meaning of the term according to which this principle deserves recognition and reverence in his possible "age."

In order to get at the significance of the expression "freedom of conscience," it is necessary to understand what is meant by the term *conscience*.

First, *"conscience"* is not identical with *moral insight*, nor even with a "capacity" for it. Whereas an evidential insight into what is good and evil cannot deceive (for the only possible deception concerns the presence of insight), *there are* "deceptions of conscience." One cannot dismiss the fact of "deceptions of conscience" (as J. G. Fichte and J. F. Fries do) by saying that there are deceptions only in our considering whether *conscience* or *another* feeling or impulse is what suggests something that we (only falsely) take to be a declaration of conscience. Of course, if "conscience" were a final *court of appeals* charged with the final say in moral matters, one would have to conclude that there is no deception in the area of conscience; and conscience would be above any criticism based on another

---

105. Jeremy Bentham evaluates this principle similarly (see his *Deontology* [London: Longman, 1834]).

insight, for instance, that of immediate insight into the objective good, and a fortiori above the insight gained from authoritative and traditional forms of economizing moral insight. But conscience does *not* have this role. "Conscience" is also more or less valuable according to its advising or not advising the objective and evidential *good*. Conscience is a *bearer* of moral values, but it is not their ultimate source. There are conscienceless men not only in the sense that they ignore the clear "voice" of conscience, or do not follow this voice in practice, but let their own drive-impulses win over the clarity of the voice of conscience, but also in the sense that this "voice" is not present at all or present only to a slight degree. The difference between not observing the stirrings of conscience [106] and a deception of conscience becomes clear in all cases when correction or reprimand by someone else *after* the action evokes an *awareness* of the evil of the action and a clear recollection that "nothing bad was seen in this action." This difference also becomes clear when, having had comportment of higher value *shown* to us by another, we subsequently feel and assess our actions "as" bad on this basis.

In addition it must be realized that conscience functions essentially in a *negative* fashion, according to the meaning of the term. Conscience represents something as bad or as something that ought not to be; it "enters a protest." When we say, "Conscience is aroused," we understand immediately that it is set against a certain action. This *never* means that conscience tells us that something is good. For this reason a "guilty conscience" is a decisively more positive phenomenon than a "good conscience," which is, strictly speaking, only an experienced lack or absence of a "guilty conscience" vis-à-vis a certain action that is morally in question. Also, if one "consults his conscience" in cases of volitional decisions, it "warns" and "forbids" more than it recommends or commands. The function of conscience is therefore only *critical*—in part one of warning and in part one of directing; it has no function of giving original, *positive* insight.

As the very core of what one's *own individual cognitive activities* and moral experience *contribute to moral insight*, conscience is only *one* form among others of the economization of ultimate moral insight—in contrast to the knowledge of this type accumulated in the past through authority and tradition. Only the *cooperation* of conscience and principles of authority

106. Ethnologists have confirmed that there are no "stirrings of conscience" among primitive peoples.

and the contents of tradition with the *mutual correction* of *all* these merely *subjective sources of cognition* guarantees the highest degree of subjective acquisition of this insight (in average cases). But *all* these *sources* of moral insight can be appealed to the insight *itself* and to the evidential *self-givenness* of what is good and not good. And if "conscience" becomes an apparent *substitute* for moral insight, the principle of "freedom of conscience" *must* become the principle of *"anarchy* in all moral questions." Anyone can then appeal to his "conscience" and demand absolute recognition of what he says from others.

Conscience obtained this supposed *role of a last court of appeals* only by way of complicated developments.

The word *conscience* first appeared in the Latin language, where *conscientia* meant both "with knowledge" and today's "conscience." Since that time the term has taken on very different meanings. These, however, have gradually moved more and more in the direction of a moral connotation. I would distinguish three stages in the development of the meaning of *conscientia*. The Scholastics identified conscience with practical reason (Aristotle's νοῦς πρακτικός) as a faculty that applies norms (of reason or authority) to an individual case (*casus conscientiae*). The second meaning of *conscience* does not connote a logical bailiff, as does the first. Rather, conscience becomes in part an admonisher and in part a judge (as in the case of Kant, who clearly distinguishes conscience from his "practical reason," i.e., "reason itself" as practical in setting forth norms). In the third meaning of the term, conscience rises above this second function and becomes an inner cognitive organ of good and bad (the character of which is either more rational or more intuitively emotive). Conscience has received its present authority in the sense of the last two meanings as a result of a religious and metaphysical *interpretation* of experiential feelings that were amalgamated *as such,* by virtue of this interpretation, into a unified cognitive or legislative organ of good and rightness that is above all possible deception and error. This interpretation assumes that the *"voice of God"* can be heard in conscience. By virtue of this interpretation (for by nature God *cannot* err or deceive himself) conscience *acquired* the character of a final court of appeals, and it was through this that the modern sense of the word came into existence. But this interpretation was not made subsequently, as if conscience apart from this interpretation could "speak" and maintain its nature as a final court! On the contrary, this interpretation *made* conscience into this supposedly invulnerable and infallible organ! Later on, during the dissolution of religious consciousness, not all people who used the term were aware of this interpretation; but the *pathos* implicit in saying, "My conscience tells me this," echoed this old and traditional interpretation. Yet this pathos would disappear with a complete and lasting elimination of this interpretation, and so also the faith in such a unified and infallible voice. Conscience in this sense is one of the many colors of the sunset of religious belief. If, however, the principle of freedom of conscience is maintained without this interpretation, as in modern times, when even atheists use it and appeal to it and raise demands in its name, it *must* consequently become the *"principle of moral anarchy."*

3. What we have said must be the case also because of another shift in meaning of the concept of conscience. There are two forms of moral insight—one pertaining to the moral value of universal norms and the other only to what is good "for" an individual or "for" a group. The two are of equal rigor and objectivity. "Conscience" in the legitimate sense is this: (1) it represents the *individual form of the economization* of moral insight, and (2) it represents this insight only insofar as it is directed to the *good as such* "for me" (i.e., only within these bounds). Of course, this individual form of the economization of moral insight can pertain to what is *universally* good and right as well. And this good "for me" can be exhibited not only *by* me but also by another (a friend, an authority, etc.) who knows me better than I know myself. But one can speak correctly of "conscience" *only* when it is a matter of the above plus the necessary moral insight which is not and cannot be contained in universal norms, and in which the process of moral cognition is completed —and when *I* come to this insight *by myself*. The issue of my increasing insight into the good (from my own life-experience) —insofar as it is "the good for me"—constitutes the essence of conscience. Conscience in this sense is *essentially* irreplaceable by any possible "norm," "moral law," etc. It only begins to work when the latter cease, and when acting and willing already satisfy norms and moral laws. The *more clearly* conscience speaks, the more it must tell each person something different for the same situation. And it would be mistaken if it told everyone the same thing! In terms of *"conscience"* in this sense, the *principle of the freedom of conscience* is unconditionally valid. According to this principle everyone is free to listen to his conscience when the question involves solutions which are *not*

regulated by the *objective and universal part* of evidential value-propositions and the norms based on them (and which cannot be regulated according to the nature of such propositions and norms). It therefore belongs by right to a moral individual qua *individual* to be protected by this principle from the false claims of merely universal moral laws. But this conscience and the freedom of conscience dissolve neither the idea of an *objective good,* for which "conscience" is precisely a cognitive organ insofar as it is the objective good "for" an individual, nor the idea and the right of a universal insight in regard to value-propositions and norms that are valid for all men. On the contrary, these are quite independent of "conscience" and are accessible through strict insight; and they possess an *obliging character* that is wholly *independent* of *recognition by conscience* on the part of anyone. "Freedom of conscience" in the true sense can therefore never be played off against a strict and objective and obliging cognition of *universally valid* and also *non-formal* moral propositions. It is therefore certainly *not* a "principle of anarchy" in moral questions.

Doubtless the predominant sense of the above formula does not correspond at all to what I just defined, but rather to what Comte has in mind. This "predominant sense" is based on the presupposition that there is no difference between the *good as such* "for" individual *A* and that for individual *B,* i.e., the presupposition that an objective good as such *must* be of universal validity! Indeed, it is the presupposition that something *becomes* "good" only through correspondence to a law that can claim universal validity! And "conscience" is supposed to be something that can "freely" affirm and deny, recognize and reject, these "values and norms," which are inherently "universally valid"! Only this "sense" of conscience, which originates in the moral individual's being *deprived* of all the individual rights and duties that are *his* alone, and which presupposes a moral degradation and denial of his *individual dignity,* is the principle of the freedom of conscience which Comte refers to as "a principle of a most subjectivistic anarchy in all moral questions" and an expression of a *désordre du coeur* raised to the level of a principle. This principle must make every *expert* discussion of such questions a priori impossible (since such discussions make sense only when there is something objective to be determined); it must also make any recognition of the necessity of an authority in such discussion impossible; and hence everything becomes a matter of subjective "taste"! Reduced to a theoretical formula, "conscience" becomes a "universal voice of reason," or even a voice of so-called instincts of the species above "individual selfishness," etc. The assertion of the "freedom" of *this* "conscience" denies the very *idea* of objective value-insight and objective ethics. Indeed, we find here the direct opposite of the *true* sense of freedom of conscience. Whenever through insight and truth there is in fact *objective and universal cognition* with ensuing norms and obligation, subjective discretion is declared permanent by an appeal to "conscience" even though joint and objective investigation and cognition are the only possibilities. But whenever in fact *"conscience"* must speak as a vehicle of individually valid insight, which therefore is not less objective, and the principle of the *freedom* of conscience also obtains, the binding of the individual by a so-called universal generic reason, or, better, by the voice of a collective imagination of a majority that resulted from a mutual contagion, is established; *and with this* both conscience and freedom of conscience are violated in principle.

4. However, if Auguste Comte is correct in demanding an objective investigation into good and evil which would have generally valid results, his analogies with mathematics and physics fail in one respect to do justice to the *peculiarity* of this area of knowledge. Comte also *fails* to see that all ethical cognition must be based on the *"value-experience" that occurs in feeling and preferring,* just as all theoretical thinking must be based on sensory experience. Like all positivists, Comte substitutes a technology of actions that are conducive to the general welfare for an ethics that is based on value-experience and in so doing presupposes that the general welfare is the basic value. But, as I have shown, the fact that ethical cognition is effected according to the strict laws of *"feeling"* does not make ethics "subjective." Nevertheless, this fact justifies a distinction between ethics and the above "sciences," and Comte's analogy does not do this justice. If in questions of ethics we do not rely on the solutions of scholars and teachers of morals as in astronomy we rely on astronomers, it is because all "ethics" presupposes moral insight as already evidential *in* feeling, preferring, loving, hating. Positivism fails to recognize this because it wants to ground ethics itself in biology and history or sociology. The subjective aptitude for this insight is, however, connected with conditions—apart from differences among so-called talents for it—which cannot be compared to the general conditions of the aptitude for scientific or even theoretical cognition. Because here

we find not only those sources of deception common to all kinds of cognition but also all those sources of deception that have their roots in the interests of individuals and groups, a subjective aptitude for moral insight *presupposes* something that can only be the fruit of moral insight: namely, a whole system of means to eliminate sources of deception so that moral insight can become possible. That is, we are confronted here with the *antinomy* of which Aristotle was already aware. Moral insight is necessary to lead a good life (to will and to act in a good way). A good life is necessary to eradicate the sources of deception in moral insight so that we can eliminate not only the sophism of our interests that obstruct moral insight but also the ever present tendency to adjust our value-judgments to our factual willing and acting (and our weaknesses, deficiencies, faults, etc.). The theoretical solution to this antinomy consists in the fact that all good *being, life,* willing, and acting presuppose the *fact of moral insight* (but not an "ethics"). But the subjective aptitude for this insight presupposes on its part a good *being* and *life.* Here we find no analogy with theoretical cognition, which does not have these sources of deception.

From this fundamental relation between moral insight and the moral life, there arises within the class of moral values the moral self-value of an arrangement by which the content of the assets of the moral insight of the best men [107] is first prescribed and advised to all (even to individuals as bearers of authority), through mere commands and advice, as a norm: the *moral self-value of authority* as such (independent of the question of in which authority this value is represented, and independent of the question of how true and false authority and forces counter to morals are to be distinguished). I need not stress that this shows the absurdity of a so-called ethics of authority that seeks to base the content and nature of "good" and "evil" on the norms and commands of an authority (Hobbes, the Scotists, Kirchmann, etc.). For this ethics denies the moral value [*Eigenwert*] of authority inasmuch as it would replace moral insight with the commands of authority. If good and evil were what authority says they are, authority could have no evidential moral value. Both command and obedience would have to be equally "blind." But the moral value of authority as such is still an *evidential* principle. Whereas there is no "authority" in the area of

---

107. I.e., of those whose personal being is grasped as good in moral insight.

theoretical knowledge, and whereas the principle of "freedom of research" can be justifiably opposed to any factual claim of authority, within the entire sphere of moral problematics the being of an authority is the indispensable condition for the entrance of evidential moral value-estimations, as well as the demands that are based on them, into the region of factual insight, for they are *first* practically executed without insight into the mere commands of an authority. But in such a case of pure obedience to authority it is presupposed that the moral value of the commanding authority, or, more precisely, the truly authoritative nature of the commanding institution, is itself evident to the one who obeys. Authority differs from mere power or force in that a person can possess authority only over one who knows by evidence that this person possesses a deeper and wider moral insight than he does. Moral *"trust"* in an authority is based on this insight, and authority is based on this trust. If this trust is removed, authority becomes non-moral power and force.

But all authority is limited by the sphere in which *conscience* rules as a *peculiar* source of insight. All authority pertains only to what is *universally* and evidentially good, not to what is *individually valid* and evidentially good. The intrusion of a command of authority into the value-sphere that lies beyond universally valid values makes the command immoral [*widersittlich*].

8. The Stratification of the Emotional Life

If one accepts Kant's presuppositions concerning the nature of the emotional life, it follows as a matter of course that every non-formal ethics is of necessity not only a eudaemonism but also a hedonism, i.e., that the relation of things and actions to sensuous pleasure (in the case of any non-formal value-estimation) constitutes the meaning of the estimation.[108] We have seen that no relation to a feeling-state of any kind, be it sensible or not, can constitute or make values—least of all, moral values. But this is not to say that both the emotional intention and the feeling-states of moral subjects are not essentially connected with the moral values of persons, their acts, willing, and deeds,

108. [Sec. 8 of this chapter is connected with the problems discussed in the introduction to this chapter and in sec. 1. The following investigations into the levels of depth of the emotional life form the basis for the essential interconnections established in secs. 9 and 10 and thus for the clarification of the "old problem of happiness and morality."—*Ed.*]

the cognition of which affords a solution to the old problem of *"happiness and morality"* that is quite different from that which Kant (and other earlier thinkers) gave.

It is not possible at this point to develop the phenomenology of the emotional life to an extent that would enable us to approach a solution to this realm of questions or even the realm of those which are also relevant to ethics. Nevertheless, let us mention some basic laws that, we believe, we have found insofar as they are of importance for the problem of ethics.

For an ethics which rejects the idea that man strives for the realization of feeling-states without having a value-consciousness of what he is striving for, and for an ethics which rejects (by virtue of the aforementioned law of preferring, according to which all values of feeling-states are subordinated to values of the person, acts, functions, and deeds) the proposition that man *ought* to strive for happiness, two questions remain. The first of these pertains to the interconnection of basic types of feeling-states with the moral value of the person and his willing and acting. It is the question of whether the being of certain feelings is connected with moral being and comportment by *essential necessity*—whether comportment of positive value is connected with a positive feeling that is of positive value, and comportment of negative value with a negative feeling that is of negative value, whether comportment of higher value is connected with feelings of a different stratum and kind from that with which comportment of lower value is connected, etc.—or whether this connection is only *empirical* and *contingent,* or whether, as Kant and the Stoics believed, there is only a connection between the *ought* and the *"worthiness"* of a good man to be, for example, happy.[109] The second question pertains to the essentially necessary role that feeling-states and their kinds play, not as *ends* of striving and willing oriented toward realizing values, but as experienceable *sources* of striving toward values of a certain rank. This question has too often been connected with the question of so-called *eudaemonism.* However, the proposition that only blissful men can will and act morally, which has been recognized by so many great men,[110] has nothing at all to do with eudaemon-

---

109. It is well known that Kant's postulates of a highest good and of a moral governor of the world are based on this interconnection of the ought.

110. This was one of the basic ideas of Luther, who surely was no eudaemonist; in addition, Spinoza's claim that happiness is not a reward of virtue but virtue itself and the wellspring of all good actions has no

ism, i.e., the theory that happiness is an end of striving and, indeed, *the* end most worthy of striving for. It may very well be that blissfulness necessarily accompanies all good personal being; indeed, blissfulness may well be the necessary "source" of good comportment. But it is not likely that blissfulness is at the same time, perhaps because *it is precisely that,* the end and the purpose of striving, willing, and acting.

We mentioned before that in the emotional life known to us there is a *stratification* that is not present in the different kinds of fortuitous emotional excitation.[111] There can be no doubt that the facts which are designated in such a finely differentiated language as German by "bliss," "blissfulness" [*Glückseligkeit*], "being happy" (the term *happy* is frequently used in the sense of "lucky"), "serenity," "cheerfulness," and feelings of "comfort," "pleasure," and "agreeableness" are not simply similar types of emotional facts which differ only in terms of their intensities, or which are merely connected with different sensations and objective correlates. Rather, these terms (like their opposites, "despair," "misery," "calamity," "sadness," "suffering," "unhappy," "disagreeable") designate sharply delineated *differentiations* among positive and negative feelings. It is, for example, impossible for one to be "blissful" over happenings of the same value-complex that are "disagreeable" to another; the differences in these feelings also seem somehow to require different value-complexes. In trying to grasp the nature of these differences, it does not suffice to admit different qualities of feeling that differ in character from pleasure and displeasure, as both Lotze and Lipps did—and in our opinion they were justified in doing so. Of course, woefulness is qualitatively distinct from sadness; but there is quite a difference between sadness (or woefulness) and a painful feeling on the skin, and in this sense the difference is not one of quality. It appears to me that the special kind of difference is made evident by the fact that both types of feeling can *coexist* in one and the same act and moment of consciousness, and this most clearly when they posses different, i.e., both positive and negative, characters. This is most clear in extreme cases. A human being can be blissful while suffering from bodily pain; indeed, for a true martyr, in his conviction of faith, this suffering may itself be a blissful suffering. On the other

---

eudaemonistic meaning. For the eudaemonist sees in virtue only a disposition to bring about happiness.

111. [See chap. 2, B, secs. 3, 5. See also the introduction to chap. 5.—Ed.]

hand one in a state of "deep despair in his soul" can experience some sensuous pleasure and enjoy it in a state of ego-concentratedness. One can also be "serene" and "calm" while experiencing a serious misfortune, for instance, a great loss of property, whereas it is impossible to be "joyful" in this situation. One can also drink a glass of wine while being unhappy and still enjoy the bouquet of the wine. In these and similar cases the feeling-states involved do not constitute a rapidly changing sequence—as is the case if one takes different value-aspects of an event into consideration—for these feeling-states are given at the same time. But they do not *blend* into the unity of a total feeling-state. Nor are they different from each other merely by virtue of differences among their objective correlates. The latter frequently disappear from consciousness while the feeling-states as essentially different from each other remain. Feeling-states are also lived and given in quite different manners. One can think of a happy smile amidst grave suffering in experience and expression. In such happiness we feelingly move from the central depth of the ego into a peripheral stratum of our psychic existence. Whether we remain in this stratum for a long time or not, this "grave suffering" remains in the depth of the ego; and it leaves a deep imprint upon the totality of our states throughout the vacillations of the feeling-states belonging to this peripheral level.[112] Expression also participates in this difference. A careworn face remains that, even in a smile. A serene face remains serene, even while crying. The fact that there is no blending into one feeling, as is the case in feeling of such diverse *levels of depth,* points to the fact that feelings are not only of different qualities but also of different levels of *depth.* It is impossible to be simultaneously woeful and sad: *one* feeling is always the result.[113]

Both feeling-functions and emotional acts, as well as feeling-states, participate in such depths. Feeling-functions and emotional acts break into experience from a deeper source in the ego, and the fulfillment of the intentions contained in them gives us —when we are concerned with values—a deeper *contentment.* Feeling-states are attached to a deeper level of the ego and at the same time *fulfill* the center of the ego in a richer way. And

112. When Luther's young daughter Magdalene died, he said: "I am happy in my spirit, yet very sad in my flesh. It is a strange thing indeed to know that she rests in peace and that she is well, yet still to be so sad." (*Tischreden, Der Tod,* 2.)

113. It is only with sensible feelings that feelings remain differentiated by virtue of their localization and extension.

in the wake of this they cast their light in varying degrees on other contents of consciousness and color them.

I find this phenomenal character of the *"depth"* of feeling to be essentially connected with four well-delineated *levels* of feeling that correspond to the structure of our entire human existence. These are (1) *sensible feelings,* or "feelings of sensation" (Carl Stumpf),[114] (2) *feelings of the lived body* (as states) and *feelings of life* (as functions), (3) *pure psychic feelings* (pure feelings of the ego), and (4) *spiritual feelings* (feelings of the personality).

All "feelings" possess an experienced relatedness to the ego (or to the person). This relatedness *distinguishes* them from other contents and functions (sensing, representing, etc.) and is in principle different from the relatedness that can accompany representation, willing, and thinking. This former relatedness belongs not only to states but also to functions. When I feel "something," e.g., some value, this felt thing is joined to me more intimately through this function than anything is through representation. The difference between this ego-relatedness proper to the emotional and an "I represent" consists in the fact that the subjective character of experience does not wax or wane with the activity that goes into it as it does in the intellectual sphere. Whereas all kinds of increased activity (both in striving and in noticing [*Aufmerken*], with its subdivisions) bind intellectual contents or volitional projects more and more to the ego, such activity tends more and more to *detach* feeling from the ego whenever it takes place and to the degree that it takes place. And with this it tends more and more to extinguish the feeling-character of the ego. Intellectual contents must be more or less "sustained" by the ego if they are not to become detached from it. Feelings are *originaliter* on the ego. They can be kept *away,* but only by way of activity. That is, they always return quasi-

---

114. [The author used the terms "feelings of sensation" (*Empfindungs-gefühle*) and "sensations of feeling" (*Gefühlsempfindungen*) in the same way in his discussion of the levels of sensible feelings (see above, pp. 60, 105). Carl Stumpf, whom the author cites here and above (p. 60), used only the term "feelings of sensation" for sensible feelings (in contrast to the higher "emotions" [*Gemütsbewegungen*]). Stumpf used "feelings of sensation" as the opposite of "imagined feelings" (e.g., a toothache as opposed to "a toothache in memory"), whereas the author did not recognize imagined feelings among the levels of sensible feelings (as purely "actual" facts). See below, p. 334. See Carl Stumpf, *Gefühl und Gefühlsempfindung* (Leipzig, 1928), a special volume comprising works of his that first appeared in *Zeitschrift für Psychologie und Physiologie* in 1899, 1907, and 1916.—Ed.]

automatically to the ego. And for this reason feelings cannot be controlled or managed arbitrarily. They can be controlled or managed only indirectly, by controlling their causes and effects (expression, actions).

Yet, this *general* relatedness of feelings to the ego is, in each of the above four types of feelings, a fundamentally and essentially different relatedness.

We find *sensible feelings* to be sharply characterized by the following factors.

1. In contrast to all other feelings, a sensible feeling is given as *extended* and *localized* in specific parts of the lived body. It is structured according to the more or less clearly experienced *units of organs* of the lived body (but not on the basis of those units as perceived from the outside). Though it is incapable of "movement" in the strict sense of the term, a sensible feeling can change from place to place. It can also "extend" itself more or less feelably and affect farther and more remote parts of the body.[115] This appears to me to be evident in all kinds of pain and sensible agreeableness, e.g., eating, drinking, touching, lust.

2. A sensible feeling cannot be separated from the contents of sensation by attention. There can be no doubt concerning which group of such contents belongs to it. It is never objectless; still, it does not "face" contents in any way and is without any "intention" toward them. This is expressed in the proposition: A sensible feeling is given essentially as a *state,* never as a function or an act. Purely sensible feelings therefore lack even the most primitive form of intentionality: "having a mind to." [116] But they can become an object of, say, enjoying and suffering and can enter into the enjoyment or suffering of value-complexes through a peculiar corelatedness. But they themselves contain nothing of those functions. Even the simplest sensible feeling is never connected with one single sensation, but always represents, in relation to the contents of sensation, a new *quality* founded on a series and an order of the contents of sensation. A sensible feeling is therefore not a property or "shade" of sensation itself,

115. Its intensity does not vary independent of extension; extension grows with intensity, but not vice versa. I believe that Henri Bergson failed in his attempt to reduce intensity to extension. See his *Essai sur les Données Immédiates de la Conscience* (Paris: Alcan, 1904).

116. The vitally important types of tickling feeling, which bear in themselves a tendency toward their increase and finally their cancellation after reaching a maximum point, and whose stimulus-object is always characterized by movement, are clearly distinct from the *purely* sensible feelings.

something that would be attached to sensation like a quality or an intensity. Its thresholds and degrees of intensity do not at all coincide with those of sensation.[117]

3. A sensible feeling has no relation to the person. It is related only to the *ego* in a *doubly indirect* manner. It is not attached to the ego as immediately as purely psychic feelings are, for example, sadness, woe, grief, and happiness; it does not immediately fill the *body-ego* as genuine lived-body feelings do, nor is it attached to the body-ego as they are. This body-ego is related to the psychic ego only by the phenomenal relational fact of "my body," including all feeling belonging to it. Nor is a sensible feeling directly related to the lived body so that I always find it present in my body-consciousness as an emotional shade. Rather, it is given as founded on the givenness of some already delineated *part* of the lived body. It is given as a state of this part, and it is through this twofold experiential relatedness that it is related to the ego. I feel a sensible feeling "where" I experience the organic unit whose state it is.[118]

4. A sensible feeling is by its nature exclusively an *actual* [aktueller] fact. That is, there is no truly emotive remembering and expecting, or, more precisely, *no "refeeling," no "postfeeling," no "prefeeling,"* and *no fellow feeling.* Its exclusive form of existence is to be at some time and at some place *on* the lived body. I can of course bring about the appearance of a similar sensible feeling in me (although to a lesser degree) by remembering or reproducing the objects that were its stimuli. But such a feeling is a *new* sensible feeling and is given as such. Apart from this, only the causes and effects of the sensible feeling proper are given in reliving, remembering, and expecting it, but it is not itself accessible to me. On the other hand, the assertion that the *entire* emotional sphere contains nothing truly analogous to representations, remembrances, and expectations appears erroneous to me. For I can *feelingly* bring to mind a *psychic* feeling that I have never experienced; I can (in fancy) feel through something that I have never felt, though this given content does not become an actual feeling-state (e.g., in understanding a novel); I can feelingly understand something that I have never felt (e.g., feelingly understand a good man as a sinner, or a sinner as a good man); I can, if I have experienced a certain feeling, subsequently

117. See Kowalewski's investigations in Loewenfeld, *Grenzfragen des Nerven- und Seelenlebens.*

118. Pain is localized in the amputated limb only because the limb is still supposedly given.

postfeel it *in an iterating fashion* and feelingly "re-experience" it as the *same* feeling, and I can feelingly *anticipate* its reoccurrence; and I can—and this is especially significant for ethics—share the "same" grief "with" another *feelingly. Sensible feelings are completely and essentially devoid of all this.* Though they can be the stimuli of emotional contagion, they can never be the foundation of fellow feeling; [119] and though they can reappear in a weaker form as similar feelings, they can never be remembered or (feelingly) represented. For precisely this reason their *stimulus-object* must necessarily be given as *"present."* Although we can take sensible pleasure in an absent object, e.g., a human being who is not present, we can do so only when we represent him or imagine him *as present.* This is not the case with the joy of love when a human being is, for instance, represented as absent; for his being nevertheless gives rise to joy. As I have shown elsewhere, all vital feelings also remain accessible to postfeeling, prefeeling, and fellow feeling.[120]

5. Sensible feelings are essentially *punctual, without duration* or *continuity of sense.* Concerning punctuality and lack of duration, I refer to what I said in part I.[121] They have no continuity of sense because there are no interconnections of fulfillment among them, and because no sensible feelings essentially belong together or are essentially opposed. A feeling like that of, say, repentance—no matter when repentance sets in—can suppress a negative feeling of oneself resulting from a bad deed.[122] There is here an obvious essential interconnection. Either fear and hope (two vital feeling-functions) are fulfilled in special feelings, or they are not fulfilled; and they disappear with such "fulfillments." But a purely sensible feeling does not "require" anything; at best it "fulfills" a striving for it, but it never fulfills another *emotional* function. It "signifies" nothing in the future and nothing in the past, and it is without any possible emotional consequence in experience. Nor is it a "lived" consequence resulting from other emotional experiences.

6. Among all feelings, the *sensible* feeling is the one least disturbed by *attention* given to it. Indeed, it seems that it does not begin to disappear, as other feelings do, when attention is given to it; it seems to increase or stand out indirectly in con-

---

119. See above, p. 93.
120. See *Zur Phänomenologie und Sympathiegefühle,* p. 27. [See *Wesen und Formen der Sympathie,* pt. I, A, chap. 3.—Ed.]
121. [See chap. 2, B, sec. 3.—Ed.]
122. [See "Reue und Wiedergeburt" (Bibliog. no. 14).—Ed.]

sciousness with increases in the clarity of the basis of sensation that always accompanies it. On the other hand, *all vital* feelings are at least disturbed in their normal course when attention is directed to them. They function meaningfully and normally only when they are beyond the sphere illuminated by attention. All *vital* feelings, which always help us to regulate our *life-activities meaningfully,* thrive only in the dark, and their fostering and fertile power is destroyed by attention. *Purely psychic* feelings tend to dissolve completely when exposed to the light of attention —to various degrees, depending on the type of attention. Thus pain becomes *easier* to bear when attention is not directed to it, for example, when one seeks diversion or occupies himself with something interesting. Sometimes pain is not even "noticed," let alone observed, e.g., in war or in the middle of a battle. In contrast to this, the *pressure* of psychic grief *grows* when attention is artificially diverted from its object; and, *conversely,* it is the attention that is strongly directed toward it, plus the mental analysis as well as the objectification of it, which has a "liberating" effect.

7. Of greatest importance for the problem of ethics is the fact that *the more* feelings approach the level of 'sensible' feeling-states, *the more* having or not having feelings is subject to *willing* and *not willing* (and consequently to practical methods of control). Even *vital feelings* are much less subject to practical and arbitrary changes, and psychic feelings still less so. Spiritual feelings of the person are not at all subject to arbitrary change. Every sensible pleasure can be produced by an application of adequate stimuli insofar as no anesthesia of feelings or sensations is involved in the production; [123] in principle, every kind of pain is subject to treatment by narcotics. On the other hand, feelings of well-being or discomfort, vitality or fatigue, health or illness, or maturing or declining life *cannot* be willed or produced in this manner. They are dependent on one's whole way of life and even more on individual and racial dispositions. One can change them only to a limited degree by some kind of practical measures. And *purely psychic* feelings, to the degree that they are pure and unmixed with vital states, are attached so intimately to the *entire* constellation of contents of the individual consciousness that they are even less subject to purposeful control than vital feelings are. Depending on the degree of depth within their

123. Concerning the separability of the two kinds of anesthesia, see H. Lotze, *Medizinische Psychologie oder Physiologie der Seele* (Leipzig, 1852).

depth-stratum, they possess their own special endurability and rhythm of fading away. In this regard they can be disturbed in their inner givenness by arbitrary suppression or the displacement of oversight, but they can never be modified. Feelings which *spontaneously* issue forth from the depth of our person are beyond *any* volitional control. The least "reactive" feelings are therefore the *bliss and despair* of the person himself. Only the *reactive* feelings, to the degree that they are reactive, are subject to arbitrary production. But the others present themselves, if I may say so, as pure "grace." Despite their significance as the *sources* of our comportment as well as our willing, it is impossible to *intend* them or even posit their being or non-being as a "purpose."

In light of these facts it is completely understandable that all practical eudaemonism—i.e., all ethical comportment in which feelings of pleasure represent goals and purposes of striving and willing, whether one's own or another's—must necessarily acquire a tendency to direct all the volitional activities in such comportment toward the mere augmentation of *sensible pleasure;* that is, it must become a *hedonism.* The reason for this is not that there are no pleasures other than sensible ones, or that all pleasure develops genetically from "sensible pleasure." It is, rather, that the *causes* of *sensible pleasure alone* are immediately subject to *practical control,* e.g., within socioethical activities, first of all within relations of property. On the other hand, in the history of ethics the pragmatic effects of social reformers frequently even led to a failure to consider non-sensible feelings of happiness, or to an insufficient consideration of them as realizing bearers of values (as in the case of Bentham), or to the assumption that all other kinds of pleasure are merely genetic developments from sensible pleasure (as in the case of Spencer). Bentham, for example, explicitly attempts in his "deontology" to measure the magnitude of the "sum of pleasure" according to the magnitude of possessions; this becomes apparent not only when he says that possession, apart from its function as an autonomous source of pleasure, is a source of pleasure that is necessarily *involved* in the disclosure of *all other sources of pleasure,* but also when he says that possession is the *only practically controllable* source of pleasure. But neither he nor any of his utilitarian followers ever comes to the insight so important for ethics, namely, that the *value* and the moral significance of feelings of happiness as sources of moral willing are *inversely proportional* to their *attainability through willing and acting.* They did not see that *originaliter* necessarily only joys of the *lowest value* can be influenced by possible "reforms" of social and legal systems and by sociopolitical actions in general, that joys (and sufferings) *necessarily* elude such influences more and more, the deeper they lie in their *strata*. It seems to me that ethicists from Socrates to Tolstoi, who again and again demanded, in opposition to such endeavors, *a communion of the person with himself*, were guided —consciously or unconsciously—by insight into this fact; that is, they called for a regress toward the deeper strata of the being and life of the person, and they found moral salvation only in the inner regeneration of the person, not in any change of mere "systems."

Let us now turn to the stratum of *vital feelings*.

First, vital feelings and their modes represent a unique stratum of the emotional life; they *cannot be reduced* to the stratum of sensible feelings, because they possess characteristics that diverge from those of sensible feelings.

The assumption that vital feelings (and their modalities) can be reduced to pleasure and displeasure as sensible appearances, that they represent only a "fusion" of pleasure and displeasure, and that all elementary conative impulses are determined by sensible pleasure and displeasure, does not hold up at all in light of a phenomenological consideration of the levels of the emotional life and the conative life.[124]

We have mentioned many of the phenomenal characteristics of vital feelings. Whereas a sensible feeling is extended and localized, a vital feeling participates in the total extension of the lived body but has no special extension "in" it and possesses no place. A feeling of comfort and its opposite, e.g., health and illness, fatigue and vigor, cannot be determined in terms of localization or of certain organs so that one can ask: Where does it ache? Where do you feel pleasure? How far does your pain extend? Is your pain piercing or pricking? Nevertheless, these feelings clearly are, in contrast to psychic and spiritual feelings, e.g., sadness, woe, bliss, despair, *feelings of the lived body*. "I" cannot "be" comfortable or uncomfortable in the manner in

---

124. As to the objective side of the appearances of life, one can by analogy also show that the theory which *exactly corresponds* to that of sensualistic-associative and psychological explanations of vital feelings and which claims that the total vital activity of an organism is the mere sum and reciprocal effects of isolated activities of the organs, tissues, and cells, i.e., the "cellular-state theory" of organic life, does *not* do justice to the facts. We deal here first with the subjective side of the processes concerned.

which I am "sad," "blissful," or "in despair." Rather, "I" can only "feel myself" so. This "myself" is this *lived-body-ego,* a unitary consciousness of my lived body, from whose totality separate organic sensations and feelings emerge only secondarily from the background, as it were, that founds them. There is no reason to assume that the extension and place of sensible feelings are merely "apparent," and that sensible feelings are in fact as extensionless and placeless as psychic and mental feelings, or that they are connected by "associations of experience" with images of individual organs, or that they are merely "projected" onto such organs. In pain and sensible pleasure we can find extension and place without any knowledge whatsoever of the respective organs (either through outer perception or through remembered images of them). What we are saying cannot be refuted by citing cases of deception, e.g., the sensations of pain in a person whose arm has been amputated and who believes that he feels pain in the amputated arm, or the migrating hysterical pains that have no peripheral basis. Such deceptions presuppose the givenness of the normal case. In the first case above a pictorial memory may overcome the factual sensation of pain in the remaining part of the limb, whereas in the second case there are emotional illusions that are different in principle from representative illusions in terms of the nature and mechanism of the illusion. To make a diagnosis, the physician must avail himself of the subjective symptom of the illness and therefore must *presuppose* the authenticity of the phenomena—at least until new phenomena give him reason to doubt the content of his patient's statements. Besides, there is quite a distance between these phenomena and the declarations in words. Pain can be present without being noticed or observed. It can be transient without being recalled (as a fact previously judged as such). It can be correctly or incorrectly subsumed under a concept, or not subsumed under a concept at all.

Second, vital feelings and their modes are a *unitary* matter of fact that does not possess the manifold form of "extensionality" belonging to sensible feelings. It would be possible to make this "unity" understandable as an amalgamation *if* there were reason to believe that a vital feeling could be reduced to sensible feelings. But this is impossible. In the presence of a certain vital feeling, the manifold of sensible feelings is *also* present to our consciousness; furthermore, a vital feeling does not necessarily change when our attention is directed to sensible feelings. If a vital feeling were an amalgamation of sensible feelings (in, say,

Wundt's sense), the latter would necessarily be *used up* in the vital feeling and could not be present *alongside* it. Moreover, a vital feeling can possess a *positive* direction with different qualities *without* manifesting the same positive characteristic in predominantly sensible feelings. For we can feel "fatigued" or "miserable" without any noticeable pain, or even with the strongest sensation of pleasure. We can feel "fresh" and "strong" while experiencing severe pain; and during a long and painful illness resulting from, say, a mere injury, we can sense an increase in vitality. It is also in this that the peculiarity and autonomy of vital feelings and their modes manifest themselves.

Whereas sensible feelings are more or less *dead states,* a vital feeling always has a *functional* and *intentional* character. Of course, on the basis of an objective examination and a relation established through *it,* sensible feelings can function as *"signs"* of certain states and processes in organs and tissues. And it may very well be that we comprehend them, on the basis of associations of experience, *as* such "signs" without the aid of relating acts of thinking. But they do not thereby lose their characteristic deadness. In a vital feeling, on the other hand, we feel our *life itself,* its "growth," its "decline," its "illness," its "health," and its "future"; i.e., something is given to us *in* this feeling. And this holds for both the vital feeling that is directed toward our own life and the vital feeling that is directed toward the outer world and other living beings through postfeeling and fellow feeling and through vital sympathy. Whereas sensible feelings never in any sense lose their punctuality, in a vital feeling we are given the peculiar *value-content of our environment,* for example, the freshness of a forest, the living power of growing trees. Of special importance, however, is the fact that vital feelings, and not spiritual feelings, first participate in the functions of *postfeeling* and *fellow feeling.* Thus vital feelings can contribute to the foundation of a consciousness of *community,* which a sensible feeling cannot bring about and to which it is blind. Everything belonging to the sphere of "passion," e.g., passionate love, is completely different from sensible feelings, but it certainly does not belong to the realm of spiritual feelings. Moreover, in the sphere of vital feelings there are genuine so-called recollections of feelings, whereas there are only feelings of recollection in the sphere of sensible feelings. If I am not content with the merely judgmental recollection that I had a certain pain, I can remember it only when a small actual pain joins the representation of the irritation involved. As we pointed out, sensible feelings are by *nature* actual [*aktuell*]. Hence they do not possess *continuity* of existence or *continuity of development* as do feelings of the vital sphere. Just as I can have true fellow feeling with the fatigue of a bird but can never have fellow feeling with its sensible feeling-states, which are completely unknown to me, so can I feel my own vital feeling later, through postfeeling, better than I can feel the state of my unitary lived organism as it was constituted at the time of the feeling.

This intentional character belonging to vital feelings is of special importance in that vital feelings can evidentially *indicate* the vital *meaning of the value* of events and processes within and outside my body; they can indicate, as it were, their vital "sense." We do not find anything like this in the entire sphere of representation, let alone in the sphere of comprehension. In other words, vital feelings can reveal dangers and advantages, not through associations of experience, but directly, *before* I comprehend the intellectual sense of such dangers and advantages. Hence vital feelings form in their totality, apart from their immediate emotive contents, a true *system of signs* for the changing states of life-processes. The value of this system consists in the fact that its signs emerge originally and *prior in time to* the factual disadvantages or advantages that the processes of life experience either through events in the body or through those in the environment. For it is through this property alone that vital feelings determine actions that avert those "dangers" and safeguard any possible "advantage." Thus the "value" of phenomena is given to us in a vital feeling before we are given the phenomena *themselves;* and so we are able to advance or retard the arrival of these phenomena. It is an empirical mistake to hold that vital feelings *originally* are *phenomena that simultaneously accompany* advantageous and disadvantageous processes in an organism, and that they only secondarily are mere signs of what we intellectually calculate or in some way expect to come. On the contrary, *precisely* this is the property of *sensible* feelings. *These* are by nature consequences of stimuli, whereas vital feelings *anticipate* the *value* of possible stimuli and their arrival. Sensible feelings, e.g., different kinds of pain, can become signs of processes in the organism that enhance or obstruct life, although only on the basis of associations of experience. Here we merely encounter "the child who learns to fear fire by burning himself." However, we encounter something very different when we study even the most simple phenomena, e.g., anxiety, disgust, shame, appetite, aversion, vital sympathy and vital aversion with regard to animals or men, feelings of dizziness,[125] and similar things. For the entire sense and meaning of these feelings consist in the fact that they point to the value of what is *coming*, not to the value of what is present, and that they are in a certain sense spatial and temporal feelings of distance, in contrast to spatial and temporal feelings of contact, which are sensible feelings.

Purely psychic feelings differ most sharply from the stratum of vital feelings. A psychic feeling does not become a state or function of the ego by virtue of my going through the givenness of my lived body and comprehending my lived body as "my own," i.e., as one belonging to the (psychic) ego. It is *originaliter* an ego-quality. A deep feeling of sorrow in no way participates in extension, which is still vaguely present in feelings of well-being and ill-being. Of course, on this level of psychic feelings there can be various distances from the ego. *Increasing* proximity to the ego is expressed, e.g., by "I feel sad," "I feel sadness," "I am sad" [*Ich fühle mich traurig, Ich fühle Trauer, Ich bin traurig*] (the first of these probably lies at the limits of what can be expressed in language).[126] But the variety of types of emotional experience that a feeling of the *same* quality and stratum can encounter has nothing to do with the variety *of the strata* to which certain spheres of qualities are connected. In addition, the changing shades that purely psychic feelings can have through different feelings of the lived body and through different feelings of life do not affect that peculiarity. For psychic feelings are subject to their own laws of oscillation, as are the types of feelings of different strata in general; and we regard it more or less as a pathological "capriciousness" when a certain shade becomes too intense, or when there are deceptions among the constituents of different *strata* to the point of confusion. A human being whose psychic feelings are not "motivated" (in the sense of the interconnections of understanding mentioned earlier) and whose continuity of feeling continually breaks away from changing emotional states of the lived body is as incomprehensible as someone who is severely disturbed mentally.

Spiritual feelings are distinguished from purely psychic feel-

125. See E. Pflüger's subtle remarks in his *Die teleologische Mechanik der lebendigen Natur*, 2d ed. (Bonn: Max Cohen, 1877). See also H. S. Jenning's elaborations on fright in his *Das Verhalten der niederen Organismen*, trans. Mangold (Leipzig, 1910).

126. This "I feel" [*Ich fühle mich*] is the *most adequate* expression for "well," "not well," "comfortable," "uncomfortable." But we can never say, "I feel agreeable."

ings, it appears to me, first by the fact that they can *never* be *states.* For in true *bliss* and *despair,* and even in cases of serenity (*serenitas animi*) and "peace of mind," all ego-states seem to be extinguished. Spiritual feelings seem to stream forth, as it were, from the very source of spiritual acts. The light or darkness of these feelings appears to bathe *everything* given in the inner world and the outer world in these acts. They "permeate" all special contents of experience. Their peculiarity can also be seen in the fact that they are *absolute* feelings that are not relative to extrapersonal value-complexes or their motivating powers. For we cannot be in despair "over something" or blissful "over something" as we can be glad or sad or happy or unhappy over something. The use of these phrases is immediately felt to be an exaggeration. It can even be said that if this "something" is given or if it is subject to explanation, we are certainly *not* yet blissful or in despair. It may well be that a number of other experiences deprive us of these feelings by motivating nexus of sense, or that they cause them to come up at the end of a series of experiences; but *if* these feelings are *there,* they *detach* themselves in a peculiar manner from these connections of motives and *fulfill,* as it were, our entire existence and our "world," to the core of our person. We can then only *"be"* blissful or in despair. We cannot, in the strict sense of the word, "feel" bliss or despair, nor can we even feel "ourselves" to be blissful or in despair. According to the nature of these feelings, either they are *not* experienced at all, *or* they take possession of the *whole* of our being. Just as in despair there lies at the core of our personal existence and world an emotional "No!" without our "person" becoming a mere object of reflection, so also in "bliss," at the deepest level of the feeling of happiness, there lies an emotional "Yes!" Bliss and despair appear to be the correlates of the moral value of our personal being. And for this reason they are the metaphysical and religious self-feelings par excellence. They can be given only when we are not given to ourselves as related to a special area of our existence (society, friends, vocation, state, etc.), and when we are not given to ourselves as existentially and valuatively relative to an act that is to be executed by us (an act of cognition or will). They are given when we are given as absolute: "we ourselves as selves." Bliss in its pregnant sense is present whenever there is no particular state of affairs or values outside or inside us that could *motivate* us feelingly to this fulfillment in bliss, and whenever the being and endurance of bliss appears phenomenally, *un*conditioned and *un*alterable by any performable acts of the will, by any deed, or by any way of life. For it is the *being and the self-value of the person himself* that is the "foundation" of bliss and despair. On the other hand, despair is present whenever all possibilities of escape from this negative feeling seem to be, as it were, *extinct,* and whenever, within the scope of our personal abilities, there is no possible act, no possible action or comportment, on our part which could conceivably alter this feeling. Since these feelings are *not conditioned* by value-complexes exterior to the person and his possible acts, it is clear that they take root in the value-nature of the person *himself* and his being and value-being, which stand above all acts. Therefore these feelings are the only ones which cannot be conceived as feelings that could be produced, or even *merited,* by our comportment. Both possibilities contradict the *essence* of these feelings.[127]

THE PROBLEM OF EUDAEMONISM

9. *The Interconnections between Feeling-States and Moral Values*

IN ANY STRIVING for something, there is, as I have shown, a *feeling* directed toward some value that founds the pictorial or meaning-component of the striving.[128] This peculiar relation is what is commonly called practical *motivation.* All motivation is an immediately experienced causality in the special sense of "causality of attraction" [129] and is to be distinguished from the *feeling-state from* which the striving and willing issues forth. This relation, in contrast to motivation, includes the phenomenon of the physical "push" (the *vis a tergo*). A state which functions in this way may also be called the *source* or *mainspring* of striving. Just as the "goal" of striving is conditioned by an experience in which the value of the content of striving is felt, so also *striving* for a goal is conditioned by its affective source. In

127. This proposition is valid independent of all religious and metaphysical interpretations of these feelings (e.g., as grace or condemnation). Yet, as Luther rightly saw, this essential interconnection also appears in religious dress. For he expressly denies that blissfulness can ever be produced or merited through works or that despair can ever be averted or suppressed through them. *This* insight, however, is quite independent of his other religious formulas (e.g., blissfulness only through faith, etc.).

128. See above, pp. 34 ff.

129. For this reason we consider a striving in which this relation is not present to be unmotivated, e.g., impulses of ire and rage.

addition to these two emotional components of all striving and willing, there is also feeling which *accompanies* the execution of striving and willing and has a special interconnection with its value. Thus, for example, the execution of all willing based on loving is, as such, always pleasant, and all willing based on hate is always unpleasant, independent of the fact that the former leads to an unpleasant state when it is not answered by love on the part of the other, and that the latter leads to a pleasant state as soon as the hatred is satisfied. Hence these moral *functional feelings* are to be distinguished from *value-feeling* (feeling of motivation), as well as from the *source* of striving and the emotional *effect* of striving.

But there are also peculiar interconnections between the *sources* and the value-directions of striving that are, in turn, foundations for certain laws concerning the processes of willing and acting. Without pretending to exhaust this theme, we have selected two of these to elaborate.

a. The Law of the Tendency toward Surrogates When a "Deeper" Emotional Determination of the Ego Is Negative

All practical eudaemonism, which, as we saw, necessarily turns into hedonism because (the plainest) sensible feelings are in practice the most easily reproduced, has its roots in the central wretchedness [*Unseligkeit*] of man. For whenever man is *discontent* in the *more central* and deeper strata of his being, his striving acquires a certain *disposition* to replace, as it were, this unpleasant state with a conative intention toward *pleasure,* i.e., the pleasure of the more peripheral stratum at hand, which is the stratum of feelings that are more easily produced. A conative intention toward pleasure is therefore a *sign* of inner *wretchedness* (despair), or, depending on the individual case, inner unhappiness or misery, inner cheerlessness or sadness, or a feeling of life that would indicate a direction toward a "decline of life." Thus someone who is at heart in despair *"seeks" happiness* in every new human experience; thus someone of very limited vital life-power seeks to accumulate individual feelings of sensible pleasure (as is the case with so many diseased persons, e.g., those suffering from diseased lungs, who increasingly long for sensible pleasure). An advanced practical hedonism is a most certain sign of vital decadence in an entire era.[130] Indeed, one can

---

130. But practical hedonism is never the *cause* of this decadence and all that belongs to it, such as a decline in fertility, as our preachers of high morals would have it.

say that the number of means designed to produce sensible pleasure and to remove sensible pain (e.g., narcotics) increases as unhappiness and negativity in vital feeling become the inner *fundamental attitude* of a society. *In addition to this* it must be stated that the more centrally seated joy is, the less its actualization requires *special* combinations of external stimuli. These combinations of stimuli become more rare as they become more complicated, and their production becomes increasingly bound up with, e.g., the possession of things.[131] The deeper and more central a feeling of pleasure is, the more *independent* it is *originaliter* of the possible vicissitudes of outer life, and the more indestructible is its bond to the person himself. For bliss and despair fulfill the center of the person throughout changes in objective happiness, unhappiness, and their emotional correlates. And the feelings of happiness and misery do *not* fluctuate with the mere alternation of joy and sorrow, which occurs in everyone's life. They encompass such changes. But any negative character of the deeper strata of the emotional life immediately enhances the orientation of striving toward a positive balance of pleasure in a more peripheral stratum. This explains why a "blissful" man can suffer misery and unhappiness with joy and can do so with no need to deaden his sensing of pain and pleasure at more peripheral levels.

No ethos has assimilated the sense of the above as deeply as the Christian. The tremendous innovation of the Christian theory of life was its presentation of a way in which one can suffer pain and unhappiness while remaining *blissful,* a position opposed to that of the Stoics and the ancient skeptics, who considered apathy, i.e., the deadening of sensible feelings, as something good. The ethics of antiquity knew only the method of deadening, or that of an *arbitrary reinterpretation* of suffering through *judgments* of "reason" (e.g., the Stoic judgment that "pain is no evil"), that is, a sort of *illusionism* and autosuggestion with regard to pain and suffering in life. The Buddhist theory of life, on the other hand, knew only the method of *objectifying* suffering through a cognition of its (supposed) basis in the nature of things themselves, and through the resignation of oneself in the face of suffering insofar as it was considered to be a *necessary* consequence and part of a world-suffering based on the essence

131. The historically variable degree of this striving for possessions as the main source of sensible enjoyment is for this reason always a sign of the vital rise and decline of those who thus strive. All vital decadence is accompanied by increased striving for possessions.

of things. All such methods are rejected in the Christian theory of suffering, and with justification. It rejected the negative ascetic methods of deadening and of *ascesis* (in *this* sense of the word) and in simple and true language called pain "evil" and pleasure "good." In the Christian theory of life the essential moment of what it calls the salvation of the soul is *positive bliss* in the center of the person—not mere redemption from suffering through the elimination of both desire and the *reality* of the world (supposedly) constituted by desire (the opposite of this reality in its fully sustained world-*content* being the very essence of Nirvana). For the Christian, the redemption from suffering and evil is not bliss—as with Buddha—but only the *consequence* of bliss. This redemption consists not in the absence of pain and suffering but in the art of suffering in the "right way," i.e. in bliss ("to take up the cross blissfully").[132]

There follows from our law at least the possibility of resolving the question concerning the status that pain and suffering do in fact have and the one that they cannot have in the "order of the way of salvation." They certainly cannot have the status assigned by a false, almost pathological, desire to suffer (a desire that is all too frequently clothed in Christian language). *All kinds of suffering* (no matter on what level they occur) are *evil*, and no suffering can be a condition of bliss. Any interpretation of suffering as a moral means of improvement or as a so-called divine training is questionable for the simple reason that it can never be shown precisely why *suffering* (an evil) is required in order to realize these objectives. The biological interpretation of pain as a sign of warning shows the purposefulness that lies in the interconnection of harm and pain in their types and intensities; but it is impossible to deduce from this teleological idea the necessity of pain, nor is it possible to explain why evolution did not bring about another system of warning. But every negative determination of feeling at peripheral emotive levels has value as the source of an act in which we become *conscious* of a deeper level of our existence into which we withdraw, as it were; indeed, we begin to *discover* that this level is deeper in the experience of withdrawal. But *what*ever we experientially find at this deeper level of our being, e.g., bliss or despair, is not at all conditioned or determined *by* pain or suffering at the peripheral stratum. No man *becomes* blissful through suffering, for through suffering he can "meditate" only on what the deeper levels of his being permit

132. [See "Vom Sinn des Leides" (Bibliog. nos. 11, 19).—*Ed.*]

him to comprehend and to notice. This particular function of suffering, which guides us to the deeper levels of our being, is acknowledged in our assigning to it the power of *"purification."* Purification does not imply moral "improvement"—still less, "training." Rather, it means a continuous falling away (in our value-estimations and spiritual observation) from all that does not belong to our personal essence. It is an ever increasing *clarification* of the center of our existence for our consciousness.

b. All Volitional Directions toward the Realization of Positive and Comparatively Higher Values Originally Arise from Positive Feeling-States as Sources

Not only in historical ethics but also in historical theories of values in general, it is maintained that diverse negative experiences of feeling, e.g., "suffering," "anxiety," "need," "feeling of deficiency," etc., are necessary conditions for the direction of willing toward the realization of both positive and comparatively higher values.[133] Although such theories appear to be very different from one another in their treatment of moral values or other values related, say, to the origin of civilization and invention, they share the same false basis. They consider negative feeling-states as *creating* values or at least as *sources* of the realization of positive values. But all these theories are based on *ressentiment*, on envy and value-deceptions connected with it, and finally on the "pride of suffering" that follows from it. However, we cannot demonstrate this in detail here.[134]

With regard to moral values, values of the person are the highest. Only the good person is necessarily the blissful person; and the evil person is necessarily the despairing person. All values of acts, especially acts of willing, and all *feelings* that accompany acts, are ultimately dependent on this inner value of the person *and* his most central emotional fulfillment. The most central feeling that accompanies the value of the person is the *"source"* of willing and the direction of his moral tenor. Only the *blissful* person can have a *good* will, and only the *despairing* person *must* be *evil* in his willing and actions. If practical eudaemonism is basically erroneous and full of contradictions, then Kant's theory, in which blissfulness and moral value are completely independent of each other in their being and are supposedly joined to one another only by a necessary rational postu-

133. One may think of sayings like "Need teaches one to pray," "Need is the mother of culture," etc.

134. See "Das Ressentiment im Aufbau der Moralen," sec. 1.

late in the sense of the ought, must seem equally erroneous to us.[135] All good volitional directions have their source in a *surplus* of positive feelings at the deepest stratum; all "better" comportment has its source in a surplus of positive feelings at a comparatively deeper stratum. This simple and great truth has been overlooked, it seems to me, only because of a desire to regard *realizability* by or in a volitional act as the essential condition of all moral value-being. When it has been (correctly) observed that bliss and despair are feelings that can in no way be produced by our *willing* (since they permeate the being of the person itself), it has been necessary to conclude that moral values *in general* have no essential interconnections with these emotional factors fulfilling a person. Moreover, these ultimate strata of depth of the emotional—even the differences among the dimensions of depths—frequently have been overlooked; and hence one could with apparent justification point to the experience of life and history, which so frequently shows a connection between the highest moral values of a person and misfortune and misery, and between the lowest moral vice and misdeeds of a person and happiness and success. But it goes without saying that what is here called "happiness" and "misfortune," i.e., events that on the average release negative feelings, including those of a certain peripheral stratum, does *not* permit any kind of inference with respect to the bliss or despair of a person in our sense of the terms. For it is precisely the independence of bliss and despair from such changes in happiness and misfortune that belongs to their *essence*. Here it is not a matter of any effects of happiness or of the success of willing and acting, but only of the *emotional source and origin* of willing and acting. Bliss and despair are feelings that permeate the being of the person himself, feelings that are beyond the will of the person; and therefore they reach into and codetermine *everything that the person acts out*.

But the very same kind of interconnection exists between values of acts and those feelings that *accompany* the execution of acts—and this quite independent of outer historical experience. For every willing that is given as good willing is accompanied by central feelings of happiness, and every bad willing is accompanied by central feelings of unhappiness [*Leidgefühlen*].

---

135. No one saw this point better than Luther, whose historically relative and questionable dogmatic statements (*sola fides* theory, etc.) do not affect *this* insight hidden among them. He always emphasized not only that "the person must be good and pious" before good acts can emanate from him, but also that the person must first be *blissful* in order to will and effect the good. How much more deeply he understood this than Kant!

The feeling-*state* that follows such willing and acting as a *consequence* does not matter to the one who acts. Only the distorted construction of these feelings as the *"self-reward"* or "self-punishment" of the good or evil will, and along with this a eudaemonistic twist to the *interpretation* of this interconnection, could have provoked the antieudaemonistic thesis that there is no such interconnection whatsoever.

There are, however, two reasons why reward and punishment cannot at this point enter into the discussion. First, the *goods of reward* and the *evils of punishment* can never reach into the centrality and the level of depth of the feeling of happiness and its opposite, which the joy *in* good willing and the suffering *in* evil willing represent. Second, every volitional intention toward these feelings suffices to make them impossible.[136] *Inasmuch as no* feeling of happiness can hover above good willing as an *end* (if this willing is to be "good"), it is *absolutely certain* that such willing carries happiness along with it.

It is necessary to add that the original source of the realization of all *other* positive values does not consist in any so-called need or feeling of deficiency, any "necessity" which "teaches us to pray," or any "mother of invention," etc. It is based on a *surplus of positive* feeling-states and is accompanied by positive act-feelings or function-feelings.

What is a so-called *need*? In contrast to a mere drive-impulse, e.g., hunger, need is the feeling (of displeasure) of the non-existence of a good of a certain kind or the feeling of a qualitatively well delineated and displeasurable "lacking" of such a good. Striving for the good is based on this peculiar experience of "lacking." It is certain that in this the positive whatness of the absent good (or the kind of goods) does not have to be represented or thought. For very often the "urge" of the need must, in our constructive fancy, form the idea and representation of the kind of good whose production can satisfy this "need." But the specific *positive value* that constitutes the unity of the goods *according to which* there is a need *must be given as prefelt* for there to be this experience of lack in the first place. It is not the case, as the need-theory of values and value-estimation assumes (e.g., according to various writers on national economics), that something ($= X$) is of value only if it satisfies a "need." The fact that something is of value does not imply that a mere lack (i.e.,

---

136. One who strives for the joy attached to good willing and thus wills "the good" *is* not involved in good willing, and therefore he is *necessarily* denied the joy that is essentially attached to *good willing itself.*

the objective correlate of an experience of lacking) is to be removed, and that an axiological vacuum is to be filled. On the contrary, the feeling of a lack presupposes that the positive value of the "lacking" goods is pregiven in feeling, that is, insofar as it is not a completely *undirected* urge that is present, which does not deserve to be called a need. A second characteristic of need is that the drive-impulse (on which every need "rests") is in some way *periodically repeated.* For if we have an appetite for something only *once* in our lives, there is no need. Finally, if such a drive-impulse, or, better, the "desire for" that rests on it, has become a "need," then it must have been satisfied in some form, and such satisfaction must have become at the same time a habit. In contrast to natural "drives" and the urgency and intensity of their impulses, *all needs* have *developed* historically and psychologically. There are no "innate needs." For this reason they are never something original according to which one could *explain,* for instance, inventions or productions of certain *kinds* of goods. For *they* always require an "explanation." We can see in our daily lives how things which first serve only as luxuries, that is, things which are enjoyed because of their agreeableness, become "needs"; not only is their existence sensed as pleasurable, but their non-existence becomes displeasurable and a "lacking." History shows us that this process has also taken place with regard to goods that we take for granted today, e.g., the so-called mass needs, like salt, pepper, coffee, etc. It is clear that the *original* production of these goods cannot be explained in terms of the drive of a need: their becoming needs presupposes production, *its* emotive sources, and the transformation of the consumption of the goods into a habit.[137] On the other hand, a most pressing necessity which is oriented in a specific direction cannot produce a "need for something." There are, for example, a great many tribes of Negroes who fall victim to famines at certain times, even though they live near lakes full of fish. Nevertheless, a "need" for fish or for the invention of ways to catch fish with nets or hooks does not arise. For needs presuppose, in addition to the feeling for the positive value of a class of things, the conviction of the *presence* of this class of things, or the conviction that there is a possibility of production. *If* all of these factors are

137. Therefore the principle of the *evocation* of needs can and must consciously guide not only the colonial work of civilizing primitive peoples (see Werner von Siemens, *Lebenserinnerungen*) but also the development of the most highly civilized economies. All of the electrical industry, for example, owes its existence to this principle.

given, or there is also a modification of the *direction* of the need with respect to similar and modified goods, these factors can then begin the activity of producing such goods, but they can *never* come to an original *"invention"* of this type of production or to a *"discovery"* of those goods which possess this positive value. The activity of inventing and discovering always occurs, considered in light of its emotional basis, through the *pleasurable surplus of power and ability* at the deeper levels of the being of man (apart from the activities of free, playful, and logical combining in fancy and its subsequent "testing"). Displeasure at the peripheral level of the emotional life, which represents no "need for" and which contains only a vague urge, *never* results in a specific positive value-direction with regard to this surplus; at best, it results in the *exclusion* of certain otherwise possible value-directions.

Since the time of John Locke, who was the first to trace the origin of striving to needs,[138] a false role has been assigned to "needs" in the origin of civilization and its progress. This has been the case because those who assigned this role to needs neglected to ask what needs are and to explain changes in needs. And so it was not observed that the clarification *presupposes* value-estimations of goods *and* the sources of their production.[139] In this undertaking, the entire productive life of the will and its emotional bases were *constructed* (in a wholly erroneous manner) from the viewpoint of a "consumer," as if the producer of goods experiences during the course of the production *precisely what* the consumer experiences when he has an appetite for such a good, namely, when he has a "need" for it. But this requires that a "need," which in fact occurs *much* later *in time* (be it by way of contagion or mutual comparison among members of a society, or by way of an immediate adaptation of striving to a certain type of satisfaction which presupposes existing goods), be erroneously placed at the point of origin of the production of goods. Thus "needs" which never existed are fabricated; they are only the *effects* of those productions for which they are taken to be the cause. Not only does this theory of need fail completely

138. It is well known that Schopenhauer derived his pessimistic conclusions and the merely negative importance of pleasure in general from this theory of Locke.

139. It must be considered an analogous error to assume that different styles of art can be explained by changes in "taste"; on the contrary, "taste" can be explained only by the types of art produced and the adaptation of the feelings of the people who enjoy art to the aesthetic values of *this* art.

in the face of an understanding of all moral values ("to make a virtue out of necessity" is justifiably recognized as a sign of a *lack* of true virtue) and all spiritual values and cultural goods (something which should stand to reason); but it also fails to make values and goods of civilization understandable. However, there is a difference here. The essential difference in production between both types of goods lies in the fact that the former goods come into existence in terms of a free surplus of the spirit *uninfluenced* by drives, whereas the latter come to be through the countereffect of an arbitrarily invented project on the drives which coconditions the character of their structure and stimulation. But neither drives nor drive-impulses are "needs for something." For drive-impulses also presuppose the production of types of goods.

We shall not consider the importance of this insight in terms of concrete problems in the formation of civilizations.[140]

140. A. Adler (in his recent writings, *Organminderwertigkeit* [Vienna: Urban & Schwarzenberg, 1907], and *Über den nervösen Charakter* [Wiesbaden: Bergmann, 1912]) has tried in another, essentially different way to prove the creative power of the displeasure that accompanies a felt deficiency (with respect to a special organic quality or psychic disposition), especially displeasure of the "defect" of which one is conscious in comparing oneself with others, and which releases "jealousy" and "ambition." Adler maintains that the feeling of displeasure evokes a tendency toward "overcompensation" and that it produces a special readiness and willingness to exercise the organs and dispositions felt to be deficient. He states that this "And now, with a vengeance!" frequently leads to a high degree of proficiency. It is especially the *idealization* of what a man desires to be or to be able to do, what "hovers" over him as an ideal of himself, that is said to stem from this contrast with dispositions felt as defective. I do not wish to deal here with the importance of this process for psychological explanations of pathological psychic phenomena. But it would be a grave error to declare that this process has explanatory value for the formation of the will and idealizations in general and to regard this process as the *normal* form in which the cultural accomplishments of man come about. Undoubtedly there is a specifically *positive consciousness of ability,* accompanied by the joy in this ability as *ability,* which functions as the (ideal) measure of the factual accomplishments of the normal person and which always leaves him dissatisfied with his present accomplishments and drives him beyond them. What lies in a person's innermost powers is nevertheless an "ideal" that may remain "unreachable" throughout his life. I do not wish to deny the fact that there are also specific idealizations which come about through the contrast with what one knows one can do (e.g., Goethe wished to be a scientific investigator of nature, Michelangelo a poet and *homo religiosus*) or, furthermore, that the value-estimations of certain areas of occupation on the one hand and the feelings of ability as applied to such areas on the other can greatly disagree with each other. But such disagreement does not lead to an idealization that corresponds to the value-estimation but not to the ability. For it is only when a consciousness of ability, either a "genuine" one in one area or the still-undifferentiated ability of the person himself, is transferred to an area

10. The Idea of Sanction and Reprisal in Relation to the Connection between Happiness and Moral Values

All who have tackled this question agree that there is some interconnection between blissfulness and the positive moral value of the person, between good comportment and the positive feelings which accompany it, an interconnection that is more than a merely fortuitous and empirical association or the lack of one. The dispute begins when a determination of the *nature* of this interconnection is sought, when it is asked, for example, whether it is an "essential interconnection" or a "law of nature" or simply a "demand of the ought," or whether it is a causal relation or some other relation and, in the case of the former, what should be regarded as cause and what as effect, etc.

Let us begin to clarify this important question by looking at the relations obtaining between *positive* or *negative* values and the *feeling* of a being for whom such values exist in striving (or against striving), i.e., obtaining independent of kinds of goods as well as of the organization of such beings.

Certain *interconnections* appear to be *a priori* because they function as interconnections of understanding for the understanding of all animated beings, and because we cannot even imagine an observation that could disprove them. They are the following:

---

where it is *not genuine,* and when an initially felt deficiency of ability is covered up by this, that the impulse of overcompensation and the special exercise of relevant dispositions can occur. In this case, the idealization follows the direction of the "supposed" ability. In this way there *never* occurs an *original* accomplishment of *positive value* but, at best, weak imitations of what those men produced with whom the person "competes" (consciously or not). There exists a specific type of man who has no naïve feeling of self-value, whose consciousness of self-value is built up only *through* comparing his value with that of another person, i.e., who is given to himself as "valuable" only when he knows himself to be "of more value than another" (or disvaluable when he is of less value). That is, he does not compare the values *given* in himself with those of somebody else (as does one who "chooses a hero" whom he wishes to equal), but his and the other's values are constituted *in* comparing itself. The active version of this type of man becomes an "ambitious person" who has as his goal only his being and doing more than others, who seeks to level in this manner the felt value-differences (his inferior value). He does not have as his goal a positive state of affairs or his own value. The passive form of this type leads to *one* kind of man of resentment, i.e., to a man who levels out felt value-differences by dragging down the values of someone else, and in the end to a perversion of the value-estimation of values of others. The type of man whom Adler describes appears to belong to the active version.

1. The felt existence of a positive value is followed by some kind of pleasure as a reaction in the being concerned. If a positive value becomes a "goal" of striving, the activity tending to transfer this value from non-being into being is accompanied by ever more contentment as this striving moves toward the achievement of its goal. If this positive value becomes a goal of counterstriving, the activity involved is accompanied by ever more discontent as this counterstriving moves toward the achievement of its goal. The felt existence of a negative value is followed by displeasure (as a reaction in the being concerned). The striving for a (felt) negative value is followed by ever more discontent as the activity moves toward its goal, and the counterstriving against a felt negative value is followed by contentment to the same degree.

Hence the being of these *feelings*, apart from their *own qualities*, is a "sign" of the *being* and *non-being* of values and disvalues (and it is indirectly their emotive expression). The being of these feelings is a sign of those values which the being concerned feelingly receives. The qualities of contentment and discontentment are at the same time "signs" of the *relation* of striving and counterstriving to the values felt by a being (in which case "discontentment" is by no means a lack of contentment, but a positive fact). No fact of inductive experience could threaten these claims. For example, the fact that diverse beings (e.g., different races of men, different animals, etc.) react differently to the same things, some with pleasure and others with displeasure, only demonstrates that these things are for some beings goods, for others evils, or that *different* values are realized in these things for different beings. The essential interconnection between reactions of pleasure and the being of positive values and between reactions of displeasure and the being of negative values is by no means affected by this. The same holds true for the interconnection between contentment and discontentment and the success of striving or counterstriving for or against positive and negative values.

The question of whether we can (or, indeed, must) admit that a counterstriving against positive values and a striving for negative values are facts of the same originality is most important here. Neither those who believe that contentment can be *defined* as an accompanying phenomenon (be it a case of striving or counterstriving) nor those who hold it to be an essential law that only positive values can be striven for and that only negative values are subject to counterstriving would admit the possibility of the same originality. They would assert that in the appearance of counterstriving against a positive value, a negative value is always felt in the thing in question, or that there is only a preference for a greater and higher value and a placing after of the positive value. But this is a pure construction which *cannot* stand up against the evidential fact that there is a counterstriving against positive values felt as positive values, and that there is a striving for negative values felt as negative values. One cannot ask about the "if" of this fact, but only about its essential conditions. And there is indeed an essential condition. For every being that feels its own *being* as having negative value and, hence, as one that "ought not to be" must strive for negative values and counterstrive against positive values. This being negates its own value-being in such practical comportment but nevertheless *in doing this* affirms the *being* of positive values. The self-destructive character of evil rests on this essential interconnection. A bad person is bad, not because he fails "to keep himself in existence," as if good = the capacity to preserve one's existence, as Spinoza says (and as Darwin and Spencer presuppose in their derivations of what is moral), but because he *must* destroy himself and his own "world." [141]

2. Every increase in positive value (of a certain value-*height*) of a being that executes acts is accompanied by an increase in pleasure as a reaction at the corresponding stratum of feeling. Every decrease in positive value is accompanied by a decrease in pleasure. Every increase in negative value is accompanied by an increase in displeasure. And every decrease in negative value is accompanied by a decrease in displeasure. These increases and decreases in positive and negative value are "*signs*" of the accompanying factors. The heights of values and the depths of feeling correspond to each other in these relations.

3. Every preferring of a higher value to a lower one is accompanied by an increase in the depth of the positive feeling. Every placing after of a higher value is accompanied by an increase in the depth of the negative feeling. And it follows from what we said earlier (that all doing and bringing about which is of positive value stems from positive and central feelings) that

141. The ultimate basis of all *value-deception* lies in perversions of striving which are present every time conation goes against the good and toward the bad. Under no circumstances can it be said that value-deceptions cause perversion; on the contrary, perversion is the cause of the value-deception in which something is *presumed* good but is nevertheless given as bad, even if it is given as bad in only a "transparent" fashion. See "Das Ressentiment im Aufbau der Moralen," sec. 1.

every preferring of a higher value to a lower one makes a later similar preferring *easier,* and, conversely, that every preferring of a lower value to a higher one makes a later similar preferring easier. In what concerns "choice" (which can occur on the basis of a higher value given in "preferring," as well as on the basis of a lower value given in "placing after"),[142] the depth of contentment increases with the choice of a *higher* value, and the depth of discontentment increases with the choice of a lower value.

In terms of their basic ideas these interconnections are not new. Such basic ideas are found, for example, in Leibniz, for whom any pleasure indicates progress in the "perfection" of a feeling subject. It is only to the extent that we maintain that perfection *cannot be reduced* to degrees of *being,* and that pleasure cannot be reduced to a kind of a confused *insight* into this "perfection," that we differ basically from this position. The familiar objections to this theory on the basis of inductive experience appeared for so long to be justified because no one distinguished the *strata* of the emotional life. Hence not every pleasure indicates the existence of a positive value for the being concerned, e.g., the person or the total organism; and not every increase in pleasure indicates an increase in positive value. The *spiritual* emotions (i.e., pure act-feelings that blend with acts of feelings) show, not some value or advancement in the *life* of the person, but values, advancements, and obstructions in the spiritual *person himself* in the achievement of his own ideal and individual value-being. Spiritual emotions measure the exact *distance* between what the person as such is and what he ought to be, but at the same time his vital feeling can be of quite a different character; for example, in an experienced enhancement of the person there can be a process of decline in his life. And, likewise, one can hardly expect *sensible* feelings to be indicators, for example, of what obstructs or furthers the *well-being* of the *total* organism. Only a person who fails to recognize the unity and autonomy of vital feelings (and other levels of feeling) and views them as mere consequences of sensible feelings can be astonished that a drink of cold water can be fatal when one feels very hot, that severe diseases of the lungs and severe mental disorders can be accompanied by sensible pleasure, and that the presence or absence and the degree of sensible pleasure and displeasure do not correspond exactly to the magnitude of

---

142. The reader will recall what was said about the types of bearers ("good" as well as "evil") of acts of preferring and rejecting in chap. 2, B, sec. 3.

damages and advancements in the life of the entire organism. But this dysteleology becomes quite evident and, indeed, is *required* when we assume that sensible feelings indicate only the value-state (and advancements and obstructions) of the specific life-activity of *organs* in which these feelings are phenomenally found—without thereby becoming measures that would indicate what this specific activity means in terms of the *unitary* life of the entire organism. Such measures are given only through *vital feelings* in their own variations. Moreover, one must not attribute *moral* significance to all feelings of pleasure and displeasure. These can be attributed only to feelings of conscience in the strict sense, i.e., those emotional variations which belong to the *preferring* and *placing after* of values, to choices, and to the relation of values to the *person himself*. All of these variations are always at the same time variations in the *depths* of feelings.

What then can we conclude with regard to the old question of *happiness and morality* on the basis of these essential interconnections?

The Foundation of Happiness in Positive Values and the Foundation of Positive and Valuable Striving and Willing in Happiness

In their pragmatic zeal, ethical theorists have almost always supposed that there is only one alternative: (1) Happiness is conditioned by morally valuable being, life, and acting, in which case it has *no* significance for "virtue," moral willing, and acting, either as a source or as a goal. Happiness is then to be regarded either as a naturally necessary consequence and at the same time as a "reward for virtue" or as a "postulate" that the good person becomes happy because he "deserves" to be happy. It is therefore better to "deserve happiness" or to be "worthy of it" than to be happy.[143] Or (2) happiness is the goal of all com-

---

143. The first theory mentioned is a theory of "moral causality" in which a good action appears at the same time to be the cause of happiness —an idea which is at the bottom of all theories of a so-called natural moral order of the world. Thus, e.g., the Fourth Commandment of the Decalogue, "Honor your father and mother *so that* your life will be long [auf dass *du lange lebest*]," should not be taken in a way in which it has often been interpreted, i.e., eudaemonistically (*so as to obtain* long life [damit *du lange lebest*]). It is to be understood in the sense of a "*natural requital*." On the view which holds that meriting happiness or being worthy of happiness is to be preferred to happiness, see my remarks on "humility" in "Zur Rehabilitierung der Tugend."

portment that deserves to be called virtuous. In this case one *ought* to strive for happiness above all (eudaemonism).

This alternative misses the very point of the problem. For all *feelings* of happiness and unhappiness have their foundation in *feelings of values*. Deepest happiness and complete bliss are dependent in their being on a consciousness of one's own moral goodness. *Only the good person is blissful.* This does *not* preclude the possibility that this very blissfulness is the *root* and *source* of all willing and acting. But happiness can *never* be a goal or even a "purpose" of willing and acting. *Only the happy person acts in a morally good way.* Happiness is therefore in no way a "reward for virtue," nor is virtue the *means* to reach blissfulness. Nevertheless, happiness is the *root* and *source* of virtue, a fountainhead, although it is only a *consequence* of the inner *goodness* of the person.

One must reject a fortiori the theory which claims that there is a so-called *sanction* for the obligating power of ideal propositions of the ought, i.e., a "ground of obligation" through which the good is subsequently "linked" to one's own interest in happiness. Such a "linking" is required only when the good is thought to be originally separated from the person, his being and nature—for example, as the content of a series of demands or legal norms which aim at the person so that he must somehow be won over to them. These demands and legal norms are required only when the nature and fact of the *deepest* feelings of happiness, which are founded in the goodness of the person himself, are not seen and observed, and when in comparison with these feelings every *possible* reward represents only a feeling of happiness at a *less* deep level. The original being-good is that of the person himself, and the deepest feeling of happiness is the blissful consciousness that accompanies it. Why do we need a so-called sanction here? It does not matter if a deed brings the agent great harm or any number of unhappy feeling-states, for the displeasure effected *by* the *deed* can never be of the same depth as the pleasure *in* this good deed itself. Nor can it be of the same depth as that *still* deeper pleasure which rendered the deed possible and which *cannot be destroyed* by the displeasure of peripheral strata, irrespective of the degree to which this displeasure sets in. No reward that is supposed to function as a reward for a moral good can ever, by essential necessity, determine happiness as deep as the *happiness itself* out of which morally good willing streams forth and which accompanies it. No evil that inflicts punishment can ever determine suffering as deep as the wretchedness [*Unseligkeit*] out of which a bad deed flows or as deep as the feeling of displeasure which accompanies this deed. Even expressions like *"The good is its own reward"* and "Evil brings its own punishment" presuppose the erroneous proposition that there must be some "sanctions" for moral being and willing.

It is precisely for this reason that one must reject the old theory of a union, *according to a law of nature,* of the consequence of happiness with good deeds and the consequence of unhappiness with bad deeds, in which "consequence" is taken to mean an immanent or transcendent *"reprisal."* One must similarly reject Kant's theory, which, although it expressly denies such a union, requires on the basis of a *"postulate"* of practical reason that there be such *"reprisal"* through the action of a "moral ruler over the order of the world," and which would base "belief" in this ruler on this requirement as a "necessity of reason."

Let us try to make clear *what* "reprisal" is. What is "done in retaliation" can only be the real or possible *effects* which morally good and bad actions have on another being, making him happy or harming him and, consequently, bringing him pleasure or displeasure. In rewards and punishments a *possible equivalence in value,* as well as an equivalence in the *depths* of pleasure and displeasure, can exist only for such effects. On the other hand, the concept of reprisal has *no* sense whatsoever for the values of good and evil implicit *in* such actions, be it as *their* properties or as properties of willing and the person himself. Here "reprisal" could only mean "to comport oneself evilly toward evil persons and evil acting." But it is *evident* that one "ought" to comport oneself in a morally good way toward an evil person and evil comportment! Indeed, the comportment of reprisal itself makes a *pretense* of being morally good! Second, reprisal could mean "to inflict upon a person who acts evilly a displeasure of the same central depth as the discontentment implicit in 'guilty conscience' itself." This, however, is impossible. For the displeasure of this depth is essentially connected with evil being and willing.

Hence the idea of *reprisal* has *no* place at all in the sphere of the purely moral. The idea of reprisal makes sense only from the viewpoint of someone *harmed* by an action or from the viewpoint of a *third* person in relation to one harmed. But this idea does *not* apply to one who *is* good or evil and *comports* himself accordingly. The idea of reprisal must be located in the *sphere of right,* not in the *moral sphere,* which is entirely different from the former. Therefore "reprisal" does not follow as a consequence from the demand that justice ought to be. Justice orders and governs only the impulse of reprisal by *adding* the idea of proportion, like for like, to the demand for reprisal (in some more determinate way). But one cannot derive the idea of "reprisal" from the idea of justice, nor can one arrive at this idea through analysis. Reprisal is *akin* to revenge, primarily the specific impulse of revenge which is postfelt by an individual *C* who cooperates with the impulse of revenge of a harmed individual *A* against a *B* who harmed him. And recompense is akin to the sympathetic postfelt gratitude of *A* toward *B*.[144] But here there is only *kinship* and not identity. Whereas revenge requires only two persons, reprisal originally requires three persons, of whom the "third person" is feelingly "above" the other two. In addition, reprisal as "demand" and as practically performed (e.g., on the part of a judge) is completely *independent* of the *type and intensity* of the feeling (and postfeeling) of revenge and gratitude on the part of the person harmed or advanced. The act of any retaliating judge is *distinguishable* from, say, an impulse of revenge on the part of a person who has been harmed by the fact that the judge acts out his office in a cold-blooded manner, uninfluenced by the feelings of the one who has been harmed. Second, the demand for reprisal occurs also when there is *no* feeling of revenge in the victim. This becomes understandable when we consider that reprisal *and* revenge have a common experience as their basis. A closer look at this experience would show it to be one of an *"atonement"* demanded by a specific *value-complex.* Revenge is as different from an immediate "offense" or "defense" against an inflicted evil as it is from a mere explosion of the affects of ire and anger manifested in totally aimless movements. The impulse of revenge, which is not directed against the guilty person alone but against any person related to him (family, gens, tribe, people) or against his goods—indeed, at the most primitive level, against any goods, whether animate or inanimate [145]—contains an act of "post-

144. It must be stressed here that it is only reprisal, and not recompense [*Entgeltung*], that has an original and positive character. The term *reprisal,* without additions, always means reprisal for a harm, not for a good deed.

145. See my remarks on S. R. Steinmetz's view that there was originally an "undirected" revenge (*Ethnologische Studien zur ersten Entwicklung der Strafe* [Leyden, 1894]) in "Das Ressentiment im Aufbau der Moralen." [See *ibid.*, sec. 1. "Über Ressentiment und moralisches Werturteil" does not contain this critique.—Ed.]

poning" factual reprisal to a later time. It also contains the experience of "tit for tat," the same emotional factor contained in reprisal. If for a moment we abstract from the harmed subject who feels revengeful as well as the third person who exercises reprisal and who always hovers "above" the person who harms and the person harmed, there remains something beyond the implicit negative value-complex, e.g., "that someone has been killed here," and, in primitive cases, that something went beyond "natural" bounds and caused an evil (e.g., devastations resulting from a flood). What remains is the "demand" for "atonement," which comes from this negative value-complex *itself*. Thus it appears to be the "spilled blood" itself that "cries out for atonement," apart from any reference to a possible agent who could be the object of revenge or reprisal. Both revenge and reprisal, however, are *equally* founded in the *experience* of this demand. No matter how "subjective" and unlimited revenge may be in contrast to "reprisal," in contrast to mere affections like ire, rage, and anger (and their discharge) it is an emotion founded in a given state of affairs of negative value. True, one who feels revenge seeks compensation for his harm as *his* harm, in contrast to one who retaliates; but he does so because this harm also appears to *demand atonement* irrespective of *his* displeasure. It is for this reason alone that a deed of revenge can sometimes be felt as a "duty," and that even the lack of a feeling of revenge can in certain cases be felt as a moral deficiency. But this could *never* be the case in the absence of ire, rage, etc. On the one hand revenge presupposes the idea of an agent, and reprisal at least the idea of a deed (though *not* the determinate or indeterminate givenness of the agent); on the other hand revenge does not necessarily presuppose guilt but only causality for the evil involved, though reprisal presupposes, in addition to causality, the givenness of guilt. But a demand for atonement is *not* connected with any of these conditions. For this reason even the accidental death of an evil-doer, that is, a death not caused by the revenging or retaliating deed of a person or by a retaliating power, can be felt *as* "atonement for" his deed. Revenge and reprisal appear to be only two *subjective methods* of satisfying the demand for atonement arising from negative value-complexes *themselves*. But the idea of *punishment* is not based on revenge; it has its spiritual origins in *reprisal* and *demand for atonement*. It is futile to attempt to derive punishment from revenge or from the idea of justice or some purpose. The consideration of purposes implies the total misconception of the *essence* of punishment. Of course punishment can, *if* it is given, be utilized for purposes in various ways. And of course the derivation of punishment from revenge can be justified historically and genetically. However, in terms of its *origin* such a derivation is insufficient. Even if feelings and impulses of revenge completely disappeared, the demand for atonement and its realization through punishment would retain their sense. Hence neither reprisal nor punishment is relative to the existence of beings that have feelings of revenge. One falls victim to another basic misconception of the essence of the idea of reprisal and the idea of punishment when one attempts to derive them from *purely* moral values and demands, especially the demand for "justice." Insofar as the pure essence of justice is grasped, it does not require the reprisal of evil through bad deeds. Only from that part of the central essence of justice according to which the occurrence of the *same comportment* on the condition of the *same value-complexes* is good and ought to be does it follow that *if* there is reprisal, it must aim equally at factors of equivalent value. But from this no demand for "reprisal" follows.

Therefore, the boast of a purely moral origin on the part of both reprisal and punishment is without any inner foundation. In fact, they do not reach into the absolute and purely moral spheres of persons and their relations, but are, in their contents, definitely *relative* to the *value of the well-being of a community of living beings.* If we clearly distinguish purely moral values and demands from everything in human nature that is added to them, the perceived fact of evil—whether it is directed against us or against others, whether it enhances or obstructs weal—can only cause sadness as well as an awareness of everyone's *co-responsibility* (as a *mea culpa, mea maxima culpa*) on the basis of the principle and feeling of moral solidarity of all men with all men. But it can *never* bring about a demand for or an impulse of reprisal. This moral insight is already present in unmistakable clarity in the Gospels. The "judgment" of reprisal (in the moral, not the juridical, sense) is clearly rejected as evil. This insight must not be affected in the least by any factual institution and its supposed "need of moral support," e.g., the one that our factual system of punishment represents. It does not matter if such a system must be acknowledged as *necessary* on the basis of *extramoral* reasons; indeed, it does not matter if it is based not only on human nature but also on the *essence of all living being* and therefore on the very heart of the order of living being, so that it must be acknowledged as extending to all mundane human experience. This does not change the fact that such a system is devoid of all sense and value for the *purely* moral sphere of values and hence also for the sphere of the deity, and that such a system does not possess any purely moral-religious sanction.

We must therefore expressly reject Kant's designation of reprisal as a postulate of "pure" practical reason as unfounded. Reprisal is a postulate of *vitally conditioned* reason, not one of "pure" reason.

As a value-idea, and as a value-idea that is relative to the value of the well-being of a life-community, reprisal must be *sharply* distinguished from the value that its realization can possess in terms of the accomplishment of certain *purposes* of a life-community, e.g., its protection, i.e., over and above the value of reprisal *as* reprisal. The value *itself* which reprisal for a misdeed or an evil by an evil has—i.e., the value itself, without further possible purposeful applications in the future—consists first in its *purification* of the soul of the harmed person with a malicious moral tenor by affording him the feeling of satisfying a demand for atonement, a feeling of "satisfaction," and therefore by recreating the *basis* of truly moral relations with others, including the evil-doer—namely, the *capacity for loving*. On the other hand, in reprisal and punishment something is accomplished with regard to the guilty evil-doer himself which enables him *also* to re-enter a basic moral relationship with the guiltily harmed person as well as with himself. Punishment does not follow from moral guilt as the value-necessary demand of an ought, nor can punishment as such free the person from *guilt* and its weight. This function and capacity can be attributed only to purely moral *repentance,* which alone can restore the positive and inward happiness whose negative counterpart, on the same level of depth, was the source of the guilty action.[146] The depth of displeasure that repentance contains, which is based on the consciousness of the moral disvalue of one's own deed, cannot be replaced by any outwardly inflicted punishment and *its* displeasure. For these feelings belong to essentially different levels of *depth.* But punishment does bring about one thing: this *"purification"* [Läuterung] which can in general be, as we have seen, the only morally important consequence of displeasure that does not belong to the deeper spheres of the person or of such suffering. Punishment directs the inner regard

---

146. [See "Reue und Wiedergeburt."—*Ed.*]

of the evil-doer to his own personal sphere and therefore makes him *see* his own moral nature. In this sense it gives him an *opportunity* to offset his evil morally by an act of repentance, though it does not thereby necessarily determine the act of repentance. The act of repentance is presupposed by the harmed person's ability to execute a true act of forgiving after he has obtained satisfaction. On the side of the evil-doer the act of repentance is presupposed by his ability to lose the malicious moral tenor that every guilty infliction of harm on a person provokes in the evil-doer as a reminder of his wickedness, and by his ability to regain his lost capacity for loving the harmed person. Under the supposition of the *extramoral* impulse of reprisal, punishment is the form through which the *possibility of a moral relationship between the harmed person and the evil-doer is restored.* Therein *alone* lies the merely *relative* moral justification of punishment, and not in a pure "moral demand for justice." On the presupposition that there are personal relations which are not purely moral, punishment diminishes the hatred in the world and the central feelings of displeasure necessarily connected with it; however, in the final account punishment adds a certain quantity to peripheral feelings of displeasure and does so without any reservations concerning some greater pleasure to be effected by this. In terms of the mere *sense of reprisal,* and not the possible effects it may have on future human comportment (improvement, intimidation), it serves the restoration of pure moral relations that have been disturbed. Indeed, it is only this *sense of reprisal* in legal punishment, and not punishment as an evil or its motivational effects with regard to future actions and being, that has this *necessary* consequence. That which *exclusively* possesses this *relative* moral significance is precisely the fact that this evil is to be established, *not* as a preventive measure, but as a *punishment,* that the evil of punishment is not to be feared (by possible evil-doers) or desired (by harmed persons) as a mere evil, but is to be feared and desired *as* punishment, and this evil as founded on the idea of *punishment.* It seems to us that this is forgotten by those who would posit a mere "measure for security" in lieu of punishment and would reduce its sense to a motivation for future comportment.[147]

From a point of view which fails to recognize the differences in depths of feelings as well as the essential differences in cor-

---

147. I can make no sense of the assertion that punishment "is" a measure for security.

responding evil deeds, punishment must be unconditionally re- jected as the positing of an evil *in addition* to hitherto existing evils.[148] Punishment then cannot be justified anew by saying that this addition of evils to extant ones would be justified, in a utilitarian manner, on the pretext that they would diminish the total sum of evils.[149] The infliction of an evil with this *intention* lacks the character of "punishment" and, furthermore, fails to have any *moral* justification. For such procedures possess moral justification only when they begin to form a part of the *educa-tional* activity and when the one who is subject to such proce- dures is not yet given as a *full person.*[150] For the evil-doer or the one who is guilty of any kind of grave crime possesses the *moral right,* insofar as he is mature and of sound mind, to demand *recognition* of his person and his dignity as a moral being. Ir- respective of what the positive law may be in any individual case, he also possesses, on the basis of *this* right, a moral right to demand *factual* and *true* punishment when faced with an il- lusory system of punishment of the kind that we have criticized. He thus possesses a moral "right to punishment" which could, for example, morally shield him from moral injustice on the part of all who would make him the exclusive object of their protec- tive disciplinary measures.[151] Above all, he possesses a right to the power of punishment *as* punishment that can purify him, and a right to its inherent power to restore his relations with the harmed person and with all who participate, through postfeeling and fellow feeling, in his harm and his negative moral tenor with respect to the evil-doer. Even the most severe true punish- ment, as seen from deeper levels of feeling, is much "milder" than the smallest, merely educative, legal or illusory punishment, which, by making an evil-doer an immature object of question- able sociopolitical experiments instead of directing itself to the deeds of the evil-doer, *precludes* the restorability of moral rela- tions. Bentham therefore has no justification for his claim that the positing of punishment would be justified if one could prove

148. Bentham rejected it for this reason.
149. As some have tried to do, e.g., Bentham.
150. Pedagogical "punishment" is only illusory punishment, just as the pedagogical order is an "illusory order" and the pedagogical question an "illusory question."
151. Much as the modern positivistic theory of protective punishment with its praxis would like to appear "humane," "human," "social," etc., it rests in fact on a deep and immoral disregard of "man" as the *person* in man; it degrades the person to the level of a mere means for purposes completely and exclusively outside the person.

that its positing would bring an increase in universal happiness of the same kind.[152] The evil of punishment is also justified as a *definitive* augmentation of evil in the world in that it can be proved to be a *condition for the restoration of moral relations* and the essentially connected deeper feelings of happiness. Despite the fact that punishment has no purely moral basis (here we agree with the so-called modern school) and no foundation in the idea of justice, and despite the fact that it depends on the presence and recognition of the merely vitally relative value of reprisal and atonement, whose impulses and willing can be overcome in an act of a higher value-level, namely, "forgiving" —and, indeed, "ought" to be overcome in a moral sense—neither punishment itself nor the impulse of reprisal, on which it rests, is something that can be genetically understood on the basis of the development and preservation of the useful, or something that can be demanded on the basis of what is useful to society. Utilitarianism cannot explain the origin of the impulse of revenge, the demand for atonement, or the impulse of reprisal in any biological or psychogenetic way. Utilitarianism fails here, as it does in the case of any truly vital feeling (or vital impulse) that cannot be reduced to a sum of sensible feelings (and tendencies). For this reason, too, utilitarianism cannot comprehend that the vital well-being of a higher value-level, namely, the well-being of a life-community, requires the drive of reprisal (and *therefore* also its satisfaction by way of punishment), even though this drive must appear to be nothing short of "harmful" from the standpoint of the value of its general usefulness to society.[153] Hence the dying out of the drive of reprisal must be regarded not as moral progress but as a token of vital decline.[154]

All of this does not disprove the proposition that "reprisal" has *no* meaning or value *outside* the vital sphere, which itself does *not* contain the purely moral values standing above it. Not only is there no demand for revenge within the realm of purely moral persons, i.e., within the spiritual "community of love";

152. A punishment is not canceled when, e.g., the punished person dies before or right after his punishment is inflicted. This holds even when we set aside its exemplary character.

153. On the distinction between well-being and usefulness, see chap. 2, B, sec. 5.

154. All law [*Recht*] must, above all, account for the facts of human nature and in particular the "feeling of right." The "sciences" cannot ignore this, either. The mere absence of a drive of reprisal is not an advantage but only a *lack* and a *phenomenon of deficiency*, in contrast to the *free renunciation* of the satisfaction of this drive through the act of forgiving.

but there is *no* demand for *reprisal,* for here there exists only a demand for *love* and *justice.* This realm is marked not by a principle of "reprisal" but by principles of *forgiveness* and *gratitude* (in contrast to reward), which are based on love, and by the principle of *moral solidarity* (or of shared guilt and shared merit).[155] Reprisal, punishment, and reward are morally required only when forgiving and gratitude are evidentially *beyond moral abilities.* Conversely, an omission of the demand for reprisal for the sake of the preservation and maintenance of sensible and utilitarian values (the values of the agreeable and the disagreeable) is, morally speaking, always of *negative value;* and the execution of this demand is of relative goodness (but is not absolutely good).

The idea of "reprisal from beyond" retains its *sense* (we are not considering its existence here) because reprisal does not have a value that is dependent on man and his organization (nor is it a fortiori merely of "historical" significance). According to its *essence* it has a value that is dependent only on life. But such reprisal is *not* required by virtue of anything purely moral.

Things are different with respect to the idea of a so-called *divine justice of reward and punishment.* This idea in *no* way corresponds, either in terms of its *essence* or its *meaning* (apart from its existence), to a refined idea of God. The attribution of impulses of reprisal to the divinity is no less erroneous than the attribution (by the ancient Hebrews) of an impulse of revenge to the divinity. This attribution only shows that the idea of the spirituality of God has not yet become a pure and clear idea with no biological connotations. In his existence and his acts, the "good" person directly participates in the nature of God, in the sense of *velle* in *deo* or *amare* in *deo,* and he is "blissful" *in* this participation. A "reward" of God could only put a smaller and lower good in the place of a higher one, and a superficial feeling in the place of a deeper pleasure. God can "forgive" an "evil" person (out of the love that is his essence) and thereby *eliminate* his evil (in contrast to a mere pardon, which does not absolutely eliminate an evil, but can only eliminate it "for" a forgiving but

155. I have touched upon this principle twice before. See *Zur Phänomenologie und Theorie der Sympathiegefühle,* p. 65, and "Über Ressentiment und moralisches Werturteil," p. 359. I must reserve a more penetrating study of the foundations involved for future studies. [See *Wesen und Formen der Sympathie,* pt. B, chap. 2 (end); "Das Ressentiment im Aufbau der Moralen," sec. 5, 3, b, 1. On the principle of solidarity, see below, chap. 6, B, sec. 4, ad 4.—*Ed.*]

finite person).[156] But God cannot "retaliate," for his essence is above reprisal; he can only abandon a person to the demands and laws of reprisal by *not forgiving* him.

The idea of a "God of reprisal" or of a God who is "required" for reprisal on the basis of a postulate of reason (and who is in this sense a "moral world-orderer"), an idea that Kant formulates in his philosophy of religion, stands in contradiction to the above. Kant is completely correct in denying the assertion that good willing can be brought together with all kinds of calculations based on divine reward and punishment. And he right-fully stresses that such calculations *"ought"* not to be. But it does not appear to us that Kant has shown that if this "neces-sary postulate of reason" concerning the being of a divine judge of reprisal has been accepted, this reprisal *must* necessarily be expected, even though motivation behind morally good comport-ment in general *can* be free of eudaemonistic speculation in terms of reward and punishment. One *cannot* argue from ought to abilities here, either. Of course, mere calculations in terms of a reward-good and the fear of the evil of punishment *can* be excluded from his theory, too. But this comportment must not be identified with the fear of *punishment as punishment* and the hope for *reward as reward* (as opposed to mere "recompense" and goods of payment). This "submissive" comportment and calculating-for, as the Scholastics call it, has been rejected as immoral by every ethics, including the ethics that Kant calls heteronomous.[157] But fear of the punitive character of punish-ment, which is different from fear of the evil of punishment, is *not* yet excluded with the exclusion of the latter. And fear of the evil of punishment *must* arise with the adoption of this postulate of reason if this postulate is to be the foundation of *genuine* faith.

This conflict of ideas can be resolved only through the in-sight that reprisal is not a demand that comes from a pure, rational idea of justice, but only a vitally conditioned demand of a finite sort.

---

156. "Forgiving" is *not* to be understood as the mere abandonment of punitive evil or punishment itself, but as the factual cancellation of evil as a non-formal value, though not, of course, of its bearers, which are factual actions that cannot be undone. Only God can "forgive" in this sense.

157. Especially by the ethics of all of the Scholastics.

6 / Formalism and Person

ONE OF THE BASIC CLAIMS OF *formal ethics,* especially Kant's ethics, is that it alone can confer upon the person a *"dignity"* which is beyond any "price." On the other hand, formal ethics claims that all non-formal ethics destroy the dignity of the person and his self-value, which cannot be derived from anything. It is easy to see that this claim is true for all ethics of goods and purposes. Every endeavor to measure the goodness of the person in terms of the degree to which his accomplishments support an existing world of goods (including even "holy" goods), as well as every endeavor to measure the goodness of the person in terms of the accomplishments of his will and actions as the means of realizing a purpose (even if this be a holy final purpose which is immanent to the world), contradicts the aforementioned law of preference, according to which values of the person are the highest of all values. But it is another matter to ask whether a formalistic and rational ethics of laws does not also *de*grade the person (although in a different manner from that of the ethics of goods and purposes) by virtue of its subordination of the person to an impersonal *nomos* under whose domination he can become a person only through obedience.

Before undertaking a separate examination of what a person is and the meaning that is to be attributed to the person in ethics, it is necessary to determine precisely the place that the person occupies in the formalistic systematic and, after that, the relation of the "person" thus conceived to moral values within formalism.

A. ON THE THEORETICAL CONCEPTION
OF THE PERSON IN GENERAL

1. Person and Reason

IT IS NO TERMINOLOGICAL ACCIDENT that formal ethics designates the person first as *"rational* person." This expression does not mean that it belongs essentially to the nature of the person to execute acts which, independent of all causality, follow ideal laws of meaning and states of affairs (logic, ethics, etc.); rather, with this one expression, formalism reveals its implicit material assumption that the person is basically nothing but a logical subject of rational acts, i.e., acts that follow these ideal laws. Or, in a word, the person is the X of some kind of rational activity; the moral person, therefore, the X of volitional activity conforming to the moral law. Instead of *first* showing what the essence of the person with its special unity consists in and then *demonstrating* that rational activity belongs to this essence, it is assumed that the being of the person *is* nothing but, and exhausts itself in, a point of departure, some X of a lawful rational will or a practical rational activity. Whatever a being called a person, for example, a certain human being (or even the person of God), may be beyond this "point of departure of lawful rational acts" cannot serve as a foundation for the being of the person. Indeed, anything beyond this would restrict, or even relatively destroy, the being of persons.

As the following will show, one thing in this definition is entirely correct: namely, the person must *never* be considered a *thing* or a *substance* with faculties and powers, among which the "faculty" or "power" of reason etc., is one. The person is, rather, the immediately coexperienced *unity* of *experiencing;* the person is not a merely thought thing behind and outside what is immediately experienced.

Apart from this, however, the above definition of the person as rational leads first to the consequence that every concretization of the idea of the person in a concrete person coincides at once with a depersonalization. For that which is here called "person," namely, that "something" which is the subject of rational activity, must be attributed to concrete persons—indeed, to *all men*—in the same way and as something *identical* in all men. Hence men are not distinguishable by virtue of their personal being alone. Indeed, the concept of an "individual person" becomes, strictly speaking, a *contradictio in adjecto*. For rational acts—themselves defined merely as acts corresponding to a certain lawfulness of states of affairs—are *eo ipso* extraindividual, or, as many followers of critical philosophy say, supraindividual. Any individually determining factors that might be added to the idea of the subject of these acts would necessarily do away with the personal nature of the being concerned. This consequence is, however, in contradiction to the essential interconnection that every finite person is an individual as a *person himself;* he is not an individual by virtue of his special (outer or inner) *contents* of experience, i.e., what he thinks, wills, feels, etc., or by virtue of the lived body (its spatial extensions, etc.) that he possesses. In other words, the being of the person is never exhausted in being a subject of rational acts of a certain lawfulness—no matter how his being must otherwise be more precisely conceived, and no matter how wrong it is to conceive of this being as a thing or a substance. The person could not even be "obedient" to the moral law if, as its executor, he were created, as it were, by this law.[1] For the being of the person is also the foundation of any obedience.

If one fixes his attention on the above erroneous definition (Kant, fortunately, did not do so), the result is an ethics that leads to anything but the recognition of the so-called *autonomy* or dignity of the person qua person. What must follow from this definition is not autonomy (a term in which *auto-* is supposed to point to the independence [*Selbständigkeit*] of the *person*) but *logonomy* and at the same time extreme *heteronomy* of the person.[2] This consequence has been drawn from the Kantian concept of the person by J. G. Fichte and to a greater extent by Hegel. For with both Fichte and Hegel the person becomes in the end an indifferent thoroughfare for an impersonal rational

1. Nor can the person as subject to the laws of the state—a derived form of the person which H. Cohen curiously enough identifies with the essence of the person—be created by a legal constitution; at best, the person can be recognized as a person by such a constitution. The right to vote, for example, *belongs* only to persons. But no one *is* a person simply because a constitution attributes this right to him. Independent of a preliminary examination to establish whether someone is a person, positive law can determine only whether someone "obtains" as a person and is to be accepted or treated as one, and this only in regard to the exercise of certain rights.

2. One should note that Kant speaks of the autonomy of reason much more frequently than he does of the autonomy of the person.

activity.[3] The results here are the same as with Averroes and Spinoza, despite their different points of departure, whether it be the contingent content of experience or the body which is to individualize this suprapersonal and supraindividual rational activity as a person.

If one does not hold strictly to the consequence of this definition but mixes some positive non-formal element in with the application of the concept of the person, that is, some element which goes beyond the mere X of rational activity, then there can no longer be any limit to the determination of *what* in man is to share in "autonomy" and "dignity," or *what* is to share in this inviolability and esteem—indeed, no strict limit on the blink of his eyes or any whimsical change in his mood. Thus the πρῶτον ψεῦδος in the definition of the person leads to a false alternative: there is either heteronomy of the person through a pure logonomy and, indeed, the tendency to complete depersonalization, or the ethical individualism of living one's life without any inner limits on its right. But the recognition of a spiritual person *and* individuality, which alone can prevent such mistakes, is at once completely precluded by this system of concepts.

It is true that in Kant's case the idea of the person acquires the appearance of an existence and full-bloodedness that transcends the X of a rational will through his identification of this X with the *homo noumenon,* i.e., with man as "thing in itself," which he opposes to the *homo phenomenon.* But, logically, the *homo noumenon* is nothing but the concept of the unknowable constant "thing in itself" applied to man. The same unknowable constant also pertains, without *any* inner possibility of differentiation, to every plant and every rock. How could *this* constant render man a dignity different from that of a rock? [4]

3. Fichte's "state of private commerce," with its complete and socialistic enslavement of the person, is the first result in the philosophy of law of this twist of the Kantian concept of the person.

4. With *freedom,* things are somewhat different. The third antinomy is supposed to demonstrate only the legal-theoretical possibility of freedom in the sphere of the thing in itself (in the negative sense of uncaused activity). But the fact that man, and not a rock, as a thing in itself is free is supposed to be given through the moral law as a categorical "you ought" by way of a postulate ("You can, for you ought"). But a number of other known contradictions result from the identification of this possible freedom (which man shares with a rock) and the postulated one (positive freedom). For the conceptual range of being-free coincides with the "being-good" or the legal character of the will, whereas "freedom" in the first (transcendental) sense is freedom to do evil or good, which is a presupposition of the moral *relevance* of acting in general. It is well

2. *Person and the "Ego" of Transcendental Apperception*

Kant holds that the primordial condition of every objective unity of experience, and therewith of the idea of an object in general (as well as of the inner "psychic" and outer "physical" object, and, we may add, of the ideal object), is an "I think" which must accompany every act of perception, representation, etc. That is, this *"ego"* is not a correlate that is added to the unity of the object; its unity and identity constitute the *condition* of the unity and identity of the *object*. "Object" here *means* only a something that is identified through the ego. *Identity* is not (as it is for us) an essential characteristic of the object, a characteristic that would be intuitable as such in any object (the intuitive basis of the law of identity, $A = A$). Rather, the meaning of the term *object* supposedly coincides with the identification of something through an ego. Hence, identity is originally in the ego, and it is from the ego that the identity of an object is borrowed.[5]

According to what we found earlier, such a condition does not exist.[6] True, essentially identical objects must correspond to essentially identical acts. But this interconnection, like that between act and object in general, is not a unilateral but a *mutual* one. For "the ego" itself is still an object (not only the individual ego but also what corresponds to the idea of the egolike manifold and unity, called the ego, in contrast to the manifold of the spatiotemporal extensionality of intuition). But an act is never an object. For according to the nature of the being of acts, they are experienced only in their execution and are given in reflection. Hence an act can never become an object through a second act or a retrospective act of sorts. For an act is not an "object" even in reflection, which alone makes an act knowable beyond its (naïve) execution. Reflective knowing accompanies an act but does not objectify it.[7] Therefore an act can never be given in

---

known that Fichte developed the first of these Kantian concepts of freedom and Schopenhauer the second in his theory of the "intelligible innate basic character" of man. Both Kantian concepts of freedom are thoroughly untenable. It was shown above that the famous "You can, for you ought" is in conflict with an evidential essential law (see chap. 4, sec. 2, c).

5. The psychological and empirical ego is supposed to have its identity and unity on the basis of the givenness of "constancy in space" (of matter) (see "The Refutation of Idealism"). But matter itself is supposed to have its identity and unity on the basis of the transcendental ego.

6. See chap. 2.

7. [See chap. 6, A, sec. 3, b.—*Ed.*]

any form of perception (or even observation), be it outer or inner perception. Nevertheless every ego is given in the *form* of only one kind of perception, namely, the act-form of inner perception and the form of the manifold corresponding to it by essential law. If we reduce these differences of forms of perception and the intuitive form-correlates of their manifolds to an act of form-less intuition, "the" ego, functioning in the execution of an act of *inner* perception (as a determinate direction of perception as act) only as the *form* of perception, remains a definite *content* of perception—but not, as Kant believes, the mere idea of the object or the idea of a "logical subject" in the form of temporal intuition.

Hence, *egoness* cannot be determined or delineated from the *being of nature* through either the idea of a "logical subject" of experiential predications or the temporal manifold, which at the very least belongs as originally to the given of outer intuition as well. Matter is, for example, also a logical subject in time (and not only a constant in space). The ego cannot be made a condition of an object in *any* possible sense of the term. For the idea of the object and its correlate, the idea of the act, are with equal originality differentiated by the addition of specific, phenomenologically demonstrable different contents of plain, formless intuition into the ideas of an "ego" and a "content" (or into the corresponding differences in direction of "inner" and "outer" perception). The ego *itself* is, rather, only an object among objects. Its identity exists only insofar as identity is an essential *characteristic* of the object. On the other hand, we can see that Kant's definition contains a contradiction. For if the object is nothing but something identifiable, the "ego"—whose own identity is supposedly the very condition of the object—must then be an object, though the ego as a "condition of an object" cannot be an object.

For this reason there is only one point in Kant's theory that we recognize, though even it is concealed by his tremendous exaggeration, namely, that comprehensibility through an act "belongs" by essential necessity to the essence of an object, and that the *identifiability of acts* belongs equally to the *essence of the identity* of acts—without regard to the identity of objects that are comprehended by acts. But to this there does not belong *in addition* an identification or an identity of an ego that executes such acts. The identity of the ego is only a special case of this essential mutual belongingness, not its basis or its "condition." Moreover, this essential mutual belongingness does not imply that objects and their interconnections must "conform" to acts and their interconnections and a priori relations of foundation ("the Copernican turn"). Hence it is not a "condition" of the world or world-being to be experienceable or knowable by an *ego* or by a knowing being bearing the essence of *egoness*. It is only the *cogitare* in the sense of the above essential interconnection (and not the *cogito*) that is a "condition," though it is no less true that world-being is a "condition" of the *cogitare*. For every essential interconnection implies that objects of such essences condition each other, and that they do so mutually.[8] This characteristic "Kantian" fear of "transcendental chance"— that objects could behave in a manner quite different from the laws of our experience (thinking, etc.) if we did not "bind" them by the laws of our experience—simply follows from Kant's failure to recognize the above essential interconnection, which precludes precisely this possibility; and he fails here, if I may say so, because he does not give objects a chance to jump over the stick of our laws of experience. But with the elimination of this "fear," the subjectivistic reaction of the "Copernican turn" with respect to these laws is eliminated.

Our argument implies that we fully recognize Kant's refutation of the *theory of the soul* that was part of the rationalism of his time, insofar as this refutation is purely negative. Like all positing of things, the positing of a soul-thing as a real substance or "bearer" of experience given in inner perception is governed not only by the above essential interconnection between act and object but also by all the many essential interconnections which constitute the nature of *egoness* and its form of manifoldness, and which are subject to exploration by (a priori) phenomenology of the psychic. It also goes without saying that egoness and, of course, the ego of individual experience must *not* be *founded* on such assumptions of the soul; at best, the opposite is the case.[9] If egoness, and not merely the individual ego of experience, is already an *object* and therefore subject to the essential interconnections which obtain among objects and which are the basis of the fulfillments of propositions of pure logic, then the "soul" as a "real basis" for an individual ego-experience

8. There is nothing of a "condition" in an "essential interconnection," only a "mutual belongingness." It is only the application of essential interconnections that leads to "conditions."

9. How could the "soul" be that which perceives the exterior? The soul and its intuitive foundation are given only in the specific form of inner perception.

must a fortiori be an object—because it is a thing. And from the fact that not even an intuitive foundation for the (possible) assumption of such a thing is phenomenally given—not even the foundation of this foundation, i.e., egoness as such a "point of departure"—it follows that the soul can never be considered the point of departure of acts.

In opposition to Kant's attempt to deny the ego of individual experience and to degrade the meaning of this term by calling it a mere "interconnection of experience in time," attached to the idea of a merely logical subject, we must affirm the intuitive datum of an *ego of individual experience* as an incontestable *phenomenon*. It is far from true that the ego of individual experience is some interconnection of experiences. For each experience is fully and adequately given only if the experiencing individual is cogiven in it.[10] It is only by way of an *abstraction* from that content of experiences which belongs to them, as experiences of an individual, by essential necessity that we can in psychology speak of "experiences" as if they were separate structures floating freely in the air—an abstraction, therefore, from the always individual experiencing of these experiences to which this positive special content in experiences corresponds. This holds for descriptive psychology, which does not consider experiences identifiable "things" or "events" that can return, be produced, join together, etc. Just as egoness is a positive datum of intuition comparable to the idea of an object in time—a datum of intuition, that is, for an act of formless intuition—so also is every individual ego an ever new givenness of intuition for an act of the form of inner perception. This givenness of intuition does not coincide with any special *content* of experience, with the *sum* of this givenness, or with *relations* and *orders* among such *contents*. Because, of all the possible and factually always more or less contingent series of experiences, every individual ego is based on a special *kind of experience,* accessible only to immediate intuition, and because this kind of experience can still be given to the act of inner intuition itself and can come to the fore in, for example, literary biography, the individual ego can, it is true, be given in intuition *by way of* [an] its factual experiences; but it can never be reduced to the interconnections of these experiences or those of intuition. The individual ego does *not* require a factual and specific bodiliness, or even a specific organic body, for its identification as this or that

10. For more details, see my essay "Über Selbsttäuschungen" (Bibliog. no. 4), esp. the end.

individual ego. Only the following is an essential interconnection, and not a merely inductive, factual state of affairs: that whenever an individual ego is given, an individual lived body is cogiven, and with the latter a body-ego.[11] We therefore need no foundational existential positing of its body [*Körper*] in order to posit an individual ego as existing. An individual ego is also contained, for example, in certain "symbols" and "traces" of its existence which works or actions have impressed in some form on matter, and in which it becomes "understandable."

Furthermore, it is an essential interconnection that *"egoness"* represents itself as existing *only in* some *individual* ego, and that it represents the "essence" of all possible individual egos, namely, their essence *as* egos, and cannot itself be thought of as "a" being. Although we are able to form the idea of an "egoness" without abstracting it empirically from individual egos, but by "finding" it in them through eidetic abstraction, we can also find the above essential interconnection between the essence of egoness and the essence of an individual ego in general. And it is precisely here that this essential interconnection assumes special significance. For it shows us that all talk of a "supraindividual ego," a "consciousness in general," or a "transcendental ego" with special lawful types of procedural activities in all men is evident nonsense. There is the essence of egoness on the one hand and the individual egos in which alone this egoness becomes extant on the other. Hence the individual ego is by no means the "limit" of egoness, as those who adopt such concepts maintain. On the contrary, every idea of an extra- or "supraindividual ego," whose limit or "empirical disturbance" the individual ego is supposed to be, and only with whose presupposition the individual ego could be such a limit, is evidentially a nonsensical assumption.[12] For if we bracket the individual egos, there remains no so-called supraindividual ego as a center of reference for the "world"; indeed, there remains no ego at all.

From this we can draw a simple conclusion: If the "world" (the inner and outer world) is something other than the content of experience of individual egos, *no* ego (and no "transcen-

11. I tried to show elsewhere that in perception this lived-body ego also functions as the "inner sense" of what the total individual can "perceive" in his being and experience. See *ibid.*, and the following.

12. That is, not a "contradictory one," in the sense of a *contradictio in terminis*, or a "senseless" assumption, because the laws of pure grammar remain unaffected here. The assumption is nonsensical because it cancels the uniformly essential *sense* of the idea of the ego. The assumption is false only *because* it is "nonsensical."

dental" or "supraindividual" one) can be the condition of the world. Conversely, every assumption of an egological condition of the world and its givenness *necessarily* leads to solipsism on the basis of the above-mentioned interconnection of essence.[13] And since solipsism is nonsense according to an evidential consciousness of transcendence, i.e., the immediate knowledge, which accompanies every act of "knowing-of," of the natural independence of things in their being from the *execution* of a knowing act (including "this" one, with regard to what we perceive of us and of the outer world), there remains only one conclusion—namely, that the ego cannot be, in any sense of this word (as either actual or merely "possible," for essential interconnections obtain also in the sphere of the "possible"), the condition of the object.

However, as all forms of "transcendentalism" claim, the *individual* ego does not coincide with the *"empirical* ego," if by the term *empirical* we mean the domain of observation and induction. Every individual ego possesses its "essence," which does not disappear with the cancellation of its existence in thinking. Essences also belong, for example, to characters in the poetic realm. And precisely this essence of an individual ego is cogiven *in all its empirical experiences,* insofar as they are given fully and adequately. But this "individual essence" is never accessible to any form of observation, nor is its cognition accessible to any kind of induction. Nevertheless, the intuition of its essence is the presupposition of all applications of "laws of empirical psychology" (both collective and individual psychology), which are possible and accessible to us through a setting aside of the individual essential differences, to any empirical event or action of the individual concerned. For essence has nothing to do with universality. That the essence of an individual ego is different from "egoness" as the essence of *the* ego hardly needs to be men-

13. With this statement we have still not said anything about the justification of assuming a communal collective ego (and, corresponding to it, a communal soul). For we are concerned here not with the opposition "collective" and "member of a collective" but with the opposition "essence" and (exemplary) "individuals of this essence." A "communal ego" would have to be an individual ego, just like the ego of any member of this communal unit. A communal consciousness has nothing to do with a "universal consciousness" or a "supraindividual ego," which we reject. A communal ego, even in its widest extension, cannot function as a "condition of the object of experience" as long as we remain serious about this matter. One cannot demand of the world that it a priori obey the "laws of some communal consciousness." I am in agreement here on many points with Max Frischeisen-Köhler. See his instructive *Wissen und Wirklichkeit.*

tioned. Hence, one who calls the "empirical ego," as the essence of all possible observational contents of an ego (be it self-observation or observation of another), a "disturbance" must at least make it clear that the empirical ego is a disturbance of the individual essential ego, and not a "disturbance" of an "ego in general" or of a "transcendental ego." And he who wants to say that something belonging to the sphere of essences is transcendental must consequently also speak of a *transcendental individual ego,* which is at the same time "transempirical" but nevertheless a non-formal content of intuition. It is therefore by no means an unknowable thing, like Kant's *homo noumenon,* or a hypothetical one, like the soul-substance.

Despite the great importance of the above for ethics, we have not advanced one step toward knowledge of *personality.*[14] For the concept of "person" cannot be gained from any of the basic facts and concepts that we have thus far found, not from the interconnections existing *between act and object,* between act-forms, act-directions, and act-kinds and their respective realms of objects, or from egoness and the individual ego, and especially not from the "soul."

However, there are *two* problems which remain, and these can be brought to intuition only by a clear break from the problems above—a break which is not found in the theories that we have criticized.

Once we have separated the *kinds, forms, and directions of acts,* having bracketed their real bearers and the natural *organization* of such bearers, and once we have demonstrated what their essences and foundational laws consist in, we are confronted with a final question: What, in fact, is it that forms the *unity* of these acts quite independent of the natural *organization* of those bearers (e.g., men) with whose reduction the essences of acts came to the fore—in other words, what forms the unity of these *different* act-essences themselves, not of the factually performed acts of a certain real individual or a species? Single temporal acts, e.g., those of my present thinking while I am writing, are performed by a certain human individual with all his factual being and whatness, not by an "ego" or even by a "soul." No further executing agent is required for this act. If (by means of a phenomenological reduction) we set aside this executing agent along with its reality and character, we have only those different *act-essences*—e.g., judging, loving, hating, will-

14. See chap. 6, B.

ing, as well as inner and outer perception—of which only *one* has an ego corresponding to it, namely, the act-essence of inner perception. Here again no executing agent is required for these acts, and not just because we have set aside the individual executing agent. Disregarding individual act-executing agents, we examine the infinite fullness of existing lawful relations, e.g., between perception and a thing perceived, between seeing and a thing seen, between feeling and values, between loving and values, between preferring and values, between willing and its projects. However, a question still remains: Which *unitary* executor "belongs" to the essence of an execution of acts that are so *different* in their kinds, forms, and directions? This question has nothing to do with the one who executes such acts or with a real being that executes them. Such a question would make no sense in the area of act-essences. And because act-essences and foundational interconnections are *eo ipso* "a priori" to all of inductive experience, we can also ask: Which executor "belongs" essentially to the execution of acts of such different natures in general? And it is precisely here—and not "earlier" within the order of problems involved—that the problem of *personality* confronts us.

A second, analogous problem arises here with regard to *objects* and their realms. For if we perform a phenomenological reduction with regard to objects, as we did with regard to acts, and if in so doing we set aside the reality or non-reality of objects in order to study their essential interconnections and the meaning of their plain whatness, i.e., their formal and non-formal whatness as based on special regions of objects, e.g., the region of values and the region of extant objects (or resistance as the phenomenal and objective correlate of striving) plus the many we are faced with this problem: Which kind of *unity* is formed subdivisions of these regions (e.g., physical, psychic, ideal), by such object-essences insofar as they generally come into being and insofar as they *are* not in this or that thing? And here again the problem of *world* as that of the *unity of world* poses itself, a problem which therefore corresponds exactly to that of the *person*.

Just as the idea of the object essentially corresponds to the idea of the act, essential kinds of objects to all essential kinds of acts, the forms of being of the psychic and the physical to the forms of acts, e.g., inner and outer perception, and an "environment" to vital acts, so also a *world* (as essence) corresponds to the *person* (as essence).

And it must be noted here that the psychic and the physical represent only two forms of being of *one world-being*. Both are determined a priori by two basically different forms of the manifold. *In this sense* all *ego-unities* and their individual essences and of course *egoness*, or the essence of "ego," *belong* to the "world." But they do not constitute a referential center of the world. Ego-unities can be meaningfully regarded as referential centers only of "nature," *not* of world, to which the entire being of the psychic also belongs. Likewise, inner and outer perception, as essentially different directions of intuiting, which is in itself pure and formless, are only two different act-directions of a possible *person*. Just as the opposition between inner and outer perception disappears *in the essence* of the person—that is, just as the *essence of the person*, like the essence of a pure act of the person, *is psychophysically indifferent*—so also is the *being of world psychophysically indifferent* if we "reduce" the forms of this being, that is, if we also make the essential differences among the manifolds, which function as "forms" of intuition, the *content* of the "given" in an act of pure, formless intuition.

3. Person and Act
The Psychophysical Indifference of the Person
and Concrete Acts
Essential Levels of Centrality within the Person

a. Person and Act

Neither the being nor the problem of the *"person"* would exist if there were beings (whose natural organization we set aside in the reduction) endowed *only with knowing* (as thought and intuition) and those acts belonging to this (specifically theoretical) sphere. (Let us call such beings purely rational beings.) Of course these beings would still be (logical) subjects that execute rational acts: but they would not be "persons." Nor would they be persons if they had both inner and outer perception and often dealt with knowledge of the soul and nature, that is, even if they found an object "ego" in themselves and others and could perfectly observe, describe, and explicate experiences of "the ego" as well as all individual egos. The same would hold for beings whose entire contents were given only as projects of willing. They would be (logical) subjects of a willing, but not persons. For the person is precisely that unity which exists for acts of all possible *essential differences* insofar as these acts are thought to be executed.[15] Hence, by saying that it belongs to the nature of the differences of acts to be in a *person* and *only* in a person, we imply that the *different logical subjects* of essentially different acts (which are different only as otherwise identical subjects of such act-differences) can only *be in a form of unity* insofar as we reflect on the possible "being" of these subjects and not merely on their nature.

We can now enunciate the essential definition in the above sense: *the person is the concrete and essential unity of being of acts of different essences* which in itself (and therefore not πρὸς ἡμᾶς) precedes all essential act-differences (especially the difference between inner and outer perception, inner and outer willing, inner and outer feeling, loving and hating, etc.). *The being of the person is therefore the "foundation" of all essentially different acts.*

But all of this depends on a correct understanding of the relation which we call foundation.

Above all, it must be made clear that in *all* investigations of acts made in pure phenomenology we are concerned with *genuine intuitive essences,* never with empirical abstractions, which always presuppose the intuition of such essences in that these essences delineate the possible scope of the inductive abstraction of possible "common characteristics." Nevertheless in all act-investigations we are also concerned with *abstract intuitive essences.*[16] These are "abstract," not because they have been "abstracted," but because they require supplementation insofar as they are to *be.* As opposed to abstract essences, *concrete essences* are a second kind of genuine intuitive essences.[17] If an

15. Therefore a *"being which thinks itself"* (e.g., Aristotle's God, according to many interpreters, although not Franz Brentano) is not a "person." For "self-consciousness" is not a person if, in this consciousness "of" itself, all possible kinds of conscious activities (e.g., the knowing, willing, feeling, loving, and hating kinds) are not uniformly contained in it.

16. A nuance of red on the surface of a cloth, for example, is truly intuitable; and, as this nuance, it is also "individual." That is, it is not individual because of the complex it enters into, but at the same time it is something *abstract* belonging to the *concretum* of this surface.

17. Just because something is concrete does not mean that it is "real." Thus "the" number 3 is a single concrete existence, but ideal and not real, insofar as it functions neither as a quantity nor as an ordinal number fulfilling all possible equations (e.g., $4 - 1 = ?, 2 + 1 = ?, 17 - 14 = ?$; or $2 + 1 = +?, 4 - 7 = -?$). The *possible fulfillments* of the 3s meant in such equations represent only *abstracta* of this concrete 3.

act-essence is to be concrete, its full intuitable givenness *presupposes* a reference to the essence of the *person,* who is the executor of acts.[18]

From this it clearly follows that the person can never be reduced to the X of a mere "point of departure" of acts or to some kind of mere "interconnective complex" or network of acts, as a form of the so-called actualistic theories which conceives of the being of the person in terms of his doings (*ex operari sequitur esse*) would have it. The person is not an empty "point of departure" of acts; he is, rather, a concrete being. Unless we keep this in mind, all of our talk about acts can never catch the fully adequate essence of any act, but only an abstract essence. Abstract act-essences concretize into concrete act-essences only by belonging to the essence of this or that individual person. Therefore a concrete act can never be fully and adequately comprehended without the antecedent intending of the essence of the person. Any "interconnective complex" will remain a mere complex of abstract act-essences if the person "himself" in whom such an interconnective complex exists is not given.[19] Of course the actualistic theory is correct to maintain that the person is not a "thing" or a "substance" which executes acts in the sense of a substance-causality. For such "things" could in fact be randomly obliterated or exchanged, if there is a multiplicity (one thinks of Kant's picture of electric spheres, which are dynamically unified), with no change at all in immediate experience. In addition, everyone would carry the same "substance" with him, which—since *every* kind of manifold, e.g., time, space, number, plurality, would be missing—could not yield differences between one and the other.[20] The conclusion that the person must be only an "interconnective complex" of acts (even if only the intentional

18. One can also form classes of persons that lead to a more complete essential cognition of the acts concerned, which cognition is completed in the cognition of the personal individual who executed an act.

19. A theory of acts which neglects this turns the person into a mosaic of acts and so arrives at another version of the atomistic conception of the mind, a version similar to that of association psychology.

20. This was Spinoza's deep insight, insofar as he broke away from the Cartesian theory of substance. Thus soul-substances became modes of the attribute "thinking" of a substance. Spinoza correctly saw that there is no place for the *person* on the presupposition that the mind's essence is only "thinking," and he saw as well that the individualization of thinking beings would have to be shifted to mere differences among human bodies (as in the philosophy of Averroes). Thus Spinoza drew correct conclusions from Descartes's false presuppositions.

interconnection of meaning) is quite false.[21] Surely the person *is* and experiences himself only as a being that *executes acts*, and he is in no sense "behind" or "above" acts, or something standing "above" the execution and processes of acts, like a point at rest. For all of this is a picture taken from a spatiotemporal sphere; and it stands to reason that this does not hold for the relation between *person* and *acts*. This picture always leads to a substantialization of the person.[22] But the *whole person* is contained in *every* fully concrete act, and the whole person *"varies"* in and through every act—without being exhausted in his being in any of these acts, and without "changing" like a thing in time. But this concept of "variation" as a pure "becoming different" implies no time that makes change possible, nor does it imply a fortiori any thinglike changes. Nor is anything given here of a "succession" in this becoming different (we can comprehend succession without comprehending a change and without comprehending a thinglike arrangement of a given material, e.g., succession in the phenomenon of "oscillation"). And for this very reason there is *no* necessity for an *enduring being* that subsists in this succession in order to safeguard the "identity of the individual person." Identity lies solely in the qualitative direction of this pure becoming different. In trying to bring this most hidden of all phenomena to givenness, we can guide the reader to the direction of the phenomenon only by way of images. Thus we can say that the person lives *into* time and executes his acts into time in becoming different. But the person does not live within phenomenal time, which is immediately given in the flow of inwardly perceived psychic processes, nor does he live in the objective time of physics. In the latter there is nothing like fast and slow, endurance (which figures here only as a limiting case of succession),[23] or the phenomenal time dimensions of present, past, and

21. Needless to say, there is no causal relationship here. For the latter exists only for real correlates of experience of what is given in inner perception.

22. Pictures of this kind also lead to questions characteristic of the seventeenth century: whether the *soul always* thinks, whether it executes acts even in dreamless sleep, etc., whether it "remains unchanged" throughout life.

23. "Objective" time is deformed and dequalified phenomenal time. Whereas duration and succession within phenomenal time are positive qualities, duration in objective time consists only in successive phases of the being of an object in which the object does not change. Although there is no "present" in objective time, since there is neither past nor future (a

future, because the past and future points of phenomenal time are treated "as" possible points of the present. Because the person lives his existence precisely in the *experiencing* of his possible *experiences,* it makes no sense to try to grasp the person in past lived experiences. As long as we look only at the so-called experiences and not at their *being* experienced, the person remains completely transcendent. But every experiencing, or, as we can also say, every *concrete act,* contains all act-essences that can be distinguished in phenomenological investigations. It contains them according to a priori orders of foundation, which are established by the results concerning act-founding. Therefore every concrete act always contains inner and outer perception, lived-body consciousness, loving and hating, feeling and preferring, willing and not willing, judging, remembering, representing, etc. All these divisions, necessary as they are, yield only abstract traits of the concrete act of the person—if we are looking at the person. The concrete act of the person can be understood as a mere sum or a mere construct of such abstract act-essences no more than the person can be understood as a mere interconnective complex of acts. Rather, it is the person himself, living in each of his acts, who permeates every act with his peculiar character. No knowledge of the nature of love, for instance, or of the nature of judgment, can bring us one step nearer to the knowledge of how person *A* loves or judges person *B;* nor can a reference to the contents (values, states of affairs) given in each of these acts furnish this knowledge. But, on the other hand, a glance at the person himself and his essence immediately yields a peculiarity for every act that we know him to execute, and the knowledge of his "world" yields a peculiarity for the contents of his acts.

b. The Being of the Person Is Never an Object
The Psychophysical Indifference of the Person and His Acts
The Relation of the Person to "Consciousness"

The "ego," as we have shown, is an object in every sense of the term: egoness is an object of formless intuition, and the individual ego an object of inner perception. In contrast to this, an *act* is never an object. No matter how much knowledge we have of an act, our reflecting on its naïve execution (in the moment of such execution or in reflective, immediate memory) contains

---

distinction which is relative to a lived body), present points of phenomenal time (and these exclusively) do correspond to points of objective time.

nothing like the objectification which marks, e.g., all inner perception, especially all inner observation.[24]

If an act can therefore never be an object, then the *person* who lives in the execution of acts can a fortiori never be an object. The only and exclusive kind of givenness of the person is his *execution of acts* (including the execution of acts reflecting on acts). It is through this execution of acts that the person experiences himself at the same time. Or, if we are concerned with other persons, the person is experienced in terms of post-execution, coexecution, or pre-execution of acts. In these cases of the execution of acts of other persons, there is no objectification.

If one understands *psychology* (in the way that it usually is understood) as a science of (the observation, description, and explanation of accessible) "happenings," and, indeed, happenings in inner perception, everything that deserves the name *act*, as well as everything that deserves the name *person*, must, for this reason, remain *transcendent* to psychology. Hence we are compelled to regard the attempt to assign to psychology studies of *acts*, for example, acts of judging, representing, feeling, etc., and to other sciences studies of *"appearances"* and *"contents"* (according to Franz Brentano, natural science; according to Carl Stumpf, "phenomenology") as completely mistaken. What is regarded as content and object, as opposed to "act," contains, among many other things, all possible facts of psychological research. In the case of that which is given according to essential laws only in the person-act of inner perception, the act must be executed-with by the researcher who "understands," for example, what his subject has perceived and observed, for it cannot be objectified. This does not imply, however, that within the series of objectively given phenomena of inner perception, the *contents* and *functions* of appearances are not to be distinguished, as they are in Stumpf's valuable studies.[25] Indeed, we regard this distinction as both necessary and irreducible. Associative psychology was mistaken in its failure to take this differentiation

24. The difference between reflection and inner perception is also made clear by the fact that an act of outer perception can definitely be given in reflection, but, of course, never in inner perception. One who does not see this is bound to declare the entire content of outer perception a partial content of the act of outer perception given (on this premise) in inner perception; i.e., he will fall victim to idealistic psychologism.

25. See Carl Stumpf, "Erscheinungen und psychische Funktionen," in *Abhandlungen der preussischen Akademie der Wissenschaften vom Jahre 1906* (Berlin, 1907).

into account. Nevertheless these *"functions"* have nothing to do with *"acts."* First, all functions are ego-functions; they never belong to the sphere of the person. Functions are psychic; acts are non-psychic. Acts are executed; functions happen by themselves. Functions necessarily require a lived body and an environment to which the "appearances" of functions belong. But with the person and acts we do not posit a lived body; and to the person there corresponds a world, not an environment. Acts spring from the person into time; functions are facts in phenomenal time and can be measured indirectly by coordinating their phenomenal time-relations with measurable lengths of time of appearances given in functions themselves. For example, seeing, hearing, tasting, and smelling belong to functions, as do *all* kinds of noticing, noting, and taking notice of (and not only so-called sensible attention to) vital feeling, etc. However, genuine acts, in which something is "meant," and which among themselves possess an immediate complex of meaning, are not functions. *Functions* can have a twofold relation to *acts.* They can be objects of acts, e.g., when I try to bring my seeing to intuitive givenness; and they can also be that "through" which an act is directed toward something objectified, though without this function's becoming an object in the process. The latter happens when I perform the "same" act of judging in both seeing an object and hearing it at another time (that is, an act of judging of identical sense and about the same state of affairs). Stumpf properly stresses that the variation of an object's "appearances" is independent of the variation of functions, that the latter is independent of the former, and that together these are *in concreto* a criterion of the distinction between functions and appearances. This criterion also holds for the differentiation of functions and acts, but with this difference: the same acts can be conjoined with all possible combinations and variations of functions, and vice versa. On the other hand, laws of acts and their interconnections of foundations are transferable, for example, to beings of quite a different *functional* character. But it is impossible for laws of functions, which are in principle empirical and inductive, to set limits on laws of acts, which are a priori in nature.[26]

This means that the opposition of function and appearance

26. See my critique of Brentano's and Stumpf's division of the psychic and the physical in "Idole der Selbsterkenntnis." [See "Die Idole der Selbsterkenntnis" (Bibliog. no. 10), sec. 2. "Über Selbsttäuschungen" did not contain the critique mentioned.—*Ed.*]

is still contained as a part within person and world and therefore does not coincide with the opposition of person and world. Stumpf's "functions" and their counterparts, "appearances," can become given only when we focus, from among the givens of the act of intuition which is separated from the concrete person-act, on the givenness "lived body" and its corresponding "environment," and think of the act of "inner perception" as having been executed.

Our claim that acts (and especially the person) do not belong to the psychic sphere does not imply that they are physical. We maintain only that both act and person are psychophysically *indifferent*. We are not at all troubled by the old Cartesian alternative, which requires that everything be either psychic or physical. For such a long time this alternative concealed ideal objects and the fact "lived body" (as distinct from thing-bodies) and thus the true object of biology, and it also led to the vain attempt to place the whole sphere of law and the state, that of art and religious objects, and many other domains into the ontological categories "recognized" by philosophers.

Still, we use the term *mind* [Geist] for the entire sphere of acts (following our procedure of many years).[27] With this term we designate all things that possess the nature of act, intentionality, and fulfillment of meaning, wherever we may find them. This of course implies at once that all mind is by essential necessity *"personal,"* and that the idea of a "non-personal mind" is "contradictory." But no *"ego"* at all belongs to the essence of mind, and hence no division between *"ego* and *outer world."* [28] It is, rather, the *person* that is the single and necessary existential form of mind insofar as we are concerned with concrete mind.

The use of the word *person* in *language* already reveals that the form of unity meant by this term has nothing to do with the form of unity of the "consciousness"-object of inner perception or consequently the "ego" (either the "ego" in opposition to a "thou" or the "ego" in opposition to the "outer world"). For *person*, unlike these terms, is an absolute, not a feelably *relative*, name. The word *I* is always connected with a "thou" on the one hand and an "outer world" on the other. This is not the case with the title *person*. God, for example, can be a person, but not an

---

27. See "Die transzendentale und die psychologische Methode" (Bibliog. no. 3).

28. Hence the spheres of person and world, egoness and outer world, individual ego and community, and lived body and environment are not reducible, one to the other.

"I," because for him there is neither a "thou" nor an "outer world." What we mean by the term *person,* in contrast to the ego, is something of a self-sufficient *totality.* A person acts, for example. He "takes a walk," etc. True, language permits such expressions as "I act," "I go for a walk." But here the word *I* does not designate a psychic fact of experience; it is, rather, an occasional expression, changing its meaning from speaker to speaker, and merely a linguistic form of address. The "I" does not speak. The man does. All of this clearly shows that *person* means something that is completely indifferent to the oppositions "I-thou," "psychic-physical," and "ego–outer world." If I say, "I perceive myself," the "I" is the form of address, not the psychic ego of experience. "Myself," however, does not mean "my I"; it does not answer the question of whether I perceive "myself" in an outer or inner fashion. If, on the other hand, I say, "I perceive my ego," again the "I" and the "ego" have different senses. The "I" has the same sense as in "I go for a walk"; i.e., it is the form of address. The "ego," however, is the psychic ego of experiencing. It is the object of *inner perception.* Hence, just as a person can "go for a walk," so also can he "perceive" his ego, e.g., when he is working in psychology. However, this psychic ego that the person perceives can no more perceive than it can go for a walk or act. Although the person can perceive his ego as well as his lived body and the outer world, it is not possible for him to become an object of representation or perception, either for himself or for others.

It *belongs to the essence of the person* to exist and to live solely in the *execution of intentional acts.* The person is therefore essentially never an "object." On the contrary, any objectifying attitude (be it perception, representation, thinking, remembering, or expectation) makes the person immediately transcendent.

The psychophysical indifference of acts is also clearly given in the fact that all acts and act-differences can have as their objects both the psychic and the physical. Thus, representing and perceiving, remembering and expecting, feeling and preferring, willing and not willing, loving and hating, judging, etc., can have psychic as well as physical "contents." I can, for instance, "remember" an appearance of nature and a psychic experience, and I can feel my own value or that of an object of the outer world, etc. We therefore expressly reject those curious theories which hold that when I remember an experience, there must be an element of the psychic stream coming from it in order to bend back intentionally to another part. Acts can be objects no more than psychic happenings or "events" can "mean" something or relate to each other intentionally. Acts either are or are not, and are of either this or that quality. On the other hand, we do not need any passageway through the psychic sphere in order to love physical appearances or to will or to do something in the physical world. As the person wills or does something, whatever happens in his psychic sphere is quite indifferent to the meaning and being of this willing or doing. But no matter how wrong it is to smuggle intentional factors into the psychic sphere, as the theories that we have criticized do, it is also wrong to deny completely the intentional factor and to say, for example, as Theodor Ziehen does, that every memory of a representation is a new representation or merely a new element in the psychic stream. The former theory falsely spiritualizes the psychic and ruins psychology. The latter psychologizes the mind and ruins philosophy.

Psychology can deal neither with (abstract) essences of remembering, expecting, loving, etc., nor with these acts as abstract parts of a concrete person-act. Even less can it deal with the a priori orders of foundation of these acts. What concerns psychology is simply what happens in the sphere of inner perception on the occasion of the execution of such acts, and the interconnections that such executions have among themselves and with the lived body (in causal terms). As in all other inductive sciences, there is no sharp distinction between description and explanation. Thus, for example, association, reproduction, perseveration, and the aftereffect of a determining tendency toward the processes of representation, i.e., as a condition of the origin of an act of representing or remembering a "content" (which is determined by its object, which is presupposed as real), become problems for psychology.[29] But the essence of remembering and representing, etc., and the phenomenology of these things remain inaccessible to psychology, and so does the origin of these acts in the person, as well as the a priori laws of this origin. For both the origin and the laws obtain for *any* imaginable phase of this stream, whose changing complexes of contents psychology studies inductively. This stream, whose parts a psychologist sees, "originates" at *every* point according to a priori laws of origin and, within the scope of these, in the concrete nature of the person. If the content of this stream could

29. [See chap. 6, A, sec. 3, f, g.—*Ed.*]

teach us anything at all about this "origin," *any* random phase and *any* random cross-section of this stream would suffice, and no "induction" would be needed. For the origin of an experience out of a person and the rise of an experience within a person are basically two different things.

If we take the word *consciousness* to mean everything that comes to appearance in inner perception, as we do when we define psychology as the "science of appearances in consciousness," (and it seems to me that this is the only usage which makes any sense), then both the *person* and his acts must be designated as *supraconscious being,* whereas the appearances in consciousness themselves divide into *surconscious* and *subconscious* ones. And all psychic real being corresponding to these appearances—i.e., so-called psychic events and processes and their causality, the psychic dispositions that are hypothetically assumed for the production of a causal nexus, etc.—must be called *unconscious.*[30] But one who uses the term *consciousness* to designate all *"consciousness of something,"* who carefully avoids contaminating the usage of the term with the introduction of the intellectualistic theory according to which "representation" must be the basis of all intentional acts (including judging, loving, hating, feeling, willing) as the basic act of objectification, and who therefore understands by "consciousness of something" (first without any theory of foundations) all intentionally directed acts filled with meaning (also feeling of something [e.g., values], willing of something [projects], judging of something [states of affairs], etc.), may also call the person the concrete "consciousness-of." But this cannot be allowed when this "consciousness of something" is taken to mean and imply (in a Cartesian fashion) only the *cogitare,* so that loving, hating, feeling, willing, and their own lawfulness have their foundations in the union of the person so defined (*res cogitans*) with a body. This is also Kant's pre-

---

30. By "subconscious" sphere of inner perception, I do not mean, say, "unnoticed" or "unrecognized." I mean everything whose presence, absence, or variation produces in the totality of what is inwardly perceived a "change" in a specific direction, but which is not necessarily given (even in an attitude of maximal noticing). For these "subconscious" facts, all of which belong to the *phenomenal* sphere, there is the real plus dispositions, just as in the case of surconscious appearances. Thus the sphere of the unconscious divides into what is unconscious in the subconscious sphere and what is unconscious in the surconscious sphere. In Benno Erdmann's terminology (of association psychology), our sphere of what is unconscious in the subconscious sphere coincides with the "dispositionally excited."

supposition with regard to all emotional and voluntary acts with the curious exception of the "feeling of reverence." [31] We shall prefer in the following to use the term *consciousness* only in the sense of either a specific consciousness-of of inner perception or appearances in consciousness (the psychic), because the term *consciousness* in the sense of "consciousness of something" is closely connected historically with Cartesian rationalism and its thousand modifications (among which, in this case, we may include Kant).

c. Person and World

In the foregoing we called the *world* the correlate [*Sachkorrelat*] of the person. Hence there is an *individual world* corresponding to every individual person. Just as every act belongs to a person, so also every object "belongs" by essential necessity to a *world*. But every world is in its essential structure a priori bound to the interconnections of essence and structure that exist for essences of things [*Sachwesenheiten*]. Every world is at the same time a concrete world, but only as the *world* of a *person*. No matter which realms of objects we may distinguish—the realm of objects of the inner world, of the outer world, of bodiliness (and thereby the total possible realm of life), the realm of ideal objects, or the realm of values—they all have an abstract objectivity. They become fully concrete only as part of a world, the world of a person. But the *person* is never a "part" of a world; the person is always the *correlate* of a "world," namely, the world in which he experiences himself. If we consider only one concrete act of a person, this act contains in itself all possible act-essences, and its objective correlate contains all essential factors of world—e.g., egoness, the individual ego, and all essential constituents of the psychic, as well as the outer world, spatiality, temporality, the phenomenon of the lived body, thingness, effecting, etc.—on the basis of an a priori and lawful structure, valid without exception for all possible persons and all possible acts of all persons. This structure is valid not only for the real world but also for all possible worlds. This correlate also contains an ultimate peculiarity, an original trait, belonging only to the "world" of this person and nobody else. This peculiarity cannot

31. His pure will is simply "reason as practical," i.e., thinking related to the realization of a content by means of actions (πράττειν). The fact that Kant actually denies a pure "will" was emphasized first by Herman Schwarz. See his *Psychologie des Willens* (Leipzig: Engelmann, 1900).

be grasped in terms of essential concepts pertaining to general essences. The fact that this is so is not empirically found,[32] nor is it this individual a priori essence itself. It is, rather, a general essential trait of all *possible worlds*. Therefore, if we reduce everything that is "given" to a concrete person in general to the phenomenal essences that are purely *self*-given to the person (i.e., to facts that are perfectly what they are), so that even all abstract qualities, forms, and directions of acts, and what we distinguish among acts, enter into the sphere of *givenness* for a pure and formless act of the person, here alone we have a world that is *not relative* to life [*daseins*-absolut], and we find ourselves in the realm of things themselves. However, so long as a *single* world exists for different individual persons, a world that is regarded as "self-given" and "absolute," its singularity and sameness are necessarily an *illusion* [Schein]. Here, in fact, only realms of objects that are relative to the types of bearers of concrete personalities (e.g., living beings, men, races, etc.) are given. Or it is "the world," i.e., the *one* concrete world encompassing all concrete worlds, that is "given"; but it is not "self-given," only meant. That is, *"the world"* becomes in this case a mere "idea" in Kant's sense of the term (but not with the token of reality that he attributes to it). For Kant believed he could degrade the nature of "world" itself to an "idea." But *"the world"* is by no means an idea. It is an absolute, always concrete, individual being. The intention toward it becomes an idea that is in principle unfulfillable, something only meant, as soon as we demand that it be "given" to a *plurality* of individual persons and thus self-given. This is also the case when we allow ourselves to believe that we can make the "universal validity" of the establishment and the determination of its being and content the condition of its own and every kind of existence through general concepts and propositions. For such a determination of the world is in principle not possible. As we showed earlier, the so-called transcendental concept of truth, existence, and object, which volatilizes the object in a necessary and universally valid combination of representations, is in fact a subjectivistic falsification. And it is this falsification which *entails* that absolute being become an unrecognizable X of a "thing in itself." Hence metaphysical truth, or "the" truth itself, *must* have a different content, within the limits of the a priori structure of world, for each per-

---

32. The "contingency" of the real world, the fact that it cannot be deduced from the laws of "possible worlds," is given with this alone.

son because the content of world-*being* is, in every case, different for each person. Therefore, the fact that truth about the world and the absolute world is, in a certain sense, a "personal truth" (as the absolute good is a "personal good," as we shall see later) [33] is due not to any supposed "relativity" and "subjectivity," or "humanness," of the idea of truth, but to the essential interconnection between person and world. The fact that this is so and not otherwise has its foundation in the essence of *Being, not* in the essence of the "truth." Of course one who from the very beginning looks on personality as something "negative," for instance, as a contingent bodily or egological limitation of a "transcendental reason," will not see this point, nor will one who regards the person merely as a factual part of the empirical world or a world in general, one who does not regard the person as having his foundation in *absolute* Being and as representing absolute Being (and world). He will always believe that in order to reach Being itself, one must set the person *aside*, "rise above" him, or "get rid" of him. In fact, he has only to "overcome" his ego, his bodiliness, and his prejudices—above all, his prejudices of genus and race—which limit the nature of his personality because he regards them all as objective, so that the absolute world belonging essentially to his person can gradually emerge from the empty web of mere "world relations." For if person and world are absolute being, and if they are reciprocally related essentially, absolute truth can only be personal. And insofar as truth is impersonal, and insofar as it is "universal" and not personally valid, there *must* be either falsehood or merely truth about objects relative to life. Only those subjectivists and transcendental psychologists who believe that they can *define* "truth" merely as the "universal validity" of a proposition hold that a personally valid truth cannot be a "truth" in the (strictest and "transcendentally" unspoiled) sense of an agreement between a judged proposition and its state of affairs, and that personally valid truth (and, analogously, a good) is a "*contradictio in adjecto.*"

If personality were a concept having its foundation in the "*ego*"—in any sense of the term—or in a "transcendental ego" or in "consciousness in general," what we call a personal truth would of course be a contradictory notion. It is Fichte's "ego" and its numerous modern forms, as well as Kant's infinitely more profound and more carefully explained "transcendental apperception," which dissolve the basis of a strict and objective

33. [See chap. 6, B, sec. 2.—*Ed.*]

idea of truth, and which represent the first steps on a path that ends in the pragmatistic conversion of all philosophy into a bog.

d. Microcosm, Macrocosm, and the Idea of God

If to every "person" there corresponds a "world," and to every "world," a "person," we must ask—because concreteness belongs to the essence of the real, not only to its empirical being-real— whether the "idea" of *one identical real world,* surpassing the a priori essential structure that binds "all possible worlds," has phenomenal fulfillment, or whether we must stay on the level of a plurality of personal worlds. We are not referring to the idea of "a" concrete, real, absolute world, one that is accessible to each person in principle as "his world." Let us call this idea of one identical real world the idea of the *macrocosm,* following an old philosophical tradition, but without committing ourselves to what various writers have meant by this notion. If there is such a macrocosm, there is something familiar about and in it: namely, its a priori essential structure, which phenomenology brings to prominence in all regions. This structure holds for all *possible worlds* because it holds for the general essence of "world." All microcosms, i.e., all individual "personal worlds," are, notwithstanding their totality, parts of the macrocosm—if there is one concrete world into which all persons look [*hinblicken*]. And the personal correlate of the macrocosm would be the idea of an infinite and perfect person of spirit, one whose acts would be given to us in their essential determinations in act-phenomenology, which pertains to the acts of all possible persons. But this "person" would have to be concrete simply to fulfill the essential condition of a reality.[34] Thus the *idea of God* is *cogiven* with the unity and identity and singularity of the world on the basis of an essential interconnection of complexes. Therefore, if we posit one concrete world as real, it would be absurd (though not "contradictory") not to posit the idea of a concrete spirit [*Geistes*]. However, only a concrete person who is in immediate communication with something corresponding to this idea, and to whom its concrete being is "self-given," can posit the idea of God as real; philosophy can never do so. The reality of "God" therefore has its only foundation in a possible positive

34. At no point in this book is there ever any question of positing the reality of the "essence" of God. [See the author's remarks at the very end of chap. 6.—*Ed.*]

revelation of God in a concrete person.[35] Without going into this question in detail, we would like to stress one point: every "unity of the world" (including all kinds of monism and pantheism) without regress to the essence of a *personal* God, and, similarly, every kind of "substitute" for a personal "God," be it a "universal world-reason," a "transcendental rational ego," a "moral governor of the world" (Kant), an *ordo ordinans* (Fichte in his earlier period), an infinite logical "subject" (Hegel), or an impersonal or self-styled "suprapersonal unconscious," etc., is an "absurd" philosophical assumption. For such assumptions do not agree with evidential essential interconnections. One who speaks of *concrete* thought or *concrete* willing posits at the same time the totality of personality. For otherwise he would be concerned only with abstract act-essences. But concreteness itself belongs to the essence of reality, not only to reality's being posited. One who speaks about and posits "the" concrete absolute world, and does not mean simply his own, necessarily posits the concrete person of God, also. If, on the other hand, the essence of personality were based in the "ego," e.g., as Eduard von Hartmann presupposes in his subtle but purely dialectical investigations of the question, the idea of a divine person would be nonsense. For to every "ego" there belongs by essential necessity an "outer world" and a "thou" and a "lived body," all of which it would be a priori nonsensical to attribute to God. Conversely, it is the meaningful idea of a personal God which shows that the idea of the person is not founded in the "ego."

If, however, the unity and singularity of world are not founded in the unity of the logical consciousness (in which only the unity of objects of cognition is founded, objects which in turn essentially require belongingness to a world), and if it is a fortiori not founded in "science" (as a special symbolic and universal type of cognition of objects relative to life) or in any other spiritual root of culture, but in the essence of a concrete personal God, then we must also say that all essential communities of individual persons are not founded in some "rational lawfulness" or in an abstract idea of reason, but solely in the possible community of these persons and the person of persons, i.e., in the *community with God*. All other communities of a moral and legal character have this community as their *foundation*. Hence, all

35. On pure types of the person, see chap. 7. [See chap. 6, B, sec. 4, ad 6. "Vorbilder und Führer" (Bibliog. no. 29) was to have been included in this work as chapter 7.—*Ed.*]

amare, contemplare, cogitare, and *velle* are intentionally inter-woven with the *one concrete world,* the macrocosm, by way of *amare, contemplare, cogitare,* and *velle "in Deo."* But this is not the place to pursue this matter further.

e. Lived Body and Environment

We have already touched upon the concepts of the *lived body* [Leib] and the *environment* [Umwelt] in our analysis of deeds. We sharply distinguished these from the oppositions of ego and external world, and person and world.[36] We are now concerned with an explanation of their relation or the relation of their corresponding givens to the givens of the person and the world. We will not, however, furnish an exhaustive explanation of these data as such.

First, there can be no doubt that the *lived body* does *not* be-long to the *sphere of the person* or the *sphere of acts.* It belongs to the *object sphere* of any "consciousness of something" and its kind and ways of being. The lived body's phenomenal mode of givenness, with its foundations, is essentially different from that of the *ego,* with its states and experiences.

In order to arrive at correct knowledge of these states of af-fairs, let us begin with a critique of major types of prevailing opinions on this matter. We will then pursue a positive investi-gation of the facts involved.

It is our contention that *"lived bodiliness"* [Leiblichkeit] rep-resents a special non-formal essential given (for pure phenome-nological intuition), which, in any factual perception of a lived body, functions as a form of perception (we can also say that it functions as a category, in the sense of the aforementioned pre-cise characteristic of anything categorial).[37] This implies that its *givenness* is not reducible to a form of outer or inner percep-tion, to a coordination of the contents of these, or a fortiori to a fact of inductive experience, i.e., the perception of an individual thing. This also implies that the lived body must never be con-sidered a primary given on whose foundation some psychophysi-cally indifferent thing that we "come upon" differentiates itself and sets itself off as "psychic" or "physical" according to different relations with the lived body. If the psychic and the physical have been shown to belong to two irreducible perceptual direc-tions (inner and outer perception), the lived double relationship

36. [See above, p. 143, n. 32.—*Ed.*]
37. See chap. 2, A.

of their series of contents to the datum "lived body" must lead to two sciences, whose proper characteristics will clearly be revealed to us at this time.

We wish to make a sharp distinction between *"lived body"* and *"thing-body"* [*der* "Leib" *und der* "Körper"], a distinction which, unfortunately, is not found nowadays in scientific terminology. If, in thinking, we suppressed the functions of all the external senses by which we perceive the external world, then all possible perception of our own "thing-body" would be abolished, along with the perception of all other different bodies. We would not be able to touch ourselves or have any access to the forms of our chest, hands, legs, etc., as in the case of external bodies, e.g., inanimate ones; nor would we be able to look at ourselves (with or without mirrors). We would not be able to hear any sounds of our voice or those otherwise produced, nor would we be able to taste anything, smell ourselves, etc. But the phenomenon of our "lived body" would by no means be annihilated in this case. For—no matter how closely one may focus on this point—in the case of our lived body we have, in addition to its possible external consciousness, an inner consciousness that we lack in rgard to inanimate bodies. There is a customary interpretation of this inner consciousness of our lived body: (1) it is identified with the sum or the product of the fusion of so-called *"organic sensations"* (e.g., sensations of muscles, of moving joints, of pain, of itching); and (2) these "sensations" are distinguished from those of our outer senses, such as the so-called sensations of colors and sounds, only with regard to *quality* and *location*. And this, in turn, leads to a terminology in the sciences—one most curious, indeed, to the unsophisticated —according to which a painful sensation in the forehead or an occurrence of "itching" is referred to as a psychic phenomenon and is thus included with woe and sadness, for instance, in a basic class of phenomena, namely, the so-called psychic phenomena. Of course, from this point of view there is no irreducible, unanalyzable sphere of consciousness which is lived-body consciousness; nor is there any corresponding phenomenon of "lived body." Rather, there is on the one hand only my own "body" [*Körper*], which I "think into" the sense-contents of optical, tactile, and other outer perceptions in the same manner in which I think other "bodies" into other sense-contents (e.g., the body of the inkwell standing in front of me into my own optical picture of it). There are on the other hand certain components of my psychic stream of consciousness which are coordinated with such sense-contents only through the outer observation of their appearance and disappearance that depends on changes in my body and changing states of certain organs (e.g., hands, legs, muscles, joints, etc.). According to this interpretation the co-ordination would, of course, result in a *justification* for calling the above sense-contents "sensations," e.g., "organic sensations," "muscular sensations," "articular sensations," etc., whereas according to their phenomenal facticity there would be nothing in them which could betray the existence of a muscle, a stomach, etc. In short, the "lived body" is reduced to the fact of an ani-mated body, and lived-body consciousness either to a mere co-ordination of psychic and corporal facticities or to a mere relation and order between them.

Who cannot at first glance see—insofar as he is still un-sophisticated and can see the visible—that this way of conjuring away the lived body is nothing but a totally empty and irrelevant construction alien to intuitive comprehension?

The first thing that remains wholly unintelligible here is the indubitable fact that there exists a strict and *immediate unity of identity* of the *inner consciousness* which everyone has "of" the existence and the "hereness" [*Befinden*] of the lived body—first of all, of one's own lived body—and the *outer perception* of one's lived body (as the body-thing [*Leibkörper*]), e.g., through the senses of sight and touch. It may be true that some *learning* and a gradual and progressive "development" are required in order to recognize my right hand, whose being, Gestalt, and finger move-ments I possess as elements of my inner lived-body conscious-ness, and which now, e.g., "aches," as the *same thing* which I now touch with my hand, and which corresponds to my own optical picture. Analogously, there is a thinglike identification of the place in which I feel hungry with what to the anatomist represents a stomach. But this process of learning refers to only two factors: (1) the coordination of the *corresponding parts* of the "sides" of this one "lived body" (seen from within and with-out), in which the *immediate identity* of the whole lived-body ob-ject, given from within and without, is already *pregiven;* and (2) not the relationship of immediately given appearances to the same objective thing as such, but only those appearances of *thinglike* significance or those which cofunction as symbols for *certain things*, e.g., this *thing* "hand," this *thing* "stomach," etc. That is, everything here is analogous to the fact that we must learn to relate the *differences* among depths in which simple things of sight are given—and, indeed, given in an original manner—to the objective proportions of distances of real bodies (including also the body "eye") as a kind of system of signs for such distances (Hering). By no means do we have to "learn" the seeing of depths themselves, nor does this seeing "originate" in so-called sensations which do not yet contain anything like depths and their differences. Hence we do not have to learn the identity of the same "*lived body*" given in inner and outer consciousness—given, we might say, in the former as a "*lived-body soul*," in the latter as a "*body-thing*." The lived body is given, rather, as a totally uniform, phenomenal fact and as a subject of "being-here" thus and otherwise. This fact is independent of and, in order of givenness, prior to any special so-called organic sensations and any special kinds of outer perception. It, or its immediate and total perception, *founds* the givenness of the lived-body soul, as well as that of the body-thing. It is precisely *this* basic founding phenomenon which is the "*lived body*" in the strictest sense of the term.

In contrast to this, the above-mentioned theory would prove that an identically meant lived body is only a fiction: that *in practice* there is only one class of purely psychic sensations (later termed organic sensations) and an increasingly more fixed coordination of them, their unities, and their changes to other classes of sensations, which have no relation to a body-thing other than what they have to inanimate physical bodies not belonging to it. The *difference* between the two groups of "sensations" lies only in a certain constancy in the first group and frequent appearances of "double sensations." (Such a double sensation occurs, for example, when I touch my body, but not when I see my body; [38] in hearing my voice, experiences in the larynx, mouth, etc., are connected with acoustical contents.) The theory also implies that an immediately given identity of the lived body, which alone makes such a constancy and coordination something meaningful, can be reduced to a mere constancy of a part of my experiences (something totally "incomprehensible") and a mere "coordination," which is supposed to be nothing more than a "fixed" association. Apart from the deficiencies in the bases of this theory, the criteria for separating sensations related to the "lived body" and to extrabodily objects are insufficient. To someone sentenced to life imprisonment, the walls of a prison are no less "constant" than, say, the image that

---

38. Insofar as one does not wish to regard as such the sensations of tension and position mediated by muscles of the eyes when the eyes are open and at rest.

he has of his hands. Yet, it is impossible for him to confuse them for an instant with his lived body. A so-called double sensation is not at all given in the phenomena on the occasion of touching; it is only by looking at a finger and by touching the palm of the hand with it that we are able to relate two functional processes of *sensing* to the *same* content. But in this the differences between a lived body (and its parts) and other bodies are already presupposed.

Let me summarize the various errors of these traditional theories. It is erroneous (1) to consider inner "lived-body consciousness" only a group of sensations; (2) to think that *lived-body sensations* are different only in degree from "organic sensations," and to hold that certain organic sensations as states of a lived body are different only in degree and content from "sensations" of sound, color, taste, and smell, rather than in the kind of givenness which belongs essentially to them; (3) to believe that the *lived-body-thing* is originally encountered in the same fashion as *other bodies;* [39] (4) to consider *lived-body sensations* "psychic phenomena"; (5) to consider inner *lived-body consciousness* something originally unarticulated which is articulated only according to the parts of the body to which it is secondarily related (the converse assertion would be equally wrong); (6) to hold that the contents of inner lived-body consciousness are more deceptive than those of outer consciousness (inner diagnostics); (7) to think that inner lived-body consciousness is originally non-extended and without any spatio-temporal order; (8) to think that there is no fundamental essential difference between volitional control over the lived body and over external objects; and (9) to hold that the unity of the lived body has only an associative character (this is erroneous because it is the lived body that first of all makes associative combinations possible).

Let us return for a moment to the first of these errors. [40]

39. Lipps's argument against an original depth-dimension of vision can be understood on the basis of the following presupposition: Every comprehension of distance presupposes that the two bodies at a distance from each other are perceived, but the eye itself is not perceived; hence . . . .

40. It is not my intention in this connection to clarify completely the difficult problem of the givenness of the lived body. But I intend to return to this in a later work dealing with a phenomenological examination of basic concepts of biology with which I dealt earlier. In the present context I am concerned only with the systematic determination of limits of the givenness of the lived body within the interconnection of the givenness of the body and the ego.

The *first* error of this theory consists in the assumption that it is possible simply to equate the inner consciousness of our lived body with the sum of sensations experienced as localized in specific organs. In fact, consciousness of our lived body is always given as a consciousness of a whole that is more or less vaguely articulated, and it is given independent of and *prior to* the givenness of any special complex of "organic sensations." But the relation between this consciousness of a lived body and organic sensations is not comparable to that between a whole and its parts, or to a relation between two "terms." It is a relation of *form* to its *content*. Just as all psychic experiences are experienced together only in an "ego" in which they are joined into a unity of a special kind, so all organic sensations are necessarily given "together" in a lived body. Just as the "ego" must accompany all our (psychic) experiences (as Kant observed), so must our lived body accompany all organic sensations. The lived body is therefore the underlying form through which all organic sensations are conjoined, and through which they are organic sensations of *this* lived body and not of any other. When special organic sensations are observed or otherwise more sharply set off, as in the case of painful sensations, the vague whole of the lived body is coexperienced as their "background"; but the lived body as a whole is cointended in any *organic sensation* as a special kind of sensation. From this it clearly follows that we do not have to "learn" by "experience"—in the sense of progressive induction—that we are *not angels*, that we possess a body. We only "learn" the orientation in the manifold of our given body, as well as the "sense and meaning" of the vicissitudes in this manifold for the states of limb-units, which are likewise given in inner fashion, of the lived body or the body organs. However, for any finite consciousness there is an essential interconnection between *"ego"* and *"lived body."* This interconnection is not an inductive-empirical or associative one. Otherwise correct observations of infants have often been falsely interpreted in this regard. An infant is certainly "amazed" when he sees his feet for the first time. He may kick his feet as if they were strange external bodies; and there may come a time when he must learn that the optical picture of the far corner of his bed does not have the same relation to his body as the picture of his feet. But the difference between the spheres "lived body" and "external world" is *presupposed* here as given. The child does not learn how to distinguish these spheres as such; he only "learns" that some *seen things* belong to this sphere, some to that one.

"Lived Body" and "Environment" Are Not Presupposed by the Distinction between "Psychic" and "Physical." Among modern scholars it was Avenarius and, quite independent of him, Ernst Mach ("coming from the idealistic camp," as he himself said) who most successfully elaborated a theory of knowledge in which it is maintained that a distinction between psychic and physical phenomena is possible only on the basis of a pregiven lived body and environment. Avenarius asserts that there is a plain *"coming upon"* [Vorfinden] (which neither presupposes nor contains either an "ego" or a distinction of act, object, and content), and that the content of this plain *"coming upon"* represents the datum of the "natural conception of the world." But this datum, he says, contains nothing more than a lived body and its environment, whose contents exhibit certain dependencies in their variations. Dependencies existing between the parts of the environment are said to represent the subject matter of the natural sciences—physics, chemistry, etc. Dependencies between the facts of the above order of dependencies and the parts and processes of the body are said to form the subject matter of biology. The subject matter of psychology is said to be the dependencies among the alterations of contents lying between environmental parts and the parts of the body, not the dependencies among the contents themselves. Avenarius further maintains that a false and "artificial" concept of the world results when the variational relationship between the content that one "comes upon" in the environment (e.g., this "tree") and a lived body (which is reduced to "system *C*," i.e., the brain with its spinal continuation) is made a special object, an object that is said to be "introjected" into the lived bodies of our "fellow men" so that in these lived bodies one imagines the "perception" or "representation" of the tree and in these new "psychic forms" or "contents of consciousness," etc., a special "subject," a "soul," etc. In this fashion, so runs the argument, there arises the "concept of the soul" and the concept of the "psychic," as well as the assumption of a special perceptual source of such fictitious objects, namely, the concept of an "inner perception." For other scholars this was the basis for the distinction between (psychic) acts and the (physical) objects corresponding to them, as well as for analogous distinctions.

These assertions (and, *mutatis mutandis*, Mach's also) do not require a serious refutation. They have been judged by their inevitable consequences: one is forced to reduce *all* feeling-states to organic sensations and their (sensible) character, and to reduce the experience of the ego, and even that of the person, to complexes and derivatives of such experiences; one is also forced to reduce all pictorial recollections to the reappearance of faint ("shadowlike") elements of the environment, and all "thinking" to mere economy, to the most parsimonious use of images and their contents. For a psychology dealing with at least some facts, such inadmissible consequences are not even debatable.

We are interested in these (now antiquated) theories only in regard to the *lived body*. Avenarius' premise is that the "lived bodies of our fellow men," their "environments," and their "statements" are all "come upon" in fully identical ways. From the outset, however, he fails to see that there is not the least clue in this primary material that we are supposed to "come upon" which would distinguish anything like *"lived body," "environment,"* or *"statement."* What is it that distinguishes the "lived body" from an "element of the environment," e.g., some inanimate object in the same sensible content? What is it that distinguishes a "statement" from any combination of sounds or noises? What makes it a "statement," or even only a "phenomenal expression"? That the "lived body" is not simply *one* thing-body among others; that it is given, rather, as a "center" of thing-bodies functioning as its "environment"; that "expressions," or even "statements," are not simple changes in thing-bodies determined by changing relationships to other thing-bodies, as is the case with the sound of a piece of steel hitting the ground, but that they always exist in terms of a twofold symbolic relation [41]—where could one find all of this in the *givenness* of such plain "coming upon"? The alternative is simple: either this plain and indifferent "coming upon" of Avenarius' is not plain at all but possesses *different modes* and *forms* for a lived body, an environment, and a statement (all of which can contain the *same* sensible material), in which case what one "comes upon" must have different (intuitive but non-sensible) structures corresponding to such forms; or the above *distinctions* cannot be accounted for at all. Avenarius makes the obvious mistake of identifying the *"lived body"* with the body-thing; and instead of recognizing an essential interconnection according to which the *same* lived body is capable of a totally different (inner) givenness (e.g., in hunger, lust, pain), he understands

41. With respect to both the expressed experience and the object meant in the expression. An object is always comeant in statements.

this latter on the basis of an "introjection" analogous to the introjection of the environmental "tree" "into" the lived body as the "perception" of the tree. Let us *suppose* that there is such an "introjection." If, on this premise, we assume that something "psychic" arises which has the fictitious structure of a thinglike "relation" in a "perception" or a "representation" belonging to an "ego," and if we further assume a special source of knowledge belonging to this "ego," namely, "inner perception," nothing like "being hungry" or "tickling" could ever be "introjected" in an analogous fashion. Where could we find the "environmental element" for this, or what would the introjected "character" be like? The occurrence of such an "introjection," which does not occur in inanimate objects, would presuppose a unity of a lived body that is essentially distinct from such environmental elements. (No animist would hold that a stone "perceives" an animal in the same way that an animal perceives a stone.) [42] We consider this "theory of introjection," insofar as it goes beyond the dismissal of the old, well-known "projection theories" of sensation, to have no basis whatsoever in fact. On one point, however, we agree with Avenarius, and not with his many critics: no matter how we arrive at the idea of the "ego," no matter how the "ego" of our fellow man is "given," the perception of a factual reality of the essence "lived-bodiliness" is *not* based on the assumption that there is an "ego" or psychic facts in what we come upon, and that this "ego" (our own or that of another) must be given to us before we can consider any appearances to be appearances of a "lived body." [43] Although every given lived body of a human being is given (to the human being himself) as "my" body or (to someone else) as "his" body, it is not this relation to the ego that makes this a "lived body," or that detaches the lived body as a unit from the manifold of other "given" contents. It is on the *basis* of the independence of the givenness of a lived body that its unity must be different in essence from that of inanimate things. [44] The facts apply analo-

---

42. Animism, as referred to by Avenarius, presupposes the formation of the idea "ego" or "soul" with regard to the inanimate world.

43. As, for instance, Lipps and Ettlinger hold.

44. The idea at the basis of Avenarius' critique of pure experience, that his system C, with all its excitations, aims at a maximum of "self-preservation" and therefore works according to the principle of the "smallest amount of force," *presupposes* "amechanical" factors. No matter how justified this may be in our view, it has no justification in his theory of knowledge, according to which the lived body is found like any other thing-body. If one were to make the quite impossible *attempt* to derive

gously to Ernst Mach's theory. According to Mach, *"elements of being"* are "sensations" if their givenness and their absence prove to be dependent on the being of an "organism." If, for instance, a sphere is "yellow," not because of sodium light, but because a person has taken santonin, the element of being "yellow" is psychic. But how does the mass of these elements *L,* representing a *lived body,* differ from other such elements *E,* representing an environment, so that the variations in *E* and their mutual "dependencies" can be differentiated from the variations in *L* and their respective mutual dependencies? What is the phenomenal difference between "sensations," which are elements of being *as* related to the lived body, and the elements *of which* the lived body is supposed to consist? There are no answers to these questions. Both Avenarius and Mach fail to see that there is an essence *"lived-bodiliness"* that is not inductively abstracted from factual lived bodies, an essence whose possible intuition in the presence of an empirical object (e.g., my lived body at this moment, that of someone else, etc.) presents the object to me as one that is different from inanimate objects and as an *essentially* different lived-body object. They both equate lived-bodiliness with the lived body (*in concreto*) and the latter with a mere body-thing, i.e. (in our terminology), the lived body as an object of outer perception alone. Avenarius maintains that there is no difference between "outer" and "inner" perception with regard to what we come upon; but his mistaken polemic against the concept of "inner perception" merely reveals that he reduces all perception to the concept of "outer perception." Avenarius tries to show that facts of inner perception consist of the same elements as the "simplest" complexities of outer perception, and, like Berkeley, he falls victim to an erroneous, one-sided artificiality. Berkeley attempted to show that Locke's "sensation" is merely a limiting case of "reflection"—as if colors and sounds (supposedly related to an ego and experienced only as ego-related) were given in the same fashion as pain or muscular tension, as if outer sense-perception were nothing but a strong representation. Avenarius also tries to do away with the perceptual *direction* of "inner perception" by assuming that

---

the logical principles from the principle of the economy of thought, which would mean, of course, to demonstrate their validity as "conditions of preservation of the lived body" (even of a "system C"), one would have to attribute to the lived body a *teleological* principle which is effective in it and which determines its *unity,* i.e., a tendency toward self-preservation with the fewest means. But then one cannot *also* be a mechanist in biology.

this expression refers to a perception of something psychic "in" an objective thing-body, and that there is no "blue in the head" or "pain in the (anatomic) arm" when one senses "blue" or "pain." These assumptions result in his theory (which later was widely accepted) that all specific lived-body phenomena, or phenomena experienced as belonging to the lived body, e.g., pain, tickling, tension, relaxing, and even all experienced active motor impulses, as opposed to so-called kinesthetic passive phenomena, are complexes of "sensations" which can also occur as "elements" of the content of outer perception. (Kinesthetic passive sensations are, in fact, only consequences of tactile sensations in sinews and joints and the phenomena of position and form built on the basis of these. They can be "interpreted" as "sensations of movements" only on the basis of previously experienced impulses of movements.) All of this also results in the opinion that there are no non-extensive psychic experiences at all—e.g., in spiritual feelings and especially the experience of the ego— which are unquestionably experiences of this particular kind. Indeed, Avenarius did not even see that the difference in direction between "inner" and "outer" perception is not at all relative to what is (in a spatial sense) "inner" and "outer" for a body-thing. But there is in fact a difference in *act-direction,* one that is essentially conjoined with a special form of the manifold of the given. This difference in direction and form remains as a residuum, even when the lived body is completely bracketed. Once this difference in direction and form is related to a uniformly "given" lived body—one that is given in principle *without* this directional differentiation of perceptual acts—it projects two entirely different "aspects" of the lived body; but it is nevertheless evident that it relates to the *"same"* facticity *"lived body."* [45]

45. The following is to be said against Avenarius' assertion that one implicitly thinks of a perception of the "interior" of something corporeal on the occasion of an "inner" perception. There is, strictly speaking, no "interior" or "exterior" to the spatiality of outer perception. There is *extensionality,* but no genuine "interwovenness" [*Ineinander*]. It is only on the basis of a lived-embodying [*Verleiblichung*] of even inanimate things, which is so typical of the natural standpoint, that we can say, for example, that a ball is "in" a box, or even that a box is "in" space. For both cases presuppose that we first *add* the spatial form of the ball to the box in intuition and then subtract the form (as belonging to the ball) from the "box." The evident a priori proposition of the impenetrability of a "body" makes every "in" merely "apparent." Hence things are just the *reverse* of what Avenarius believes. Any *interwovenness* is analogous

It is equally erroneous to assume, as both Avenarius and Mach do, that the difference between the "psychic" and the "physical" is a difference in the *"connection"* and "order" of the *"same"* contents and *elements*. In fact, they always consider physical elements the primary factors of givenness (as elements of *outer* perception which are not yet comprehended as thing-like or a fortiori as corporeal). Much as Mach, like Hume, endeavors to derive the thing-category from his "elements of being" as a relatively stable complex of them,[46] his "elements of being" are in fact true and genuine *physical things* (i.e., things of the senses of sight, touch, etc.), having all the phenomenological determinations of essence belonging to things (like Hume's "impressions"). As *"sensations,"* i.e., as "related to an organism," such "elements" are not pure "contents" of sensation, but are already things-of-sensation. It is precisely at this point that we encounter the formal "materialism" of this philosophy; and it is as much a qualitative materialism as any. Moreover, every other possible form of an *"order theory,"* which would have to avoid this mistake, would also fail.[47] An "element" of sorrow or woe can never occur "also" as an element of a physical appearance (even if this concept were expanded to include so-called organic sensations). Nor can it ever occur as a "character" of, say, a landscape. For what is qualitatively identical in the feeling-state of sorrow—when "I am sad"—and in the "character" of a "sorrowful landscape" represents no *real* element in either case. If the order theory were to hold only that the "psychic" and the "physical" are not *empirically definable* objective unities (i.e., definable *per genus proximum* and *differentia specifica*), then it would be completely correct. For these unities taken in that sense would not imply a difference in *essence*. The criterion of such essential differences is precisely this: in attempting to define them, we must presuppose them, and we therefore are necessarily trapped in a *circulus in definiendo*. The above assumption does not afford a reason to posit *two different modes* and directions of perception instead of one kind of perception plus two different empirical concepts of objects (as in "I perceive trees," "I perceive houses,"

---

to the way in which elements can be with one another in the manifold of inner perception. This "analogy" holds even when we say: My heart is "in" my lived-body-thing [*Leibkörper*].

46. E. Mach, *Die Analyse der Empfindungen* (Jena, 1903), Vol. I, sec. 7–8.

47. [See "Über Selbsttäuschungen" ("Idole"), secs. 2, 4.—*Ed.*]

etc.).[48] However, it does not follow from such a negatively correct assertion of the "order theory" that there are no non-formal differences at all in the phenomena of the psychic, the physical, and the lived body, or that we are concerned only with *differences in order* from a logicoformal point of view. For it merely follows that different non-formal contents already residing in the essence of psychic and physical objects are essentially connected with both perceptual directions.[49]

It is therefore out of the question to think that *"egoness" itself* and *"individual ego-being"* are somehow based on genetically and historically explicable processes like that of *"introjection,"* instead of considering them data of immediate intuition (corresponding to the "materiality" of objects of outer perception, which does not presuppose any hypothetical positing of a specific thinglike "matter"). The thousands of beliefs and superstitions concerning a substantial soul can be reduced to analogous processes—but only on the *assumption* of intuitive facts. The essence "egoness," however, is *constitutive* of the essence "psychic" and is *essentially connected* with the direction of inner perception; this interconnection is given in both factors in formless, *pure* intuition itself. The "projective theory of sensations," which Avenarius rightly refutes, and the quite similar "empathic theory" of "values," "characters," forces, and phenomena of life are invalid and cannot establish a basis for the phenomenon of an "external world" (with or without the unconscious causal inferences subscribed to by Schopenhauer and Helmholtz), just as "introjection" cannot make the assumption of a psychic sphere, an ego, etc., comprehensible. Whenever such processes in fact occur, they presuppose both spheres and regions of being, as well as their essential contents, which are projected, empathized, and introjected into.[50]

Although we emphasized that *"lived-bodiliness"* "can be given" without regard to a psychic ego belonging to it (we are

48. If there were a property X that physical objects could have, but psychic objects could not, one could maintain only that there is one and the same perception of physical objects on the one hand and psychic objects on the other, like a perception of tables and chairs; one could not maintain that there are two different perceptual directions, like inner and outer perception.

49. Just as Husserl's "noema" and "noesis" are mutually interdependent in their qualitative nature.

50. The old theory of projection and its opposite, the theory of introjection, make the same basic mistake of not distinguishing between psychic, physical, and lived-body phenomena and the types of perception which belong to them.

in agreement with Avenarius on this point), we must point out on the other hand that we do not in principle have to *pass through* any givenness of the *lived body* in order to comprehend an *egoness* in each psychic experience, and that a fortiori we do not have to pass through the perception of another, alien lived body or that of a fellow man. Nor is there any need to pass through the perception of one's own ego and lived body in order to comprehend another's ego and lived body as such.[51] Even if in imagination we reduce organic sensations of our lived body to a zero point, the ego and, for example, its spiritual feelings remain "given" (for there are in fact moments in our lives when only the schema of our lived body immediately exists for us— almost without positive contents—moments in which we seem to be lifted "from all earthly heaviness" [*Erdenschwere*], and there are also cases of deeply pathological anesthesia of bodily sensations and feelings). There is an essential difference between the manner in which I "am sad," i.e., the way in which sadness is related to the ego and "fills" it, and the manner in which I "feel *myself*" weak or strong, hungry or appeased, ill or healthy, or even the way in which I "feel my leg hurt" or "feel my skin itch." The modal diversity of the givenness in the phenomenal essence is not affected in the least by the fact that it is often difficult, sometimes even impossible, to distinguish *in concreto* the modes of the vital feeling-states belonging to a concrete global state and to lived-body sensations from a fact that is experienced as an ego-determination or one that is immediately related to the ego. Although self-deceptions are obviously possible here (especially regarding affections, which are always admixtures of the psychic, the body, and outer sensations), again, the modal diversity of the givenness in the phenomenal essence is by no means affected by this. One could come to believe that he finds a "bridge," e.g., from colors and sounds to feelings of hunger, or that he understands facts like "to be hungry" in exactly the same terms as sensations of the inner body, since sensations of colors are supposedly "sensations" of extrabodily objects. But one could do this only by making an insufficient distinction between inner bodily sensations of touch (possessing the quality of contents of touch), e.g., sensations of joints or sinews, which belong to the exterior sphere of the senses, and genuine bodily sensations

---

51. See *Zur Phänomenologie und Theorie der Sympathiegefühle* (Bibliog. no. 6), app. [See *Wesen und Formen der Sympathie* (Bibliog. no. 18), pt. C, chap. 3.—*Ed.*]

and feeling-states, as well as drive-impulses, e.g., pain, tickling, and the feeling and impulses of hunger. However, the experienced *states* of the lived body are absolutely distinct from the contents and qualities of functions of the outer senses, and these (e.g., colors and sounds), in turn, from their "sensing" and its main types (e.g., seeing and hearing). Although the same contents of touching, for example, can serve as the basis for phenomenal body-determinations, such as smoothness, softness, and hardness, which are the phenomena to which we refer when we say that something feels "soft," "hard," "rough," or "smooth," as well as the basis for experiences that are more than sensuous states, this is *totally impossible* with respect to pain, tickling, and being hungry. These can never be "given" as determinations of inanimate bodies, but, at best, as experienced effects on a lived body. There are also no "elements" in them which can be given as such determinations.

Of course, what is always and by evident necessity given in an act of the essence of *inner perception* is only the essence and individuality of the ego and "any" of its *experiences* and *determinations*. For every factual comprehension of these and their special contents, the following proposition holds: All contents in the sphere of inner intuition also become, *in all degrees of clarity and distinctness,* contents of real perception only insofar as their being or non-being and their being-so or being-other-than-so posit some *variation* of the *lived body*. This fact is described in the following manner: All *inner perception is executed through an "inner sense,"* according to which all contents of possible inner perception that do *not* posit a variation of the lived body remain in the sphere of the "subconscious," [52] and according to which it is not the inwardly perceived itself but the form of givenness of "appearances" presented in factual perceiving that acquires the forms of the manifold that are essential for facts of a phenomenal "*lived body*." Hence the factual perception of the ego and of the sphere of "pure" psychic facts is *not* an immediate perception that gives such facts themselves; it is, rather, a perception that is *mediated* through a *sensible lived body*. Factual perception of the ego and of psychic facts is, for this reason, as subject to deception as factual outer perception through outer "sensibility" is.[53] In both cases "sen-

---

52. We have discussed this concept above, on p. 392.
53. The failure to see that factual psychic self-perception is mediated by the lived body and sensibility leads to difficulties in understanding the

sibility" neither "creates" nor "produces" anything at all. It only suppresses or selects in accordance with the significance of psychic experiences (or possible contents of outer perception) for a lived body and the immanent goal-direction of its activity.

From this it becomes clear why the pure *"interwovenness"* [Ineinander] of experiences in the ego acquires, for factual perception, a *sequential* and *extensional* character [Nacheinandersein und Aussereinander*sein*], which already belongs to the manifoldness of the phenomenal lived body (but without any trace of temporality or spatiality); and it also becomes clear how psychic experiences divide into "present," "past," and "future" ones.

No characteristic distinguishes all essentially *lived-body* phenomena from purely psychic phenomena more sharply than their being *extensive* and *non-extensive*. Moreover, both types of phenomena have a "position" that is "different in kind" in relation to the ego; this also holds for their subdivisions. For instance, pain is clearly extended: it "spreads" "across the back" or changes its place. "Hunger" is something that occurs in the area of the stomach and the chest. Even "fatigue," though it has no specific area of localization, as does tickling or, for example, "tiredness in the legs," is "spread" over and in the extended whole of a lived body. Such characteristics are completely nonsensical with regard to "sorrow," "woe," "serenity," etc. Nevertheless, such lived-body phenomena are by no means "in" space, neither in an objective space (e.g., in an arm as an anatomic, objective form-unity) nor even in a phenomenal space. On the contrary, they share "non-spatiality" with everything belonging to the purely psychic.

However, not only are lived-body phenomena of an extended nature. They also reveal *"extensionality"* [Aussereinandersein] and, within this form of manifoldness, in turn, a *side-by-side* as well as a *sequential* character [Nebeneinander- *und* Nacheinander*sein*]. There is also an appearance of *"oscillation"* within this form of manifoldness. Neither the side-by-side nor the sequential character is a relation in space and time, i.e., in *one* space and *one* time; and a fortiori they are not measurable relations. There is here, however, something like a "more" or "less" of this extensionality in terms of the side-by-side and

---

cognition of the alter psychic. I have shown this in *Zur Phänomenologie und Theorie der Sympathiegefühle*, p. 133 (app.). [See *Wesen und Formen der Sympathie*, pt. C, chap. 3.—*Ed.*]

sequential characters of, e.g., the tickle coming from a pain. But there are no spatial or temporal lines that would serve to connect these phenomena. Nor is there any fixed order in space or time. Pain may "alternate" with tickling in the same area. But in such a case it is senseless to say that a specific area of the body "changed" from a painful one into a ticklish one. Pain spreads "out" or afflicts first this and then that limb (e.g., in a case of gout), but there is no trace of "pain moving from one area to another." This particular manifold is therefore totally different from that of *extra*-lived-body phenomena.

This manifold is no less different from the above "*inter-wovenness in the ego*," which (purely) *psychic* facts possess. It would be senseless to assert that a thought, a spiritual feeling, or an expectation is "extensional" or "sequential," or that thoughts, etc., stand "side by side." The fact that one attributes a "sequential" character to them more often than a "side-by-side" character is only a consequence of identifying the type of *given-ness* through which they come before the inner sense with an *element* of their content. It is not the "purely" psychic phenomena, from which every state of a lived body that is the condition of their factual perception is taken, but their *appearing in this and that content* of a plurality of acts of the type and form of "inner intuition," that brings about the "sequential character." Doubtless an act A of inner perception can possess more fullness in its content than another act B. But this difference in *fullness* is not the manifold of the "sequential." True, a third act C of inner intuition may even *encompass* the fullness of A and B in its content. In this case the fullness of A and B (F and F_1) may appear "sequentially" within the fullness of act C (F_2), but this is because F and F_1 were coordinated to *factually sequential* states of the lived body. This sequence of F and F_1 within the act C is only a part of the *content* of this act's fullness, whereas F and F_1 possess no existence as separate units of fullness. Thus the inner field of view overlooking one's own (or another's) ego may wax and wane, but without any manifestation of sequence in the contents of this field. It is therefore not what appears there but *how* it appears that reveals a "sequence." If a light is moved along a dark wall (the source of light being unknown), various areas of the wall are successively illuminated; however, there is no sequence of parts of the wall, but only the sequence of their illumination. One who is ignorant of the mechanism involved is led to believe that there is a sequence of parts. In this manner the factually sequential lived-body states illuminate interwoven determinations of the ego for inner perception according to specific laws of direction. It may seem that these determinations are *in themselves* sequential, but they are only coordinated to different, successively appearing lived-body states and are at the same time conditioned by them.

In this sense all that we experience (and also all that appears from the point of view of a given lived body as past) is experienced as *"together and interwoven"* in the ego. We cannot say that what appears as "past" lasts in objective time and is simply not perceived now (or that a "disposition," a psychic disposition, of it lasts). Nor can we say that it does *not* last but is annihilated, or that what lasts is only a physiological disposition to bring it back to life (epiphenomenalism of the psychic). Although these theories are strongly opposed to each other, they suffer from the *same* πρῶτον ψεῦδος: they construe the ego and its determinations and manifoldness as originally *sequential,* whereas in reality we are concerned with a totally different, positive manifoldness, namely, that of an *interwovenness* whose elements, as the elements which appear in inner perception to an embodied being, are coordinated by this being to the sequence of its lived-body states and are in their appearance conditioned by these states. These theories are bootless precisely because each psychic experience determines the *totality* of the "ego" in a *different* manner. The ego itself, however, which is neither sequential nor extensional, neither endures nor ceases to be (i.e., it cannot be or cease to be in a second point of time— *if* it existed in a preceding point of time).

f. Ego and Lived Body (Association or Dissociation)

It is only on the basis of an essential connection with the being of a lived body that (inner and outer) intuition, which is itself unitary, separates into differences of act-qualities (sense-*perception, remembering, expecting*), which are, however, encompassed by intuition as such. The spheres [*Sachsphären*] of being-*present* (*hic et nunc* sphere), being-*past*, and being-*future,* which are not found in objective time, correspond to these act-qualities. The proposition stating that "perception" as an act-quality in which something is given, but in terms of a *lived body,* simultaneously *is bodily-sensible* and *can give only what is "present"*—hence, only content of (inner and outer) *sense*-perception—is not analytic but synthetic. Only someone who wishes to define perception in terms of the concepts of sense and sensation, and who thus ignores the special quality implicit in the act, could deny this.[54]

If we were to consider inner and outer intuition (whose differences in direction and form-differences are absolute and not relative to a lived body) to be performed independent of any simultaneous givenness of a lived body or any dependence on it, they would yield the inner and outer worlds of the person to the extent that such worlds exist independent of these extensions. It is only the (essentially necessary) interposition of a *lived body*, its "sensibility" (which varies among different living organizations), and its "movement" (which is "free" with regard to the laws and the causality of inanimate nature) that determine the *dissociation* and *selection* of the unities of intuition which are possible as such according to specific laws. All investigations of individual dependencies must therefore be guided by the proposition that inner intuition, like outer intuition, is connected to "sensibility" and to the structure of the movements and drives of the lived body in its factual execution. There is in inner perception no less mediation by sensibility and stimuli than there is in outer intuition.[55] It is executed through an "inner sense."

The functional specialization of the sensibility of the lived body (i.e., the functions of seeing, hearing, etc., which possess their *own proper* lawfulness independent of peripheral and central organs) is in principle *identical* for both inner and outer intuition, no matter how rigorously one must differentiate the concepts of psychic "function" and physiological "function." Functional laws of senses are independent of the structure, order, stimulability, etc., of sense *organs* and their corresponding "sensations." They are also antecedent to their lawfulness. The inner world, too, gets the structure of the animation of its givenness from the twofold selection of factual psychic being and life. This selection takes place in sensible functions and on the basis of the meaning of psychic being as a stimulus-value for the lived body and its organic sensations. In a precisely analogous manner the same uniform and *identical structure* of tendencies of the lived body serves as the foundation of functional structures

---

54. For further remarks on this point, see "Über Selbsttäuschungen" and *Zur Phänomenologie und Theorie der Sympathiegefühle.*

55. A detailed proof of these points will be given in a future study. I make mention of this in this context only to complete the picture of the matter in question.

of movement of the body-thing and of the drive-structure of the body-psyche.[56] But the lawfulness inherent in this structure is as independent of organs of movement and their corresponding systems of motor impulses as the lawfulness of functional sensibility is independent of the sense organs and their corresponding sensations. Finally, within the entire sphere of the lived body and of life there exists a lawful relation between the structure of tendencies of movement and the functional structure of sensibility; namely, the latter remains *dependent* upon the former. This is because only such sensible functions (and a fortiori their corresponding sense organs and sensory capacities) come to develop which, in terms of objects situated within the goal-direction of kinetic body-tendencies, can serve as a fitting means of conveyance for possible intuition as such.

Among the many detailed answers to the question concerning the fundamental determination of the relationship between the manifoldness of the ego and the lived body, there are—if we set aside the metaphysical theory of two substances—only two that differ in principle. According to the first, the uniform inner interwovenness of the ego is *dissociated* by the lived body in terms of what is found as a given individual experience of inner perception. According to the second, basic psychic facts, originally differentiated, are *associated* by the lived body into one unitary form and, finally, into the complex associative combination of an "ego."

According to the second view, the ego represents a conglomeration of objects [*Sachen*] and processes which are univocally connected to some special excitations of the lived body. All forms of psychic unity are said to depend on the connections and types of connections of these excitations in the unity of the lived body (theory of association).

According to the first opinion, the *ego* is the *unity* of a manifoldness of *pure interwovenness*. It represents something whose *fullness alone* can wax or wane, insofar as it is conceived purely through a reduction of the lived body. The units of the observable *"experiences,"* however, are said to be *consequences of the dissociation* of the unity of the ego that occurs for and through a lived body only by expression in the body and by the utilization of purely psychic contents enclosed in the ego-manifold. The lived body, then, does not "assemble" but splits up and

56. "Tendency" is a qualitatively identical element of drives and lived movements.

divides this manifold into different parts, namely, *empirical experiences.*

The understanding of this view is, above all, dependent on our learning to see that pure *psychic facts* possess a special form of manifoldness, namely, that of *interwovenness in the ego.* This unity escapes intuition if one thinks of the "ego" as somehow "opposed" to psychic experiences, "opposed" in the sense of an unchangeable object lasting through time, and as an object by which such experiences pass—just as this unity escapes intuition if one considers it this stream *itself* (a "stream of events"). In the first case the ego becomes something totally empty and "simple," *without* a manifold. It becomes petrified as a substantial X to which one can attribute equally unknown "psychic dispositions." In this case one says that "past" experiences have no being, although they have had effects on the "ego" (= soul) and have left "psychic dispositions." These dispositions can be excited in the soul by certain stimuli of the body. However, in contrast to this, "past" experiences do not have to cease to exist or cease to have effects. They *exist* in the ego and *"in"* the ego. Any removal of experiences would, in principle, *vary* a present, total experience to a certain degree. Past experiences are not just inwardly perceived, since a bodily excitation is necessary for this *perception,* just as a bodily excitation was necessary when they were experienced in the past. These past experiences are, however, encompassed by a pure inner intuition and are effective in their totality within pure psychic effectiveness. And they "would be" given as "present" experiences of the ego *if* it were not for the inner meaning, essentially connected with a lived body, which separates them with regard to the perception of their being and effectiveness by specific laws. If one recognizes the basic errors in the theory of a substantial soul but cannot at the same time see this interwovenness of a genuine manifold *in* the ego, he posits the interwovenness as something initially *asunder.* This "in the ego" passes out of sight, and he is led to identify the *present* momentary content of inner perception with the psychic in general. "Past experiences" will not exist, nor will their "psychic dispositions"; thus, according to its *nature* the psychic appears merely as a *present* appearance, which disconnected (psychically) from an antecedent present experience, and which forms an interconnective whole through the continuous existence of the body-*thing* in objective time and through its inherent physiological causality (epiphenomenalism). According to this view there are only "physiological dispositions." Without a doubt, the very assumption of something psychic extending beyond a present and concrete moment becomes here philosophically absurd, and the fact of remembering becomes incomprehensible.[57]

Such conclusions result from the refusal to see that there is a psychic manifold, as well as types of combinations, which represents a genuine *"interwovenness in the ego"*—a genuine being of experiences "in" the ego and not outside it. If one were to ask how past experiences "are," I would answer that they "are" in my ego, which *"becomes"* different in all experiences, though without "changing" as a thing would change. Therefore they are not in a mystic area of the past, like bloodless shadows that sometimes knock at the door of my present to taste the blood of my life. Nevertheless, it would be equally wrong to assert that they do *not* exist as experiences, that they exist only as "dispositions" of the soul or the body. Something psychically unexperienced (even subconsciously unexperienced) would be a purely transcendent assumption, a purely removable symbol for which there could be no fulfillment in intuition. Past experience is present "in" the ego, and it is also given as "effective" in inner intuition insofar as each variation of one of these experiences varies the present *total content* of this intuition in a certain direction. Past experiences "speak to me" from all points of my life; they "motivate" all my oncoming experiences in one uniformly experienced efficacy. Yet their special, articulated, positive content is not present in inner, sensibly conditioned perception, which is, like all sense-perception, restricted to a lived body and to something "present." This is entirely similar to the case of outer perception inasmuch as we do not find in articulated fashion everything that codetermines, as a part of the "unity of the situation" in the "environment" of a lived body, each experienced content.[58] Hence epiphenomenalism mistakes the "physiology of the inner sense" for psychology itself. For the assertion that my past ego-experiences *are* not, that they do not exist, is as nonsensical as the assertion that the sun of my milieu does not exist because I do not see it at the moment.

The main point, then, is to bring to one's intuition the purely

---

57. The very assumption of a past psychic life is rendered totally groundless by this premise. For it is clear that I can set aside all past psychic life, if only physiological dispositions of former effects of excitation remain, without the slightest change in the content of my present experience.

58. Concerning the concept of "environment," see above, pp. 138 ff.

psychic manifold, the interwovenness of the ego, in its peculiar character, namely, this interwoven, non-extended structure that can both wax and wane in its fullness in such a manner that the phenomenon of "waxing" is a non-temporal becoming. The first task before us is to elaborate a phenomenology of "having oneself" in order to see this phenomenon.

There are states in our existence that one calls *"ingathered-ness"* [Sammlung]. This term refers to a concentrated being-in-oneself, or "living deeply in oneself." In such a state our total psychic life, including our past, is grasped as *one* and is effective as *one*. These states occur very rarely in our lives; e.g., one may occur before we make a grave decision or when we are compelled to take a crucial step. Everything is somehow "present" and "effective" at such a moment, and no "isolated particulars" of our past are remembered. We are not empty but entirely "full" and truly "with ourselves," "in ourselves." Effective experiences speak to us from all points of our lives, and at the same time a thousand "calls" reach us from both the past and the future. We "look over" our *entire* ego in its total manifold, experiencing it as a whole entering into *one* act, one deed, one action, one work. Yet we do not come "upon" any singular past experience here, nor do we direct our attention to any such thing, not even "to our ego." But we "experience" the ego-totality in a peculiarly concentrated manner. One who knows this phenomenon also knows the unmistakable character of the *given-ness of lived body* connected with the phenomenon at this moment. One's own lived-bodiliness is given here as something "belonging" to this concentrated totality, something that can exercise *"power"* over it and something that can sway it. Our lived-bodiliness is given here as "only present," as a moment that is enclosed as a part in our given "enduring" existence. The contents of this bodiliness appear to "float by" this enduring existence. There are also states of an opposite nature, a totally *reversed* phenomenal relationship between the ego and lived-body givenness. These states occur when we "live in our body," as it were (e.g., with increasing fatigue and tiredness, with high indolence, by losing ourselves in empty pleasures, "diversions," etc.). The level of our experienced existence peculiarly *oscillates* between the ego-totality, with the interwovenness of its contents, and the body-ego, with its character of extensionality. Here we live near the *body*-periphery of our being, with the extensionality and the sequential character of its states. It is precisely here that everything which before was "full" now becomes *"empty."* And this "emptiness" remains given to us. Here we are also living *"in the moment"* to the extent that we are living in the lived body, to the extent that it is *this* lived body that occupies the "place of the ego." "To live in a lived body" does not mean to possess it objectively. This is completely out of the question. It means "to be in it" through one's inner experience, or to "imagine" oneself [*sich wähnen*] in it. In the latter case it becomes exceptionally clear that the purely psychic begins to acquire the appearance of "floating away," although it remains given and present. Thinking and feeling, etc., appear only as a "small movement" that "passes through" one's head and body. Although the lived body in the case concerned is present and is given as present (with its states), it is not "our own" and "subject to our sway"; neither is it given "only momentarily." Rather, the lived body is, or appears to be, the ego itself, and at the same time a *solid, enduring,* and *continuous* Something that fills out objective time. The psychic floats by it like something "transient."

It is not primarily facts of observation and their theoretical elaboration, nor is it arbitrary assumptions of "methodological goals," that provide the intuitive grounds for more materialistic (and epiphenomenalistic) *theories* or more spiritualistic *theories* (which affirm a causality unique to the psychic). It is, rather, the phenomenal kinds and modes of the *immediate givenness to oneself* that oscillate between these *poles*. These particular *kinds of experiences precede* all observation and theory. Depending on the kinds of experiences in question, very different classes of facts may result for *possible* observations.

There is a *plurality of such levels* or of such *differences of levels* throughout the depth-ranges of our ego-experiences, and these levels are subject to a precise determination.[59] Each possesses its special basic type of *connection* with the manifold or with things and events appearing in it, a connection symbolically located at the basis of such levels by explanatory psychology. At the most peripheral level there is the connection through "association by contiguity"; at a deeper level is the connection of "similarity"; at a still deeper level is the connection of genuine "assimilation." This is followed by ample levels of different forms of attention (instinctive and volitional, passive and active, sensible and spiritual). These are followed by directions of attitudes, which are the foundation of directions of inter-

---

59. I am reserving a more exact determination of these for future studies that I have planned.

ests.[60] The most central level is the uniformly waxing and waning efficacy of the purely psychic ego *itself* in its manifold.

These levels and their changes represent at the same time the levels of the *relativity of existence* [Daseinsrelativität] of objects of inner intuition or inwardly experienced efficacy, i.e., levels of the relativity of existence of the ego-totality. But the *vacillations* [Wechsel] of these levels are not subject to any form of psychic causality: *these changes follow the acts of the person,* which are *"free" from all psychic causality,* and so they follow only the nature of a person's "self-positioning" [*Selbststellung*].

In the final analysis, therefore, psychic causality is always ego-causality, i.e., the experienced efficacy of a uniform ego. As such it is by essence *individual* causality, i.e., one in which the "same causes and effects" never recur. Hence, every change in the ego is dependent upon all experiences of the ego up to this change. We can call this *purely psychic causality* the *causality of motivation.* It forms the foundation of the humanities. *Objective psychology* [verstehende Psychologie] must investigate this area from all angles. This psychology does not "explain" but seeks to "understand" all singular processes of individual and typical psychic units in terms of their individual or typical contents. It does *not* set aside the "individuality" or the "types" of ego-totalities; rather, it *sticks to them,* making them special objects from which it derives an "understanding."

Although this psychic causality determines all *pure* psychic being and events, no single *concrete* psychic event, as it is given in inner observation, is straightforwardly determined by this causality. For this requires, in addition, knowledge of the psychophysiological mechanism of the *"inner sense,"* i.e., the laws of division and resolution according to which ego-totalities, which develop purely by themselves in a comprehensible fashion, become divided and *dissociated* in their relationship to a bodily organization. It is only by our explicitly *setting aside* the being and efficacy of the always individual ego-totalities that we can investigate these laws according to principles of reproduction, assimilation, association, determination, etc. This problematic *alone* is the object of psychology as a "science," i.e., the "physiology of the inner sense." For every "level," however, there are non-inductive principles of explanation. Psychology in the latter sense does not bring anything to "understanding"; it only *"explains."* It establishes psychophysiological causal laws of ob-

60. The concepts "interest" and "attitude" were delineated in chap. 3.

jectively factual elementary processes that are as "non-understandable" as the facts of free-falling bodies.

A clear determination of *concrete* psychic happenings results, then, only from the *superposition* of the concrete causality of motivation and understandability on these psychophysiological laws—with the "free" acts of the person still bracketed. This is analogous to the case of outer perception, for its concrete object with its properties requires both physical and physiological explanations.[61]

The failure to recognize this complex state of affairs and the belief that there is only a physiology of the inner sense, which has its a priori non-formal presuppositions in the principles of association, result from the same illusion that led to the adoption of the world view of classical mechanics, which supposedly presented a picture of absolutely real nature. There are two factors involved in this: first, the failure to see that the objects of *both* associative psychology *and* classical mechanics are *relative* to an *embodied being* with its tendencies to utilize its psychic experiences (i.e., the contents of its outer intuition) in terms of body-tendencies; second, the failure to recognize the principles of the technical positing of purposes (for psychology, educational purposes, political purposes, medical purposes, etc.), through which only *those* elements are selected from the givens of inner (and outer) intuition which are directly dependent on possible stimuli of the body and which are therefore also determinable by way of possible outside effects on the lived body (or technically controllable by body movements in an outward direction). But within *"pure"* psychic causality neither "prediction" nor calculation is possible. Here, a cause has an effect only *once*. Although the formal a priori proposition—same causes, same effects—is true, it does not "obtain" in this context. There simply are no "same causes"! The absence of these makes all "control" impossible. "Modern" man, eager to "control," wanted, first in the case of outer reality, to recognize as real in the psychic life only what could be controlled. He was inclined to recognize only the associative-mechanical side of the soul as the true soul, and hence his eyes became blind to its non-mechanical side. He came to think of the soul as a "bundle of associations" among derivatives of sensations because, owing to his technological attitude, he was interested only in what is

61. See above, pp. 143 f. The term *physical* is used here not only for physics but for all of the sciences of inanimate nature. *Physiological* is used for all of the sciences of life in general.

dependent on the body and what is both calculable and change-able by means of outer effects. But, in fact, there is no physical mechanism capable of absolutely determining a concrete natural event, for there is a multitude of other conceivable mechanisms that explain such natural events equally well. Nor is there any concrete psychic event that is absolutely determinable by the associative mechanism, which functions only in its appearance before the inner sense.

g. Non-Formal A Priori Principles of Explanatory Psychology

A purely psychic experience is therefore primarily deter-mined only by the fact that it is the *experience* of this or that *individual ego*—independent of all possible questions concern-ing the time of its occurrence or which lived body is the specific correlate for its perception. Through its belonging to a specific individual ego, it finds its *place of being* in the totality of all possible "inner worlds" and the entirety of what is accessible to inner perception.

Hence the two "images" that are used most often to represent the ego, namely, an enduring point set over a flowing movement, a point which perceives this movement as a man in a tower views a stream flowing by below, and something identified with the "interconnective whole" of this stream, are equally erroneous analogies in view of the factual state of affairs. The error of the second image is only a reaction to that of the first.[62] The in-dividual ego does not "endure"; it is, rather, *"modified"* [ändert sich], without damage to its egoness, *in* every one of its ex-periences.[63] And it is modified only *"in"* its experiences. This is not to imply that experiences "cause" such modifications in the ego, as if the ego and its experiences were at first separate ele-ments. Indeed, this *"becoming different" in* its experiences, as well as this becoming different in an individual manner, is the total *content* of the ego's "existence." During the continuations of the ego's becoming different, experiences do not remain "somewhere" in a mysterious area of the ego's "past" so that, say, things can be retrieved from it. Likewise, the ego's "future" experiences do not come to it from an area or sphere of the

---

62. [See above, p. 418.—*Ed.*]
63. It would be too much to say that the ego has changed. Change presupposes both succession and duration. Modification implies only a becoming different or a being-different in becoming. "Becoming," how-ever, does not imply time, but only the continuity in the transition from being-so to being-other-than-so.

"future" as if they were already there. It is in this being-different that the entire experiencedness of experiences *consists*. One cannot say that a past experience belongs to *being*, but only that it belongs to past being; one cannot say that a past experience leaves behind a disposition (a psychic disposition) in this enduring ego, leaves it hovering above this stream, so that this experience represents a "causal factor" for the "present ego"—for example, for its future possible experiencings, including recollections *of* this "past experience." This *image* is wrong. First of all, an "experience that cannot be experienced," i.e., an experience that is essentially only a "disposition," does not exist. One must be clear on this point above all. How in all the world could even the existence of such a "past experience" (and its existence is the *presupposition* for positing a "disposition") be *possible* if remembering a past experience (or "reliving" it) consists only in the actualization of that "disposition"? A past experience is, in this case, only a pure "thing in itself" that one can arbitrarily obliterate or posit without changing the total experience of an individual in the least. Moreover, the experiences of the ego that we call "past" ones would leave the ego entirely unaltered insofar as it does not remember them, an assumption that flies in the face of all experience. No wonder that a second image of the ego has been set up against the former one. This image connects the psychic generally and essentially to the *present*, and not, as we do, to an actual [*aktuelles*] individual ego. Indeed, this image connects the ego to the present and implies that there is originally nothing but what I am conscious of at present and what I am conscious of as present, e.g., what I now sense, think, etc. Everything else is supposedly a modification of the lived body, or even of the body-thing, or a "physiological disposition" for some new content to enter into an interconnection of the psychic present. In this case the ego is entirely canceled *out*, and in its place we find the *lived body* as the only factor of continuous endurance, its changing modifications possess experiences as epiphenomena which *among themselves* lack any interconnection and any autonomous form of unity. Who cannot see the basic phenomenological error here? It obviously consists in making "what I am conscious of at present" into "what I am conscious of as present" without further ado—as if it were not true that *every* moment of consciousness (in the sense of "what I am conscious of at present") is, according to essential laws, *constituted* of what I am conscious of *as* present, what I am conscious of *as* past (in the act of remembering or reliving), and what I am conscious of *as* future (in the act of expecting or anticipating experiencing). One speaks here as if the acts of remembering and expecting, plus their "contents," are "first" taken only as parts of a "content" of which I am conscious "as present," or as if, in remembering, one "comes upon" a present "picture of remembrance," or, in expecting, a "picture of expectation," which subsequently enters into a sphere of the past or the future through various manipulations (such as projections, rejections, simple judgments about the "symbolic functions" of these "pictures"). But this is nothing but an empty construction of a naturalistic conception of the soul, a construction that turns facts upside down. Neither acts of remembering or expecting *nor* their positive contents are given "as present"— the acts, because they are not at all experienced as filling time; the contents, because they are from the very beginning immediately given as past or future. Apart from this, to designate the acts as "now executed" (in a non-phenomenological sense) makes sense only because in this case we are concerned with acts of the ego, and because to every ego there belongs a lived body that is and can be given only as present.[64] Furthermore, it becomes an *a priori* proposition of explanatory psychology that there must also be *processes of correlates of the lived body* for the real execution of acts of this special type, as well as for the selection of precisely *these* and not the *other* contents out of all possible contents that in general encompass an ego-individual's remembering and expecting (for remembering, a cause "reproducing" the *special* content of remembering; for expecting, a tendency "determining" the *special* content of expecting). And precisely the same holds for the act of (inner) perception and its purely psychic content given "as present." This act is not experienced "as present," but it is a "present act" for the same reason that the acts of remembering and expecting are. But the "as present" of its given content is in essence only a *partial content* of the full and concrete *total* content of a moment of consciousness and is therefore always surrounded by a *being-past*

---

64. Suppose I remember something that was present to me some time ago, say, when, as a child, I was standing before a lake. The "being-present" of this content belongs to the encompassing content of remembering, which itself is given "as past." Hence we must distinguish two quite different things: remembering the (then) present of an experience and remembering the experience. In the first case there is always the phenomenon of the lived body as a part *in* the content of remembrance (in remembering, I see "myself" in front of the lake), whereas in the second case "I remember when I was standing before the lake."

and a *being-future*. And no matter *which moment of conscious-ness* of my whole life it is that inner intuition meets, *every* moment contains again this threefold division of being-present, being-past, and being-future. It is therefore *not a supposed multiplicity of moments of consciousness following one another like a stream* that yields these elongations with their spheres. Rather, *every single one of these moments of consciousness* bears them *in* itself, even if we think of such a moment as fulfilling an indivisible point in time—not the "stream," but each of its "cross-sections." [65]

When we say that a psychic experience given as present is always part of the *total givenness* that reaches into the direction of the being-past and the being-future, we imply that "the ego," which is always cogiven as experienced in experiences, is *not* a "*synthesis*" of egos given "first" as "egos of the present." For there is no such thing as an "ego of the present" as a *phenomenal* fact. Everything that is experienced as present is by essential necessity given against the *background* of this *total* givenness in which the *whole* of the individual ego is intended as temporally undivided. Thus all experiences, no matter if they are given within this total givenness as "present," "past," or "future," appear by essential necessity against the background of the *whole life* that this intended ego experiences, no matter how much or how little of this "whole" life is given.

It is therefore clear, first, that the so-called identity of the ego is *not* constituted through *identifying acts* that pertain to *contents of experience* and the relations of meaning among them. The identity of the ego is, rather, the individual mode of *experiencing* all such contents. This mode is immediately given as the same. This immediate *identity of experiencing* is the presupposition of all identifications of *contents* which we find in diverse qualities of acts (e.g., remembering the "same" thing that I "perceived"; perceiving now what I previously only "represented"; "knowing" now what I previously only "guessed,"

65. Such a *"moment of consciousness"* does not exist as a phenomenal fact. The unity of consciousness concerned can be called a "present" only by virtue of the belongingness of an (inner) *"unity of consciousness-of"* to an (essentially present) instance of the lived body's givenness. But, even with this, no "moment of consciousness" is given. The instance of the givenness of the lived body can be (indirectly) coordinated to objective time and in a *twofold sense* (indirectly) thought to fulfill its own unity of consciousness as a "moment of this time" only through a further dovetailing of the objective body "belonging" necessarily to this instance of lived-body givenness in the objective time of mechanics, which contains nothing like present, past, or future.

"doubted," or "left unsolved," etc.). Second, it follows that a special *consciousness of continuity* is present and experienced during acts of mediate "remembering something," for instance, acts that conjoin phenomena that are still given in immediate remembering (first, values, as we showed earlier). (This would be recollective consciousness of continuity.) This "consciousness of continuity" is not, say, a "*continuous consciousness*" that fills time continuously. Something like this is *not at all* necessary. For in deepest sleep, in a fainting fit, etc., there is perhaps no consciousness at all. But wherever and whenever "the same" is remembered, an immediate consciousness of the same relational sense of former acts of remembering "the same" must be cogiven with the new act of remembering. Otherwise one would think that a series of events of the *same* content had been experienced earlier.[66] What we said above about a plurality of acts of the same quality (acts of remembering or expecting "the same," etc.) also holds analogously for acts of different qualities, such as perceiving, representing, remembering, expecting, judging, desiring, loving, etc. All popular attempts which, instead of regarding this identity of content as an ultimate phenomenon, try to "explain" it (as it is found in expressions like "I imagine now what I previously perceived," "I now remember the C that I earlier perceived," "I like it as I thought I would"), so that one assumes "first" a series of experiences separated in time and supposedly similar to one another only in direction, *tear apart* the unity of the ego. This unity cannot be reconstructed by any "hypothesis," no matter how subtle or complicated.

The problem is *not how* the identity of meaning of such temporally and qualitatively different acts comes about. This is the primordial phenomenon and is not to be questioned. The problem is *how* an explanatory psychologist comes to assume that there is, for example, *now* an experience of remembering and an "image of remembrance" and three minutes ago a perceptual experience "of the tone *C*," embedded in objective time and conjoined by something like "reproduction," by something that we do not find in the phenomenal. The problem is also how people come to regard processes of perception, representation,

---

66. The case described by one of Pick's students, a case that one could call reduplicating paramnesia, seems to me to rest on an absence of the above "recollective consciousness of continuity." (See Specht's *Zeitschrift für Pathopsychologie*, Vol. II, no. 4). [The work under discussion is Maximilian Rosenberg, "Die Erinnerungstäuschungen der reduplizierenden Paramnesie und des déja vu."—*Ed.*]

recollection, etc., as different classes of processes. How does this *tearing apart* of what is immediately unified in meaning come about? Indeed, we must enlarge this problematic.

We are not always aware of the identity of the relational sense of an act that we have just executed with previously executed acts having the same or different natures. We are not aware of this in a manner that would allow us to localize these acts in time. We cannot point to their quality in terms of different directions of possible qualifications, nor can we always determine the diverse appearances of what is identically meant in a former act of the same quality, for instance, a face. Frequently there is, for example, an experience of the simple "*sameness*" of something that is perceived and something that was "somewhere," "at some time," or "somehow" "given," without the fulfillment of such undetermined places by contents. Sometimes we do not even know whether we "represented" *or* "perceived" "the same," or whether we have only been told about it; sometimes, when we "perceived" the same, we also do not know whether we "heard" *or* "saw" it. Indeed, this "sameness" can cover the content with its presence; and, though we have no idea of any former experience or of any possible recollection ("being-able-to-remember"), this recollection occurs solely on the *basis* of the phenomenon of "sameness." Such simple experienced relations as "the same as X," "similar to Y," "different from Z," "distinguishable from A," "analogous to B," "prettier than C," "as good as G," etc., turn our attention first to the direction of a more certain fulfillment of X, Y, Z, etc. The tone C in the above example—for instance, when gradually fading away—can be given without its being cogiven whether we actually hear it or only hear it in an "inner ear" in immediate remembering. In a startling event we can also experience an immediate "totally different from . . ." which makes us aware for the first time that a certain expectation already existed, an expectation, that is, which is opposite in direction to this content. One cannot dismiss these facts and many similar ones of the same type—indeed, as many as you will—by saying that the contents belonging to X, Y, and Z have simply been "forgotten." Apart from the difficulties contained in "forgetting" (as distinguished from merely not remembering), the question here is why the relational sense of the given, with respect to that which figures as not actually given, is not *also* canceled out for consciousness, but, indeed, must be there. Not the present content alone—for example, the remembered tone C—nor the act-quality in which this content is present, nor the subsumption of the relation "same as" or "identical to" under the concept of the relation "sameness," "similarity," etc., can explain these experiential facts. Furthermore, the assumption that something abstract is remembered here, something without the appropriate concreteness, explains nothing. For one must either admit that the abstract does not have to be "abstracted" from the previously given concrete, i.e., that the content of the abstract can also be originally given as independent content, thus appearing "as" abstract only in relation to the concrete (but then this assumption is not sufficient to shake our position), or reduce the abstract to a mere fact of attention, a "disregarding" (in which case we are led back to the question of "forgetting"). These and other similar facts do not show that the sense-relations among act-contents (despite their differences in quality and time) represent conscious *diminutions* of different, concrete experiences that originally are variously localized in time. On the contrary, these facts show that these sense-relations are original, given so originally and so independently that they can be present even *without* the experiences in question, and that it is *they* that determine from the beginning the givenness of *these* and no *other* experiences (which would be equally reproducible), even in cases where the X, Y, and Z are given as filled with experiences that are fixed in time, quality, and content.[67]

This enlargement of the problematic, which we juxtaposed to the falsely formulated problem in which the tone C of a present recollective experience is identified with the perceived tone C, can now be formulated in this fashion: How can we get from a *timeless interconnection of meaning* and from a *timeless continuity of meaning* of all acts executed by *one* personal being (we were only concerned with acts of the ego), and how can we get from an *identical individual experiencing*, despite different act-qualities and apparently different acts in objective time, to the *image* of this *flux* of act-experiences in time if we can*not* regain the undoubtedly present interconnection of meaning when this flux is posited in its originality?

Once again we will take a synthetic look at the case. No matter how little of myself and my life is given at this very moment

---

67. "Directions of meaning" or directions of possible "*meaning* of something" also determine the temporal course of an individual's pictorial representations or the course of the interconnection of sense of a plurality of intersecting directions of meaning, in which the meanings of values are revealed as primary factors in the determination.

of inner perception, there is contained in this: (1) the intention toward the totality of my individual ego, which does not require any patching together of this and earlier egological moments, and which knows itself in every experience as what is experiencing; (2) along with the sphere of the present, a sphere of pastness (the sphere of remembrance of immediate remembrance) and a sphere of futurity (the sphere of expectation of immediate expectation); [68] and (3) in these givens, again, all types of

---

68. If someone were to hold (a) that "remembrance" is nothing but the possession of a present picture with the judgment that something corresponding to this picture lies in the past, and (b) that this judgment is true if, as an anticipatory judgment, it fulfills a possible effect coming from what one assumes to have been in the past, or even only fulfills the expectation of the recurrence of a similar event, I would raise the following objection: (1) How could one who holds this view make a distinction *within* remembrance between the mere judgmental remembrance, e.g., when I judged that "I saw this landscape," on the one hand, and the "seeing" of the "landscape" in remembrance, or when I make the judgment that "I saw this landscape" *within* remembering seeing, on the other? (2) How does he get, in addition to the present "remembered picture" and the judgment, the datum "being-past," in which he must set what is supposed to correspond to the present picture? Moreover, how can the "symbolic function" of the picture contain, in addition to a "symbol of something," a symbol of things past? If this man were to answer that the word *past* means nothing but the duration of the temporal process up to 4 o'clock, assuming that my clock "now" shows 4 o'clock, one would have to reply that clocks which measure time have no traces of "past," "present," or "future." This, in turn, would pose the question of why he calls this and no other temporal duration "past," since from any arbitrarily chosen point of objective continuous time (every point of time is arbitrary in objective time) every duration runs up to 4 o'clock. Surely things must be different: The existence of past, present, and future is *not* a relative but an *absolute* fact precisely because what is of objective temporal duration and is represented in its content as "present," "past," or "future" is totally relative to a "present" lived body and, therefore, to the implicitly given spheres of the past and the future. For my life prior to 4 o'clock *is not* my past life; rather, my life given in the immediate dimension of the past coincides with 4 o'clock in that it is "simultaneous" with the content of this time, i.e., simultaneous in absolute time, which is different from objective, measurable time, and in which my lived body occupies a specific point. (3) How could the man holding the above view expect a recurrence of a similar experience (similar to the one in the past) when he does not *know* (in immediate evidence of remembrance) that he lived this experience? For our question is whether there is or is not remembrance to be confirmed *by* a fulfillment of this expectation. In practice we expect such a recurrence of the similar only when we evidentially at least believe that the experience concerned is given to us as a past one in remembrance. But this givenness does not *consist* in a fulfillment of the expectation (see "Über Selbsttäuschungen" for an analogous example). [See *ibid.* sec. 4—Ed.] (4) Expectation presents an analogous case. Or should there be an "immediate expecting of something" and no remembering? This would be tantamount to the grave error of basing remembrance on expectation. Should it be the case, for instance, that a historical event is historically

interconnections of meaning of that which is given as *no longer*
actual [*aktuell*], but which is nevertheless affected and touched
in directions of both pastness and futurity by the experience of
these interconnections—no matter at which points in time "my"
body in objective time and all other bodies having a causal connection with it are coordinated with the actuality of the experience concerned.

This is certainly an essential fact given in any inner world.
But how do we respond to the above problem?

Natural experience of psychic being as such knows *nothing*
about the associative-psychological dissolution of the living unity
of the ego into moments that are only temporally separated objectively; nor does it know anything about this dissolution of
the unity of meaning of the manifold of experiences. This is
beyond doubt. But natural experience as such knows *no more*
about a non-temporal interwovenness of this manifold, nor does
it know in which form individual experiential groups form unities of meaning other than the temporal divisions; nor does it
know how these groups possess among themselves *one* unity of
sense within the total sense of an experiencing ego. Natural
experience yields only a kind of *mixtum compositum* of these
two kinds of interconnections. Just as natural experience customarily places the ego with its feelings and thoughts vaguely
"in" the lived body or the "head," etc., and makes it move through
space—for example, along with a walk that I take—so does it
place experiences vaguely in time and let them flow by, although
it affirms the identity of the ego with its contents and duration
in an equally vague manner. Empirical descriptive *psychology*,
too, i.e., the strictly empirical one, which is as different from
the constructive psychology of association as it is from any other
theory of the soul, recognizes predominant connections of meaning in addition to associative ones. And it is only in the pathological disintegration of psychic life (e.g., in morbid imagination)
that associative connections become predominant over those of
meaning. We owe much to Külpe's school of psychology, which
on the whole gives us such a picture. This school has succeeded
in exposing the complete artificiality of old associative-psychological descriptions of processes of thinking, in the sense of
"thinking" understood as "thinking of something," and "process"
as the process of sequences of thoughts. But it, too, has stuck to

---

real only if we may expect some effect of it in the future? This would be
the plainest of pragmatistic dilutions of history!

occurrences of pure associations. No wonder genuinely empirical psychology holds as strictly as the empirical natural sciences (e.g., experimental physics and chemistry) to the basic forms of natural experience, even though the observation and description of its contents are much more subtle than those of everyday life. But the very facts of natural experience and their basic forms are *not* ultimate givens for *phenomenology* and philosophy. Phenomenology or phenomenological seeing does not dwell *in* these basic forms. On the contrary, phenomenology makes these forms givens of pure intuition. And this pertains to the natural experience of the outer world, as well as to the natural experience of the inner world. Whatever "structure" there is in natural experience with its objects, though it cannot be explained within natural experience or by positive empirical sciences (which are confined to those basic forms), can be brought to light and explained in detail in phenomenology.

Proceeding in this manner, we will see that natural experience with the essential repertory contained in all of its experiential units, when considered from the viewpoint of the units of act-meanings, which phenomenology shows to permeate our whole psychic life, and from the viewpoint of the concrete unity of act-meanings of a concrete ego (in which such essential interconnections of such a separated, abstract act-being are fulfilled in a singular manner), is already *on the way* to giving us a kind of associative picture of the psychic life. This unity of act-meaning, as I said, "permeates" this psychic life, which temporally flows by in natural experience, structured in certain vacillating units (which contain units of meaning although they appear to lack them here and there), and it does so in a completely nontemporal way, in strict, essential form. Does not this *"natural psychic life"* of natural experience—as measured against what phenomenology can find of the permeations [*Verwebung*] of pure units of sense—already appear here as a mode of the *relative dissolution* of this concrete unity of meaning, as a disintegration of it into pieces in which the lines of this pure unity of meaning of the whole are still visible, but which, when separated from this whole and placed into the extensionality of a temporal process (with this or that piece possibly missing), look as if the "natural course" were governed by completely *different principles,* principles that are as decisive for the structure of natural experience as the interconnections of meaning are? It is as if the "natural course" were governed by these in addition to being governed by the inner interconnection of the concrete unity of acts, independent of the latter but superposed along with it. "Natural experience" originally contains a *tendency*, although nothing *more* than a tendency, to prompt an associative picture of the ego and its experiences. This picture, in its most ideal form, would have a *single* connection between experiences: association by contiguity (at least as an elementary kind of connection) in a pure extensionality that can be both temporal and spatial as the case may be (or which can be so interpreted).[69] But, on the other hand, if one measures the facts of the "natural" structure of experience against the ideal picture of a *perfect* psychology of association—the picture toward which these facts, as compared with the concrete complex of meaning of a psychic life, have a mere "tendency"—they appear to acquire the *opposite:* namely, a tendency toward this concrete unity of meaning. And this "picture" changes so that the attempt of a strict associative-psychological construction appears to make a farce of what is given factually in this structure. It evidently "lacks" something that would *somehow* bring a unity of meaning to the combinations of elements of the experiences in pure extensionality, something that would rebuild unities of meaning—even those units of experience implied in natural language, those belonging to the psychic (experiences of "woe," "joy," "commiseration," a goal-determined conation toward something, etc.).[70] In any case one can see that *something* like a unity of meaning, which does not enter into the so-called association by contiguity (and which the so-called association by contiguity and the assimilative connection as we find it already in sense-memory oppose so that this unity will not be arbitrarily constructed), must be there; i.e., there must be something that the phenomenology of psychic life establishes which makes the production of this associative mechanism impossible.

69. Here we cannot discuss in greater detail the levels of the psychic situated *between* the pure interwovenness, with its sense-units, and the picture of the absolute dispersion of elements of experience; nor can we discuss further the connecting forms in each of such levels, namely, the assimilations reaching into the lower areas (the "chemicism" of psychic life) and the sense-units of vital feelings, drives, and instincts reaching into upper areas.

70. Here one often returns, as Herbart, for example, does, to a "soul-substance" in which associations could "meet." A reasonable psychologist of associations ought to be inclined to accept this view the more *consistently* he sticks to his principles (a point that Herbart's first disciples stressed); or he should allow an apperception (in Wundt's sense of the term) or dark forces of "synthetic activities" so that a whole of an experienced substance is built up from the dusty piles of "impressions" and "representations."

And here we can attempt to answer our question. This attempt, if completely thought through, would open up a huge field of investigation, whose parts we can only touch upon in this context.

Let us try to reduce the structure of the "natural" experience of psychic being and life to phenomenological interconnections of essence. We must show that there is in the whole of empirical psychic life, as it is presented in observation, description, and inductive generalization in terms of empirical rules, a plurality of strict *"principles."* These principles go back to evident interconnections of essence and represent the non-formal a priori of all *inductive* experience of the psychic, but at the same time they yield this structure only in their *superposition* with *complexes of meaning.*

The concrete meaning-complex of act-intentions of a concrete ego (as a content of pure and formless intuition in general) is of necessity, as we saw, given in *inner intuition,* to which the manifold of "interwovenness" corresponds. If we take the act of inner intuition *alone,* and as wholly unqualified by "direction," "form," "quality," etc., then we must ask if the *elongation* of the *content* of any inner *"consciousness-of"* in terms of present, past, and future is still given. And we must further ask if the *run-off* of the contents of any acts of the ego that are already qualified would be given. Would the always intended ego-totality, which "surrounds" these elongations and their contents like a "background," and which is never self-given in natural experience but only "meant" in perception like a concrete corporeal thing of the physical world, be *self*-given? Would the complexes of meaning contained in the actually given (in the three elongations), which point to all possible points of the temporal total life of the concrete ego, "begin to address" them without what is addressed actually being present? In this case would those givens be actually given with their *missing* elements?

For many reasons the answer to the first of these questions is no. The essential differences in temporal directions and their act-correlates—the act-qualities of perceiving, remembering, and expecting—are *not* parts of the nature of a person looking purely at his concrete ego. To be sure, these are differences in essence. And for this reason it is impossible to reduce them to the mere "sequence" of experiences that lie in them. It is also impossible similarly to "reduce" this "sequence" taken as a phenomenon, as certain theories in the genetic psychology of a so-called sense of time would have it. Nor, for example, can one get gradual, qualitative differences from pictorial contents which are supposedly simultaneous, and which, by going forward and backward, result in a consciousness of so-called time perspective (as in the theory of "time signs," which is copied from the theory of locality signs).[71] And it is equally impossible to doubt that perception, remembrance, and expectation are genuine act-*qualities*. But this is denied in every theory that reduces remembering to a representation connected with content that symbolically goes back into the past, or to an immanent "characteristic" of this representation, or to the "symbolic function" of such content. For representation exists without remembrance (and the simple addition of a characteristic to representational content never results in a recollective consciousness of something),[72] and remembrance—indeed, the recognition of something again *within* the sphere of remembering [73]—exists without "representation." [74] A critique of attempts to reduce remembering to a reproduction of perception (for example, to weakened perceptual content) or of attempts to reduce perception to a strong and compelling representation (which, according to Berkeley, God produces magically) is for this reason redundant. In the merely imagined formation of a special content of perception, "reproduction" plays the *same* role that it plays in the formation of a recollected content (or an expected one).[75] Nor can one reduce "expecting" to a representation of something future plus attention to its content. But we do not wish to demonstrate this at this time.

It does *not* follow from this that the temporal directions and

71. Such "qualitative differences" have never been detected. Indeed, even if they existed, they could not be detected because they would have been used in the production of the appearance of the time perspective.

72. The representation that something took place in the past is, of course, no remembrance of this something.

73. Re-recognition is not restricted to remembrance, still less to reproduction. Very often it is the consciousness "the same as . . ." that *founds* an act of remembrance.

74. This is the case with remembrance that stays within the spheres of meaning and judgment, e.g., a remembrance of thoughts, as K. Bühler showed. But even when the remembered content is a pictorial one of a representative type, remembrance can immediately aim at this pictorial content without its being represented. Thus I now remember Zeus, whom I represented yesterday; and this "represented yesterday" is co-given, but without any present representation of Zeus.

75. Thus remembered colors, for example, undoubtedly have the character of a perceived content, not of a content of remembrance (or of a "content of representation"); but they do have as their condition a "reproduction."

the act-qualities corresponding to them would remain if we were to bracket the lived body, i.e., the essence of bodiliness. What alone follows is that the elongations of past, present, and future, with their corresponding act-qualities, are independent of the time that the body-thing (as an object of outer perception) occupies in mechanical time. Therefore, if we reduce the lived body as bearer of the ego plus the inner intuition given with the ego (i.e., not merely as this or that *specific* body-thing), the elongations and act-qualities, too, will *as such* disappear. They become mere types of relations that are contained in the pure interwovenness of the psychic manifold of the ego in relation to a possible lived body. If, however, we were to take *only* the act of inner intuition, which is necessarily implicit in any factual human inner perception, the ray of this intuition taken purely by itself would hit *every* psychic experience of this concrete ego with the *same* immediacy, and would bring the contents of past and future to givenness with the *same* immediacy, as the contents of the present. And this is impossible only because *lived-bodiliness* is in essence connected with an ego.[76] On the other hand, with this connection with the lived body, the identity of the act of inner intuition (in the strict sense of the term) remains in all act-qualities of acts of this unity and form, just as the identity of what is intended and "meant" in those acts remains given. It is not only the *concept* of the act of inner intuition that remains the same in every quality, but also the act itself. Therefore the immediate identity, for example, a tone remembered and a tone previously heard in perception, as well as the immediate identity of the expected with the perceived, etc., *is itself given*. I know of no presupposition or theory that could make such basic facts understandable other than these, which are also *presupposed* by the concept of possible deception.

If the fission of the act of inner intuition (into the above qualities, etc.) does not lie in the nature of an ego in general, but only in its essential connection with a lived body, we can draw the one conclusion that is commensurate with the facts: namely, only in the *unities of coincidence* of perception, remembrance, and expectation can a *replete* intuition and the complete *fullness* of the respective contents meant in them be given, and

---

76. This essential nexus, however, does not bring about the interconnection of the ego and the time dimensions as an essential interconnection. There is only the necessity of this nexus. But it rests on an *inference* that is made on the basis of positing something with a lived-body nature.

only in these unities of coincidence can this complete fullness be *constituted*.

Anyone who holds that the contents of remembering (and expecting) "stem" from the contents of perception (e.g., in Hume's theory, every "idea" is supposed to be a "copy" of an "impression") must always arrive at this curious theory: (1) that remembrance *as* remembrance (and expectation *as* expectation) cannot yield its givens as "immediately" as perception can, or that it cannot in the same sense give the object "itself"; (2) that the contents of remembrance (and those of expectation), according to their nature, are "poorer" than those of perception, and that they contain in themselves something "less" than the contents of perception; and (3) that, accordingly, every insertion of the content of remembrance (and that of expectation) into the total intuited content of a perceived object (if the same characteristics of the object are concerned) can only falsify the intuition of the object and will not allow a *deeper* penetration into its objective content.

None of these sensualistic presuppositions is in any sense justified. The content of *im*mediate remembering does not "stem" in any way from the content of perception.[77] And it is only for mediate remembrance (which is always founded on an immediate remembrance of a certain direction in a "sphere," limited by meaning, into which mediate remembrance always directs itself) that there is the *essential law* that a possible mediate remembrance "belongs" to every possible perception. This proposition is based on an essential interconnective complex of mediate remembrance and perception. It is *not* based on psychological empiricism. In this respect any empiricism *presupposes* this. For the psychologist *starts* with the facts of the run-off of psychic experiences in objective time. All his possible "observations" demand the immediate identifiability and the essential interconnection of the mediate remembrance and perception of the experience observed. But this proposition does not hold at all for the content of immediate remembering. It is evident, rather, that perception can never give contents having the same charac-

77. [In the following elaborations on the three essential laws which underlie the principles of association as their phenomenal basis (pp. 438 f., 440 f., 444 ff.), the author has chosen to expound his thesis against the sensualistic theory in terms of the relation between perception and remembrance. However, as has been noted elsewhere, these remarks obtain analogously for the relation between perception and expectation.— Ed.]

ter as those given by immediate remembering, nor can it give what "immediate expecting of . . ." gives. It is not because of, say, our "human organization" (and time sense) that we cannot also perceive the contents of immediate remembrance, as if an *elongation* of our time sense could make this possible. Rather, perception, remembrance, and expectation are given with specific contents in *every* indivisible moment of consciousness (which corresponds to a point in objective time). Imagined beings whose fields of perception and "presence" (as well as the fields of their "functions," e.g., hearing, seeing) are larger or smaller because of their different organizations could *never* have the same content given to them in both perception and immediate remembering (in the case of a larger field) or the same content in both remembrance and perception (in the case of a smaller field). To such imagined beings (in the case of a larger field of perception) there would be given, e.g., *more* things and events, *more* movement and change, or parts of these (i.e., in the same spatiotemporal unity). But the fact that "things," "events," "movement," and "change," i.e., facts of these essences, could be given at all to these beings presupposes the immediate identification of something meant in the various contents of the perceived and the immediately remembered and expected in *every* one of these beings' acts of intuition. It belongs to the nature of these phenomena to be comprehended only in the unity of acts of this quality, independent of real or illusory thingness (as in hallucination), real or illusory movement or change. It stands to reason, therefore, that there is *no reproduction* of the perceived (or even of merely sensory content *in* the content of the perceived), whether through assimilation or association, that could, given a different organization, furnish a substitute for what immediate remembering and expecting give.

The *content of mediate and possible remembrance* does not "stem" from the content of possible perception, either. However, in addition to the aforementioned essential interconnection, mediate remembrance "belongs" to every perception and vice versa (the proposition of reproduction): Every occurrence of mediate remembrance is connected in the order of time with a perception of the same object and content preceding it in this order of time.

This proposition follows from: (1) the proposition of the immediate identity of every possible recollected object with a perceived object, a proposition that makes possible the idea of recognizing something; [78] (2) the proposition of the mutual belongingness of one content of perception and one content of remembrance; and (3) the proposition that the content of mediate remembrance can only be situated in the sphere at which immediate remembering is aimed and directed according to its meaning (i.e., in the experienced "past").

This is not an empirical proposition of psychological observation. It is an *essential law* based on the nature of mediate remembrance and perception. But this proposition in no way implies that the content of mediate remembrance "stems" from a factual, antecedent perception, or that it is only a "remnant" of such perception. What is meant here, what alone can be meant, is the *temporal sequence,* not some possible "origin" of the content, and the *order* of the sequence, not the sequence in terms of succession as opposed to endurance. All psychological observation, however, presupposes this proposition in this particular sense, because the object of *this* psychology, the psychic event in objective time, is constituted in the acts concerned.

It is only with this that the purely phenomenal content of the concept of *"reproduction"* is given, and thus the evidential proposition that a reproduction (of any kind) of something "previously" perceived belongs to every mediate remembrance (of an embodied being). To introduce into this "reproduction," say, a real recurrence of perceptual content in weakened form, etc., or a "stemming" of the mediate content of remembrance from the content of perception (as if the former were to be regarded as a minus in terms of the content of perception) is not merely wrongheaded; it is to mystify the concept of reproduction. And thus the limits of what "reproduction" can *"explain"* become clear. That it can in no way explain "remembrance" goes without saying. The concept of "reproduction" has *eo ipso* no significance for immediate remembering and its content in the "having-been," nor has it any significance for the "directions" of the values and meanings of immediate remembering, from whose already *structured* darkness all mediate recollective con-

78. Re-recognizability is *not,* say, identity (as pure psychologism holds), nor is the mode of consciousness involved (in the sense of "consciousness-of") a condition of or even identical to an "immediate consciousness of identity." For *one* remembrance of a certain event in my life can give the sameness of this event with something actually experienced in the past. "Recognizing something again" implies a plurality of acts, whereby recognizing something again in a plurality of mediate acts of remembrance can constitute itself *within* a mediately given sphere of remembrance without any givenness of a perceptual act of the event.

tent comes to the fore in these directions. Not only does mediate remembrance in its general nature presuppose immediate remembering and its implicit essence of "having-been," but content that is not encompassed by the sphere of meanings and values of the sphere of immediate remembering of a certain individual can*not* enter into the mediate remembrance of this individual ego! That is, *immediate* remembering fixes the very field for the *mediate* remembrance of possible contents, and its elements alone can become factual contents of mediate remembrance! Reproduction only determines the *kinds* of elements, *within this field* of possible contents, that will be mediately remembered. (Such fields vary with individuals, but in them the general laws of the foundation of acts, for instance, of striving, representing, loving, etc., remain valid.) Reproduction therefore possesses only a *selective* significance with regard to such fields; it has *no* determining significance for the pure *what* of contents.[79]

Let us also note that *"forgetting"* belongs only to mediate "remembrance," but that this "forgetting" must still belong to the field of what is at least given in immediate remembering.[80] "For-

79. The fact that in "trying to remember something" we still *experience* an "approximation" and (as it were) the "distance" of that toward which mediate remembrance (a mode of this "trying to remember") is directed (in the sense of a mere "thinking of . . .") shows that the content which we are trying to remember is not sought after like the X of an equation, and that its consciously experienced belongingness to the immediate content of remembrance is still involved. In many cases we do not even try to remember—even when we judge that we have experienced certain things in the past on the basis of the statement of one whom we believe. We do not do so because we believe (at this moment) that the *ability* to try is missing since the things to be remembered do not at all "come to address" the content of immediate remembrance.

80. What is here called *immediate remembering* corresponds in its content, according to its essence (if all individual egos are set aside), only to the sphere of a having-been in general as an extension of the time background which is always brought along in any consciousness of the psychic. In investigating an individual's immediate remembering of something, we realize that the distinction between immediate and mediate remembrance does not presuppose that mediate remembrance pertains to what is far away in the past and immediate remembering to what has *just* passed, e.g., the "disappearing of a sound," the sinking of an actual experience into the past, or even the sinking of a content into the "time just past." Rather, this distinction rests only on the essential differences of the modes of givenness involved.

We find here the following phenomenal characteristics. [These remarks on the essential difference between the manners of givenness of immediate and mediate remembrance obtain also for immediate and mediate expectation.—*Ed.*] (1) In the execution of the act of *immediate* remembering, the quality of this act itself (= remembering) is *not* experienced as given. Here

getting," which is not at all the same as not remembering, always pertains to something that is still addressed within the contents of immediate remembering. When we approach what

the experience dwells entirely in the *content,* which is only cloaked by the sphere of the "having-been." This is clearly the case, e.g., in the kinds of daydreaming which possess a character of detachment until something is "ripped" out. Thus, I begin "to see again" the lake, the landscape, and the mansions where I played as a child, I see the people who were there at that time, and I see and experience myself as a child placed in this whole. I may see this or that and can, by directing myself toward a house at the lake, for example, *mediately* remember something that was connected with that house. In *mediate* remembrance, however, the *act*-quality of "remembering something" is itself *experienced,* and it is not the past-quality of that in which I dwell that allows me to know *that I remember.* Only in mediate remembrance is there the experience of "I remember" in the strict sense of this term. (2) In *immediate* remembering, "remembered contents come upon me," or the "changing contents of something" reach into my active [*aktuelle*] consciousness in such a way that they are given "as reaching into" it; i.e., "parts" or "aspects" of something more encompassing and still intended are *co*given. This often happens in the flash of a moment. Here may be the basis of the concept of perseveration. In *mediate* remembrance, on the other hand, the *starting point* in what is given "as present" (or "as past" in immediate remembrance) is always cogiven, even if I do not in fact know *what* this starting point is. I may not know, e.g., that it is the smell of tar around me that makes me remember the ships and the sea that I once saw. But this starting point is cogiven all the same, which makes this markedly different from immediate remembrance. The *content* of this starting point is often found later (e.g., this smell). But when this mode of consciousness is missing, any assumption that there *must* be something (a hidden association) is an arbitrary prejudice. Therefore, in *immediate* remembrance the time *direction* is always past → present: what is given as having-been "continues into" my present, and I am given to myself as "living into" my present (as, analogously, I "live into" my future in immediate expectation). In *mediate* remembrance, however, the time direction of experience is always present → past: here things flow from the present "back into" the past, and between present and past there is a deep gap. From the viewpoint of my present, I live into the past (no matter if I do so actively, e.g., in trying to remember something, or passively, when the past becomes booty of mine by way of an automatic process). (3) It should be clear that it is only with regard to *mediate* remembrance that one can speak of "pictures of remembrance," i.e., of remembrances whose contents are given only in the mode of a "representation of . . . ," as opposed to "the thing itself." For it is only in mediate remembrance that the lake is given as "merely represented," or otherwise "as itself," as in perception, but in this *one* way only, in a veiled manner. Hence one who (arbitrarily) defines the word *perception* as an act in which something is given as "itself there" should be consistent enough to speak of "perception" in *this* case and to make a distinction between perceptual remembering and representational remembering. The content of a so-called picture of remembrance (i.e., apart from "representation") is never the *full* content of remembrance. It is, rather, an *assimilation* of the *starting point* and *inception* of mediate remembrance and the remembered content *itself.* Here I understand assimilation to be a combination of contents *not* reducible to an *association by contiguity* of similar initial elements, i.e., a combination of contents such that all partial similarities among contents (and *not* all similarities of

is thus "addressed," there occurs a deviation of the mental gaze (in remembering) which constitutes the positive act of "forgetting." Hence one can hold a person responsible for "forgetting,"

---

parts of contents) increase according to the degree of their similarity and cancel each other according to their dissimilarity. [On "similarity," "partial similarity," "association," etc., see the remarks that follow in this section.—*Ed.*] One can reduce all (genuine) "tradition"—viewed macroscopically—to such "pictures," in contrast to *"living history,"* in which immediate remembering unifies the phases of historical processes, distinct from the objective succession of natural processes, into *one* consciousness; and, again, in contrast to all *knowledge* of "history," which is based wholly on mediate remembrance. Therefore, it is the *taking apart* and the *analysis* of this "picture" or the content of tradition that returns in *one* and the *same* process on the one hand to the content of a pure present, i.e., the pure content of perception, *and* on the other hand to the content of a pure past, i.e., the pure content of remembrance. The analysis of this "picture" liberates, as it were, the one from the other. (4) The question of whether we are in this division of *immediate* and *mediate* remembrance concerned with something "just past" or at any distance in the past plays no role here. This division has nothing to do with either an "immediate continuation of experience" or anything like "continued pictures" [*Nachbilder*] or so-called pictures continued in remembrance. If one were to hold this view, a completely false limitation would be imposed on the *sphere* of immediate remembrance; then, too, our proposition which states that all mediate remembrance must be located within the scope of the immediately remembered would be, of course, nonsense. The "facts," however, which allegedly support this view—without any *definition* of "immediate remembrance"—are false interpretations of the facts. Let us give an example. First, if I check to see how many beats of a metronome I can hear simultaneously when there are equal intervals—without any mediate remembrance of them—I do *not* establish anything with regard to a so-called immediate domain of consciousness. What is established concerns the domain of the immediate retained hearing which enters into "hearing of . . . ." This retained hearing differs from the beats given "as present"; it also differs from the immediate remembrance of retained hearing and what is heard in it. For in immediate remembrance the successive contents of retained hearing are themselves unified again into an immediate unity of consciousness along with what has just been heard. Second, I can establish something about the given in perception, i.e., in hearing, only *if* the test subject grasps the given as tokens of real natural processes—not as "beats of the metronome," but as the number of the units of sound coming from things. But in this case I have not established anything about qualities of sounds or qualities of resonance or about sounds and resonance, i.e., *without* this grasping. Nor have I established anything about how far immediately retained hearing reaches into melodious *form-units,* rhythmic Gestalten, and their various overlappings, which can be given in retained hearing *without* any cogivenness of the sounds. Even when the sounds have already entered mediate remembrance, the individual place-values [*Stellenwerte*] which they occupy in the immediately given rhythm and melodic form and in which they realize themselves have not done so. Such place-values are *autonomous* objects of intuition, i.e., of hearing. They are not to be regarded as relations of rhythm and melody. How could a musical performance of, say, one and a half hours be "understood" were there not some kind of immediate consciousness of the whole of the musical sense?

which would be senseless if he lacked the mechanism of reproduction.

There is, finally, an essential law concerning the condition to
which the occurrence of a possible reproduction is essentially
connected: the *principle of similarity.*

Not only is a possible same thing given in mediate remembrance, as is the case in remembrance and perception in
general; but, despite this same meant object, there is by essential
necessity a content that is *different* in both perception and remembering. This is the case because all contents of mediate
remembrance *must* have been contained in the sphere delineated
by the direction of contents of possible immediate remembering,
and because all contents of mediate remembrance represent the
selection of elements from this sphere. The content of mediate
remembrance can never coincide with that of immediate remembering. We have seen that the content of immediate remembering is necessarily and absolutely different from perceptual content, and that this difference is not merely factual and relative
to points in objective time and its content. For every thing
and every possible part of a thing (even the smallest), every
event and every possible real part of an event, every motion
and every part of a motion, etc., are constituted by (among
other factors) essential necessity in immediate remembering and
expecting. And this is quite independent of all thresholds of the
comprehension of these phenomena and their reality or appearance. Therefore all content of mediate remembrance must be
different, in its specific *kind* and *direction,* from the perceptual
content that necessarily belongs to it and necessarily precedes it
in the order of time, despite its essential and necessary identity
with the object of reference of perception.[81] This specific kind of
difference is the *similarity* of both contents, to which we now
will turn.

Rationalists and empiricists have always taken different
stands on the phenomenon of similarity (e.g., the similarity between red and orange), and they have done so in various ways.
Some have tried to *reduce* similarity to the *identity* and *difference* of a number (however large) or "aggregate" of parts
(*identitas partium*) in things given as "similar" (e.g., Herbart).
Others have attempted to do the opposite. Proceeding from similarity as a *basic* phenomenon, they regard identity as the "limiting case" of similarity, i.e., the case wherein similar objects are

81. [Compare the above remarks with those on pp. 438, 441 ff.—*Ed.*]

no longer distinguishable, but "indistinguishable." And in so doing they regard "difference" not as a presupposition of similarity (its species) but as non-identity (e.g., Hume and all specific nominalists for whom "concepts" are only names applicable to areas of similarity among objects). But this is logical arbitrariness. In orange and red we find neither spatial nor merely extensive "parts," which would be in some cases different and in others identical so that the orange-red similarity would differ from, say, the greater purple-red similarity only in terms of number or type of distribution. Does, for example, the number 2 have more similarity to the number 3 than to the number 10, even though it cannot be "numerically" identical with them in parts yet cannot be "not identical with" (different from) them because they are numbers? Is not the same true for aggregates? On the other hand, with regard to the second attempt mentioned, it is evident that similarity *presupposes* that similar objects are identical but, at the same time, mutually different (both logically and in the phenomenal givenness of similarity). But it is too much to demand that there also be an identical "respect" in relation to which different objects can be similar so that similarity can be objectively possible and comprehensible. Of course, there is a similarity which emerges only with this presupposition and which is determinable and communicable in this and that "respect." Thus different bodies can be similar and dissimilar with "respect" to size, form, and chemical composition, and this can be the case to various degrees. But to this *"mediate"* similarity, which presupposes a conceptual grasp of objects that are similar, there corresponds an *immediate* similarity, which is the presupposition of mediate similarity. The latter we find only among simple qualities, e.g., between rose and purple (as opposed to green). This similarity, however, is not presupposed when one grasps the redness in both colors, or when one dissociates them in terms of their tones, brightness, and saturation—which, by the way, one cannot do with pure qualia except when one grasps them at least as fulfillments of previously seen area units. But even when there are such "respects," and when a comparing "with respect to" *can* precede the comprehension of similarity (which is not necessary in all comprehensions of similarity), being-similar, i.e., the state of affairs that *A* and *B* are similar, is frequently given to us; and it is *this* givenness that *determines* the consideration of the "respect" in which similarity occurs. Finally, similarity is by essence "similarity of something, an *X*, and something else, a *Y*," and no similarity can be *given* unless its relation to two bearers is cogiven. It would, however, be a mistake to assume that X and Y must be given in some way other than "only meant" for their similarity to be comprehended, or that *both* must be self-given or given in some positive degree of adequation. On the contrary, that a plainly given Y is similar to an X can be given even when this X is merely meant and nothing more, that is, when the intuited similarity between Y and X consequently determines the content of X. This fact is of the utmost importance for the theory of similarity. Not only is it necessary to distinguish strictly between the intuited *essence* of similarity and its *concept;* it is also necessary to admit differences among intuited similarities *themselves*—i.e., not on the basis of differences between the bearers of similarity. The differences among intuited similarities are, objectively and in their givenness, independent of differences between their pairs of bearers. The *similarities* between purple and rose and between purple and orange or rose and orange are in themselves *qualitatively different* intuitional similarities (even though both relations fall under the same concept of similarity). These similarities can be given as different similarities even when only one of the two terms is given. And, finally, the similarity of A to B and the similarity of B to A are intuitively different cases of similarity of the same quality, though the a priori proposition holds: that is, if A is similar to B, B is similar to A.

As far as the *givenness* of similarity is concerned, it has a peculiar essential relationship to immediate remembering. We find hints of this in certain expressions: we say, for instance, that this or that thing "reminds us" of this or that other thing, or that we do not know what this reminds us of. These are linguistic forms that express a phenomenon which is undoubtedly quite different from that which lies behind "I remember on this occasion," etc. The comprehension of similarity is constitutively tied up with an act of immediate remembering. Similarity is given when identical sensual contents [82] of two perceiving acts, A and B, are connected with two different contents of immediate remembering, β and γ, within the total content of an intuitive act surrounding the perceiving acts. We then say that the two perceived objects are similar to each other. Thus that which gives the objects as *"similar"* when they are meant in two total acts (and meant as the same in both perception and remem-

82. [I.e., when identical sensual contents, a . . . , are connected with two different contents of remembering, β and γ.—*Ed.*]

brance) is the difference between the content of immediate remembering and the identical sensual content of perception, or,
as we may add, the difference between the content of immediate
expecting and the identical sensual content of perception. If, on
the other hand, there are identical contents of immediate remembering and expecting plus identical contents of sensual perception in two total acts, "*sameness*" is given.

It clearly follows from the above that to reduce similarity to
the *identity of simple parts* (or the differences between other
simple parts) of an object, as the old rationalism does, can *never*
be correct. For the object or any part thereof is given only in a
total act that already contains perception, immediate remembering, and expecting. This is true even for the content of a completely simple point in space or time and also for any indivisible
phase of a process, motion, change, etc.[83] And it is no less evident
that the givenness of similarity presupposes nothing like comparison, and that it can be given prior to and independent of the
content of its bearers. The fact that there is comparability in the
world presupposes the *similarity* of objects. It is also clear from
the above that similarity is not a so-called category which can
be impressed upon contents at random or, if not at random, on
the basis of (factually wholly transcendent) signs of the given
which declare the applicability of this category; that the concept
of similarity differs intuitively from its intuitive essence, and
that similarities differ intuitively from each other without these
differences consisting merely in the differences and inequalities
of their bearers; and that the choice of a "respect" with regard
to which objects are similar only pertains to these different intuitive similarities (in the mediate establishment of similarity)
but in no way *constitutes* similarity. All of these rationalistic
prejudices are based on the confusion of immediate similarity
with mediate similarity, or on the confusion of the similarity
whose establishment presupposes mediate remembrance with
the similarity whose establishment presupposes immediate remembering alone.

83. For this reason the "rest" of a point differs completely from the
mere continuous being of a point in time, and so also "motion" differs
completely from "continuous change of place." A point in motion, or, in
other words, something moved, is "in motion" at *any* indivisible point of
its path. On the other hand, an object which continuously changes its
place and is given in this process as the same object can in principle be in
a state of rest at any point. This phenomenon can, as we know, be produced in a series of continuously succeeding processes of the disappearance and origin of the same object (i.e., without motion).

It becomes equally clear that *sameness* and *identity cannot* be "reduced" to similarity—as if sameness were only the maximal limit of similarity, and identity "reducible" to the indistinguishability of what is the same. There is an essential difference between similarity and sameness, and not merely a quantitative or relative one. Whether it is sameness or only similarity that appears in a given case depends on the thousands of ways in which we are able to make distinctions, ranging from the difference-thresholds of sensation to the higher and most subtle abilities to make distinctions. For this reason the difference between sameness and similarity remains an absolute one grounded in their essences! The same is true of the difference between identity and sameness. Of course, we often *identify* objects that are, in fact, only "the same." There are many well-known deceptions in the sphere of the immediate intuition of identity and the immediate intuition of sameness. But all this pertains solely to the application and not to the essence. The fact that "sameness" presupposes the identity of the terms of the relation with themselves as well as their differences, and that similarity, in turn, presupposes precisely this and inequality as well, are evidential propositions that cannot be called into question by any investigation of our human ability to make distinctions. These propositions also apply to, among other things, the "making of differences" itself.

The errors of empiricism concerning the question of the givenness of what is similar, etc., correspond to its logical errors. It is impossible to hold that a statement like "I now remember the tone C that I perceived" (say, five seconds ago) is inadequate, strictly speaking, to the immediate fact because only two different and temporally distinguished similar *experiences* are involved (the experience of perception and the experience of remembrance). It is also impossible to hold that any perception of an object lasting longer than one indivisible moment would be indistinguishably similar to the perception of the following moment, and that they would therefore be taken as "identical" (= indistinguishable similarity). It is impossible to maintain that the previously assumed "identity" of the members of a series would be obliterated only if, in a series of indistinguishable and temporally adjacent perceptions, two other terms of the series more remote from each other were to become distinguishable. Finally, it is impossible to hold that this contradiction (or contrariness) between the assumptions of identity and difference concerning the terms of the series would lead to the division between perception as "act" and the perceived as "object"—as if the "acts" were merely similar and temporally differentiated in the sense of "succession," and as if the "objects" were taken as identical and continuously "enduring." All of this would supposedly lead to the assumption of an existing substance that is separated from and independent of all experiences.[84]

First, it is erroneous to treat psychic experiences (e.g., experiences of both perception and remembrance, or two immediately successive perceptual experiences), which are taken as the point of departure, as thinglike (or processlike) objects exactly like the objects and thing-unities that they are to explain genetically; and it is erroneous to treat the problem of the *inner* perception of experiences and their "observation," as well as the possibility of statements about them, etc., as if it were in *no* way different from the problem of the object of outer nature. Second, this theory would proceed from the similarity of experiences that take place at different times, but would do so without showing even the possibility of the consciousness *of* this similarity. The task, however, is to show how one can arrive at the assumption of two different perceptual *experiences* from the consciousness of the immediate identity of an object perceived now and in the moment that immediately follows (whereby these experiences possess the same content under otherwise identical circumstances), and how the intentions of perception and remembrance directed immediately to the "same" tone (at the same point in time) can be broken up into two, merely "similar," "psychic" experiences. It is now clear that every psychic "*experience*" is "given" only within a total act of perception, immediate remembering, and immediate expecting. "Same" experiences are those which reveal the *same content* of two total acts in *one* act of inner intuition encompassing the two total acts, but which do so in the immediate consciousness of the difference of their content from the content of the encompassing act. "Similar" experiences are those which, given the identity of only the perceptual content, result in different *total contents*, that is, "*immediately different*" contents, for the contents of the two total acts. Between perception and immediate remembering, therefore, there is *no* need for *mediation* through *similarity*. There is no need for a "principle of association by similarity" to explain the fact that something is given to us as "the same," something

---

84. E.g., the well-known schema according to which Hume "explained" the "belief in identical objects separated from consciousness." See *A Treatise of Human Nature*, pt. I.

that we sensibly perceive and immediately remember. This is required no more than some "reproduction." The immediate *similarity* of objects, i.e., of the reproducing perceived object and the one remembered that was previously perceived, is a constitutive condition for the occurrence of a mediate remembering act—i.e., for mediate remembrance (and expectation) and a mediate identification through it, be it a matter of two observations of stars or two contents of the inner perception of the same psychic experience, etc.

Thus we come to the following propositions: The occurrence of *"reproduction,"* which according to proposition 2 [85] belongs essentially to the mediate remembrance and expectation of any embodied being, is tied to the *similarity of previously perceived objects of remembrance and expectation* with the object of perception that reproduces such objects. This proposition is not based on the nature of the psychic in general, nor is it an inductive proposition of empirical psychology. It is, rather, an *axiom* for empirical psychology that can be neither verified nor denied through observation. Still, it is a proposition that can be understood in phenomenology by way of the essential nexus between an ego and a *lived body*. And to this extent this proposition is evidential, non-formal, and a priori; but nevertheless it is true only for objects that are *given as relative* [daseinsrelativ] to a possible *lived body*. There would be nothing like "similarity" for a disembodied spirit; for such a thing there would be only identity and difference. Its *intuition* of the inner and outer worlds would *not* be split into perception, remembrance, and expectation, nor would its content be divided into the elongations of present, past, and future. But the fact of similarity and immediate remembering, which belongs to its comprehension, is not relative to any empirical facts of bodily organizations, for example, that of man. And the principle of similarity of reproduction is also an a priori principle for all possible experiences of man (in the sense of observation and induction). It is a principle of *both* inner and outer intuition.

If we formulate this more precisely, we can also say that the *principle of "association by similarity"* is the principle according to which an intuiting and cognizing being in general, one that comprehends objects through an outer and inner sense of a possible lived body, selects these objects and their contents. In

85. [The proposition concerning reproduction (p. 440).—*Ed.*]

this sense one can also call this principle the *form* of this being's (inductive) experience.

The principle of similarity is also the presuppositional *foundation* of all possible *association by contiguity;* indeed, it is the foundation for the formation of the intuition of manifolds in which such "contiguity" is possible, and it is the foundation of these manifolds themselves (as the principle of the fact that there are similar things and, therefore, things that can be associated in the world). One therefore cannot derive this principle from a presupposed fact of space and time or from the principle of contiguity.[86] For any such derivation presupposes the proposition that we rejected, namely, that similarity is the partial identity and difference of simple parts of the similar.

Furthermore, the principle of the similarity between objects of cognition, as well as between the formations of possible representations of them, is also a condition of the assumption of the so-called *lawfulness of the causal nexus of nature.* It is not a possible consequence of this assumption, as Kant, for example, believed he could show. By "lawfulness of the causal nexus of nature," we mean, as is customary, the following: In time there are recurring events and changes of identical content; these are causes and effects in the sense that a Y as effect is always conjoined with an X as cause in the immediate temporal sequence. And there are things of identical content which can occupy different places in space and which are related to each other as cause and effect in such a way that a thing X can have an effect on a thing Y only when they are spatially contiguous.[87] In contrast to this, the truth and validity of the so-called *principle of causality* is totally independent of the principle of similarity; according to this principle of causality, all becoming real is the effect of a cause, and all *variation* (here this word means the "being-different" of something vis-à-vis something else and also "becoming different") of an object is evidentially conjoined with a variation of another object in mutual dependency. This latter proposition does not imply any division between the real and the ideal, nor does it presuppose space and time. But *both* of these,

86. [See below, pp. 460 ff.—*Ed.*]

87. Max Planck has recently drawn attention to the nexus between the condition of temporal succession and contiguity on the one hand and the condition of spatial contiguity on the other (and the elimination of the idea of attraction as a basic concept of science with respect to the idea of thrust). See the end of his *Das Prinzip der Erhaltung der Energie* (Leipzig: Teubner, 1887).

the causal principle and the "principle of the mutual dependence of all variations of possible objects," are strict *presuppositions* of the principle of the *lawfulness of the causal nexus of nature,* which only represents a special application of them. But without the help of the *principle of similarity* it cannot be derived from them. Whereas the causal principle obtains for real objects in general, and whereas the "principle of dependency" (as we prefer to call it) obtains for all objects in general and is therefore a *pure* logical principle, the principle of the *lawfulness of the causal nexus of nature* obtains only for objects that are *relative* to a possible *lived body,* its apriority for all possible inductive experience notwithstanding.[88]

Finally, the "law of the causal nexus of nature" has two methodological subdivisions, for which the same phenomenological basis in the extensionality of the lived-body manifold is to be shown: (1) the principles of the mechanical theory of nature— all changes of extrabodily natural things are to be regarded as dependencies of a combination of constant space-occupations that touch each other; (2) the principle of association by contiguity—all changes of the ego are to be considered as dependencies of association by contiguity, and all psychic complexes are to be regarded as simultaneous modifications of a possible lived body, which are, depending on the case involved, sensations, drive-stimuli, etc.

Let us first restrict ourselves to mediate remembrance (and expectation), reproduction, and similarity. Here the following questions are posed: *What* must be similar so that a perception may lead to reproduction? Is this similarity "given," and, if so, how? What can in principle "explain" this similarity? Is there an association by similarity which is as original as association by contiguity and which "explains" certain occurrences of mediate contents of remembrance and expectation? Or does this association by similarity depend on association by contiguity? What is the actual relationship between association by similarity and association by contiguity? Is association by similarity a presup-

88. Thus the principle of the lawfulness of the causal nexus loses all validity in *biology,* in contrast to the principles of causality and dependency of variations. In biology there obtains a totally *autonomous* principle of causality within the framework of the principles of causality and dependency, which I intend to discuss in another study. I also will show in my forthcoming "Phänomenologie und Erkenntnistheorie" (Bibliog. no. 29) how the reality of objects subject to mechanical explanation is relative to a lived body. [See "Massstäbe der Erkenntnis," *ibid.,* sec. 4, and *ibid.,* sec. 5.—*Ed.*]

position or a consequence of the general vital phenomena of practice and habit? Is there a conceivable "correlate" of association by similarity in the body and its parts (e.g., in the brain)? Finally, does association by similarity play a constitutive role in the *mode* of forming the natural view of the world concerning the ego and the world of bodies, or does it have these givens as its presupposition?

As to the first of these questions, there is, it appears to me, only one sensible and clear answer. In order for a perception to lead to the reproduction of a mediate remembrance or the mediate remembering of a certain object, the *object* of *this* perception (as this object is meant in this perception) must be *similar* to the *object* of a previous perception that "belongs" to this remembrance and whose occurrence in the order of time is the presupposition of this remembrance. (The same holds analogously for perception and the reproduction of a mediate expectation.) It is therefore solely the *objects* meant in those acts which have to be similar, not the "acts" or their "contents." To say that "similar representations" enter into the association is basically wrong. True, I can have a mediate recollection "of" representation, fantasies, dreams, etc. (so-called recollections of representations). In this fashion I can also remember representations of recollections that I experienced previously. In this case they are the *objects* of an earlier inner perception and immediate re membrance and are "similar" to the objects of a present inner perception and are mediately remembered. The "similarity" that is the condition of reproduction is therefore exclusively a *similarity between objects*. It is out of the question to maintain that these similar objects must be given, known, represented, etc., as similar objects within specific contents in order to condition reproduction, or that the characteristics and properties by virtue of which they are similar must be given generally or, furthermore, given as those which provide the basis for similarity. For reproductively *effective* similarity evidentially precludes an intuition of its bearers, as well as the basis of similarity in their characteristics and properties. If, for instance, reproduction is to bring about, in mediate remembrance, an object (e.g., a lion) that is similar to another perceived object (e.g., a tiger), how could this object (the lion) have been given before so that *by this means* alone the similarity of the objects could be *experienced? In this case there would be no need for reproduction.* One would have to reduce *all* so-called association by similarity to experiences of similarity previously experienced wherein the same objects were simultaneously given, and this is an entirely unsatisfactory solution to the problem. Of course, if reproduction has become effective "on the basis of" the similarity of the objects, the similarity between the remembered object and the perceived one can also be known from their *contents* (as bases for similarity). But this, too, *need* not be so. Whenever similarity is *not* known, true association by similarity leads not to a judgment of similarity but to a judgment of equality, indeed, in certain cases to a judgment of identity. Things that are merely similar, e.g., a bird and a butterfly, appear to a child as "equal," and the child says of the butterfly, "This is a bird," instead of, "This is like a bird." And, if reproduction does lead to a judgment of similarity, this is not to say that the properties and characteristics of the object according to which the object is similar to the one now perceived (or represented) must have been given in the perception to which remembrance goes back and to which it "belongs." It is, rather, very much the rule that properties and traits of the formerly perceived object first "appear" in the object of mediate remembrance *because* they are the basis of the similarity with the object now perceived. These are characteristics that did not previously appear in the contents of perception. In remembering, not only can we "pay attention to," "notice," "observe," etc., properties of something perceived—that is, properties that were not noticed or paid attention to when we perceived the object (also, of course, when we loved, hated, desired, or detested it)—and not only can we find similarity, equality, etc. (e.g., in two faces), which were not contained in perception; we can also have contents which never entered into the previous perceptual content, but which all the same belong to the "possible perception" of this thing, on the basis of the similarity between the object now perceived and the part of the content of the earlier perception on "whose basis" the object now perceived is "similar" to the previously perceived one. It is only *by virtue of* the similarity with the object now perceived that through remembering we can gain knowledge of properties and qualities that we did not perceive earlier. And it is *here* that an earlier judgment of equality or identity is replaced by one of similarity (or equality). Thus, for example, I grasp (in inner intuition) a feeling-state through recollective refeeling and (in outer intuition) a landscape through recollective seeing *ever more richly* by virtue of their similarity to a present feeling and a landscape now perceived (and similarly by virtue of their similarity to immediately remembered contents), and I feel more of the state and see more of the object than was given to me at some time before. The opinion that these are subsequent false additions is merely a consequence of the sensualistic prejudice that remembrance must always be poorer than the perception that essentially belongs to it and that reproduction is "nothing more than a mysterious" iteration of an old perception with its content "weakened"—not to mention other ridiculous mysticisms of vulgar psychology. In fact, remembering the same thing that we perceived represents an *advance* into the *entire* intuitive fullness of the object which is intuited as identical in the acts of perception *and* remembering, and which is identically meant in its content. Thus the intuition of this object is necessarily divided into remembering and perceiving only for an *embodied* being. It is certain, of course, that no new *thing* or new real thing-part that was not given in perception ever comes to intuition in remembering. A sparrow sitting on a roof which I did not see when I perceived the roof will not be seen in remembrance. It is also true that there are no objective properties or qualities of a thing (or an event) which I could remember just because these properties or qualities in a perceived thing make the first thing similar to the one perceived. Rather, they must have been encompassed by the content of the total act, with its total *intention*, in which the perceived thing is constituted (thus also by immediate remembering and expecting). This, however, does not prevent their obtaining in later recollection an intuited fullness surpassing their *merely* "having been meant."

Is it the case that similarity must somehow be *"given,"* or is that which we call association by similarity a pure hypothesis, without any experienced basis? Is there a phenomenal basis in *immediate experiencing* for the concept of association by similarity itself? If there were no such basis, that is, if it had been established through observation alone that series of representations follow each other and that they or their objects are "similar" to one another—just as one can order a series of associations of a test subject according to all points of view, e.g., cause-effect, means-end, part-whole, etc.—one would have to ask why similarity was made a strict condition of reproduction (instead of a mere member in the systems of the types of factual sequences of representations and conations, etc.). Is not similarity, according to the views of all psychologists, *more* than a possible point of view for the classification of series of representations? If, however, it is a strict condition of possible reproductions, we must ask how it is possible to establish this proposition by observation, and whether it makes any sense at all to establish something like this through observation. During his research, the psychologist is subject (although he easily forgets this) to all the propositions, laws, etc., which he establishes concerning psychic processes and which, he asserts, enter into such research. Psychology dare not assert anything which (if it were true) would make the discovery of this truth appear evidentially impossible or contradictory. But how can the psychologist establish through self-observation that a condition of the reproduction of a certain (mediate) recollected content is the similarity between the recollected object and a perceived object? Apart from "conditions," how does he know anything about this similarity? He does know about his perceived object and what he perceives in it. He also knows about the object of his recollection. But how does he know about a previously perceived object or a previous perception of this object? By recollection? But the content of this object is supposed to be explained by the reproduction of the previous perceptual content! And this phenomenon is a *part* of the *declarandum*. He asserts that its content is "similar" to an object of an earlier perception. But in this case is not his *own* recollection, which alone can lead him to this object, conditioned by "reproduction through similarity"? In other words, he should say, "I know only that the object of the present recollection is similar to a perceptual object of which I know only that it is similar to the recollected object!" He would go around in circles, or else he would admit that the similarity is essentially unascertainable! At this point we must note what we said before about immediate similarity, that the being-similar of one perceptual object to another perceived earlier is in fact "*given*" as an experienced fact. And it is *this* that is a condition of the fact that the object of earlier perception becomes the object of a mediate recollection. Hence an *immediate experience* forms the basis of association by similarity.

But what (in principle) can this similarity as a condition of reproduction "*explain*"? First, it can *never* explain the *content* of mediate recollection. Second, it cannot explain the act of *remembering* this content. Recollection is directed toward the object of an earlier perception, and not toward the perception of this object, despite the essential interconnection between every mediate recollection and a perception "belonging" to it, one that precedes it in the order of time (this interconnection leads to the assumption of the concept of "reproduction").[89] The content of recollection does not "stem" from the content of this perception, but only from the content of the object *itself*. This also obtains, of course, when I remember a psychic experience that is the "object" (of an inner perception). I always look, in remembering, at this object. This perception was hardly a "picture" of the object, a picture that could eventually come back again. Nor is there any foundation for the assumption of a "disposition" (whether psychic or physiological) which was left by perception and which now must be "stimulated." For this perception is completely annihilated. Nothing of it remains, i.e., nothing "somewhere" in a so-called soul or in the "brain"! If, then, neither the content of recollection *nor* the remembering of the content can be "explained" through similarity, only one possibility remains as the sole factual *declarandum:* what similarity *can* explain, and what it does explain, is the arrangement of what lies within the sphere of the above-mentioned immediate recollection in the context of my life in the fortuitous present. In other words, one can explain the fact that the object concerned is factually remembered just *now* and not at another time; that is, one can explain the *relation* of the recollected world of a person to his given *"present,"* or, as we can also put it, to his *body-givenness.* This relation is subject to regulation by the principle of reproduction through similarity in that the *similarity* between both perceptual objects (now and earlier perceived) is a *conditio sine qua non* for the arrangement of what can generally be remembered in the nexus of life "given" as present. If such a similarity has become reproductively effective (i.e., a specific *qualified similarity*, a qualification that it has independent of the properties of its bearers) one may—indeed, one must—assume a disposition for the *iteration* of the association (taken here as a process) that has already taken place. It goes without saying that such an "associative disposition" has nothing to do with that wrongheaded theory which would explain association *itself* through mysterious dispositions of perceptions and representations, and thus would conceive its "possibility." We can also state

---

89. Of course, *mediate* remembrance (in contrast to immediate remembrance) contains a consciousness of the "already having experienced" by essential necessity. But this is not the object of the remembrance, nor is it a part of the content. It is only when a "recognizing again" comes into play that the object as the same object is given as an "already experienced one." Here identity as sameness is a part of the *content*. But the *consciousness of already having experienced* that accompanies the remembrance is a component of the act-quality of remembering.

what similarity can explain in another, equivalent form: of all the factual and mediate contents of recollection which an individual has at moments of a specific present, similarity can explain why this individual factually remembers *this* and not *that* object among all the objects which he perceived and experienced and which are reproducible in recollection. Thus similarity explains *selection* through mediate recollection within the scope of immediate remembering.

Here we must make one *additional comment: by itself,* the principle of similarity *never* explains a concrete happening, precisely because this principle rests on an evidential interconnection of essence and is a true *"principle,"* not an inductive rule stemming from observation. It is a principle of a present becoming conscious of past experiences. It is not a rule derived from that of which I am at present conscious. Mediate recollection *operates in conformity to and according to* it. It is a principle of the manner in which mediate recollection is formed. It is therefore only a *statement* of *one* necessary but nevertheless nonsufficient condition of what is factually remembered. It is only a *conditio sine qua non,* a wholly general condition without which the placement of a previously experienced object into the present nexus of life would not be possible. This clearly follows from the fact that *similarities* between perceived objects, including objects of present inner experience of psychic recollections, and what has previously been perceived and experienced are *different* from each other both *qualitatively* and *in degree* and are numerically *incommensurable.* In order to explain what is *factually* remembered from the sphere which posits this *conditio sine qua non* of similarity as a condition of reproduction, it is necessary to consider *all* qualities and directions of acts occurring in the recollections of an individual, his act-directions of love and hate and taking-interest-in, and, finally, all types of mental, sensory-functional, active, and instinctive attention (which we will not distinguish in detail), all of which penetrate the distinctions among perceiving, remembering, and expecting. But we will not pursue this point further.

The "principle of similarity" is not only a "condition of reproduction" in mediate recollection but also an equally original condition of the *determination* of mediate expectation. Whatever is given in immediate expecting—of course, as future—does not require determination, just as the content of immediate remembering does not require reproduction. Determination in general, however, is a concept going back to the immediately experienced and its interconnective nexus, which is as *original* as reproduction.

It would therefore be completely wrong to reduce the determining and experienced "power" of a given of immediate expectation, that is, the power directed to *present* emerging representations, drive-impulses, acts of the will, etc., or the power that a prefelt *value* of a project of willing has for my present actions—one of the cases of an immediate and feeling expecting of something—to a previous reproduction. Rather, a perception of the same object "belongs" to each expectation, and to "mediate" expectation there belongs the perception that follows an immediate expectation of the same object in the order of time. No recollection or reproduction of this perception or its object belongs to this perception. If, for instance, I am in a bad mood early in the morning and find myself unable to do certain things because I must give a lecture on formal logic at six o'clock in the afternoon (an example from William James), the object of the immediately expected lecture determines my present emotional state. It is not the recollection of a previous lecture which determines this mood,[90] nor is it the representation of the content of my having to give this lecture. There is just this immediate expecting, quite independent of the expected content being represented or judged "as" such. Immediate expecting also exists *without* such act-qualities. It does not matter whether this state of affairs agrees with genetic theories that were formulated beforehand. For "theories" must conform to facts. The essential nexus only implies that a perception of the same object "belongs" to immediate expecting. And in our case this is the perception or the actual experience of the six-o'clock lecture which was given earlier. All "determinations" of "tasks" posited from outside, and all determinations of one's own "deliberate intentions" and orders and promises, etc., independent of the recollection, reproduction, and representation of the occurrence of their positings, are in principle of the *same* type: there is no reproduction that pushes itself between them and their effects! My past as immediately remembered continues to have immediate effects in the present nexus of my life, and so also my "future" as an immediately expected content. I am happy, for instance, when the future before me is "open" and "bright," and I am unhappy when it is "narrow" and "dark." In this case it is

---

90. See my treatise "Die Psychologie der sogenannten Rentenhysterie" (Bibliog. no. 10).

not my present feeling that colors the content of expecting. It is this content that colors my present feeling. There belongs to mediate expecting (in which something expected in the future is also given "as expected") [91] something which previously was immediately expected and which has been realized as an object of perception. And it is the *similarity* between the present object of perception and the object of an earlier perception that conditions the *selection* of the mediately expected within the scope of the immediately expected. This is analogous to the above case of recollection.

Our proposition that reproduction and determination (in the above sense) are evidentially conditioned by the *similarity* between objects of perception and those of mediate recollection (and expectation) would appear to be rendered invalid or questionable by those theories which assert that association by similarity is to be reduced to so-called *association by contiguity*.

The *motive* behind the attempts at such a "reduction" is quite clear; for it is thoroughly unthinkable to assume that association by similarity has a *correlative process in the nervous system and the brain*. It is possible, of course, to assume such processes for the subsequent *repetition* of an association by similarity that has been performed, but not for the establishment of an association by similarity. It is *inconceivable*, irrespective of the extent of our positive knowledge of the nervous system, because it is evidentially impossible for the similarity between two things, which is *not* connected with the basic condition of the natural law of causes, i.e., the contiguity of C and E in space and time, to manifest an efficacy or even to possess a mechanical analogue which is coordinated to it and which manifests this efficacy.[92] For if there *is* an autonomous association by similarity, it represents a negative proof that there cannot be a *mechanical correlate* for recollected contents or for remembering or for the oscillations of contents conditioned by association. And it represents a positive proof that in the immediate experience of similarity—setting aside the lived body—the extant *unity* and the *identical* objective content of what is meant in perception and recollection become, as it were, *phenomenally transparent* in that the similarity of things can still become immediately effec-

91. [See above, p. 441, n. 80.—*Ed.*]
92. This reductive motive is clearly present in H. Ebbinghaus, *Grundzüge der Psychologie* (Leipzig, 1902), and it is described as a "postulate" by H. Münsterberg (whose strong belief in it does not make it any less arbitrary).

tive when these things, or one of these things as a term, are *not* given. The basic motive behind the aforementioned "reduction" is *therefore* the *mechanical and parallelistic prejudice*.

The "reduction" of association by similarity to association by contiguity is erroneous also for the simple reason that it presupposes a faulty concept of similarity. This reduction implies that similarity in general can be reduced to the partial identity and partial difference of the "simplest" parts of similar objects. For it is only with this presupposition in mind that one can say: If the actual perception *P*, whose object *O* has the qualities *a b c d e*, determines the recollection of an object whose earlier perception P_1 possesses an object O_1 with the qualities *a b c g h*, it is *not* necessary for the similarity between *O* and O_1 as a whole to become effective in order for the recollection of O_1 to appear. The *identical* qualities *a b c*, which are in "contact" with *g h* in O_1, suffice for *a b c g h* = O_1 to be remembered without further ado. This is of course the well-known schema of the "reduction" which Lehmann, Ebbinghaus, Münsterberg, and others have explored.[93] And if this reduction is to be realized, it is necessary for the "simple" on whose partial identity and difference the similarity is supposed to rest to be capable of any kind of "contact" in a spatiotemporal manifold. But not only are these presuppositions unfounded; they are essentially impossible. For "similarity" is not exclusively a relational phenomenon between mere "complexes." It can also exist, or not exist, between strictly *simple* parts of any complex. And although there are degrees of increase within similarity, i.e., within the relation among objects in which the essence of similarity (which is, like any other essence, absolute in character) can be found—in other words, although there can be "more" or "less" similarity—this does not mean that there is merely a quantitative relation between similarity as essence and the fact that the two complexes contain identical and different parts. And the identical elements in the above example are not capable of "contact." For anybody will admit that the identity in the case mentioned is not between the *a b c* of object O_1 and the *a b c* of object *O*, which are different from each other both in time and by their belonging to *O* and O_1 and are at best merely equal. Identity concerns only the *conceptual objects*, "the *a*," "the *b*," and "the *c*," which are, like "the number 3," or "the red," timeless ideal objects, i.e., true "species"

---

93. See Otto Selz, *Über die Gesetze des geordneten Denkablaufs* (Stuttgart, 1913), esp. chap. 2, in which he argues against such attempts.

(in Husserl's sense). It is *eo ipso* senseless to predicate "contiguity" of them in a spatiotemporal manifold. Strangely enough, it is precisely this hypernaturalistic theory which falls victim to the hypostatization of the species that constitutes the very essence of false Platonism! Of course this reduction has also been rejected here and there for the wrong reasons. It has been maintained, for instance, that if I remember Adam and Eve as I look at a tree in a beautiful garden, I must do so on the basis of the similarity of this tree to the tree in paradise, because the "representation" of the latter "must be reproduced first" if Adam and Eve are to be remembered on the basis of "contiguity." For it is only with this tree in paradise, not with the seen tree, that there can be "contiguity" (Höffding). This theory obviously assumes the erroneous concept of reproduction that presupposes a mysterious "iteration" of the representation of an earlier perception or the stimulation of a "disposition" left over from such a perception, which in turn prompts this argumentation. If one sees that there is no such mysterious iteration and that perception does not return and does not leave any "disposition," he can hold that an association by similarity which mediates this contiguity is unnecessary, and that it is precisely the identical in both "trees" that gives rise, through contiguity, to recollection. But such mysterious assumptions (which differ only in degree, not in kind, from belief in ghosts) do not preclude this reduction; what precludes it is the evidential insight that similarity cannot be reduced to the identity and difference of simple parts. Even the mediate recollection of the *most simple* parts of a perceived or represented object requires similarity with the most simple parts of the actually given. If one tries to analyze the total similarity of two complexes, say, of two faces, one finds that what alone can be analyzed are the partial similarities that are immediately given with their terms in the parts or partial objects of the total complex. It is only the partial similarities (which, of course, are *not* similarities of the parts) that lead, through the mediation of the "terms" belonging essentially to them, to the parts whose similarity constitutes the similarity of the total objects. It is necessary to intuit partial similarities in order to grasp similar cases.[94] No imaginable analysis can go from total similarity to

94. As intuitive terms of the establishment of the identity of an object or the differences of objects, both sameness as an immediate phenomenon and "being different from," or, better, non-sameness, precede any such establishment. Only the following essential interconnections are involved here: where there is sameness, there is also an identical object;

sameness and its opposite—still less, to identity and difference of parts. Nevertheless, there is an important essential difference for the relation between contiguity and similarity, namely, the difference between the way in which similarity between objects becomes a condition of mediate recollection and the reproduction belonging to it and the way in which it becomes a condition for the comprehension of thingness in a concrete thing.

Let us note that there is also a similarity among similarities, one that cannot be divided into larger or smaller similarities. Similarities can be intuited independent of similar objects (bearers) and a fortiori independent of any possible indication of the place wherein (i.e., in which parts of the objects) similarity exists, and *different similarities* are thus intuitable. (For example, the three similarities of a face A to a face B, of face A to a face C, and of face B to face C are also intuitable in themselves as different from each other, and not on the basis of the different pairs of objects concerned. Hence we frequently recognize the difference between one face and another on the basis of the different similarities of these faces to a third if we are dubious about whether or not we are dealing with the same man.) The mode of givenness of the phenomenon of similarity among similarities (given what we said earlier) consists in the fact that an object meant as the same [*als selbig*] in both perception and *immediate remembering* possesses the same perceptual content in two *total acts;* and though there are two different rings of immediate contents of recollection and expectation around the perceptual content, the two total acts A and B are nevertheless unified (in immediate recollection of the content of A on the occasion of B). And in the act encompassing the two total acts, we have only one object meant as the same object. Yet, in a complete phenomenological analysis of the four partial acts involved (the first perceptual act and the first immediate act of remembering, the second perceptual act and the second immediate act of remembering), we have four partial objects (and not four parts of an object) of this one object (and *eo ipso* of any of its parts), among which there are and must be similar similarities. If the object presents such different "aspects" in

---

where there is non-sameness, there are also differences of objects; where there is partial similarity, there are also similar parts. Moreover, in all similarity, terms by virtue of which objects are similar are given. In all differences of similarities, different terms are given. All terms belong to objects. But it would be basically wrong to maintain that, e.g., different similarities also imply differently similar pairs of objects.

both total acts, these are to be analyzed as two different immediate phenomena of similarity. And it is this case alone that may be called "*assimilation*," in contrast to *association*, in the strict sense of the term. The essence of assimilation is therefore such that when it occurs, only *one* object is intentionally given— not two, as in the case of mediate recollection and expectation. Hence assimilation cannot be reduced to an association of elements. And it stands to reason that assimilation presupposes the thinghood whose comprehension is, as we saw, constituted in perception, immediate remembering, and expecting, and thus in *each* of the two total acts.[95] Assimilation cannot be reduced to an association by similarity of simple elements or parts, or to an association by contiguity of these parts. For what is assimilated through similarity are "partial similarities," *not* similar parts.

What are the constitutive conditions of the possibility of "association by contiguity"? But first, what is "*association by contiguity*"? According to this principle, what is experienced "*together*" in objects has the tendency, when one of these objects is given, to provoke the recollection of the other objects. But what does this "*together*" mean? Is it synonymous with "simultaneity" or "immediate succession"? Is it a condition of experiencing objects or of experienced objects? Should "temporal" contiguity have priority over spatial contiguity? Is this proposition an empirical rule, or is it an evidential principle? What is its relation to the principle of similarity?

"Simultaneity" and "immediate succession" have no meaning for us when they are applied to the givens of *inner intuition;* in those givens we find neither objective time nor objective space, indeed, no simple extensionality in general (with its qualities of being-side-by-side and being-sequential). We find simple extensionality only *in* the givenness of the "lived body" as the "now-here." What is "together" "in consciousness" is, in the first place, that and only that which is experienced together, i.e.,

---

95. Thus the form of being of a thing cannot be reduced to association (as Hume would have it), to a nexus of expectations or "possibilities of perception," to a "law of appearances," etc; nor can this form of being be reduced to assimilations of antecedent perceptual contents, or their reproductions reduced to given contents. Rather, the phenomenal sameness of the thing, whose sensual contents of perception supposedly assimilate antecedent sense-contents, is the condition for speaking meaningfully about assimilation. See the recent work by W. Specht, "Zur Phänomenologie und Morphologie der pathologischen Wahrnehmungstäuschungen," *Zeitschrift für Pathopsychologie*, II, no. 4, 516.

that which is given in *one* act, or one unitary act, of inner intuition. This can be anything: something simultaneous or something not simultaneous, something perceived now or something perceived ten years ago. In *outer intuition* there is always a manifold of extensionality, but according to its essence it is not tied to the now-here of the lived body; and in such an act (of outer intuition) what is "together" is everything thought or represented in this manifold, and not merely what is simultaneous or spatiotemporally contiguous. It is only through the positing of a lived body, to which a now-here belongs *essentially*, as well as the being-side-by-side of its parts and the sequential character of its sensations in the entirety of its extensionality, that it makes any sense to say that something is simultaneous or in immediate succession or spatially contiguous; and we say that something given as "being contiguous in a manifold of extensionality" is also given to "consciousness-of" because all these cases are contained as special cases in the latter. Everything that is thus given (as a part of what is given to consciousness in general) is what is experienced as immediately effective on a lived body and as coordinated to its now-here. Here there is not yet any *separation of space and time* or even spatiality and temporality. Thus there is no separation of spatial and temporal contiguity.[96] The separation of spatiality and temporality is given only through the different orientations of two elements of extrabodily, physical phenomena insofar as these elements are spatially reversible and temporally irreversible with respect to the givenness of the body's now-here. This separation is, of course, also presupposed for the body-thing itself.[97] Therefore

96. It is erroneous to hold that the spatial manifold is based on the temporal manifold. Berkeley tried to show this in his theory of the acquisition of the intuition of space; and Leibniz tried to establish this in a metaphysical way. Berkeley asserted that the reversibility of a sequence of impressions yields a line; Leibniz (in a metaphysical way) obtains "extension" through "quelque chose, qui s'étand." Kant shares this error, for he asserts that the manifold is "first" given in time as the manifold of the "inner sense," implying that the points of a line are first temporal sequences of the acts that grasp them. But it is no less erroneous to hold that temporal succession is based on the spatial manifold. We find this error in the theories of Descartes and Spinoza. And H. Bergson recently tried to show this, for he declares that space is the *only* homogeneous milieu, and he says that he can understand time, which, in contrast to his *durée*, contains extensionality of parts, only on the basis of given space.

97. This pertains also to the division of the phenomenon of motion and the phenomenon of change on the basis of the "phenomenon of oscillation" [*Wechselphänomen*], which is the phenomenon on which both motion and change are based.

the "contiguity" involved in association by contiguity may *not* be defined in terms of either spatial or temporal contiguity. Nor may it be defined in terms of "simultaneity"; for this concept presupposes space and time as separate, and designates only the relation of points in space and time. Simultaneity therefore can never serve as a foundation for the idea of spatiality, as if space were "a mode of the simultaneous" (Leibniz). What is essential to this contiguity is that it be in a *pure* extensionality whose contiguous elements assume the character of points in either space *or* time (as variable determinations), and whose "contiguities" can acquire the variable determinations of successiveness or being-side-by-side without possessing them *originaliter*. The consciousness of spatiality and temporality in the givens of outer intuition in general, as well as the consciousness of the differences between them, *presupposes* the principle of association by contiguity. Association by contiguity does not follow from the assumption that the lived body is like any other body in space and time (and with the same mode of givenness as the latter), and that other bodies have effects on it, producing spatial contiguity among the stimuli that touch it and temporal contiguity among the stimulative processes that are in its inner processes. If one connects all facts of consciousness *originaliter* with such stimuli and their effects in the body (be it in the sense of causality or parallelism), the principle of association by contiguity is reduced to an arbitrary *definition* that can be neither true nor false.[98] The consciousness of spatiality and temporality is therefore essentially interconnected with lived-bodiliness and its "now-here." It is in no way a content of a "pure transcendental consciousness." This difficulty does not exist for God. Naturally, the consciousness of this difficulty remains absolutely inexplicable for all positive science, for the physiology and psychology of the senses. For this givenness with its essential interconnections (and thus every possible science of spatiality, i.e., all of geometry) *precedes* the diversity of sense-functions and their possible contents and a fortiori the contingent sense organs and their functional laws, which as organs they presuppose. The lived body itself, however, is not "in" space and time as inanimate bodies essentially are. The lived body is, rather, the *center of reference* of space and time and all causality of contiguity in them (which coincides in extension with the essence of formal

---

98. As is the case in Münsterberg's psychology. His "establishments" are plainly factors outside the domain of the true and the false.

mechanical causality). Yet the lived body is not merely extensive; it is in the *same* manifold of extensionality as extrabodily physical phenomena and is subject to the many laws and principles which are valid for material manifolds of that kind. But we will not discuss these further at this time.[99]

Hence the *consciousness of* a "succession" in our experiences (as well as a "being-side-by-side") is *presupposed* by the concepts of temporal sequence (and spatial line), because the grasping of these objects is constituted in this consciousness. Therefore one cannot derive the consciousness of a succession from such a temporal sequence of conscious experiences, as empirical psychology must presuppose. Nevertheless this peculiar "consciousness-of" is subject to phenomenological explication, which follows from what we said earlier. The phenomenon of the succession of experiences occurs when in the same total act of inner consciousness we see the "same" object that is given in perception, immediate remembering, and immediate expecting *turn* from a perceived object into an immediately remembered one, or from one immediately expected into one perceived, with the consciousness of sameness remaining throughout. Thus we see a perceptual content "go by" and its immediately recollected content "come about" without any change in the object, but, on the contrary, with the evidential sameness of the object. In this manner its perceptual content "becomes" a content of immediate remembering in any indivisible phase that we may choose from its perception (which has a certain objective duration), therefore, in any momentary point of objective time. Hence this "succession" would be given even if *nothing* outside us or in our lived body changed. It is the basis for any grasping of change.

Thus it becomes clear that in *every* unified conscious act, i.e., not first in a plurality of such acts, there is cogiven the evidential insight that what is given in this act is part of a *stream*

99. See the chapters on the foundation of a phenomenology of biology in my forthcoming book on phenomenology and epistemology. Here it is necessary to include, from a formal point of view, the disciplines of set theory and the theory of functions and, from the point of view of content, certain principles of a philosophically well founded physics based on the theory of relativity in which only "world-points" and "world-lines"—in Minkowsky's sense—are presupposed; and, in addition to these, irreducible, pure biological principles that obtain for all life independent of the earthly life that we know because they are founded in the phenomenon of life itself. [Among the author's papers no manuscripts were found for the planned section of this frequently cited work (Bibliog. no. 29). An extensive older manuscript on the philosophical foundations of biology (1909) contains parts of a phenomenology of living things.—*Ed.*]

that flows in one direction, a stream that does not terminate in the direction of recollection or expectation, and in whose "succession" every special content of inner intuition is constituted. The *phenomenon of streaming*—itself the presupposition for the secondary arrangements of experiences as processes in objective time, to which our body-thing, along with other bodies, belongs—must therefore not be reduced to any kind of "synthesis" or even to an association of contents of particular acts of consciousness. Rather, this phenomenon is evidentially *co-given* in *every* possible content. In every experience that I know to be my own, it is evidentially given that every one of my experiences belongs to this indivisible stream. This does not follow from inductive investigations of this stream-content. Thus it is not because this experience is contained in this stream, whose components represent a real or non-real nexus, that this is the experience of a specific ego; rather, because it is an experience of this specific ego, it *must* belong to such a stream.

But the acts in which the experience is experienced [*er-lebt*] belong in no way to the content of the stream. Only the experienced life, and not the experiencing of this life, is "in this stream." This stream as a form of this experiencing of the experience of the ego belongs in essence to the *lived body,* not to the ego itself.[100]

"Association by similarity" and "association by contiguity" are therefore essentially dependent on the fact that a *lived body* stands in a nexus with the ego-individual. What is presented to us as an "association," as a connection between unities which were thought of earlier as separate, phenomenologically is, in principle, only a continuous *reinstitution* of the *original unity* of the *ego* and the pure *"interwovenness"* of its experiences, a reinstitution of that unity in this interwovenness which, to use an image, has been split and broken by the diverse significations that egological experiences have had for the presence of the lived body in question. And therefore neither principle is a rule that can be established through observation of experiences and induction; both are conditions for the observation of what is psychically experienced and for an inductive experience of it.

100. The acts of the ego as non-temporal acts may not be regarded as occurring in terms of a point in time. For a point in time presupposes the givenness of an infinite temporal run-off. Considered according to their general nature, however, they do have an order of origin in the domain of time, and as acts of a concrete person (or as ego-acts of a concrete ego), they have a concrete order of origin "into time" which must represent itself as the temporal location of the contents of these acts.

They are essential conditions for the manner in which the ego and its experiences can alone come to *givenness* in a being endowed with a body. They are not, however, conditions for this ego and its own experiences.

But each of the principles is an essential condition in its own way; and so we return to the relation between association by similarity and association by contiguity. Thus far we have shown only that the principle of similarity cannot be reduced to that of contiguity and, similarly, that one cannot speak about a "reduction" of the principle of contiguity to that of similarity.[101] But one can ask whether there is an association by contiguity among contents, one that is not conditioned by an association by similarity of *unities* of consciousness encompassing these contents.

Let us proceed from the fact that the contiguity among objects that becomes the condition of reproduction in association by contiguity is dependent upon the fact that those objects were given in a conscious act (given as represented or only meant, or with one object represented or perceived and the other only meant), and that they were given as contiguous in *one* now-here. In this case it is clear that there can be no passage from the content of one now-here to the content of another now-here through association by contiguity. This can be accomplished only through association by similarity or "amalgamation" or assimilation. We must be very careful to avoid a determination of the "contiguity of objects," which is the condition for such association, that is either too narrow or too wide (as was the case with association by similarity). One point is clear: neither the purely objective, temporal sequence nor the spatial proximity of

101. Note that David Hume's attempt to reduce spatial representation to a mosaic of qualitative contents of sensation also implies a reduction of spatial contiguity to similarity. Each of such qualitative points has its extension only as a determination of its quality; this follows from his proposition that "where there is no color or tactile content there is no extension, or all extension is intuitively based on a quality," a proposition which Berkeley shares with him. Berkeley expresses this in the terms, "no extension without color." This is the opposite of Kant's (also false) proposition, "no color without extension." What alone can yield the phenomenon of homogeneity and the smallness below the lower-limit sensibility of the idea of a geometrical point is the indistinguishable similarity of points. But the continuity of a line or a plane is to result from a representation in fantasy in which the structure is a partial content of a greater one in which each part grows beyond the sensible minimum; yet the structure is to appear again as identical with the initial structure. The same holds for the theory of time. All later theories that mix all of these factors together, e.g., those of Herbart and W. Wundt, presuppose such a reduction.

objects, insofar as these are thought to be causally effective on the organism, is sufficient to permit, on the occasion of the givenness of one of the objects, mediate remembrance of the other object. No matter how one object *A* spatially and temporally touches another object *B*, if *B* has not been perceived in any sense of the term, the perception of the same *A* and the same content of this perception (if the latter were possible) cannot bring *B* into mediate remembrance. If, however, *B* has been perceived, it is not necessary for *A*'s being-side-by-side with *B* or its successiveness with *B* to have been given in a special spatial or temporal intuition of relation (or for a judgment about this to have been made) in order for an association by contiguity with the same *A* to become possible. *A* must have been in the extensionality of a now-here (i.e., of a "unity of situation"); it must also have been given (intuitively). In this case it is not necessary for *B* to have been perceived in a special content of perception and therefore to have been contiguous with *A* in this perception. It is sufficient if *B* was merely meant or represented or presented in fantasy, etc. These contacts among objects which are experienced together are also peculiar, qualitatively changing, relational facts, different from case to case, and they are not necessarily founded on the qualities of perceptions of contiguous objects. For example, in the contiguity of parts of a situation lived as a whole, there are always qualitatively peculiar contacts which together result in a *"constellation of contacts"* that is independent of the types of objects which are contiguous and whose recurrence can bring this concrete situation back to consciousness. It is not in recollection itself that the being-side-by-side and the succession of these objects is comprehended anew.

These peculiarities of this "meeting together" of things and processes in the unity of a "situation" within the totality of the present "environmental content" [102]—*these* above all, and not the identity or sameness of the objects meeting together—appear to me to be the still-phenomenal starting points of association by contiguity. They are experienced facts and, indeed, the intuitive foundation for the concept of *"association by contiguity."* It is through them alone that one can establish an association of this nature as a fact. For if association by contiguity were only the association of an object that had previously been

102. According to what we said earlier, environment is what is experienced as effective by an individual (see above, pp. 138 ff). Its content unfolds in a sequence of "situations."

in contact with a perceived one in perception, and if, in addition, this association were a condition for mediate recollection, how could a psychologist establish such "contiguity"? The fact that an object was there, beside or after an identical object of the initial perception, does not suffice! Had this object not been *co-experienced* in some way, it might as well have been hidden on Sirius. But the fact that the object was coexperienced as contiguous with the now given cannot again be given through association by contiguity. For this would mean: through the contiguity of A and B, I remember B when A is given; and this contiguity "consists" in the fact that I remember this B through Λ. One can see that it is impossible to reduce the reproductive signification of this "constellation" to a complex of associations by contiguity. It is, rather, *this constellation* which conditions the possibility of this kind of association of individual objects!

Objects must therefore already be contained in the unity of the environment of an individual (and the "structure" of this environment) in terms of an elementary unity of *one* "situation," and they must form a peculiar constellation of contiguity with one another if an object given later, one that is given as the same as that given "at an earlier time," is to determine an *association by contiguity* with the other objects contained in the situation.

But on what does the givenness of a consciousness of constellation, which alone makes association by contiguity possible (the givenness of a "constellation of consciousness" does not do this; to say that it does is to presuppose the consciousness of constellation), depend? It depends on the *similarity* of these constellations, because the constellation of every present of a situation (no matter what its special present contents may be) is a unique and peculiar one, and not "peculiar" merely as the univocal consequence of the nature of the objects hidden in it and what is experienced *of them* or of their sum. Hence, in response to our question we assert: It is only the *experience of the similarity* of the *constellation* of a now-here content (in the "extensionality" where there are not yet spatiotemporal differences) with the *constellation* of an earlier now-here content that makes an "association by contiguity" possible. *And to this extent every possible occurrence of an "association by contiguity" is conditioned by the occurrence of an association by similarity.*[103]

103. In other words, we emphatically deny that everything objectively experienced as "simultaneous" or "in immediate succession," e.g., muscular sensations along with thoughts about polygons, psychic sufferings with

What can make *both principles of association* understandable, and what can they help to "explain" in empirical psychology?

Concerning the range within which such principles obtain, it follows from what we have said that by no means do they obtain only for "man." The positive sciences, too, would never accept such a restriction, although they would have to accept it if these principles were to be established only through the empirical observation of man, and not in terms of the essential interconnection between a consciousness and a lived body. For we would have no right at all to presuppose them in the case of the psychic life of animals, although this is done everywhere, and correctly so. These principles are factually evidential propositions that obtain for all possible beings having an existence endowed with a lived-body and spiritual nature.[104] But it is *for this reason* that they cannot make even *one* concrete psychic experience fully understandable. For the interconnection of meaning of *mental acts and their contents*—not only the interconnection of meaning of general act-essences established in general phenomenology but also the interconnection of *any* concrete individual life—remains a completely autonomous problem and is therefore independent of these principles. Indeed, these interconnections of meaning remain the very *presupposition* of the meaningfulness of questions about laws of association and their application. It is evidentially senseless to try to explain the meaning-content of even one act, or its interconnection with another meaning-content, through laws of association. What these principles regulate is not the content of inner or outer intuition, but simply the *givenness* of such content in some now-here of our lived body, or, as we may put it, the kind and mode of the dependency which the mere givenness of a

---

itchings of the skin, etc., reveals a tendency to reproduction if anything of these experiences is "again there." Apart from the vagueness of such opinions, they are *complete nonsense* and defy all practical experience! For what is objectively experienced simultaneously (or successively) has no more tendency toward reproduction than a thing not perceived or meant behind a wall that is once perceived and then perceived again.

104. ["Lived-body and spiritual nature," in the sense of the "essential connection between a consciousness and a lived body," includes the psychic life of animals. In later works (see *"Die Stellung des Menschen im Kosmos* [Bibliog. no. 23]) in which the author sharply distinguishes pure "spiritual" activity from all activity bound to the vital lived body, including the activity of higher animals ("intelligence," "associative memory"), "lived-body and spiritual nature" in the above sense is no longer found.—*Ed.*]

uniform sense of life and the givenness of the interconnection of sense of its being-experienced—but not these things by themselves—possess in connection with a *lived body*.

A wholly definite and concrete interconnection of meaning and a definite, organized lived body and body-thing are always presupposed by all sciences of observation, description, and explanation. And any description and explanation of this kind must therefore start with the presupposition that a *superposition* of meaning and meaning-lawfulness *and* association and associative lawfulness is already contained in the object to be observed. Empirically there are no "pure associations" or pure interconnections of sense. There are only concrete facts which are to be analyzed with respect to *both* viewpoints, and which can be fully conceived only by a superposition of both types of lawfulness.[105]

Still more important is the question of the peculiar "place" of the so-called principles of association. There is no clarity concerning this question. The peculiarity and incomparability of their place, as we can see from the above, lies in the fact that the associative principles obtain for the objects of outer intuition that are relative to a lived body (thus, in principle, for "physical

105. Hume proceeds on the basis of his principles as if they were pure ontological *axioms* and through them explains the ideas of identical object, thing, and causality. Mill compares their significance to the law of gravity. (For Hume, the principle of gravity is, like any "law of nature," only a special case of laws of association.) Wundt attributes to the principles a role analogous to that of the principles of mechanics, but he restricts their powerful function of explanation by his "apperception." Again, others consider them empirical rules of only statistical importance which are to be explained through physical laws of outer nature and the physiology of nerves and the brain, i.e., derivatives of purely physical laws. Natorp arrives at a similar stand, following Kant, and the same can be said for Ebbinghaus and Münsterberg (see Ebbinghaus, *Grundzüge der Psychologie* [Leipzig: Veit & Comp, 1911], Vol. I). The latter view becomes necessary when one reduces the principle of similarity to the principle of contiguity, and contiguity to objectively simultaneous or immediately successive organic excitations through objects of perception. But this does not prevent Ebbinghaus' reduction of the idea of *laws of nature* to our predominant interest in what is similar in successive contents of perception (see *Einleitung in die Psychologie*), so that the principle of similarity as conjoined with this interest is to explain laws of nature, whose presupposition, however, served earlier as an "explanation" of this principle by way of the principle of contiguity! Bergson, on the other hand, futilely attempts to reduce the idea of similarity on the grounds that different complexes of "pure perception" tend to become identical because they equally satisfy drives and needs of the body. Apart from this basic mistake, Bergson comes closest to the truth in this area. In comparing all these views with what we described above, the reader will see that our stand does not coincide with any of these theories, which are so far apart.

objects"), as well as for objects of inner intuition that are relative to a lived body. If a name were desired, one could call them "noosomatic principles," thereby indicating that they regulate the way in which *acts of the mind* and contents, no matter if they pertain to physical, extrabodily objects or to psychic processes and experiences of an ego, fit themselves into a *lived-body present*. They therefore play the *same* role for the understandability of the objects and the objective structure of the "natural view of the world" in the case of the outer world as they do for the understandability of the natural view of the psychic (i.e., the flow of psychic "events" past a constant ego). These principles, because they are not based on observation and induction, do not presuppose the natural view of the world or the natural view of the psychic. Nevertheless, according to these principles, the *mode of formation* of both kinds of natural views can be grasped. If we call the peculiar science dealing with the mutual relationships between the lived body and the environment biophysics, and the science dealing with the mutual relationships between the lived body and empirical psychic life biopsychology, the noosomatic principles are to be regarded as *axioms* for both sciences. The *principles of association* therefore have a mediating position between the content of pure intuition, like a *bodiless spirit's* intuition of the ego and of nature, and the factual content of the natural view of a spirit connected with a *lived body* having an organization of some sort. They are therefore not only "psychic" principles but no less originally "physical" ones, too. They do not obtain in *both* directions in the sphere of absolute objects, as if they were given to pure intuition without a body; they so obtain only for objects that are, in their *existence and effects, relative to a lived body.*

These questions concerning basic relations between the purely psychic ego and the lived body have led us to the phenomenological foundation of these principles of association—in other words, to the threshold of explanatory psychology. We have dealt with these questions at great length because, for us, the concept of the *person,* which is fundamental in ethics, can be disclosed in its full meaning only when we are not merely in a (negative) position to reject the claims made by associative psychology in explaining the unity of the person—claims which are indeed fatal to ethics in general—but also in a (positive) position to assign to these associative principles their well-delineated meaning, and to all their explanations a subordinated area of validity in which they obtain with full justification. This may serve to justify the inclusion of these final investigations, which seem to be far removed from problems in ethics, in an investigation dealing with basic ethical questions. But the justification for the basic concept of the person which we have submitted here would receive its final touches only if we were to subject the principles and basic concepts of the mechanical theory of nature, which offer explanations in the sphere of outer intuition, to a phenomenological inquiry concerning their intuitional foundations, and if we were to do this in a way that corresponds to what has been done for explanatory psychology with regard to associative principles. This, however, would go beyond the bounds of this treatise and will be dealt with elsewhere, in a work containing additional points of importance for what we submit here.[106] These two investigations, the present one and the one just mentioned, will provide the reader with a full demonstration of the fact that an associative-psychological explanation of psychic being and a mechanical explanation of outer natural phenomena (which historically originated for analogous reasons) possess, in addition to their special presuppositions, one common assumption: they claim to give a symbolic image to things in such a way that, of the full givenness of intuition, only *those elements which are immediately controlled and directed by a personal-embodied being,* plus the possible connections and relations among these elements, are to be made independent variables of being and events or "principles" of their explanation. Here *both* images are *relative* [daseinsrelativ] to a possible person *and* a possible lived body, as well as possible vital movement; hence neither one of these two types of explanation nor both taken together can *ever* "explain" vital bodily unities, much less the unities of persons; *both* of these are centers of reference for the objects of these images.[107]

This ends our investigations concerning the theoretical meaning of the concept of the person and its place in these contexts, without which the following would have had no foundation.

---

106. See my forthcoming treatise "Phänomenologie und Erkenntnistheorie." [See *ibid.*, sec. 5.—*Ed.*]

107. Here we cannot even touch on the far-reaching consequences of this state of affairs in terms of the establishment of principles and basic concepts of biology. These can be developed only with a rigorous phenomenological grounding of the knowledge of living beings. Nor can we treat here the matter of how the problem of freedom should be investigated.

We now turn to the question of the role that the *person* plays as a bearer of *ethical values,* and to the question of the meaning of the word *person* in ethical contexts in general.

B. THE PERSON IN ETHICAL CONTEXTS

1. *The Nature of the Moral Person*

LET US FIRST SEEK what lies in the meaning-intention of the term *person,* but without making use of the phenomenological theory of mind that we presented before. Several points strike us immediately:

1. The word *person* cannot be applied to every case wherein we *assume* something like animation, egoness, or even consciousness of the existence and value of the ego (self-consciousness, consciousness of self-value). Animation, for instance—and undoubtedly an egoness of some sort—belongs to animals, too. But they are not persons. Animals have had legal proceedings instituted against them, and they have even been sentenced to death. But in closely examining such cases, we find that it was assumed that the animal was a bewitched person, or that extrahuman personal units, such as "evil spirits," expressed themselves through the animal and that the creature was believed to be "possessed" by a person.[108] But "man" qua man never has determined the limits within which beings are to be taken as persons. The concept of the person is applicable only to a specific *level* of human existence. Even if, after we have come to see the phenomenological essence of the person, we broaden the concept of the person and grant that there are seeds of personhood in still-undeveloped levels of human beingness (e.g., in children or imbeciles), there remains the fact that the place, as it were, in which the nature of the person first flashes before us is to be sought only in a certain *kind* of man, not in man in general—a kind, that is, which varies considerably in its positive historical delineation.

One of the *first* conditions is the possession of a *wholly sound mind*—in contrast to madness, for example. This I hold in the phenomenological sense rather than in the positive scientific one. A phenomenally sound mind is given when we attempt to "*understand*" the expressions of a man without further ado, in contrast

108. See J. Bregenzer, *Tierethik* (Bamberg, 1894).

to our seeking to *explain* them "causally." In this "understanding," the fact that psychic processes take place in the other person, processes which have causes and whose life-expressions are "effects," is never present as a state of affairs. What is essential for "understanding" is that out of the *spiritual center* of the other, which is cogiven in intuition, we experience the acts of the person (speech, expressions, deeds) with respect to us and the environment as intentionally *directed* toward something, and that we re-execute such acts, i.e., that we "rejudge" his spoken propositions and the corresponding judgments, "refeel" his feelings, and "relive" his acts of will, and that we attribute to all of this at once the unity of some "*sense.*" Of course, this "rejudging, refeeling, and reliving" is not a "cojudging" in the sense of "agreeing with" or making the same judgment as the other, nor is it a feeling of the same or similar feelings. It is only a reforming of the "sense" contained in a number of acts with random temporal distribution of their execution, acts that are directed toward *changing variations of sameness.* This continuity of sense in the course of the acts of the other is, in all understanding, the continuous intuitive background of *single* acts of comprehension. This is independent of the question of whether this sense is true or false, good or evil, a question that belongs to a sphere other than that of this "sense." This sense is also the "background" of "misunderstanding." And only when we encounter obstructions to this intention of understanding that prove to be unalterable, even if we assume misunderstandings on our part, does our *attitude* toward the other *change* in a characteristic manner. Someone tells us a somewhat curious and extravagant story that seems "hard to understand." We are in the attitude of "understanding." Then someone comes and whispers into our ear, "This man is mad." Our attitude changes at once in a characteristic manner. An empty spot replaces the previously given spiritual center out of which we relived his acts with him. Only his body- and life-center and his egoness remain in the givenness of intuition. We cease to see meaningfully directed intentions that end in his life-expressions. What remains given are movements of expression and other movements behind which we begin to look for psychic processes as causes. A band of "causality" or of environmental stimuli which releases his expressions replaces the "band of sense" of his former expressions. "Objects" that we saw *with* him in understanding now become "stimuli"; intentions become "processes"; the "nexus of sense" becomes a nexus of causes; the personal act-center becomes an objective unity of body and ego; "understanding" becomes "explaining"; and the "person" becomes a piece of nature. If someone with whom I find myself in an understanding attitude says, "It is a nice day today," I do not make the judgment, "Mr. X is telling me that we have a nice day today," or, "X experiences the process of judgment pertaining to the state of affairs of its being a nice day." His saying so is only the occasion on which my *intention* is directed toward the *being of a nice day* (as *a state of affairs*), and I may perhaps merely correct his assertion with regard to the reality of this. But it is quite different when something given is not "meaningful." In this case I make the following judgment *first:* "X *says* that it is a nice day today," "X *judges* that it is a nice day today," "He says first this and then that." And it is this *process* in him that I now bring into a *causal relation* with other psychic processes and the environment.[109] It does not matter in either case whether the proposition of judgment is true or false. A human being can always "be mistaken," but he does not thereby lose his sound mind. Even if an insane man happens to find the most original truth, he remains insane.

Two things follow from the above: (1) Every psychological objectification is identical with *depersonalization.* (2) The person is given as one who executes intentional acts that are bound by a unity of sense. Psychic being therefore has nothing to do with person-being [*Personsein*].

2. A second factor involved in the application of the word *person* is this: it is ascribed only to a certain level of development in man. A child manifests egoness, possession of a soul, and consciousness of self, but this does not make him a person in the moral sense. Only a child who has "come of age" is a person in the full sense. But this *"coming of age"* is based on certain phenomena—no matter when it is believed to come about in an individual according to changing positive law, and no matter which varying conditions, true or fictitious, have been established concerning its onset. The basic phenomenon of coming of age consists in the ability to experience insight into the difference between *one's own* and *someone else's* acts, willing, feeling, thinking, an insight which is already given in the immediate experiencing of any experience itself (the insight into the difference is *not* based on the content of the experience). And, furthermore, this insight must occur without any *necessary* reference

109. [On "understanding" and "explaining," see chap. 6, A, sec. 3, f.—Ed.]

to whether it was another's lived body or one's own through which the act-experience was externally made known. If such a reference is constitutionally necessary—if, for example, only in remembering can one recognize that it was another who bodily externalized a thought, that is, if one can recognize a thought or volition as that of another (as opposed to himself) only through the recollective image of the expression and what is expressed (e.g., his mouth saying these words, his face, etc.) or through the *image of his deed*—then he has not yet "come of age." In plain language this means that a man is not of age as long as he simply *coexecutes* the experiential intentions of his environment *without* first understanding them, and as long as the forms of *contagion,* plain *cooperation,* and *tradition* in a wide sense are the basic forms of the transference of his own mental state to others. He is immature as long as he plainly wills what parents and educators or anybody else in his world-about want him to do without recognizing, in willing these specific contents, the will of someone else or a person *different* from himself. It is for this reason that he takes an "alien" will for his "own," and his "own" for the "alien" one. Still, the immature human being can differentiate his will in general from the will of *others,* but not by referring to the pure willing of the volitional content with its interconnection of meaning with other contents. He can do so only by referring to the expressions and enunciations of the will in different, spatially separated, lived bodies. And when this point is missing (e.g., in recollection), the immature human being's own will and an alien will become indistinguishable. Of course, it may happen that the immature person is subject to suggestion and therefore takes someone else's will for his *own* in unconscious reminiscences. For this reason I say that the essence of maturity lies in the immediate *being-able*-to-differentiate and in the immediate consciousness of the ability to differentiate, not in the factual possession of distinctions. We can also say that it lies in "the genuine being-able-to-understand."

3. The phenomenon of personality, however, is not merely restricted to human beings who are essentially sound in mind and who are mature. It is further restricted to those men in whom *domination over the lived body* appears immediately, who feel, know, and live immediately as *masters* of the lived body. Of greatest importance in this regard is the phenomenal relation of man to his lived body. One who lives predominantly in his lived body and, as a result, identifies himself with its contents is not a person. Only he who experiences his lived body, identifi-

able in outer and inner perception, as *"belonging"* to *himself* through the bond "my lived body" (a phenomenon that forms a condition for the idea of property) is a person. The unity of the lived body (as opposed to that of the person) is an objective one, although it is not necessarily given as *thing* (still less, as object-body). But it is a given unity as a *"something"* [Sache].[110] And it is only when the body is given in this fashion, i.e., as being "owned" by something which operates in the body and recognizes itself as doing this, that this "something" [*Etwas*] is a person. Inanimate things are property only insofar as they are bound to the person through the most original "property," i.e., through the *mediation of the lived body.* Hence a *"slave,"* the opposite of a master, cannot be an owner; he is property. But, above all, it is important to observe that the person is given only when a being-able-to-do is present (to oneself and others) as a simple phenomenal fact, a being-able-to-do "through" the lived body. And this being-able-to-do must not be based on the remembrance of organic sensations and experiences of activity caused by movements that have already taken place. This being-able-to-do must *precede all* factual actions. Not only willing but also the immediate consciousness of the *power of willing* belong to the person. And one who does not have this power and the immediate consciousness of it *is* not a person. Thus he cannot own his lived body, but he can *be* the property of someone else; i.e., he can be given as a something [*Sache*]. So the *"slave"* is not a social person, and a true slave (not merely a slave according to positive law) is given both to himself and to others as a something. Nevertheless the slave has an ego, a soul, and a consciousness of self,[111] which proves that these have nothing to do with the person. Killing a slave was considered "murder" no more than killing an animal, for the destruction of thinglike entities, including living ones, is not murder. Nor could a slave be *punished* by a death sentence; for punishment is, as we said earlier, the infliction of an evil and the taking away of a good that presupposes the *existence*, independent of these things, of the one who will be punished. One can "care for" a slave in any number of ways: the slave can be showered with kind deeds. But he cannot be "loved"—only enjoyed and used. Nor can he "obey," "promise," "take an oath," etc. He cannot "obey," for "his will is in the

---

110. See above, p. 20 f.
111. Nor are these denied him as a social being.

master" (as Aristotle aptly said), who owns the slave's lived body and his ego. The slave *cannot "promise"* (i.e., execute the basic act which every idea of contract presupposes), because a man who is not a person cannot have any *continuity* between willing and being-able-to-do which is in principle independent of the states of his lived body. For *"promising"* is not an "artificial" act based on convention, as psychologism (e.g., Hume's) teaches; that is, it is not simply an act having the content "I will do this if you will do that" (and vice versa) so that a *contract* becomes the root and foundation of this act (and not a consequence of it). Promising is a *natural act* in which the person posits, in the present act of willing, a state of affairs "to be realized" (and not merely "represented" or "judged" as to be realized and willed in the future). Only the *action* belonging to the realization of the act is given to him "as" in the future. For this to be possible, the being-*able*-to-do the willed must be *experienced independent of possible experiences of the lived body,* and in this the person must experience a possible continuity of willing with this being-able-to-do.[112] But the slave lacks the experience of this being-able-to-do. Therefore the institution of slavery is not an institution permitting the enslavement of persons, or permitting the circumstances under which *"persons* can be *property."* The opposite is the case: because the slave represents himself to *himself,* or even to *others, not as a person* but as a human entity, an ego, a psychic subject, etc., i.e., still as a *"thinglike entity"* [Sache], it is *allowed* that he can be killed, sold, etc. In contrast to this, the *serf* [Leibeigene] already functions as a person, and he is restricted to his lived body only in exercising his right to property.

It is well known that *women* have long fought to be recognized as persons, and in the history of their struggles we see the fulfillment of all the essential interconnections that we have discussed. One can clearly distinguish two phases. There is, for example, a clear, essential nexus between monogamy and the recognition of the woman as a person. When polygamy was dominant in Turkey, for example, the institution was essentially interrelated with the teachings of the Koran, according to which women do not possess a "soul," which obviously means "person" here. Christian culture, on the other hand, recognizes a religious

---

112. [On person and lived body, see chap. 6, A, sec. 3; on the relations among willing of the person, being-able-to-do, and doing, see chap. 3; on personality and "murder," see chap. 5, sec. 6, ad 3; on "punishment," see chap. 5, sec. 10.—*Ed.*]

personal nature in women, and through the Mother of God it even attributes this nature to angels (i.e., pure, finite persons— *formae separatae,* in the language of Scholasticism). And women can be "holy," too, whereas in the Muslim afterlife a woman remains only a personless houri. The custom of burning widows in India is also based on the fact that a wife is not a person with regard to her husband, but only a thing of sorts [*Sache*]. Yet in the Christian culture, too, the *social and legal personality of women* is generally recognized only in private law, not in state or public law, and only very slowly did they gain full recognition in marriage laws. *Even* for Kant, let it be added, the married woman is by law (but not morally) a "thing of sorts" [*Sache*]; for he includes matrimonial law in his discussion of laws pertaining to things [*Sachenrecht*].

These facts show that the very *idea of the person* has *nothing* to do with ideas of the ego and the soul and analogous concepts in ethical and legal domains. Just as there can be ego-being and a soul (including the human soul) without any personality (in the strict sense), it makes perfect sense to assume a personality where there is neither ego nor soul (e.g., when we speak of the *person* of God, who can confront neither an outer world nor a "thou").

4. For the same reasons one also must sharply distinguish the idea of the person from all those ideas, based on experiential phenomena, which correspond to the above concepts. These are the real- and thing-concepts of the *"soul-substance"* and the so-called *character.*

Though we ignore the question of the justification of the assumption of a *soul-substance,* we can at any rate say that the soul-substance is thought to be a real and thinglike object that supports the individual ego-experience given in inner intuition. This object consists of hypothetically attributed properties, forces, faculties, dispositions, etc., so that one can causally explain the run-off of experiential contents of the individual ego in terms of the changing conditions of real effects of stimuli on the "soul." But all of this lies in a direction completely different from that in which the essence of *person* is to be found. The person is, among other things, the concrete subject of all acts of the essence of *inner* intuition, in which everything psychic becomes objective; and for this reason the person can *never* be an object, much less a real "thing." The person "is" only as the concrete unity of acts executed by the person and only *in* the execution of these acts. The person *experiences* [er-lebt] all being and life

—including so-called psychic experiences—but the person is never an *experienced* being and life.[113]

For this reason also, the well-known problem of the interaction of soul and body lies on a plane entirely different from that of the relation between the *person* and his *actions*. It is completely unjustified to bring the difficulties and issues concerning this interplay of soul and body into the question of the person and his actions. Since the person is not to be identified at all with the psychic, an issue like "How can a person act?" does not exist at all in this form. For the idea of action coincides with experienced efficacy on the environment of the lived body, on the lived body, and on the ego. The person acts as immediately on the outer world as on the inner world. The latter kind of action includes, for example, acts of self-overcoming and personal interventions in the psychic automatism.

It therefore is not necessary for the person to act *first* on his inner world and then, through this, on the outer world. The person is no nearer to one than to the other, and he experiences the "resistance" of both in equally immediate ways. Thus such action is, as shown in part I, an indivisible phenomenal unity that cannot be analyzed into a composition or sequence of psychic experiences and body-movements and body-processes.[114] The problem of the so-called interplay (in the widest sense), with which the seventeenth and eighteenth centuries were so intensely preoccupied, has, when seen in a correct perspective, lost its metaphysical significance, given our presuppositions (which here coincide with Kant's, at least with respect to the major point of this matter).

If the concepts of soul and body do not represent species of absolute objects, it makes no sense to ask how they could act upon each other. In other words, this famous problem turns out to be one that has been "fabricated," as Kant aptly remarked. And it is only of epistemological interest. All possible interconnections between psychic and bodily processes are possible and understandable because they are mediated by the *uniform* and *indivisible* efficacy of the person. That is to say, for any uniform action of a person there are two forms of intuition, the inner and the outer, and in both of these the difference, sameness, and similarity of the "actions" in question must mirror themselves. And, of course, all that we have said obtains for every considera-

---

113. [See chap. 6, A, sec. 3.—*Ed.*]
114. [On "deed," see chap. 3.—*Ed.*]

tion of the personal actions of others. These are never given in such a way that there first occurs a "causal inference" from given movements to the effecting soul. All such considerations are necessarily preceded by an *understanding* of the person and of the unity of his actions, an understanding that proceeds from the *center* of the other person.

What we call *character* has nothing to do with the idea of the *"person"* if we take "character" to mean enduring dispositions of the will or other "dispositions," e.g., those of the mind, intellect, and memory of a person, and thus move into the entire range of problems of characterology and differential psychology (the term *character* would have to be reduced to dispositions of soul *and* body if a soul-substance were assumed). In particular, the action of a person is not a straightforward consequence of the sum of his dispositions and his changing external life-situations. On the contrary, the person, as well as his actions, can be thought of as freely varying, notwithstanding the same dispositions of soul and body and the same situations. Any attempt to reduce the freedom of the person to the mere causality of character (in contrast to the causality of single so-called motives, as Lipps tried to do) would fall far below the plain meaning of the problem of freedom. For such dispositions and character require a causal (biological and historical) explanation and are as causally necessary as the product of character and action. If in this *sense* we could have knowledge of the innate and acquired dispositions of a man (in an ideally perfect manner), and if we could know all effects of the outer world on this man (in an equally ideal manner), his action would nevertheless remain as different as the *person* to whom this character and these dispositions belong. The problem of freedom (which we will not discuss here) therefore lies on a much deeper plane than this solution.[115]

On the level of epistemology the person is given to us in a manner which basically differs from what we have called *character*. For character is nothing other than a hypothetical, more or less constant X that we posit in order to explain single observed actions of a person. And if a man acts in a way which does not correspond to the deductions that we made in a specific case from our assumed hypothetical "picture of his character," nothing can follow save that we have reason to change this "picture" of his character. But then the concept of an (objective) *change* in character, which is evident, e.g., in all facts of con-

115. [See above, p. 203, n. 31.—*Ed.*]

version, would be impossible (because it would be contradictory). Nevertheless, such "changes in character" certainly exist. But the situation is very different with regard to our cognitive relation to the other *person*. This is shown most clearly by the fact that we can understand the individuality of the person both from a single action and from any phenomenal expression of his.[116] And we can (ethically) measure his deeds not only by moral laws of a *general* sort but also by the ideal intentions of the person *himself*. Given an action, for example, that is beyond the normal bounds of the known intentions of a person, on the basis of our comprehending-intuitive knowledge of him we are able to tell with certainty that these actions, different in kind, rest on factors which "disturbed" the realizations of his intentions. If, for example, someone tells us certain things about a friend whose person, we believe, we understand—things that go beyond the sphere of possibilities which results from our understanding his personal intentions—we will not, as in the former case, simply change our image of his person. Rather, our evidential knowledge of his individuality will induce us to criticize either the correctness of the story or his understanding of the action. And if what we have been told withstands this twofold challenge, we are induced to assume a change in character (e.g., of a diseased nature), and this always implies some form of obstruction of the person's possibility for expression and his capacity to act.

It is therefore of extreme importance for ethics, and for the separation and subtle differentiation of concepts like "morally good," "psychically normal," "morally bad," and "pathological," that *person* and *character* be distinguished. What psychiatry says about so-called changes in character in certain psychic illnesses can never pertain to the *person* of the other, even in the most severe cases (e.g., paralysis). It is only the *givenness*-to-others of his person that disappears. In severe cases one can only say that his person was made *invisible* by the illness and that a judgment about his *person* is therefore no longer possible. But this statement itself is possible only because we still assume the existence of a person behind the character changes, an existence which is *not* affected by them. And it is for this very reason that we attribute *"imputability"* to the actions in question, but do not charge the subject with *"responsibility"* for them in such

116. Every action *also* has a symbolic value of expression. But every act of expression does not have a value of action.

cases. Apart from cases in which the person appears to be completely invisible by virtue of changes in character, our experience gives continuous testimony that the character changes described in psychiatry are *completely* independent of the moral and other mental intentions of the person. The same hysterical character can, e.g., in the case of Joan of Arc, lead to true heroic greatness and, in other cases, to actions of malicious annihilation of values. And the same traits of the "hysterical character" can be attached to both actions. Therefore, in psychiatric analyses of the pathological character, one should carefully avoid terms that express moral approval and disapproval. If this is not done, one can be sure that the psychiatrist will not succeed in extracting the pathological change in character from the special, individual contents of life with which he is faced in his analyses.

For this reason psychic illness nullifies the *"imputability"* of the actions concerned *with regard to* the person, but it does not nullify the *responsibility* of the person in general. For the latter is essentially connected with the being of the person. One must *sharply* distinguish between moral "responsibility" and the imputability of actions or the "accountability" of a man, i.e., the ability of a person to be the subject of imputable actions. The nullification of accountability simply implies that the effectiveness of *"motives"* deviates from the *normal effectiveness* of these motives, and that it is therefore impossible to *decide knowingly* whether or not a given action belongs to the *person* of the man. But there is no *nullification of the responsibility* of the person in the strict sense. An animal, for example, is not responsible for its deeds. The sick person is only unaccountable. This means that no one can attribute an action to his person or *determine whether* he is responsible for such an action. But he remains *responsible* for all of his truly personal acts. Hence responsibility is the *presupposition* of "accountability," but they are not identical. Nor does responsibility follow from accountability, as a number of deterministic theoreticians believe (e.g., Theodor Lipps, who identifies responsibility with normal motivational effectiveness).[117]

To affirm the accountability of a man is simply to say that *certain* of his actions can be coordinated with *certain* acts of his

---

117. Hence we must deny that there is necessarily a relatedness "to someone" in the experience of responsibility (as the word may suggest). It is only because we know ourselves to be "responsible" in our acts that we can feel responsible "to someone."

person. A statement of his unaccountability denies this possibility. It does not deny responsibility, but simply the determination of responsibility for *certain* actions. Both concepts (accountability and unaccountability) are formed from the outside, from visibly executed action. It is quite otherwise with the concept of moral responsibility! *In* the execution of his acts the person experiences himself as *"responsible"* for his actions in his reflection on his having done the actions himself (here it is not necessarily a matter of actions alone, but also acts of the moral tenor, potential moral tenors, intentions, things done on purpose, wishes, etc.). *This* concept of responsibility has its roots in the experience of the person himself and is not formed on the basis of external consideration of his actions. It is in this reflection alone that the concept of responsibility is fulfilled.[118] The concept of moral responsibility has its roots in one's immediately knowing that he is the author of his deed and its moral value-relevance, not in any subsequent connection in thought of an executed and completed act or action with the self. The experience of *"self-responsibility"* as an absolute experience is the presupposition of all responsibility "before" someone (man, God), i.e., of all relative responsibility.

For these very reasons "illness" and "health" are not possible predicates of the *person,* though they are predicates of the *man,* the *soul,* etc. There are "psychic diseases," but there are no "personal diseases." One who fails to see the essence of the person,[119] as all psychologistic (and vitalistic) ethics does, must come to the conclusion that there is *no essential difference* between "morally evil" and "sick," between evil and "atavism" or lower stages of development.

As we have already observed, the difference between person and character manifests itself so clearly and sharply that we are able to measure a factual person and his life-expressions and actions by the *value-intentions immanent to the person himself,* i.e., by his own ideal value-essence (both in the case of oneself and in that of another), and not merely by general moral norms. This would be impossible, however, if the person were given to us inferentially as the constant cause of his expressions, which is the case with "character." For if these intentions were merely

118. Hence the person is responsible for all acts of his absolute intimate being, not merely for acts of the person as a social person. But he can be held accountable only for the latter. [On "intimate person" and "social person," see chap. 6, B, sec. 4, ad 5.—*Ed.*]

119. Herbert Spencer, for instance.

given as hypothetically assumed causes *x, y, z* of his actions, it would be impossible to compare a person's ideal value-essence with his actions and to know whether it is "fulfilled" in these actions or whether the value-essence and these actions "conflict" with each other. But precisely this *is* possible. For every moral assessment of another consists in the fact that we measure his actions *neither* exclusively by universal norms *nor* by an ideal picture that hovers above us through our own doing, but only by the ideal picture that we form by bringing to their end, as it were, the *basic intentions* of the other person which have been obtained through a central understanding of his individual *essence* and which we unite with the *concrete ideal value-picture* of the person given only in intuition. And it is by this picture that we measure his empirical actions.

What mediates the intuition of the person's ideal and *individual value-essence* is, first of all, the *understanding* of his most central source, which is itself mediated through *love* of the person. This understanding love is the great master workman and (as Michelangelo says so profoundly and beautifully in his well-known sonnet) the great *sculptor* who, working from the masses of empirical particulars, can intuitively seize, sometimes from only *one* action or only *one* expressive gesture, the lines of the person's *value-essence*. This essence, which is concealed more than it is revealed by our empirical, historical, and psychological knowledge of the person's life, never comes to complete appearance in *any one* action or life-expression, but is the condition of *any* full understanding of either of them. Hence this value-essence *cannot* be reached by *any inductive procedure*. Even ideally perfect inductive knowledge of all factual experiences and all inherited and acquired dispositions of a person would not suffice to determine this essence. On the contrary, it is the light streaming from the intuition (even though inadequate) of the person's essence onto all of his empirical experiences that raises the cognition of him far above a mere sum of *general concepts* of which—whether taken individually or together—one can always find *another* person as a "case of application" or an "example." It is only when I know to which *person* the experiencing of an experience belongs that I can have a full understanding of this experience.

All psychology—even so-called differential psychology and so-called individual psychology—secures its object only by *abstracting from and disregarding* the person. Hence the person is totally *transcendent* to psychology. What psychology yields, even in ideally perfect fashion, is merely possible *material* of the person's life that can be structured in one way or another.

2. *Person and Individual*

It is necessary to give a more precise definition of what we understand by *individual-personal value-essence.*

Essence, as we mentioned earlier, has nothing to do with *universality.* An essence of an intuitive nature is the foundation of both general concepts and intentions directed to *particulars.* It is only when we refer an essence to an object of observation ("the essence of something") and inductive experience that the intention through which this reference occurs becomes something that pertains to either a universal or a particular. Therefore there are essences that are given only in one particular individual. And for this very reason it makes good sense to speak of an individual essence and also the individual value-essence of a person. It is this value-essence of a personal *and* individual nature that I also designate "personal salvation." It would be a complete mistake to identify this "salvation" with a personal-individual *ought,* or to say that it is given in the experience of such an "ought." There is, of course, an individual ought—an experiencing of the ought-to-be of a content, an action, a deed, or a project through *me,* and, in certain cases, *only* through me as this individual. But this experience of my obligation—no matter if I share this obligation with others or not, no matter if it is recognized by others or not, no matter if they "can" recognize it or not—is *based* on the experience of my *individual value-essence.* If, on the other hand, we begin with the ought (as G. Simmel docs in an instructive essay),[120] we cannot distinguish between *true oughtness* and mere capricious impulses on the individual (covered up by the form of an "ought" and a "duty" in self-deception) unless we agree with Kant and regard the *true* ought as one whose content can be a *universal principle* of the ought. For just as a subjectively valid connection of representations can, according to Kant, be distinguished from an objectively valid one by virtue of the fact that the former is "only individual" and stems from habit whereas the latter is universal and necessary, so also can the ought of duty be distinguished from mere compelling impulses of the individual character only by its possible universality and its "supraindividual" necessity. Thus

120. Simmel, "Das individuelle Gesetz," *Logos,* Vol. IV, no. 2.

Simmel's interesting attempt to adhere to Kant's theory that "good" is what ought to be and, at the same time, to oppose Kant's theory concerning the necessary universality of duty appears to me to be hopeless; for on *this* basis it becomes impossible to formulate what Simmel correctly held (against Kant) in a manner that distinguishes it from an individualistic *subjectivism*, which would of course imply on Simmel's part an even *more* deeply mistaken position than Kant's.

If, however, an ought becomes a moral and genuine ought whenever it is *based* on *insight into objective values*—i.e., in this context, into the *morally good*—there is also the possibility of an evidential insight into a good whose *objective* essence and value-content contain a *reference* to an individual person, and whose ought therefore comes to this person and to him alone as a "call," no matter if this "call" is addressed to others or not.[121] This, therefore, is to catch sight of the value-essence of my person—in religious terms, of the value-picture, so to speak, which God's love has of me and which God's love draws and bears before me insofar as this love is directed to *me*. This peculiar individual *value-content* is the basis on which a consciousness of an individual ought is built, that is, the evidential knowledge of a "good-in-itself" but precisely in the sense of a "good-in-itself-for-*me*." The latter does not contain any logical contradiction. Its being good "for" me (in the sense of my experiencing it) does not make it a *good-in-itself*. In *that* case there would be an evident contradiction. It is good precisely in the sense of being "independent of my knowledge." For this includes the *"good-in-itself."* Yet it is the *"good-in-itself"* for *"me"* in the sense that there is an experienced *reference* to me which is contained (descriptively put) in the special non-formal content of this good-in-itself, something that comes from this *content* and points to "me," something that whispers, "For you." And precisely this *content* places me in a *unique* position in the moral cosmos and obliges me with respect to actions, deeds, and works, etc., which, when I represent them, all call, "I am for you and you are for me."

It is—to refer once again to this state of affairs—precisely this theory which claims that there is a true good-in-itself which not only allows but also *demands* that there be a *good-in-itself*

---

121. See the following concerning the ideas of a "calling" ("vocation"), "mission," and "election" for a task. All these ideas have as their basis the above fundamental experience. [These ideas are not discussed by the author in the remainder of this work.—*Ed.*]

for *each* person in particular. On the other hand, one who does *not* recognize a "good-in-itself," but would join with Kant in basing the idea of the good only on the *universality* (and necessity) of a *willing*, must find it impossible to recognize a good for me as an individual person.

But if the act through which the ideal value-essence of a person is revealed is the full *understanding* of the person based on love, this pertains equally to the revelation of this essence through oneself and through others. The highest form of self-love is therefore the act through which the person *reaches* full understanding of himself and thus the intuition and feeling of *his salvation*. But it is also possible for another person to show me the path to my salvation through *his completely understanding love of me*. Through a love which is deeper and more true than the love that I have toward myself, the other person reveals to me an idea of my salvation that is *clearer* than the one which I have by myself. The claim that "each is necessarily the best judge of his salvation" is absolutely groundless. This "salvation" has nothing to do with pleasure and happiness. Kant completely misunderstands the religious idea of salvation when he detects "eudaemonism" in one's own "salvation" in the correct sense.[122] Although the distance between the person and his salvation is *measured* by personal feelings of blissfulness and despair, salvation does not *consist* in this blissfulness.

What, then, is the relation of *universally valid* values and their dependent, universally valid norms to the *personal* essence and the ought founded on it? In the past ethicists have for the most part given the answer which Kant has set forth in its most extreme form: the person acquires a *positive moral value* only by realizing universally valid values or by *obeying a universally valid moral law*. Kant goes one step further. For him, not only is all oughtness universally valid, with the consequence that a

122. In religious terms: In the domain of the *infinite fullness of the good* spread out *before the eyes* of God, there is in *one* special "place" a good that is a good "for me," my own ideal value-essence that, empirically, I "ought" to become. Or this individual value-essence becomes an "ideal" for me because it lies not only in the direction of *love of the Divine* but also in the direction of divine love directed *to me*. It is not the case that this image empirically *grows* out of "my *life*" (Simmel), or that it is an X in the direction of an individual *necessitation of the moral ought*. Rather, all empirical life happens and is formed under the influence of the *goal* of this value-ideal of the individual person, through which the unique place of the person in the realm of the extant good is *fixed*. And founded on this is the place that the ideal of the person occupies in the divine plan of salvation.

personal, i.e., individual, "ought" (as opposed to "inclination") does not exist, but the *content* of this ought urges one to act so that the maxim of his action can become a universal principle for all rational beings. That is, the universalizability of a will, its fitness as a principle, is, for Kant, the *reason* [Grund] for its moral *goodness*. Kant does not say, "Will the good, and then see that others will it, too." No, he says, "*Good* is that of which you can will that everybody else (in your situation) will the same." [123] The last point has been rejected in what we have said. But the former point is to be rejected, too. According to our earlier analyses, the following obtains: all universally valid values (universally valid for persons) represent, in relation to the highest value, i.e., the sainthood of the person, and in relation to the highest good, i.e., "the salvation of an individual person," only a minimum of values; if these values are not recognized and realized, the person cannot attain his salvation. But these values do *not in themselves* incorporate all possible moral values *through* whose realization the person attains salvation. Any deception concerning universally valid values, and any action contrary to norms derived from them, is therefore evil or conditioned by evil. But true cognition and recognition of them, as well as obedience to their norms, are *not* at all the positive good as such. The latter is fully and evidentially given only insofar as it implies individual-personal salvation.

The true relation between *value-universalism and value-individualism* remains preserved only when every individual moral subject submits those value-qualities which he alone can grasp to a special moral cultivation and culture, though of course without neglecting universally valid values. However, this pertains not only to *individuals* but also to spiritual *collective* individuals, e.g., cultural units, nations, peoples, tribes, and families. Thus we are given this important insight: the *fullness* and *variety* of the types of moral ideals of life that we find in peoples and nations are by no means objections to the *objectivity*

123. There is a well-known objection which begins with the claim that "similar conditions" must include "everyone similar to my individuality" and ends with the claim that Kant's principle must mean that everyone should act differently in similar situations on the grounds that no one has an individuality similar to mine. This is *not* what Kant had in mind. This meaning is artificially forced upon him. But the objection is meaningless because Kant does not speak of the "individual person" in the strict sense, as we have shown, but only of the empirical individual who can become a "person" only by way of his participation in a supraindividual reason.

of moral values. They are, rather, essential consequences of the fact that only *the coincidental grasps and the interpenetration* of *universally valid* moral values with those of *individual validity* can yield complete evidence *for the good-in-itself*. And an analogous state of affairs obtains for the historical development of each individual and each collective individual. For example, the Kantian rule stipulates that a maxim is justified only if it *can become* for any moment in life a principle of universal legislation, i.e., one that applies to all fortuitous moments of life. Sidgwick established an analogous axiom: "Willing is good only if it is independent of the differences in time which willing has in the nexus of life." [124] We must expressly reject this axiom, too. *Every moment of life in the development of an individual* represents at the same time a possibility for the individual to know *unique* values and their interconnections, and, in accordance with these, the necessitation of moral tasks and actions that can never be repeated; such tasks and actions are predetermined, as it were, in the objective nexus of the factual-moral value-order for this moment (and for this individual, for example) and, if not utilized, are lost forever. The complete evidence with respect to the good-in-itself can be given only in the *coincidental grasp* of values which temporally are universally valid and of "historical," concrete situational values, i.e., in the frame of mind in which one continuously surveys the whole of life and listens for the unique *"demand of the moment."* [125] The essential *consequence* of *essential moral values* and their corresponding *tasks* is to be seen not only in the fullness and variety of moral values of individuals, peoples, and nations, but also in the *manifoldness and fullness* of *historically* changing moral systems, which are denied in principle by rationalistic moral systems. And it is precisely because it belongs to the essence of extant values to be *fully* realized by only a variety of individuals and collective individuals and a variety of levels of concrete and historical development of these that the existence of these historical *differences* in morals is not an objection to the *objectivity of moral values,* but is on the contrary required by it. On the other hand, the boundless tendency toward the universalization of values and norms was the *consequence* of the *subjectification* of values, as in Kant's case. So even though we cannot abstract moral values from *positive history* and *its* goods, the *"historicity"* of their

124. See his *Methods of Ethics* (London: Macmillan, 1907).
125. The "demand of the moment" (Goethe) is quite definitely an essential category of ethics.

comprehension (and the cognition of their order of ranks and laws of preferring) is as essential to them as is the historicity of their realization or their realization *in a possible "history."* That is to say, if the relativism that abstracts *values* from *historical goods* and regards them as made in history or as produced in its workings is erroneous, then the idea that the *total fullness* of the realm of values with its extant value-order *could be given* to *one* individual, *one* people, *one* nation, or at *one* moment in history, is erroneous also.

In this fullness there are qualities and relations of preferring that can be known by all at any time. These are simply the *universally valid values* and *laws of preferring.* There are, however, qualities and relations of preferring that suit only *individuals.* They are originally syntonized only with individuals and are therefore experienceable and realizable only by these individuals. At the same time these qualities and relations can be seized only at a *unique* moment in historical development, so that ever new values and relations of preferring become visible with every new stage of development. If this does not happen, there is a stagnation of "moral culture." Still, every rule of preferring, once known, remains in existence.

It stands to reason that *ethics* as a philosophical discipline can never exhaust moral values. Ethics deals only with the universally valid values and their nexus of preferring. And it is the point of ethics to show expressly and to make understood this indubitable fact, i.e., it is its task to *explain*, that there is an ethical cognition through *wisdom* which lies wholly above ethics and without which all immediate ethical knowledge of universally valid values (a fortiori the scientific description of what is thus known) is essentially *imperfect.* Ethics can never replace individual conscience, nor should it.

3. *The Autonomy of the Person*

We have come to the point where we must establish a foundation for the ethical *autonomy of the person.*

As we said earlier, all true autonomy is first and foremost a predicate of the *person*, not a predicate of reason (Kant) or of the person only as an X that participates in the lawfulness of reason.[126] But here we must distinguish two sorts of autonomy: the autonomy of personal *insight* into good and evil and the

---

126. [See chap. 6, A, sec. 1.—*Ed.*]

autonomy of personal *willing* of what is given as good and evil. The first kind of autonomy has as its counterpart the heteronomy of *blind* willing without insight; the second, the heteronomy of the *forced* willing that is very distinctly present in all kinds of volitional contagion and suggestion. In this twofold sense of autonomy the value of morally relevant being and willing in general can be possessed only by the autonomous person and his acts. But the autonomous person is by no means already a good person. Autonomy is the presupposition of the moral *relevance* of the person and of his acts insofar as these acts are to be considered as belonging to this person. If, for instance, an action that is good in itself is willed by *A* without insight and under constraint (e.g., on the basis of heritage or tradition or blind obedience to authority), this action is not any less a "good action"—but it is not to be attributed to *A* as a person. An action willed in the same way remains evil if it is evil in itself. Therefore, the basic condition of all act-units bearing value-predicates is that they be, in general, units of autonomous acts of *those* individual persons who execute these act-units. Thus both the theory of natural determinism, which holds that because it can be proved that an action can be reduced to inherited dispositions, it can also be proved that the action cannot be evil or good, blameworthy or praiseworthy, for this reason, and the theory of autonomy, which declares the autonomy of the acting agent to be the presupposition not only of the imputability of a good (or evil) action to the person but also of the moral relevance of actions in general, are false. In both theories the ideas of inherited good and inherited evil (and, with them, the idea of inherited guilt) become contradictory: in the first, because the inherited cannot be good or evil (blameworthy or praiseworthy); in the second, because good and evil cannot be inherited.[127] But in

127. One must express gratitude to the predominantly positivistic thinkers who, in opposition to the proponents of individualistic morality, have broadly demonstrated on a factual basis the biological, historical, and social causal-conditioning of morally valued kinds of comportment. But these thinkers, who still *value* individualistically, hold that one can entirely eliminate the concept of moral guilt. So one must ask how these thinkers know that every evil and therefore guilty action must always be attributed to the person and not, e.g., to a collective whole of persons to which the respective person belongs, or even to his ancestors. One must also ask how they know that bad attitudes as *consequences* of originally bad acts are not subject to transmission through heredity and tradition. The entire uncertainty of our age on these questions simply follows from the fact that we have, on the one hand, learned to think historically and socially but, on the other, are still stuck in the individualistic modes of valuation of the eighteenth century.

practice the idea of an evil of which the acting person is nevertheless not guilty, or of a good which brings no merit to *this* person, as well as the idea of a guiltiness of which the individual is not guilty, are completely meaningful ideas, and not contradictory ones, within the entire realm of acts.[128] This alone is the essential interconnection here: all evil presupposes the autonomous guilt of some *person*, though not necessarily the guilt of the individual person to whose action this evil is attached. The subjectivistic interpretation that Kant has given his concept of autonomy, according to which moral insight and willing are not even distinguished,[129] and in which the sense of the words good and *evil* is reduced to the law that the rational person gives to himself ("self-legislation"), precludes at once every transfer, *heteronomous* for the individual, of the value-content of an earlier autonomous personal act. If this Kantian interpretation of "autonomy" is considered to be identical with autonomy in general, the idea of an "autonomous" ethics must be rejected. But we hold this terminology to be useless and mistaken; for it prompts one to overlook the fact that everything that is objectively and morally valuable is essentially connected to "autonomous" acts of the person, no matter how difficult it may be to determine the specific individual person to whom such acts originally belong.[130]

There is an important difference in consequence between our concept of autonomy and Kant's. Our concept at least does not preclude the principle of the moral *"solidarity of all persons"* and, given the help of evidential propositions that we have set forth elsewhere, even requires it, whereas Kant's concept necessarily precludes such solidarity. The principle of solidarity in good and evil, in guilt and merit, states that there is a *collective* guilt and a *collective* merit in addition to and independent of the guilt of which an individual is guilty and the merit that is "self-merited."[131] Collective guilt and merit do not represent sums of

---

128. Thus "tragic guilt" especially is always "guilt of which we are not guilty" because it is already attached to the sphere of choosing, i.e., the domain in which we must choose, but not, however, to the act of choosing itself. See "Zum Phänomen des Tragischen," (Bibliog. no. 10).

129. See above, pp. 45 ff.

130. Dispositions toward evil of a certain kind (vice) can also occur in one's individual life by way of originally autonomous acts. These can then be realized by habit. But they do not lose their morally negative qualities by virtue of their being habits.

131. Collective guilt and collective merit may possess a form that is either more historical or more social; but they possess both of these forms at the same time. Their bearers are "willing, loving, and hating with one another," which are autonomous phenomena of experience, as I have

individual guilt and self-merit in which every individual partakes (in determined and changing ways). This principle further states that every personal individual is not only responsible for his own individual acts but also originally *"coresponsible"* for all acts of others. It states, therefore, not that the moral coresponsibility of each person with others rests solely on mutual obligations resulting from promises and contracts in which responsibility for the accomplishment or omission of moral value-complexes has been "freely" assumed, but, on the contrary, that one's self-responsibility is originally accompanied by coresponsibility for such accomplishment and omission.[132] Of course, the application of this principle to a *specific* case of coresponsibility always requires a positive demonstration of some factual and volitionally causal cooperation of the "coresponsible" person in question with the realization of the events. But this *demonstration only determines and localizes*, as it were, coresponsibility. It does not *create* it! The degree of coresponsibility, too, can increase or decrease according to the type of participation. Coresponsibility does not result from this demonstration of participation but is cogiven with self-responsibility and lies in the essence of a moral *community* of persons in general. Coresponsibility cannot be regarded as having sprung from self-responsible acts of "recognition" of this community, that is, recognition that would result from the requirement of the moral law which the person puts upon himself. For it is the identical personhood of every individual in a community, not the individuality of the person, that founds responsibility along with autonomy.

The idea of a moral community of persons (whose highest form is a religious community of love) would not be possible according to the (Kantian) principle of autonomy rejected earlier.[133] For Kant, all esteem for the other person (or his personal dignity) is founded on the subjective autonomy of one's own person, as well as on self-esteem or esteem for one's own

---

shown (see *Zur Phänomenologie und Theorie der Sympathiegefühle*), and are not to be considered as sums of individual volitions with the same content. See also chap. 6, B, sec. 4, ad 4.

132. All freely assumed moral obligations, insofar as they are moral and not merely legal, have their foundation in coresponsibility for the acts of the person with whom such obligations are shared and, therefore, also in coresponsibility for the act by which this person has obligated himself to the other (i.e., in mutual obligation) or has "accepted" the other's obligating promise. Accepting a promise to do something that is in itself evil is as originally evil as making the promise.

133. See above, p. 114, and chap. 6, B, sec. 4, ad 4.

"dignity"; in other words, if, on the basis of what we said before, we consider love to be moral comportment of maximal value, love for the other is founded on self-love.[134] But, in fact, love for the other is *not* founded on self-love (much less on self-esteem, as Kant would have it). Rather, love for the other and self-love are equally original and valuable; and both are founded ultimately on God's love, which is always a coloving of all finite persons "with" the love of God as the person of persons. Hence it is *God's love* through which the fundamental individualistic and universalistic moral values, "*self-sanctification*" and "*love of one's neighbor*," ultimately are inseparably and organically united. Neither can serve as a foundation for the other! Rather, the mutual nexus of essence between love for the other and self-sanctification requires that all *love for others* be *regarded as pure and genuine* only to the degree that it sanctifies the *loving person*, and that all *self-sanctification* be regarded as pure and genuine only to the degree that it is confirmed in acts of *love for one's neighbor*.[135]

As we mentioned, it is no less important to distinguish the autonomy of moral *insight* (in the sense defined in part I) from the autonomy of a person's *willing* the evidentially good (and his other morally relevant ways of comportment).[136] The relation

134. In fact, it is evident that one's own dignity as the value-correlate of self-respect is to be placed after the salvation of the other person (but not after his dignity) as it is grasped in purely personal loving; one's own dignity is not to be preferred here, despite what Kant holds. See "Das Ressentiment im Aufbau der Moralen" (Bibliog. no. 10), where I argue against this view, which Luther shares with Kant. [See *ibid.*, sec. 4, "Über Ressentiment und moralisches Werturteil" (Bibliog. no. 5), sec. 3.—*Ed.*]

135. E. Troeltsch, in his *Soziallehren der christlichen Kirchen und Gruppen* (Tübingen, 1912), claims that the unity of individualism and universalism of Christian ethics lies in the fact that "altruistic commandments belong to those commandments according to which self-sanctification in God takes place"; he maintains that "those who sanctify themselves for God in a common goal will also meet in God" and, therefore, will accomplish God's loving will. In this view, however, the value of the love of the other person is founded in that of self-sanctification. We have rejected this view as a false kind of "individualism." A true "union" of individualism and universalism would not occur here, because individualism remains primary. Troeltsch's views on the Christian idea of community seem to us to be incorrect also from a historical viewpoint. This "meeting in God" is not merely a fortuitous thing coming about through the self-sanctification of anyone; rather, it is originally *conditioned* by love of one's neighbor, and not merely by self-sanctification. The love of one's neighbor is distinct from self-sanctification in that it has a value that is not founded in self-sanctification and is independent of it. See my treatise, "Liebe und Erkenntnis," *Weisse Blätter*, July, 1915. [See "Liebe und Erkenntnis" (Bibliog. nos. 11, 19).—*Ed.*]

136. [See above, pp. 67 f., 80 f.—*Ed.*]

between these two sorts of autonomy (which constitute the necessary presupposition for all morally relevant acts to be imputed to the individual person in question) is such that a fully adequate autonomous and immediate insight into what is good *necessarily* posits an autonomous willing of the comprehended good. But it is not the case that autonomous willing also posits a full and immediate insight into what is meant as "good" in willing. The one thing which is precluded is that autonomous willing can be completely "blind willing"; this would imply a contradiction, as we saw before, or that a merely instinctive impulse has been confused with willing. But between such impulses and willing that is characterized by immediate, adequate, autonomous insight, there are all the cases of merely mediate knowledge of the goodness or badness of the volitional project concerned. But, without doubt, *all* of these cases *can* be connected with autonomous willing and choice without the givenness of fully autonomous insight into the value of the willed. Thus autonomous and immediate insight into the moral value-content of the value-complex that is commanded to be realized is not given in *any* act of *"obedience."* If we assume that there are things like "obeying oneself" or obedience to a self-posited norm of the will, such things also lack *this* autonomous insight. Nevertheless, *willing* that "is obedient" can be fully *autonomous* if it is expressly based on the will "to obey." For *"to obey"* is the exact opposite of comportment whose extreme is action from suggestion and contagion. One who is obedient does not will what another wills only "because" the other wills it, whether this "because" is meant in a purely objective or causal sense, as in pure contagion and suggestion, or in the sense of the conscious motivation of one's willing by another's such that another's willing translates itself into one's own in the form on an experienced continuity—in the absence of mediating acts of understanding— which is the case in all specifically slavish comportment. One who renders obedience wills "to obey"; i.e., the *positive act* of obeying becomes an immediate volitional project in which the willing of what is commanded is formed. A distinct awareness of the difference between one's own and another's willing, together with the understanding of another's willing "as" that of another, is the necessary condition of genuine obeying. Willing by suggestion and slavish comportment in the above sense are as heteronomous as the willing of the obedient person is *autonomous*. However, according to Kant's concept of autonomy, which does *not* differentiate between autonomy of insight and that of

willing, any obedience to others would be nothing but heteronomous and compelled willing. But in fact the heteronomy in
obedience (and if there were self-obedience, it would be necessary to make the same point against Kant) consists in the fact
that the *insight* into the moral value of the volitional project of
one who obeys is determined heteronomously, not autonomously.
This is not to imply that there is no insight here at all. When
insight is completely missing, we speak of "blind obedience,"
which, in the strict sense of the term, is no longer obedience at
all but slavish comportment. But morally valuable obedience
exists whenever, despite the *lack* of insight into the moral value
of a commanded state of affairs which characterizes obedience
as obedience, the insight into the moral goodness of willing and
willing persons (or their "office") is evidentially given, the goodness becoming manifest in the making of the commandments or
(*in concreto*) in the ordering of the orders. In this case there is
autonomous and immediate insight into the moral value of
commanding, heteronomous and mediate insight into the value
of the commanded value-complex, and at the same time complete
autonomy of willing in rendering obedience. Moral obedience to
God's commandments, too, must be based on *insight* into the
essential goodness of the law-giving will of God; if slavish
comportment is to be avoided, the act should not follow simply
because God commanded it. If insight into the goodness of the
commanding authority or person is not fully adequate and therefore subject to possible deception, the commanded realization of
the value-complex on the part of the obedient person can represent the realization of a moral evil. Although in this case the
willing and acting in the execution of what is commanded on the
part of the obedient person is bad and culpable, it is the person
commanding, not the one obeying, who is *guilty* of realizing this
evil; and the moral value of the obedience remains unaffected.

And since we can come to the insight that another person is,
in his individual nature, morally better and higher than we are,
it would be quite senseless to make the results of our own insight
into the assessment of any special volitional projects of ours a
condition of any good practical comportment for which we are
accountable. A concept of autonomy like Kant's, which, strictly
speaking, requires this, would exclude as "heteronomous" all
moral education and instruction,[137] the idea of "moral obedience,"

137. As Herbart has correctly stressed.

the far higher form of the moral determination of other persons (that is, following the pure and good example that the good person gives), and, finally, the immediate evidence of the unity of meaning of our willing and God's willing that is given in the loving union with God, not in obedience to a "divine command." The correct principle of autonomous insight for all morally valuable being and autonomous comportment does not at all require that the individual reach factual moral insight into good and evil by his own subjective insight into what is evidential. The individual's *way* toward insight into values and their relations can still be mediated by *authority, tradition,* and *fidelity.* His comportment nevertheless remains autonomously evidential if he has clear insight into the different cognitional values of these possible *sources* of moral insight, and if he respects these sources—in addition to the source of his own individual life-experience—according to their evidential and general value.

4. Our Concept of the Person in Relation to Other Forms of Personalistic Ethics

With the above results concerning the nature and value of the person, we are now in a position to assess the very different *forms of ethical personalism* which came about during the nineteenth century and which correspond to the more or less influential general currents of the age. Here we will briefly outline the points which our personalism shares with these other forms and the points in them which we reject.

The present forms of ethical thought of this sort can best be divided in terms of the following points:

1. Either the *being of the person* (or of the person of the highest value) is regarded as the *end* of all community and historical process, or, on the contrary, the being of the person is considered valuable only to the degree that he effects something particular for the community and the progress of history (e.g., to the degree that he furthers cultural development).

2. Either the conscious intention of the person toward his own highest value obtains as required, or, on the contrary, the person can in fact reach his own highest value only by not intending his own value in any volitional act. ("Only one who loses himself will find himself.")

3. Either the person (in the above sense) is regarded as the bearer of a highest value only as a rational person (Kant and

classical idealism), or the individual spiritual person is regarded as the bearer of the formally highest value to the degree that he is individual and unrepeatable (Schleiermacher). The former of these two assumptions precludes the idea of persons who are of different non-formal values; for this idea is not possible without the assumption of an original individualization of the person qua person (i.e., as independent of the lived body and the empirical content of experience). Taking the opposite presupposition into consideration, only one point remains valid: a man becomes all the more moral as he becomes a person—in other words, as he allows himself to be moved by a law of reason.

4. Either the concept of the collective person (e.g., the personality of a nation or a state) is attributed a reality independent of our conceptualizations (in addition to the reality of the concept of the individual person), or it is not; and if it is, these theories can be divided in terms of the manner in which the categorial relation between individual and collective persons is understood (whole and part, participation, membership). The important problem of the moral solidarity of individual persons within the collective person belongs to the realm of these questions.

5. Either the *intimate* person, i.e., the person as he exclusively experiences himself, is said to be the bearer of the highest moral values, as well as the main arena of moral processes, *or* the *social* person, i.e., the person (individual or collective) as he experiences himself in terms of any social acts, which pertain to other persons (individual or collective), and knows of this experience, is considered to be this bearer.

6. Finally, the different forms of assessing the person which correspond to these currents can be sharply distinguished on the basis of which of the above value-modalities they regard as the central value-content of the person—in other words, whether the ideal of the saint (modality of sainthood), the ideal of the genius (modality of values of the spirit), the ideal of the hero (modality of the noble), the ideal of the "leading spirit" (modality of the useful),[138] or the ideal of the *bon vivant* (modality of the agreeable) is predominant—and on the basis of the order of ranks thought to hold among these non-formal types of personalities.

138. [Here the author establishes a special "modality" for the useful. (He did this also in his Cologne lectures.)—*Ed.*]

ad 1. The Being of the Person as Self-Value in History and Community

If we consider the first of the above issues, we find two extremely dissimilar pairs of opinions in the cultural currents of
the last century. On the one hand, Kant and Nietzsche (and
lesser figures as well) are on the side of the self-value of the
being of the person. On the other hand, the "great man" theory,
set forth in so many different ways, as well as the entirely opposite ethos of socialistic and communistic currents, declares
that the value of the person is derived from and dependent on
what he achieves in an impersonal community or an impersonal
historical process (development of culture, civilization, state,
etc.). (For example, we find this thesis in W. Wundt's ethics.) [139]

Kant and Nietzsche, however different their concepts of the
person may be, assess the value of a community or society, and
the value of a historical process as well, according to the degree
to which these are able to provide the *being of the person* with
the most appropriate foundation for his existence and action
(for Nietzsche, the being of the most valuable persons, i.e., the
"great personalities"; for Kant, the being of the rational person
in *every* man). The goal of human history is, for Nietzsche, the
"greatest exemplars" of men and, for Kant, a community that
makes rational persons of free will possible. Neither Kant nor
Nietzsche recognizes a *supra*personal *highest* bearer of value
(be it the community, culture or its development, a moral world-
order, the state, etc.). There is no "devotion" to such a bearer on
the part of the person which could give him a value that he did
not already have (even though this value may necessarily express and manifest itself in such devotion). Both theories are
therefore sharply opposed to all theories of post-Kantian German
idealism, especially to Fichte's and Hegel's, which impose devotion to a suprapersonal and supraindividual "moral world-order,"
or to a state of this kind and a cultural revolution of this kind,
as the highest bearer of value on the value-being of the person
and make this devotion the latter's condition. As a consequence
of all of this devotion, the idea of God becomes depersonalized
(pantheism).

At *one* most important point both theories coincide with the
laws that I have discovered concerning ranks of values: although
values of things [*Sachwerte*] are higher than values of feeling-

---

139. [See the critique of Wundt's cultural ethics in "Ethik" (Bibliog.
no. 8), sec. 2.—*Ed.*]

states (e.g., the feeling of well-being), values of the person are, as such, higher than values of things, and so, for example, spiritual values of the person are higher than spiritual values of things. To whatever degree the absence of the person's volitional intention toward his own value remains the first basic condition of his *factual* value,[140] the value of the *person* remains the highest value of the values, and the glorification of the person, ultimately the person or persons, i.e., God, remains the moral meaning of all moral "order."

The ultimate measure of community and history is therefore the idea above them that shows to what extent they provide the basis of existence and life for the pure ontological value [*Seinswert*] of the maximum of most valuable persons (both individual and collective persons, as we shall see).[141]

In contrast to this theory of ours, it is a presupposition of both the exaggerated "great man" worship (Carlyle, Treitschke, and others) and a great part of German philosophy (W. Wundt is but one of its recent representatives) that the person's value is determined by his service to community and history—indeed, only by his contribution to their progress. This is also the presupposition of all variations of socialism and communism having ethical overtones. However deep the differences among these currents, they have *one* common denominator in the *above* point, a point that must be underlined because it has so rarely been noticed among all the differences. The reason why this point has so rarely been noticed is that *value*-personalism and historical *causal* personalism, as well as value-collectivism and historical causal collectivism, have not been distinguished with enough care; this has resulted in the assumption that a value-personalism must always correspond to a causal personalism, and a causal collectivism to a value-collectivism. But this is not at all true.

The "individualism" of the theory of "great men," who are called "great" because they exercised great influence on the course of history or because they raised the whole of a people to a higher level of existence, is, in contrast to Nietzsche's and Kant's theories, a distinctive value-collectivism. The value of man is measured by the enhancement of an extrapersonal "development" or an extrapersonal "community." The theory represents a causal personalism and at the same time a value-collectivism. The "great man" is valued as "great" merely as the X of the point

140. See chap. 6, B, sec. 4, ad 2.
141. [See chap. 6, B, sec. 4, ad 4.—*Ed.*]

of departure of a strong historical effectiveness, not as the fullness of existence that fills this X.

But *ethics* must vigorously protest this standard, which might have certain significance for the narrow purposes of a historian (and here only for a political historian). Ethics must stick to *value-personalism,* for which the ultimate meaning and value of community and history lie precisely in their providing conditions within which the most valuable persons can come to the fore and freely bring about their effects. For value-personalism, all history has its goal in the *being and activity of persons.*[142] This proposition would remain unaffected even if causal personalism were held to be completely erroneous, that is, even if in the course of history the driving forces behind historical change were to shift more and more from persons to the masses.[143] One can accept this proposition—which we hold to be correct, though we will not demonstrate it here—without accepting any value-collectivism. Indeed, one would have to ask whether it is not rather the *same* processes which, by their relieving persons from service to an impersonal community and history all the more as they touch by this service the central being, the deepest levels of being and value of persons, put more and more of the powers that drive history forward into the extrapersonal factors of mass movements and "relations." The united powers of increased solidarity of interests through the division and organization of labor ("organization") and all types of production techniques represent such processes. They relieve the deeper levels of the "spirit" in general from tasks that by nature can be realized by non-personal and non-spiritual powers. They make causal factors in historical events gradually shift from the person to the masses. As we go further back into primitive times, the *person becomes* more and more the basic *cause* of historical events, their *efflorescence,* and their *meaning.* One can even say that what is truly personal and spiritual in man is, during the course of history, ever more thoroughly liberated from the power and ties of history in an unending process; in the course of time it becomes detached from time, and in the course of history more and more *trans*historical. It is more and more relieved of the mere role of being cause and effect within historical causality.

For *ethics,* this singular nexus results in a principle no less

142. I.e., individual persons *and* collective persons, as the following will show. See *ibid.*

143. [See "Probleme einer Soziologie des Wissens" (Bibliog. nos. 20, 22), chap. 1.—*Ed.*]

important than those propositions which are the basis of the
independence and freedom of the person from all formal and
mechanical causality. This principle is as follows: All positive
values that *can* be realized by *extra*personal and *extra*spiritual
powers *ought* to be so realized. Or, more briefly, everything that
can be mechanized *ought* to be mechanized. Needless to say, this
proposition does not coincide with the orientation of thinking in
positivistic ethics, e.g., the ethics of H. Spencer, which sees in
the progressive exclusion of love, sacrifice, conscience, duty—
and finally the person and spirit in general—a growing "progress"
in history. But this proposition does establish a clear boundary
between all truly ethical personalism and idealism and their
truly reactionary and "romantic" copies, which would artificially
maintain and fix the personal principle *at the expense* of a *possible* mechanism, e.g., love and sacrifice at the expense of a
possible solidarity of interests, spiritual personal activity at the
expense of a possible collective organization and mechanism.
These copies do not serve to liberate the personal in men; on
the contrary, they serve to maintain the servitude of the personal.
Here we will not elaborate on the range of applicability of this
principle but will only point out that it is valid for all forms of
personal spirit, not only singular but also collective forms, for
instance, for nations in relation to the international mechanism
of civilization. Increasing mechanization in actualizing values
that are *at all* mechanizable lifts the *peculiarity* and *self-value*
of personal forms of spirit to ever purer heights; it does not
destroy them, as both positivism and false personalism assume,
though with opposing assessments.

ad 2. Person and the Intention of One's Own Value

In regard to the second point mentioned, the ethical personalism presented here rests on the proposition that the nature
of any possible enhancement of personal value is such that the
person must *never purposely intend* his own moral value. A
great misunderstanding of true personalism occurred when
many forms of the ethical orientation called "individualism,"
as well as many of its opponents, accepted the claim that
personal values must be *willed* if they are to be realized. But
this being-willed is the only type in which the value of oneself
and the value of the other are never realized, indeed, cannot
come to givenness. Concentration on possible self-esteem, all
kinds of "moral pride," and volitional directedness toward one's
own "dignity," not toward a thing-value or a value of a feeling-

state that is to be realized, are not forms of comportment which coincide with the principle that values of the person are the highest values.[144] Clearly, the opposite holds, namely, that these attitudes must obstruct and hinder the actualization of the otherwise *possible* value of the person, i.e., actualization in and by virtue of act-activities in the person. Because it belongs to the essence of the person as the concrete subject of all possible acts (as opposed to ego, soul, lived body) *never* to be *objectified*, it is only a deception for him to believe that he can become objectified. Still, our proposition does not imply that the enhancement of the person's value is exclusively objective in the sense that this enhancement is not *lived* by the person. This experience is the timeless *consequence* of his activity, a consequence that is *not* immediately directed toward him, and thus it is not an intended content. It is, on the other hand, a mistake on the part of antipersonalistic ethics to assume that the person's directedness *beyond* himself, essential for any ethically positive posture, and the *absence* of his intending his own value would contradict the fact that the person realizes his value *in* precisely this posture and that the values of the person are above all other values in terms of rank. This mistake stems from the prejudice that the *highest* values (or value-contents, e.g., being-good, being-perfect, etc.) must be projects or determining factors of the projects of willing. But we have already seen that the possible realizability of values through willing and actions is necessarily inversely proportional to the heights of the values.[145] For we are at the upper limit when the value of the person as the highest value is maximally excluded from this *immediate* realizability through willing, i.e., absolutely excluded. Even concepts like "care for your own salvation" and the higher concept belonging to it, "self-sanctification," and even the concept of "self-perfection" stemming from world morals, must, when viewed from the above principle, be put within the proper bounds of their validity. They have full validity (corresponding to the order of ranks among values) as long as "soul" and "self" in these word-combinations are sharply distinguished from the *person* (as possible objects for the person and as a field of ac-

144. On the subjects of humility and pride, see my essay, "Zur Rehabilitierung der Tugend" (Bibliog. no. 10). This thought is also clearly developed in the Christian idea of God (when correctly grasped): God glorifies himself *in* the act of his world-creating will of love. But he does not intend his glorification in the act of creation.

145. [On the relation between the value-height of a feeling and its realizability, see chap. 5, sec. 8.—*Ed.*]

tivity for the person). They are invalid, however, when "soul" and "self" are identified with the person. This does not preclude a person's having the intention to sacrifice his own "salvation" for another person out of love for him, or even his finding *in* this *actus* the summit of his own value. This is the case at least when and insofar as this "salvation" is considered to be the destiny and value of a certain objective *thing*. If one understands the terms "salvation," "self-perfection," etc., to mean salvation and self-perfection of the person, then these values belong to the class of values, hitherto insufficiently studied, whose *necessary* condition of realization is precisely their being *non-intended* in willing.

The above also holds, of course, for the totality or collective person, e.g., for a nation. A nation can develop its *peculiar* best (in culture, ethos, etc.) only when its members rigidly banish from their intentions the idea that as members of this nation they must act, be efficient, build, and create in a specific direction; they must let themselves be guided only by the thing-values [*Sachwerten*] lying within the span of comprehensibility of the national spirit and ethos.[146]

ad 3. Person and Individual (Personalism and "Individualism")

At no point does the ethical personalism to which our investigation has led us reveal its distinctiveness from other present ethical currents to a greater degree than in the position that it allocates to the becoming and being of the spiritual *individuality* of the person as the bearer of moral value. For us, the value of the person is the highest value-level; and it is superior to all those kinds of values whose bearers are willing, actions, and properties of the person, just as it is superior to all values of things and of feeling-states. The "willing" of the person can never be better or worse than the person in question. At the same time, however, every man is, as we saw, an *individual* and therefore a unique being, distinct from all others to the *same* degree that he is a *pure* person. And, similarly, his value is a unique value. (This, of course, also pertains to both the individual person and the collective person, e.g., the Greek or Roman people.) Accordingly, in addition to the universally valid objective good (and the con-

146. See my essay, "Das Nationale in der Philosophie Frankreichs," *Der Neue Merkur*, August, 1915. The proper national character of spirit is *lost* precisely when the spirit is not simply effective (as a push, as it were), but effective only through reflection on it (as a pull). [See "Das Nationale im Denken Frankreichs" (Bibliog. nos. 11, 19).—*Ed.*]

tent of oughtness resulting from it), there is for every person (individual or collective) an *individually valid* good that is no less objective and evidential, and for whose comprehension we utilize "conscience" (in the pregnant sense of the term).

Hence all *ultimate* bearers of moral value, to the degree that they are conceived as *pure* persons, are *different and unequal* not only in their being but also in their value. Either an assumption of their equality in value (and of their equality in terms of duties resulting from their equality in value) is a pure fiction, or else it arises (in this case correctly) from consideration of a special area of *tasks* that is anchored in the idea of the universal good. "From consideration of" this area of tasks, e.g., "as" economic subjects, "as" bearers of civil rights and duties, etc., ultimate bearers can and must "obtain" as "equal" in a given case (which would be the object of a special investigation). Hence in terms of the moral "ideal" *each person must comport himself as ethically different and different in value from every other person under otherwise similar organizational, psychic, and exterior circumstances*—and he must do so without violating the universally valid series of norms coming from the idea of the value of the person in general. It remains to be seen how and to what extent the extant differences and differences in value among persons can be shown as given or even be "established." If this were not possible, such differences would in any case be present before the idea of an all-loving and all-knowing God. Persons and their individual values must be considered different precisely "before God." We must not assume any so-called equality of souls before God, which some interpret to be the teaching of historical Christianity—though, we believe, without justification.[147] Indeed, the following may be regarded as the result of our analyses: men should become all the *more* equal and therefore "obtain" as equal in value, as those goods and tasks in relation to which these men are taken to be subjects of "possession" (for the goods) and subjects of obligation (for the tasks) become *lower* and *more relative* within the ranks of the value-order. To put it plainly, aristocracy "in heaven" does not preclude democracy "on earth." Indeed, democracy on earth is *required* by it. If the satisfaction of instinctive needs in the order of their level of urgency is a condition, not of the being, but of the coming to appearance of persons, in themselves individual and of

---

147. Such a doctrine could be explained as a distortion produced by Stoic philosophy.

different value (in acts, actions, and works), then both goods and tasks corresponding to the more urgent needs *ought* to become more *equal* for men. They ought to become more equal, for *precisely because of this*, their differences do not remain concealed and hidden with regard to *absolute* or less relative values of being and with regard to the higher goods and tasks connected with faculties of *higher* value.[148]

When I compare these results with prevailing ethical currents, it seems to me that the "individualism" of eighteenth-century philosophy, which is still effective today, is the complete opposite of the truth. According to this doctrine, men and their values are to be regarded all the *more* equal, the *more* their being approaches the *absolute* level of being (as "rational entity") and the *more* their values are compared to values of the *highest* ranks (salvation and spiritual values); and they and their values should (or at least may) appear all the more *unequal*, too, the more their being approaches sensible states of the lived body and the more their values are compared to values of the *lowest* ranks. This connection between transcendental *universalism* and empirical aristocratism and individualism is the exact *opposite* of our opinion. As we have seen, this connection has its philosophical basis in the premise of *one* so-called supra-individual transcendental reason, which is supposed to concretize itself in a plurality of persons, be it by virtue of the *lived body* (a new form of Averroism) or by virtue of the special *content* of psychic life which can be established only by induction. The notion of a spiritual individual *qua* spiritual and the notion that the *individualization* of being and value increases with the purity of spirituality have no place in this way of thinking. In addition, this so-called individualism in part confuses the idea of the *single* person (as opposed to the whole) with the totally different idea of the *individual* (as opposed to the universal or the universally human) and in part still believes both to be bound up with one another. In contrast to this, our "individualism" excludes neither the reality of the collective person (and, of course, the individual) nor the moral consequences of this assumption. This way of thinking (to which Kant's theories by all means belong) identifies everything good that is merely *individually* valid with the merely "subjective," i.e., with what is merely fancied as good.

148. Here we cannot develop the many important applications of this principle to theories of society, politics, and law.

In this line of thought the individual person is reduced to the *social* person without any consideration of the fact that every individual person can be looked upon as a social person and, with equal originality, as an *intimate* person, both being merely sides and views of the person's undivided totality.[149] Moreover, in this line of thinking some (especially Kant) preferred the person as subject of the state, the *citizen,* in the whole of the social person, for the anchor of the ethically relevant concept of the person *in general,* and at times (especially in English philosophy) some preferred the social individual person as an economic subject that is capable of making contracts according to *private law.* It is *this* person who received the highest estimation in the ethics of this orientation.

Yet we must side with Kant on the *particular* question of how the social person as *citizen* is related to the social person as *subject of private law.* In every man the latter must be *subordinated* to the former because the state achieves the highest meaning of its existence in the rational regulation of the will to live and the reasonable distribution of the goods of life (of a community, of a people), whereas private law has to do with the values of the useful and the agreeable, which are subordinated to the vital series of values, or with the will directed toward values of the useful and the agreeable (and the goods encompassed by these value-qualities) in terms of reasonable regulation. According to our order of values, it is especially the *economic subject* that must be *subordinated* to the person as citizen so that all laws concerning simultaneity and temporal succession in economic processes, laws that can be derived under the fiction (explicitly adopted by Adam Smith) of a purely economic subject, i.e., a subject who is selfish and equal and, with respect to the events of the market place, all-knowing and continuously working (i.e., without sleep, indolence, etc.), are only *technical rules* for the person as a member of the state, i.e., for the will of man as *citizen,* rules to be applied to freely variable purposes.[150]

---

149. [See chap. 6, B, sec. 4, ad 5.—*Ed.*]

150. Just as on the small scale the uniform *centers of life* (with normal regulation of movements) restrict all conation aimed at the agreeable and the useful, and order it with respect to the "ends" in such centers, so on the large scale the state restricts society, and man as a citizen restricts the economic and consuming subject. *Abstention* from intervention on the part of the will of the state in lawfully regulated economic processes by way of the above fiction must be considered a positive act of the will of the state. If, for example, a state pursues free trade instead of a policy of protective duty, this is not for the sake of the "principle" of free trade.

Still, Kant's (and his successors') deep insight does not lessen the basic conceptual *error* in identifying the merely social person with the person in general, the rational person with the spiritual individual person, and the idea of *equally* "obtaining" rational persons, presupposed by the idea of all law (private and church law included), with the idea of persons of the *state*.[151]

On the basis of the above there can be no doubt that the core of the individual person (in relation to which the "rational person" and the "social person" represent *abstract* contents only through their relations to certain spheres and tasks) is *far above* all states and all mere personality as citizen, and that his ultimate salvation is totally *independent* of his relation to the state. Seen from above, the idea of the *state* is founded on the solidarity of individual persons in general (*not* on a contract among them) and on a possible community of love comprising such persons. Seen from below, the state is founded on a possible *life-community* based on vital sympathy (*not* on a society of purposes), a community that forms its material.[152] As a member of an always individual and in itself *un*equal realm of free spiritual persons, a realm that is in itself also unequal in value, the person is therefore in *all* respects *above* the state and, we may add, above law.

Hence the state can (in extreme cases) demand the sacrifice of the person's *life* (e.g., in war); but it can never demand the sacrifice of the *person* in general (its salvation and its conscience), nor can it demand the person's limitless "devotion" to the state.[153]

It does this because it considers the abstention from intervention in free competition to be expedient.

151. Kant's definition of the "highest good" on earth as a free constitution of world citizenship, according to which everyone is both citizen and subject and everyone's purpose is to harmonize with the purpose of everyone else in one system, is only a consequence of this.

152. A *life-community* (plus its conditions, such as a territory, etc.) is not only material for the will of the state (Kant) but also a coconstituent of the nature of the state. [See chap. 6, B, sec. 4, ad 4.—*Ed.*]

153. I cannot but regard as excessively banal and childishly simple the recent ideas of certain thinkers—among them, thinkers of note—who would oppose the "individualism" of the liberal "mechanical" conception of the state (which in their eyes is wrong) to the "universalistic," "organic" conception and would then consider the state a "supraindividual" good for which the individual must be prepared to make *any* sacrifice. I regard similarly the views of those who would glorify our German conception of the state as an inheritance from antiquity. All "ancient" conceptions of the state were abolished *once and for all* by Jesus.

Just as the economic person is *below* the state and the individual person in general is *above* it, the entire sphere of the intimate person is *outside* the state.[154] The principle of original solidarity also holds for the *intimate person* (because it holds for the spiritual person in general). And the intimate person as a person is only the spiritual core of the intimate *side* of the unity of levels of the sensible-vital-spiritual being which man represents. For this reason man as a relatively intimate person possesses a peculiar form of connection with men as relatively intimate persons. If the individuality of the intimate person and differences, including differences in value, between him and other persons are disregarded, and if he is taken to be equal and equal in value to others, he becomes subject to ecclesiastical law. The idea and essence of the church rest on this unity of connection insofar as the church is directed to the solidary value of salvation of a realm and totality of persons.

Having thus established the relation of our "personalism" to that of the philosophy of Kant and his followers, we would like to consider briefly its relation to other forms of this ethical point of view.

At least with regard to the point under discussion, Schleiermacher appears to have come closest to the view that we consider correct. Against Kant's rationalistic theory he re-established —although on a subjectivistic basis that is *not* our own—the ideas of the individual salvation of every individual and collective person, of the good according to individual conscience, and of a spiritual individuality.[155]

Max Stirner has criticized rationalistic theories in a *false,* but nonetheless correctly motivated, manner, and he has developed his own anarchistic "individualism." He correctly saw that the "rational person," which is the same in all and not the same in all (see the preceding), is an *impossible* concept, and that individuality belongs essentially to the person. But because, without further examination, he *shared* with his opponents the

---

154. Concerning this concept, see chap. 6, B, sec. 4, ad 5.
155. With the assistance of Herder (who, in turn, followed Leibniz), Schleiermacher introduced not only the idea that there is also an individual ethos of a people and a nation which is not merely a negative limitation of a general ethos of "mankind," but also the idea in ethics that there is in each nation a peculiar "national conscience" and ethos, and that it is only the cooperation of *all* nations (each following its own ethos) that can bring forth the highest good within the framework of what is universally valid. The same holds for cognition.

opinion that individualization of the person occurs by virtue of the *lived body* alone, his value-individualism resulted in a theory that morally vindicated limitless "living it up" in terms of *bodily drives*. Moreover, his version of anarchism resulted from his connecting this individualism with an epistemological skepticism, following Fichte's errors, and from his identifying his "individual" with the "single" person. The *source* and *kind* of Stirner's errors are most instructive for every "individualism of living it up," despite the insignificance of this theory. For the theories of Stirner, Kant, and their successors have at bottom the *same* deficiencies: the *disregard of spiritual individualism* and the assumption that only the lived body individualizes the person. No wonder that this conception of "drive-individualism," so common in the realities of modern life, leads *in fact* to something that is quite contrary to this kind of "individualism": large-scale *objective uni*formity of the being and life of these "individualists" to the extent that one can almost predict the nature and actions of others from only *one* example. For it is the bodily drives and their structure that make up the most *general* processes within human nature, processes which man even shares with higher animals. Thus there is a conspicuous contradiction here between the *subjective* consciousness of such an "individualist" intending to be a "unique" individual and the factual absence of *objective* individuality. The "individual," a category whose *sense* is such that in all cases where it obtains the individual hits upon something unique, and different from others, becomes for these "individualists" the *extension* of a concept for which the individualist and his companions represent only "examples" that are, as such, not at all different from each other. And this contradiction is repeated for the same reasons in all cases in which the individuality of a *collective* reality comes into question. A national "chauvinist" shows the *same* habitus in all countries; he makes the *same* speeches, the *same* gestures. The fact that his people, too, are an example of a nation makes him forget that the individual of any nation demands in each case a different "nationalism." Given its presuppositions, this type of individualism must come to forget that precisely what it disregards—namely, the inner and outer powers of ordering and uniting human drives (which pertain to what is more or less *general* in human nature according to *universally valid* norms of men or the state or a people, and which are effective as consciousness of duty, as state or church authority, as mores, etc.)—is what creates the very *condition* for the *liberation* of the *true* seat of individuality, i.e., the spiritual personality of an individual or a people.

As a final type of ethical "individualism" we shall consider one of a very different sort, one which regards the being and activity of the *"rich"* and *"great" individuality* to be the bearer of maximal value, and which designates the establishment of the best conditions for the existence of these "highest exemplars" of mankind as the basis for the orientation of moral tasks.[156] Friedrich Nietzsche became the foremost representative of this philosophy. Apart from all the colorful and changing garments with which he clothed his idea, we find aspects that both affirm and deny a number of our opinions. We agree that the *being of the person* (and not his willing, actions, etc.) is the bearer of maximal value, that the individuality of the person is to be viewed *not* as something which destroys or "limits" his possible positive value but as the *orientation* of its increase, and that there exists an *irreducible difference in value* among persons.[157] For Kant, the manifestation of the person (as the autonomous rational person) in every man, as well as the measure of this manifestation [*Auswirkung*], is the final goal of morality and the measure of the good that is present in the world. But this person cannot be *good* or *evil,* nor can he be of *higher* or *lower* value. For Kant, the "good" person *is* precisely the autonomous person. A non-formal difference in value among persons, as well as the only possible bearer of this difference in value, i.e., the person's non-formal individuality, is excluded here. On this one point our ethics sides with Nietzsche's. For persons *themselves* are *originaliter* different in value; it is not the *relation* of the rational person (the same in each) to any of his acts (or to only his volitional acts) that brings about a differentiation in ethical value. It is only by *disregarding* the original difference in value for the purpose of realizing a universally valid good that one is led to the *assumption* of the equality of persons before a universally valid moral law and the consequences of this with regard to law and state.

On two other points Kant and Nietzsche stand together on *one* side, a side from which we are far removed. To both Kant and Nietzsche, not only is the person the bearer of moral value (although they differ on this, as we can see from what we have said about Kant); but they also posit this value as a value. Both

156. [See chap. 6, B, sec. 4, ad 1.—*Ed.*]
157. On this point Nietzsche and Schleiermacher are in agreement.

tie their "individualism" to subjectivism and value-nominalism: Kant ties individualism to transcendental subjectivism; Nietzsche ties it to empirical subjectivism. But, for us, the person alone is the ultimate *bearer* of value, but in no respect whatsoever is the person a *positor* of values.[158] Furthermore, for Kant and Nietzsche, the person is *exclusively self*-responsible; he is not simultaneously and with equal originality "*coresponsible*" for the comportment, willing, and actions of any other person. For both, personalism is at the same time *singularism:* Kant's personalism is rational singularism; Nietzsche's, empirical singularism. Both philosophers deny the principle of solidarity.

Although Nietzsche was far removed from cheap historical cults of "great men"—cults with value-collective, and not value-individual, foundations—he nevertheless shares *one* trait with such cults because of his predominantly historical orientation; and this trait, I wish to emphasize, is thoroughly opposed to our own principles. For the manner and degree in which the moral quality of persons enters into human experience in general, and, within it, that sector called "historical experience," in *no* way determine or limit the *existence* of these persons and their *qualities.* Perhaps the old Christian principle that, *ceteris paribus, the good remains more unknown than the evil,* that good blossoms silently whereas evil makes noise for all the world to hear, can be philosophically justified. In particular, the degrees of *conspicuousness,* under otherwise equal conditions, of different positive and negative moral qualities in general to historical consciousness has not yet been sufficiently investigated. All this must be forgotten as long as an ethics is oriented toward the "great person." For to this "greatness" there belongs (at least as a cocondition) not only a broad, factual, and visible *effectiveness* on human affairs but also some sort of image of this effectiveness in the continuity of historical consciousness, even if this be that minimum of "historical consciousness" which constitutes *objective* "history" (and not, first of all, knowledge of this history in some form of historical *cognition*) in contrast to the merely objective succession of states in nature. For I can imagine many *good* men whom no one knows or has known. But I cannot imagine an unknown *great* man. True, this so-called greatness has its *ultimate* foundation in qualities of the person that are in themselves valuable; for the effectiveness and the image of the

---

158. Essential goodness precedes all "moral legislation" in God's case, too.

effectiveness represent the grounds of *cognition,* not of being.[159] But this foundation, which makes possible the distinction between true and apparent "greatness," is only a *conditio sine qua non* of possible "being-great"; it is not its fully sufficient ground. A certain *breadth of feelable effectiveness* and an *image* of it belong equally to "greatness." Being, image, and effectiveness are thus interwoven in a peculiar way in the idea of the "great" person. And so all further purely empirical conditions that are necessary for this possible breadth of effectiveness and for the becoming of the image and Gestalt in historical consciousness belong also to the condition of the being of the great person (which must be distinguished from the condition of the knowledge of the historian). In order for someone to become "great," "times," "situations," and "tasks" that respond to his personal qualities and allow his active explication must be *given.* And the becoming of the *image* requires a spectator, a bard, a man who writes history, etc.

These two unavoidable factors of *selection* of the *possible* greatness and the *factual* greatness of given persons and personal qualities would not have *moral* significance even if we were to suppose that the goodness of a person is the foundation of his "true" greatness.[160] In this case one would have to be a good man in order to be a great one, but not a great man in order to be a good one. Ethics would have *no* reason to regard the "great" personality as the highest value-being on earth (in Nietzsche's sense). Rather, ethics would have to recommend, with respect to the past, the veneration of the inner spiritual structure of all mankind in whose personal center moral values are originally located—that sublime spiritual structure of which only a few varied points and visible consequences enter into *the* sphere in which not only our known "history" but also all possible "history," including all greatness, happens. Yet, these presuppositions give ethics the right to establish the ideal norm: it *ought* to be that the conditions of life are so created that good men (and not evil men) can *become* great.

Nietzsche headed in a somewhat different direction, though

159. Both Carlyle (see the introduction to his *Hero-Worship*) and Jacob Burckhardt (see his *Weltgeschichtliche Betrachtungen*) correctly stress this point.

160. But I believe that we must do this in the sense that this goodness is a necessary condition of all other greatness, for instance, in art and statesmanship. A predication of greatness in general appears to me to be tied up with this, without clarity concerning the location of greatness (e.g., greatness in an artist).

one connected with his fascination with "great" men, when he fell victim to the *pragmatic* prejudice, which we rejected earlier, that the realization of the highest moral values can and must be a task of our *will* and our *actions*. This view caused him to see in the being of the (great) person not only the highest *value* of world events but also an immediate *volitional goal* for our actions. Witnesses to this error in principle are his immature racial ideas in ethics and politics and aspects of the ideal personality that is to be produced in the *future* in the form of the "overman." Hence he failed to see the *character of grace* in all historical greatness. And within this framework of ideas we find the root of his passionate criticism of the ethos of his time as a false "democratism." [161] We also find here the root of the ridiculous spectacle of those who thought that they could use his ideas in support of themselves, but who, as representatives of narrow classes and parties,[162] had nothing to do with the excellence of his view on the human and moral subjects about which he had so seriously thought. But, as we have said, it is precisely a correctly conceived value-ethics of personality that must come to the conclusion, in applying itself to the questions of the *normalization* of the will, that only the establishment of maximally *uniform conditions for the being and life of persons,* in terms of a *distribution of goods subject first to the value of utility* and second to the value of life, can bring to the fore the *inner* differences of the bearers of *higher* values and furnish the basis for their self-explication in actions and works. And only the direction of willing toward goals of *these* kinds of goods can mediately reach what cannot be posited immediately as a "purpose": the being of the *best*. Had Nietzsche realized this, his criticism of his era and his conclusions concerning the factors *in which* equality and inequality among men consist, and the factors in which they *should* consist with respect to the distribution of all kinds of goods and rights, would have been different from what they are. But this is a subject for applied ethics to investigate.

Finally, the *value*-content of Nietzsche's idea of personality (insofar as this content goes beyond the still-formal values of the maximal richness and fullness of the personality as simultaneously realizable with the highest concentration, *ceteris pari-*

161. On the difference between democratism and democracy, see my essay, "Der Bourgeois" (Bibliog. no. 10).

162. See, for example, Alexander Tille, *Von Darwin bis Nietzsche* (Leipzig, 1895).

bus) is one-sided and fails to correspond to the genuine ranks among the order of values. This is the case because his idea of the person is determined by the *heroic* type. If Nietzsche was unable to do justice to the ideas of *genius* and *saint*—in relation to the hero—as guidelines for human becoming and as the fruit and the most concentrated *meaning* of basic types of human communalization, it was because of the erroneous *biological* foundations on which he sought to place *all* ethics.

ad 4. Individual Person and Collective Person

Just as the person discovers every psychic experience against the cogiven background of a stream of such experiences, and every object of outer perception against the background of and as a "part" of a nature that is spatially and temporally endless,[163] so also in every execution of an act is the person given to himself in self-experience as a *member* of a *community of persons which encompasses* him. Whatever the type of this community, simultaneity and succession (of generations) are at first still *undifferentiated.* From an ethical viewpoint this experience of a person's necessary membership in a social sphere appears in the *coresponsibility* for the total effective activity of the sphere. With regard to the possible factualness of community, it appears in *re-experiencing and coexperiencing, refeeling and cofeeling,* as the basic acts of inner perception of the other. At least the very *sense* of community and its *possible* existence is not an assumption that requires empirical establishment, because in certain classes of acts the intention toward a possible community is cogiven *by essential necessity* with the nature of these acts themselves. It is, rather, an assumption that is conjoined with the sense of a *person as originally* and *essentially* as it is with that of the *outer and inner worlds.*

A great deal of importance rests on this *equal originality.* For the existence or the position of "community" in general is neither ethically nor epistemologically conjoined with the existence (or the position) of a *world of bodies* (as I have shown in the appendix to my work on sympathetic feelings). And this is also the *highest* philosophical reason why the sciences of community and history and their basic givens are not dependent on the natural sciences and *their* basic givens; the former are "autonomous" with respect to the latter. The constitution of the concep-

---

163. [See chap. 6, A, sec. 3, g.—*Ed.*]

tual unities of these human sciences—the unities of simultaneity as well as those of succession, e.g., family, tribe, people, nation, cultural unit, or age, period, etc.—does not require any regression to existing scientific unities of reality, for example, to those of geography (territories), or to scientific-biological theories of race. Basic details in this regard must be more closely investigated in the philosophy of history and sociology. Only a mundane *correlate* is necessarily in the essence of a social unit. But the assumption (G. Berkeley and J. G. Fichte) according to which the existence and assumption of an objectively real world of bodies with their own laws can be *founded* only on the existence and assumption of a social unit—an X, for example, identical and identifiable for the members of a social unit, or the mere "material" of a consciousness of duty leading primarily to the assumption of a community—is untenable.[164]

However, as we have shown, the existence and assumption of a community is not founded on the existence or position of an objective *inner world* or of something psychic.[165] Understanding and coexperiencing (including the inner self-perception of the other) necessarily preclude such objectification, although they are the first condition of knowledge of the other's psychic sphere. And one's own psychic sphere is constituted only in differentiating it from that of the other.

Hence both community and history are psychophysically *indifferent* concepts.

Thus not only does everyone discover himself against a background of, and at the same time as a "member" of, a totality of interconnections of experience which have somehow become concentrated, and which are *called* in their temporal extension *history*, in their simultaneous extension *social unity;* but as a moral subject in this whole, everyone is *also* given as a "person *acting with others*," as a "man with others," and as "coresponsible" for everything morally relevant in this totality.

We must designate as *collective persons* the various *centers* of *experiencing* [Er-lebens] in this endless totality of living with one another, insofar as these centers fully correspond to the definitions of the person which we gave earlier.

---

164. Such a deduction can be found in Fichte's *Naturrecht*. Hugo Münsterberg has followed him on this point.

165. See *Zur Phänomenologie und Theorie der Sympathiegefühle*, app., and what I have said on W. Dilthey in my essay, "Versuche einer Philosophie des Lebens" (Bibliog. no. 10). [See *Wesen und Formen der Sympathie*, pt. C, chap. 3.—*Ed.*]

As we said above, according to its meaning a social unit is a totality *without an end*. Just as it belongs to the essence of every finite person of a social unit, and to the nature of any social unit, to be a partial manifestation of a concrete collective person, so also does it belong to the essence of any given *social unit* to be a *member* of a social unit encompassing it, and to the essence of any kind of a given *collective person* also or simultaneously to be a *member* of a collective person encompassing it. These are strictly a priori propositions that compel us, by virtue of their apriority, to transcend in spirit any given, factual, earthly community, i.e., to see it as a member of a community encompassing it. Whether or not this transcending act finds "fulfillment" in a factual experience is of no consequence for the sense and nature of this "consciousness-of." An imaginary Robinson Crusoe endowed with cognitive-theoretical faculties would also coexperience his *being a member of a social unit* in his experiencing the *lack* of fulfillment of acts of act-types constituting a person in general.[166] For it is by virtue of their intentional *essence*, and not on the basis of their contingent *objects* or what they empirically have in common, that these acts are factual acts, that is, *social* acts, acts that find their fulfillment only in a possible community. Among these acts are acts of the true *kinds* of love (which are listed in the above-mentioned work); such acts are capable of and require "fulfillment," and I have distinguished them from all differentiations of love resulting from the nature of factual and experienced objects.[167] Acts of commanding, obeying, ordering, promising, vowing, and cofeeling also belong to this class. In contrast to these are acts of a *singularizing* nature (consciousness of self, self-esteem, self-love, scrutinizing one's conscience, etc.) and acts that are indifferent to these two directions (e.g., judging). Therefore, the being of the person as individual person is constituted within a person and a world in general in the special essential class of singularizing acts; the being of the collective person, in the special essential class of social acts. The

---

166. For more details, see *Zur Phänomenologie und Theorie der Sympathiegefühle*, pp. 96 ff. [See *Wesen und Formen der Sympathie*, pt. B, chap. 6, sec. 3.—*Ed.*]

167. For example, a mother's love, sexual love, love for one's country and home, and also love of humanity and God. These kinds of love are essentially different from one another independent of their objects and the discovery of their objects; they only find their "fulfillment" or "nonfulfillment" in such objects. See *Zur Phänomenologie und Theorie der Sympathiegefühle*, pp. 73 ff. [See *Wesen und Formen der Sympathie*, pt. B, chap. 4.—*Ed.*]

world of a community is the *total* content of all experiencing of the kind "experiencing with one another" (in relation to which "understanding" is only a secondary kind). This is the *collective world,* which has as its concrete subject on the act side the *collective person.* The world of the individual, the *individual world,* is the content of all experiencing in singularizing acts and acts of experiencing-for-oneself. This is the *singular world,* which has as its concrete subject on the act side the *individual person.* Hence an individual person *and* a collective person "belong" to every *finite* person. Both factors are essentially necessary sides of a concrete whole of person and world. Thus individual and collective persons can be related to each other *within* every possible concrete finite person, and the relation of one to the other is experienceable. The collective person with its world is not the result of any kind of "synthesis" which it or even an individual person must undertake; it is, on the contrary, an experienced *reality.* The collective person is not a kind of "sum" or a kind of artificial [168] or real collection [169] of individual persons, nor are its properties composed of properties of individual persons; the collective person is not contained "first" in individual persons, nor is the world of the collective person the sum of the worlds of individual persons, not even in some first stage. Hence *no inference* of any sort and no act of constructive "synthesis" are required in order to arrive at the reality of a collective person. Such acts come into question only for the establishment of the special world-*content* of a collective person.

It is therefore *in* the person that the mutually related *individual person* and *collective person* become differentiated. The idea of one is not the "foundation" of the other. The collective or group person is not composed of individual persons in the sense that it derives its existence from such a composition; nor is the collective person a result of the merely reciprocal agency of individual persons or (subjectively and in cognition) a result of a synthesis of arbitrary additions. It is an experienced *reality,* and not a construction, although it is a starting point for constructions of all types.

If one asks whether the collective person has a "consciousness-of" that is *different* from and *independent* of the consciousness-of of the individual person, the answer depends on the meaning of the question. No doubt the collective person does

---

168. Like a statistical unity.
169. Like the collective *thing* of the heaven of stars.

possess a "consciousness-of" that is different from and independent of the consciousness-of of the *individual* person.

This proposition will appear paradoxical only to someone who would base the differentiation of consciousness in general on the separation of lived bodies or to someone who would base the concept of the person on the concept of a soul-substance.[170] The mistake of such assumptions was shown before. Inasmuch as the collective person is constituted in mutual coexperiencing of persons, and inasmuch as the person is the concrete act-center of the experience *in* this mutual coexperiencing, the consciousness-of of the collective person is *always contained* in the consciousness of a total finite person as *act-direction*. It is not something transcendent to it. Yet it is not the case that a certain finite total person must also have a reflective consciousness of the contents that he contingently experiences in mutual coexperiencing. Nor is it the case that his experience can encompass the *collective content* which is experienced by the collective person and to which the person *also* belongs as a member-person. Indeed, the person's peculiar awareness that he can never encompass the total contents of the experience of the collective person to which he belongs is a part of the *essence* of this experienced relation in which both member-person and collective person are given. The collective person with its world is *not fully* experienced in *any* of its member-persons; it is given as something going beyond the member-persons in terms of duration, content, and range of effectiveness. Indeed, it belongs to the essence of all collective persons to have member-persons who are *also* individual persons; but the collective person's existence, with its strict continuity as a collective person, is not connected with the existence of the same individual persons. In relation to the collective person the latter are freely variable and, in principle, replaceable. Through death and in other ways they lose their membership in the collective person.[171] And the same individual

170. A collective soul-substance is, of course, nonsense.

171. Above all, one must be careful not to regard the collective person as an individual person of only wider scope, whether consciously or implicitly, and thus attribute to it the kind of consciousness which can be attributed *only* to individual persons. If one does this, it is easy to show that the collective person cannot have a consciousness, or that this assumption is but a "mysterious" assertion. This mistake would be analogous to the one with which Husserl rightly charged Berkeley. Berkeley maintained that it is necessary to represent to oneself "one" triangle which is neither right-angled nor oblique-angled and yet both at the same time in order to demonstrate the existence of the species. If one does not consider the fact that special singular acts are necessary to reveal the

persons can also belong to different collective persons, for example, to a nation and to a church.

It would appear that in making these statements we have simply sided with Aristotle in the old philosophical dispute between the Aristotelian doctrine, according to which man as a rational being is by nature a ζῶον πολιτικόν,[172] and the doctrine first formulated by the Epicureans, according to which community is first constituted by some form of *contract*. But this is true only in a negative way inasmuch as we must reject the theory of a contract in any of its three possible forms: as a genetic theory, as a theory of origin, or as a theoretical standard (according to which only the type of order of a community is to be assessed against the idea of a contract). But in a positive sense our views do not confirm Aristotle's. For Aristotle, the individual person is not equal in origin to the whole. He is, rather, derived from it—essentially, not historically. The person becomes a person by being a member of a community (first of all, the state) and does not have an independent value of his own apart from his value as member. In our view, however, all persons are, with *equal* originality, both individual persons and (essentially) members of a collective person. And one's own value as an individual person is independent of his value as a member-person. Second, Aristotle does not recognize the concept of a collective *person*. Also, *logos, form,* and ratio are, for Aristotle, *over and above* the idea of a *person,* a principle that is typically held by the ancients (even in their theories about God). The state, too, is viewed not as a sovereign personal will but only as the form and rational order of a people's community based on laws. However, we remain convinced that the community has its ultimate foundation in the idea of the *person;* and we maintain that it is not values of the community but values of the *person* that are the highest values, and that the highest values *among* values of the com-

---

givenness of the individual person, one is easily led into a metaphysical hypostatization of the individual person which does not allow one to accept a collective person unless the latter is falsely interpreted simply as an individual person of wider scope.

172. Aristotle's expression means something very different from what historians and economists (especially those of the historical school), with their complete lack of knowledge of philosophy, say that it does: the mere trivial recognition of the (questionable!) fact that there is no isolated living man—a fact never denied by the subtle representatives of the theory of the contract. Aristotle means that it belongs to the essence "man" = bearer of νοῦς (*anima rationalis*) to be a member of a state-community and to know himself as such, no matter to what extent he may *in fact* live alone.

munity are those belonging to the collective *person*. And so the relation between the collective person and the individual person does not represent a special kind of relation between the universal and the individual; the collective person (apart from the concepts of it, such as state, nation, church) is as much a spiritual *individual* as the individual person, e.g., the Prussian state.[173] From an ethical point of view there is for us no relation of subordination between the individual person and the collective person. Rather, both have a *common* ethical subordination to the idea of an infinite person in whom the division between individual persons and collective persons, necessary for finite persons, *ceases to be*. Therefore the Godhead, according to its very idea, cannot be conceived either as an individual person (which would be henotheism, and not monotheism) or as the highest collective person (pantheism). It can be conceived only as *the* ("singular," not numerically "one") infinite person.

From this it follows, of course, that not *all* kinds of social unity are unities that may be called collective *persons* (insofar as we use "social" to designate the most general and undifferentiated combinations of men).

One must fully develop a *theory of all possible essential social units* to be applied to the understanding of factual social units (marriage, family, people, nation, etc.). This is the basic problem of philosophical sociology and the presupposition of any social ethics. As we mentioned in the Preface, we are planning to develop this discipline in a special work. Let it suffice here to mention the principles of division of such a theory of the essence of the social and its chief result, so that we may get to the deeper foundation of the concept of the collective person. The first such principle deals with the essentially different *kinds of being with one another* and experiencing one another through which a specific kind of social unity is constituted. The second principle deals with the kind and rank of *values* in whose direction the member-persons of a social unit see "with one another" so that they may act according to norms that conform to those values. As is the case with all non-inductive concepts and propositions,

173. It is the tension between Christianity (especially its theory of individuality and the infinite value of every "soul," as well as its incorporation of each person into *two* basic communities, state *and* church) and the ancient idea of community and partnership that historically led to the *depth* of this problem—a depth which those who want to return to the ancient idea of the state in some form and those who want to renovate the theory of contract in some form on Christian bases (e.g., the Calvinists) completely miss.

these essential social units and their interconnections are never purely and fully realized in factual experience; but since they function as the *condition* for the objective possibility of this experience, they serve in their being understood.

According to the first of these principles, we make the following distinctions in conformity with the detailed, but not quite sufficient, preliminary work, *Zur Phänomenologie und Theorie der Sympathiegefühle*, especially its appendix.[174]

1. A social unit is constituted (simultaneously) in so-called contagion and involuntary imitation devoid of understanding.[175] Such a unit of animals is called the *herd*, of men, the *mass*. With respect to its members, the mass possesses a reality of its own and has its own laws of effectiveness.

2. A social unit is constituted in *that* kind of coexperiencing or reliving (cofeeling, costriving, cothinking, cojudging, etc.) which reveals some *"understanding"* of the members of this unit (distinguishing it from the mass). However, this understanding is not that which would precede this coexperiencing as a separate act, but that which occurs *in* coexperiencing *itself*. In particular, here there is no "understanding" in whose acts a member coexperiences his individual *ego*ness as the starting point of such acts; still less is the other being *objectified* (which distinguishes this unit from society). It is in this immediate experience and understanding, in which (as I have shown in the work mentioned) there is *no division* of any kind between the experience of self and that of the other or between bodily expression and experience in the comprehension of member *A* and that of member *B*, that the basic social unit which I call the *life-community* (in the pregnant sense) is constituted. The *content* of this coexperiencing is, in the "community," truly *identical* content. Any attempt to "explain" this peculiar phenomenon of "coexperiencing something" by saying that *A* experiences something that is experienced by *B*, and that both, in addition, *know* of their experiencing it, or that they only "take part" in their experiences in terms of a mere "cofeeling-with," would be a fully erroneous construction.[176] If one looks away from the *uniform actus* of coexperiencing and toward (objective) individuals and their experiences, this *actus*

174. [See *Wesen und Formen der Sympathie*, pt. C, chap. 3.—*Ed.*]
175. On the psychological mechanism of these processes, see the above-mentioned work. [See *Wesen und Formen der Sympathie*, pt. A, chap. 2.—*Ed.*]
176. See *Zur Phänomenologie und Theorie der Sympathiegefühle*, p. 9. [See *Wesen und Formen der Sympathie*, pt. A, chap. 2.—*Ed.*]

(and the ever changing structure) of coliving, cohearing, coseeing, cothinking, cohoping, coloving, and cohating hovers between these individuals like a *stream of experience which has its own laws* and whose subject is the reality of the community itself.[177] Hence, given the basis of the "community," mutual understanding among members requires *no inferences* from expression to experience; their common knowledge of the truth, no *criteria of truth* and no artificial terminology; and the formation of the common will, no promises and no contracts.

Whereas there is no solidarity in the social unit of the mass because the individual does not exist at all as an experience and therefore cannot possess solidarity with others, there is a special *form* of solidarity in a life-community which, in contrast to another higher form (as we shall see), may be called *representable solidarity*. This solidarity arises on the basis of the fact that, although the experiences of the individual are given *as* such experiences, they vary with regard to course and content in their total dependency on the variations of collective experience. True, the experiences of an individual are given to him as single experiences, but only on the basis of a special singularizing act that clips him, as it were, out of the communal whole. *This* solidarity implies that self-responsibility, when it is experienced, is *built upon* an experience of *coresponsibility* for the willing, acting, and effecting of the whole community. And for this reason the individual is in principle "representable" by other individuals according to law, in conformity with the firm, but nonetheless changing, structure of forms which correspond to different areas of tasks of the community, and which are called caste, class, dignity, occupation, etc., depending upon the kind of structure.

Whereas we can explain the unity of the mass, with the assistance of principles of association and their derivatives, on the basis of a common, sensible complex of stimuli, this is not possible in the case of the life-community. The life-community is a *suprasingular* unit of life and body that possesses a (formally) non-mechanical unity and lawfulness, as does any unity of this essence, whether considered objectively or subjectively, i.e., whether considered in inner or outer perception. Nevertheless,

177. The colorful and changing hypostatizations of communal subjects in history, such as units of family gods, tribal gods, and gods of common people, exist as long as religion is tied to community, i.e., to the *vital* (factual blood-communities can always be replaced by the many kinds of *symbolizations* of them).

the life-community is far from being a *personal* unit, i.e., a collective *person*. True, there is one and the same goal-determined *striving* and *counterstriving*, with a certain structure of involuntary and subconscious preferring and rejecting of values and goals of striving in the form of traditional mores, customs, cults, and costumes. But there is *no* will which can be called purposeful, which is able to choose, which is unitary and morally responsible, all of which would belong to a person. Accordingly, the life-community's *values*, i.e., both the values which it experiences as the same (especially in the natural language or its dialects) and the values of which it is the bearer, belong to the class of *thing*-values [Sach*werte*], not to the class of *personal* values.

3. The social unit of the *society* is basically different from the essential social unit of the life-community.[178] First, the society, as opposed to the *natural* unit of the life-community, is to be defined as an *artificial* unit of individuals having *no* original "living-with-one-another" in the sense described above. Rather, *all* relations among individuals are established by *specific conscious* acts that are experienced by each as coming from his *individual* ego, which is experientially given *first in this case*, as directed to someone else as "another."

The plain experience of what goes on in the "other," or what he thinks, wills, etc., presupposes a clear *distinction* between "self-experience" and "understanding" and, consequently, between the self-experienced and the understood (with primary retention of one's own judgments), as well as the primary experienced attribution of these contents to two *different* single men. Understanding presupposes a distinction between *bodily* gestures of expression (not given *as bodily* in the life-community) and the experience in the other. It also presupposes an *analogical inference* from the self-experienced to the experienced of the other (or some logically equivalent mental process), an inference that is made on the basis of the former distinction. Moreover, common cognition, enjoyment, etc., presuppose some *criteria* of the true and the false, the beautiful and the ugly, which have been agreed upon beforehand.[179] Every kind of willing together and doing together presupposes the *actus* of *promising* and the

178. It is to the credit of Ferdinand Tönnies to have first established the difference between life-community and society as essential forms of human togetherness. But the above characteristics of these two social forms deviate a great deal from his; in our opinion he does not sufficiently separate a priori and historical factors.

179. All philosophy using criteria is essentially philosophy of *society*. [See "Probleme einer Soziologie des Wissens."—*Ed.*]

phenomenon [*Sachgebilde*] of the *contract* that is constituted in mutual promising—the basic phenomenon of all private law.

From ethical and legal points of view there is no longer *any* original coresponsibility. All responsibility for others is based on unilateral *self-responsibility,* and all possible responsibility for others must be regarded as having come from a free and singular act of taking over certain obligations. There is no true solidarity (in some form of "one for all" and "all for one")—either representable or unrepresentable [180]—but only the similarity or dissimilarity of individuals' *interests* and the *"classes"* resulting from such interests. As a whole, the essential social unit of society is not a special reality outside or above individuals. It is simply an indivisible fabric of *relations* that represent "conventions," [181] "usage," or "contracts," depending on whether they are more explicit or more tacit. Hence there is nothing to be found in society *in* which individuals can know themselves to possess solidarity. Just as boundless *trust* in one another is the basic attitude in the life-community, unfathomable and primary *distrust* of all in all is the basic attitude in society. If, however, the society is supposed to "will" something that is to be "common" to all of its individuals, it can do so only by *fiction* or by *force* unless it has the assistance of *other* essential social units. It is the so-called *majority* principle which functions here in constructing the fiction that the "common will" is (and must be, if things are to go on without force) the fortuitously identical volitional content of *all as individuals* (because the majority comes closest to this ideal). Force, however, consists in imposing the will of the majority on the minority.

In contrast to the life-community, which encompasses people who are *not of age* (as well as domestic animals attached to it), the society is a unit of *mature* and *self-conscious individual persons.* Whereas the personal form of unity in general does not appear in the mass or the life-community, it does appear throughout society. But it appears *exclusively* as the *individual* person who obtains in society as the person, i.e., as the individual person who is related to the value-modalities of the agreeable (society as sociability) and the useful (society as the bearer of civilization), which are relative to the sensible and are, by nature, not

180. See the following.

181. Hence conventions and mores, like fashions and costumes, must be sharply distinguished. Conventions and fashions belong entirely to society; mores and costumes, to the life-community. [See "Probleme einer Soziologie des Wissens."—*Ed.*]

unifying, but *divisive*.[182] The "elements" of society, however, are not individuals in the sense of the individual spiritual person described above. The elements of society are *originaliter equal* and of *equal value* because they enter the picture as such "elements" solely by virtue of their formal character as *single* persons, not by virtue of their *non-formal* [materialen] contents of individuality. Differences in society and differences in value between its elements come about only through different values of *accomplishment* of the individuals in the value-direction of the agreeable and the useful, the value-correlates of society. To this extent there is a peculiar law that applies to the elements of society, namely, that they are formally (as single elements) entirely unrepresentable, but non-formally (as individuals) representable because they are originally *equal*. Although every individual being in a life-community is representable by another one who occupies the same position in the community (standing, office, rank, occupation), these positions themselves are not representable, nor are the individual beings insofar as they exercise functions in different positions.

However, this peculiarity of the societal structure does not preclude the possibility that the single being *as* single being, and not as an "element" of the society, perfects an awareness of his incomparable *individuality*. This occurs in a manner that is impossible in the life-community. On the level of the pure community the individualistic principle is realized only for the concrete *community*, not for the individual being. In a (pure) society it is realized *exclusively* for the *individual being*. An individual being of a life-community is *primarily* given to himself as an *X*, a *Y*, or a *Z* of mutual living-with-one-another or of a specific form of this. In society these *X*-, *Y*-, and *Z*-places are filled with an original content, so that instead of mutual living-with-one-another, there is *mediate mutual accord* concerning what is experienced by anyone "for himself." The primary seat of all moral responsibility is the *whole* of the communal reality in a life-community (the real subject of mutual living-with-one-another), and the individual being is only coresponsible for the will, actions, and doings of the whole.[183] By contrast, it is in (pure) society that

182. "Divisive" in contrast to "unifying" higher value-modalities of vital values, spiritual values, and values of the holy. It is the localizable relatedness to a lived body that accounts for their being essentially "divisive." See chap. 2, sec. 3.

183. All institutions, mores, and moralities conforming to the principle of solidary responsibility, for example, blood-revenge (within families,

the principle of the *exclusive self-responsibility* of each for his actions is realized.

Yet there are interconnections of a quite determinate character *between* society and life-community (as essential structures of social unity). The basic nexus is this: there can be *no society without life-community* (though there can be life-community without society). All *possible* society is therefore *founded* through community. This proposition holds both for the manner of "accord" and for the kind of formation of a *common will*. Mutual living-with-one-another and *its* content are the origins of the non-formal premises that serve in society as bases for analogical inferences establishing the "inner" life of the "other." These premises cannot be derived from any inferences.[184] In what concerns the obligating character of *"promising"* as the *actus* of formation of the will and as the ideal ought-to-be of "promising" in the sense of *what* has been promised, the (former) duty does *not* have its source in *other* acts of promising (e.g., in the promise to keep one's promise), but solely in the moral *faithfulness* whose roots are in the norm according to which original willing-with-one-another cannot be changed without an additional and sufficient reason of value. For the ought-to-be of what has been promised and of what has been accepted as such by the one who has been promised something has its foundation in the ought-to-be of this content as something *identical* for a willing-with-one-another. And the duty to keep mutual promises that are in a contract, the basic form of the formation of a uniform will in society, does *not* have its source in *another* contract to keep contracts. It has its source in the *solidary* obligation of the members of the community to realize the contents that ought to be for the members. A so-called contract *without* this foundation would be nothing but a fiction. It would be only the expression and statement of a momentary, hypothetical volitional readiness to do something on the condition that the other do something, while the other expresses this momentary and hypothetical readiness. But the content of the *genuine contract* (as something to be realized in the future) is *plainly* willed by the contractual partners, and not in terms of this merely hypothetical volitional readiness. And the hypothetical obligation of *A* to do something

---

tribes, and clans), belong to the predominantly communal ethos. The community itself is responsible, while every one of its members remains coresponsible to the degree of his importance within the community.

184. See *Zur Phänomenologie und Theorie der Sympathiegefühle*, p. 144. [See *Wesen und Formen der Sympathie*, pt. C, chap. 3.—Ed.]

when *B* does something belongs to the mutually willed *content* of the contract, not to the will of one of the partners.[185] Furthermore, what is mutually *willed* in the contract is plainly given as something to be realized (and thus it is not given as present or future); only the *execution* lies in the sphere of the future within specified dates. Just as the contractual principle has its *roots* in the principle of solidarity, so also conventions and artificial terminologies that support the societal form of *mutual cognition* have their *roots* in the *natural language,* where they can be established in the first place, and on whose *categories* of meaning they remain dependent.[186]

To say that all societal unity (in all walks of life, religion, art, knowledge, commerce) has its foundation in the unity of the life-community is not to imply that the *same* groups of real individuals bound together in a society must also (in another direction) form a community. This law of foundations obtains only for the two *essential structures* of social unification. However, in its application to *factual* relations, this law means two things. First, individuals who enter into societal relations must at some time have gone through a union of the structure of the community in order to be able to enter into the forms of mutual accord and volitional formation that characterize the societal unit. For *A* to be able to make a contract with *B*, it is not necessary for *A* to be communally related to *B;* but he must have been so related to *C, D,* or *E* at some time (e.g., in terms of the family in which he grew up) in order to be able to understand the sense of "contract." Second, all societal combinations of individuals *A,* *B,* and *C* or groups *G, G_1,* and *G_2* can occur *only* when *A, B,* and *C* or *G, G_1,* and *G_2* simultaneously belong to another totality *G_3* of a community—one which is not necessarily formed by *A, B,* and *C* or *G, G_1,* and *G_2*, but which nevertheless contains them as members. Thus the individuals of all families of *one* lineage [*Stammes*] form a community vis-à-vis the individuals of all families of another lineage; within the lineage they form a community

185. Naturally, willing with reservation is to be clearly distinguished from the willing of reservations.

186. There is an analogous relation between natural symbols and artificial allegory, between artistic willing and works of art in a community and in a society, between a traditional, communal, religious content of faith and religious education, etc. But the *criteria* which must be presupposed in collective cognition in a society if an understanding of the sameness of something is to be possible must themselves be seen by all in terms of συμφιλοσοφειν. Otherwise an infinite series of criteria would be necessary to establish the sameness of a proposition as a criterion. [See "Probleme einer Soziologie des Wissens."—*Ed.*]

only as members of their families, and among themselves they form only a society. Thus all nations belonging to the cultural circle "Europe" form a community in relation to all nations of the Asian cultural circle. The members of each cultural circle are coresponsible for the well-being of the whole of the circle; but within Europe and among themselves the same nations form only a society. In this case and analogous ones our proposition implies that the character of obligation and the sanction of the contracts into which individuals or groups enter always presuppose a *further* communal whole to which they simultaneously belong, and that this sanction stems from the unitary collective will of this whole. The idea of the contract thus does not presuppose the unit of the *state* [187]—as some have erroneously maintained in criticism of the contract theory—but a *further* community to which the partners to the contract belong.

4. From the essential types of social unity thus far mentioned, namely, mass, society, and life-community, we must distinguish the highest essential type of social unity, with whose characteristics we began this chapter: *the unity of independent, spiritual, and individual single persons "in" an independent, spiritual, and individual collective person.* We assert that this unity, and it alone, is the *nucleus* and total *novelty* of the true and ancient Christian idea of community, and that this Christian idea represents, so to speak, the historical discovery of this unity. In quite a peculiar manner, this idea of community unites the being and indestructible self-value of the individual "soul" (conceived in terms of creation) and the person (contrary to the ancient theory of corporation and the Jewish idea of "people") by means of the idea of the salvational solidarity of all in the *corpus christianum,* which is founded on the Christian idea of love (and which is contrary to the mere ethos of "society," which denies moral solidarity).

For on this level any finite person is an individual person *and* at the same time a member of a collective person. It simply belongs to the essence of a finite person (fully known as such) both to *be* so and to *experience* himself so. Thus responsibility-for (someone) and responsibility-to (someone) are *essentially* different in orientation. In the life-community the bearer of *all* responsibility is the reality of the community, and the individual is coresponsible for the life-community; in the collective person every individual *and* the collective person are *self*-responsible

187. The idea of a contract *between* states is for this reason precluded.

(= responsible for oneself), and at the same time every individual is also coresponsible for the collective person (and for every individual "in" it), just as the collective person is coresponsible for *each* of its members. Hence coresponsibility between the individual person and the collective person is *mutual* and does not preclude self-responsibility on the part of both. As for the responsibility-to (someone), it must be said that there is *neither* an ultimate responsibility of the individual to the collective person, as is the case in the life-community, *nor* an ultimate responsibility of the collective person to the individual (or to the sum or a majority of individuals), as is the case in the society (principle of the majority). Nevertheless, *both* the collective person and the individual person are responsible to the person of persons, to *God,* and, indeed, in terms of self-responsibility *as well as* coresponsibility. But here the principle of solidarity, which diminishes and disappears in a pure society but obtains *exclusively* in the life-community, takes on a new sense. It changes from a principle of *representable* solidarity into one of *unrepresentable solidarity:* the individual person is coresponsible for all other individual persons "in" the collective person not only as the representative of an *office,* a *rank,* or any other positional value in the social *structure,* but also, indeed, *first of all,* as a *unique personal individual* and as the bearer of an individual conscience in the sense defined above. In moral self-examination at this level, not only must everyone ask, What of positive moral value would have occurred in the world and what of negative moral value would have been avoided if I, as a *representative of a place* in the social structure, had comported myself differently? But everyone must also ask, What would have occurred *if I, as a spiritual individual, had grasped,* willed, and realized the *"good-in-itself-for-me"* (in the sense described before) in a *superior* manner? The principle of solidarity is thus not *precluded* by the proposition that there is, in addition to the universally valid good-in-itself, an individually valid good-in-itself. On the contrary, this proposition raises the principle to the *highest* level that it can possibly attain.

Hence in *this* sense the principle of solidarity is for us an eternal component and a *fundamental article of the cosmos of finite moral persons.* The *total* moral world—no matter how far its sphere may extend in space and time, here on earth or on discovered and undiscovered planets or even beyond these—becomes *one encompassing whole* through the validity of this principle. This whole *rises and falls as a whole* whenever this principle suffers the slightest change, and as a *whole* it possesses at every moment of its existence a *unique* moral *totality-value* (a total evil and total good, a total guilt and total merit) that can *never* be regarded as the *sum* of individuals' evil and good or as the sum of their guilt and merit. But *every* person, both the individual person and the collective person, participates in this according to his special and *unique* membership. Suppose that we find ourselves in a world court. No one *alone* would be tried by its highest judge; all would have to answer to him in the unity of *one* act, and all taken together would have to listen to this judge in *one* act. He would not sentence anyone until he had heard, understood, and valued *all* others *with* this one. In *each* he would cosentence the *whole* no less than the whole in each.

What are the essential elements on which this great and sublime principle rests?[188] Ultimately it rests on two propositions. The first is a proposition that we stressed before, namely, that a community of persons belongs to the evidential *essence* of a possible person—regardless of the real and, by essential necessity, fortuitous causes of the *empirically real connections* between certain persons and certain others—and that the possible unities of sense and of value of such a community possess an a priori structure independent in principle of the kind, measure, place, and time of the realization of these unities. This is the *foundation* that makes moral solidarity *possible*. What makes moral solidarity *necessary* is the formal proposition concerning the (direct or indirect) [189] *essential reciprocity and reciprocal value-ness* of all morally relevant comportment and the corresponding non-formal propositions concerning the essential nexus of the basic *types* of social acts. This reciprocity is *not* based on the contingent reality of these acts, on specific persons who execute these acts, or on the presence of real mechanisms and factual forms of conveyance in which this reciprocity gains *reality*. It

188. See *Zur Phänomenologie und Theorie der Sympathiegefühle*, pp. 65 ff., and "Das Ressentiment im Aufbau der Moralen," pp. 217, 241–74. Since I do not wish to repeat myself, I must ask the reader to consult these passages. [See *Wesen und Formen der Sympathie*, pt. B, chap. 2. See also "Das Ressentiment im Aufbau der Moralen," sec. 5, and "Über Ressentiment und moralisches Werturteil," sec. 4.—*Ed.*]

189. By virtue of the co-originality of individual and collective persons in the nature of the uniform finite person, the individual acts mentioned earlier (self-love, self-perfection, self-happiness, etc.) "indirectly" possess this essential reciprocity and reciprocal valueness, and all social acts "indirectly" possess an essential relation to self-sanctification and self-ruin (in the end)—without any *intention toward* community or one's own self in either case.

rests on the ideal *unity of sense* of these acts as acts of the *essence* of love, esteem, promising, giving orders, etc., acts that require as ideal correlates responses of love, esteem, accepting, obeying, etc., in order to bring about a fact of uniform sense. These and analogous propositions *cannot* be established by inductive methods for two reasons: first, because they are presupposed by every possible understanding of these acts (including every inductive investigation of their factual occurrence); and, second, because they could not in the least be as well founded inductively as inductive propositions are required to be. The possible understanding of a love—for instance, of an act of kindness to me—at least implies coexperiencing the *requirement* of a response of love which belongs to the nature of this act and which is realized psychically (be it in terms of an actual response or a real tendency toward its execution which is disturbed by other motives, or in terms of a merely emotionally represented response of love).[190] It is, I say, the mere *understanding* of this act that implies this. One who does not see this does not look with precision at the *experience*. However I may deny esteem to him who esteems me and whose esteem I understand, however I may refuse any response of love to a felt love, or obedience to an understood command, or acceptance of a promise, I must somehow *"deny"* this to him and *"refuse"* this. I cannot on the one hand understand the sense of his intention and on the other comport myself as if nothing had happened. Of course it may be that the responding act of love and esteem, based on the experienced demand for an act of response, remains a mere act-*stimulus* or, if executed, hits an empty spot, so to speak, in which no *value* of the other person is given that would *correspond* to this act of response. I am then not "able" to esteem and love the other despite *his* esteem and love. But in this case this tendency or this inability or the non-fulfillment of this responding intention in the value of the other is experienced as something positive. Of course this does not in the least mean that in love and esteem there is an *intention* toward a response of love or esteem, or any conditional act with a reservation such as "I will esteem and love you *if* you love and esteem me." For precisely this is *evidentially* precluded by *true* love and esteem of the person. And even the sight of such an intention *destroys* the *experience* of

190. We have discussed so-called emotive representations earlier. [See above, pp. 331, 332, n. 114. See also "Idole," chap. 4 (in *Vom Umsturz der Werte* [Bibliog. no. 31], p. 266).—*Ed.*]

the demand for response in love and esteem. The demand for the response to love lies in the *sense* of love *as* love, *not* in subjective intentions and desires (which may accompany love in X or Y); and in the mere understanding of this sense of love one finds the stimulus of the act of response to love, without which not even the experiential *material* for such understanding would be given. This holds analogously for correlative negative acts of hate and disrespect, when they occur. This *fact alone* grounds the coresponsibility of every (otherwise variable) bearer of these acts for the moral values and disvalues of the acts of the (otherwise variable) bearers of responding acts. One who loves not only realizes a positive act-value in himself but also realizes, *ceteris paribus,* such a value in the beloved. Responding love, *as* love, also bears the positive act-value of love.[191] He who refuses an act of love of ideal oughtness, which is to correspond to the other's *worthiness* to be loved, possesses *coresponsibility* for the negative value lying in the non-being of the positive value of responding love.[192] He does not simply possess self-responsibility for having refused this act. In addition to this there is another proposition, also stressed before, which confers upon the principle of solidarity the *complete* fullness of its *extension.* Because the spiritual person, as the concrete act-center of all his executions of acts, is related to his acts, not as an unalterable substance to its changing properties or activities or as a collective whole to its members or as a whole to its aggregate parts, but as the concrete to the abstract,[193] and because the whole person is and lives in *each* act without exhausting himself in one act or the sum of these acts, there is no act whose execution does not change the content of the person's *being,* and no act-value that does not increase or decrease, enhance or diminish, or positively or negatively determine the value of the person. In every moral individual act of positive value the ability for acts of the kind concerned increases; in other words, there is an increase in what we designated as the *virtue* of the person (which is very different from the habituation and practice of *actions* related to the virtue in question), that is, the experienced power to realize the good that ought to be. Thus mediated, every moral act effects changes in the being and value of the person himself. In relation to our question, this

191. Even though this act, as a reactive act, would not be equal in height to the spontaneous act. See above, p. 101.
192. See the formal axioms given above, on p. 26 f.
193. See chap. 6, A, sec. 3.

means that it is *not* by virtue of *fortuitous* causes or circumstances but by virtue of the *essence* of the state of affairs concerned that the virtue-value implicit in *B*'s act of love in response to *A*, or the increase in personal value, obtains not only for *A* but also for *any other persons C, D, E,* . . . *X* and can become fruitful for them. This also means that *A* possesses original coresponsibility for the presence or absence of *this*, quite apart from the fortuitous causes that lead *C, D, E,* . . . *X* to meet in space and time. One who has become more lovable in responding to love with love, or one who has become more filled with hate in responding to hate with hate, will become so, *ceteris paribus*, for all *possible* "others," not according to rules of experiential association, but according to essential laws.[194]

If one takes a look at the *relation* of this idea of the highest form of social unity—as the idea of a solidary realm of love of individual, independent spiritual persons in a plurality of collective persons of the same character (this unity of collective persons among themselves, as well as the unity of the individual person and the collective person, is possible in God alone)—to the ideas of life-*community* and *society*, one can see that life-community and society as essential forms of social unity are *subordinated* to this highest essential social form, and that they are determined to serve it and to make it appear, but, to be sure, in different manners. Although the idea of the highest form of

---

194. In *Zur Phänomenologie und Theorie der Sympathiegefühle*, I also showed that neither spiritual acts of love nor the genuine *kinds* of love are genetic products of drive-impulses or empirically contingent feeling-states, and, furthermore, that drive-impulses have only a *selective* significance for the contingent real objects that become the factual object of love or the type of love concerned. Accordingly, I showed, too, that real history, in which there occurs a gradual enlargement and extension of the domain of objects of love and its types (family, tribe, people, nation, etc.), only "fulfills" original intentional goals, which do not grow out of real history itself. As to the first of these two points, it follows, concerning the principle of solidarity, that not only the act of hate (bad *in itself*) but also the *absence* of the act of love determines coresponsibility for all evil deeds and for all that happens—and this *prior* to any empirical demonstration of even the possibility of a factual and indirect cooperation in the realization of evil. Yet these principles are maxims that obligate us always to *find out* the evil that would not have happened in the world had *we* only comported ourselves differently. The second point has this consequence for the principle of solidarity: that its sense and validity are not somehow *produced* by history or by changes in communities in factual contact with each other, that this sense is, in part, *fulfilled* only in history, and that this principle itself is a *moral a priori of all possible history and all possible community*. [See *ibid.*, pt. B, chap. 6.—*Ed.*]

social unity is not a "synthesis" of life-community and society, essential characteristics of *both* are nevertheless cogiven in it: the independent, individual person, as in society; and solidarity and real collective unity, as in community. If one asks what the societal form and the communal form mean and achieve in terms of the establishment of the highest moral ideal, one can do justice to *both forms* only by refusing to measure one against the other as its supposed superior. One must measure both society and life-community against this uniquely factual *highest* form. The philosophical, ethical, and sociological currents that have dominated the past two centuries show the errors to which the first of these alternatives leads. From the viewpoint of society as the highest unitary person, the *life-community* (with its ethos) appears only as a more *primitive* developmental form of society, not as an *enduring* essential type of human association in which essential values of specific ranks are represented, indeed, the only place in which they *can* be represented. This alternative dominated almost all philosophy of the eighteenth century; Kant, as well as positivists like Hume, Comte, and Spencer, adopted this view more or less consciously. The peculiar nature of community as an *essential kind* of social unity is not grasped at all here. In order to explain the origin (i.e., the *form* of the genesis, not the positive historical genesis) of all social structures of the spirit (the state, economic corporations, the church, law, mores, myth, language, etc.), it is necessary to return to the idea of a contract that is consciously concluded, or, in the case of Hume, for example, to a contract that is automatically established; and in order to have a *standard* by which to assess the legal order and the degree of development of any extant social structure, one is forced to suppose that it is "as if" its origin were contractual.[195]

195. In the appendix to *Zur Phänomenologie und Theorie der Sympa-thiegefühle,* I showed how the structure of these ideas is, in the final analysis, also borne by the theory of a pointlike soul-substance (like an atom) of the individual person—a theory so characteristic of this type of philosophy—as well as by the theory of analogical inferences as the basis of the positing of other persons. Other *consequences* stemming from these false principles include the theory of exclusive self-responsibility in ethics, the disintegration of the idea of the church as a form of a (historical or simultaneous) *solidary* path to God in favor of a basic relatedness of "every soul to its God," the ideal of an "eternal peace" on the basis of con-tracts among states (the ethos of peace is predominantly societal, that of war predominantly communal), the educationally one-sided intellectual-ization of the individual through "enlightenment," the economic system of free competition, and many other factors. [See *Wesen und Formen der Sympathie,* pt. C, chap. 3.—*Ed.*]

If, on the other hand, one takes the life-community's form of human association, with *its* ethos, to be the "highest" as well as the basic form—as is done in various ways in the doctrines of the old and the new romanticisms (the "historical" schools of the sciences of the spirit)—*society*, like life-community in the case above, no longer appears to be an *enduring* essential form of possible social unity in which, and in which alone, essential values of a specific rank can be and are represented. Here society appears to be a *phenomenon of dissolution,* i.e., a merely *historical* phase of the life-community. If this presupposition were true, this *would* in fact be the form of societal existence and its ethos. Here there is an exact *analogy* with the value-relation among the vital-organic good, the mechanical-instrumental good, and the cultural good (ultimately the good of salvation) that I have demonstrated elsewhere.[196] Measured against the vital-organic good (which cannot be reduced to the instrumental good, just as life cannot be reduced to mechanisms), the instrumental good appears to be a miserable surrogate and at the same time the consequence of a *fixation* of vital development or of the subordination of values of development to values of preservation—and so an *evil*. But in relation to the cultural good, the instrumental good as the means of release and liberation of the spirit and the individual person to their immanent goal-directions is a good of *positive* value. From the point of view of the life-community and its ethos, society is analogously a mere phenomenon of *dissolution* of negative value, although society represents an *essential basis* for a possible spiritual community of persons in a collective personality and an unavoidable essential condition for the latter. And for this reason it represents a *positive* social essential value. Hence the romanticism and the rationalism (as well as the "liberalism") of the eighteenth century are *equally* wrong. Their errors have two principal components in *common*: first, disregard for the *highest* form of possible social unity and therewith disregard for the ultimately subordinated and mediating nature of *all* other social forms vis-à-vis this highest form; second, and following from this, the erroneous opinion that life-community and society are historically contingent stages of development which differ from one another only *in degree,* and that they are not *essentially* different, *necessary,* and *lasting*

196. See my essay, "Zur Idee des Menschen" (Bibliog. no. 10). My treatment of the same point in my essay, "Das Ressentiment im Aufbau der Moralen," in the chapter entitled "Organ und Werkzeug," was one-sided because I did not consider cultural goods.

forms of *all* possible association which are to be differentiated as elements in *every* kind of real, concrete social unity.[197]

But in fact all historical development possesses strict *limits* set by these essentialities of social unity and their essential relations. This "development" does not give birth to them but occurs *according to them* and within their *framework*. What is historically variable is simply the special *content* of mass, life-community, society, and collective person; the ties that these forms have with factual groups and their changing magnitudes, their properties, their human material, and the specially dominant ideas about them; and the passage of positive historical structures, e.g., Christianity, the European economy, *through* these forms. *But these essential units themselves correspond to the idea of the social unity of a sensible-bodily-spiritual being in general,* of which the factual nature of *man* is only a "special case." There was no real development of any sort *from* one form *to* another, as if man entered first the form of the mass or the herd, *then* the form of the community, and finally the personal-communal form.[198] On the contrary, at all places and at all times *all* of these forms and their corresponding ethoses have in some measure been present in various *mixtures*. The only law that can be maintained here with regard, not to the succession itself, but to the *order* of the stages of their succession is that a positively determined historical totality, *ceteris paribus*, shows the tendency to pass through these forms in the following direction: *predominantly* mass (or herd) existence, vital-communal existence, societal existence, and personal-communal existence. Analogously, every concretely historical *moral tenor* of a group would manifest itself as a *mixture* of the ideally typical forms of mass comportment, which is without ethos and responsibility, and the *ethos* of life-community, the ethos of society, and the ethos of the community of persons. That is, a special bearing toward goods of the values of well-being and the noble (the positive values of the life-community), goods of the agreeable and the useful (the positive values of society as sociability and civilized society), and goods of spiritual values and the holy (the positive values of the community of persons in its two basic forms, the cultural community and the religious community) was present *at all places and at all times* in some measure and in some order.

197. The intersubjective form of the mass is also in some measure in *all* factual social units.

198. As, for example, the sociology of Spencer would have us believe. He does not consider the last of our social forms at all.

The only changes occur in the real subjects of this bearing, the sizes of the groups that fulfill these communal forms, the world of *goods* in which these types of *values* are represented, the organizations of communal groups, etc.

If the forms of life-community and society are ultimately in the service of the spiritual community of persons, the same also holds for the variety of ethoses of these forms, which Herbert Spencer designated as either predominantly *warlike* (status) or predominantly *peaceful* (contract). On the basis of *his* assumptions the former would have to *disappear* in the face of the latter. According to our view the direction of *development* from status (community) to contract (society), which Spencer assumes, does *not* exist, because both forms (i.e., in their service to the third one) are equally essential factors in any factual social classification of mankind. We must expect for *all* times a peculiar admixture of these two forms of human ethos and a rhythmic alteration of the states of war and peace in which they express themselves most often and most purely.

What alone is true in Spencer's construction is that the ethos of *Western Europe in modern times,* in comparison with the ethos of the Middle Ages and the ethoses of other modern cultures, has been *predominantly societal* in all special value-regions (religion, state, commerce, etc.). But it is equally certain that there are visible hints that the *principle of solidarity,* which conflicts with this ethos, will win *new reality* in both experience and theory on the grounds which prepared the way for this predominantly societal period and in the relations among individual persons within the collective person and in the relations among collective persons within a collective person encompassing them.[199] This is not the place to pursue these clues empirically. We will simply say that to expect a simple return from the new ethos to the predominance of the ethos of the life-community is, in our view, an error as basic as Spencer's. I have shown that the representation of *one* moral total ideal anchored in the objective order of values not only *allows* different forms of ethos but also *requires* them, and that these different forms must express themselves both in the dimension of simultaneity (as diverse types of ethos among peoples, nations, cultural units) and in the dimension of succession (as diverse forms of ethos of the so-called spirit of the times). In this case we may assume that one should not

199. On the labor movement, see Eduard Bernstein, "Die moderne Arbeiterbewegung," in *Die Gesellschaft.* A proof of this proposition in relation to the factual tendencies of our era belongs to another context.

regard a societal ethos prevailing within Western Europe in modern times as a segment of a curve which one could extend (in Spencerian fashion), according to an inherent orientation, to all humanity, but that one must regard such an ethos as a special *direction of preferring* which lasted for a time in the development of one (relatively small) part of humanity, as opposed to the rest of humanity and other historical periods in which the ethos of the life-community is predominant. Appearances of such directions reveal a world-historical division in all of man's moral work, the final result of which will be something unique, something greater than mortal eyes have ever seen.[200]

We have sharply distinguished the reality of a community in general from that of the collective person. But what are the most general *characteristics* that distinguish a collective *person* from the other kinds of *non*-personal communal reality? These are characteristics which make a collective person primarily a unity of a *spiritual* act-center—not primarily a unity of place (territory), time (tradition), or descent (blood), or a unity of a collective *purpose*, which always presupposes the existence of such an act-center with its special values and special ends, and which does not determine any collective *reality* at all. Second, a collective *person* must be directed toward goods of *all* modal types of values, not only toward goods of only *one* type among them, and it must be directed toward these modalities in accordance with the order of its individuality. Hence the collective *person* must possess this autonomy of being and superiority of will with respect to all other particular social units directed toward only one value-modality, i.e., both the society and the life-community. And this we call its *sovereignty*. Only insofar as the collective person is sovereign in this sense is it a genuine person with a peculiar *total world of values* with its own peculiar gradations. But this sovereignty of the collective person does not at all imply that the collective person is responsible "only to God," nor does it imply that the characteristics of free and autonomous existence and volitional determination implicit in its sovereignty with regard to particular social units also belong to all other genuine collective persons. Rather, the collective person is always *co*-responsible for these other collective persons because it is in each case *also* a member of a collective person encompassing several collective persons. The collective person does not even

200. [See "Der Mensch im Weltalter des Ausgleichs" (Bibliog. nos. 26, 27).—*Ed.*]

have sovereignty (apart from particular social units) with regard to collective persons of one and the same group of membership, *for* whom it is coresponsible. Still less does it have sovereignty with respect to the collective persons encompassing it, for which it is coresponsible and *before* which it is, in addition, responsible.[201] Whether it can be called into account before a *court of law* does not matter, because legal and a fortiori moral responsibility is not dependent upon the existence of such a court.

If the collective person is sovereign to this extent, and *only* to this extent, then it is always sovereign *over* one or more *life-communities* and one or more *societal* units. The life-community is in principle related to the collective person as the lived body is related to the individual person. The life-community can therefore be called the *collective lived body* of the collective person. But we never reach the individual by attempting to reach a simple unit of the lived body of a collective person, no matter how it is to be divided.[202] The individual and all units of groups of individuals are always *members* of *society*, which, above all, lacks the characteristic of a total reality. Society is always subordinated to the collective person, not in an immediate and direct way, but only through the *mediation* of the life-communities (and their special organizations) to which the elements of society belong. Societal "purposes" and "interests" are subordinated to the growth and well-being and the values of development and preservation of the life-communities to which societal elements belong, and are thus subordinated *independent* of the collective person. The task of the collective person begins only when the values of growth and well-being of the specific life-communities subordinated to the collective person are to be balanced in the idea of collective growth and well-being (of "its" lived body).[203]

Among the essential characteristics of the collective person,

201. It was Jean Bodin who first formulated the concept of sovereignty that is opposed to ours. His concept, applied to the state, implies responsibility on the part of a "sovereign subject" "only before God" (in Bismarck's words, "We Germans fear God and nothing else in this world"), or it even denies responsibility on the part of the sovereign because he is the "creator" of what is good, evil, holy, unholy, etc. (Thomas Hobbes). Hobbes later carried Bodin's concept to extremes. It can be easily seen in this context that Bodin's concept is only an application of an exclusively societal ethos to a collective person (the state).

202. Whether the family or marriage is this elementary unit does not have to be decided here.

203. This could serve as a basis for a general principle of *self-administration* for life-communities over social conflicts of interest within their territories. We will not deal with this point in detail here.

which is itself a concrete and spiritual act-center, we have found that it must possess both the goods of *all* value-modalities and the factual social units of *all* essential forms. But this does not mean that there is only *one* kind of collective person; it means, rather, that *supra*vital values belong only to the collective person, i.e., neither to society nor to the life-community, that the collective person is directed in some way toward all types of values, and that it must possess a peculiar *consciousness* of them and have *consideration* for them. But here it is not yet decided which values are to be realized in *preference* to others in a certain kind of collective person. This last point provides the basis for another possible *essential differentiation* within the idea of the collective person.

One cannot simply base this differentiation on one of the spiritual values, namely, *right,* because a just order exists and should exist for *all* external actions and all distributions of goods, no matter to which class of non-formal values they may belong. Hence *all* collective persons can in principle become establishers and administrators of a positive order of laws, which, in order to be just, must satisfy all essential propositions that found possible law.[204]

Among the spiritual culture values, we have already distinguished the special divisions of *collective* values and the value of the holy as *collective* salvation. *Two* types of collective persons correspond to these basic values that must be realized: to the former, the *cultural collective person*, which de facto can be a *nation* or a *cultural unit;* and to the latter, the collective person of the *church*. Only these two types of collective persons can be called *purely* spiritual collective persons.

The *state* may not be called this. It is not a concrete and perfect person, because it does not perform *all* acts of an essentially spiritual nature, despite its total reality of a *spiritual* nature. The state, as seen by itself, is simply the highest center of the spiritual collective *will*, i.e., the will of *control* over a natural life-community (people) or a plurality of such communities. The values toward which the controlling will is directed are implicit in: (1) the establishment and realization of a positive *order of laws* for life-communities subordinated to it (legislation and jurisprudence); (2) the furtherance, regulation, and guidance of the natural extensive and intensive *growth* of the life-com-

204. It is a mere *partisan* principle of no philosophical or historical importance that the state is the *sole* source of positive law, and that the **state** *bestows* all right of legislation through corporations, churches, etc.

munities and the production of vital goods for the communities which it governs (realization of the "values of development"), i.e., extensive growth through a military organization, intensive growth first through qualitative and quantitative policies for population and health; (3) the preservation and furtherance of the *well-being* of the whole of the community, both within and without (administration, "defense" of the community against attacks).[205]

Among the kinds of values to which these three kinds of goods can be reduced, only the values of *right* are of a *purely* spiritual nature. The other two kinds of values, the values of *power* and *well-being*, are vital in nature. The state remains a *spiritual* subject-of-will having value *in itself* in regulating the realization of the goods corresponding to the values of power and well-being. But the *ethos* by which the state fulfills all its basic tasks does not stem originally from the state itself. It stems from the spiritual collective persons behind and, as it were, *above* the state, i.e., immediately from the cultural personality of the *nation* or the cultural circle which stands behind it and to which it belongs, and mediately from the collective person of the religio-ecclesiastical unity. Only when nation and state coincide, the nation giving the state its essential unity and limits (and not vice versa, as in the so-called state-nation), does the idea of a perfectly spiritual collective person arise [206]—the idea of the national state, which, although it is nowhere fully realized and is not drawn from experience, nevertheless remains a *standard* for everything present in this direction.

The *people*, in contrast to the nation, are primarily or predominantly a real *life*-community. And the *state*, in relation to the people, is, as a *spiritual* collective reality, a form surpassing them in value. Hence the state is by no means an "organized

---

205. The positive task of the realization of "culture" can*not* be attributed to the state, and this according to the essence of the state. What the state has to accomplish for schools and lower and higher education as organized by the state can be assigned in part to legislation for *all* institutions of activities of the state's communities and in part to the task of the preservation and enhancement of the general well-being. As to spiritual culture, in the strict sense the state has the merely *negative* function of sustaining the conditions of the possibility of culture and protecting itself from within and without against forces *hostile* to culture. The *creative* forces of culture reside with the nation and the individual, not with the state.

206. I call this personal unit perfect, as opposed to the state, which is not a subject of culture, and the nation, which in itself is not a subject of a real collective *will*.

people" (Paulsen), but the highest real organizing will of control over a people or a plurality of peoples.[207] In a certain sense, therefore, the state is, in the ranks of values, *above* the people [208] but *below* the nation: [209] in the former case, as a spiritual structure; in the latter, as the mere unity of a will of control. In summary we may say that the state is a personlike, real, spiritual total subject with sovereign control over the life-community, but that it is neither a "perfectly" spiritual collective person nor a "purely" spiritual collective person. The state, like the merely cultural collective person (as opposed to the national state), is an "imperfect" person, and it is also a personlike reality in which the spiritual and the vital are mixed.

The *church* is distinguished from the *state* because it is related first of all to the realization of another basic value, namely, that of collective *salvation*, and because it is related to all other values only insofar as the realization of these values *conditions* the realization of collective salvation (according to the church's variable positive contents of faith and doctrine). Man partakes in this *collective salvation* of a realm of love of *all* finite persons (this salvation being distinguished from the salvation of all), not primarily as a member of a life-community (family, tribe, people, etc.) or as an element of society, but as a *purely spiritual individual person*, who can be a single *and* a collective person. "Leave your father and mother and follow me" is the advice here; and, I add, leave your home, people, fatherland, state, nation, and cultural circle, if necessary, for the collective salvation of the world of finite persons. The immediate substrate for the church as an essential idea is therefore not mankind as divided into life-communities (families, tribes, peoples), societies, states, or cultural units; still less is it mankind as a real species in nature. It is the *realm of finite persons*, which can be greater or smaller than this species (a fortiori its known part), for it also

207. The fact that the term *people* is used to designate the uneducated and lower classes ("a man of the people," "people's art," etc.), and also in the sense of "the Bavarian people," is *not* a matter of pure chance. A unit of people in the last sense, in contrast to a national unit, which rests, above all, on the *minority of the educated*, is determined essentially by the unit in the first sense, also.

208. *Nationality* pertains to a predominant community of *natural* language which does *not* yet condition a specific cultural unit or represent a predominant life-community, as the people do. This is in contrast to the *nation*, which has its unity in a specific cultural idea.

209. For this reason, only the nation has the *moral* right to change the constitution of the state beyond those changes provided for in the constitution, i.e., the moral right to revolution.

includes the *deceased*, if immortality is assumed, as well as finite personal beings unknown to us, but only *insofar* as it encompasses their *personal* form of existence, or insofar as we may assume with good reason that it *can* do so. If it belongs to the nature of a cultural person to produce *collective works of the spirit* in accordance with its specific inner cultural temperament, and if it belongs to the nature of the state to *rule* in accordance with the ethos of the cultural unit to which it belongs, it belongs to the nature of the church to serve: *to serve the solidary collective unity of all finite persons*. The church may develop structures of control *within itself*, but the whole of such a structure will serve the end of total salvation. And the state may develop structures of service, but, again, the whole will possess the sense of *ruling*. The church also performs its service in checking on the moral tenors, wills, and deeds of both individual and collective persons, so that *nothing happens* which is contrary to the collective salvation of the person-totality. On the other hand, in determining *what* (positively) is supposed to be and what is supposed to happen, *only* individual persons as members of the realm of persons (and not as persons as such) are subject to the church's norms, not collective persons. Hence collective persons determine, according to their own immanent *ethoses*, what should happen in their own spheres. Since the *pure* state possesses *no* ethos of its own, as we have shown, but receives the ethos that it is obliged to follow from the collective person standing behind it, the essential relationship between church and state is such that the church does not control the state directly, but controls it *through* checking on the ethos of the cultural unit to which the state belongs. In what concerns the ethos,[210] the church, according to its nature, exercises direct control *exclusively* over the ethos of purely cultural persons.

The basic relationship between the church and the life-community and society is completely different. The life-community by nature has *no* ethos. It has only *mores* and *customs*. If these mores and customs touch upon the conditions of collective salvation by autonomous decree of the church, they are subject to a *direct* action of the church (through positive legislation, jurisdiction) that is not necessarily mediated by the state. Likewise, those forms and values of forms inherent in a life-community which, by virtue of their structure and inner constitution, *necessarily* touch upon the conditions of salvation are sub-

210. In the sense defined above. See chap. 5, sec. 6.

ject to *direct* ecclesiastical regulation, though the state's simultaneous regulation of these matters (mores, customs, and certain forms of the life-community) is not thereby precluded but demanded.[211] Forms of the life-community of this type are, above all, *marriage, family,* and the *home-community.* These require regulation *as such* and as forms of the development and formation of men toward possible mature persons, i.e., as the primary factors in education and instruction, insofar as these touch upon the values of salvation. However, in contrast to its relation with the life-community, the church exercises *no* influence on *society.* The social form of unity of *society* is subject both to the will of control of the *state* through the life-communities to which society's elements belong and to the *ethos* of these cultural units through the cultural units to which society's elements belong, insofar as nothing in society must be or happen contrary to this will and this ethos. Apart from this, society and its goods follow their *own* laws (for example, private law, classes, economic exchange, technological development, etc.), and within these two restrictions society pervades *all* life-communities, units of culture, and states as an international, intercultural, interstate, and interpeoples social structure. The church has no direct relation to it; it can have significance for society only through the mediate exercising of direct and indirect forms of influence on the life-community and the units of the state and the culture.[212]

There is another, basically different relationship between the church and the spiritual collective persons of *cultural units.* First, the cultural domains (art, philosophy, pure science, etc.), which are divided on the basis of the divisions of spiritual values, follow their own special and universally valid laws of values (and the norms derived from them). Second, they follow the special, *individually valid* value-ideal of the cultural person concerned. This person's universally valid and, for the cultural person in question, individual form of *growth* and *decline* possesses its *own* types of *laws* which are pertinent to the essences of these

211. A positive act of abstention concerning this regulation can occur, be it on the part of the state or on the part of the church, for the benefit of the other party. But this is *positive act.*

212. Every ecclesiastical-religious ethos always contains a fixed "economic tenor." See "Der Bourgeois und die religiösen Mächte" (Bibliog. no. 10). But this economic tenor can become effective in societal development in only the indicated indirect manner. Direct involvement of a church in societal processes—for instance, ecclesiastical *legal norm-giving* for economic life, or bringing together economic interests and ecclesiastical ones—is contrary to the nature of the *two* value-areas concerned.

cultural areas vis-à-vis the analogous forms of *progression* and *retrogression* possessed by civilizational values directed toward society (and which obtain interpersonally for cultural persons).[213] Cultural domains do not require any so-called completion by some religious reality. The act-essences that construct them do not require any "completion" by a form of religious consciousness, either. Nor do these domains by themselves lead in a conclusive way toward the positing of some religious idea of value and its act-correlate. For neither religious values in general nor religious collective values, as they determine the ecclesiastical consciousness, "stem" from cultural values or cultural collective values or from a "synthesis" of these; nor is the source of religious experience the undifferentiated unity of the source of that world experience which is at the bottom of all cultural production. Rather, religion possesses its *own* domains of value and being, its own source of experience, which is called "grace" with regard to the individual person and "revelation" with regard to the collective person. True, philosophy can and should uncover the essence of this form of experience and the essence of its corresponding objects. But from its *own* form of experience and its own objects, philosophy has no access to the positing of the reality of a religious object or to the positive content factually experienced. Nevertheless, philosophy *itself* can show that it has not been a matter of historical accident that in all previous histories the structural forms of the worlds meant by world views of cultural units had their foundation in the structural forms of the domain meant by religious views of God, i.e., the domain of objects taken as holy.[214] And it can show that *all* meant world ethoses (including the ethos of society) have had their foundation in the ethos meant by religious views with regard both to types of acts and to act-correlates,[215] and that this relation is rooted in the nature of these objective domains and the corresponding forms of experience (including philosophical experience).[216] The *sociological*

213. [With regard to both the text and the preceding and following footnotes, see "Probleme einer Soziologie des Wissens." See also "Vom Wesen der Philosophie" and "Probleme der Religion" (Bibliog. no. 14).—Ed.]

214. Since, as I maintain, philosophy *itself* can show this, it sets itself off autonomously from religion and church; i.e., philosophy is not heteronomously determined in its delineation by the church.

215. It is for the philosophy of religion to show this in a special study.

216. In particular, I believe that I can show (1) that all existence of objects is founded in their value-being; (2) that all cognition of an object and all willing of a project are founded in the love of the common contents of this object *and* this project; (3) that historically and nationally the

forms in which production of culture occurs (cognitional activity, artistic practice), among which the most dominant have thus far been the communal form of solidary positive cooperation and the societal form of individualistic and critical competition, are conditioned by primary changes in the sociological form of the *religious* spirit and its objective institutions, i.e., the church.[217] If we find community predominant *here,* then we also find it predominant in cognition and art; and if we find "society" (i.e., religious *sects*) predominant *here,* then we also find the predominance of *schools,* etc. (e.g., of philosophy).

A twofold task for the church could follow from this relationship between church and cultural collective person. First, there is the essentially *negative* task of immediately controlling all cultural collective activity and its works in order to see that the ethos of this activity and the guiding structure of the preferring of the values of the domain in question (style in the arts, the methodological structure of science) *do not conflict* with the conditions of a possible collective *salvation* and, if necessary, of issuing an authoritative declaration on the matter.[218] Second, there is the *positive* task of *inspiring* all cultural activity toward collective salvation through the spirit invested in the church as a holy collective person. But this "inspiration" is *not* a matter of *willing* and *not*-willing, and thus it is not dependent on the will of any ecclesiastical organ. It is an immediate *consequence* of this "spirit" itself, so that the degree and kind of such an inspiration become in certain cases a touchstone for measuring the authenticity and fullness of the spirit which is *present* in a

varying structures of worlds intended (meant) in all world views follow the structures of prevailing "moralities," and that the selective forms of given data follow so-called categories of directions of the love present; (4) that all possible love of the world is founded in the love of God, and all varying directions of love of the world in independently changing directions of the love of God.

217. Predominant traits of a communal form of cognition, as in the Middle Ages, are traditionalism (in the dimension of succession), unity of the language of learning throughout different nations, and, above all, the spiritual endeavor to build a *universal cognition* bridging ages and peoples. These traits are opposed in character to the predominantly *societal* form of cognition of modern times and the dominance of national languages in the sciences. [See "Probleme einer Soziologie des Wissens." —*Ed.*]

218. *Philosophy* should be the means of such a correction, e.g., in (positive) science and art, because philosophy is a part of culture and has as its object the nature of all other areas *plus* the nature of religion and the church. Hence philosophy provides a possible *dialogue* in this sense (and only in this sense) between church and cultural systems. Of course, philosophy is not an *arbitrator* in this.

certain church, but which cannot be attributed to any disobedience or guilt of individuals. It is *not* in the nature of the church to give positive and moral *volitional* guidance or to settle objectives with respect to culture, which unfolds according to its own universally and individually valid laws. If a church attempts such interference, it claims control that contradicts its nature.

Hence the relationship between church and culture is essentially different from the relationship between *state* and culture. For the state has a task with respect to the concrete *goods* of culture only insofar as the values of right, well-being, and power are mirrored in cultural forms, and insofar as the cultural education of a people touches upon the realization of these values of the state and upon the basic civil tenor directed toward them (civil education, the art of government, the formation of offices)—that is, only insofar as culture is *not pure* culture, but culture that is *useful* in terms of the aims implicit in the nature of the state. In our terminology, the state has *no positive* task in realizing *cultural values as such.*[219] But the role of the state is all the more fundamental as the negative condition, and the *conditio sine qua non,* of the possible existence of a factual world of cultural goods, or, more precisely, of the *realization* of its collective cultural person's positive world of values as a collective world of goods, wherein the structure of the world of values determines the structure of the collective world of goods.[220] The following propositions obtain in this context: (1) The freedom and independence of the state in relation to other states is the condition required for the cultural person, situated behind the state, to produce, according to its own proper spirit, a world of cultural goods corresponding to the state. This freedom and independence is also the condition required for this world of goods as a whole and for its *peculiarity* to receive recognition and adequate evaluation in the world.[221] Hence

219. Above all, the state has *no* task with regard to inspiration. A state culture is a contradiction in terms, and one should not speak of a cultural state.

220. Here, of course, we are not referring to the education of the individual. Education has a value totally independent of the conditions of the culture as a *whole* since it is independent of the state as well as changes in the conditions of the state.

221. This relation does *not* hold at all for goods pertinent to a civilized society. This kind of good can also be enhanced by slaves. The ability to enhance it is not dependent on a consciousness of freedom, on one's being a free citizen in a free state. Besides, these values are international and interstate, and men who produce them are always *replaceable,* irrespective of their nationality.

neither the singular *cultural works* belonging to this "world" (or their recognition) nor the culturally productive ability of the cultural person or the spiritual peculiarity of this ability perishes with the state. What perishes is the peculiar *world* of the *collective* power to effect this ability and its peculiarity. These collective values possess a value of their own. (2) Whereas it is true that extension of the domination of the state enlarges the field for propagating the cultural style of its cultural person, and that decreased domination restricts this style, this does not affect the peculiar cultural style either in its nature or in its value; nor do these events affect the ability of the cultural person. It is the factual distribution of these *styles* of collective values in real worlds of goods, which are found by the historian to be *already there,* that is, essentially affected by these processes. Each of the various realizations and distributions of possible cultural styles for and in real worlds of goods possesses its own autonomous (positive or negative) value, which is independent of the values of the *contents* of these styles. (3) The relations of power among life-communities within a state codetermine which special act-directions in the spirit of the cultural collective person will factually manifest themselves in cultural works. They also codetermine the selection of *what* will become real from possible "tastes" and from possible collective recognition of knowledge and a national form of sciences. (4) Collective well-being is essentially the condition of the *existence,* not of the quality, of the *possible* whole of cultural goods already selected according to (the consequences of) the first two conditions, i.e., according to the qualities of the collective cultural person and its peculiar world of values. (5) The forms of laws established by this state and pertaining to cultural goods codetermine the form of distribution of the participation of the state's population in the total culture. The state will do a *better* job in its task, which belongs essentially to it, of *realizing* culture, the *less* it claims autonomous guidance and leadership in cultural activities, the *less* it claims to inspire this activity, the *less* it follows a direct cultural policy (instead of a policy of power) toward other states, and the *less* it orders the relations of power among people living in its life-communities according to cultural points of view (propagation of education) rather than the point of view of justice.[222] Again, we find a case wherein the possible realization

222. I.e., the state must give life-communities equal or unequal rights according to their degree of significance with respect to the whole of the state.

of a certain value is tied to the condition that this value not be intended in an immediate fashion.

There are also certain a priori propositions which are founded in the essences of the types of collective persons (and other social units). These propositions deal with the *diversity* of these types.

Let us recall what we said about the simplicity and divisibility of value-modalities in part I of this treatise,[223] i.e., their inherent ability to be identically experienced commonly, and let us see what follows from these propositions and from those that we can discover concerning the value-relatedness of forms of social unity. The highest modality in the order of ranks of values —the holy [*das Heilige*] as the value of the person [*Personwert*], and "salvation" [*das Heil*] as the value of the collective person, i.e., (solidary) collective salvation—is the most indivisible of the value-modalities and, for this very reason, the one that can be shared with others to the highest degree. The collective person to which collective salvation is directed can therefore only be *one* according to its *nature*. The unity of the church vis-à-vis the simultaneous plurality of collective cultural persons (a fortiori the other collective persons) is an a priori principle.[224] The solidary inclusion of *all possible finite* persons in my salvation and of my salvation in the salvation of all finite persons belongs to the essence of the collective intention directed toward the value of all things lying in the absolute sphere of being and value. On the other hand, a *plurality* of *cultural* collective persons, in the sense of both simultaneous and successive plurality (in cultural units, nations, and cultural periods), belongs to the essence of this type of collective person in general. This plurality therefore does not belong to factors of race, milieu, nationality [*Volkstum*], etc., which obstruct the mere representation of the idea of culture and can be considered surmountable by history and possible progress in methods and social organizations. Plurality belongs to the *essence* of the idea of culture. The idea of a plurality of individual cultural collective persons as the bearers of individual collective cultural values is an idea that is constitutive of values of this type. The idea of *one* so-called world culture is therefore a priori "contradictory"; it is not a goal (not even a "utopian" one) that our spirit is supposed to posit for a form of history.[225] The idea of a world-*state*, which Kant

223. See chap. 2, B, secs. 3, 5.
224. "Unity," as opposed to plurality, must not be confused with the number 1; number is only a measure of plurality.
225. There exists a "cultural unit" when there is an identical structure

had to require because of his presuppositions, is even more contradictory than the idea of a *world culture*. Since every state,
according to its essence, has a unitary cultural person as the
background of its possible existence and ethos,[226] and since the
cultural person as a unit does *not* require a *state* as a unit for its
existence, the plurality of states is *larger* than the *plurality* of
collective cultural persons according to the essence of both the
state and the collective cultural person.[227] The same follows immediately from the mode of divisibility of the values to which
the state is essentially directed. For these values are in essence
values of the vital value-series, despite the spirituality of the
state. Analogous relations of plurality obtain further for the
state, for the people or groups of a predominantly life-communal
character,[228] and in the ultimate case for the life-community and
society. The last point holds insofar as there are as many "real"
units in a society as there are single persons. It is *because*
society is in no way a collective reality that society itself and its
subdivisions (e.g., classes) can penetrate all other collective
realities; and it is because of this, too, that the idea of society
as an artifact is the idea of a thing [*Sache*] that can be only *one*.
The values to which society is directed are, however, the most
divisible and the least subject to sharing. Indeed, there is
absolutely no possible mutual living-with-one-another in such
values, because each can have only *his* sensations of agreeableness and *his* interests, no matter how many people there may be
who have the *same* interests. This similarity never creates
solidarity, but at best a contractual working together on the part
of many with the aim of realizing *one* purpose.

According to these central propositions concerning the theory

---

in the ways in which people look at the world as well as in the corresponding forms of being, and when there is an identical "ethos," but only when
a reflective consciousness *of* this identity has *not* yet developed. This lack
of reflection characterizes a nation. The existence of a national group of
people always presupposes that they belong to *one* "cultural unit." Thus
there cannot be more nations than cultural units.

226. This does not have to be a nation; it can also be a cultural unit.

227. The perfect national state is not a reality but only a guiding idea
implicit in the essentially continuous transitions between social cultural
units and in the essentially discontinuous cultural units among states.
(No person can belong to two sovereign states!) Even if we imagine mankind divided up into a plurality of perfect national states, our proposition
would hold true because there would be no cultural units.

228. One can conceive of a state with a plurality of life-communities,
but not of a life-community which does not belong to a state. The possible
plurality of life-communities is therefore larger than that of states.

of social diversity (not elaborated in detail here), there are also certain essential relations *among* and *within* social units. The *one* church is, according to its essence, both a *supranational* [229] (and supracultural) collective person and, at the same time, a collective person *immanent* to all possible cultural units and nations. The church is non-national in a certain positive sense, in that it is simultaneously supranational and inherent in *all* cultural units. Society, on the other hand, although sharing with the church the formal moment of a potential unity = non-plurality (in the above sense) and non-nationality, is both *infranational* and *international*.[230] That is, society is immanent to *no* nation and *no* cultural unit, whereas the church is immanent to *each* nation and *each* cultural unit. Although formally similar to society, the church is the most *extreme* counterpart of society imaginable. In one we find solidarity, a collective person, and *one* collective salvation; in the other, contract and convention, a sum of individuals, and interests of many which fortuitously coincide or intersect.

Still, the (imperfect) collective cultural person of the cultural unit is both supranational and immanent with respect to nations, and the nation is in principle above and immanent to the state. Of course, the church is both above and immanent to the state (but only as *mediated* through the nation or the cultural unit).[231] Because the church is at the same time an intrastate institution, the state has the duty and the right to preserve its independence in all matters that are of a state-church "admixture" (the *jus circa sacra*), and the state has the duty to protect the church from attacks on the values and goods that the church represents. Finally, the cultural unit, the nation, the state, and the church are *jointly* above the life-communities (e.g., the peoples) in which they have their ordered places. Hence they

229. A national church is therefore an a priori contradiction.

230. All internationalism has its roots in international society. Internationalism is correctly referred to as "formal." To it belong the purely formal parts of so-called international law (to be distinguished from the "international law" of a cultural unit, for instance, of Europe), international private law, as well as all formal conventions concerning measures, weights, coins, etc., and all international "agreements" on technical and scientific symbols, terminologies, means of communication, etc. [See "Nation und ihre Querschichtungen," in "Soziologische Neuorientierung und die Aufgabe der deutschen Katholiken nach dem Kriege" (Bibliog. nos. 11, 19).—Ed.]

231. Hence a state church is a contradictory idea on the assumption of monotheism. The same holds for theocracy, as well as for a church which claims to be a state or to *govern* other states.

are in principle structures above peoples, but they are also immanent to peoples.[232]

Finally, these social units have a peculiar essential relation to the contents of the *spatial* and *temporal* manifold.

Each life-community possesses a common *environment* which each of its members can overlook and feel together. The life-community is adjusted to this environment not only in its vital feeling and vital striving but also in an objectively physiological sense, in that any transfer of a member of the life-community to another environment can be experienced, even without objective knowledge of this transfer, as a "yearning for" or "longing for" of a certain qualitative coloration. This environment, depending on the kind and complexity of the life-community in question, is called "dwelling place" (family), "home" (local commune), or "fatherland" (people).[233] If values and disvalues as targets of this yearning and longing (which is consciously set off only by a *change* in the common environment) become especially clear, and if this whole, founded in values, is comprehended, there springs forth *love* for the abode (for "tent" or "house"), *love* for one's home, and *love* for the fatherland.[234] What is essential to the state at each moment of its existence is a so-called *territory* and its frontiers. Of course the unity of the *state* is not established through natural determinations of spatial extension. The territory is the field of its will of domination and is *posited* by the state itself. The territory is the solid surface belonging as an objective corporeal correlate to the *common* environment of the life-communities governed by the state.[235]

232. See what I have said in the January, 1916, issue of the monthly journal *Hochland* on these fundamental relations among social units. [See "Soziologische Neuorientierung."—Ed.]

233. On home and fatherland, see *Zur Phänomenologie und Theorie der Sympathiegefühle.*

234. These types of love are quite independent of the *positive* value-content of the environment. I.e., one loves one's home and country, not because they happen to be "beautiful," "fertile," "rich," etc., but *because* they are home and country. This vital emotive and conative basis of these types of love certainly belongs to higher animals.

235. All of this would hold also for a migrating horde or for a group divided up into statelike units and living on ships. In the first case the territory would continually change, but would nevertheless exist. In the second case the decks of the ships would form the territory. Many have tried to deny the essential necessity of a territory with regard to the state. To us this is a hopeless undertaking. If one were to pursue such an attempt consistently, it would lead to anarchism, i.e., to the dissolution of the state into a society that would exist only in terms of legal contractual relations. But the territories of more than one state can coincide in the case where a plurality of states is unified into a so-called federal republic so that the

The different environments can *overlap,* but territories cannot, for they exclude each other as every section of space excludes every other section. On the other hand, the cultural collective person, the nation, and the cultural unit require *neither* an environment *nor* a territory. Their member-persons can change their residence, home, fatherland, and state without unbinding their national ties. Thus the nation is shown to be a predominantly *spiritual* reality. Yet one cannot say that the cultural collective person is ubiquitous. It essentially possesses a certain *field of effectiveness* that is at every moment spatial, but in such a way that the fields of a plurality of nations can intersect in the same objective segments of space (and their content). They do not exclude each other, as territories do; nor do they necessarily change along with migrations of the lived bodies of their members, i.e., *through* the migrations, as environments of life-communities do. The church, as the pure and perfect collective person in which the salvation of all finite persons is solidary, has a unique relation to space. Its field of effectiveness is both supraspatial and intraspatial. It is supraspatial because it encompasses not only all finite living persons but also (in given cases) non-humans (the idea of angels) as well as deceased persons. And it gathers the latter, together with all finite persons living in inner space, into a solidary unity. Hence the church, by virtue of its *essence,* lacks the essential parts of the life-community, the state, and the nation: a *special* environment, a *special* territory, and a *special* spatial field of effectiveness. But it *sanctifies* every territory into which a finite person may enter, every environment, and every field of effectiveness.[236] And precisely because the church encompasses the realm of finite individual persons, it is not necessary that *one* of its historical forms also encompass all "humanity" precisely as "society" does. A historically positive church therefore must not tend to go in a dangerous direction leading away from its true essence, namely, to assume structures (in contents of faith, ethics, and institutions) that *can* encompass "all humanity." Such a tendency

---

territory of the member-state is at the same time a territory of the republic. We will not discuss the question of whether the member-state, no longer sovereign, can still be called a state, i.e., the problem of the state in a republic.

236. However, this does not rule out the fact that the places in which a church manifests its effectiveness for the sake of a common salvation (e.g., "churches," "holy places," etc.) still assume a special character of the value of the "holy" which is not yet given with general religious observance.

necessarily leads to a false and pernicious adaptation of the church to the "universal" human nature of a humanity that has *not* yet been religiously transformed. A church that pursues this course will finally *drown* in the sphere of society and ultimately in the mass and will move away from its true goal, which is to *elevate* everything human according to its present dispositions [*Anlagen*] to the sphere of solidarity in love among all finite persons. The church must not assume a priori that everyone who belongs to the natural species "man" is also *necessarily* an individual person, i.e., one who belongs to the church's field, or that every such man must be able to understand the doctrines of the church.[237] This depends on the church's missionary experiences and is no a priori principle.[238] In this respect society is quite different from the church. Because society is the social unit that can penetrate all other social units, it has no spatial ties other than those which are posited by the resident beings who can make contracts about matters concerning their individual interests and the essentially singular values of the agreeable and the useful. And since society *consists in* the validity of such contractual relations alone, it has a *non-spatial* character. And it is only insofar as the ideas of society and contract presuppose the life-community in general that society indirectly partakes in the environment of the widest life-community existing between beings of such a nature. This life-community is mankind as a *real* species [*Gattung*], which is of course different from the sum of men and the concept of man. The environment of this life-community is the earth. Society is therefore, when viewed from its spatial field, the *earthly* social unit par excellence.[239]

Analogous essential relations obtain between social units and the *temporality* of their spheres of being and effectiveness. No matter how long or short the objective time which a factual social unit occupies may be, each social unit has a necessary claim to a longer or shorter *duration* with respect to other units. We saw in part I that there are "durabilities" proper to the natures of the value-modalities themselves, and that the higher the values, the more they can endure. The social unit of society is *without* duration; and, as opposed to all other social units related to values,

237. The degree to which the church in fact encompasses humanity has no bearing on how much the essence of the church can be purely exemplified in humanity.

238. At best, this principle could belong to positive dogma, but not to philosophy.

239. [It appears to us that Scheler should have said that *community* is this, but in every edition the word used is *Gesellschaft.—Trans.*]

society has *no* temporal dimension to its existence. Hence society only encompasses men living at the same time. Contracts with the deceased or with men of the future do not exist.[240] The validity of contracts (and not only the conclusions of contracts) presupposes the simultaneous existence of their subjects, no matter to what extent the contractual content may relate to specifications for what will or will not happen in the future. In contrast to this, life-communities possess by nature a duration that goes beyond the duration of existence of any of their members. In the family, the tribe, the home, and the people there live a peculiar "spirit" (love and hate, "prejudice") and will which have continuity in comparison with the discrete times of the members of a life-community.[241] This spirit, with its structure, has its own value or disvalue independent of the value of the sum of the acts of its members. The state is more enduring than the life-communities corresponding to the sphere of its will of domination. The cultural unit and the nation are more enduring than the state. And the church is more enduring than the cultural unit and the nation. The sequence from life-community to church shows an increasing concentration, preservation, and deepening of the sense of collective acts, themselves separated in time, of real social units. It is as if the collective life of a lower social unit were preserved in higher units according to its value for the collective life of the realm of persons. Only the church, and not merely its origin but also its sphere, is at the same time *supra*temporal and *intra*temporal. Its claim to "eternal" duration belongs to its essence. But the historical change of cultural collective persons and of the worlds of goods which they encompass belongs to the essence of these collective existences. An "eternal nation" is *contradictory* (not merely "impossible" in reality). Still more contradictory is an "eternal state." [242] For inasmuch as the

240. When one of the partners to an agreement concerning succession dies, the agreement does not become a contract *between* the survivor and the deceased. According to its content, it only defines the capacity of the one upon the death of the other.

241. This continuity is of the same nature as that of vital feeling in relation to changing sensible feeling-states.

242. The false assumption of such an eternal nation or state would also lead to a deadly conservatism that would obstruct a total explication of the inner possibilities of the spirit which forms culture and states. Every ethics of state or culture is therefore *eo ipso* "reactionary." Rather, there is a *moral* right to both cultural revolution and revolution against the state —the former on the basis of a new level of the collective consciousness of religious and ecclesiastical matters, the latter on the basis of a new cultural idea.

state is related to essentially "temporal" goods, the state's own existence necessarily partakes in this temporality. But it does so in a way that differs essentially from the case of the existence of the cultural person. The cultural collective person and the state are basically related in such a way that the cultural person can "survive" the state.[243] The collapse of a state's organization does not entail the collapse of the cultural person. Indeed, the latter may bring about new state structures to replace the old, collapsing ones.[244]

ad 5. Intimate Person and Social Person

No matter how rich and diverse the memberships through which *each* person is enmeshed in the whole of the moral cosmos, and no matter how diverse the directions of the various kinds of coresponsibility by which the person is tied to this *whole* and its direction and sense, the person is never exhausted by these kinds of membership, nor is his self-responsibility reduced to various coresponsibilities, nor his duties and rights to those duties and rights which derive from such memberships (duties of family, office, vocation, citizenship, class, etc.). For behind all experience that enters into these memberships and obstructs or furthers the person as a whole by realizing these memberships, everyone feels (in some measure)—if he attempts to have a clear view of the whole of these kinds of membership and of his own being—a *peculiar self-being* (similarly, a self-value and a self-disvalue) which towers above this whole and in which he knows himself (descriptively speaking) *alone*. And what comes to givenness in this essential form of possible self-experiencing is what I call the *intimate person*. I wish to distinguish this sharply from the contents of experience of all forms of self-experiencing that occur with an explicit or somehow cogiven reference to the mere bearer-being of some personal membership, i.e., the *social person*. We can say, therefore, that every finite and complete person possesses an intimate sphere and a social one. The *col-*

---

243. On the very peculiar (and little-investigated) relation of the idea of the afterlife of the person in general beyond death to the idea of the afterlife of the individual person beyond his lived body, as well as to the idea of the afterlife of the collective person beyond its member-persons, see my essay, "Die Idee des Todes und das Fortleben." In this essay I discuss the vast difference between Leibniz (Herder) and Kant on whether all moral life consists in a movement of infinite perfection of the individual soul beyond life or in devotion to the collective persons which survive the earthly life of the individual. [See above, p. 302, n. 78.—*Ed.*]

244. [See "Probleme einer Soziologie des Wissens."—*Ed.*]

lective person also possesses these two spheres. For one must distinguish between the manner in which a nation experiences itself as an isolated form and the manner in which it experiences itself as a member of the realm of collective persons. The same holds true for a family, a marriage, etc. But one must keep in mind that this difference is relative not through self-experiencing but through factual application to persons that are themselves already collective ones. This is so because every collective person is both the counterpart of the intimate personal spheres of member-persons and the subject of an intimate person. This differentiation is absolute only when applied to the individual person.[245] His intimate person is no longer the counterpart of an individual person, but the intimate person, purely and simply.

It is only the absolutely intimate person who cannot possibly participate in a social association with other persons (through the mediation of a collective person). Thus the absolutely intimate person occupies a place of absolute *solitude* within the total realm of finite persons,[246] and this solitude is a category that expresses an *indestructible* essential relation of a negative kind among finite persons. This solitude can be filled with very different contents by different persons. It can escape the interests and attentions of individual persons and entire epochs, but the *sphere* of solitude is necessarily there and, as such, is always coexperienced to some degree. It is therefore a mistake to assume that the sphere of solitude can be completely annihilated by possible historical changes in social relations

245. Needless to say, the differences (in any form) between the intimate person and the social person have as little to do with the individual person and the collective person as with the differences between the psychic and the physical or with those between man's individuality and man as a species. The person has an intimate sphere and a social sphere, both with respect to his lived body and the psychic. Individuality is both social and intimate individuality. Bergson is mistaken in confusing the intimate person in part with individuality and in part with the psychic in general. If this were true, it would follow in ethics that man becomes a person only by stepping out of all lived social relations in experience, that he must move closer to the inanimate and the mechanical the more he is a member of social units. This mistake is no less grave than the opposite error of, e.g., Hermann Cohen, who wants to establish the personhood of man only in terms of his properties as a subject of law in a possible social nexus.

246. Solitude has nothing to do with objective "being-alone." The former occurs most purely and more frequently in societal relations and, indeed, in the relatively most intimate communal relations (friendship, marriage, family). For it is precisely here that the absolute limit of the self-communicability of the person to another can be seen most impressively. The famous saying, "Solitary am I, but not alone," distinguishes between the two notions.

(increasing socialization and solidarity) and so be made to disappear. Since the sphere of solitude is an *essential* social category, this is quite impossible. Only shifts in the experiential content that occupies, as it were, the existential form of the person in a typical single person living in a certain developmental stage of social formation can frequently occur. However, solitude does *not* exclude one communal relation, namely, the relation to God, who by definition is neither an individual nor a collective person, but one in whom both individual and collective persons are solidary.[247] Thus it is in God alone that the intimate person may know himself to be condemned or saved. But he cannot do even this without his becoming indirectly aware of his solidarity (at least "in God") with the collective person *in general* and, in the first place, with the church. And without *this* certitude there would be no God but merely a deceptive object of the highest nature, i.e., an illusory god. On the other hand, it would be tantamount to a theory coinciding with the (unjustified) denial of the *essential idea* of the church itself to hold that the individual person can reach the idea of solidarity "only" and "exclusively" as founded in his solitary relation to God, i.e., solely through this "necessary" detour.[248]

An analogous relation also obtains between the relatively intimate *collective* person (with the exception of the church) and the idea of God. Cultural units and nations,[249] in their intimate spheres of being and value, have not only the relation to God mediated by the church but *also* an immediate relation to God, for they experience the same religious objects. And the

247. Mysticism tends to exaggerate *this* particular relatedness of every person to God (e.g., Meister Eckhart's writings) to such an extent that the idea of solidary salvation in the church becomes secondary, and the source of experience, which for religious subjects resides in historical revelation, is reduced in value vis-à-vis the so-called inner illumination and grace of the intimate person. But just as one must not reject a special source of religious experience in the case of the intimate person—lest his nature be denied and dissolved—one cannot hold that this "mystic" subordination corresponds to the *true* order of religious values and their sources in experience.

248. There are many forms of such denial. It is implicit historically in the doctrine of predestination (as one of its consequences), as well as in the theory of justification through faith. For in both theories a solidary community of love and salvation is not considered as original and as necessary a road to God as the immediate liaison between the intimate person and God. In both theories the community of love and salvation is derived from this intimate relatedness.

249. The state, however, is an exclusively social person, even though it can possess an *intimate ethos* by virtue of the cultural person to which it belongs.

more perfect and adequate this experience, the more its coloration corresponds to the individuality of *their* collective spirit. To this extent they know themselves to be *immediately* related to the Godhead. The church as a social person has no right either to deny these colorations their legitimate religious value or to deny the *possible* immediate relation between collective persons and God. On the other hand, nations do not have the right to make the content of this relation the *foundation* of a church (national church). There is a relation of subordination, however, between the intimate spheres of the faith and salvation of the spirit of collective persons and the holy spirit of the intimate collective person of the church. This relation is such that none of these colorations and immediate relations between non-ecclesiastical collective persons and the Godhead may conflict with the relation of the intimate collective person of the church to God.

Finally, there are different *levels of approximation* between the absolutely intimate person of an individual and the types of collective persons to which he belongs. These levels are based on the essences of these types. Despite the existence of the absolutely intimate sphere of being of every individual as a person—indeed, only upon the assumption of the existence of such a sphere— there are also *relatively intimate* spheres of being which everyone *as a member* of a collective person *A* possesses in relation to his simultaneous membership in a collective person *B*. The individual as an element of society (which is not a collective reality in any respect), as well as everything based upon this form of social unity, does not possess any *intimate* person at all, nor does he have any intimate sphere of being. It is exclusively as a social person that he enters the world of "society" in speaking, making contracts, abiding by contracts, and enjoying himself. Doubtless he knows at every moment (in the sense of a vague coliving with others) that the "other" may "have" an intimate sphere as the *X* of a possible fulfillment. But no *content* of this *X* extends into society.[250] If there is an attempt to invade the relatively intimate sphere, the ethos of society correctly considers this an "indiscretion"; if, however, this same conduct were

---

250. Thus one is fully justified in considering society a *stage*, the subject of society a *role*, and the whole a "social illusion" [*sozialer Schein*], i.e., the *most illusory* level of social existence. But the experience in which this particular value-character is given is, in actual social life, *least* present. It is by way of a glance back to the intimate spheres that this character comes to the fore.

omitted, this would be considered false "reserve," culpable "lack of care" for the other person, or "egoism." Within the life-community, however, the individual as a member shares with the other *as* such a member a mutual sphere that is *relatively intimate* in comparison with the situation in society. The more there is an experienced inwardness in a life-community, the more this sphere is filled with richer contents. But with this the personhood of the experiencing subject recedes. The maximum amount of the relatively intimate experiential content of the person as such enters into the *religious* community, i.e., the church. Thus in the church an experiential level that is even "closer" to the absolutely intimate person—closer, that is, than in any other collective person, e.g., a nation or a state—can become open and communicable (and also subject to criticism). This experiential level is also to be defined as *independent* of state and national factors, and it would be an *encroachment* on the part of the state and the nation (and their organs) to interfere with this person. As a member of my nation, too, I possess an experiential level that is *independent* of the state, and with this I possess an original right to exchange opinions and beliefs and to use the conditions of interchange (right of natural language), a right that contains the will of the state within fixed limits and has its roots in essential relations.

The above, relatively intimate, experiential levels of the individual nevertheless have *one* thing in common. Although they are of an intimate nature, they are also of an essentially *general* nature. The forms, however, that pertain to the most intimate being and experience and at the same time to the *most individual* experience are friendship and marriage.[251] Both forms are *accompanied* by a religious community and a community of culture and state, as is required by the highest perfection of the ideas of these forms, and so represent forms of the most intimate proximity and community which finite persons can share. No finite power can rupture them. And it may well be that this factor is what gives true experiences of marital and amicable love a *transcendent* touch and the sense of eternity in the contents of the intention directed to their essence, which poets of all ages have experienced and praised.

The difference between the intimate person and the social person and between their respective content spheres must not be

251. On these forms, see *Zur Phänomenologie und Theorie der Sympathiegefühle*. On friendship, see the still-classic essential explications in Aristotle's *Nicomachean Ethics*.

misconstrued in such a way that the "social" person of an individual X *consists*, say, only in the content of perceptions, representations, judgments, etc., that other persons may have or make with respect to this X. This difference is not epistemological but *ontic* in character. Because everyone *has* both a social and an intimate sphere of his person, it does not matter whether he or others can "imagine" or "think" this, or a fortiori whether he or others have *adequate* representations of the social and intimate spheres, or whether they make inadequate, correct, or incorrect judgments about them. Further, to hold that the social person is only the social mirror-image of each in the other is wrong, because everyone experiences *himself* as a social person and as an intimate person with equal originality. One who executes an action of his office, for instance, executes it also *in* experiencing, *in* willing, *in* doing, etc., "*as*" a social person. In other words, he is given to himself during this action as a certain type of social person, e.g., as a judge. Moreover, everyone can direct his intentions toward the intimate as well as the social sphere of another person.

This is equally important for an ethical value theory and theories of goods, duties, and virtues dependent on it. The social person first appears as the *bearer* of a peculiar group of *values* whose nature is missed entirely if one attempts, as most do, to derive these values psychologically from the comportment and judgments of the individual's fortuitous social environment. Depending on the nature of the single person's membership in his social unit, these values are, e.g., good or bad "*name*," "*reputation*," "*esteem*," "*honor*," "*dignity*," "*fame*," "*sanctity*," etc.[252] The possession or non-possession of these values is not a consequence of a *judgment*, or of esteem or reverence or the lack of these, on the part of the environment. The possession of these values *obtains independent* of the environment, but they "exact" and "require" specific acts of recognition, esteem, praise, etc., on the part of the environment. If there are types of comportment which contradict the requirements emanating from these values, we speak of a violation of honor, of a refusal of "due" esteem and praise, etc.[253] This group of values, whose unity lies

252. As social persons, collective unities and collective persons (with the exceptions of mass and society) also bear such values, e.g., the honor of the family or the tribe, national honor, "prestige," etc.

253. The degree of violation is determined by the absence of the social acts that the person concerned expects from others. It is determined by the nature and magnitude of the conflict between requirement and act; but a violation of honor is *not* determined by the social *consequences* that

in the exclusive bearer, the social person, and which is also feelably unified in quality, is well differentiated by both the *type* of the social unit in question and the *value-modalities* toward which it is originally directed. Man as an element of society has a so-called *civil honor* that is necessarily individual and not collective. Hence the groups into which society can be divided, for instance, classes, groups of common interests, business enterprises, or certain "businesses," possess as such *no* honor. There is no "class honor," but there is honor of profession, social rank, and party. There is *no* business honor, but only commercial "repute." *Collective* honor is found only in the life-community and the collective person. "Civil honor" differs sharply from all other values of the social person in that it can be *only* "violated" or "disallowed," never "extended" or "bestowed." It is also characterized by the fact that only its *violation* and its *loss* can be felt by the individual and the environment, not its untouched possession. Civil honor is therefore a *positive* quality of the individual as an element of society. But it is at the same time also the minimum and the presupposition of all other social personal values that a man can possess.[254] Civil honor is, as we said, *singular* and at the same time completely *non-individual*. For everyone possesses the *same* exemplar of "civil honor." Very different from civil honor are all the types of "honor" which require of their bearers not only mere omissions but also spontaneous and positive acts of *"maintenance,"* [255] and of the environment not only non-violation but also spontaneous and positive acts of *recognition* and demonstrations and exhibitions of respect. The types of honor in question are nobility, profession, social level, and office, as well as all types that follow from certain possessions of dignity, for example, the dignity of a prince, a priest, etc. The original bearers of these kinds of honor are those membership slots which an individual social person can occupy in the framework of a collective person, i.e., so-called offices and dignities. The individual person receives these honors derivatively through the possession of such an office or dignified

---

it has for the harmed person (e.g., damage of credit, economic damage), nor is it determined by the degree to which one "feels" one's honor violated. Honor is a *solid* objective value-fact, as opposed to the changing degrees of "feelings of honor."

254. There are many positive contents of intuition and feeling that become more noticeable when they disappear. See my essay "Idole." [See *ibid.*, sec. 4.—Ed.]

255. Civil honor can be "maintained" [*gewahrt*] in a reactive act only on the basis of an already experienced harm.

position. He is a bearer of these honors, neither as an individual nor as a singular man, but only as a form-specific member of a total unit. The individual as a social person merits the esteem and respect due his office and dignity *only* as the bearer of this office and dignified position—but *as* the bearer.[256] Finally, there are values of the social person that belong to their bearer, the social person, exclusively as an *individual,* whether as the agent of a unique deed, the creator of a unique work, or an example of singular individual perfection of value in personal being. In the first two cases the value is *"fame"*; in the third, *"sanctity."* These values do not arise from acts of recognition on the part of the environment and future generations, say, acts of praise or declarations of sainthood by the church, etc. Such acts only fulfill the *requirements* stemming from the object of the representation of the person in question *himself,* and they can be correct or incorrect, adequate or inadequate. It is for this reason alone that one can distinguish true fame and sanctity from merely illusory fame and sanctity.[257] This distinction could not be made if these values consisted only in factual recognition, adoration, or fame. Every one of these values of the social person, with the exception of civil honor, which expires on the death of its bearer, endures beyond the existence of its bearer as a living organism.[258] They elevate the single person, who is by himself extrahistorical, into the sphere of history, and they make him worthy of remembrance and respect. They also augment the solidary collective good of the moral cosmos. The series of those who performed well in office or who held a dignified position allows anyone who assumes the office or dignified position to partake of the honors of his predecessors. And this series obligates every successor in a special way to preserve this level of honor. Analogous requirements are set by the ancestry of a family and the fame of a

256. It is a pernicious Byzantinism to transfer reverence and honor to the *individuality* of the person or to the intimate person or to all those qualities of the person that have nothing to do with him *as* a bearer of an office or some dignified position. This is as objectionable as the failure to recognize "due" reverence and honor because of negative values of the person as an individual or an intimate person apart from his execution of an office. See the wonderful passages on "living with nobility" in Pascal's *Pensées.*

257. On another level one similarly distinguishes genuine nobility from the illusory (e.g., a *title* of rank given on the basis of an arbitrary elevation to the status of nobility).

258. Thus a violation of the honor of a deceased person can be punished only insofar as it touches upon the honor of a family or the honor of a living person.

military regiment or a nation. The attitude toward this whole value-series takes on the character of vanity, which is negative in value, only when it is not these values of the social person but the mere *picture* that the environment has of them which becomes a codetermining factor for comportment.[259] Only those who, erroneously, would have these values spring from such a picture must assume that all love of honor, fame, etc., is different only in degree from vanity (or only in terms of the value-quality toward whose picture conation is directed). But one can be called vain only if he intends mere acts that grant honor and fame, not if he intends honor and fame.[260] For he posits a merely illusory picture in the place of true honor and fame.

If all these values have a positive character and are higher and lower in relation to each other according to their durability and according to the value of the personal qualities that found honor and fame, then one must not forget for a moment that only the whole and *undivided* concrete person is the bearer of truly moral values. And the intimate person belongs to this whole no less essentially than the social person. Intimate peace of conscience, intimate bliss, and intimate goodness, for example, are quite different from the consciousness of having completely fulfilled the duties of one's office or one's duties as a father. They are quite different from the socially visible "happiness" of the social person and his goodness that can be felt socially. In intimate peace, etc., everyone has his *own* value, which is not merely auxiliary to the value of the social person. And for this very reason the *harmony* of the intimate person and the social person is also a bearer of a positive value of the person as a unity. And the disharmony of both is the bearer of a negative value of the person.

Let us not forget that the absolutely intimate person is eternally transcendent to all possible cognition and valuation of

259. The only one of these values that presupposes for its possible realization an *absence of intending it* (*without conditions*) is the value of sanctity. This is because holiness alone is a pure value of the person, whereas fame is attached to one who performs a deed or to one who creates a work (see above, p. 568). Love of fame may very well be justified, but it is genuine love of fame only when it is directed toward the spiritual effectiveness of the deed or the accomplished work on posterity. If it is directed toward recognition by future generations, it becomes a case of (higher) vanity. The analogous case is love of honor and ambition.

260. Concerning life as seen by others in both normal and pathological cases, see "Idole," pp. 159 ff., as well as *Zur Phänomenologie und Theorie der Sympathiegefühle*, p. 20. [See "Idole," sec. 4; *Wesen und Formen der Sympathie*, pt. A, chap. 3.—*Ed.*]

the other (and therefore also transcendent to all historical cognition).[261] And precisely for this reason every ethics that would measure the moral value of man on the basis of the individual's relation to a historical collective world of goods, a collective will, or a collective *logos* must be false and erroneous.[262] From the outset every ethics of this type considers only one-half of man and, when applied, necessarily gives a thoroughly wrong picture of the factual distribution of values. Of course the opposite error, according to which only the intimate person is the original bearer of moral values, must be rejected with equal vigor. This error is to be found (as we have already remarked) in the ethical consequences of H. Bergson's theory. This error is also contained as a most wonderful consequence indeed in the works of Leo Tolstoi, who knew better than anyone how to shake the ethos of our present culture.[263] If his theory and conception were correct, the eremite would be the exemplar of moral perfection, and communal life would *in itself* be stained with evil.

Only the uniform, whole, and concrete person is the original bearer of the moral values "good" and "evil," and every man evidentially knows that every other finite person has an absolutely intimate sphere and, with equal evidence, knows that the contents of this sphere remain eternally *transcendent* to his own possible cognition. With this, we come to a *principle* that

261. Duties of absolutely intimate self-examination on the basis of self-love "in" God and duties of such self-criticism are quite *independent* of the degree to which they indirectly become of importance for the being and willing of each social person. Duties of relatively intimate self-examination with respect to the community of a church or friendship are independent of the degree to which they contribute to the being and acting of other social units (state, society, nation, etc.). By analogy, the good quality of the intimate sphere of a collective personality or of a community, for example, a *family,* is a self-value which is independent of the meaning that it may have for the being or non-being of more encompassing spheres, for example, humanity.

262. This judgment pertains without restriction to, e.g., Hegel's and Wundt's ethics. It also pertains to all those false positivistic theories in which the mere progress of society is considered progress toward the good, say, progress toward an increase of love. See my criticism of Darwin's and Spencer's theories of the origins of sympathetic feelings in *Zur Phänomenologie und Theorie der Sympathiegefühle*, p. 31. [See *Wesen und Formen der Sympathie*, pt. A, chap. 8.—Ed.]

263. In Tolstoi's world, for example, every official is bad, evil, or ridiculous, and every tendency toward the good begins with the official's ridding himself of his office and assuming more and more a direction toward the intimate person. This ethos stems from a mind of orthodox religiosity, no matter to what degree Tolstoi has opposed the idea of the church. [See "Über östliches und westliches Christentum" (Bibliog. nos. 11, 19).—Ed.]

is most important for ethics. I will end this chapter with its formulation. This principle states that every ultimate judgment of the finite person which concerns the moral value or disvalue of the other is self-contradictory. *Of necessity* there is no cognition of the absolutely intimate personal sphere of the other, which belongs essentially to the cobearer of moral values. Only the social person and the *relatively* intimate person can be subjects of a (possibly) evidential value-comprehension. Thus, to *withhold* the ultimate moral assessment of the other is the *duty* of all finite persons; [264] indeed, any such assessment (whether it be positive or negative) implies at once a violation of the other person and an evil act. This proposition and this duty obtain independent of another proposition which has as its content not the evidence but only the adequation of the possible cognition of finite persons, and which obtains for the person in his own intimate personal sphere (and also in his own and the other's social persons).[265]

This duty to withhold moral judgment also holds *mutatis mutandis* for the collective person insofar as its members possess absolutely intimate personal spheres or (in relation to their membership in other social units encompassing something that is nearer to their intimate person) at least relatively intimate personal spheres. Even the church's judgment of the whole person can in this sense be made only "with reservations," since "only God can see man's heart—adequately and evidentially." And since a social unit that is encompassed by a larger one can be known by the latter only with respect to the former's social side, not with respect to its intimate sphere, all legal institutions that subject the moral sentencing of men by men to negative norms and legal threats of punishment must be structured so that the judgments which are made on this relatively intimate sphere by those who are outside the community in question but who are, at the same time, members of the encompassing social unit can also be legally punished *without* proof of the true and the false. For it is not the possible falsehood of the judgment but the judgment itself that is blameworthy. The fact that this pertains only to sentencing, and not to positive value-judgments, is

---

264. It seems to me that this alone is the sense of "Do not judge others lest you be judged."

265. On this last proposition, see "Idole." See also "Das Ressentiment im Aufbau der Moralen," in which I cite Paul's words, "He dare not judge himself." [See "Idole," sec. 4; "Das Ressentiment im Aufbau der Moralen," sec. 3. See above, p. 182 f.—*Ed.*]

due to the limits of law, whose purpose is not to realize morality but only to make it possible.

ad 6.
a. The Law of the Origin of the Prevailing Ethos
Model Persons

An ethics which, like the one developed here, locates the highest and ultimate moral meaning of the world in the possible being of (individual and collective) persons of the highest positive value must finally come to a question of great significance: Are there specific *qualitative types* of persons within the idea of the person of highest positive value which can be differentiated in an a priori fashion, i.e., without recourse to positive historical experience; and if there are such types, to what extent do they exist? This question becomes all the more important in our ethics because of the insight that we gained earlier, namely, that all norms have their foundation in values, and that the (formally) highest value is not a thing-value [*Sachwert*], a value of a feeling-state, or a value of law, but *a value of the person*. It would follow syllogistically from this that the idea of the person of highest non-formal value is also the norm for moral being and comportment. But the ideal ought which originates as a requirement in the intuited personal value of a person is not called a norm, a name pertaining only to universally valid and universally ideal *propositions* of oughtness which have as content a valuable *action*. This ideal ought is called *a model*, or *an ideal*. A model is, like a norm, anchored in an evidential value of the person. But a model does not pertain to mere action, as is the case with a norm. It pertains first of all to a To-Be. One who has a model tends to *become* similar or equal to it, in that he experiences the requirement of the ought-to-be on the basis of the value seen in the content of the model person. In addition, the *individual* value-essence of the person who serves as a model is not extinguished in the idea of the model, as is the case with a *norm*, which is universal by virtue of its content and validity.

We can now ask, What is the essential relation (of *value* and *origin*) between norm and model?

It stands to reason that the answers to this question must differ, depending on whether an ethics maintains that good and evil are originally attached to lawful acts and acts contrary to laws, *or* whether it holds that good and evil belong to the being of persons. In the former case we would have the following: A model is by itself of positive or negative value, depending on whether the acts of will of which the person seen in this model is given as an executor (X) are, with respect to a moral law, either lawful or unlawful. This is precisely Kant's position. With regard to one's following the evangelical ideal, he expressly states:

> Imitation does not occur in the moral world, and examples serve only as encouragement; i.e., they put the feasibility of what the law orders beyond doubt, and they make pictorial [*anschaulich*] what the practical rule expresses in universal terms. But examples never give a justification for one's setting aside their true original, which resides in reason, and conforming to the example [*Metaphysics of Morals*, pt. II].

The answer to the above question is quite different for one who locates the highest sense of all moral acts, not in the realization of a supreme *law* or in the production of a specifically *structured order*, but in a solidary *realm of best persons*, and who considers the person, not as a mere subject (X) of possible acts of reason, i.e., "a rational person," but as an individual and concrete act-center of self-value.[266] One who gives this answer has first of all determined that norms can be of positive or negative value, and that ideal norms can be good or bad, depending on whether they ultimately advance or hinder the possible becoming of good or bad (individual and collective) persons. He has also determined that the positing of ideal norms as norms of duty is an act that is itself good or evil, depending on the essential goodness or badness of the person executing this *actus* of positing. Thus, above all, there can be *no norm of duty without a person who posits it,* and no non-formal rightness of a norm of duty without the essential goodness of the person who posits it. There can be no norm of duty at all without positive insight, that is, when the person "for" whom this norm should be valid lacks the insight to see *by himself* what is good. There can be no "reverence" for a norm or moral law that is not founded in reverence for the *person* who posits it—founded ultimately in love for this person as a model.[267]

266. See chap. 6, A.
267. This pertains also to all regions of norms. Reverence for the laws of the state has its roots in reverence for the total *person* of the state from which the laws came, but the state is not the empty X of these laws which, *as such*, ask for "reverence." A father's orders addressed to his child are subject to reverence on the basis of reverence for (or "love of") the social person of the father as a member and the head of a family. These orders are not subject to reverence simply because they have this content. One

And so the following holds generally: all norms have their value and disvalue in accordance with the possible positive or negative value of the *exemplariness of the person* who posits them; and the positive or negative value of the model's content is determined by the positive or negative value-essence of the person who functions as model.

Model persons essentially are, from a genetic viewpoint, also *more original* than norms. For this reason one must return to the systems of models and finally to prevailing and recognized *ideal types of persons* in all positive historical understanding of a system of norms (a "morality" in the sense defined earlier). If one does not find any models at first, one must look for them. For our proposition is rooted in the essential relation between norm and model, not in a positive, changing historical experience.

The experienced relation that a person has with regard to the content of the personality of his model is *fidelity* [Gefolg-schaft], based on love for this content, in the becoming of his morally personal *being*. This relation cannot be reduced to executing the same acts as the model has executed or merely imitating the model's actions and ways of expression. This relation is of a unique nature and requires an investigation of its own.[268] For it is, above all, the *only* relation in which the morally positive personal values of a person *A* can *immediately* determine the origin of the same personal values for *B*, i.e., the relation to the *pure and good example*. Nothing on earth allows a person to become good so originally and immediately and necessarily as the evidential and adequate intuition [*Anschauung*] of a good person *in* his goodness. This relation is *absolutely superior* to *any other* relation in terms of a possible becoming good of which it can be considered the origin. It is superior to *B*'s obeying the orders and commands of *A*, because this obedience (including the case of so-called obedience to oneself) can never follow from an autonomous and immediate insight into the value of what is commanded, and because this obedience can aim only at *action*, not at the moral tenor and not at all at the being of the person. This relation is also superior to all so-called moral education,

---

who believes in the commandments of God reveres them because they are commandments of the person of *God* (and because their content corresponds to his personal benevolence). He does not revere first of all the moral law, and God only as the empty X who gives this *law* or institutes this *order*.

268. [Concerning what follows, see "Vorbilder und Führer."—*Ed.*]

because, as we have seen, this can never make one moral, but can only bring about the empirical development of a personal being and moral tenor (with their value or disvalue), and because such education becomes immoral (as the very essence of educative acts) whenever it is pursued with the intention of "improving." [269] In this relation *alone* can both the autonomous insight and the autonomous will of the person who achieves fidelity be preserved, *despite* his being determined by another person. His autonomous will is preserved because the primary transformation toward the good first concerns not willing and acting but the *being* of the person who achieves fidelity as the root of all acting. One can therefore say that the highest *effectiveness* of the good person on the moral cosmos lies in the pure *value of exemplariness* that he possesses exclusively by virtue of his *being* and *haecceity,* which are accessible to intuition and love, and not in his will or in any acts that he may execute, still less in his deeds and actions.

Let us ignore for a moment the question of what functions as an evidentially good model and turn to the *factual effectiveness* of the model person throughout the growth and decline of moral being and life. We can then see that the principle of exemplariness is everywhere the primary vehicle for all changes in the moral. And models can, of course, be good or bad, superior or inferior; and the place of a *model* (in the narrow sense) can be filled by a *countermodel*—i.e., an image of a moral person constructed in direct opposition to a prevailing model, whereby the dependence of the value-structure on the content of the model remains visible in the countermodel's content.[270] But the proposition that is the foundation of all effectiveness of the model, namely, that the moral person is always set into the motion of moral transformation by a person or by the idea of one (prior to all effectiveness of norms and education), remains valid in the case of the effectiveness of a countermodel. In this sense parents, and primarily "the father," are the first models (or

<hr>

269. Both relations have their foundation in the pure exemplariness of the subject or educator who gives orders.

270. In all movements that are reactive to values, e.g., Protestantism, the Counter Reformation, romanticism, there is always a tendency to create *countermodels* against prevailing models. Thus, in romanticism the "beautiful soul" is the countermodel of the citizen of the eighteenth century, who is valued and hated as a Philistine. But in all such cases the dependency on the existing ideal remains. Such pictorial countermodels are structurally similar to the existing exemplary models. On *ressentiment* as a source of countermodels, see "Abhandlungen und Aufsätze" [Bibliog. no. 10].

countermodels) for their children; [271] and the "head" of the family or the "chief" is the model (or countermodel) for families and tribes, each as a member of a series of ancestors in which *one* ancestor emerges as the (typical) "good" one. And, again, in a community or a homeland there is an exemplary man or minority that functions as an example of what is "good," "right," "honorable," and "wise" in such a communal life. These models (as the non-formal content of the collective intention of communal life) function as that at which *everyone* looks; they are a measure for assessing oneself and others. And for a member of a people, the place of exemplariness is occupied by the social person of the "prince," [272] or (depending on the social structure in question) the type of the dominant nobility, the type of the "man of the people," of the "man of confidence," of the "president," of the "deputy." And, analogously, for a party member there is the image of the "leader"; for a pupil as a member of a school, that of the "teacher" or "master"; and for a member of a nation, that of the typical national "hero," "poet," "bard," etc. For the citizen and official there is the image of the currently highest statesman; [273] for the businessman, that of the "business leader"; [274] for a member of a church or sect, that of the founder, a reformer, or a saint; and for the sociable person, that of the "lion" of society, the exemplary man of fashion or tact, the *arbiter elegantiarum*. It is not our aim to deal with the empirical to the fullest extent. We only want to demonstrate that in every factual social unit there are entire *systems of exemplary, ideal types of social persons* from which, in each case, a primary exemplary or counterexemplary effectiveness emanates into all

271. "The father" is of course meant here as the content of a child's venerating, loving, and revering (or hating and negating) intentionality, i.e., not the "real" father. This or that "father" and this or that "mother" are still undifferentiated *pictorial sources* of all possible personal values. They are, as it were, the concrete value-individuals representing everything that is "higher" or "good." They are not yet people, nor is the father a "man," the mother a "woman," etc.

272. Thus, in terms of a model, the king of England is the highest gentleman, the German kaiser the highest warlord, the czar the foremost religious-ecclesiastical patriarch ("little father"), etc.

273. When Bismarck ruled Germany, the picture that people had of him was an extremely powerful factor of selection and imitation among German officials. One could find "little Bismarcks" everywhere—later on, little Bülows and Bethmanns. Who cannot see the same thing in philosophical schools?

274. I stressed in my essays on resentment and the bourgeois (see Bibliog. no. 10) that a transformation of a "prevailing" economic state of mind always originates with a minority that is effective as an example.

moral becoming, into the good as well as the bad, the superior as well as the inferior.[275] The primary effectiveness of the model and its opposite is on factual *collective persons* in their reciprocal relations and their spheres of influence over mankind in all areas, *not* in their political actions, the measures they take, their legislation, etc. It is the pictorial type of *the* Frenchman, for instance, or *the* Englishman or *the* Russian,[276] that carries a certain degree of exemplary effectiveness (or its opposite), primarily on mankind, by way of conformity and transformation; this pictorial type codetermines the moral constitution of mankind in terms of the power that affects other formal types through countereffectiveness.[277]

We must now specify what a *"model"* is ontically, and the mode and manner in which it originates and becomes effective.

One must be clear on one point above all: acts in which something—first in the structure of the unity of the person—becomes a model have their foundation in acts that we have designated as acts of *value*-cognition (and in this case acts of cognizing another's value, such acts as feeling, preferring, loving, hating), therefore *not* in acts of willing or striving or in acts of the cognition of being and still less in acts of deed or expression or in voluntary or involuntary acts of imitating deeds and expressions.[278] Hence all acts of striving and willing presuppose the content of the model and are *founded* in *love* for the object of the model (and in hatred for the object, in the case of a counterimage). In striving and willing we "follow" the person

275. There are, of course, exemplary models that the individual person makes of the individual person as such.

276. Friedrich von Wieser (*Recht und Macht* [Leipzig, 1910]) holds that the model and fidelity to the model are the basic principles of all sociological understanding. But his "law of the small number" implies only that the basic form of all sociological *acting* is leadership and fidelity, and that this leadership is always of a "small number" (even within democracies). More essential to us than the validity of this law for acting is its validity for the formation of prevailing systems of *valuation* and *ideals* of a social unit.

277. This formal type is secondarily the formal type of goods (ranging from a work of art, a house, etc., to merchandise) which pertain to the nation in question.

278. Since Kant did not introduce any ethical cognition into his ethics, and since he did not even include value-cognition among his basic concepts (see above, pp. 67 ff.), the relation between a model and fidelity to it had to remain hidden from him. It is quite characteristic of Kant that the passage cited ("Imitation does not occur in the moral world") confuses autonomous and evidential "fidelity" with blind and completely heteronomous "imitation." Perhaps he was misled by the traditional version of the *imitatio Christi*.

whom we love, but not vice versa. Acts in which the exemplary model and our following are lived have nothing at all to do with imitation (or "copying"). The exemplariness of the person does not originate in our imitating him. At best we tend to imitate what is already before us *as* a model person. There are alpha animals in the herd and the mass, but no models. Nor can one hold that value-free cognition of the model object (or the model person) is the basis of exemplariness. For here also values are in principle *prior* to the pictorial content and the meaning-content. "Father," "mother," "uncle," "prince," etc., first are value-persons of a certain quality, and it is around this nucleus of value alone that both pictorial content and meaning-content group themselves. Judgment (assessment) and acts of choice are therefore not at all a condition of something's becoming a model. Our consciousness of a model is entirely *pre*logical and *prior* to the comprehension of even possible *spheres* of choice. This consciousness determines judgment and the direction of choice. It would be most naïve to assume that one must judge whether something is or is not a model in order for it to become a model, or that one must judge and state what and who are supposed to be models before they can be models.[279]

What then is the model ontically? We may now say that it is, in its content, a structured value-complex in the form of unity of the unity of the person, a structured thisness of values in the form of the person—but according to the exemplariness of the content, the unity of a requirement of ought-to-*be* that is based on this content. But how are we to understand the manner of givenness of the model and its content in its being a model? In what concerns the first part of our question, it is a fact of greatest importance that this requirement of ought-to-be is experienced as an "it obliges me to follow," not as an "I am obligated to follow." We can also say that this requirement is experienced as a powerful tug which comes from the individual or collective person in whom the model-content appears as exemplary, or as a gentle tug or an "enticement"—but in any case as a *tug* which originates in the model. Models draw persons

---

279. Statistical experiments are guilty of this tremendous naïveté when, for example, pupils are given a questionnaire and are asked to list their model persons. It is precisely the model with the power of attraction that cannot come to the fore here. For, under like conditions, that model which has been judged as such, in comparison with the one that has not been judged as such (but which is nevertheless *effective*), is a model of definitely less power of attraction. Besides, we will soon show that a model, in its effectiveness as a special content, does not have to be given.

toward them. One does *not* actively move toward them. Models *become* goal-*determining;* the model is not a goal after which one strives or an end that one posits. But this tug does not appear in the form of a blind compulsion, say, the "suggestive powers" of a certain person. Rather, it possesses a consciousness of the ought-to-be and the being-right as its foundation.[280] As to the second part of the question, it is of equal importance to realize that in having a model, the givenness of the exemplary content is not to be identified with a singular content—be it perception, representation, or fantasy—but, as I have so often described, with one's experience of "being-delimited" [*Eingegrenztseins*].[281] In other words, this content is experienced in such a fashion that it becomes given only as a special content in the *totality* of experiences of fulfillment and non-fulfillment (or contrariness) through a possible exemplar. It is through delineated experiences of the form "This is what I love," "This is not what I love," "This is what I hate," etc. (and precisely *because* these experiences constantly fulfill our consciousness of the moral tenor), that our reflective consciousness notices the model's content as a peculiar succession. And in this way the model penetrates the differentiation of perception, representation, and fantasy—without being specially given in any one of these act-qualities as a single content. Therefore the content of the model and the act-correlate of the content function as a *form* of apprehension and existence for all these individual acts and their objects.[282]

280. Consciousness of goodness and rightness can of course be as deceptive as the comprehensions of value-complexes which found it, as in all cases of bad models. But then we are concerned with *deception*, and not with blind compulsion. For a bad model is a model, and not an object of the blind compulsion of imitation. Therefore, in all consciousness of exemplariness there is at least a *tendency* toward insight.

281. On the kind of givenness of the aesthetic laws that an artist obeys without having to know them, and the practical recognition of law on the part of the "criminal" in contrast to the breaker of the law, see above, pp. 141 f.

282. For this reason it is of course most difficult to know reflectively *what* is effective or posteffective as a model both in our own case and in that of the other. In individual cases this requires difficult technical methods. These cannot be developed here; but psychoanalytic techniques (though they still have poor theoretical foundations and are laden with superfluous baggage) offer much in this regard. Ethics proper demands only that bad models be raised to the level of human awareness, which holds for both good *and* bad countermodels. For good contents of countermodels *as* countermodels can be bad, e.g., the countermodel which arises in opposition to a father who claims exemplariness but who is also a bad father. Illusory models must also be destroyed. As I understand it, an il-

In what concerns not only the immediately lived effectiveness of the model, or the model in its effectiveness, but also the morally relevant *transformation* that comes from exemplary content, which we call *fidelity* [Folge, Nachfolge, Gefolgschaft], such transformations truly are basically different, depending on the rank of the value of the model, though in such a way that an identical moment of essence remains. This transformation is neither obedience nor imitation. It is, rather, *growth* of the *being* of the person and growth of the moral tenor according to the structure and traits of the model, growth encompassed by an attitude of *devotion* to the exemplary model. The model, for example, the lovingly intended exemplar, draws and invites, and we "follow." This "following" is not to be understood in the sense of willing and acting, which aim only at obedience to true commands or pedagogical pseudocommands, or at copying. Willing and acting can consist in this and can be partially heteronomous. "Following," however, is to be understood in the sense of *free* devotion to the content of personal value that is accessible to autonomous insight. For we become *like* the exemplar as a person. We do not become what he is. The new formation or, as the case may be, the transformation of the moral tenor, its alteration, and the change in the person's sense are only consequences of the growing adaptation of the person to the model. That is, we learn to will and do *as* the model wills and does, not what he wills and does (as in psychic contagion, imitation, and, in a different fashion,[283] obedience). The "moral tenor" encompasses not only willing but also all ethical value-cognition and preferring, loving, and hating, which are the foundation of all willing and choosing.[284] An alteration in the basic moral tenor is a moral process; commands (including self-commands, if there were such), educational directives (which do not reach

---

lusory model is one that is codetermined by an intention toward the "higher" or toward "giving a good example," i.e., one that arises in the pharisaical calculation of a mere social picture of effectiveness. Models which one imagines are also to be destroyed, e.g., one which one imagines to be one's model when another model is the genuine and effective one. It is even more difficult to ascertain the origins of a "morality" of an entire age and a totality (e.g., a cultural unit, a nation) in terms of model persons, as well as to ascertain the origins of these model persons in certain minorities. This is a task through which the science of history could *liberate* itself from the effectiveness of bad model persons in such totalities. See my essay "Der Bourgeois."

283. I.e., in the sense of doing something that somebody else wants done.

284. [See chaps. 2, 3.—*Ed.*]

the moral tenor), and advice and counsel cannot determine such an alteration. What alone can determine it is fidelity to a model. And such an *alteration* of the moral tenor [*Gesinnung*swandel] (different from a mere change in it) comes about primarily through the alteration of the direction of love in coloving with the love of the exemplar.[285]

The essence of the effectiveness of the model, as we just tried to show, is the most pure, the most immediate, and the highest form of this effectiveness. We will soon see, however, that associated with this are other *mixed* and *indirect* forms of this effectiveness, depending on the kind of ideal non-formal ideas of the person which become guidelines for the concretization of factual model persons, and depending on the type of social units in which the model persons live. There are three forms in which a model person can be handed down from *A* to *B*, from generation to generation, and so become indirectly effective: cultural-scientific knowledge, tradition, and the hereditary transmission of dispositions toward structures of preferring, through which a model person who prevailed among ancestors is revived. True, arbitrary imitation (without insight), which, as we said, is devoid of the *creative power* of the model, plays a significant role in *tradition*. A child, for instance, certainly "obeys" his parents without insight (i.e., "behaves"), no matter if they are good or bad exemplary models of "the" father and "the" mother.[286] Imitation certainly plays a determining role here. However, the fact that in this case imitation [287] (or copying of a higher sort) automatically *mediates* the exemplariness of parents

285. This is the case according to the basic character that belongs to a pure act of love in connection with all forms of ethical cognition and, indirectly, to willing and acting. In my study on resentment I presented a historical example of such a fundamental alteration of the moral tenor. The model person of Christ gave rise to a primary alteration of the direction of love (away from that of the ancient world).

286. Note that the concept "well behaved" coincides in meaning with "following a personal model," with readiness to obey and perform commanded *actions*, and finally with a positive value-predicate (this is a "well-behaved" child). Here "well behaved" does not mean "obedient," but "*ready* to obey" on the basis of fidelity-to-model.

287. In "imitation" (including involuntary imitation) the expressive *sense* of a gesture or action is given as the substrate of imitation (see the appendix to *Zur Phänomenologie und Theorie der Sympathiegefühle*). [See *Wesen und Formen der Sympathie*, pt. C, chap. 3.—*Ed.*] Contrary to Lipps's opinion, this sense is *not* given through imitation. In the mass and in herds, however, there is no imitation but only the similar movements of members according to the mere picture of movement which mediates this simple moving. Only secondarily does this similarity of movement *effect* similar experiences (the herd in relation to the alpha animal).

does not remotely imply that this exemplary effectiveness *consists* in processes of imitation and copying,[288] or that the exemplary content, insight into the exemplary content, insight into (or deception over) its value, or its transformative effectiveness comes about through these processes. We are concerned here, as well as in the case of hereditary transmission, only with differently structured vehicles or selective forms of exemplary effectiveness proper, or with more or less automatically mediated types of this effectiveness.[289]

Let us now turn to the question of the *laws of origin* of all factually *historical* models and countermodels, good as well as bad, superior as well as inferior. It is certain that factual models originate for man *in* [an] other factual men as objects of some kind of experience. Yet these men, as they are experienced, *are* not the exemplars themselves. Although we frequently say, "This X is my model," what we mean by "model" is not at all this factual man in his flesh and blood. We mean that this X is an *exemplification* of our model proper—perhaps the only one, perhaps evidentially the "uniquely" possible one. But even in this case he functions merely *as* exemplar. The model itself is seen *in* [*geschaut* an] men who function as exemplars; that is, it is seen more or less adequately (in terms of deception or insight). But the model is not extracted or abstracted from the empirically contingent natures of such men, nor is it found as a real or abstract part of the exemplars.[290] If the essence of the model and

288. Or counterimitation, in the case of a countermodel.
289. The reason why the immense significance of the effectiveness of models for the (positive and negative) moral formation of personal being and the will has been overlooked in ethics for such a long time is what I have frequently called the pragmatistic prejudice of all normative ethics. Of course, if there were moral value only in what we will, choose, do, command, regard as norms, etc., or in what can be taught, all that we have said would have *no* moral significance. Model persons and models for *being* a person cannot be "willed," "created," "chosen," "commanded," or established as "norms." For they "are" and "become," one "grows" into them, etc. It is time to stop talking about these problems from the standpoint of a sergeant!
290. Expressions like the "idealization" of empirical men as models or their "sublimation" by drive-impulses not yet guided by values, or their blind inclination to such impulses, say *nothing* about the origin of the model. For what could direct the arbitrary and fortuitous activities of idealizations, feignings, and sublimations toward a specific *value-goal*? Could factual wishes or inclinations, etc.? But how could these obtain the supraempirical content of a goal if the empirical theory of the will were valid (see chap. 3)? If it is the case that a man *has become* our model person, then, of course, it is also possible for us to idealize this model in the direction of his exemplariness. But neither the model-content nor the fact that this man became our model is due to any "idealization." [On "subli-

the essential relation between model and exemplar *cannot* be derived from contingent, inductive experience, we must ask the following: Are there, for the factual formation of factual models in men and for the factual comprehension of these by men, universally and individually valid pure *types of models* which, though they be non-formal structures in the intuition of value-complexes in the *form*-unity of the person, function as model *forms* in the formation and structuration of all factual models and their factual acquisition by man; and if there are such types, to what extent do they exist? And can we find ordered ranks which obtain in themselves among these pure types of the value-person?

b. The Idea of Ordered Ranks among Pure Types of the Value-Person

Thus far we have established only the important law of all moral growth (and decline) of values: namely, that moral growth (and decline) occurs through the effectiveness of models and countermodels in the form of the person, and not through acts of obedience and disobedience with regard to norms, etc. But we have not specified what a *good* or *bad* model (or countermodel) is, or why the grasping of a model is accordingly justified or unjustified.

First of all, it is clear that the person who functions as an exemplary model and in whom the model first and foremost comes to givenness for us is in *intention* necessarily and always "good" (or, in the case of the countermodel, "evil"). It is not possible to seize as an exemplary model the person who is given as evil. It is possible, however, for us not to follow our "model" in *practice*, and in such cases we deceive ourselves in taking this or that person as our model. Finally, the act of preferring in which we make a person the exemplar of our model can lack evidence. The first of these cases (not following the model in practice) is possible only if one of the other cases is present,[291] inasmuch as

mation," see *Wesen und Formen der Sympathie*, pt. B, chap. 6, esp. sec. 5, "Zu Freuds Ontogenie." See also *Die Stellung des Menschen im Kosmos.* —*Ed.*]

291. It is quite possible consciously to will the bad as the bad. We do *not at all* agree with Thomas Aquinas' claim, "Omnia volumus sub specie boni." But it is *not* possible consciously to *prefer* what is given as bad to what is given as good. Our will can consciously *resist* the (believed-in) will of God *as* this will of God. But "God-hate" is not possible (in a conscious intention). And our will can no longer resist the divine will after the union of our value-being with the essential goodness of God in God's love.

evident and adequate cognition of what is good *necessarily* determines the will.[292] But it is necessary to distinguish all these cases of intentional content from the *objective* being-good and being-bad of the whole which originates in the *actus* of the exemplification of the model type in a specific factual person (i.e., the model in the sense that "This *A* is my model"). *This* model is *good* only when the order of ranks of pure model types is maintained in it. And the act of preferring in which one person is preferred as an exemplar over another is "correct" only when the a priori non-formal laws of preferring are fulfilled in this act. Of course, an objectively bad model necessarily *corresponds* to *deception* in preferring (but never to mere inadequation, which leads only to deficient practical consequences). But one must not say that *by definition* a model corresponding to such a deception *is* bad. Hence we can establish the goodness and badness of prevailing models (in the above sense) without regard to any acts of their comprehension or their origin. But we *do know* that deception in preferring is the origin of bad models. If, for instance, such a person or group of persons becomes exemplary for a person, period, or group which by moral tenor prefers the useful to the noble, vital values to those of the mind, etc., we know that the positive models originating in this person, period, or group are objectively bad ones, and that this person, period, or group must have had bad models.[293]

We also know what good and bad models are when we know the *pure types of value-persons* (and their ranks) which are at the same time, and on the basis of their type-characteristics, pure models for all factual models. If these types and their ranks are "fulfilled" in factual models, the factual models are (objectively) good. If these models contradict these types and their ranks, these models are bad.

Of these pure types of value-persons, universal *ethics* can

292. [See above, pp. 68 ff., 191 f.—Ed.]
293. This proposition is important for the genealogy of prevailing "types of ethos and morality," and it prescribes a specific method for these studies. We tend to prefer "first" empirical persons to other empirical persons, empirical goods to other empirical goods, as well as norms to other norms. But we do this *because* the preferred persons become models or countermodels through such rules of preferring. Hence the deceptions that occur in preferring things *originate* in deceptions in preferring values of the person. A whole prevailing system of such deceptions (a bad ethos), however, originates in the representative prevailing class of persons who function as exemplars (to the common mind). On the application of this to historical investigations of various kinds of ethoses, see "Der Bourgeois" and "Der Bourgeois und die religiösen Mächte."

determine only those which are *universally valid*, not those which are individually valid. The latter are situated in the frame of the former but nevertheless cannot be derived from them. The individually valid types can be intuited in the historically factual.

The universally valid, pure types of value-persons result from the connection of the idea of the value-person as the highest value [294]—an idea that we arrived at earlier—with the order of ranks of the modalities of values.[295] We discovered this order without deception in part I,[296] and thus we have the *saint,* the *genius,* the *hero,* the *leading spirit,* and the *bon vivant* as the highest types of all positive and good models according to the order of ranks of this series.[297]

Although these ideas are obtained in a deductive fashion, nevertheless, when considered in themselves by setting aside their ordered ranks, they are remarkable enough. For no moment of image or meaning from outside the sphere of values penetrates the objects of these ideas. They are ideas of genuine *value-persons,* ideas that are related to values whose bearers are already determinate persons according to their being in the same way that goods (= value-things) are related to values of things.[298] Here the value of a specific rank fills the *formal unity* of personality *primally* as the value-essence of the personality. This value of a specific rank constitutes the unity of the type. This value is therefore no mere characteristic or property of a group of persons which is already unified independent of this kind of value, as is the case with the statesman, the general, etc. Hence there are good and bad statesmen, generals, etc., but not good and bad heroes, saints, etc. For the unity of the person-type itself is *constituted* by a positive value. Just as we do not originally discover the triangle as a property of corporeal surfaces, but only call *those* surfaces triangular whose forms correspond more or less adequately to the pure triangle, so we cannot discover these ideas by looking at common properties of men. A heroic man is precisely one who corresponds (more or less adequately) to the type of the value-person as a model, not one who has

294. As opposed to values of the person (virtues), values of things, and values of feeling-states.

295. See chap. 2, B, sec. 5.

296. If we had not discovered this order, the theory of the ideas and origin of these types would nevertheless be dependent on it.

297. See my final remarks, on p. 595.

298. See above, p. 19 f.

some namable properties in common with other empirical men. (With regard to the act, it is not pictorial representations or meanings, which could have only exemplary sense *for* these types, that correspond originally to these types when held before the mind's eye, but specific directions of intentional feeling, preferring, loving.) [299] There is proof of this in the fact that when we apply the concepts of these types, e.g., in history, we analyze the empirical value-complex of a man *according to* these types, and at the same time we depict any such value-complex that does not adequately exemplify *one* of these as an admixture of types or as a complex which lies between types.[300] This would not be possible if these ideas were inductively abstracted from positive historical material.

Finally, for these very reasons one must not "*hypostatize*" these types of the value-person in a historically factual person in such a way that they are confused with their mere exemplars. This mistake is at the root of all false *traditionalism*, which prefers values of the past to those of the present and the future. This false traditionalism has a counterpart in false "*idealism*" and "*utopianism*," which mistakenly attempt to conceive of the types of the value-person *originaliter* as mere "ideals" of an ought-to-be (or even as an eternal so-called task). In so doing they attribute lower values not only to the factual past (which can at times be justified) but also to the phenomenological just-past, i.e., the field of everything given "as past," in favor of the phenomenological present and future.[301] And if such hypostatiza-

---

299. Hence the *idea* of the value-type of the hero is to be clearly distinguished from the pure value-type.

300. Thus, e.g., St. Francis is a good example of the value-person of the saint (faithful to a model), whereas Augustine exhibits a mixture of holiness and the heroic. Similarly, Frederick the Great reveals a mixture in which heroism dominates, but in which there is an element of the genius (the philosopher and poet Frederick), etc. This also obtains for the *types of men of personal value* derived from the *pure types of value-persons*. Such men are, for instance, the statesman, the general, the "great ecclesiastic," the philosopher, the artist, the sage. The heroism of Alexander, Duke Eugene, and Napoleon is mixed with the traits of the statesman and the general, in contrast to Blücher, whose heroism blends with the traits of the general. Pascal revealed the trait of holiness, that of the genius (as philosopher and mathematician), etc. These types are still a priori; but they are not value–a priori, as are the pure types of value-persons. [On the types of men of personal value, see "Vorbilder und Führer."—Ed.]

301. This trait appears as the predominant ethos of a whole people among the Jews, for whom the Messiah is always "coming" (though *not* expected at a certain time). The Jewish ethos is therefore one of "progress," and it retains this *structure* even when its *content* becomes other than re-

tion is avoided, it becomes clear that there *can never* be a *pure* or *perfect* hero, genius, etc., as a fact. Hence, if the type of the value-person functions correctly, the totality of this model is related to time in a twofold manner. As a model for personal becoming, it is an image of anticipation and, at the same time, one of hope, and derivatively an image of striving. In this case its content is related to the phenomenal future. But if the model has been acquired *in* [an] (not from) a historically factual person, it is an image of recollection and, at the same time, one of adoration, and derivatively a cult-image. Here its content is related to the phenomenal past, i.e., to what is given in every case "as past."

The hypostatization of the types of the value-person can also lead to another error: namely, the simple transfer of *their* objective order of ranks to certain *factual* groups of men that are definitely conceptualized and represented, e.g., occupations, classes, offices, dignities, nations, etc. In principle, every group of this type represents only a sphere for the appearance of certain types of the value-person, and each has its own peculiar ideas of these types.[302] The ideas that various classes and occupations have of the "heroic," for instance, are quite different. They are different among farmers, citizens, knights, physicians, technicians, and soldiers. But the heroic, as well as its idea, can in principle come to the fore in any individual person. Only the conditions of its coming (objectively) to the fore are essentially different among various classes, occupations, etc. But there is the law that even these possible fields, within which the heroic may come to the fore in certain groups, are greatest for the exemplary

---

ligious. The Messiah is in such cases replaced by other contents of the spirit of the time. The same basic idea can be found in Hermann Cohen's ethics. This deception, by the way, is connected with another: namely, that only *willing* is "originally good" (Kant). For everything present in this act is essentially (phenomenally) related to the future (even if it is a matter of factually past willing). The roots of this deception can be found already in the case of Kant. It is pushed to an extreme by Fichte, for whom the good is *in essence* a "task." Hegel's criticism, justified as such, overshot its goal, and so he was led into the opposite error of traditionalism (see esp. *Die Phänomenologie des Geistes*).

302. Hence there are German, English, and French ideas of the hero, the genius, and the saint. These cannot be judged one against the other without difficulties. Similarly, there are national and epochal pictures of the "gentleman," the *gentil homme*, the *homme honnête*, the *Biedermann*, the *cortegiano*, the Japanese *bushido*. All of these contain admixtures of types of personal values and are permeated by the individual spirit and ethos of the national collective personality.

saint and become smaller and smaller as we go down the scale of exemplary types.[303]

Before we undertake the essential characterization of these types,[304] we must ask how they are related to the *idea of God* as the idea of an infinite person. It should be clear that the idea of God, unlike the ideal types of the person discussed above, does not function as an *exemplary* model [Vor*bild*]. For it is senseless to say that a finite person takes the infinite person as a model or even as the pure type of his model persons.[305] Nevertheless, the essential goodness of God expresses an idea in which the universally valid types of the value-person (although not "as" models) are in their order "co-"contained in infinite perfection as fully exemplary. But the Godhead also contains individually valid essences of the value-person. This "cocontaining" means that the essential goodness of God does *not* exhaust itself in the infinite exemplariness of the universally and individually valid being of the value-person. It means that the essential goodness of God is primally infinite as an *indivisible* essential value-quality. It is *only through* a possible experiential and cognitive relation of a finite person to the infinite person that divine goodness divides into unities of value-essences = value-types and their declining sequence of ranks.[306]

It is for this reason that a factual, novel comprehension of these ideas and their ordered ranks (or, in deception, their reversal), as well as the positive historical outlines of their contents, expressed in historical pictorial contents, does not lead to those

303. The slave and the king, the poor man and the rich man, all have an equal chance to be an exemplary saint. But in the case of a slave there is less probability of his being a genius, and still less a hero. Very improbable indeed is a case of a poor *bon vivant*. Obviously, the role of the social condition of the realization of value-models increases as we go down the scale of value-modalities.

304. [The "essential characterization of these types," referred to here and later, was not included in *Formalism* owing to concern for the size of the work. See the author's final remarks, p. 595.—*Ed.*]

305. It is even greater nonsense to degrade the idea of God *itself* to an ideal in which humanity is to find its unity, as Hermann Cohen and Paul Natorp do.

306. Thus the idea of God implies that the all-loving God is also the all-saintly God; as the omniscient God, divine artist, law-giver, and judge, also the all-knowing God; and as the almighty, also the all-heroic God. But the values relative to life, i.e., the values of the useful and the agreeable, have no place in the idea of God. The value of life, whose personal actualization is the "hero," is, of course, *not* "relative" to life itself. It is possible to observe a group's *ethos* in nuce *and compressed*, as it were, in terms of the foundational structure of the essential determinations and value-attributes of the idea of God which is "believed in."

variations in the idea of the Divine which we find in the history of religion. Rather, the opposite is true. It is the *primal alteration of the positive content of what has been intended as "divine"* that allows the coalteration of the factual model types and the laws of construction of the factual models.[307] And in this sense we may say that the intended Divine (factually) becomes the point of departure for all other functioning model types—a proposition which is equally significant in investigations concerning the connection between the history of religion and the history of ethos and culture. This proposition also holds for *counter*types formed in reactionary movements against a prevailing idea of the Divine, which in extreme cases are called, in relation to this idea, *atheism*. Such countertypes remain entirely *dependent* on the prevailing idea of God, for their mere denial of a reality[308] does not change anything in the inner *value-structure* of the denied content of the idea of God. One can even say that all so-called atheism originates of *necessity* as a countertheism against the content of the value-structure of the prevailing idea of the Divine.[309]

We have maintained that the plurality of types of the value-person, in their relatedness to the uniform and simple essential goodness of the Divine, rests on acts of a lawfully ordered analysis of this goodness, and that this idea of goodness does not rest

307. The history of religions shows that such changes in the idea of God and the personal model occur everywhere. Now God is conceived predominantly as the omniscient God (Aristotle), now the heroic God, the law-giver and judge (Judaism). One could show how the assumptions of the unity or the plurality of the Divine, as well as the sense and meaning of his intended personality or non-personality, change along with the essential interconnections of the value-qualities that are predominantly intended in the various cases. For example, God as the all-heroic God is *in essence* a God of the people. This is the case with the ancient Jews, who associated God with the most important possessions of the people, namely, the herds; later, after the people took up residence, God became "the God of battles," Zebaoth.

308. This negation of reality, as a theoretical negation, is founded in the emotive "rejection" of the value-structure present in the content of the prevailing idea of the Divine. We reject the reality of a specific "God" because we reject the divine character of such an assumed reality.

309. No matter how well taken the points of the supporters of atheism as contratheism against a *prevailing idea of God* and its object may be, atheism, in the strict sense, is always based on the *deception* of mistaking a rejection of the essence of the Divine (which is an act thoroughly different from an act of not *positing* the Divine and from the act of negating the reality of a posited "prevailing" God) for what is in fact only a rejection of a certain historical idea of God with the accompanying *inability* to see another positive content of the Divine (in simple fashion). [See "Probleme der Religion."—*Ed.*]

on a synthesis of previously *given* types of the value-person. In this sense one can call the pure types of the value-person perspectival sides (structured by ranks) of the simple and undivided Godhead, sides which are constitutive for the possible *modes of givenness* of the Godhead (as value-being) in a finite person, but not constitutive for the being of God. And we have maintained that the divine goodness itself becomes *indirectly* a possible model-content only in the forms of these types of the value-person.

On the basis of this phenomenological state of affairs, especially insofar as it implies a plurality of types, there is the phenomenon which I call *the essential tragic of all finite personal being* and its (essential) moral *imperfection.*[310] The former is based on the latter. It is essentially, not contingently, impossible for one finite (individual or collective) person to represent simultaneously an exemplar of the saint, the genius, and the hero. Therefore no possible opposition of *will*, that is, no possible "strife" between the exemplars of types of the value-person (as models), *can be settled* by a finite person. For this "strife" could be settled in a *just* manner only by a finite person who was the exemplar of all three models in identical ways. Hence strife is tragic whenever the judgment of the Godhead is the *only* just solution that can be presented. We can also say that the idea of law presupposes that persons are of equal value before the law.[311] And because *inequality* in value also necessarily exists among the most perfect, good finite persons of highest value, the value-rank of the type in question, for whom persons are examples, can still be known. But the mere cognition of this relation among the value-ranks of the persons involved in strife does not justly settle their possible strife, i.e., a contrary relation of *wills* in relation to the same good or evil. For this to happen, both the value-equality of the conflicting persons before a conceivable *law* and the possible idea of a *judge* who could understand and value those persons are presupposed. "Understanding" and "valu-

310. I am assuming that the reader is familiar with my essay "Zum Phänomen des Tragischen." The idea of the tragic is an ethical category, no matter to what extent the tragic also serves as material for literary works. It is through "inherited good and evil" (see above, p. 495 f.) and their possible clash in the will and in action that the tragic becomes "fate," a concept which requires a separate study.

311. This proposition does not rule out so-called laws of exception for certain positive groups (they have existed for centuries), but only the value-inequality of persons before a certain law which pertains to them as members of one social unit.

ation," however, presuppose at least the phenomenal encompass-ability of the sense and value of the conflicting volitional acts on the part of the judge, which is clearly impossible in this case.[312] Only the hero fully values the hero; only the genius fully values the genius.

Who should value both wills [313] when it is impossible to be both perfect hero *and* perfect genius? [314]

Our assertion concerning the essential imperfection of the finite person and the consequence of this, the implicit essential tragic of certain moral conflict, must not be confused with another idea that has played a great role in the history of both philosophical and theological ethics up to the time of Kant, an idea which we must expressly reject. This idea can be expressed in two essentially related propositions: namely, that the finite person *qua* finite person is *necessarily evil* (not merely "im-perfect" and therefore "radically" evil), and that there is no as-sessment of a person in terms of the degree of his moral perfec-tion, which is distinct from the assessment of his volitional acts in terms of the idea of a norm. The false idea that evil is con-

---

312. "Understanding" (comprehension of the other's sense) and "valu-ation" (comprehension of the other's value-sense) do not at all presuppose the prior experience of a like experience (see *Zur Phänomenologie und Theorie der Sympathiegefühle*, app.). [See *Wesen und Formen der Sym-pathie*, pt. C, chap. 3.—Ed.] For otherwise only thieves could judge thieves; and only murderers, murderers. But they do presuppose that sense-units and units of value-complexes are common to both the understanding and valuing subject and the understood and valued, i.e., the types of value-persons of the individuals concerned as we described them earlier. And it is only to this extent that only like can judge like.

313. Note that the sense and value of a volitional act can be *fully* given only on the basis of the comprehension of the willing person (see above, p. 28). And it is not at all correct to hold that law is concerned only with actions, and ethics only with the basic moral tenor of the per-son. Ethics has something to do not only with the moral tenor (or actions as expressions of it) but also with actions themselves (see chap. 3). Law, too, has something to do not only with actions but also with the moral tenor expressed in such actions. The difference between the two must be seen in the fact that law (in itself) has to do with the *social* moral tenor and *social* actions, and not with the tenor and actions of the relatively or absolutely intimate person. In addition, law deals only with the existing relative *differences* in value among the moral tenors and actions of legal subjects who "function as equal" (but who do not exist as equal) with regard to the "law" concerned, through which the order of right is realized.

314. Analogous "tragic" conflicts of the will belong also to the essential relations among collective persons and among states, to the relations be-tween church and state, nation and state, and among nations themselves. *If* sexual relations reached the finite sphere of the *person* (i.e., not only the spheres of the lived body and of the psychic), such conflict would also occur between woman and man.

nected with finitude can (curiously enough) emerge from two quite different and opposite errors concerning the nature of good and evil (and history shows this). First, it emerges from the attempt to reduce the ideas of good and evil to mere "degrees of perfection" or the opposite of perfection, imperfection (this attempt was made by Spinoza, Leibniz, and Wolff, and Kant *rightly* rejected it).[315] In this case the essential imperfection of the finite person *must* of course coincide with his radically evil propensity. And we encounter the same error in Kant's attempt to deny *entirely* the originality of the dimensions of perfection and imperfection of moral qualities, or to reduce the idea of moral perfection to that of the goodness of the will and to reduce this goodness to dutiful willing out of duty. From this the false theory of the so-called infinity of duty (the correlate of the denial of a dimension of perfection), as well as the illusion that the mere fact of an essential *imperfection* of the finite person is the same in meaning as the given radical *"propensity" for evil*, necessarily follows.[316] But in fact both moral imperfection and moral

315. This kind of reduction has its exact analogue in the theory of cognition that tries to reduce the true and the false to degrees (or types) of adequation and inadequation in cognition (Spinoza). We find the same error *today* in the attempt to reduce differences of adequation in cognition to truth and falsity of judgment. This is equivalent to denying degrees of perfection in ethics.

316. Historically, this theory of Kant's is of course a continuation of the old Protestant theories of original sin and the Fall of Man (both the Lutheran version and the somewhat different Calvinist version). In these theories sin is already located in the *fact of a finite lived body and its drives* (a point similar to the views of some Gnostics), not in the comportment of a finite *spiritual* personality and his volitions with regard to excitations of drives. Kant's theory, however, is also a *logical* consequence of his premises, especially his premise that the individuality of the person is located not in the spirituality of the person *himself* but in the lived body and in the empirical content of his psychic life; i.e., individuality is a mere disturbance of autonomous transcendental reason. But one can also ask how there *can* ever be evil on Kant's presuppositions (i.e., whether it is possible, not whether it factually is). The moral law is in itself and for rational beings a "natural law of reason," the law of "pure reason itself." This means that man "as" a rational being cannot be evil. Drives, on the other hand, are morally *indifferent* and *cannot* be the basis of evil. (Kant only recognizes the "chaos" of moral drive-excitations; see pt. I.) It remains completely *incomprehensible* how their acting together in the moral life could be evil *if* the moral life is to originate from these two factors alone! Kantian moral philosophers frequently cover up this fact by a circular argument: the "natural law of pure reason" becomes "duty" (and norm) only in the *clash* with drive-impulses, and the drive-impulses become "evil" in the clash with the lawfulness of reason. But for Kant himself, individual drive-excitations, which yield possible material for the form of the moral law, are not at all evil or radically evil. Only the *fact* that there is something like "drives" is evil. (See his *Kritik der Religion*

perfection consist (independent of good and evil) in the *poverty*
and *fullness* of moral qualities (imperfection of degree) and
modalities [317] (imperfection of kind) that encompass the person
in the field of his moral being and experience and, secondarily,
in moral cognition, understanding, and valuation [*Würdigen*]
and, only *thereby, also* in his possible (good *or* evil) acts of
willing and acting. The devil, too, has his own kind of perfection. He is, however, perfectly evil.[318] The *peculiarity* of the tragic
must disappear in the theory that we reject here, which either
locates an essential tragic in the nature of the person's relation
to himself and to God, thereby conceiving the finite person as
perpetually involved in a *struggle* between duty and inclination
and as *necessarily* sinful, *or* completely denies, in the sense of the
Spinozistic reduction, the phenomenon of the tragic.[319] And the
peculiarity of the tragic disappears precisely because either all
moral being or none of it contains the character of the tragic. In
contrast to this theory our propositions imply that the phenomenon of the tragic has its peculiar sense and origin in the
essential *type* of imperfection (not in its degree) among good
exemplars of value-persons. In the tragic conflict, *equally justified provinces* of duty clash, each "province" receiving its objective field from the value-being and value-kind of the persons
themselves who participate in the conflict.[320] (This clash is not
one of duties with inclinations or of duties with duties.)

The tragic is recognized in the above as an essential moral
category (not as a merely historical category) of the world of
finite persons, but it has no possible predicative meaning either

innerhalb der Grenzen reiner Vernunft.) The many followers of Kant who
for one reason or another cannot buy this, who simply dispose of his theory
as a "whim" or take it as, at best, only "historical" (i.e., as residue of the
old Protestant dogmaticism), must be considered most naïve.

317. [See chap. 2, B, sec. 5.—*Ed.*]

318. But the devil remains (in intention) a "lord of rank," the "principle" of hell, and is therefore quite distinct from the sphere of the "base,"
"common," and "bad." As a countermodel to the believed "Divine," the
"devilish" still shares in the *formal* structure of perfection of the Divine
(belief in the devil is only *one* specific historical manifestation of this
countermodel). But the devil shares in this only insofar as this formal
structure is not *equal* to the Divine. Thus the difference between finite
and infinite perfection remains.

319. Pantheism, which is essentially interrelated with this theory,
denies the nature of the tragic and is forced to reduce it to deficient morality or deficient "progress." (Whether philosophers have always proceeded consistently on this point is not to be settled here.)

320. A demonstration of the fact that it is not acts of choosing but the
spheres of choosing that become (objectively) "guilty" can be found in my
treatise "Zum Phänomen des Tragischen."

"for" God or "before" God.[321] The tragic remains relative to the value and existence of the finite person. It has no transcendental meaning. For a possible judge of *tragic* (and not merely moral) conflict is also implied in the idea of God. And, as was the case among the Greeks, it is only when the Divine is represented in a plurality of finite persons that the εἱμαρμένη can also be considered a power "over gods and men." In this way the tragic acquires a value and existence-*absolute* and therefore a transcendental character.[322]

With this general theory of the effectiveness of models and their counterparts as the *original form* of moral becoming and alteration, and with the explication of the idea of the order of ranks for pure types of value-persons, these investigations into the *foundations* of ethics come to an end. But it is not difficult to see that two additions are needed.

1. Because the idea of God is originally determining for all models and their counterparts and for types of the value-person governing their formation, the natural continuation of our investigations requires a theory of God and also an investigation into the types of acts in which the essence of God comes to the fore (theory of religion). However, this involves the question of whether, in the basic religious acts of having faith (not belief) in something, the positing of the reality of the being of the Divine is possible or necessary, and, if this positing is possible or necessary, how it takes place. And since such an investigation would especially require a treatment of the original saint and the saint as follower (with the manifold subdivisions of "divine man," "prophet," "seer," "teacher of salvation," "God's delegate," "the called," "savior," "healer") as types of the value-person, we could not present our theory of the types of value-persons, finished some years ago, without expanding the present work to include both the theory of God and the philosophy of religion. I

321. Hence, despite what E. von Hartmann suggests, it is nonsense to consider God a "tragic hero."

322. Therefore the phenomenon of the tragic as presented in the literature of Aeschylus and Sophocles reveals a depth, irreconcilability, and absoluteness in comparison with which all other historical forms of so-called tragedy appear to be mere *lugubrious dramatizations* [Trauerspiele] of this phenomenon (i.e., presentations of the tragic that remain relative to and based on the finite subject itself). There are "historians" today who still believe that the phenomenon of the tragic occurred in Greece simply because Sophocles, Aeschylus, and Euripides lived there, men who invented the "form of the tragedy." I include this remark only for the amusement of future generations who will confront the conception of ancient tragedy of our all-too-"historical" age.

prefer a separate publication of my investigation into the connection between ethics and the theory of God because I believe it is better not to burden the results of this other investigation with a basic theory of ethics that is *independent* (and valid independently) of all philosophical investigations into religion and *religious* ethos. Hence I will present this work soon in a special volume.[323]

2. The present investigation requires a concrete elaboration of the theory of *all types of the value-person,* their order of ranks, and their subdivisions. This investigation, which I wanted at first to include here, and which I usually do include in my lectures on ethics, I withhold for another reason. It will obtain its full meaning and fruitfulness only if it is immediately followed by an investigation into the essential roles which types of the value-person play in the basic forms of *socialization* and *history.* And this requires an elaboration of the basic forms of association which is much more concrete than the one that we have sketched here. Only on such a basis can the theory of types of the value-person with his societal and historical functions be enlarged into an essential theory and ethics of human "occupations," a theory in which constants and historical variables of occupations are distinguished, and in which certain directions and laws of their alterations and their structuration within the total structure of a positive age and society can be detected.

This *second* addition to the present work will be presented much later than the above-mentioned forthcoming addition. It will be entitled "Types of the Value-Person and the Sociology of Human Occupations." [324]

323. Under the title *Vom Wesen des Göttlichen und den Formen seiner Erfahrung.* [See "Probleme der Religion." A major manuscript which deals with the problems of "faith" and "belief," the real positing of God, and the relation between metaphysics and religion, and which came about in connection with *Formalism* (ca. 1915), was found among the author's papers. This was published in *Collected Works* (Bibliog. no. 31), Vol. X. —*Ed.*]

324. [No major manuscripts dealing with a "sociology of occupations" were found among the author's papers. The writings on social philosophy and the philosophy of history which stem from the period of *Formalism* and later are to be published in a forthcoming volume of the *Collected Works.*—*Ed.*]

Bibliography

(NOTE: The following works by Max Scheler are listed in chronological order according to the date of first publication. Those accompanied by "C.W." in parentheses also appear in Number 31, *Collected Works*.)

1. "Beiträge zur Feststellung der Beziehungen zwischen den logischen und ethischen Prinzipien." Ph.D. dissertation, Jena, 1897. Jena: Druck Vopelius, 1899 (*C.W.*, Vol. I).

2. "Arbeit und Ethik." *Zeitschrift für Philosophie und philosophische Kritik*, Vol. CXIV, no. 2 (1899) (*C.W.*, Vol. I). (See Bibliog. no. 19.)

3. "Die transzendentale und die psychologische Methode: Eine grundsätzliche Erörterung zur philosophischen Methodik." Habilitationsschrift, Jena, 1899. Jena: Verlag Dürr, 1900. 2d ed., Leipzig: Verlag Felix Meiner, 1922 (*C.W.*, Vol. I).

4. "Über Selbsttäuschungen." *Zeitschrift für Pathopsychologie*, Vol. I, no. 1 (1911) (*C.W.*, Vol. III). (See Bibliog. no. 10.)

5. "Über Ressentiment und moralisches Werturteil: Ein Beitrag zur Pathologie der Kultur." *Zeitschrift für Pathopsychologie*, Vol. I, nos. 2–3 (1912) (*C.W.*, Vol. III). (See Bibliog. no. 10.)

6. *Zur Phänomenologie und Theorie der Sympathiegefühle und von Liebe und Hass: Mit einem Anhang über den Grund zur Annahme der Existenz des fremden Ich.* Halle: Verlag Max Niemeyer, 1913. (See Bibliog. no. 18.)

7. *Der Formalismus in der Ethik und die materiale Wertethik: Mit besonderer Berücksichtigung der Ethik Immanuel Kants.* Pt. I: *Jahrbuch für Philosophie und phänomenologische Forschung,* Vol. I (1913). Pt. II: *Ibid.,* Vol. II (1916). 1st ed. (with a Preface), Halle: Verlag Max Niemeyer, 1916; 2d ed. (with the subtitle *Neuer Versuch der Grundlegung eines ethischen Personalismus* and a second Preface), 1921; 3d ed. (with a third Preface and an index), 1927 (*C.W.,* Vol. II).

8. "Ethik: Ein Forschungsbericht." *Jahrbücher der Philosophie,* Vol. II (1914), Eine kritische Übersicht der Philosophie der Gegenwart, edited by Max Frischeisen-Köhler (*C.W.,* Vol. I).

9. *Der Genius des Krieges und der Deutsche Krieg.* Leipzig: Verlag der Weissen Bücher, 1915; 2d ed., 1916; 3d ed., 1917 (*C.W.,* Vol. IV).

10. *Abhandlungen und Aufsätze.* 2 vols. Leipzig: Verlag der Weissen Bücher, 1915; 2d ed. (under the title *Vom Umsturz der Werte*), Leipzig: Neue Geist Verlag, 1919; 3d ed., 1923 (*C.W.,* Vol. III). This work comprises the following essays: "Zur Rehabilitierung der Tugend," "Das Ressentiment im Aufbau der Moralen" (an expanded version of "Über Ressentiment und moralisches Werturteil" [see Bibliog. no. 5]), "Zum Phänomen des Tragischen," "Zur Idee des Menschen," "Zum Sinn der Frauenbewegung," "Die Idole der Selbsterkenntnis" (an expanded version of "Über Selbsttäuschungen" [see Bibliog. no. 4]), "Die Psychologie der sogenannten Rentenhysterie und der rechte Kampf gegen das Übel," "Versuche einer Philosophie des Lebens," "Der Bourgeois," "Der Bourgeois und die religiösen Mächte," "Die Zukunft des Kapitalismus."

11. *Krieg und Aufbau.* Leipzig: Verlag der Weissen Bücher, 1916 (*C.W.,* Vol. VI). This work comprises the following essays: "Der Krieg als Gesamterlebnis," "Über östliches und westliches Christentum," "Das Nationale im Denken Frankreichs," "Über die Nationalidee der grossen Nationen," "Bemerkungen zum Geiste und den ideellen Grundlagen der Demokratien der grossen Nationen," "Über Gesinnungs- und Zweckmilitarismus: Eine Studie zur Psychologie des Militarismus," "Soziologische Neuorientierung und die Aufgabe der deutschen Katholiken nach dem Kriege," "Vom Sinn des Leides," "Liebe und Erkenntnis." All of these essays except

the first were subsequently published in *Schriften zur Soziologie und Weltanschauungslehre*. (See Bibliog. no. 19.)

12. *Die Ursachen des Deutschenhasses: Eine nationalpädagogische Erörterung.* Leipzig: Kurt Wolff-Verlag, 1917; 2d ed., Leipzig: Neue Geist Verlag, 1919 (*C.W.*, Vol. IV).

13. "Von zwei deutschen Krankheiten." *Der Leuchter,* Vol. VI (1919). (See Bibliog. no. 19.)

14. *Vom Ewigen im Menschen: Religiöse Erneuerung.* Leipzig: Neue Geist Verlag, 1921; 2d ed. (in 2 vols., with an expanded Foreword), 1923; 3d ed. (unabridged popular edition), Berlin: Neue Geist Verlag, 1933 (*C.W.*, Vol. V). This work comprises the following essays: "Reue und Wiedergeburt," "Vom Wesen der Philosophie und den moralischen Bedingungen des philosophischen Erkennens," "Probleme der Religion," "Die christliche Liebesidee und die gegenwärtige Welt," "Vom kulturellen Wiederaufbau Europas."

15. "Universität und Volkshochschule." In *Zur Soziologie des Volksbildungswesens.* Schriften des Forschungsinstitutes für Sozialwissenschaften in Köln, edited by Max Scheler, Vol. 1. Munich: Duncker & Humblot, 1921 (*C.W.*, Vol. VIII). (See Bibliog. no. 22.)

16. "Die deutsche Philosophie der Gegenwart." In *Deutsches Leben der Gegenwart*, edited by P. Witkop. Berlin: Verlag der Bücherfreunde, 1922 (*C.W.*, Vol. VII).

17. *Walter Rathenau: Eine Würdigung.* Cologne: Marcan-Block-Verlag, 1922 (*C.W.*, Vol. VI).

18. *Wesen und Formen der Sympathie.* Bonn: Verlag Friedrich Cohen, 1923; 2d ed., 1927; 3d ed., 1931; 4th ed., Frankfurt: Verlag Schulte-Bulmke, 1948; 5th ed., Bern: Francke Verlag, 1973 (*C.W.*, Vol. VII). This work is an expanded version of *Zur Phänomenologie und Theorie der Sympathiegefühle*. (See Bibliog. no. 6.)

19. *Schriften zur Soziologie und Weltanschauungslehre.* 4 vols. Leipzig: Neue Geist Verlag, 1923–24 (*C.W.*, Vol. VI). Volume I, *Moralia*, includes the following essays: "Weltanschauungslehre, Soziologie und Weltanschauungssetzung," "Über die positivistische Geschichtsphilosophie des Wissens," "Vom Sinn des Leides" (a considerably expanded version of the previously published essay [see Bibliog. no. 11]), "Vom Verrat der Freude," "Liebe und Erkenntnis," "Über östliches

und westliches Christentum." Volume II, *Nation*, includes the following essays: "Über die Nationalidee der grossen Nationen," "Das Nationale im Denken Frankreichs," "Der Geist und die ideellen Grundlagen der Demokratien der grossen Nationen," "Über Gesinnungs- und Zweckmilitarismus," "Von zwei deutschen Krankheiten" (see Bibliog. no. 13). Volume IIIA, *Christentum und Gesellschaft: Konfessionen*, includes: "Der Friede unter den Konfessionen," "Soziologische Neuorientierung und die Aufgabe der deutschen Katholiken nach dem Kriege." Volume IIIB, *Christentum und Gesellschaft: Arbeits- und Bevölkerungsprobleme*, includes: "Prophetischer oder marxistischer Sozialismus?," "Arbeit und Ethik" (see Bibliog. no. 2), "Arbeit und Weltanschauung," "Bevölkerungsprobleme als Weltanschauungsfragen." A number of these essays were first published in *Krieg und Aufbau*. (See Bibliog. no. 11.)

20. "Probleme einer Soziologie des Wissens." In *Versuche zu einer Soziologie des Wissens*. Schriften des Forschungsinstitutes für Sozialwissenschaften in Köln, edited by Max Scheler, Vol. II. Munich: Duncker & Humblot, 1924. (See Bibliog. no. 22.)

21. *Die Formen des Wissens und die Bildung*. Bonn: Verlag Friedrich Cohen, 1925. (See Bibliog. no. 27.)

22. *Die Wissensformen und die Gesellschaft*. Leipzig: Neue Geist Verlag, 1926 (*C.W.*, Vol. VIII). This work comprises the following essays: "Probleme einer Soziologie des Wissens" (an expanded version of the previously published essay [see Bibliog. no. 20]), "Erkenntnis und Arbeit: Eine Studie über Wert und Grenzen des pragmatischen Motivs in der Erkenntnis der Welt," "Universität und Volkshochschule" (see Bibliog. no. 15).

23. "Die Stellung des Menschen im Kosmos." *Der Leuchter*, Vol. VIII (1927). 1st ed., Darmstadt: Verlag Otto Reichl, 1928; 2d ed., 1929; 3d ed., 1931; 4th ed., Munich: Nymphenburger Verlagsanstalt, 1948; 5th ed., 1949; 6th ed., Bern: Francke Verlag, 1962; 7th ed., 1966 (*C.W.*, Vol. IX).

24. "Mensch und Geschichte." *Neue Rundschau*, Vol. XXXVII (Nov., 1926). (See Bibliog. no. 27.)

25. "Idealismus—Realismus." *Philosophischer Anzeiger*, Vol. II (1927) (*C.W.*, Vol. IX).

26. "Der Mensch im Weltalter des Ausgleichs." In *Politische Wissenshaft (Ausgleich als Schicksal und Aufgabe)*. Berlin: Veröffentlichung der Deutschen Hochschule für Politik, 1929. (See Bibliog. no. 27.)

(NOTE: The following works were published after Scheler's death. Numbers 28–30 were compiled from unpublished manuscripts found among his papers.)

27. *Philosophische Weltanschauung*. Bonn: Verlag Friedrich Cohen, 1929. Reprinted in *Dalp-Taschenbücher*, Vol. CCCI (1954) (*C.W.*, Vol. IX). This work includes the following essays: "Philosophische Weltanschauung," "Mensch und Geschichte" (see Bibliog. no. 24), "Der Mensch im Weltalter des Ausgleichs" (see Bibliog. no. 26), "Die Formen des Wissens und die Bildung" (see Bibliog. no. 21), "Spinoza: Eine Rede."

28. *Die Idee des Ewigen Friedens und der Pazifismus*. Berlin: Neue Geist Verlag, 1931.

29. *Zur Ethik und Erkenntnislehre*. Edited by Maria Scheler. Schriften aus dem Nachlass, Vol. I. Berlin: Neue Geist Verlag, 1933 (*C.W.*, Vol. X). This work includes the following essays: "Tod und Fortleben," "Über Scham und Schamgefühl," "Vorbilder und Führer," "Ordo Amoris," "Phänomenologie und Erkenntnistheorie," "Lehre von den Drei Tatsachen."

30. "Metaphysik und Kunst." *Deutsche Beiträge*, Vol. I, no. 2 (1947).

31. *Collected Works*. 13 vols. Bern: Francke Verlag, 1954–. Vol. I, *Frühe Schriften*, edited by Maria Scheler and Manfred S. Frings, 1971; Vol. II, *Der Formalismus in der Ethik und die materiale Wertethik*, edited by Maria Scheler, 1954 (4th ed.), 1966 (5th ed.); Vol. III, *Vom Umsturz der Werte*, edited by Maria Scheler, 1955; Vol. IV, *Politisch-Pädagogische Schriften*, edited by Manfred S. Frings, forthcoming; Vol. V, *Vom Ewigen im Menschen*, edited by Maria Scheler, 1954; Vol. VI, *Schriften zur Soziologie und Weltanschauungslehre*, edited by Maria Scheler, 1963; Vol. VII, *Wesen und Formen der Sympathie*, edited by Manfred S. Frings, 1973; Vol. VIII, *Die Wissensformen und die Gesellschaft*,

edited by Maria Scheler, 1960; Vol. IX, *Späte Schriften*, edited by Manfred S. Frings, forthcoming; Vol. X, *Schriften aus dem Nachlass*, edited by Maria Scheler, 1957; Vols. XI–XIII, *Schriften aus dem Nachlass*, edited by Manfred S. Frings, forthcoming.

(NOTE: The following works by Scheler have been translated into English.)

On the Eternal in Man. Translated by Bernard Noble. London: SCM Press, 1960. (See Bibliog. no. 14.)

Man's Place in Nature. Translated, and with an introduction, by Hans Meyerhoff. New York: Noonday, 1961. (See Bibliog. no. 23.)

"Metaphysics and Art." Translated by Manfred S. Frings. In *Max Scheler: Centennial Essays.* The Hague: Martinus Nijhoff, forthcoming.

The Nature of Sympathy. Translated by Peter Heath, with an introduction by W. Stark. Hamden, Conn.: Archon Books, 1970. (See Bibliog. no. 18.)

Philosophical Perspectives. Translated by Oscar Haac. Boston: Beacon Press, 1958. (See Bibliog. no. 27.)

"Problems of a Sociology of Knowledge." Translated by Ernest Ranly. *Philosophy Today*, Vol. XII, no. 4 (Spring, 1968), pp. 42–70. (See Bibliog. no. 22.)

Ressentiment. Translated by William Holdheim, with an introduction by the editor, Lewis A. Coser. Glencoe, Ill.: Free Press, 1961. (See Bibliog. no. 10.)

Selected Philosophical Essays. Translated, and with an introduction, by David R. Lachterman. Evanston, Ill.: Northwestern University Press, 1973. This volume comprises the following essays: "The Idols of Self-Knowledge" (see Bibliog. no. 10), "*Ordo Amoris*" (see Bibliog. no. 29), "Phenomenology and the Theory of Cognition" (see Bibliog. no. 29), "The Theory of the Three Facts" (see Bibliog. no. 29), "Idealism and Realism" (see Bibliog. no. 25).

"On the Tragic." Translated by Bernard Stambler. *Cross Currents*, Vol. IV (1954), pp. 178–91. (See Bibliog. no. 10.)

For further bibliographical information, see:

FRINGS, MANFRED S. *Zur Phänomenologie der Lebensgemeinschaft: Ein Versuch mit Max Scheler.* Meisenheim: Verlag Anton Hain, 1971. (Secondary works published since 1963.)

HARTMANN, W. *Max Scheler—Bibliographie.* Stuttgart: Friedrich Frommann Verlag, 1965. (Primary and secondary works published before 1963.)

RANLY, E. W. *Scheler's Phenomenology of Community.* The Hague: Nijhoff, 1966. (Primary works.)

Name Index

Subject Index